THE LOSS OF JAVA

This publication has been made possible by the Corts Foundation, Almere, The Netherlands. The research was done as part of the Research Program of the Netherlands Defence Academy (NLDA), Breda, The Netherlands.

THE LOSS OF JAVA

The final battles for the possession of
Java fought by allied air, naval and land forces
in the period of 18 February–7 March 1942

P.C. Boer

NUS PRESS
SINGAPORE

© P.C. Boer

Published by:

NUS Press
National University of Singapore
AS3-01-02, 3 Arts Link
Singapore 117569

Fax: (65) 6774-0652
E-mail: nusbooks@nus.edu.sg
Website: http://www.nus.edu.sg/nuspress

ISBN 978-9971-69-513-2 (Paper)

First Edition 2011
Reprint 2013

National Library Board, Singapore Cataloguing-in-Publication Data

Boer, P.C., 1948–
    The loss of Java: the final battles for the possession of Java fought by allied
air, naval and land forces in the period of 18 February–7 March 1942 /
P.C. Boer. – Singapore: NUS Press, c2011.
    p. cm.
    Includes bibliographical references and index.
    ISBN-13: 978-9971-69-513-2 (pbk.)

    1. World War, 1939–45 – Campaigns – Indonesia – Java.
    2. Java (Indonesia) – History, Military – 20th century. I. Nederlandse
Defensie Academie. II. Title.

D767.7
940.5425982 — dc22   OCN649274484

Typeset by: Scientifik Graphics
Printed by: Markono Print Media Pte Ltd

Contents

Part 1B: A description and analysis of the deployment of the bombers

PART 2: The Battle of the Java Sea

PART 3:   The Battle of Kalidjati

PART 4:   The Battle of the Tjiater Pass

PART 5:   Conclusions   503

List of Maps

List of Illustrations

A 4-cm Bofors anti-aircraft gun of the KNIL during a night exercise in 1940. During these exercises ML reconnaissance aircraft were the target. (Private collection, P.C. Boer)

Preface, design of the study, aim and research questions

Preface

The subject of this study is the final battle between the allied and Japanese armed forces for Java, the principal island in the former Netherlands East Indies, as it was fought after the fall of Singapore (15 February 1942) and the evacuation by the allies of southern Sumatra (16 and 17 February 1942) in the period from 18 February up to and including 7 March 1942. It began with an air battle to attain air superiority over Java (18 February–27 February) and a naval battle, the Battle of the Java Sea (27 February), during which the allies sought in vain to prevent a Japanese invasion of Java. This invasion came in the night of 28 February on 1 March. The main effort of the struggle that ensued lay in western Java and it can be divided into two battles involving land and air components: the Battle of Kalidjati (28 February 1942–3 March 1942) and the Battle of the Tjiater Pass (5–7 March 1942), respectively.

Many people cherish a peculiar, but erroneous, idea of this final battle for Java. In brief it comes down to the following: after the fall of Singapore the Dutch lost interest in continuing the fight and as result they barely put up as much as a token resistance once the Japanese had invaded Java. In this accepted version there is only one important engagement between Allied and Japanese forces in this period: the Battle of the Java Sea on 27 February 1942. After this the Koninklijk Nederlands-Indisch Leger–Royal Netherlands East Indies Army (KNIL) retreated, only to capitulate a little more than a week later, as the story goes. It is this simplified, mistaken, impression which I am trying to put right by means of this book.

There is very little knowledge about the allied air campaign fought between 18 and 27 February 1942, and hardly anyone is aware of how hard the allied air and land forces fought in the period of 28 February–3 March 1942 for possession of the strategically vital Kalidjati air base. Nor do many people know why the KNIL in the later stages of the struggle only fought one major battle with the Japanese, the Battle of the Tjiater Pass from 5–7 March 1942. The fact that this was a consequence of a well-devised plan of defence and that the battle for Java comprised not one (the Battle of the Java Sea) but four major engagements with the Japanese, is one of the central themes of this book.

Apart from the battle for air superiority, *Air Power* also played a major part in the three other big engagements with the Japanese. In the literature there is remarkably little, almost no, attention for the interplay between the operations of the land and air components and naval and air components, or the different effects of the use of Air Power, including the psychological ones. The great impact of Air Power on the outcome of the various major engagements with the Japanese is one of the leading themes of this book.

In this publication I have attempted to lend the *Combined* and *Joint* character of the struggle on the allied side some more perspective. There is substantial documentation on the fall of Java in March 1942 and the rapid demise of the KNIL and the allied forces. As was said above, there is, however, virtually no attention for the operational cooperation between the land, air and naval forces. The final battle for Java, however, is one of the first instances in military history of *Combined* (several nationalities together) and *Joint* (several Services together) operations. As military historians have so far almost exclusively documented the battle for Java from a single-Service perspective, I am convinced that there has been absolutely insufficient attention for the coherence of allied (*Combined*) naval and air force and allied land and air force operations. Even the battle for air superiority over Java was *Combined* and *Joint* on the part of the allies.

The generally accepted idea is that the allies were rather ineffective in their battle against the Japanese invaders. In fact, the Japanese were made to suffer truly serious losses, but the Japanese commanders consciously took several heavy risks that turned out well for them and which put the allies under great time pressure each time. As a result of this, the KNIL and the allied forces capitulated on 8 March, effective the following day.

I would like to express my appreciation to all those who have helped me in my research for this book and the process of writing it, in particular the many veterans. I would like to mention especially (in random order): A.E. van Kempen, P. van Meel (+2003), P.A.C. Benjamins (+2000), P.A. Hoyer (+2001), G.M. Bruggink (+2005), and O.A.O. Kreefft (+2009). Jos Mulders helped me with the data and documents on the British anti-aircraft artillery units in Java, Mark Haselden provided me with data from operations reports and orders of battle of the allied air forces in Java from the *Public Records Office* in London, which could not be found in Dutch archives. The following colleagues and ex-colleagues of the Royal Netherlands Military Academy and the Netherlands Defence Academy were helpful in reading the proofs and editing the various parts of this book: Prof. Dr. W. Klinkert, A. Rosendahl Huber, M.A. and R.L. Erhardt. C.H. Murre, LL.M gave the book a final perusal for "incomprehensibles". This English language edition is a revised and updated version of the original Dutch edition titled "Het verlies van Java: een kwestie van Air Power" (De Bataafsche Leeuw, Amsterdam, The Netherlands, 2006) and was made possible by the Corts Foundation of Almere, the Netherlands. The translation work was done by H. Kirkels, M.A.

The design of the study

The above-mentioned air, sea and land battles will be described and subsequently briefly analysed as much as possible from a *joint* operations perspective. Part 1 of this book deals with the battle for air superiority over western Java, from the allied perspective. A central position is taken up by the *Counter-Air* operation of the allied air forces in the period between 18 and 27 February 1942, where Part 1A describes the deployment of the allied fighters and allied anti-aircraft artillery (the defensive component of the air operation), and Part 1B discusses the involvement of allied bombers (the offensive component of the air operation). In view of the great importance of *Air Power* also the following parts of the book feature detailed descriptions of allied and Japanese air forces operations. For the convenience of the reader the concept of *sortie* (though not yet in use in February and March 1942) is used as a measure for operational involvement of the aircraft (one mission carried out by one aircraft is one sortie; one mission carried out by two aircraft is two sorties, etc.). Part 2 describes the actions of the allied sea and air forces (in their reciprocity) during the days preceding the battle of the Java Sea and the battle itself (though the actions at sea are only briefly sketched), as well as the events of 28 February 1942 immediately following it. Parts 3 and 4 present the descriptions and analyses of the battle of Kalidjati in the period between 28 February and 3 March 1942, and the battle of the Tjiater pass in the period between 5 and 7 March, respectively. Part 5, finally, presents a summary of the main conclusions. I have introduced small text overlaps for the benefit of the "quick and dirty" reader, to enable reading the different parts (including 1A and 1B) of the book separately. The five parts are preceded by an introduction chapter titled *The Japanese advance: Java given up by the allies*.

Aim and research questions

The aim of this study is to provide an insight into the (major) role the air forces played in the final battle for Java in the period between 18 February and 7 March 1942. The research questions are the following:

1. How realistic was the assessment by the staff of Major-General Van Oyen (Air Officer Commanding Java Air Command) with regard to the chance of preventing a Japanese invasion by making use of the allied air forces. Was there indeed a small chance of making the Japanese postpone and subsequently cancel the invasion, and if so, how well was this opportunity used?

2. What role did Air Power play in the failure of the allied naval forces to eliminate the so-called 'eastern' invasion fleet of the Japanese?

3. What role did Air Power play in the failure of the KNIL to defeat the Japanese troops that had landed near Eretan Wetan, and, in particular, the units that had occupied Kalidjati and Soebang?

4. What role did Air Power play in the failure of the KNIL to deny the Japanese troops that landed near Eretan Wetan access to the Bandoeng plateau?

The following parts of this study will present detailed historical reconstructions and the concise analyses of the results of the deployment of the allied armed forces will provide the answers to the research questions formulated above. The allied *Counter-air* operation carried out from and over central and eastern Java and the battles of the land forces that took place there will not be discussed here; nor will the actions of the naval forces, other than those in relation to the battle of the Java Sea, described in Part 2. The focus with regard to the land battle in western Java lies on the actions in the area of the so called Bandoeng Group. All times mentioned are local time (MJT).

Reliability and validity

In order to guarantee optimal reliability and validity in this case study, I have made historical reconstructions, as complete as possible, which will be presented in full. These reconstructions are based on four different types of sources: written sources from 1942 (documents, such as operations reports, log books, diary entries, etc.), reports and statements written after WWII by former KNIL service personnel involved (mostly drawn up in 1946 and varying greatly in accuracy), interviews and correspondence I had with ex-servicemen involved, mainly from the ML and the KNIL, in various periods between the beginning of 1975 and late 2003, and relevant literature (books, articles, reports, papers, etc.). I have always tried as much as possible to use the various types in mutual combination, taking as a framework the (scarce) sources from 1942, complemented with surveys and reports, exclusively based on original sources, published shortly after WWII (such as *Army Air Force Historical Studies* and *Japanese Monographs*). Furthermore, reliability and validity of the study is based on *peer reviews* and *member checks*. The vast majority of archive material used, including all the reports written shortly after WW II by ML and KNIL servicemen, are in the Dutch language and are mentioned in the notes using their original title in Dutch, the reports by servicemen being named "Verslag".

As there is an almost complete lack of sources from March 1942, the description of the operations of the land forces of the KNIL is mainly based on reports and statements of those involved, dating from the period between 1945 and 1948 and relevant literature. In this I have made intensive use of the still excellent study of the land battle by J.J. Nortier, P. Kuijt and P.M.H. Groen, *De Japanse aanval op Java* [*The Japanese attack on Java*] (Amsterdam, 1994). As the authors of this book (*Java*, for short) also based themselves on the reports and statements mentioned above, I have limited myself to references to the relevant pages of this book as much as possible in the notes. I have referred to the original reports and statements insofar as my own text is more elaborate, deviates from theirs or when I arrive at different conclusions than the authors of *Java*. In order to clarify or solve uncertainties and discrepancies in the original research material a limited number of interviews were conducted with authors (former KNIL service personnel) of articles in the *Stabelan* periodical (1974–99). A number of these interviews were conducted with the help of a questionnaire on my behalf by one of the editors of the Stichting Vriendenkring Oud KNIL Militairen (Stichting Stabelan–Stabelan Foundation), P. van Meel. On his request, references to *Stabelan* articles in the notes are made in 'plain language', mentioning date or month and year of publication.

I have been in correspondence with some authors of books I used as sources in order to resolve issues, check what their original sources had been, etc. From Chr. Shores I received logbook and diary entries and information coming from correspondence with RAF and RAAF ex-servicemen. Colonel (ret.) J.J. Nortier provided me with a number of tables of unit strengths of the KNIL. The Military History Office, the present-day Military History Department, of the National Institute for Defense Studies in Tokyo answered a number of questions I had on the Japanese operations and made available several parts from war diaries of units and other additional information.

Reading guide

In this book I tried to isolate my main findings and present these in the summary chapters at the end of each part of the book. The larger part of the book, however, concerns a day-by-day detailed account of the battles described (in conformity with the original NLDA research project). The reader who is not interested in details about the actual operations is advised only to read the introduction chapter "The Japanese advance: Java given up by the allies", the first chapters (1A.1, 1B.1, 2.1 [Introduction paragraph only], 3.1 and 4.1) and the final chapters (1A.9, 1B.12, 2.4, 3.7 and 4.6) of each part of the book plus Part 5: Conclusions. Readers interested in only one of the described battles are advised to read the chapter "The Japanese advance: Java given up by the allies", the first chapter (in the case of chapter 2.1, the Introduction paragraph only) and the final chapter of the part(s) of the book preceding the part about the battle, the complete part about this battle, the first (in the case of chapter 2.1, the Introduction paragraph only) and the final chapter of the part(s) following this part, plus Part 5: Conclusions. Readers interested in the ground battles are also advised to read Attachment 3 which explains the KNIL basic unit structure and the names used for subunits in the KNIL.

INTRODUCTION

The Japanese advance: Java given up by the allies

Introduction

On 8 December 1941 the Netherlands declared war on Japan. Nine days later the Militaire Luchtvaart–Army Aviation Corps (ML) of the Koninklijk Nederlands-Indisch Leger–Royal Netherlands East Indies Army (KNIL) flew its first combat missions. After its attack on Pearl Harbor and the American bases in Hawai, Japan had simultaneously attacked the Malayan Peninsula and the Philippines. The final destination of the Japanese forces, however, was the Dutch East Indies with its important oil fields and refineries and large supplies of rubber and raw materials, such as tin. Once its forces had made good progress in Malaya and the Philippines, Japan embarked on the second phase of its war of conquest. On 7 January 1942 the first invasion fleet left port for the Netherlands East Indies.

Three Japanese forces advanced on Java, via Banka and Sumatra (the western force), via Tarakan and eastern and southern Borneo (the central force), and via Celebes, Ambon and Timor (the eastern force), respectively. The attack on Banka and Palembang in southern Sumatra began on 14 February 1942, one day before the surrender of Singapore and it coincided with the arrival of allied reinforcements. On 16 February Palembang fell, followed by Bali, directly east of Java, on 19 February. Timor was attacked the next day. In spite of often fierce resistance from mostly the Militaire Luchtvaart, assisted by the Royal Air Force (RAF), the Royal Australian Air Force (RAAF) and the United States Army Air Force (USAAF), Java was in a tight situation and shipping military reinforcements to the island had become virtually impossible.

The final battle for Java already began on 18 February 1942 and came to consist of four major engagements with the Japanese. It began with an air battle to attain air superiority over Java (18 February–27 February) and a naval battle, the Battle of the Java Sea (27 February), during which the allies sought in vain to prevent a Japanese invasion of Java. This invasion came in the night of 28 February on 1 March. The main effort of the struggle that ensued lay in western Java and it can be divided into two battles involving land and air components: the Battle of Kalidjati (28 February 1942–3 March 1942) and the Battle of the Tjiater Pass (5–7 March 1942), respectively.

Apart from the battle for air superiority, *Air Power* also played a major part in the three other major engagements with the Japanese. All four battles further share a *Combined* and *Joint* character on the allied side. Indeed, the final battle for Java is one of the first instances in military history of *Combined* (several nationalities together) and *Joint* (several Services together) operations.

The allied command structure

The *Combined* and *Joint* forces meant above fell under the command of an allied coordinating general HQ, ABDA Command (ABDACOM), at the time usually referred to as *Unified Command*, established in Java on 15 January 1942. This allied *joint combined headquarters*, which was staffed with American, British, Netherlands East Indies and Australian personnel from all Services, was commanded by British *Supreme Commander* (present-day *Joint Forces Commander* or *Theatre Commander*) General Sir Archibald Wavell, whose formal superiors were the *Combined Chiefs of Staff*, but who in fact had two bosses, the British and the American Chiefs of Staff. There were three subordinate headquarters including the allied air force headquarters called ABDA-AIR, or ABDAIR, for short, where ABDA stood for *American, British, Dutch and Australian*. This *combined operations centre avant la lettre*, just like its allied naval (ABDA-FLOAT) and land forces (ABDA-ARM) counterparts, resorted directly under ABDACOM.[1]

The allied area of command initially comprised the Philippines, Malaya and Singapore, Burma, the Dutch East Indies and (from 5 February 1942) northern Australia. After 20 February it had shrunk to little more than Java, several as yet unoccupied parts of the East Indian archipelago, such as northern Sumatra, northern Australia, the still unoccupied part of the Philippines (where the rearguard battles, however, were fought entirely outside ABDACOM's scope) and Burma. This latter part of the area of command was transferred to the British *India Command* on 21 February 1942.

Java given up by the allies

On the basis of analyses of the Japanese advance and information acquired from intelligence channels, General Wavell was convinced that Java could not be held after the evacuation of southern Sumatra. On 16 February 1942 he expected a Japanese invasion within ten to fourteen days, an estimate, which, as we now know, was fully in keeping with the Japanese plans. On 16 February Wavell gave the advice to deploy an Australian army corps on its way to Java to an alternative theatre, and to refrain from reinforcing Java at the expense of the defence of Burma and the Australian main land. Wavell's staff had (rightly) concluded that the Australian corps with its two divisions could not possibly be made operational within the time available. Wavell was convinced that it would be irresponsible to try it anyway.[2]

The *Combined Chiefs of Staff* in Washington concurred with Wavell's assessment of the situation and his advice in the matter: Java was to be defended exclusively with the available resources already in situ. The only reinforcement that could be expected came from the allied air forces, fighters and bombers that were already on their way, augmented with the units of the British and Australian armies and RAF that had been sent to southern Sumatra in the middle of February, only to be evacuated immediately.[3]

On 19 and 20 February Wavell was confronted with serious military setbacks. The Japanese occupied Bali, carried out a heavy air raid on Darwin in northern Australia and landed on Timor. Moreover, the 19th marked the beginning of the expected Japanese air offensive to attain air superiority over western Java, with heavy raids on the airfields of Semplak and Andir. In central and eastern Java the Japanese continued their air raids (commenced on 3 February) on airfields and the port of Soerabaja. The allied air forces lacked the numbers to put up a strong defence. There was insufficient anti-aircraft artillery and there were too few fighters. In particular allied bombers were destroyed on the airfields in bombing raids and strafings (low-level attacks) of Japanese fighters.[4]

New instructions from the *Combined Chiefs of Staff* followed on 22 February. Aircraft that could operate more effectively from bases outside the island (American heavy bombers already on their way would still be based in Java, however) were to be pulled back from Java, just like air force personnel for whom there were no aircraft, and troops, mechanics, in particular, that could not contribute to the defence of Java. Wavell himself received orders on 22 February to go to India in order to assume the position of *Commander-in-Chief India*.[5] His ABDACOM Headquarters (*Unified Command*) at Lembang was dismantled on 23 and 24 February, with only a few specific elements remaining intact, such as the *Combined Operations and Intelligence Centre* (COIC), the allied combat intelligence centre (in a down-sized form).[6]

Under Dutch command

The allied command structure remained as it was, with the top positions taken up by Dutch personnel, but the overall general ABDACOM Headquarters was disbanded on 25 February. The KNIL commander, Lieutenant-General H. ter Poorten, who was already the commander of the allied land forces, now became *Commander-in-Chief ABDA Area*. To this end he extended his own Headquarters, the Algemeen Hoofdkwartier–General Headquarters (AHK), using Dutch personnel and small numbers of allied specialists and liaison officers from *Unified Command*. The Governor-General of the Netherlands East Indies, in fact, took over as Supreme Commander but only in a largely formal sense as all military-operational matters were immediately delegated in full to Ter Poorten.

The allied naval Headquarters ABDA-FLOAT also already had a Dutchman as its commanding officer, the Dutch Navy Commander in the Netherlands East Indies, Vice-Admiral C.E.L. Helfrich. As the principal force, the Navy could dispose of the *Combined Striking Force*, an allied naval squadron, consisting of American, British, Australian and Dutch cruisers and destroyers. Incidentally, for logistic reasons this squadron was temporarily divided over Tandjong Priok (the *Western Striking Force*) and Soerabaja (the *Eastern Striking Force*), only to be recombined into one squadron at Soerabaja on 26 February. It then consisted of five cruisers and nine destroyers, commanded by Rear-Admiral K.W.F.M. Doorman.[7]

The allied air force Headquarters ABDAIR was renamed to *Java Air Command* (JAC) and on the night of 22 February 1942 the commander of the KNIL Army Aviation Corps (ML), Major-General L.H. van Oyen, took over command from RAF Air Marshal Sir Richard Peirse. JAC, which was much smaller compared to ABDAIR, consisted of three subordinate HQs, the British/Australian BRITAIR (the former *West Group*) and the Commando ML–ML Command (*Central Group*) in western Java and the American *East Group* (EASGROUP) in central and eastern Java. These HQs controlled the operational squadrons and *afdelingen*. Furthermore, JAC encompassed the staff of *Reconnaissance Group* (*RecGroup* or RECGROUP), a tiny staff that managed the flying boats of the Marine Luchtvaart Dienst–Dutch Naval Air Service (MLD), the RAF, U.S. Navy and the RAAF in the operational area, the Air Defence Commands Batavia, Bandoeng and Soerabaja and all anti-aircraft artillery units of the KNIL and the British Army. The COIC also came under Van Oyen's command.[8]

JAC, BRITAIR and COIC were accommodated in the same building, that of the Royal Netherlands Military Academy (KMA) in Bandoeng, which was situated on the eastern edge of north Bandoeng, a few kilometres away from the evacuated Technical University complex on the northern edge of Bandoeng, where the AHK and ABDA-FLOAT were seated. These HQs were organized in a rather modern way for those days, and the operational air support for naval and land forces was arranged effectively by JAC. Thus, modern procedures for requesting and granting air support, derived from the British experiences in the battles in northern Africa, were used.[9]

From the moment Dutch officers became fully responsible for the allied command in Java, the general strategy was entirely directed at keeping the island for the allies. General HQ (AHK) thought simultaneous landings by the Japanese in western and eastern Java the most likely. The invasion fleets were expected to approach through the Macassar Straits, east of Borneo, and through the Karimata and Gaspar Straits, west of Borneo. Landings in central Java were deemed unlikely, and in view of a shortage of troops, it was decided to carry out large-scale troop movements in order to reinforce western Java, in particular, where the main effort of the battle was expected. The intended general strategy (which was also actually followed) can be summarized as follows:

a. By means of long-distance reconnaissance with RecGroup's flying boats, complemented with submarine patrolling/surveillance, search as far north as possible for Japanese invasion fleets.
b. Attack detected invasion fleets with all available bombers, and as much as possible also the reconnaissance planes, as soon as they come within range.
c. The *Combined Striking Force*, the allied naval squadron, leaves port to engage on the main threat, as soon as it is located.

d.   No spreading out of the land forces over possible landing sites, but positioning them in such a way that they can be concentrated quickly with a view to counter-attacking any possible hostile landing operation.

e.   In case of a successful Japanese invasion, the troops fall back on the Bandoeng plateau in the west and the Malang plateau in the east.[10]

Java Air Command

As the above-mentioned overall strategy indicates, the objective was to prevent a Japanese invasion of Java. The two major instruments available for this were the allied air force and the allied naval squadron. The allied air force would get the first opportunity to try and prevent an invasion. The allied fleet would not go into battle until the Japanese invasion fleet or fleets had been discovered, and they would be held in reserve, unless a good opportunity presented itself to carry out a successful hit and run action. This last possibility, however, was considered academic, as the size of the allied air force had already been reduced so much on 22 February that the *Counter-air* operation, which had been embarked upon four days earlier (see below), would use up all capacity. A successful action of the allied naval squadron without (daylight) fighter support was considered impossible.

On 18 February 1942, almost simultaneously with the start of the Japanese air offensive for air superiority over western Java, the allied air campaign began, intended to make the enemy postpone his invasion of Java. In the present-day jargon it was a *Counter-air* campaign, directed at attaining and maintaining a required air superiority of one's own. From 19 February onwards, there were in fact two campaigns; one executed from bases in central and eastern Java by the USAAF, and one carried out from western Java by the ML, RAF, and RAAF. The latter was the more intensive one, and it is one of the objects of study of this book. As the allied air operation for the retention of Java is all but forgotten nowadays (in contrast to, for instance, the Battle of the Java Sea), it will be discussed in some detail below.

Although devised in a few days' time, the *Counter-air* operation carried out by ML, RAF and RAAF, was well-conceived. On the basis of operations reports and intelligence analyses ABDAIR and COIC had drawn the conclusion that the Japanese air force was extremely vulnerable with regard to its logistics. Supply lines were very long and transport capacity by sea was limited. It was assumed that for the Japanese vanguard units the available aircraft fuel would be a bottle-neck. Apart from that, the intelligence specialists concluded that by now the Japanese air force would have depleted its reserves of fighters and (for their battle for western Java) would have to rely on available resources at Palembang. Both assumptions, we now know, were correct.

The strategy of the allied *Counter-air* operation, therefore, was directed at degrading as much as possible the enemy's ability to carry out operational sorties (for air operations in the west), by:

a. making aircraft fuel a scarce commodity (by means of bombing raids on aircraft fuel stocks captured by the Japanese in southern Sumatra and on ships en route to or lying at anchor in Palembang), and

b. reducing the number of operational Japanese combat aircraft (by means of bombing raids on airfields near Palembang and inflic-ting losses over western Java by allied fighters and anti-aircraft artillery).

The objective of this strategy was to extend the period the Japanese would need to attain air superiority, and thus to force them to post-pone the invasion. This would create enough time for the allied air force in Java to be reinforced, with extra fighters, for a start.[11]

In contrast to his predecessor, Van Oyen was convinced that there was still a slim chance that deployment of the allied air force could save the island, and that this chance must be taken. Analyses of the Japanese advance showed that it was completely dependent on the results of the deployment of the air forces. Naval forces were not de-ployed without air superiority and any invasion was routinely accom-panied by intensive air actions to achieve local air superiority. So, preventing the attainment of enemy air superiority meant fending off an invasion. Where Peirse held the opinion that the numbers of allied fighters and bombers had dropped below a critical point to attain this objective, Van Oyen was convinced that by employing all available resources, the allies might just pull it off and force the Japanese to postpone their planned invasion.[12]

The JAC commander continued the air campaigns in the west and east. As ML commander, he had been closely involved in the planning of the western campaign. The only change he made was the way in which fighters were deployed. For the time being, he assigned only air defence tasks to the few allied fighters he had. This involved the protection of the major air fields in Java, the principal ports and where possible the allied fleet.

He agreed with Peirse that western Java and southern Sumatra would be the main theatres and that there lay the best chances of doing damage to the Japanese. The battle to attain air superiority over western Java had only just begun, but in central and eastern Java the Japanese had already partly reached their objective. If the battle in the west could be turned around, the Japanese would certainly cancel their planned invasion, in spite of their successes in the east, Van Oyen was convinced. The resources at JAC's disposal were small, however, and on 22 February they comprised some 35 operationally serviceable fighters and 25 operationally serviceable bombers, apart from the anti-aircraft artillery.[13]

The overall defence plan for an invasion

From 22 February onwards, by order of Ter Poorten, the General Staff of the KNIL had begun to develop the defence plans for Java, which had in fact been given up by the allies. Apart from what was on its way, they could not count on any further allied reinforcements. The promised Australian army corps, had been given a different destination, except for the units that had already arrived in Java. Two locations, in particular, were suitable for the defence against the expected Japanese superiority. These were Soerabaja naval base and 'Bandoeng Army base', that is, the Bandoeng or Preanger plateau with its great concentration of military installations. Next to KNIL barracks, warehouses and workshops (amongst which the Artillerie Constructie Werkplaats–Artillery Ordnance Workshop, ACW, a large ammunition factory on the edge of Bandoeng) the plateau was also the location of the large ML Andir air base, with its warehouses of the Warehouse Service and Technical Service workshops. The Technical Service at Andir in fact constituted a large technical depot (called "the factory") for second and third echelon maintenance and repairs of military aircraft and it was the largest in the entirety of south-east Asia.[14]

For military (defence of the naval base) as well as political (support for the retention of Dutch authority in eastern Java) reasons the choice was made for a partial (though relatively heavy) concentration of military resources in western Java. The 6th Infantry Regiment (6-R.I.) was to remain in eastern Java for the defence of the naval base. Central Java, however, was to be abandoned as much as possible by ground forces for the defence of western Java. It was here that, correctly, the main effort of the battle was expected, also because all the main military and civilian headquarters were concentrated at Bandoeng. The defence was not only to be limited to the Bandoeng plateau which could be defended well, but was to encompass the entirety of western Java, and also the port of Tjilatjap on the south coast. The defence was founded on as much an all out offensive effort of KNIL and allied forces as could be mustered against the Japanese landing operations.[15]

West Group and Bandoeng Group

The KNIL area of command of western Java was split up. In the westernmost part of western Java (with a 75-kilometre line east of Batavia and Buitenzorg as the easternmost boundary) a West Group, under command of Major-General W. Schilling, was formed on 22 February 1942. Apart from the 1st Infantry Regiment (1-R.I.) and some KNIL artillery and cavalry units Schilling commanded the so-called *Blackforce*. This brigade consisted of two Australian infantry battalions, one Australian infantry battalion (minus), a British squadron of light tanks and two American field artillery batteries. The formation of the *Blackforce* brigade had only begun on 24 February, but it was operational on 1 March. In the West Group area of command the strategic reserve of the allied land forces, consisting of the 2nd Infantry Regiment (2-R.I.) and the Ist Afdeling Bergartillerie–Ist Mountain Artillery Battalion (A.I Bg.) of the KNIL, was positioned. Including this reserve, West Group totalled some 21,200 combat-ready mobile troops.[16]

In the eastern part of western Java the 'Bandoeng Group' was formed for the defence of the Bandoeng plateau and the area adjacent to it. On 26 February Major-General J.J. Pesman assumed command of several units already present on the plateau itself, at Cheribon and Kadipaten, as well as the 4th Infantry Regiment (4-R.I.) and IInd Mountain Artillery Battalion (A. II Bg.) from central Java. The Bandoeng Group comprised some 5,900 combat-ready mobile troops. In his command area was also located the so-called *Mobile Unit*, part of the general army reserve and consisting of 24 light tanks and an infantry company in light armoured vehicles.[17]

The discovery of the first Japanese invasion fleet

In the late morning of 25 February Van Oyen concluded that the race against time had been lost. *RecGroup* discovered a Japanese invasion fleet in the roadstead of Balikpapan bound, no doubt, for eastern Java. Although there was no trace of a similar operation in the west, it was clear from intelligence channels that such a fleet was assembled. In spite of some JAC successes, the Japanese had not (or hardly) postponed their planned invasion and the expected American P-40s and British Hurricane fighters would not arrive in time to fend off the invasion in the eleventh hour. The allied *Counter-air* operation had bought Java two more days. The Japanese commanders had adjusted their plans on 23 February and postponed the invasion with two days to the early hours of 28 February.[18]

In consultation with Van Oyen and Vice-Admiral Helfrich, Lieutenant-General Ter Poorten decided on the following course of action:

–   The allied fleet is to assemble immediately at Soerabaja in order to attack the reported invasion fleet; to this end as many ships as possible need to be relocated from Tandjong Priok to Soerabaja.
–   The allied air force is to relocate as many fighters as possible to Ngoro (eastern Java) in order to give maximum protection to the *Combined Striking Force*.
–   After carrying out an attack the naval squadron is to relocate to western Java to engage the Japanese invasion fleet (there was certainty that there was such a fleet, even though it had not been discovered yet) bound for western Java. The fighters that have been directed to Ngoro are to relocate to western Java for support.[19]

In spite of this, the JAC *Counter-Air* offensive continued. The JAC fighters in western Java, however, were partly committed to the protection of allied war ships in the east, together with the American fighters that were already present there. The bombing offensive against Japanese objectives in southern Sumatra slowly petered out as more and more bombers were committed in the search for the 'western' invasion fleet from 26 February onwards.[20]

After several previous fruitless search operations, the allied naval squadron put to sea in the afternoon of 27 February 1942. JAC aircraft had re-discovered the approaching 'eastern' invasion fleet and the *Combined Striking Force* prepared to attack the Japanese transport fleet. It was impossible, however, to come close enough and instead Rear-Admiral Doorman was engaged by the covering squadrons. Although JAC managed to maintain local air superiority over the allied squadron in the afternoon, forcing the adversary to do without artillery observation from reconnaissance float planes, the naval battle, which had been not altogether unsuccessful during the afternoon, continued into the evening and night of 27 February when the *Combined Striking Force* was defeated with great loss of life.[21]

The final battles

The naval battle and the discovery of a number of allied war ships in the west by a Japanese reconnaissance float plane led to a day's postponement of the invasion of Java. In the night of 28 February on 1 March the Japanese troops landed in eastern Java near Kragan and in three different locations in western Java, one of which was Eretan Wetan. Near this small town north-east of Bandoeng the so-called Shoji detachment (a regiment-sized battle group, commanded by Colonel Shoji) landed unexpectedly, an extremely dangerous development, as not far from this landing site in the plane north of the Bandoeng plateau the major Kalidjati air base was located.

The battle of the Java Sea had been lost and it was now up to the land forces, with the help of the air forces, to foil the Japanese landings. The most important attempt at doing so was the so-called battle of Kalidjati (28 February–3 March 1942), a series of clashes, involving land and air forces for the possession of the strategically important Kalidjati air base. That battle was lost. It was the beginning of the end.[22] The KNIL and allied land forces fell back on the Bandoeng plateau, exactly according to the general strategy. During this retreat the Japanese Shoji regimental battle group tried to force access to the plateau through the Tjiater pass, but met with fierce resistance of the KNIL. The so-called battle of the Tjiater pass (5–7 March 1942), however, was also lost, which made capitulation unavoidable.[23]

Although the Japanese forces were made to suffer truly serious losses during the period from 18 February 1942 onwards, the Japanese commanders at different levels consciously took several heavy risks that turned out well for them and which put the allies under great time pressure each time. This was, in fact, also the case at the strategic level as there was no strategic reserve of ground forces that could be transported quickly to West Java in case anything went wrong after the landings of 28 February–1 March 1942. As it was, the KNIL and the allied forces capitulated on 8 March 1942, effective the following day.

PART 1

⸙⸙

The Battle for Air Superiority over western Java from 18 February 1942 up to and including 27 February 1942

The Counter-air operation of the KNIL Army Aviation Corps, the Royal Air Force, the Royal Australian Air Force and the anti-aircraft artillery of the KNIL and the British Army for the retention of western Java

PART 1A:
A DESCRIPTION AND ANALYSIS OF THE DEPLOYMENT OF FIGHTERS AND ANTI-AIRCRAFT ARTILLERY

※※

CHAPTER 1A.1
The Air Defence Plans and the Balance of Strength on 18 February 1942

Introduction

On 18 February 1942 the offensive component of the allied *Counter-air* operation commenced with bomber missions directed at objectives at Palembang. At the same time, the defensive component of the operation became fully operational. It involved allied fighters and anti-aircraft artillery units in western Java, which, for their operational control, were organised in the Batavia and Bandoeng Air Defence Commands. This had necessitated quite a few urgent actions and temporary measures as developments were several weeks ahead of the existing planning, laid down in ABDAIR's air defence plan (see below). The various logistic services of the KNIL and the ML did a fantastic job, together with the completely over-burdened logistics headquarters of the RAF/RAAF *West Group* at Soekaboemi (the British Army had not yet established a logistic organisation in Java), supporting the somewhat disoriented and shattered British and Australians who had been evacuated from Singapore and southern Sumatra.

On 18 February *RAF Station Tjililitan*, with two Hurricane squadrons and the reorganised Batavia Air Defence Command, now

Air Defence Sector Control Batavia, were the last to become operational. The air defence of western Java had only two tasks in the context of the allied *Counter-air* operation: eliminating as many Japanese combat aircraft as could be managed and protecting its own airfields and along with that the capacity for the offensive part of the operation. The air defence of western Java was *combined* (NEI, British) and *joint* (the ML and RAF, as well as the KNIL and British Army anti-aircraft artillery).

ABDAIR's air defence plan

Shortly before the Japanese attack on southern Sumatra, on 12 February 1942, the allied air force headquarters issued a new force planning for the short term and force requirements to bring the air defence of Java up to the mark. It was the intention (with regard to western Java) to station 32 fighters each at Pondok Tjabe, Tjisaoek, Bandoeng (Andir-Kalidjati) and Tasikmalaja, with a minimum requirement of 16 fighters,

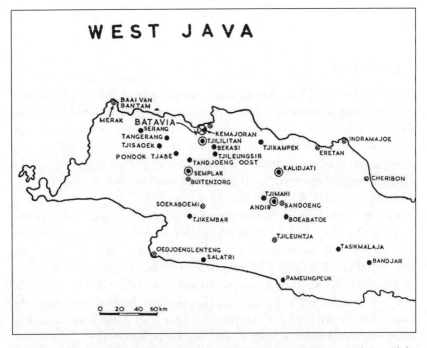

Western Java with the military main airfields (Andir, Tjililitan and Semplak) and civilian airfields and military landing sites (black dots)

8 of which were to be available at immediate notice on a daily basis, at each of the 4 locations. Pondok Tjabe and Tjisaoek were so-called shelter airfields carefully integrated with the surrounding foliage and hardly recognisable as airfields from the air. Andir, Kalidjati and Tasikmalaja were 'main fields', large bases, which nowadays would be called *main operation bases*. Only the latter two bases had wooded dispersal areas. At Andir there was a large concentration of workshops and warehouses of the Technical Service and Warehouse Service of the ML.

Pondok Tjabe was to get two RAF Hawker Hurricane squadrons by mid-March, which were on their way on board the British aircraft carrier *Indomitable*. Tjisaoek was to be turned over to the USAAF in early March with two USAAF Curtiss P-40 Warhawks fighter squadrons, and by the same time the ML was to station two fighter afdelingen (squadrons) at Tasikmalaja, a large base still under construction. Furthermore, British radar and direction finding installations (the latter for taking bearings of friendly fighters with the help of radio communication) were on their way to Java by sea to be integrated into the existing reporting and warning system of the Air Defence Commands at Batavia and Bandoeng.[1]

A Brewster B 339C fighter of the ML afdeling 2-Vl.G.V, photographed at Semplak near Buitenzorg in 1941. (Private collection, P.C. Boer)

This planning was adjusted because of the evacuation of southern Sumatra. The Hurricanes evacuated from Palembang, together with the RAF Hurricanes already available in Java prior to the evacuation (25 in total, most of which, however, were not operationally serviceable as yet), were now to be stationed at Pondok Tjabe. For the time being the ML was to retain afdeling 2-Vl.G.V (10 Brewster B 339C and D fighters) at Tjisaoek, which meant that for the defence of the Batavia-Buitenzorg area there were available at least 16 fighters. Furthermore, with the help of the RAF, which had also evacuated several Brewster B 339E fighters to western Java, the strength of 2-Vl.G.V. was to be increased to 16 fighters.[2] The ML afdelingen were all grouped under administrative corps, called Vliegtuiggroep–Aircraft Group (Vl.G.). These corps belonged to air bases; thus, the Ve Vliegtuiggroep (Vth Vliegtuiggroep, Vl.G.V) was stationed at Semplak in western Java. The designation 2-Vl.G.V indicated the 2nd Afdeling of the Vth Vliegtuiggroep. The statutory strength of an afdeling of fighters was 18 aircraft, lowered to 16 aircraft around 14 February 1942.

Initially, only the ML at Bandoeng met the new strength requirements of ABDAIR. At Andir, the Boeabatoe road (a 900-metre stretch of new road in the southern edge of the town of Bandoeng) and at Kalidjati 32 fighters were stationed: 14 'Brewsters' plus two Curtiss H-75A Hawks of 1-Vl.G.V, five Curtiss-Wright CW-21B Interceptors of 2-Vl.G.IV (plus an unmanned maintenance reserve) and 11 Hawker Hurricanes Mark IIB of 2-Vl.G.IV. For the time being, however, the Hurricanes were not fully operational yet as their radios could not be used and the crews were still in the middle of a type transition. There were also limitations with regard to the deployment of the Interceptors, while the Hawks were not suitable for air defence tasks at all. Experiences in eastern Java had shown that the Interceptors could absorb only relatively little battle damage and were quick to sustain structural damage when hit by 20-mm shells. Because of this the Air Defence Commands of the KNIL had been ordered to employ these fighters, if possible, exclusively for the interception of enemy bombers.[3]

The RAF built up its squadrons at Tjililitan, as Pondok Tjabe proved to be soggy. Tjisaoek was expanded for the USAAF, getting an extra dispersal area, amongst others, and a store of 100-octane fuel for the expected 32 P-40 fighters.[4] The British radar installations, two so-called *Transportable Radar Units*, originally intended for the RAF in Malaya, arrived in Batavia in the first half of February 1942. At the same time a further three British Army gun laying radars arrived, which brought the number of installations that could be set up on the north and west coasts of western Java up to five.[5] Shrouded in great secrecy, the stations were made operational, which was a major technical feat and for which only limited numbers of specialists were available. Not until 25–26 February 1942 were the first two stations, Batavia East and Batavia West, become operational.[6]

On 22 February 1942 a convoy departed from Fremantle in Australia consisting of, amongst others, the American tender *Langley* (a former aircraft carrier used as mother ship for flying boats) and the freighter *Sea Witch*, with on board the two USAAF squadrons destined for Tjisaoek, with 32 Curtiss P-40E fighters mounted on deck, and 27 P-40Es in crates, respectively.[7] The latter had been intended by ABDAIR mainly to re-equip 1-Vl.G.IV (destined for Tasikmalaja) and 605 Squadron RAF at Tjililitan (temporarily equipped with six Hurricanes).[8] *Langley* and *Sea Witch* were due in Tjilatjap on the Java south coast on 27 and 28 February respectively. The ABDAIR air defence plan, which was sound and adequate in itself had by now, however, been overtaken by events.

On 19 February 1942 Japanese troops occupied Bali, directly east of Java, and a day later they attacked Timor. The shipping lane from Australia to Java became vulnerable as a result of this with Japanese bombers and fighters from Bali being able to attack convoys and provide cover to Japanese warships during operations south of Java against the convoy routes. Furthermore, the air route for single-engine aircraft from northern Australia to eastern Java was cut off. This made it impossible for the USAAF to ferry fighters (and dive-bombers) from Australia to eastern Java any longer. Flying across bombers was still possible (from the USA via India, as well as from Australia) and small numbers of American four-engine bombers already on their way arrived in Java in the week after the occupation of Bali. A substantial reinforcement of allied bombers, however, could only begin in the course of March 1942.[9] At ABDAIR, and subsequently *Java Air Command*, which took over ABDAIR's tasks as of 23 February, it was assumed that *Langley* and *Sea Witch* with the American P-40s would make it safely to Java, and that the 48 British Hurricanes on their way on board the aircraft carrier *Indomitable* could still be 'flown off'. This would mean an important reinforcement of the air defence as of early March 1942.

The reorganisation of the RAF at Batavia

Some of the British fighter squadrons evacuated from southern Sumatra and Singapore were concentrated at Tjililitan in February 1942, where between 14 and 19 February 488 Squadron (a number of pilots and the almost complete '*ground party*') arrived, along with a number of pilots from 232 Squadron, coming from Singapore, with 19 new Hurricanes Mark IIBs. Twelve of these fighters, which had arrived by ship earlier in February, were, however, handed over to the ML on 15 February by order of ABDAIR. The new fighters were assembled by an assembly team of the Technical Service of the ML and the Koninklijke Nederlands-Indische Luchtvaart Maatschappij–Royal Netherlands Indies Airline (KNILM) at Batavia and subsequently made combat-ready by RAF personnel at the civilian airfield of Kemajoran.[10]

From 17 February 1942 onwards 14 out of 17 Hurricane IIBs evacuated from Palembang (southern Sumatra) arrived at Tjililitan, mostly from Kemajoran. For the time being, the pilots of the flying echelons of 232 and 258 Squadrons from Palembang were accommodated in hotels and civilian homes in Batavia. The ground crews of these provisional Hurricane squadrons evacuated from Palembang (largely composed of men from 232, 242 and 605 Squadrons) were accommodated in requisitioned encampments or a transit camp in the neighbourhood. 258 Squadron's own ground echelon arrived at Oosthaven just before the Japanese attack on Palembang, only to re-embark straight away with the personnel of other squadrons.[11]

In total the RAF at Batavia had eight new Hurricanes, one of which was under repair at Kemajaron, in addition to the 17 evacuated from or via Palembang. Of the latter, three were in such disrepair that they, at least the engines and some components, were sent by rail to 153 Maintenance Unit (153MU) at Djocjakarta. By the end of February 1942 these planes gradually became available again for service in the squadrons at Tjililitan.

Initially, only the seven serviceable Hurricanes of the new batch at Tjililitan were deployed. On 16 February 488 Squadron had five operationally serviceable fighters there and the next day the unit flew its first operational sorties in western Java. A section of four fighters plus a Hurricane that happened to be on a test flight from Tjililitan tried in vain to intercept a high-flying Japanese Ki-46 strategic reconnaissance plane.[12] On 18 February *A Flight* of 488 Squadron was put on (official) *Readiness* for the first time with six out of the total of seven Hurricanes assigned to it.[13]

On 27 February 1942 the small freighter *Kota Gede* evacuated approximately 2,500 allied troops, mainly coming from disbanded RAF squadrons, to Ceylon. (Private collection, P.C. Boer)

On 17 February 1942 the RAF formed a second Hurricane squadron at Tjililitan, designated 232 Squadron for the first few days and 242 Squadron as of 22 February. It was composed of the evacuated pilots of 232 Squadron and the 'ground party' of 242 Squadron that had arrived several weeks earlier in Java and that had been deployed at Palembang I (the former civilian airfield of Palembang) as of 9 February. This latter squadron had arrived in Java without pilots. Together with a number of wounded pilots of its squadron, the 232 Squadron ground crew were designated for evacuation to Ceylon a few days later. They left Tjililitan on 27 February on board *Kota Gede*, together with 258 Squadron (less a number of pilots) which had been disbanded on 17 February at Batavia. Although 232 Squadron had 12 Hurricanes on 17 February and 19 pilots assigned to it, the unit was initially operational only to a limited extent.[14]

On 16 and 17 February also two *Troops* of 242 *Battery* of 48 *Light Anti-Aircraft Regiment* (48 LAA) of the British Army became operational at Tjililitan, with eight 4-cm Bofor anti-aircraft guns in total. Besides, a section of the 1st Battalion Anti-Aircraft Artillery of the KNIL remained stationed at Tjililitan with two 2-cm guns. 48 LAA Battery also had at least ten Brenguns for low-altitude air defence. Furthermore, a detachment of 242 Battery was stationed at Tandjong Priok, to defend the naval air station there. This detachment had two 4-cm guns and several Brenguns.[15]

It took the RAF several days to become fully operational again at Tjililitan. The KNIL and ML, however, immediately lent a helping hand. Evacuated RAF personnel were accommodated and if necessary given new clothing and footwear, the supply of 100-octane aircraft fuel was expanded (the ML fighters used 91-octane fuel), oxygen for use in the Hurricanes was shipped in, the ML supplied parachutes, hydraulic oil, etc. As of 19 February 1942, 232 Squadron began to do *Readiness* shifts with eight "available" aircraft, and the unit was considered fully operational. On that day 19 pilots were in strength.[16]

488 Squadron was deactivated at the end of the day on 21 February 1942. The squadron personnel present in Java were designated for evacuation and left Batavia two days later on board *Deucalion*. Only a number of pilots remained behind. Two pilots of 232 Squadron (as CO and deputy CO), six pilots of 258 Squadron, six pilots of 488 Squadron and several non-assigned replacement pilots, together with the 605 Squadron ground echelon coming from Palembang, went on to form the new 605 Squadron on 21 February. Just like 242 Squadron, 605 Squadron had arrived in Java without any pilots and had been deployed at Palembang I as of 9 February.

For a start the new 605 Squadron got the six still serviceable Hurricanes from 488 Squadron and it became operational (with five deployable fighters) on 21 February 1942 at the end of the day.[17] At that moment 232 Squadron had 12 operationally serviceable Hurricanes and a further three aircraft in repair or scheduled maintenance at 81 *Repair and Salvage Unit* (81 RSU) at Tjililitan. With 21 Hurricanes, 17–18 of which were serviceable, assigned to the two squadrons the RAF at Tjililitan was at peak strength. According to a temporary table of equipment of *West Group* each squadron had a statutory strength of 16 first line fighters.[18]

The RAF built up its own support organisation for its fighter squadrons in Java. At Buitenzorg an *Air Stores Park* warehouse was set up for unit supply and the above-mentioned 81 RSU was sent to Tjililitan. This was a second-echelon maintenance unit for scheduled maintenance and minor repairs, which had been in the process of moving to southern Sumatra in mid-February, only to re-embark immediately due to the Japanese attack on Palembang. For major maintenance (overhauls and major repairs) of RAF engines a Maintenance Unit had already been established in central Java in January 1942 — the above-mentioned 153 MU at Djocjakarta.[19]

The Air Defence Commands

The Air Defence Command Batavia of the KNIL consisted of a central command post at Batavia, which commanded the anti-aircraft artillery at Tjililitan and Batavia (for their operational deployment) and had operational control of the fighters at Tjililitan and Tjisaoek (insofar as they had been assigned for air defence). It was here that the information was gathered from visual observations of two rings of aerial observation posts at different distances from the cities of Batavia and Buitenzorg, several posts on the northern and southern coasts of western Java and a post in one of the Duizend Eilanden, north of Batavia. The air defence commander Major R.S. Soeria Santoso, CO of the 1st Battalion Anti-Aircraft Artillery (A. I Ld.) of the KNIL and his permanent personnel belonged to the KNIL anti-aircraft artillery, but the aerial observation posts, organised in sectors, and the command posts of the 'rings' were almost exclusively manned by volunteers of the so-called Luchtbeschermingsdienst–Air Surveillance Service (LBD). This air surveillance, too, came under the command of Air Defence Command Batavia.

The Air Defence Command Batavia was passed on to the RAF on 18 February as (*Air Defence*) *Sector Control Batavia*. The British established a new command post after the British model, and it was staffed entirely by RAF and some British Army personnel, with the exception of one ML liaison officer. For the Plotting Room a number of local young ladies from a volunteer corps of the KNIL were recruited. In command was Air Commodore S.F. Vincent (former CO of 226 (*Fighter*) Group, disbanded on 18 February), who had direct operational control of the RAF squadrons at Tjililitan with regard to air defence tasks.

Major Soeria Santoso came under operational command of Vincent and remained CO of the aerial surveillance organisation and air defence of the KNIL, which comprised the main body of A. I Ld. at Tandjong Priok, in permanent positions, with four 8-cm guns, two 4-cm guns, four 2-cm guns and eighteen 12.7-mm machine guns, and the section mentioned above at Tjililitan and a section of three 12.7-mm

machine guns at Kemajoran. In addition, there were two British anti-
aircraft Batteries, 242 Battery of 48 Light Anti-Aircraft Regiment and
239 Battery of 77 Heavy Anti-Aircraft Regiment. The commanders
of 242 Battery (at Tjililitan, with a detachment at Tandjong Priok, as
mentioned above) and of 239 Battery at Tandjong Priok (eight 9-mm
guns) also came under operational command of Vincent. The ML
Commandant Luchtstrijdkrachten–regional Air Officer Commanding
(CL) for the sector Batavia-Buitenzorg, Kap C. Terluin, was formally
under command of the ML. His main task, however, was coordinating
the operational activities with those of the RAF at Tjililitan.[20]

The Air Defence Command Bandoeng had been organised along
the lines of the original Tjililitan command, with rings of aerial surveillance posts around Bandoeng and Soebang and on the north and
south coasts, and it controlled the fighter units at Andir, Boeabatoe
road and Kalidjati insofar as they had been assigned to air defence tasks.
The anti-aircraft artillery under this command comprised the IIIrd
Battalion Anti-Aircraft Artillery (A. III Ld.) of the KNIL. This battalion
consisted of three companies (minus), in permanent positions, viz. the

A 4-cm air defence gun (Bofors) of the KNIL. These guns had a high rate
of fire and could also be used as anti-tank guns. The Light Anti-Aircraft
Batteries of the British Army in Java were equipped with the same type of
gun. (Private collection, P.C. Boer)

Andir North position (two 2-cm, four 4-cm and four 8-cm guns, plus three 12.7-mm machine guns), the Andir South position (four 2-cm, two 4-cm and four 8-cm guns, plus nine 12.7-mm machine guns) and the Artillerie Constructie Werkplaats–Artillery Ordnance Workshop (ACW) position at Bandoeng (two 2-cm, two 4-cm and four 8-cm guns, plus three 12.7-mm machine guns). In addition, there were two 4-cm guns and six 12.7-mm machine guns located at Kalidjati.

The reorganisation of the ML fighter afdelingen

On 16 February 1942 the ML had completed the reorganisation of its fighter afdelingen. What was left of 1-Vl.G.IV and 2-Vl.G.IV after the heavy air battles of Soerabaja and Madioen (eastern and central Java) that had taken place shortly before, had been pulled back on Andir in western Java. The air defence in eastern Java had been passed on to the American 17 *Pursuit* Squadron. On 15 February 1942 2-Vl.G.IV took over 12 Hurricane IIBs from the RAF at Tjililitan and flew them to Kalidjati the next morning. The ground crew of the afdeling, with the exception of the chief mechanic, went directly from Andir to Kalidjati, where the afdeling was to become operational with the new equipment and with the help of a RAF detachment.[21] This unit was destined for Tasikmalaja.

A patrol (= section) of 2-Vl.G.IV was stationed at the shelter air-field Boeabatoeweg–Boeabatoe road with six Curtiss-Wright CW-21B Interceptors (including one unmanned maintenance reserve). Operations were largely conducted from Andir, as there were no maintenance facilities and aircraft ammunition stores at Boeabatoeweg.[22] 1-Vl.G.IV was disbanded on 16 February and was temporarily removed from the order of battle, only to lead a purely administrative existence from then on. Two of the five Curtiss H-75A Hawks from 1-Vl.G.IV were transferred to 1-Vl.G.V, one other made a belly landing during a test flight at Andir. The other two Hawks went to the ML Technical Service (TD) and were flown back to Madioen to be held as a reserve.[23]

When the Japanese air offensive started on 19 February 2-Vl.G.IV at Kalidjati had ten Hurricanes, two planes having crashed during training flights. Furthermore, there were 1-Vl.G.V, stationed at Andir, with 14 Brewster B 339C and D fighters plus the two Curtiss H-75A Hawks, and 2-Vl.G.V at Tjisaoek, with ten B 339C and Ds.[24] In total the ML had 42 assigned fighters at its disposal. In reality, however, the two Hawks had been declared unfit for air defence duties and one of the CW-21s was an unmanned maintenance reserve, which brought the actual strength down to 39 aircraft. Of these, furthermore, the ten Hurricanes were not yet operational. Not until 22 February 1942 did 2-Vl.G.IV at Kalidjati become partially operational.

The Japanese build-up at Palembang and Muntok

On 15 February 1942 the 3rd *Hiko Shudan* (3rd Air Division) of the Japanese Army air force began the transfer of units to the conquered Palembang I, the former civilian airfield of Palembang. Late in the afternoon of that day eight Ki-27 fighters of 11th *Sentai* (11th Combat Unit) of the 12th *Hiko Dan* (12th Air Brigade) arrived for local air defence. After refuelling with taken aircraft fuel this 2nd *Chutai* of the 11th *Sentai* became operational on 16 February. It should be noted that the terms Air Division and Air Brigade are only rough translations of the Japanese unit designations.[25]

The Japanese combat units or Sentais consisted of a Staff-Chutai with several aircraft and three or four Chutais with (statutory) seven to nine aircraft each, a structure roughly comparable to that of the ML Vliegtuiggroep and the USAAF Group. From 16 February onwards the supply of Palembang I got going and on 17 February a large number of planes could be flown in from Malaya. Apart from the staff of the 3rd Hiko Dan, that afternoon saw the arrival of 20 Ki-27 fighters of the 11th Sentai, seven Ki-51 assault aircraft of the 27th Sentai (a Chutai), and one Ki-46 reconnaissance plane of the 50th Chutai of the 15th *Dokuritso Hikotai* (15th independent air force unit).[26] Late the next morning some 20 Ki-43 fighters of the 64th Sentai, eight Ki-27 fighters of the 11th Sentai, eight Ki-27s of the 3rd Chutai of the 1st Sentai and nine Ki-51s of the 27th Sentai (a second Chutai plus a few Staff Chutai planes) landed. In the afternoon of 18 February there followed about 20 Ki-43 fighters of the 59th Sentai, the first seven or so Ki-48 bombers of the 90th Sentai and some reconnaissance planes of the 50th Chutai. Except for the Ki-27s of the 1st and 11th Sentais, coming under the 12th Hiko Dan, whose staff also arrived at Palembang on 18 February, all transferred planes belonged to the air groups of the 3rd Hiko Dan.[27]

On 18 February 1942 the reconnaissance activity over western Java was started from Palembang I. The next day the battle for air superiority over western Java commenced as a preparation for landings in that area. However, only limited bomber operations were possible for the first few days, partly due to problems with the supply of bombs and fuel. Besides, the capacity of Palembang I was insufficient to accommodate still more planes than were already stationed there. Thus, the dispersal facilities for planes had to be expanded first. It was for this reason that the arrival of the 90th Sentai, with 27 Ki-48s in total, was spread out over a number of days and that the 75th Sentai was kept in Malacca for the time being. Not until 23 February did the latter Sentai arrive at Palembang I with 27 Ki-48s (other bombers of the 3rd Hiko Dan remained in Malacca). Around the same day the 81st Sentai, which came directly under the 3rd Hiko Shudan, was transferred to this airfield with a number of Ki-15 and Ki-46 reconnaissance planes. The headquarters of the air division arrived at Palembang I on 21 February 1942.[28]

As stated above, on 17 and 18 February most of the fighters of the 3rd and 12th Hiko Dans of the Army air force arrived at Palembang I. Of the 3rd Hiko Dan a total of 42 Nakajima Ki-43 Army 1 'long-distance' fighters of the 59th and 64th Sentais. Three Ki-43s had been added to these fighter groups shortly before this transfer to make up for losses sustained earlier. The Nakajima Ki-27 Army 97 fighters of the 1st and 11th Sentais of the 12th Hiko Dan had only a limited range, approximately 850 kilometres, and were therefore less suitable for operations over western Java.[29] These fighters were therefore brought forward as much as possible and stationed mostly at Tandjoengkarang in the southernmost tip of southern Sumatra.

In the late afternoon of 24 February a part of the 11th Sentai, some 20 Ki-27s, left for Tandjoengkarang. As of 25 February this Sentai flew combat air patrols in order to fend off enemy attacks on southern Sumatra. Tandjoengkarang was a military airfield still under construction, which had accidentally been discovered by the Japanese army advancing south. The remainder of the 11th Sentai and the Chutai of the 1st Sentai remained at Palembang I with together about 20 Ki-27 fighters (several had been lost in the meantime in allied attacks) and was tasked to protect Palembang I, the ships in the River Moesi and the oil installations near Palembang. In the last few days of February 1942 planned operations over western Java from Tandjoengkarang were cancelled due to the bad condition of the airfield as a result of heavy rainfall and insufficient drainage.[30]

The Japanese Navy air force was to give fighter support in the operations for the attainment of air superiority over western Java with the *Yamada Kokutai* (Yamada air group). Initially operating from Kuching in British Borneo, this group arrived at Muntok (the island of Banka) on 23 February with 15 Mitsubishi A6M Navy O fighters and three Mitsubishi C5M reconnaissance planes. With this addition the total fighter strength suitable for missions over western Java had been brought up to 57, a number not much higher than the total of 50 fighters (suitable for air defence tasks) of the ML and RAF in western Java. The Yamada air group, however, flew only one mission to western Java.[31]

Allied Prospects

By 18 February 1942 the air defence of western Java had been prepared as well as possible for the coming battle for air superiority over western Java. The available resources were few: 50 fighters suitable for air defence; the main body of A. I Ld., a Battery of 77 HAA and a detachment of 48 LAA at Batavia and Tandjong Priok, a Battery of 48 LAA and a section of A. I Ld. at Tjililitan, a section of 12.7-mm machine guns at Kemajoran and at Bandoeng (for the protection of the Artillery Ordnance Workshop) and Andir airfield three companies (minus) of A. III Ld. A detachment of A. III Ld. was at Kalidjati.[32] New British and American fighter planes were on their way, however, and although there were no extra anti-aircraft units available, there were still two Batteries of 48 LAA, returned from southern Sumatra, which were to be stationed at Andir and Kalidjati airfield. The arrival of the fighters would be in the nick of time. It would be sink or swim.

* * *

CHAPTER 1A.2

The Fighter Operations on 19 February 1942

Introduction

On 19 February 1942 the units of the 3rd Hiko Dan attacked airfields in western Java for the first time. Their targets were Andir and Semplak. At Tjililitan as well as Tjisaoek and Andir fighters were on *Readiness* to meet the attackers. Already on 17 and 18 February there had been quite some Japanese activity over western Java, especially by Ki-46 reconnaissance planes. These fast two-engine strategic reconnaissance planes initially flew at an altitude of about 9,000 metres, while the ceiling for the ML Brewster fighters (in ideal circumstances) was 8,500 metres. The Ki-46s flew at an altitude the Hurricanes and Interceptors could reach, but they were so fast that also the RAF and 2-Vl.G.IV failed to intercept them.[1]

On 18 February 2-Vl.G.V twice sent a patrol of four Brewsters to Batavia to support the RAF. The first time it was tried to intercept a Ki-46 together with four Hurricanes of 488 Squadron, the second time there were two Ki-15 reconnaissance planes. In both cases the effort of the eight fighters was in vain. From Andir eight 1-Vl.G.V Brewsters in cooperation with two Hurricanes from 242 Squadron, tried to intercept a Ki-46 flying at an altitude of about 6,000 metres, the normal operational ceiling for the Brewster. The Japanese pilot pulled a joke on them, decreasing his speed so much that the allied pilots had to slow down and then giving full throttle. The Ki-46 proved to be so much faster at 6,000 metres that it could not be overtaken and not a single shot was fired.[2]

The numbers of assigned and operationally serviceable fighters at the beginning of the day on 19 February were as follows:[3]

Table 1

Unit	Assigned	Operationally serviceable	Type of fighter
232 Squadron	12	12	Hurricane
488 Squadron	7	7	Hurricane
2-Vl.G.V	10	9	Brewster
2-Vl.G.IV	6	5	Interceptor
1-Vl. G.V	14 (+2)	10 (+2)	Brewster (+2 Hawk)
2-Vl.G.IV	11	0	Hurricane
Total	60 (+2)	43 (+2)	

The attack on Semplak

On the morning of 19 February the first Japanese air raid took place on Semplak airfield. At around 08:00 hrs the Air Surveillance Service warned that Japanese fighters and bomber formations were flying past the Duizend Eilanden towards Batavia, upon which *Sector Control Batavia* scrambled the *Readiness Flight* at Tjililitan. The eight pilots of 488 Squadron and 232 Squadron subsequently patrolled a line north-west of Batavia, fully realising that the Japanese aircraft might be missed completely because of extensive cloud formation, which was exactly what happened. Then, small numbers of enemy aircraft were reported in the east and north (Tandjong Priok), upon which at 08:30 hrs a further four Hurricanes of 232 Squadron were scrambled. They had barely taken off when four Nakajima Ki-43 fighters flew over Tjililitan at low altitude, but, not finding any targets, they left after just one pass.[4] Now 2-Vl. G.V, which had been kept in reserve, was alerted and directed towards Batavia. Due to the heavy clouds that morning the Japanese formations remained unnoticed for a long time.

While the RAF Hurricanes were flying over Batavia and Tandjong Priok and 2-Vl.G.V was taking off with nine fighters from Tjisaoek to support the British, five Ki-48 bombers of the 90th Sentai, together with 19 Ki-43 fighters of the 59th and 64th Sentais for top cover, under the general command of 64th Sentai commander Major Takeo Kato, attacked Semplak at 08:40 hrs.[5] On their climb out towards Batavia 2-Vl.G.V encountered the Japanese fighters on their way back from the raid. After their take-off the ML pilots had seen the black pillars of smoke rising up from Semplak in the distance. When the nine Brewsters were at an altitude of about 2,000 metres, the pilots spotted the Japanese bombers with the fighters above them north-west of Buitenzorg, flying at an altitude of between 2,500 and 3,000 metres. About 15 Ki-43s (taken for Mitsubishi Navy Os by the ML pilots) dived for the ML planes, but then remained flying some 500 metres above the Brewsters for several minutes. The ML formation consisted of three patrols, composed of the following pilots:[6]

Patrol Deibel: Elt A.G. Deibel, Vdg J.F. Scheffer and Sgt G.M. Bruggink

Patrol Hoyer: Tlt P.A. Hoyer, Vdg F. Pelder, Vdg P.R. Jolly and Sgt P.C. 't Hart

Patrol Kuijper: Vdg J. Kuijper and Sgt N.G. Groot

On command of Lieutenant Deibel the patrols immediately broke off their climb to gather speed. When, at about 08:50 hrs, the Brewsters turned away a bit in order to get a better position, the Ki-43s attacked. In spite of their unfavourable starting position and the

Japanese superiority in numbers the pilots of the Brewsters engaged in combat. The battle lasted for about 15 minutes, during which four Brewsters were shot down. The ML formation quickly disintegrated, whereas the Japanese managed to hold their patrol formation of three fighters, flying according to the book, strongly echeloned in height, so that the patrols could provide cover for each other.[7]

Ensign Kuijper and Sergeant Groot attacked three enemy fighters before diving away quickly. However, before the two Brewsters were able to build up speed, three other Ki-43s opened fire on them, riddling the full length of the fuselages, from cockpit to tail with bullets. Witnesses on the ground saw the two fighters steadily picking up more speed and, still in formation, crash into the bank of the Tjisedane river, both pilots probably having lost their lives before they hit the ground.[8] Ensign Pelder had to withdraw from the fight rather early on, after receiving hits in one of his fuel tanks and engine fuel lines. In normal flight petrol came gushing from his plane. Skidding and flying in circles he returned to Tjisaoek where he made a successful belly landing. Ground crew immediately covered the fighter with branches, but the emergency landing was not noticed by the Japanese.[9]

Deibel fired twice at a 'Navy O' with his fuselage machine guns only, both his wing machine guns having jammed after the first few shots. After a turning fight of about ten minutes his B-398 was extremely heavily damaged by the 12.7-mm high explosive bullets fired by the Ki-43s. He carried out an emergency landing on Semplak, which was not easy, his Brewster having become almost uncontrollable with the rudder fabric and a rudder fitting blown away. On top of that, burning Hudson bombers and fuel drums hindered his view and the runway contained several bomb craters. On his third attempt he managed to land, after which he had to be freed from his plane with a crowbar due to a jamming canopy. He had had all the luck in the world. On inspection it appeared that the control wires had almost completely been severed. In his opinion Deibel had hit the enemy fighter on both occasions when he had got a chance to fire, but there were no visual results. He claimed two probables.[10]

With severe burns Sergeant 't Hart bailed out from his B-3133, whose left fuel tank had been hit, from 1,500 metres near Paroeng (a village two kilometres from Tjisaoek) after about 13 minutes of fighting. He had fired at a 'Navy O' for just a flicker too long.[11] Vdg Scheffer, lightly wounded in the thigh, jumped at virtually the same moment, when a lucky hit in the oil system of his fighter made his windscreen completely untransparent; on top of that he smelled a strong smell of burning.[12]

Tlt Hoijer, Vdg Jolly and Sgt Bruggink landed their lightly damaged or undamaged aircraft on Tjisaoek. They had all fired at 'Navy O's, but without visual result. Pelder, too, had not been successful. Scheffer was convinced he had downed one 'Navy O' and hit a second before he was forced to jump. Also 't Hart had had several opportunities to fire and had used one very well. He saw bits of sheet metal come off the enemy fighter, whose pilot broke away in a steep dive. The firing opportunity, however, almost became his undoing. On the basis of eyewitness accounts Scheffer and 't Hart got a 'Navy O' as a *probable*.[13] No wreckage of the Japanese fighters was found.[14]

According to the 3rd Hiko Dan report of battle nine 'P-36s' were encountered north of Buitenzorg, which were 'immediately' shot down. The 64th Sentai war diary also gives a somewhat simplified account, stating that seven out of nine 'P-36s' were shot down 'with ease'.[15] In fact, the air battle lasted for about fifteen minutes, most pilots of 2-Vl.G.V held out until the end and only four Brewsters were downed, two sustained heavy damage and one light damage.

Tlt Hoyer's B-3117 was lightly damaged, with no structural but some bullet and shrapnel damage to the sheet metal and rudder fabric. His plane could be repaired at the afdeling itself and was serviceable again on 24 February. Deibel's B-398 was pushed to a corner in the maintenance hangar at Semplak and transferred by telephone to the Technical Service (TD) at Andir. The damage was so severe that it was out of the question to make it airworthy at the afdeling by carrying out some temporary repairs and then fly it to Andir for major repairs. Hits had damaged the cockpit severely and the instrument panel had come undone. The fuselage had dozens of holes and dents in the sheet metal from high explosive bullets. Pelder's B-3111 had survived the belly landing and underwent makeshift repairs. The aircraft would be flyable a week later.[16]

Two pilots had lost their lives (Kuijper and Groot) and one was in hospital with severe burns ('t Hart). Two had sustained lighter injuries. Scheffer was flying again a few days later. In hospital the splinters in Deibel's head from a high explosive bullet that had exploded inside his cockpit some 50 centimetres from his head were removed as best as possible. He was not allowed to fly for two weeks and became temporary adjutant to the Semplak airfield commander.[17]

With the burning bombers and fuel drums on its perimeter, the damage to Semplak airfield looked worse than it was, but, nevertheless, three RAF and RAAF Hudson bombers, two Sikorsky S-43 amphibious planes of the Koninklijke Nederlands-Indische Luchtvaartmaatschappij– Royal Netherlands Indies Airline (KNILM) and a Ryan STM-2 trainer of Vl.G.V were total losses.[18] The 90th Sentai had carried out a low-altitude bombing raid on the aircraft dispersed along the perimeter of the field and the three hangars. One of the hangars was hit, causing the one Hudson to go up in flames and explode. Debris from the explosion hit the Sikorsky's and together with the hangar also the Ryan was reduced to ashes.[19] On the platform near the hangars a bomb hit a fuel filling pit, which set fire to one of the dug-in fuel tanks. The Japanese were careful during this first raid and the bombers only made one run. Afdeling commander Kap J.H. van Helsdingen followed the battle from Semplak, where he had taken his Brewster B-3110 the day before for repairs on the ignition system. His fighter was not hit.[20]

When 2-Vl.G.V engaged into combat requests for support were made to the RAF at Tjililitan as well as the ML at Andir. However, *Sector Control Batavia* and Air Defence Command Bandoeng left their Hurricanes and Brewsters that were on *Readiness* over Batavia or kept them on the ground, respectively, as it was not clear whether the attacks would be directed at Batavia or Bandoeng. At first it seemed that Batavia would be the main objective of the Japanese, and the Tjililitan *Readiness Flight* and a further Hurricane section had been sent up. Groups of Ki-43 were carrying out armed reconnaissance sorties of Tjililitan and Kemajoran and seemed to be preparing the way for the bombers. The allied command seriously reckoned with an attack on Tandjong Priok, Batavia's harbour, as a variety of ships carrying units and equipment evacuated from southern Sumatra had been arriving there since 17 February 1942.[21]

After a 15 minutes' wait it became obvious that the Japanese air-craft that had been observed by the aerial surveillance posts had been heading for Semplak only and that there were no further bombers. The Tjililitan *Readiness Flight* still tried to intercept the returning Japanese formations, but to no avail. The section of four Hurricanes of 232 Squadron that had also been sent up, was ordered to intercept a Japanese fighter that had in the meantime been reported flying over the Bay of Batavia and Tandjong Priok.[22] This was probably a C5M reconnaissance plane of the Yamada Kokutai (air group) from Kuching.

After three days of bad weather the 3rd Assault Group of the Japanese Navy air force at Kuching (to which the Yamada Kokutai was assigned) had finally been able to reconnoitre Batavia. By the time the Hurricanes arrived over Priok, the reconnaissance plane had vanished again.[23]

Four Brewsters of 1-Vl.G.V took off from Andir at about 09:15 hrs and were directed towards Buitenzorg. When they arrived the battle was already over. On their return flight the four Brewsters intercepted a single bomber near Bandoeng, which opened fire at 1,000 metres, upon which the Brewsters attacked. It appeared to be an American B-17.[24] This was one of the many incidents in which allied crews took the orange triangles on the ML aircraft for orange-red Japanese signs. This prompted the issue of a regulation on 23 February stating that all triangles as national signs had to be replaced by red-white-blue flags.[25]

The raid on Andir

Afdeling 1-Vl.G.V was accommodated at Andir in the so-called Noordhangaar (North hangar), the only and detached hangar in the northern part of the airfield. The planes were dispersed to an extent (not in so-called pens, U shaped earthen walls for shrapnel protection) in the direct vicinity of the hangar, close to the beginning of the north-south runway, Andir's 'short runway' or emergency strip. Every 30 minutes the mechanics and assistant-mechanics warmed up the engines. In case of an alarm the pilots could be inside their cockpits within a minute and be airborne within three. Take offs were always in southerly direction, across the main runway. After the evacuation of southern Sumatra there were eight Brewsters, or four Brewsters with four Interceptors of 2-Vl.G.IV, on *Readiness* every day between 05:00 hrs and 19:00 hrs.[26]

On 19 February 1-Vl.G.V carried out three emergency take offs between 09:00 hrs and 14:00 hrs. The first, however, was aborted. Just before take off the deputy afdeling commander Elt P.G. Tideman got the order, "do not take off, we are waiting until we know what the attack is directed at". After a quarter of an hour's wait it appeared that only Semplak was targeted and four out of eight Brewsters were still sent up. Led by Tideman, the patrol headed for Buitenzorg to support 2-Vl.G.V in their battle with the Japanese fighters, as described above. On the other two emergency take offs no enemy planes were found.

On the fourth emergency take off, however, it was clear that a large enemy formation was approaching Bandoeng and 1-Vl.G.V as well as the 2-Vl.G.IV patrol were ordered to take off with all available fighters. Tideman had 12 pilots in and, by now, 12 operational aircraft to match. The 2-Vl.G.IV patrol, however, had only three deployable aircraft left after an earlier emergency take off.[27]

The scrambled ML patrols were composed as follows.[28]

Patrol Van Rest: Kap A.A.M. van Rest, Sgt L.C. van Daalen, Elt H.H.J. Simons and Vdg C.A. Vonck.

Patrol Tideman: Elt P.G. Tideman, Sgt A.E. van Kempen, Elt P.A.C. Benjamins and Sgt A. Bergamin.

Patrol De Haas: Elt G.J. de Haas, Elt J.J. Tukker, Sgt G. van Haarlem and Sgt J.P. Adam.

Patrol Boxman: Elt W. Boxman, Sgt H.M. Haye and Sgt O.B. Roumimper.

In the course of the afternoon Lieutenant Tideman felt a sense of doom and foreboding and kept the pilots of the patrol that was not on *Readiness* close by. Alerted by Air Defence Command, he took off at about 15:30 hrs with 11 instead of 8 aircraft. Sgt P. Compaan, the youngest pilot of 1-Vl.G.V was left at home, afdeling commander Captain Van Rest taking off in his aircraft several minutes later. Once airborne, Van Rest took over command from Tideman and the afdeling climbed out to 3,500 metres just south of Bandoeng. The Interceptors, which had taken off just behind the Brewsters from the main runway at Andir, joined them during the climb. The 15 fighters then flew in a curve east of Bandoeng and somewhat north of the town in westerly direction. Suddenly, the fighters, by now at an altitude of 4,000 metres, saw far below them Japanese bombers attacking Andir airfield from the direction of Padalarang. The Air Defence Command requested support from RAF Batavia, but it could not be granted. The 2-Vl.G.IV patrol was called back to Andir to chase the enemy bombers away.[29]

A few minutes later the Brewsters saw two groups (they thought) of 'Navy Os' heading towards them, one at a lower and one at a slightly higher altitude. Over Lembang the fighters engaged. In a shallow dive the Van Rest patrol attacked the "bandits two o'clock below". The Tideman and De Haas patrols turned away somewhat and attacked the "bandits nine o'clock". The encounter came as a surprise for both sides. The formations of the 59th and 64th Sentais (28 Ki-43 fighters in total) as well as that of 1-Vl.G.V (12 Brewsters) broke up. The Japanese, however, mostly managed to keep the patrol formation of three aircraft intact, whereas the ML patrols quickly broke up in pairs and subsequently individual aircraft. Within ten minutes the Japanese had downed three Brewsters. De Haas and Tukker managed to surprise a couple of 'Navy Os', but in doing so they were attacked in their turn by several 'Navy Os'. De Haas landed safely by parachute. After the first burst of fire the machine guns of his fighter kept on firing and still did when he had to bail out. His wingman Tukker was injured and had to leave his heavily damaged aircraft by parachute on the way home. He landed in a river and passed away shortly after being rescued by some villagers. Sergeant Van Daalen bailed out from his Brewster badly burned but landed safely by parachute.[30]

Simons got a fantastic firing opportunity when suddenly a 'Zero' "was hanging dead in an Immelman". He throttled back and hit the enemy fighter in the wing and fuselage. Bits of sheet metal were flying around and fuel came gushing from the aircraft. Tideman fired at three different 'Zeros' at least, but without any direct visual result. Besides, after one or two bursts of fire it was necessary to immediately set in an evasive action, for hanging on an opponent's tail for too long often meant being fired at by his wingmen. One of the first 'Zeros' Tideman fired at had a wingman who was flying at an angle behind his leader and who immediately attacked Tideman's Brewster. A high explosive shell hit his right wing making a large hole in the sheet metal.[31]

Adam wrote, "… It was a matter of one against three and operating in pairs was out of the question. It was just going from one (enemy) aircraft to the next. I was after two Japs, but suddenly I had lost them both. But I was then being chased by three 'Navy Os' and the only way to escape was to go down." When Adam had climbed out after his dive, the battle was over and the sky empty.[32]

Because they were outnumbered by the Japanese Van Rest radioed his pilots to retreat from the fight and landed with three others on Kalidjati. Five of his pilots did not hear him in the heat of battle or could not hear his message due to atmospheric interference. They kept on fighting until the Japanese retreated after some twenty minutes in northerly direction. They were Tideman, Simons, Benjamins, Van Kempen and Adam. Simons was the only one to get one 'Navy O' as a probable to his name after the debriefing and accounts from eyewitnesses on the ground. The claim was confirmed the same night. KNIL infantrymen reported the hit Japanese fighter had crashed and gone up in flames near the Tjisomang fortification. With Warrant Officer Koshio Yamaguchi dead, the 59th Sentai lost one its most experienced pilots.[33]

The CW-21s of 2-Vl.G.IV were too late to help the Brewsters. Boxman with his trailing pilots had just manoeuvred into a good position to attack the bombers (by that time on their way back) when the patrol was called back. When the pilots approached the given location, they saw a tremendous confusion. The Japanese retreated from the fight, however, and they had disappeared when the Inteceptors arrived. Here and there a lonely Brewster was flying around but the Japanese fighters were nowhere to be seen anymore. The CW-21s were running out of fuel, their range being a mere 90 minutes using combat cruising speed, and Boxman returned to Andir. Shortly after landing the Brewsters came in one by one.[34]

A pre-war picture of Andir airfield near Bandoeng. From bottom left hand to top right (the south side), it shows the so-called KNILM complex, the complex of the Radiodienst (Radio Service), a wooded area with a village and the complex of the Technische Dienst (Technical Service) and the Magazijndienst (Warehouse Service). (Private collection, P.C. Boer)

The losses of 1-Vl.G.V were relatively heavy. Three Brewsters were completely lost (De Haas', Tukker's and Van Daalen's), two were badly damaged (Tideman's and Simons') and three aircraft were so lightly damaged that they could be repaired at their own afdeling. One pilot had died (Tukker) and one had been seriously injured (Van Daalen).[35]

The Japanese bombers, nine Ki-48s of the 90th Sentai, wrought havoc at Andir. Several hangars and sheds of the ML Technical Service and Warehouse Service were severely damaged. On the platforms of the Technical Service two American B-17s were hit, one of which (on its way to eastern Java and just arrived) went up in flames and one was badly damaged. Also two Ryan STM trainers, recently arrived from Tjililitan, were lost. At the Depot Vliegtuigafdeling–Depot Squadron (D.Vl.A), the ML transport afdeling, the hangar was hit, burning down a Lockheed L-12A and a Walraven W2 twin-engine civilian aircraft that had been hoisted to the roof. Three parked militarised private aircraft of D.Vl.A. and a Bucker Jungmann *aerobatics trainer* (in maintenance at D.Vl.A. for 1-Vl.G.V) were also total losses. The KNILM lost the PK-AKV, a De Haviland DH-89 *Dragon Rapide* twin-engine transport plane that was undergoing major repairs at the ML Technical Service. Another, about to be militarised, private aircraft, under repair, was also lost.[36]

During this action Sergeant Haye flew Tlt Dekker's plane because his own Interceptor was at the Technical Service at Andir for problems with the operating mechanism of the undercarriage. The Technical Service had put the aircraft on jacks but could not find anything. They had returned the plane to him that same afternoon. Haye made a short test flight, which ended in a belly landing at Andir. Probably because he was severely tired the pilot had failed to notice that switching the lever of the undercarriage into the OUT position had not been accompanied with the lowering of it. The plane was hauled off the runway to be returned to the Technical Service, after which it would go to the Technical Service at Maospati for major repairs by train.[37]

Results on both sides

On 19, 20 and 21 February KNIL and police patrols, sent out to investigate 11 reports of crashed airplanes in the area of West Group of the KNIL, found the wreckage of 6. After inspection they appeared to be from four Brewsters of 2-Vl.G.V, crashed on 19 February, one single-engine Japanese plane crashed at Bantam on 20 February and one RAAF Hudson bomber crashed about fifteen kilometres north-west of Buitenzorg on 21 February. Furthermore, on 19 and 21 February, respectively, two Japanese fighters had flown at low altitude and clearly hit over the coast in the Bay of Batavia in the direction of the Duizend Eilanden. According to coast guard personnel and the Aerial Surveillance Circle one had crashed into the sea on 19 February 1942. Apart from the fighter that had crashed near Tjisomang, patrols in the sector of Group Bandoeng of the KNIL found the wreckage of two Japanese Ki-48 bombers (hit by anti-aircraft artillery at Kalidjati), three crashed Brewsters of 1-Vl.G.V and the wreckage of one American B-17 bomber. On the basis of these investigations the claims of the pilots of 2-Vl.G.V remained probables.[38]

According to Japanese data all aircraft returned safely to their bases from their raid at Buitenzorg. There will certainly have been Ki-43s returning with bullet damage, but no data on this have survived.[39] Thus, both Scheffer and 't Hart indicated in their debriefings that they had fired at a Ki-43 at close range and seen the bullets hit the enemy plane. 't Hart could give a detailed description of the enemy plane, its markings and where the bullets had struck. During the raid at Bandoeng the Japanese did have several losses. As said above, the 59th Sentai lost a Ki-43 and a pilot in the fight with the Brewsters and an unknown number of Ki-43s of the 59th and 64th Sentais returned at Palembang I, damaged. One of these planes crashed on landing due to the battle damage it had sustained and had to be written off.[40] Furthermore, Sergeant-Major Akeshi Yokoi (64th Sentai) had been forced to land on the sea near one of the Duizend Eilanden as a result of return fire from one of two B-17 bombers (going to eastern Java via India) that had been attacked near Bandoeng and between Batavia and Bandoeng respectively by both Sentais on their way back to Palembang. Yokoi was picked up by the Japanese Navy air force with a float plane.[41] One of the two B-17s was shot down but the crew could bail out apart from one who died in the plane during the attack. This bomber had already arrived at Andir for a stop-over but had taken off again when the air raid alert sounded. The other B-17 landed on Andir, damaged.[42] The Japanese report of battle on the raid on Bandoeng states, ... "The squadron came into contact with an enemy P-43 formation of about 20 aircraft above Bandoeng airfield and engaged in mid-air battle.... The squadron shot down 10 aircraft (including

3 unconfirmed) in the air-battle...."[43] The report is very concise and
it was only after the capitulation during the interrogations of the ML
pilots that it became clear why this was so. The Japanese Sentais had
had great trouble dealing with the 'P-43s'. The air battle had lasted
exceptionally long, some 20 minutes, and on this first day of operations over Java there had been several losses and near-losses that had
somewhat affected their self-confidence. The officer of the 3rd Hiko
Shudan questioning Tideman, among others, refused to believe at first
that the opponent had only consisted of 12 Brewsters and for a large
part of the battle even only 5.[44]

For the ML this first day of the air battle over western Java had
been a disastrous one. At Buitenzorg 2-Vl.G.V encountered a numerical
superiority of Ki-43s (nine versus about 15), with an advantage of
height of 500 metres or more, on top of that. All but two of the pilots
of the ML afdeling were very experienced; nevertheless, the battle
circumstances were too unfavourable for them. The requested help for
assistance from RAF and 1-Vl.G.V did not come. In the afternoon
1-Vl.G.V also encountered superior numbers at Bandoeng (12 versus
28), with a virtually inexperienced crew (7 out of 12 fighter pilots had
only started their fighter pilot training in December 1941), but under
more favourable conditions. Help requested from RAF could not be
given. During the raid on Bandoeng the RAF Hurricanes were not
available as they were patrolling over Batavia and Tandjong Priok after
alarms and were short on fuel.

In total three ML pilots lost their lives on 19 February and two
were badly injured. The ML lost seven Brewsters in the air battle, the
Hiko Dan lost two Ki-43s, one of which on landing at Palembang I.
A third was lost as a result of the attack on the two B-17s. The Japanese pilots showed extremely good discipline in the air and managed
to maintain their combat formation and echeloning in height. What
was striking was the extent of damage the Brewster could take, along
with its manoeuvrability. Several pilots reported that the turning circle
of the Brewster was even smaller than that of the 'Navy O'. A disadvantage was that the manufacturer's manual prohibited the use of
'tracers' in the machine guns. Because of this the pilots, in spite of their
reflector gunsight, had a tendency to creep too closely on an enemy
plane, which cost dangerously much time. It was not until 23 February
1942 that this ban was lifted.[45]

***

CHAPTER 1A.3

The Fighter Operations on 20 February 1942

Introduction

The losses sustained on 19 February had reduced the total of assigned allied fighters by as much as 20 per cent. At the beginning of the day on 20 February the strengths of assigned and operational fighters were as follows:[1]

Table 2

Unit	Assigned	Operationally serviceable	Type of fighter (Remarks)
232/488 Squadron	18	14	Hurricane
2-Vl.G.V	5	2	Brewster
1-Vl.G.V	9 (+2)	7 (+2)	Brewster (+ Hawk)
2-Vl.G.IV	5	4	Interceptor
2-Vl.G.IV	11	0	10 Hurricane, limited serviceable
Total	48 (+2)	27 (+2)	

The Japanese air activity was relatively light that day and enemy forces carried out only one raid (on Kalidjati). Apart from that, both the Japanese Army and Navy air forces carried out several reconnaissance flights of targets in western Java.

A first success for 232 Squadron

From the early morning eight Hurricanes of 232 and 488 Squadrons had been on *Readiness* at Tjililitan. Six of the fighters (of 232 Squadron) had been sent up shortly after sunrise to intercept several enemy planes over the Bay of Bantam. Led by Flt Lt I. Julian, five Hurricanes engaged the Army 97 fighters (Nakajima Ki-27s), or so it was thought.

In fact they were probably three Mitsubishi Ki-15 single-engine reconnaissance planes, on a mission to reconnoitre the coastal area and the
roads leading to Batavia and Buitenzorg. The sixth Hurricane, flown
by Sgt I.D. Newlands, returned after take off with engine trouble.
Julian claimed one aircraft and another was jointly claimed by Plt Off
T.W. Watson and Sgt G.J. King. There were no losses and only Sgt D.
Kynman damaged his Hurricane when he landed too far on the runway
instead of making a go-around.[2] The wreckage of a single-engine
Japanese aircraft of unknown type was later found in the vicinity of
Serang (Bantam).[3]

From Andir 1-Vl.G.V tried in vain to intercept the twin-engine
Ki-46 reconnaissance plane on its daily recce run early in the morning.
These strategic reconnaissance planes operated from Palembang I,
photographing targets near Batavia and Bandoeng before and after the
attacks of the 3rd Hiko Dan. At the same time their crews gathered
the weather information necessary for the attacks. At Andir six still
operational Brewsters of 1-Vl.G.V had been on *Readiness* since 05:00
hrs, with a seventh plane as unmanned reserve, while at Boeabatoeweg
and later Andir 2-Vl.G.IV was on stand-by with four Interceptors.[4]

Hurricanes of the *Readiness Flight* at Tjililitan went up again
late in the morning to intercept one or two Japanese reconnaissance
aircraft over the Bay of Batavia and Tandjong Priok. They were
unsuccessful. It probably was a C5M land reconnaissance plane of the
3rd Assault Group of the Japanese Navy air force from Kuching (British-
Borneo), whose crew on their return reported 5 cruisers, 8 destroyers,
more than 50 merchantmen, 10 flying boats and 3 reconnaissance
floatplanes.[5] Incidentally, the 3rd Assault Group could do little more
than reconnoitre, as upcoming transfers of units from Kuching to
Muntok (Banka island) and Palembang II (P II, the large military
airfield in the jungle south-west of Palembang recently discovered by
the Japanese) made it impossible to carry out any operations that day.[6]

The two operationally serviceable Brewsters of 2-Vl.G.V, flown
by Vdg P.R. Jolly and Vdg F. Pelder landed at Tjililitan in the early
morning, followed somewhat later by the mechanics and assistant-
mechanics who arrived by truck. These 2-Vl.G.V personnel had only
just arrived when a Japanese Ki-15 single-engine reconnaissance plane
made a quick run over the field, firing several shots at a bowser and
personnel of 232 Squadron, one of whom got wounded. By order of
Kap C. Terluin the pilots reported at the British command post.

Deploying the few remaining Brewsters from Tjisaoek was pointless and operating together with the Hurricanes with the two planes from Tjililitan was the most efficient option.[7]

Terluin was "Commandant Luchtstrijdkrachten" – local Air Officer Commanding (CL, and in this position the operational commander of the ML fighters in the Batavia sector) and with a small staff he co-ordinated the deployment of ML fighters with the RAF from a native village shack along the road from Buitenzorg to Tjililitan airfield.[8] He was also the airfield commander of Tjililitan and he took care of many things for the RAF *Station Commander*, such as the provision of aircraft fuel and construction work for the RAF by KNIL engineers. His contacts with Air Commodore S.F. Vincent, the RAF commander of *Sector Control Batavia*, initially went through the latter's liaison officer, Elt E.H.C. Cleuver of the ML, who had held the same position with the RAF before at Palembang I. However, with the disbanding of *Unified Command*, this officer was reassigned to the ML Command at Bandoeng.[9]

From 12:00 hrs Jolly and Pelder had been on *Readiness* together with eight pilots of 232 Squadron. Around 14:00 hrs the two Brewsters took off together with the Hurricanes. Their objective was the interception of a Japanese formation off the north coast of Java that had carried out a raid on Kalidjati. The formation was not found. In the evening the Brewsters and the ground crew of 2-Vl.G.V returned to Tjisaoek.[10]

The Japanese raid on Kalidjati

The raid of the 3rd Hiko Dan on Kalidjati, the first attack on this base, took place at around 13:00 hrs and was carried out by ten Ki-48 bombers accompanied by 24 Ki-43 fighters of the 59th and 64th Sentais. The Japanese aircraft were not intercepted. The Hurricanes of 2-Vl.G.IV at Kalidjati were not operational yet and remained on the ground. The Brewsters of 1-Vl.G.V at the nearby Andir did go up when the Air Defence Command Bandoeng reported a Japanese formation approaching Bandoeng from the direction of Cheribon.

The six fighters, however, were kept by the Command at an altitude of 5,000 metres over the Tankoebang Prahoe volcano, waiting for support requested from the RAF in case the raid was directed at Bandoeng. This could not be granted. Bearing in mind the Japanese

reconnaissance activities *Sector Command Batavia* (mistakenly) concluded that the Japanese could attack Batavia at any moment. In the
meantime the Interceptor patrol of 2-Vl.G.IV had been alerted and sent
up. Tideman did not get permission to engage, even though the pilots
from their position over the Tankoebang Prahoe could see how Kalidjati
was being bombed. When the Interceptors arrived, the Japanese had
already left. In view of the enemy's numbers the order for 1-Vl.G.V
not to engage was the only right one, which an angry Tideman had to
admit after landing.[11] Kalidjati airfield itself only suffered little damage,
but the bombs fell on top of and near a number of pens with Glenn
Martins. Two of the bombers went up in flames, one was heavily
damaged and one lightly. Furthermore, a Lockheed L 212 trainer of
the Vliegschool (Flight school) was lost.[12]

Afdeling 2-Vl.G.IV at Kalidjati was about to become partially
operational. The initial logistic difficulties and problems with the
equipment of the Hurricanes (with the exception of the aircraft radios)
had been largely solved. The supply of Kalidjati with 100-octane
aircraft fuel, hydraulic oil, Glycol cooling fluid for the engines and
various types of 303-inch ammunition had got going by now, the ML
Technical Service had mounted oxygen tubes and masks (spares for
the Brewsters) in the aircraft and had supplied some 'English' tools to
complement the 'American' tools of the mechanics of the afdeling. Pilot
Officer John David, commander of the RAF detachment, and Sergeant
mechanic C.A.M. Koopmans picked up some spare parts at the warehouse of the RAF Air Stores Park at Buitenzorg, which ensured the
regular carrying out of operations.[13]

Before, on David's advice, the sand filters of all aircraft (the fighters
had originally been intended for northern Africa) had been removed.
Dependent on the altitude this gained them some 30 kilometres in
speed. The pilots of 2-Vl.G.IV had almost completed their type con-
version and were very happy with the flight performance and fire power
(eight 303-inch machine guns) of the Hurricane. There were only some
comments on the somewhat cramped and chaotic cockpit in comparison to American fighters. Within ABDAIR the idea had been proposed to locate 2-Vl.G.IV temporarily at Tjisaoek, rather than 2-Vl.G.V.
In the *Air Defence Sector Batavia* the afdeling, together with the RAF
squadrons, could be used for air defence tasks, whereas this was not
possible in the air defence sector Bandoeng due to the absence of the
right crystals for the aircraft radios. Although the ML and RAF agreed,
such a deviation of the air defence plan for western Java came up

against problems within ABDACOM. Vice-Admiral C.E.L. Helfrich, the commander of the allied naval forces ABDA-FLOAT, held on to the agreed plan, because it provided for the positioning of fighters at Tasikmalaja and radar stations along the south coast of western Java for the protection of the port of Tjilatjap and the shipping lanes towards it.[14]

Summary

The Japanese Army air force carried out a first major raid on Kalidjati airfield in the afternoon of 20 February 1942. It was not intercepted by allied fighters because raids were also expected on Bandoeng and Batavia. That morning the Japanese had reconnoitred, amongst others, Andir, Tjililitan, Tandjong Priok harbour and the coastal area near the Bay of Bantam and the roads leading from there to Batavia and Buitenzorg. Of the probably three Ki-15 reconnaissance planes carrying out the latter of these missions, at least one had been shot down by Hurricanes. ABDAIR only suffered losses on the ground at Kalidjati, where two Glenn Martin bombers and a Lockheed L 212 trainer had been lost and one Glenn-Martin had been badly damaged.

*** *** ***

CHAPTER 1A.4

The Fighter Operations on 21 February 1942

Introduction

The Japanese Army air force used 21 February 1942 to launch a third major offensive against the airfields in western Java. Because of the extremely bad weather in the vicinity of Batavia, heavy clouds and showers, only Andir and Kalidjati qualified as targets. The strength of the allied fighter units on the morning of 21 February was as follows:[1]

Table 3

Unit	Assigned	Operationally serviceable	Type of fighter (Remarks)
232/488 Squadron	18	13	Hurricane
2-Vl.G.V	5	3	Brewster
1-Vl.G.V	9 (+2)	7 (+2)	Brewster (+ Hawk)
2-Vl.G.IV	4	4	Interceptor
2-Vl.G.IV	11	0	(10 Hurricanes, limited serviceable)
Total	47 (+2)	27 (+2)	

The Japanese raid on Kalidjati and Andir

On 21 February, at about 10:30 hrs, the fighters at Andir were scrambled to intercept an enemy formation consisting of about 30 fighters and some 20 bombers. The formation had crossed the coast near Batavia and seemed to be on course for Bandoeng. The bad weather made an attack on the airfields or the harbour of Batavia unlikely, anyhow. The warning was well on time and the report of the Air Defence Command Bandoeng was accurate with regard to the enemy formation. The likely target was Andir or Kalidjati. The Japanese planes flew along the northern edge of the Preanger (Bandoeng) Plateau towards the east, circumventing an area of bad weather and heavy clouds. From the direction of Cheribon the formation then turned back towards Kalidjati. Several of the accompanying fighters, 12 in total, flew on to Andir.[2]

The available fighters of 1-Vl.G.V, seven out of the nine remaining assigned Brewsters, flown by Elt P.G. Tideman, Elt P.A.C. Benjamins, Sgt A. Bergamin, Sgt A.E. van Kempen, Res Elt H.H.J. Simons, Vdg C.A. Vonck and Sgt J.P. Adam, were airborne within two and half minutes and initially headed east to gain altitude. Three of the four serviceable CW-21B Interceptors of the patrol of 2-Vl.G.IV, flown by Tlt D. Dekker, Sgt H.M. Haye and Sgt O.B. Roumimper joined them during the climb. However, Dekker lost his patrol in the heavy clouds and subsequently returned to Andir probably because of engine trouble. Mechanics had already pointed out a loss of oil to Dekker, but apparently there had been no problems during engine run-up before take-off.

Lieutenant W. Boxman, the patrol commander, was on his way to ML Command on his motorbike. When he heard the air raid alarm he turned back immediately, knowing that there was no other pilot available for the fourth Interceptor kept in reserve. In the end he did not take off because the heavy clouds would have made it virtually impossible for him to find his patrol.[3]

The second air battle near Andir

Having arrived at an altitude of 6,000 metres, the normal combat ceiling, the nine remaining ML fighter pilots set course once more for Andir airfield. Shortly after this and about half an hour in flight they spotted the 'Navy Os' approaching from the north-east. Amid the towering cumulus clouds the Brewsters were the first to dive onto the Japanese formation, and a turning fight lasting some five to ten minutes evolved.[4]

The opponents consisted of Nakajima Ki-43s of the 59th and 64th Sentais, 14 and 15 planes, respectively, accompanying 15 light bombers of the 90th Sentai. Overall commander of the mission was Major Tateo Kato, the commander of the 64th Sentai. Because of the bad weather over Bandoeng, reported by the crew of a returning Ki-46 reconnaissance plane, the target (Andir) had been changed into Kalidjati just before take off of the Japanese units at Palembang. Only the 64th Sentai was going to try and attack Andir. The 59th Sentai and two fighters from the 64th Sentai, flown by Kato himself and his wingman Lieutenant Yohei Hinoki, covered the bombers during their attack. The other 12 Ki-43s continued for Andir.[5]

Clearly, the Japanese were surprised. Tideman wrote in 1946, "Encounter over Oedjoeng Broeng. Formation broken up with dive attack, then brief turning fight, attack fended off". A Japanese report of battle states, "The Kato Sentai met an enemy squadron over Bandung but recognised the superiority of the bullet-proof American aircraft", and, "They persistently attacked our force from a higher altitude but finally the Sentai escaped to safety." This last remark is an understatement, for a Ki-43 collided with its wing tip into Sgt Adam's Brewster and crashed near Oejdoeng Broeng. The (unknown) Japanese pilot died. Adam landed by parachute in a high tree, reported back for duty the next day and was grounded for two days to recuperate somewhat.[6]

Adam wrote, "Suddenly a Navy O came straight for me in a slow roll. At a short distance we both opened up fire in passing." Both pilots repeated the action once more, opening fire almost simultaneously.

This time neither turned away, both pilots probably thinking the other would; until it was too late. With a loud clatter the wing tips of the Ki-43 and Brewster hit each other. The Ki-43 lost a wing and tumbled uncontrollably out of the sky. Adam looked out and to his horror he discovered that about a metre of his right wing tip was missing. He dived to get out of the fight, but when he did so his plane, which had been reasonably controllable at first, got into a spin of which it was impossible to get out again. Adam climbed onto his seat to bail out, but he did not succeed. Pushed backwards by the flow of air and half inside, half outside his plane, he was stuck, until he was hurtled from it a bit later. He had unconsciously pulled his parachute.[7]

Tideman fired successfully at a 'Navy O'. The plane caught fire (so it seemed) over Tjitjalenka and went into a sheer dive, a big black plume of smoke behind it and disappeared among the clouds. Bergamin stayed on his opponent's tail for just too long and thought he had scored some hits, but his own fighter was hit by fire from one or two other 'Navy Os'. His plane sustained bullet and shrapnel damage in the wing, amongst others. Simons, Vonck and Van Kempen did not have any results; nor did the two Interceptor pilots.[8]

Van Kempen fired at a 'Navy O', without any visible result, and began to climb again to gain height once more. He wrote, "To my utter surprise a Jap came flying next to me, also climbing. We looked at each other. He passed me in triumph." The Ki-43, at altitude a much faster climber than the Brewster, turned around and attacked Van Kempen from above. Both opened fire simultaneously. In order to get his opponent in the arc of fire Van Kempen had to 'lift' the nose position of his Brewster somewhat, which made the slowly climbing plane go into a stall and tumble into a spin. It felt as if the Brewster went down almost vertically, losing almost 3,000 metres in altitude. When the ML fighter pilot had climbed out again, the battle was over and among the high cumulus clouds he could see neither enemy nor friendly planes. Van Kempen returned at Andir with only a bullet hole in one of the wings. This was quickly taped over and the Brewster was operational again.[9]

After the initial air battle the ML fighter pilots flew back individually or in loose formations. Tideman with Simons and Benjamins went north of Andir among the towering clouds. The three men relaxed somewhat, cruising around a bit before landing and waiting for the all clear signal from ground control. Suddenly, both Tideman and Benjamins came under attack. To his dismay Simons spotted a

'Navy O', a bit lower but almost coming alongside him, which began to fire at Tideman's plane in front. He tried to warn Tideman over the radio but he missed the hand microphone and dropped it. Benjamin's Brewster, which was flying on Simons' tail, was also suddenly fired at from behind and received a hit in the fuselage.[10]

The three Brewsters were taken by surprise by Kato and Hinoki. Kato had met no opposition over Kalidjati and decided to fly back via Andir when the Ki-48 bombers were on their way back, escorted by the 59th Sentai. The 64th Sentai were nowhere to be seen anymore but the two pilots spotted four 'Republic P-43s' and engaged them. Hinoki probably fired at Tideman's plane and Kato went for the trailing plane in the patrol, Benjamin's. Tideman's Brewster received hits through the wing and the explosive bullets exploded in his cockpit, against the armour plates behind his seat. Tideman dived and made ready to bail out as a fire had started. The flames were extinguished, however, and he managed to make a normal landing with the badly damaged plane.[11]

Benjamins described the incident as follows, "Suddenly, completely out of the blue, I felt and heard a series of heavy explosions at the back of the fuselage and there was a strong smell of gun smoke." He pushed his Brewster with 'everything left front' (full throttle, stick left front and left rudder pedal flat down) into a very steep spin, a manoeuvre which the Japanese fighter could not follow. During the recovery he saw his ambusher flying above him in a right turn. The Japanese pilot had followed him down, but did not engage and set course for the north-west.[12]

The ML pilot used his velocity surplus after the dive to cut him off and he got "a few fine chances for firing", without any visible result, though. Apparently short of fuel, the Japanese pilot tried to retreat from the fight as soon as he could. Near Poerwakarta Benjamins had to let his opponent go as his own fuel supply had become dangerously low. He got a probable to his name, but almost lost his own plane.[13]

Benjamins managed to reach the downwind leg in the Andir circuit when his engine gave out thumping and spluttering and he was forced to turn in across the (east-west) runway for an emergency landing on the short runway. The aircraft which was very light by now glided very far and headed straight for its own hangar. He narrowly escaped because both main wheel tyres had been punctured. Heavy braking and the flat tyres caused the Brewster to come to a standstill just in time. Benjamins was lucky the plane did not overturn. Closer inspection revealed that there were a few big holes in the fuselage and the fabric of the rudder was torn to shreds. The plane was heavily damaged, but at the Technical Service it proved to be in better shape than it seemed at first. Except for the tyres, the undercarriage was completely intact.[14]

The results on both sides

KNIL and police patrols found the wreckage of two Japanese bombers that had been shot down by the anti-aircraft artillery at Kalidjati, but with the exception of the Japanese aircraft crashed at Oedjoeng Broeng (from which the dead body of a pilot officer was recovered) and Adam's plane, blown up on the ground, no wreckage of fighters was found. Japanese records show that both Major Kato and Lieutenant Hinoki made it to Palembang. The two, incidentally, were very successful pilots and aces. In the battle over China Kato had already downed nine planes and until 22 May 1942, when he was shot down, he had reached a score of around 18. The much younger Hinoki had scored 12 kills from December 1941. After the debriefings and statements of witnesses on the ground Tideman got a 'Navy O' to his name and Benjamins a 'Navy O' as a probable. Several witnesses reported a Japanese fighter at low speed and with a smoking engine heading from the vicinity of Tjitalenka for the coast near Batavia. Some crew members from the Aerial Surveillance Circle Batavia and a coastal surveillance post saw the plane, which appeared to be on fire, cross the coastline in the direction of the Duizend Eilanden. They assumed it would not make it to its home base.[15]

The Japanese report of battle, cited above, describes the incident as follows, "Later the Sentai found four enemy fighters over Bandoeng and tried to storm them. Because of the clouds the Sentai was not able to confirm the results. We shot down one fighter in a surprise attack...." Apparently the Japanese pilots had missed the fire in Tideman's Brewster. Earlier an unknown Japanese pilot had shot down the CW-21B of Tlt Dekker of 2-Vl.G.IV, killing the pilot.[16]

In his diary Hinoki complained about the bullet proofing of the American fighters, because he had seen his 12.7-mm explosive bullets hit the wing of one of the 'P-43s', but this plane did not go up in flames. In fact, the bullet proofing consisted of sheets of natural rubber imported from the United States, which the Technical Service had applied to the wing tanks of all the Brewsters. The rubber on top and under the tanks usually sealed off any perforations of bullets and pieces of shrapnel. This limited loss of fuel and the cutting off of air reduced the incidence of fire or quickly extinguished any fires that did occur. Incidentally, this modification was not possible with the ML Curtiss-Wright Interceptors as they had integral fuel tanks.[17]

The Japanese Army air force lost a Ki-43 of the 64th Sentai, while several other planes of this unit were damaged. The ML lost one Interceptor and a Brewster; two other Brewsters (Tideman's and Benjamins') were heavily damaged and two or three lightly (Simons' and Bergamin's, and possibly Vonck's).[18] During one of the first attacks the 64th Sentai also lost a Ki-43 as an operational loss. The pilot did not make it to Palembang and had to make a forced landing due to fuel shortage. This landing probably took place on 21 February 1942.[19]

After the battle the strength of 1-Vl.G.V was down to seven Brewsters, three of which were in repair with the afdeling itself. The strength of 2-Vl.G.IV had fallen to four aircraft. Although on this day a CW-21B arrived from Maospati in exchange for Vdg L.A.M. van der Vossen's plane that had been handed over for repairs the previous day, the total strength of the patrol did not increase due to the loss of the plane of Tlt Dekker.[20]

The squadrons at Tjililitan

The RAF Hurricanes at Tjililitan did not come into action on 21 February, probably because of the very bad weather at and around Batavia. In the morning 232 Squadron had eight operational aircraft and 488 Squadron had five. The KNIL engineers finished the construction work at Tjililitan airfield, where they had been extending dispersal areas in the growth along the perimeter on the west and south side. The fighters on *Readiness*, however, remained dispersed along the perimeter of the actual flight area to be able to take to the air as soon as possible in case of an alert. 605 Squadron got shape on 21 February at the end of the day, the unit taking over six Hurricanes and the tasks of 488 Squadron, which had been designated for evacuation.[21]

Summary

On this day the ML fighter pilots got their own back. Although the Japanese raid on Kalidjati could not be prevented, 1-Vl.G.V and the patrol of 2-Vl.G.IV had managed to keep the Japanese fighters from attacking Andir. Two Japanese fighters were believed to have been shot down, one of which was a probable, while a third had crashed after a collision with a Brewster. The own losses amounted to two fighters and one pilot, while two Brewsters sustained heavy damage. Sgt Adam, who had been missing, showed up the next day. The RAF Hurricanes were unable to give support.

* * *

CHAPTER 1A.5

The Events and Fighter Operations on 22 and 23 February 1942

Introduction

The weather was bad over most of western Java on 22 February 1942, which increased the possibility of the aerial surveillance posts of the air defence commands not noticing any approaching Japanese formations. The British radar posts on the north and west coasts of western Java were not yet operational. Tandjong Priok harbour and the Bay of Batavia were full of ships. On the one hand, these were vessels that belonged to a British convoy, originally destined for Singapore, which had been stranded at Batavia on 3 February, together with ships from several smaller convoys that had arrived shortly before and after that day. On the other hand, there were also ships that had fled Singapore and southern Sumatra. In total there were over a hundred vessels, mostly British, Australian and British Indian, among which there were several freighters loaded with badly needed and valuable munitions.[1] Furthermore, there were the warships at Tandjong Priok, five cruisers and six destroyers of the allied *Western Striking Force*. Heavy Japanese air raids on the port as well as the airfields of Batavia were expected any moment now.[2]

The strengths of assigned and operationally serviceable fighters at the beginning of this day were as follows:[3]

Table 4

Unit	Assigned	Operationally serviceable	Type/remarks
232 Squadron	12	10	Hurricane
605 Squadron	6	6	Hurricane
2-Vl.G.V	5	3	Brewster
1-Vl.G.V	5 (+2)	3 (+2)	Brewster (+ Hawk)
2-Vl.G.IV	4	3	Interceptor
2-Vl.G.IV	11	10	Hurricane, limited serviceable
Total	43 (+2)	35 (+2)	

Problems for ABDA-FLOAT at Batavia

Tandjong Priok harbour was utterly congested. Unloading the ships went painfully slowly and a ship would have to wait for days before its turn came up. If it could be unloaded at last, where a lack of quays with sufficient depth sometimes necessitated transferring onto smaller ships or lighters, the absence of enough storage capacity and a railway system completely inadequate for transporting the goods caused the loads to be somewhat haphazardly dumped along the roads in the dock area.[4] The allied naval command ABDA-FLOAT therefore unceremoniously sent large numbers of ships on their way, usually changing their destinations to Australia or Ceylon. Some went to Tjilatjap on the south coast of Java.[5]

Regular reconnaissance missions of ABDAIR's *Reconnaissance Group* (ML and RAF flying boats) showed that the Soenda Strait continued to be "free of enemy", which made the risk of the passage to the Indian Ocean slight. Bombers regularly reconnoitred Oosthaven in southern Sumatra and the road leading from this harbour to Palembang and here, too, the enemy was not active yet. There was, however, regular Japanese air reconnaissance of Batavia and any moment a big air raid on the ships at Tandjong Priok could follow. On 21 February ABDACOM Intelligence warned of a possible Japanese naval operation. Speed, therefore, was of the essence. It was decided to send away as many of the remaining ships as possible on 22 and 23 February, with some troop transport ships evacuating British and Australian servicemen, and to close the harbour for incoming civilian shipping. The other ships would then be sent away from 24 February onwards, alone or in small convoys.[6]

As described above, a number of the ships at Batavia held cargo which was badly needed in Java, such as bombs and ammunition, spare engines and aircraft parts for the RAF and RAAF. These vessels were sent as part of a convoy through the Soenda Strait to be unloaded at Tjilatjap. The other ships in these convoys went on to Colombo and Australia. Because of these ship movements and the protection of the ships en route from Australia or elsewhere to Tjilatjap, 205 Squadron RAF (with three Catalina flying boats) was transferred from Tandjong Priok to Tjilatjap in the early morning of 21 February in order to reinforce the Marine Luchtvaart Dienst–Dutch Naval Air Service (MLD) there. Japanese submarines were active south of western Java and armed with four depth charges the MLD and RAF flying boats carried out several patrols per day.[7]

On 21 February six ships left Tandjong Priok in convoy, three for Colombo and three for Australia. Two further KPM ships left out of convoy, one of which was heading for Tjliatjap. The next day two convoys left, one for Tjilatjap and one for Colombo. Several other ships put out to sea on their own, among which the large troop ship *Orcades* around midnight of 21 on 22 February. This fast ship evacuated the personnel of disbanded bomber and fighter squadrons, 2,000 RAF and 700 RAAF servicemen in all. On 23 and 24 February still many ships left in convoys or on their own, among which *Deucalion* on 23 February with 488 Squadron on board. All in all, this exodus continued up to and including 26 February 1942.[8]

The Air Striking Force

On 22 February warships of the *Western Striking Force* also guarded the entrance to the Soenda Strait and MLD flying boats made regular seaward reconnaissance flights from Tandjong Priok between Banka and north-western Java and above parts of the Strait. Escorted by naval vessels the ships sailed through, but due to a great shortage of escort ships in ABDA-FLOAT the emphasis during the passage was on protection from the air. For this purpose an *Air Striking Force* had been formed, consisting of ML and RAF fighters and ML, RAF and RAAF bombers.[9]

The fighters were supposed to fend off any air raids on the ships and to investigate reports of unidentified airplanes and possible submarines. The RAF at Tjililitan normally had eight Hurricanes on *Readiness* for the air defence of Batavia. On 22 February 1942 there was only one section of four fighters. In addition, there were six fighters on *Readiness* as part of the *Air Striking Force*. The ML at Tjisaoek had two of the three 2-Vl.G.V Brewsters on *Readiness*, which brought the total of fighters directly available for the protection of ships up to eight. RAF Tjililitan had a further six Hurricanes on stand-by and flew a number of *standing patrols* (nowadays called *combat air patrols*) with these aircraft for the protection of the airfields and harbour of Batavia. Occasionally, one fighter would fly a seaward reconnaissance mission.[10]

In the early morning of 22 February two Hurricanes were scrambled for the first time when a convoy reported possible submarines. The fighter pilots reported several suspect dark spots in the water. Subsequently, three Blenheims took off from Kalidjati for closer inspection and a possible attack. One of the bombers returned immediately after take off due to engine trouble and the others after a fruitless search over the sea area north of St. Nicolaaspunt.[11]

The two Brewsters of 2-Vl.G.V were also sent up several times for reconnaissance missions around the ships in the Soenda Strait. One of these missions was delayed as Elt R.A. Sleeuw was troubled with a paralysis of his right arm just before take off. On inspection it appeared that this was the result of an undiagnosed vertebra fraction he had sustained in a crash at Tjililitan a month earlier. The ML fighter pilots did not find anything during their reconnaissance missions.[12]

605 Squadron at Tjililitan had become fully operational as of this day and it had six operationally serviceable Hurricanes available. The unit consisted of an A flight with New Zealand pilots coming from 488 Squadron and a B flight with pilots from 258 Squadron. On the morning of 22 February this squadron was on stand-by. Between 10:00 and 11:00 hrs *A Flight* took off on a standing patrol and familiarisation flight.[13]

Japanese air raids on Kemajoran and Semplak

While the allied fighters were busily engaged in the protection of ships, the Japanese Army air force attacked the airfields of Kemajoran and Semplak between 11:30 and 11:50 hrs with 15 bombers in total of the 90th Sentai, escorted by 26 Ki-43 fighters of the 59th and 64th Sentais. The Japanese formations had not been noticed during their flight over western Java. Nine Ki-48 bombers escorted by 12 Ki-43 fighters attacked Kemajoran, several hits rendering the east-west runway partially unfit for use. The fighters carried out *strafings* (low level attacks with their guns) and damaged several bombers dispersed along the perimeter of the airfield. The damage to hangars and buildings was limited. Kemajoran did not have any anti-aircraft artillery, apart from a section of three 12.7-mm machine guns of the KNIL. The two Troops of 242 Battery 48 LAA of the British Army that had originally been stationed on the airfield had been transferred to Tjililitan on the night of 15 to 16 February and 16 to 17 February, respectively.[14]

Six Ki-48s of the 90th Sentai, with an escort of 14 Ki-43 fighters, flew on and attacked Semplak for some twenty minutes until 11:50 hrs. This airfield had no anti-aircraft defence at all and the possibilities to disperse the planes were relatively few on top of that. Six Hudson bombers and an ML Lodestar transport plane went up in flames and three further Hudsons were so heavily damaged that they had to be written off. A fourth Hudson was badly damaged, but could be repaired. On top of that a KNILM Fokker transport plane was damaged beyond repair.[15]

A Flight of 605 Squadron was up in the air at that moment and was directed by the British *Sector Command Batavia* towards the returning Japanese formations. On approaching the north coast of Java Flt Lt F.W.J. Oakden, Flg Off N.C. Sharp, Plt Off H.S. Pettit, Plt Off G.P. White, Sgt W.J.N. MacIntosh and Sgt E.E.G. Kuhn spotted the formation that was flying back from Semplak via Bantam to Palembang. The pilots pursued the Japanese aircraft until they were forced to return due to lack of fuel, without being able to carry out an attack.[16] At first, the fighters on *Readiness* were not committed, until it was certain that the Japanese attack was only directed at Semplak and Kemajoran. Then, four Hurricanes took off, but to no avail.[17]

In the afternoon the operations to protect the ships were continued and *A Flight* of 605 Squadron with the same crews flew another standing patrol. Further Japanese attacks, however, did not take place. Two Brewsters of 2-Vl.G.V made another seaward reconnaissance flight over the Soenda Strait but found nothing; nor did the *RecGroup* flying boats report any enemy activity there.[18]

The results of the missions of 22 February 1942

Unified Command considered the convoy protection operations of this day a great success. A number of ships had been conducted safely through the Soenda Strait en route to Australia or Ceylon. Several thousand British and Australian servicemen had been evacuated successfully and some ships with urgently needed munitions and spares reached Tjilatjap unharmed. On 22 February also some ships that carried military and civilian evacuees from Benkoelen or Padang (west coast of Sumatra) reached this harbour, among them a British cruiser of the *Western Striking Force*, which had picked up RAF personnel, amongst others, at Padang.[19]

Meanwhile, the RAF had stationed a detachment of an Air Stores Park at Tjilatjap with the help of the KNIL and civilian authorities. This unit distributed ammunition, spare engines and other materiel for RAF units in Java from the warehouses by rail and truck.[20] The ML had been doing this for some time now and the Inspection ML, the non-operational staff elements of the ML, which controlled, among others, the Technical Service and the Warehouse Service, even prepared for the transportation of new airplanes to Bandoeng by rail.

For ABDAIR the day was considerably less successful; the bad weather had allowed the Japanese to close in on Kemajoran and Semplak unnoticed. At the latter airfield nine bombers and two transport planes were lost, while allied fighters had been unable to do anything about it. The bombers were badly needed for air attacks on Japanese targets in southern Sumatra, the offensive part of the air campaign, and the loss of so many Hudsons therefore meant a serious blow.

The convoy protection operation described above was ABDAIR's last action. Within the framework of the reorganisation of the allied staffs and the discontinuation of the coordinating Unified Command Air Marshal Sir Richard Peirse transferred his command to Major-General L.H. van Oyen on the night of 22 February. This did not take place in a very cordial atmosphere. Van Oyen disagreed with Peirse's policy, which in his view came down to "British interests first". In his new position Van Oyen was usually designated as *Air Officer Commanding*, the present-day *Joint Forces Air Component Commander*. Colonel E.T. Kengen, the CO ML Command, also became the acting ML commander. One of the first orders to be issued by Van Oyen was the reversal of his predecessor's order regarding the availability of an

Air Striking Force on 23 February 1942. In his own order the number of bombers involved was considerably reduced.[21]

Java Air Command

On 23 February Major-General Van Oyen quickly organised his headquarters. In the early morning he took over ABDAIR's location and installed his own staff there. Furthermore, he moved the RAF's *West Group* headquarters at Soekaboemi to Bandoeng, and subsequently incorporated part of the personnel into *Java Air Command*, as ABDAIR was now called. With the exception of a few Americans, the command got a combined Dutch-British-Australian Operations Staff, consisting of ML and Marine Luchtvaart Dienst (MLD), RAF and RAAF personnel.[22] As in the ABDAIR days, the staff was responsible for the central mission planning and in that context issued operational orders (in western Java) to ML Command and BRITAIR, the new name for the downsized and reorganised *West Group*.

BRITAIR was accommodated in the same building as JAC. This headquarters was expanded with personnel of a small British staff no longer needed (225 *Bomber Group*) and as of 24 February it assumed not only the existing administrative and logistic responsibilities, but also operational control of the RAF and RAAF Squadrons. Within the ML, operational command was in the hands of ML Command, the operational ML staff, also located in Bandoeng.[23]

In the same building where JAC and BRITAIR were located there was also the *Combined Operations and Intelligence Centre* (COIC), the allied inter-service combat intelligence centre. The COIC, too, was expanded with surplus RAF staff personnel. Originally coming directly under *Unified Command*, COIC was controlled by Van Oyen as of 24 February. While Ter Poorten's General Headquarters determined the overall objectives and issued general directives to subordinate commanders, JAC took care of mission planning, selection and prioritisation of targets, etc. Furthermore, JAC coordinated all kinds of logistic matters with the KNIL and between the ML, RAF/RAAF and USAAF, such as the supply of lubricants and air transport.[24]

The JAC commander continued the air campaign in the west and east, as before. He had been closely involved in setting up the western campaign as ML commander. He only made a change in fighter deployment. For the time being, he gave the few allied fighters only air defence tasks. This involved the protection of the major airfields in Java, the main harbours and, where possible, the protection of the allied fleet. Contrary to Peirse, Van Oyen was determined not to commit the fighters offensively over southern Sumatra and Bali. The fighters were too scarce a commodity and the risk of losing them was too great. On 20 February four USAAF Curtiss P-40s were lost in an air raid on Bali airfield.[25]

The Japanese activities on 23 February 1942

On 23 February there was only very limited Japanese air activity over western Java. Fighters and bombers of the Army air force were deployed in the protection of Japanese ships supplying the units in Palembang and Banka and the protection of oil installations and Palembang airfield. Only the 50th Chutai executed a number of flights with Ki-15 and Ki-46 reconnaissance planes to drop anti-Dutch leaflets. From Tjililitan as well as Andir Hurricanes and Brewsters, respectively, made several alert take offs. Neither the RAF nor the ML managed to intercept the reported Japanese aircraft (Ki-15 or Ki-46 reconnaissance planes).[26] Furthermore, a reconnaissance float plane of the Japanese navy, possibly from Toboali (on the south coast of the island of Banka), reconnoitred Batavia harbour. The first five reconnaissance planes of the 1st Air Group, coming from two tenders (mother ships for float planes) had arrived at Toboali the previous day.[27]

Late in the morning six Hurricanes took off from Tjililitan. Among the pilots were Sgt T. Kelly of 605 Squadron and Sgt R.L. Dovell and Sgt T.W. Young of 242 Squadron. Several enemy planes were reported over the Bay of Batavia and in a widely spread formation it was attempted to discover these planes. A pair, consisting of Dovell and Young spotted a float plane at an altitude of 3,000 metres. Sgt Young managed to hit it already from a large distance with his first shots, and the Japanese pilot in his smoking bi-plane came flying headlong at Youngs' Hurricane. The two planes narrowly missed each other, upon which the Japanese disappeared. Young got the plane to his name (possibly erroneously).[28] No wreckage was found.[29] Although the Japanese air force did not carry out any attacks on targets in western Java, one allied fighter was lost as a result of an accident on the morning of 23 February. After a training flight Vdg C. Busser of 1-Vl.G.V, (not having flown for several days due to illness) crashed into the tail of a Glenn Martin bomber on landing. The Brewster was a total loss and the Glenn Martin got badly damaged. The unfortunate pilot was sent away the next day and transferred to the 4th Reconnaissance afdeling at Bandjar.[30]

Transfers

The remaining six serviceable RAF and RAAF Hudsons at Semplak were flown to the better defended Kalidjati in the early morning of 23 February 1942. This base had spacious, partially wooded, dispersal areas and, apart from a section with two 4-cm Bofor guns and two sections of three 12.7-mm machine guns each of A. III Ld. of the KNIL, a complete Battery (49 Battery of 48 LAA) of the British Army with ten 4-cm Bofor guns was stationed there.[31]

The Interceptors of 2-Vl.G.IV had been flown to Andir the evening before and operated permanently from there as of 23 February. The patrol operated from pens near the KNILM hangar in the south-eastern part of the base. The office of the KNILM, which by now had been largely evacuated to Australia, functioned as the day location for the crews.[32] The strength of the patrol was four aircraft.[33]

The Boeabatoe strip was designated for operations of the transport planes of the Depot Vliegtuigafdeling (D.Vl.A.) of the ML. On this strip six Lockheed Lodestars could be parked below the trees. The D.Vl.A. had Andir as its base until 23 February but had dispersed its planes as much as possible over the airfields in western Java. In the Japanese air raids of 21 and 22 February 1942 the afdeling lost altogether three Lodestars at Semplak and Kalidjati.[34]

The results of the convoy protection on 23 February

2-Vl.G.V and the RAF squadrons at Tjililitan, also carried out several missions on 23 February 1942, each time with two planes, over the Soenda Strait to protect ships passing through to the Indian Ocean.[35] As mentioned above, Van Oyen had rescinded the order of his predecessor, which had also specified an *Air Striking Force* for 23 February. Virtually all available bombers were committed to targets in southern Sumatra on this day, and, apart from eight fighters at Tjililitan and Semplak, only three Blenheims were held ready at Kalidjati for any eventualities. These planes undertook another (unsuccessful) attempt at tracing the submarines reported on 22 February. There were no Japanese actions directed at allied ships.[36]

* * *

CHAPTER 1A.6

The Fighter Operations on 24 February 1942

Introduction

The strengths of assigned and operational fighters on 24 February 1942 were as follows:[1]

Table 5

Unit	Assigned	Operationally serviceable	Type/remarks
242/605 Squadron	18	14	Hurricane
2-Vl.G.V	5	3	Brewster
1-Vl.G.V	4 (+2)	4 (+2)	Brewster (+ Hawk)
2-Vl.G.IV	4	3	Interceptor
2-Vl.G.IV	11	9	Hurricane, limited serviceable
Total	42 (+2)	33 (+2)	

On 24 February the fighter strength at Andir was augmented with the transfer of 2-Vl.G.V from Tjisaoek and Semplak (the maintenance section of the afdeling). This afdeling had three serviceable Brewsters left. With this small number the only sensible thing to do was to deploy them together with the RAF squadrons from Tjililitan or with 1-Vl.G.V from Andir. In view of the strongly reduced number of fighters at Andir JAC chose the latter option. Two damaged fighters of 2-Vl.G.V were left behind at Tjisaoek with a small repair team. Furthermore, the Brewster B-398 that had been transferred to the Technical Service was still at Semplak. JAC now designated Tjisaoek airfield as a diversionary and reserve airfield for the RAF squadrons at Tjililitan instead of Tjilleungsir.[2]

2-Vl.G.V had been reinforced the previous day with three New-Zealand RAF pilots of the deactivated 243 Squadron. They, however, arrived without the promised six Brewster Buffalos that were to have been transferred by the RAF to the ML. The three went along to Andir, but were designated for evacuation (probably) the next day. The ML had no shortage of fighter pilots itself.[3]

A new Japanese air raid on Andir and Kalidjati

Around 08:50 hrs Andir was alerted and 1-Vl.G.V and the 2-Vl.G.IV patrol were scrambled to intercept a bomber formation with fighter escort approaching Bandoeng from the north. The readiness patrol of 1-Vl.G.V on this occasion consisted of four Brewsters flown by Res Elt G.J. de Haas, Vdg B. Wink, Sgt G. van Haarlem and Sgt P. Compaan. The patrol commander of 2-Vl.G.IV was Vdg L.A.M. van der Vossen, with Sgt H.M. Haye and Sgt O.B. Roumimper manning the two other fighters.[4]

A short time later two further Brewsters of 2-Vl.G.V, flown by Vdg P.R. Jolly and Sgt G.M. Bruggink took to the air. The planes of this afdeling had just arrived at Andir from Tjisaoek. Kap J.H. van Helsdingen, the CO of 2-Vl.G.V, was on his way to the ML Command in his car, so his fighter remained on the ground. 2-Vl.G.V was accommodated in the Noordhangaar and in commandeered billets in Bandoeng.[5]

The weather was bad, with heavy clouds over the Preanger (Bandoeng) Plateau. The alarm came rather late. The fighters had the order to engage the Japanese bombers if they got the opportunity. These, however, were escorted by Ki-43s of the 59th Sentai. The ML pilots managed to gain height in time north of Bandoeng, but they were then faced at roughly the same altitude by nine Japanese fighters from the escort. De Haas engaged immediately and the two formations came racing headlong at each other and then passing through each other, after which a confused turning fight ensued among the towering cumulus clouds over Mount Boerangran and Mount Tankoeban Prahoe, north of Andir and Lembang.[6]

The ML pilots managed to hold their own in the fights and again showed that the Brewster (with wing tanks half filled and ammunition bays filled two-thirds in the wings) and the Interceptor had a turning circle to match that of the Ki-43s. For the first time the Brewsters had tracer ammunition in their wing machine guns, one tracer in every five to eight bullets, just like the Interceptors that had for much longer.

A formation of Nakajima Ki-43 fighters of the type operated over Java by the 59th and 64th Sentais. (Private collection, William H. Bartsch, via Bernard Millot)

In combination with the modern American reflector gunsights in the Brewsters this meant a greatly increased chance of hits.[7]

On 24 February the instruction to the Air Defence Commands with regard to the commitment of CW-21s (as much as possible only against bombers) was rescinded. This was the result of the inspection of the wreckage of a Japanese fighter found near Oedjoeng Broeng. It appeared that the Japanese employed two types of fighter and that the fighters used in western Java were armed considerably lighter than the Navy Os operating in eastern Java. In contrast to the Navy Os, the Ki-43s did not have any 20-mm guns and only had one 7.7-mm machine gun (firing conventional ammunition and tracers) and one 12.7-mm machine gun, which fired high explosive bullets, though. The Japanese themselves called it a 'machine canon'. The ML had tried out the same type of explosive ammunition at Samarinda II (East-Borneo) in January 1942, but the barrels of the 12.7-mm Colt machine guns of the Brewster used in the tests had burst.[8]

The pilots of 1-Vl.G.V and 2-Vl.G.IV were unlucky. Although several of them managed to score hits, a visual result was usually lacking, and only Sgt Van Haarlem was confident enough to claim an aircraft afterwards. The Japanese fighter he had hit disappeared smoking and seemingly out of control in the clouds. Wink, who had seen this, supported his claim and Van Haarlem got the plane to his name, even though wreckage was not found afterwards. The claim was probably justified, for when the Japanese formations had flown on to Tjililitan to carry out a second attack there were only 13 instead of 14 Ki-43s (see below). Sergeant Compaan received hits in the wing of his Brewster and made a precautionary landing at Pameungpeuk with a perforated fuel tank. The other fighters of 1-Vl.G.V and 2-Vl.G.IV received no or only very light damage. Just like on 21 February the Japanese fighter pilots retreated from the fight after ten to fifteen minutes. After the battle the Andir fighters were directed towards Tandjong Priok, but some pilots did not hear the order and others returned to Andir because of the damage their planes had sustained. Only two of the Interceptors reached Batavia, but the only planes they saw there were British Hurricanes; a meeting which almost ended fatally (see below). Pilots were Van der Vossen and Roumimper.[9]

Jolly and Bruggink got into a fight with five (other) Ki-43s, but could not score any hits in the turning fight. Bruggink fired at a 'Navy O', but after about two seconds all four machine guns of his aircraft jammed. His aircraft received several hits, but afterwards the damage appeared to be limited and was classified as light. Jolly's plane was undamaged.[10]

The opponent consisted of 14 Ki-43 fighters of the 59th Sentai, escorting 17 Ki-48 bombers of the 90th Sentai. The latter attacked at 09:10 hrs and they were able to bomb Andir undisturbed from an altitude of about 1,000 metres, albeit amid intense anti-aircraft fire,[11] hitting mainly buildings and platforms with aircraft in the south-western part of the field. There, at the Technical Service, three American B-17 bombers, in for repair work, sustained damage. Furthermore, an ML Glenn Martin bomber, also at the TD was lost, while a second received damage. An old Fokker F-VII, the FT-901 of the D.Vl.A., used as a trainer for wireless operators, was also destroyed.[12]

In the northern part of Andir also a number of bombs fell, but the only damage there was from a direct hit on a row of dummy planes arranged east of the Noordhangaar. There was one casualty in the raid, a day labourer belonging to the working party which was doing construction work for the KNIL Engineers on the air defence batteries located along the north-eastern perimeter of Andir.[13]

The anti-aircraft artillery of the KNIL and the British Army, the Andir North position (a company minus of A. III Ld.), Andir South (ditto) and 95 Battery (48 LAA), fired with intensity their 2-cm, 4-cm and 8-cm guns around Andir at the attacking bombers and got (near) hits on at least nine of the Ki-48s. Three Japanese planes were actually hit, as the gunners could well see through their telescope sights and range finders, but they just kept flying on in formation. It was assumed, mistakenly, that these bombers would not make it to their home base. No wreckage was found and afterwards it was (rightly) concluded that the Japanese formation had flown on to Tjililitan after the raid. This base was attacked about half an hour later by 17 Ki-48s.[14]

About ten minutes after the raid on Andir, around 09:15 hrs, 16 Ki-48s (out of a formation of 20) of the 75th Sentai attacked Kalidjati airfield. The escort consisted of 13 Ki-43s of the 64th Sentai. Two Hudson bombers were totally lost and several were lightly damaged. The damage to the airfield was so extensive that Kalidjati had to be temporarily closed down.[15]

The Japanese fighter pilots reported a battle with seven Hurricanes and two 'P-43s' near Bandoeng, five (sic) fighters of which were shot down. Apart from anti-aircraft fire they met no resistance over Kalidjati. 49 Battery (48 LAA) of the British Army, with nine operational 4-cm Bofor guns, and the section of A. III Ld. of the KNIL at Kalidjati with two 4-cm Bofor guns, claimed hits on three bombers, with a possible fourth. Three planes were seen to crash, whose wreckage was afterwards found.[16]

2-Vl.G.IV at Kalidjati with its Hurricanes was not operational as yet for defence tasks, due to the lack of the right crystals for the aircraft radios. Patrols of three or four Hurricanes did make some training flights and all the pilots had by now done firing practice. A patrol of three fighters, led by Elt J.B.H. Bruinier, happened to be airborne when the raid on Kalidjati began and diverted to Bandoeng. Andir had been closed as well, and almost out of fuel the Hurricanes landed on the Boeabatoeweg. There were several casualties among the RAF personnel attached to 2-Vl.G.IV at Kalidjati.[17]

New raids on Tjililitan and Tandjong Priok

The RAF *Readiness Flight* at Tjililitan was also airborne. In the morning first a section was scrambled to intercept two Japanese airplanes flying over Batavia, probably two Ki-15 reconnaissance planes from Palembang. Plt Off J.A. Campbell (605 Squadron) later thought that he had shot one down, but he had probably fired at the Interceptor of Vdg Van der Vossen of 2-Vl.G.IV, who made an emergency landing with his damaged plane at Kemajoran after an attack by a Hurricane. When a formation of Japanese bombers was reported, the second section of the *Readiness Flight* was sent up, with, amongst others, Flt Lt J.C. Hutton (second in command of 605 Squadron) and 242 Squadron pilots 2 Lt N. Anderson (SAAF), Plt Off T.W. Watson and Sgt G.J. King.

Having been alerted in the meantime, the pilots of the *Stand-by Flight*, consisting of six Hurricanes, took off soon after that. They were, amongst others, Flt Lt F.W.J. Oakden, Flg Off N.C. Sharp, Sgt W.J.N. MacIntosh, Plt Off H.S. Pettit and Sgt E.E.G. Kuhn, all 605 Squadron. All 14 available Hurricanes were airborne now. They could, however, not give any support to the ML, as they were warned soon after take off that a Japanese formation was approaching Batavia from the direction of Bandoeng.[18]

Flt Lt Hutton and several other pilots of the *Readiness Flight* attacked a formation of (unescorted) bombers and claimed to have shot down three of them. They were probably the Ki-48s of the 75th Sentai passing Batavia on their way to Kalidjati. Of these probably one was shot down, as 21 Ki-48s had left Palembang I, while a formation of only 20 was seen at Kalidjati.[19]

At about 09:45 hrs 17 Ki-48s of the 90th Sentai, escorted by 13 Ki-43 fighters of the 59th Sentai, attacked Tjililitan airfield. The formation that had attacked Andir earlier had flown on to Tjililitan and dropped quite a number of bombs there. What is striking is that the formation of Ki-43s (according to Japanese records) was one short now. Hutton's section had only just returned when the Japanese bombers attacked. Hutton was wounded by bomb splinters, while 2 Lt N.R. Dummet (SAAF, a pilot working in a ground position) temporarily lost his eyesight due to bomb blast.[20]

In the meantime, the *Stand-by Flight* had engaged the fighter escort of the 59th Sentai. The Japanese fighter pilots reported a fight with some ten Hurricanes, two of which they (rightly) believed to have shot down. Sharp hit a Ki-43, but was then shot down himself. He successfully used his parachute and reported back to his unit a few days later. An unknown pilot crash landed his Hurricane, which had been hit, on Tjililitan, being pursued by a Ki-43, that subsequently fired at the grounded plane which had to be written off. One or two other Hurricanes received minor damage and could land safely. The British fighter pilots claimed three 'Navy Os' as probables. It is not known whether the 59th Sentai suffered any losses during this fight, but this was probably not the case.[21]

The anti-aircraft artillery, 242 Battery (48 LAA) of the British Army and the section of A. I Ld. of the KNIL, fired intensely at the attackers and shot one Ki-48 down, after a large part of its wing had come off, upon which it crashed. Two other Ki-48s were hit and, losing altitude, they flew at a relatively low altitude into the direction of the coast. They were claimed as probables. The damage on the ground was not too bad. There were quite a few craters, but the runway could still be used.[22]

Almost simultaneously with the raid on Tjililitan some of the bombers that had first gone to Kalidjati now attacked Tandjong Priok, Batavia's harbour. These four Ki-48s of the 75th Sentai were escorted by all 13 fighters of the 64th Sentai. At low altitude the Japanese fighters fired their machine guns at targets in the harbour area. Here, too, the anti-aircraft artillery of the KNIL and the British Army fired intensely at the attackers, but they scored no results.[23]

The afternoon attack on Tandjong Priok

At about 15:20 hrs the 75th Sentai attacked Tandjong Priok harbour once more, this time with 16 Ki-48s and again an escort of the 64th Sentai (13 Ki-43s).[24] In the first instance seven Hurricanes took off; four were flown by pilots of 242 Squadron, among whom Flt Lt B.J. Parker and Sgt G.J. Dunn, and three by pilots of 605 Squadron, among whom Sgt A. Lambert and Sgt J.G. Vibert. Sqn Ldr E.W.

Wright, the 605 Squadron CO, acted as the commander of the *Readiness Flight*. During formation, just after take off, two planes collided. Lambert successfully used his parachute at low altitude, and the other (unknown) pilot of 242 Squadron managed to make a safe belly landing, but his Hurricane was a write off.[25]

Because of the accident and the necessity to have one airplane circle over the location of the crash (in order to guide a rescue team towards the spot) Sqn Ldr Wright remained where he was. Parker and his number two Dunn saw two other Hurricanes turn away after take off, and continued their mission, later followed by one or two more pilots. Near Tandjong Priok, from an altitude of 6,000 metres, Parker and Dunn spotted an approaching formation of 12 to 15 fighters at a somewhat lower altitude and carried out a dive attack on three planes that turned away. The attack was a partial failure as the armament of Parker's aircraft did not work. Dunn hit a Ki-43, and saw bits of sheet metal come off the aircraft, and immediately dived away. The Japanese fighter was probably only damaged.[26]

The 16 Ki-48s first bombed the harbour from a high altitude (about 5,000 metres), after which some of the planes made another run from 2,000 metres. At the same time three Ki-43 fighters attacked targets in the dock area. The harbour did not receive any damage worth mentioning, as most of the bombs fell into the sea, but the fighters set fire to a large BPM storage tank for shipping fuel in their low-level attacks. This caused a serious reduction of the available fuel for the allied navy. The KNIL and British Army anti-aircraft artillery at Tandjong Priok fired fiercely at the Japanese aircraft and damaged a number of the attacking Japanese bombers.[27]

Parker and Dunn, it was later learned, were the only ones to encounter any enemy. For unknown reasons one of the Hurricanes (pilot unknown) landed at Andir, somewhere between 16:30 and 17:00 hrs. The plane hit the runway hard and in an angle, turned around it axis and came to a standstill next to the runway, the undercarriage damaged. The plane was sent to the ML Technical Service for repairs.[28]

On his return at Tjililitan, Parker ran into Air Commodore S.F. Vincent, who was on a visit and who fulminated when he heard that the armament of Parker's plane had failed. He was so angry because he thought that the pilots should not rely blindly on their ground crews and should try out their planes themselves before take off and test their guns on their way to the target. Vincent was in a bad mood, probably because that morning he had driven in vain to Tjisaoek to see Kap Van Helsdingen. 2-Vl.G.V had left without him being informed about it.[29]

The 64th Sentai claimed to have shot down two four-engine flying boats on their way back from Tandjong Priok to Palembang near Noordwachter, the northernmost island of the Duizend Eilanden. In fact it was one of a pair of triple-engine MLD Dornier flying boats that had bombed the roadstead of Muntok. A second Do-24 had been attacked a bit earlier by Navy Os of the Yamada air group operating from Muntok. Both flying boats were lost and one of the crews was killed.[30]

Apart from the Japanese bomber that had crashed near Tjililitan, no further wreckages were found of Ki-48s or Ki-43s and there were no reports afterwards of crashed airplanes, either. Dunn, too, was convinced that the fighter he had hit had only been damaged and Parker had not been able to score any hits due to the problems with his guns.[31]

Summary

In the morning the Japanese Army air force attacked Andir, Kalidjati, Tjililitan as well as Tandjong Priok. Nine Brewsters and Interceptors managed to engage the Japanese fighters escorting the bombers for Andir and to shoot one Ki-43 down, but the bombers succeeded in attacking Andir unhindered. Two ML planes were lost there. The attack on Kalidjati could only be met with anti-aircraft artillery and cost two allied bombers. RAF Hurricanes probably shot down one of the Ki-48s on their way to Kalidjati near Batavia. The anti-aircraft artillery at Kalidjati shot down three Ki-48s.

At Tjililitan two Hurricanes were downed by Ki-43s, one of which made a crash landing at the airfield. This plane was subsequently destroyed by strafing. The anti-aircraft artillery at Tjililitan shot down one Ki-48. In the afternoon the Japanese Army air force carried out a second attack on Tandjong Priok harbour. Two Hurricanes engaged the fighter escort but without success, two others crashed during take off. For the Japanese Army air force 24 February 1942 was not a good day, with the loss of one Ki-43 and five Ki-48 bombers. For the RAF, which lost four scarce fighters, it was even worse.

* * *

CHAPTER 1A.7

The Events and Fighter Operations on 25 February 1942

Introduction

On 25 February 1942 the Japanese Army air force concluded its offensive against western Java for the attainment of air superiority with several large raids. For the first, and last time, the Japanese Navy air force joined in the offensive and apart from an attack on Tandjong Priok carried out a raid on Tjililitan airfield. The Japanese Army air force carried out two attacks on Kalidjati airfield. The number of available ML and RAF fighters had been reduced considerably as a result of the Japanese actions on 24 February. In the morning RAF Tjililitan had eight operationally serviceable Hurricanes, the ML at Kalidjati had nine. The ML fighters at Andir did not carry out any operations on this day due to bad weather.

The allied decisions

In the late morning of 25 February Major-General Van Oyen, the JAC commander, concluded that the race against time had been lost. In the morning *RecGroup* discovered a Japanese invasion fleet in Balikpapan roadstead, which was doubtlessly heading for eastern Java. There were no signs yet of a similar Japanese operation in the west, but intelligence channels had revealed that such a fleet was being assembled. The Japanese had not (or at best only minimally) postponed their planned invasion, and the expected American P-40s and British Hurricane fighters would not arrive in time to fend it off.[1]

     As before in eastern Java, the Japanese air forces had been successful in their battle for air superiority in western Java. Bad weather and the failure to make the British radar stations operational quickly enough had put ABDAIR and JAC at a disadvantage. Nevertheless, the fighters had been able to hold their own quite decently in the west, but in a week's time about one third of the fighter strength had been lost. Furthermore, the local balance of strength had been so disadvantageous for the allied air force that Japanese bombers had been able to attack airfields (and also Batavia harbour) virtually unhindered, and a large number of ML, RAF and RAAF bombers had been lost in the process. As a result, the possibility to exert pressure on the Japanese by bombing them in southern Sumatra, in particular Palembang I airfield, had been greatly reduced. Still, the allied bombers scored considerable successes (see Part 1B below).

In consultation with Van Oyen and Vice-Admiral C.E.L. Helfrich, commander of the allied naval forces (ABDA-FLOAT), Lieutenant-General H. ter Poorten, the Commander-in-Chief *ABDA Area*, decided on the following measures in the late morning of 25 February.

–   The allied fleet is to assemble immediately at Soerabaja in order to attack the reported invasion fleet from there; to this end as many warships as possible will relocate from Tandjong Priok to Soerabaja.

–   The allied air force is to relocate as many fighters as possible to Ngoro (eastern Java) to provide cover for the *Combined Striking Force*, the allied naval squadron.

–   After carrying out an attack the fleet is to go to western Java to launch a second attack on the invasion fleet, which (it was assumed) is on its way to western Java. The fighters transferred to Ngoro are to relocate to western Java to provide cover.[2]

In spite of these measures, the *Counter-air* operation went on as usual. The JAC fighters, however, were mostly committed as cover for the allied warships. The bombing offensive against Japanese targets in southern Sumatra and Banka petered out, as from 26 February onwards it became more directed at searching for and attacking the expected 'western' invasion fleet.[3]

The raid on Tandjong Priok and Tjililitan

The Japanese Navy air force carried out a raid on Batavia on 25 February 1942. To this end a C5M-reconnaissance plane had reconnoitred Tandjong Priok harbour and Kemajoran and Tjililitan airfields the previous day. Tandjong Priok harbour as well as Tjililitan airfield was a target. For the attack the Japanese committed 27 G3M bombers of the Genzan Kokutai stationed at Palembang II (the military airfield south-west of the town of Palembang) and 13 Navy Os and one C5M reconnaissance plane of the Yamada air group at Muntok. The latter unit had been transferred to Palembang II in preparation of the attack. The attacks took place between 10:30 and 11:00 hrs. The Japanese G3Ms bombed ships in the harbour and the roadstead. The fighters were supposed to attack Tjililitan airfield, but were engaged by RAF Hurricanes before they got there.[4]

Thanks to the radar warning of the British cruiser Exeter stationed at Tandjong Priok, the only allied warship equipped with radar, the *Readiness Flight* at Tjililitan took off well in time. It was virtually impossible for the aerial surveillance posts to follow the enemy formations due to the poor view and thick clouds. The radar stations at Batavia were not quite operational yet that day. The RAF *Readiness Flight* took off with eight Hurricanes in total, five flown by pilots of 605 Squadron and three with pilots from 242 Squadron. More Hurricanes were not available that day.[5]

The two sections of the *Flight* became separated due to the bad weather. The 605 section got into a fight with the Navy Os over the coast north-east of Batavia. From an altitude of about 8,000 metres the Hurricane section dived onto the Japanese formation of about 15 aircraft. In spite of all the warnings about the performance of the Navy O, section leader Flt Lt H.A. Dobbyn engaged in a turning fight and was shot down, losing his life. It is possible he thought he was dealing with Ki-43 Army 1s instead of Navy Os. Plt Off J.A. Campbell also got into a turning fight. He shot one Navy O down, but had to leave his badly damaged Hurricane by parachute. A KNIL patrol recovered him later, lightly wounded. The Japanese Navy pilot Suehara Ide lost his life. The other two pilots of the section, Sgt T. Kelly and Sgt P.M.T. Healy, each fired at a Navy O and immediately dived away. Although Kelly thought he had scored hits, there were no further visual results.[6]

The section of 242 Squadron, three pilots of 242 Squadron and Sqn Ldr E.W. Wright of 605 Squadron, who acted as the commander of the *Readiness Flight*, made no contact with the enemy over the Batavia area and returned. Sgt J.A. Sandeman Allen lost contact with his section again through the bad weather and subsequently attacked several Navy Os he had spotted. He thought he had damaged one, but he got one 'Navy O' to his name, as Sqn Ldr Wright had seen a Japanese fighter go down.[7] Very likely this was the C5M reconnaissance plane. According to anti-aircraft artillery personnel at Tjililitan, however, the reconnaissance plane, which they believed to be a Navy O, crashed after a hit from the British 242 Battery. The anti-aircraft gunners saw one 'Navy O' catch fire during an attack and crash.

The section of A. I Ld. of the KNIL and 242 Battery (48 LAA) of the British Army, two 2-cm and eight 4-cm guns in total, fired intensely at eight Japanese fighters (probably seven Navy Os and one C5M reconnaissance plane) attacking the base. The British also fired with six Brenguns at the fighters that carried out low-level strafings on the anti-aircraft gun positions along the perimeter of the airfield. Two fighters were hit by the Brengunners of 242 Battery. One of the British gunners, who was firing at the Japanese fighters from a trench with his rifle, was hit in the head by a machine gun bullet and died. He was the only casualty in the attack.[8]

The British pilots claimed one Navy O, a figure that was doubled the next day when Campbell (who returned to Tjililitan in the early hours of 26 February) had been debriefed. The Japanese pilots claimed three 'Spitfires' and a fourth as probable. In reality the air fight had cost the British two Hurricanes. At Tjililitan the Japanese fighter pilots set fire to two parked single-engine planes, possibly light communication aircraft of the MVAF. The Yamada air group lost one Navy O and one C5M had gone missing. The Japanese bombers that had attacked Tandjong Priok harbour and the roadstead escaped, but the KNIL and British Army anti-aircraft artillery had put up such stiff resistance that 11 of the 27 G3Ms had sustained damaged and two crew members had been wounded.[9] The Japanese bomber crews were convinced they had scored a direct hit on the aft deck of a British heavy cruiser, but in fact they had hit a British tanker. The rest of their bombs fell into the sea.[10] A number of Navy Os also attacked the harbour after the air combat and the Japanese fighter pilots set fire to a number of storage tanks with shipping fuel.[11] The loss of the tanker and the storage tanks caused a serious shortage of shipping fuel for the allied warships. The warships themselves had been cruising at sea, pending the all-clear of the air alert and were not hit.[12]

In the afternoon two allied cruisers and three allied destroyers left Batavia for Soerabaja, where ABDA-FLOAT was assembling a *Combined Striking Force*. They arrived the next day. As mentioned above, these relocations were motivated by the discovery of a Japanese invasion fleet in the Balikpapan roadstead by *RecGroup* in the morning of 25 February.[13]

The raid on Kalidjati

On this day the 3rd Hiko Dan of the Japanese Army air force attacked Kalidjati airfield. In the early afternoon two missions from Palembang I attacked with short intervals. First to arrive, at about 11:55 hrs, were 16 Ki-48 bombers of the 75th Sentai, escorted by 12 Ki-43 fighters of the 64th Sentai, followed by 16 Ki-48s of the 90th Sentai, escorted by 12 Ki-43s of the 59th Sentai at about 12:45 hrs.[14] The ten Hurricanes of 2-Vl.G.IV at Kalidjati had not been committed in previous Japanese air raids, as they could not be employed for air defence tasks due to the absence of the right crystals for the radios. Patrolling the extensive sector of Air Defence Command without radios, often in heavy clouds, was deemed to be pointless by ML Command and a waste of scarce aircraft and engine hours. This seeming passivity created some irritation among the British units at Kalidjati, in particular. As a result, BRITAIR even cautiously enquired whether the Hurricanes could be returned. This, however, would mean that the most experienced ML fighter pilots would have no aircraft, which was unacceptable for Major-General Van Oyen. Moreover, the ML Radiodienst (Radio Service) expected to be able to supply the crystals on the short term. An outcome of the discussion was that it was (again) considered to locate 2-Vl.G.IV at Tjisaoek and the afdeling was ordered to fly standing patrols (nowadays known as *combat air patrols*) after being alerted, which it did for the first time in the morning of 25 February 1942.[15]

On the first warning of the Air Defence Command Bandoeng 2-Vl.G.IV took off with the eight Hurricanes at readiness. The Japanese planes approached Batavia via the Duizend Eilanden and might be destined for Kalidjati. The pilots were Elt R.A.D. Anemaet, Vdg W. Hamming, SM P. Boonstoppel and Sergeants F.J. de Wilde, N. Dejalle, A. Kok, H.J. Mulder, and J.C. Jacobs. For almost two hours the fighter pilots were cruising in a much spread out formation between 4,000 and 7,500 metres (with the lone top cover plane at about 7,500 metres) in a large semi-circle round Kalidjati and were then forced to return for lack of fuel. Above the mountains surrounding the Preanger (Bandoeng) Plateau they saw heavy clouds and showers. If the Japanese showed up, and that was taken for granted, no help would come from the fighters stationed at Andir.[16]

Anemaet and Kok had just landed when minutes before 12:00 hrs the first Ki-43s appeared over Kalidjati. Both pilots taxied off the runway as fast as possible and made their escape. Landing third in line, Jacobs was surprised to see his colleague Kok jump from his plane and sprint away. He gave full throttle and tried to fly for safety at low altitude. It did not work. Although one of the two Ki-43s pursuing him aborted the chase, the remaining Ki-43 shot him down in the end. His plane had sustained hits in the engine and he belly-landed on Kalidjati. Sgt Jacobs was taken to hospital with a large number of metal splinters in one of his legs.[17]

Two other ML fighter pilots engaged the enemy in a turning fight over Kalidjati and the surrounding plantation woods, but retreated as soon as they could because of their fuel shortage. Subsequently, the Japanese Ki-48 bombers released their bombs on the airfield from high altitude. Mulder, Hamming and Dejalle landed at Kalidjati on their last drops of fuel, just when the attack was over. Boonstoppel and De Wilde diverted to Tjikampek, where especially for Hurricane operations a small supply of 100-octane fuel was stored. The engine of Boonstoppel's fighter went dead when he was taxiing to the end of the landing area. Just when the two pilots had returned to Kalidjati, the Japanese attacked again, barely an hour after the first attack. This time small formations of Ki-48s bombed from a low altitude and Ki-43s carried out strafings. Kok's Hurricane, and also Jacobs' plane, were fired at by Ki-43s and were total losses after the second air raid. Also the Hurricane of either Hamming or Dejalle, which stranded with a main wheel in a fresh bomb crater after landing, was lost. The other fighters, however, were by now well dispersed, far away from the runway.[18] The Japanese fighter pilots of the 64th Sentai claimed (correctly) one Hurricane. The pilots of the 59th Sentai claimed three enemy fighters, one of which had in fact been shot down earlier by the 64th Sentai.[19]

The attacks of the 3rd Hiko Dan cost the 2-Vl.G.IV three Hurricanes and of the remaining seven the unit had six serviceable aircraft left the next day. Most of the damage at the airfield had been caused by the first (high) altitude bombardment. The second, from a relatively low altitude, preceded and followed by strafings carried out by the Ki-43s, was a partial failure due to intensive fire from the British and Netherlands East Indies 4-cm Bofor guns. The gunners of 49 Battery also fired with Brenguns at the Ki-43s and ML and RAF personnel did the same with the 7.7-mm machine guns located along the perimeter in concrete rings. Anti-aircraft gunners of the KNIL fired their 12.7-mm machine guns, probably hitting one Ki-43 during low altitude manoeuvring. Hitting the fast fighters was extremely difficult, though. Not only were parked allied aircraft attacked, but also several smaller depots with drums of aircraft fuel along the perimeter of the field were set ablaze, the water supply of the base was destroyed and several buildings and hangars were damaged or destroyed. Apart from a number of wounded, there were no fatalities among the ML, RAF, RAAF and the British Army. Two British Blenheim Mark I bombers were lost.[20]

During the first raid the 3rd Hiko Dan lost no aircraft and reported that all bombers and fighters of the 64th and 75th Sentais had returned safely at Palembang. The 59th and 90th Sentais had been less fortunate. The anti-aircraft artillery claimed hits during the second attack on altogether seven of the Japanese bombers and two Ki-48s had been seen to crash. One of them was in flames after a direct hit. Later the Air Defence Command Bandoeng confirmed that the wreckage of two bombers had been found. I Division of the KNIL and the Aerial Surveillance Circle Batavia further reported that, after the afternoon raid, a damaged single-engine plane had crossed the coastline near Batavia and had ditched into the sea. This is in line with information from the Japanese Navy air force. On 25 February a float plane, escorted by a Ki-43, picked up a ditched fighter pilot near one of the Duizend Eilanden, whose Ki-43 was destroyed.[21] The absence of radio contact between the Hurricane pilots and the ground station of the Air Defence Command Bandoeng cost JAC three of its scarce fighters. Although it became clear very early on that the first reported Japanese formation was heading for Batavia, 2-Vl.G.IV — once airborne — could not be informed about this. Due to the weather in the area of Batavia, which had deteriorated very much, it was not noticed that a second formation was flying in the direction of Cheribon (northeast of Kalidjati). *Exeter*'s radar was not available anymore. Only when the first Ki-43 fighters appeared over Kalidjati, was the air raid alarm sounded on the base. Because the weather over the Preanger Plateau (where the city of Bandoeng and Andir airfield were located) was also very bad, the fighters at Andir could not take off in support of the Hurricane pilots. What the afdeling commander had warned about with regard to the risks of deployment without radio connection, happened. Low on fuel and partially landed, the Hurricanes were taken by surprise by the Japanese fighters.[22]

Protection of the allied fleet

When the bad weather had lifted somewhat in the early afternoon, a detachment of three Brewsters without ground crew of 1-Vl.G.V left Andir for Ngoro in eastern Java. The fighters and their pilots had been seconded to the American 17 Pursuit Squadron (17 PS) that was down to only ten operational P-40s the previous day. Two other P-40s were still being repaired.[23] Two of the Brewsters (the B-3160 and the B-3161) were reserves, the very last, only recently assembled by the Technical Service. The fighters were flown by Res Elt H.H.J. Simons (in a Brewster that had just received a replacement wing), Vdg B. Wink (B-3160) and Sgt G. van Haarlem (B-3161). The planes arrived at Ngoro at the end of the afternoon.[24]

Two patrols of 1-Vl.G.V stayed behind at Andir; I patrol with Elt P.G. Tideman, Sgt A.E. van Kempen, Elt P.A.C. Benjamins, and Sgt A. Bergamin and II patrol, with Res Elt G. J. de Haas, Sgt P. Compaan, Vdg C.A. Vonck and Sgt J.P. Adam.[25] Initially, the two patrols only had five serviceable Brewsters available. Later that day, however, the Technical Service delivered two more aircraft that came out of major repairs. 2-Vl.G.V, with three Brewsters at Andir (two of which were operationally serviceable), also received one additional aircraft on 25 February when Sgt H. Huys flew the repaired B-3117 over from Tjiasoek. Furthermore, that day saw the arrival from Tjililitan of the first of four British Buffalo fighters that were transferred by the RAF to the ML on 25 and 26 February 1942. For the time being, the fighters were parked near the Noordhangaar, because (without radios) they were not fully operational and still needed to be fitted out with Dutch equipment. The Technical Service was also going to carry out some modifications to bring them up to the ML standard as much as possible. This was not to be, however.[26]

The Japanese results

The raids carried out on 25 February were meant to be the last in the context of the operation for the attainment of air superiority over western Java, prior to the invasion of the island. As of 26 February the emphasis came to lie more on the protection of the ships in the invasion fleet intended for the landings in western Java and the bases in the conquered southern Sumatra that were so vital for the logistic support. The Japanese Army air force was excited about the great successes achieved in the battle over western Java.

The Japanese Navy was much more careful. On 23 February the landings were postponed with two days on the initiative of the Navy until the (very) early hours of 28 February, because the air superiority over both eastern and western Java was deemed to be too tenuous.[27] On 25 February the 3rd Hiko Shudan worked out the results of the offensive that had been going on over western Java since 19 February. It was reckoned that up to and including 25 February, 33 enemy airplanes had been shot down, 53 had been destroyed and more than 150 were assumed to have been damaged.[28]

The Japanese Navy liaison officer at Palembang had his doubts about the report. Thus, 3rd Hiko Dan's own losses reported in it only referred to direct combat losses of the Ki-43 fighters over western Java, whereas there were also 'operational losses' and losses of other types of aircraft, on top of that. This was not explicitly mentioned in the report, however. If their own losses were presented in such favourable light, what could be expected of the losses inflicted on the enemy? The liaison officer was right, as in reality only about 65 (instead of 86) aircraft had been shot down or destroyed on the ground by the 3rd Hiko Dan, and this included a number of transport, training and communication planes; a hefty over-claim. Nevertheless, there was no question that the losses inflicted were serious.[29]

The commander of the 3rd Hiko Shudan stuck by the analysis, but on 26 February the 3rd Assault Group of the Navy air force (air groups at Kuching and Muntok) presented its own analysis on the basis of reconnaissance results. It was concluded that there were still strong enemy air forces present in the Batavia area. On the basis of this report the Japanese Navy decided on 27 February to augment the forces for the assault on western Java with the 4th Air Group at St. Jacques in Indo-China (consisting of a light aircraft carrier with F1M fighter-reconnaissance planes on board, a destroyer and several auxiliary vessels).[30] Further postponement of the invasion on the basis of the air situation was no option because of the obstinate attitude of the army, which had agreed on 23 February 1942 to a two-day delay on condition that this would be the last.[31]

Summary

On 25 February 1942 the last Japanese raids took place on western Java within the context of the operation for the attainment of air superiority in preparation of the invasion. These attacks cost JAC several planes. At Tjililitan the RAF lost two Hurricanes in the air battle and one fighter pilot was killed. The ML and RAF at Kalidjati lost three Hurricanes and two Blenheim bombers. On the Japanese side one Navy O and a C5M reconnaissance plane were lost in the raids on Tandjong Priok and Tjililitan. In the raid on Kalidjati the 3rd Hiko Dan lost a Ki-43 and two Ki-48 bombers. In the context of the formation of a single *Combined Striking Force* at Soerabaja by ABDA-FLOAT, the air defence of this naval squadron was to be reinforced to a maximum. 17 PS at Ngoro (eastern Java) was augmented with three Brewsters of 1-Vl.G.V on 25 February 1942. More were to follow.

***

CHAPTER 1A.8

The Events of 26 and 27 February 1942

Introduction

On 26 February the Japanese air forces in the west were very busy protecting the convoys of the approaching 'western' invasion fleet (as yet undiscovered by the allies) and there were no air raids on airfields in western Java on this day. There were, however, some reconnaissance activities over the area carried out by both the Army and Navy air forces. The allied fighters at Tjililitan and Andir made several unsuccessful attempts at intercepting the reported Japanese reconnaissance planes. On 26 February 1942 JAC once more transferred some of the Brewster fighters at Andir, along with 2-Vl.G.IV (Hurricanes), to Ngoro in eastern Java. The Japanese invasion was imminent and the protection of the allied fleet at Soerabaja had to be stepped up as much as possible.

The Japanese invasion of Java had originally been planned for the night of 27 on 28 February 1942 and the Japanese Army air force carried out a few final air raids on the airfields at Batavia and Buitenzorg as well as Tandjong Priok harbour on 27 February, as a preparation for the landings of the Japanese army in the Bay of Bantam and at Merak in the west of western Java. 242 Squadron at Tjililitan intercepted one of the Japanese formations in the morning, but, just like the anti-aircraft artillery, was not successful. The afternoon brought new Japanese air raids.

The fighter protection for the Combined striking Force at Soerabaja

On 26 February 1942 a considerable number of the ML fighters at Andir and Kalidjati left for Ngoro in eastern Java to reinforce the American 17 Pursuit Squadron (17 PS). In the morning the first to leave were four Brewsters of 1-Vl.G.V and 2-Vl.G.V, flown by Res Elt G.J. de Haas, Vdg C.A. Vonck, Sgt G.M. Bruggink and Sgt H. Huys. Two of the Brewsters had come out of major repairs the day before, and Bruggink's B-3117 had been flown from Tjisaoek to Andir by Huys on 25 February and had been assigned again to 2-Vl.G.V. Six Hurricanes, led by afdeling commander Elt R.A.D. Anemaet, left Kalidjati in the early afternoon. A seventh Hurricane followed the next day. One of the Brewsters, flown by Sgt Huys, returned with a malfunction and finally arrived at Ngoro from Maospati on 28 February.[1]

The three remaining Brewsters arrived around 14:00 hrs and, just like Res Elt Simons' patrol before (see the previous chapter), they were seconded to 17 PS. The aircraft of 2-Vl.G.IV arrived at Ngoro at about 16:00 hrs. This afdeling did take along its own maintenance personnel. Only the RAF detachment was left behind, its personnel to be transferred to Bandoeng and mostly designated for evacuation. The Hurricanes were still not operational for air defence tasks due to the absence of the right crystals for the radios. The ML Radiodienst (Radio Service) at Bandoeng was, however, busily engaged in acquiring the required crystals and had just concluded a successful search for them all over Java, and even as far as Australia through the NEI trade representative there.[2]

The air defence of Bandoeng on 26 February 1942

At Andir remained stationed one patrol of 1-Vl.G.V (five Brewsters), one patrol of 2-Vl.G.V (three Brewsters plus one aircraft in repair at Tjisaoek) and one patrol of 2-Vl.G.IV (four Interceptors, three of which were serviceable and one was at Kemajoran awaiting repairs). In total there were 13 assigned fighters left at Andir and Kalidjati, only eight of which, however, were operationally serviceable at the end of the day.[3]

In the afternoon of 26 February three Interceptors were flown to Maospati (Madioen), where in the Technical Service workshop the fighters were subjected to a modification and inspection. That maintenance was badly needed, for the engines of the fighters were leaking oil and they were beginning to lose power. In the afternoon of 27 February the patrol returned to Andir with the three aircraft.[4]

Four Brewsters of 1-Vl.G.V were at the Technical Service at Andir for major repairs, but only one of these aircraft was expected to be ready the next day. Two heavily damaged Brewsters were being made flyable at Tjililitan and Kemajoran, respectively, but they would not take part in the battle anymore, just like several Interceptors in major repair at Maospati. A reserve Interceptor was flown from Maospati to Andir on 1 March 1942.[5]

Four Brewsters took off from Andir that afternoon, led by Kap J.H. van Helsdingen, commander of 2-Vl.G.V. In this section there was also an RAF pilot. This was Sgt W.J.N. MacIntosh (605 Squadron, but ex-488 Squadron at Kallang, Singapore), who had come to pick up a Hurricane at the ML Technical Service. As his plane was not ready yet, he had paid a visit to the Noordhangaar in the morning to see some old friends of 2-Vl.G.V who had seen service at Kallang earlier in the war. Subsequently, he made a patrol flight over the Bandoeng Plateau in the B-395 of 1-Vl.G.V, with a pilot from 2-Vl.G.V as pair leader. In the afternoon the section led by Van Helsdingen (including MacIntosh again) was sent up to try and intercept a Japanese reconnaissance plane. Nothing was found and the section cruised about in vain for two hours over the Bandoeng Plateau.[6]

During the evening of 26 February the Intelligence department of AHK, as well as COIC, gave a warning to prepare for an invasion in the early morning of 27 February. Neither the allied naval units, nor the allied flying boats and bombers found anything, however. A flying boat did find the 'eastern' invasion fleet in the early afternoon of 27 February, its course and speed predicting an invasion of East Java at midnight of 27 to 28 February 1942.[7]

The fighter strength in western Java on 27 February 1942

Because of the transfer of a large number of ML fighters to Ngoro in eastern Java the number of allied fighters in western Java had been greatly reduced since 25 February. After the air battles on 24 and 25 February 1942 the RAF had only six serviceable fighters left in the afternoon of the latter day. This number had, however, risen again to 11 aircraft in the early morning of 26 February and came up to 12 later that day. At the beginning of the day on 27 February the ML and the RAF had the following number of assigned and operationally serviceable aircraft at their disposal.[8]

Table 6

Unit	Assigned	Operationally serviceable	Remarks
242/605 Squadron	13	11	Hurricane
1-Vl.G.V	5 (+2)	5 (+2)	Excl. fighters at Ngoro (+ Hawk)
2-Vl.G.V	4	3	Ibid.
2-Vl.G.IV	4	0	At Maospati with Technical Service + 1 in repair
Total	26 (+2)	19 (+2)	(+ Hawk)

New Japanese bombardments at Batavia

On 27 February 1942, between approximately 09:00 and 10:00 hrs, two Japanese formations attacked the Tandjong Priok harbour area and Kemajoran airfield, respectively.[9] Reconnaissance flights of the Japanese Navy air force had shown that there were still allied warships and flying boats operating from the harbour of Batavia. Both Japanese formations consisted of 12 Ki-48 bombers with an escort of 12 to 15 Ki-43 fighters. The *Readiness Flight* at Tjililitan took off with eight Hurricanes of 242 and 605 Squadrons when the first Japanese formation was approaching the north coast of Java.[10]

Thanks to the Batavia East and Batavia West radar stations, which had become fully operational on 26 February, the alarm came well in time. The two sections climbed out to an altitude of about 7,500 metres. When after a brief period of patrolling a Japanese formation came in sight at a lower altitude, the fighters carried out a dive attack on the Ki-43s of the Japanese fighter escort. Bombers were nowhere to be seen. The engagement only lasted for a couple of minutes. Amid heavy clouds the pilots returned individually to Tjililitan.[11]

In the early morning of this day Air Commodore S.F. Vincent arrived at Tjililitan to say farewell and to introduce his successor Wing Commander H.G. Maguire. Vincent was commander of the Air Defence

Command Batavia (*Sector Control Batavia*). The group of visitors saw the fighters of the *Readiness Flight* take off and were watching the explosions of the anti-aircraft artillery shells at Tandjong Priok. Suddenly, without prior warning about 15 Ki-43s carried out a low-altitude attack on Tjililitan. This was probably the escort of the Ki-48 formation that was attacking Kemajoran. The Japanese fighter pilots fired at the personnel on the ground and the anti-aircraft positions around the airfield. All serviceable planes at Tjililitan, however, had already been sent up.[12]

The anti-aircraft artillery, 242 Battery of the British Army and a section of A. I Ld of the KNIL, could not deliver fire. Sgt P.M.T. Healy (605 Squadron) arrived at Tjililitan at the moment when the Ki-43s were still carrying out their attack and with his Hurricane he pursued one of the Japanese fighters at a very low altitude right across the airfield. The Ki-43s, however, were already breaking off their attack and quickly disappeared. Only when Healy returned for his landing, did several 4-cm Bofor guns open fire but his plane was not hit. There were no casualties at the airfield.[13]

The British squadrons suffered no losses either and claimed (incorrectly) two probables. The anti-aircraft artillery of the KNIL and the British Army fired intensely at the Japanese bombers, which were attacking the harbour from as low an altitude as 1,500 metres, due to the low clouds. The anti-aircraft gunners reported that they had hit three Ki-48s, which did not crash, however.[14] The warships that had stayed behind at Batavia were at sea, but there was much damage in the harbour area. There were no planes stationed at Kemajoran anymore and apart from the KNILM complex (where there were in maintenance or repair a few transport planes of the KNILM and a Brewster and an Interceptor of the ML) the airfield presented not many more targets for attack than the runway. The anti-aircraft defence consisted of just one section of three 12.7-mm machine guns of the KNIL. It is therefore likely that it was the Japanese Army air force's intention to destroy the runway prior to the invasion of western Java. It was indeed damaged, but it was operational again the next day.[15]

Air Commodore Vincent left in the afternoon for Bandoeng to sign out at BRITAIR and JAC. Together with seven personnel of his staff he then went to Tjilatjap to be evacuated by ship to Australia. He left on 1 March 1942 on board *Zaandam*. His successor, Maguire, had fought in the battle for Palembang I and had made good his escape via the port of Benkoelen on the west coast of southern Sumatra. He had arrived at Tjilatjap on 22 February 1942 on board a coaster.[16] In the period leading up to 1 March 1942, in accordance with the instruction of the *Combined Chiefs of Staff* (see the introduction chapter, *The Japanese advance: Java given up by the allies*) thousands of allied service personnel were leaving Java, flying and ground personnel of squadrons that had no aircraft left anymore, anti-aircraft artillery gunners of the British Army whose equipment had been lost, maintenance personnel of the USAAF, etc. In the same period the ML evacuated its Vliegschool (Flying School) to Australia, including almost all instructors and trainees. Also on board *Zaandam* there was a detachment of the Vliegschool.

An attack on the allied fleet at Tandjong Priok

In the early afternoon the 3rd Hiko Dan carried out a second attack against Batavia. The bombers that had carried out the morning attack on Tandjong Priok and Kemajoran were sent on a new mission soon after their return to Palembang I. At about 12:30 hrs the first aircraft left Palembang I. In the morning a reconnaissance float plane of a Japanese cruiser had discovered an allied fleet (the remnant of the *Western Striking Force)* north of Batavia and the Japanese Navy had insufficient resources for an attack. This was caused by a lack of fuel and bombs at Palembang II and extremely bad weather over Kuching.[17] The discovery of the allied fleet provided a reason for the Japanese Navy commander responsible for fleet operations near western Java to postpone the invasion of western Java with one more day, until the very early hours of 1 March 1942.[18]

The allied warships, the Australian cruiser *Hobart*, the British light cruisers *Dragon* and *Danae* and three destroyers arrived safely at Tandjong Priok around 14:20 hrs. The eight G4M bombers of the Japanese Navy air force that had finally taken off from Palembang II (at about 12:00 hrs) bombed the ships at about 13:00 hrs with 60-kilogramme bombs. Heavier bombs had not been available. The bomber crews thought they had hit a heavy cruiser, but in fact the cruiser *Hobart* sustained light damage with several wounded on board.[19] The Army bombers could not locate the ships and after a search returned amid heavy clouds and showers. On the return trip a number of Ki-48s attacked several allied corvettes and patrol ships near Merak.[20]

A final bombing of Semplak

In the course of the afternoon the Japanese Army air force attacked Semplak airfield with about 12 Ki-48 bombers. In probably two runs they put the runway out of action for two days, and furthermore caused heavy damage to the airfield. An RAAF detachment that had been left behind on Semplak was cannibalising parts from written off Hudson bombers and repairing a Hudson that had been damaged on 22 February and still had to be flown to Kalidjati. This aircraft received renewed damage in the attack, but could still be repaired. Two parked ML planes, a Lodestar transport plane of D.Vl.A and a Brewster fighter plane that had fled to Semplak during a test flight because of an air raid alarm at Andir, received moderate and light damage, respectively. The Hurricanes at Tjililitan did not take to the air, probably because of the bad weather.[21]

Protection of the allied fleet from Andir

The ML Brewster fighters at Andir were on radiness the entire day for covering tasks during any operations the allied fleet might undertake along the north coast of Java. The aircraft had been withdrawn from air defence tasks, but did not come into action at all on 27 February. The Brewsters of 1-Vl.G.V and 2-Vl.G.V had been designated to carry out an attack on Palembang I in the early morning together with three Glenn Martin bombers of 3-Vl.G.III, but the assignment was cancelled and the Glenn Martins left on their own, unescorted.[22]

Major-General L.H. van Oyen, the JAC commander, wanted to employ the ML Brewsters that had been left behind in western Java for escort tasks of the Glenn Martin bombers (the heaviest bombers that JAC had available) heading for Palembang I, as they were the only fighters with a sufficiently large range and capable, moreover, of carrying along light bombs. In order to degrade the Japanese air force there in any meaningful way, precision bombings in formation were necessary. With an escort there was a chance that they could indeed be carried out. Previous experiences had shown this to be impossible without one because of the Japanese standing patrols (the present-day *combat air patrols*) over southern Sumatra. On 26 February there were too few fighters available at Andir because the Interceptors had been sent to Maospati for badly needed maintenance. As a result of this situation the first mission of Glenn Martins and Brewsters had been scheduled to take place in the early morning of 27 February. However, the protection of allied war ships was given priority.[23]

In the afternoon of 27 February the Battle of the Java Sea began in the eastern part of the Java Sea. It was a naval battle which lasted until deep into the night, during which the allied naval squadron lost important assets and suffered a major defeat in the battle with the covering squadrons of the Japanese 'eastern' invasion fleet. The naval battle also caused the Japanese landings in the east to be postponed with one day. The *Counter-air* operations of the JAC were terminated on the night of 27 February 1942, after which all efforts were directed at fighting off the Japanese landing operations.

Summary

On 26 February 1942 the Japanese air forces were heavily involved in convoy protection, but on 27 February the Japanese Army and Navy air forces carried out a few last raids on Tandjong Priok, Semplak and Kemajoran and on allied warships on their way back to Tandjong Priok. This was done in preparation of the landings of the Japanese Army in western Java, planned for the night of 27 on 28 February 1942. Except for a few probable cases, the allied air defence did not manage to inflict any damage on the aircraft of their Japanese attackers. The fighter pilots at Andir were on readiness the entire day on 27 February in order to cover any possible operations of the allied warships off the north coast of Java, but they did not come into action. Incidentally, a major part of the fighter fleet at Andir and at Kalidjati had already been relocated to Ngoro in eastern Java in order to provide cover for the allied naval squadron from there. This squadron engaged into battle with the Japanese in the east, but was defeated in the Battle of the Java Sea in the night of 27 February 1942.

*** *

CHAPTER 1A.9

The Results of the Air Battle over western Java and a Brief Analysis

Introduction

In terms of numbers of eliminated allied fighters the Japanese air offensive over western Java, which began on 19 February 1942, achieved its greatest successes right on the first day. This did not come as the result of an element of surprise, for that had been lost due to previous Japanese reconnaissance missions. It was more due to the fact that the reporting system of the air defence commands could not provide timely warnings and correct predictions of the Japanese targets as a result of bad weather and the absence of radar at that time. Consequently, a timely concentration of ML and RAF fighters was not possible on 19 February, which resulted in the pilots of 2-Vl.G.V and 1-Vl.G.V (the RAF did not enter into combat) being confronted with superior numbers near Buitenzorg as well as Bandoeng, respectively.

In the early fights, moreover, there were relatively many inexperienced ML fighter pilots involved, some of whom had begun their training on the Brewster B-339 as late as December 1941. On 19 February 1942 this was true for as many as 7 out of 12 in 1-Vl.G.V. The fighter control personnel of the Air Defence Command Bandoeng (anti-aircraft gunners of the KNIL) were inexperienced, too. The ML and KNIL learned quickly, however, and just as in the RAF squadrons, there were hardly any losses during the air combats after 19 February 1942. In spite of this, the defensive part of the allied *Counter-air* operation did not become a success, the reason being that the losses inflicted on the Japanese were not heavy enough. The Japanese operation for the attainment of air superiority over western Java was successful, though, albeit that the superiority attained was not as complete by far as had been hoped for.

The Japanese losses

The 59th and 64th Sentais of the 3rd Hiko Dan arrived at Palembang I airfield on 18 February 1942, together with 42 Ki-43 fighters. By the end of the month 35 Ki-43s were still operational, in other words a loss of 17 per cent.[1] On the basis of the causes, this loss can be specified as follows.

–   Three fighters shot down or missing after air combat on 19 February, 21 February and 24 February, respectively.
–   Two fighters ditched into the sea near the Duizend Eilanden on their return flight to Palembang, on 19 February and 25 February 1942, respectively, as a result of battle damage.
–   One fighter crashed at Palembang I on 19 February 1942 as a result of battle damage.

–   One fighter, on (or around) 21 February 1942 crashed during the
     return flight in southern Sumatra as a result of battle damage.

The Yamada air group of the Japanese Navy air force lost one
fighter of its original number of 15 Navy Os at Muntok (Banka), but
flew only one mission over western Java. So, all in all, of a total of 57
fighters committed over western Java eight, including the one Navy O,
were lost (14 per cent).

Except for fighters, the Japanese Army air force lost at least one
Ki-15 single-engine reconnaissance plane in air combats with British
Hurricanes on 20 February 1942 and one Ki-48 bomber on 24 February
1942. Furthermore, the allied anti-aircraft artillery shot down at least
eight Ki-48 bombers, two at Kalidjati on 21 February, three at Kalidjati
on 24 February, one at Tjililitan on 24 February and two at Kalidjati
on 25 February, as well as a C5M reconnaissance plane of the Japanese
Navy air force at Tjililitan on 25 February 1942.

The British and Dutch East Indies losses

On 27 February 1942 at the end of the day the RAF had 19 Hurricanes
left. In the period covered six aircraft were written off. On the basis
of the causes, this loss can be specified as follows.

–   Four fighters shot down in the air battles on 24 February 1942
     (two) and 25 February 1942 (two).
–   Two fighters crashed as a result of a collision immediately after
     take off on 24 February 1942.

The losses of the three ML fighter afdelingen in western Java were high
and amounted to 13 fighters in the same period.

–   Nine fighters were shot down in the air battle on 19 February
     (seven), on 21 February 1942 (one) and on 25 February 1942
     (one).
–   One fighter was lost after a collision with a Ki-43 on 21 February
     1942.
–   One fighter was lost in an accident at Andir on 23 February
     1942.
–   Two fighters were lost in a strafing at Kalidjati on 25 February
     1942.

In total, 19 ML and RAF fighters out the original 66 available allied fighters were lost in the period between 18 February 1942 and 27 February 1942 (29 per cent). This percentage is much higher than the total losses of the Japanese air forces (14 per cent). The direct combat losses during and losses as an immediate consequence of air battles lie closer together, viz. 14 ML and RAF fighters against 8 of the Japanese air forces. The allied fighters had certainly not been wiped out of the sky, but the losses were serious. In ten days' time almost a third of the fighter strength had been lost, while there were hardly any replacements available.

In spite of the often fierce attacks on the allied anti-aircraft artillery no guns were lost. There were a number of dead and wounded, though, in the anti-aircraft artillery units. There were no reserves of anti-air artillery resources at all. In spite of the successes of the fighters and anti-aircraft artillery, the results of the defensive part of the *Counter-air* operation, in terms of own and inflicted losses, were considerably worse than JAC had hoped for.

ABDAIR's and JAC's strategy

After the evacuation of southern Sumatra ABDAIR's and JAC's strategy consisted of degrading the enemy's capability of sending out sorties through the commitment of its own bombers, fighters and anti-aircraft artillery; an *attrition strategy* in present-day terms. To this end a *Counter-air* operation with a defensive and offensive component commenced on 18 February 1942.

Without escort of their own fighters and by making use of cover of cloud and smoke of oil fires, the bombers in western Java carried out attacks on three primary targets in the occupied part of Sumatra. They were the tank park of the oil refinery at Pladjoe near Palembang (filled with aircraft fuel and shipping fuel), Japanese ships on the Moesi river en route to and at Palembang and at the Muntok roadstead (Banka) and Palembang I airfield, where the Japanese air force had established itself. The intention was to disrupt the Japanese supply (in particular that of aircraft fuel) as much as possible, to cause maximum destruction of the aircraft fuel supplies the Japanese had captured at Pladjoe and to eliminate as many aircraft as possible that might be pitted against western Java by the Japanese. In other words, to bring down as much as possible the number of sorties that the Japanese air forces could fly against western Java.

The scarce own fighters were primarily, and, from 23 February 1942 onwards exclusively, given an air defence task for the defence of the major air bases in western Java, the harbour of Batavia and, inasmuch as this was possible, the allied fleet. The fighters, too, in cooperation with the allied anti-aircraft artillery, were supposed to degrade as much as possible the sortie generating capability of the enemy by inflicting maximum losses. As a result the Japanese would need more time to attain air superiority; time which the allies would need for a further reinforcement of western Java, with extra fighters to begin with.

The strategy in itself was sound and would also today stand the test of criticism if it were related to the principles of modern *Air Power* theory. ABDAIR had identified two *centres of gravity*, against which it directed a *maximum effort offensive*. The assessment that the availability of aircraft fuel would be the most limiting factor for the Japanese advance was correct. It was also correctly assessed that the Japanese air forces had exhausted their reserves, and that, in any case with regard to their fighters, they would have to make do with the aircraft that (for their battle over western Java) had been moved forward to Palembang.[2]

In how far, however, were the ML, RAF, and RAAF's own means sufficient to attain the objective aimed at? An air campaign on the basis of attrition takes time to make the enemy clearly feel the effects and a successful execution requires large reserves of aircraft. The ML, RAF and RAAF lacked both the one and the other. The available anti-aircraft artillery of the KNIL and the British Army in western Java was insufficient. One advantage the allies did have, however; it was the fact that the Japanese could disperse the targets for the allied bombers only to a very limited extent. Thus, in the first instance, all Japanese aircraft were concentrated on the relatively small airfield of Palembang I and the bulk of the fuel supplies the allies sought to destroy was stored in a well-known part of a tank park of an oil refinery.

Furthermore, it would be possible to concentrate the allied fighters with the help of British radar stations in case of a Japanese attack, or that was how it had been planned.

Bottlenecks in the execution

After the evacuation from southern Sumatra the air defence of western Java was reorganised. Of the two existing sectors the Air Defence

Command Batavia was transferred to the RAF on 18 February 1942. The existing air surveillance systems, consisting of rings of aerial surveillance posts around Batavia and Buitenzorg and Bandoeng and Kalidjati, respectively, a number of posts on the north and south coasts of Java and a post in one of the Duizend Eilanden, were expanded with British radar posts on the north and west coasts of Java. It was assumed that warning times would be increased and, in principle, this would create the possibility to concentrate the RAF and ML fighters in the Batavia-Buitenzorg sector and the ML fighters in the Bandoeng-Kalidjati sector in order to intercept major attacks.

Several basic problems proved to be impossible to solve, however. The battle took place in the 'wet period'. It was the monsoon period with often bad weather, heavy clouds and showers. This brought about a considerable number of failures in the electrical systems of the aircraft, in particular the starting systems. The monsoon period created limitations in particular for the functioning of the (visual) aerial surveillance posts. Although the rings of surveillance posts were complemented with radar stations, the first two of which had become operational at Batavia as of 25–26 February 1942, radar at the time was limited in range and use in the monsoon period. Heavy showers and (electro-magnetic) storms near the stations would cause no, or extremely poor, reception. Besides, the Japanese formations usually approached Java in such a way (via the Duizend Eilanden) that even with a radar warning it became clear at a late moment in time whether Batavia or Bandoeng was the target area. As a result, a timely concentration of the ML and RAF fighter planes never materialised in the period covered. This was a major setback, for concentration was assumed to offset the initial shortage of fighters.

Overcoming this problem by physically concentrating all available fighter planes at Batavia came up against a number of serious objections. The limitations of the warning systems during the monsoon period might lead to a situation in which the fighter concentrations were caught by surprise on the ground. Therefore, dispersing the scarce allied fighters over at least four airfields was deemed a necessity by ABDAIR and later JAC. However, apart from Tjililitan and Tjisaoek, there were no other suitable airfields available around Batavia. The other airfields were either too small, did not offer any cover for parked aircraft or were too soggy for operational use.[3]

Incidentally, a concentration of fighters in the vicinity of Batavia would not automatically have meant that flying regular standing patrols (the present-day *combat air patrols*) in order to block the Japanese approach routes would have become possible. The total number of allied fighter planes was too small for that, as standing patrols cost many flying hours and especially engine hours, which would mean that more aircraft would be withdrawn from the operational strength for maintenance.[4]

As was said above, in practice it proved to be impossible to make the relative balance of strength with regard to the number of ML and RAF fighters more advantageous by concentrating them. The consequence was that the Japanese air forces could attack the airfields in western Java almost unhindered. The allied fighters were effectively bound and the quantity of the anti-aircraft artillery at the East Indies airfields, at Bandoeng (Artillery Ordnance Workshop) and Batavia (Tandjong Priok) was only small. In the Japanese air raids not only a number of fighter planes were lost, but also bombers. This also affected the allied possibilities to degrade the Japanese capability to send out sorties by means of their own bombardments.

The shortage of anti-aircraft artillery could not be solved. There were no units left that could be sent to Java. As for the fighter aircraft, this was different. American P-40s were standing ready in Australia, but in order to get them operational in time, it was vital to force the Japanese to postpone their planned invasion. A week would suffice. On 22 February 1942 *Langley* and *Sea Witch* left port at Fremantle in Australia with on board a total 63 P-40 fighters destined for Java. Everything was tried to somehow bring about some postponement of the Japanese invasion. The results of the allied bombers, fighters and anti-aircraft artillery, however, were insufficient to make the Japanese commanders consider such a postponement. The Japanese Army could not afford too much delay because of logistic problems and therefore it suited the commanders very well that the 3rd Hiko Dan reported extremely favourable results of its own air offensive over western Java.

The balance of strength

Taking into account the orders of battle there was, overall, no Japanese superiority in fighters, if the Ki-27 fighters that took care of the local air defence over southern Sumatra are left out of the equation. The Japanese Army air force, however, was able to concentrate its fighters for an attack and, in doing so, create a local superiority of one to two or three. As said above, the allies were not able to concentrate their fighter force in Java. The local shortages of fighter planes that were the result of this prompted BRITAIR to ask for the Hurricane fighters transferred to the ML to be returned.

The RAF asked the Hurricanes of 2-Vl.G.IV back on 24 February, as they were not committed operationally (due to the absence of the right crystals for the aircraft radios), whereas they could be used as such in 605 Squadron. With the ML Hurricanes the RAF stood a good chance of 'hanging on' until the arrival (in mid-March 1942) of the Hurricanes on their way on board an aircraft carrier. JAC did not want to go along with this, as returning the fighters would mean that the ML's most experienced pilots would end up without any planes, while the required crystals were being collected at that moment by the Radiodienst (Wireless service) of the ML. Besides, Vice-Admiral C.E.L. Helfrich (ABDAFLOAT) resisted the return (see below). 2-Vl.G.IV at Kalidjati did get the order, though, to begin flying standing patrols and it was considered committing the ML Hurricanes from Tjisaoek until the arrival of the USAAF with its P-40s. This plan, however, was overtaken by the necessity to transfer the aircraft to Ngoro in eastern Java for the protection of the *Combined Striking Force* of the allied navies.

In fact, 2-Vl.G.IV, which had become partially operational on 22 February, was not able to make any contribution whatsoever to the air defence of western Java. ABDAIR had already suggested earlier that the afdeling, which was destined for Tasikmalaja, should be stationed at Tjisaoek for the time being, because it would be possible to fly air defence sorties with the RAF from this base. The radio station of *Air Defence Sector Control Batavia* worked on RAF frequencies, because there were no crystals available for the British Hurricanes to tune the radios in to the frequencies used by the ML and the KNIL. There were, however, 'RAF crystals' available for the ML fighters. However, committing the fighters from Tjisaoek would mean a deviation from the air defence plan for western Java, which was unacceptable for Vice-Admiral Helfrich. He adhered to the plan because it provided in stationing fighters (among others, those of 2-Vl.G.IV) at Tasikmalaja and in establishing radar stations on the south coast of Java for the protection of the harbour of Tjilatjap and the shipping lanes to it.

Furthermore, the ML did not want to commit the remaining Curtiss-Wright CW-21B Interceptors and Curtiss H-75A Hawks against enemy fighters, after the heavy losses sustained by Vl.G.IV in eastern Java in their battle against the Mitsubishi A6M Navy Os of the Japanese Navy air force. Yet, the Interceptor was certainly a match for the Nakajima Ki-43 Army 1s of the Japanese Army air force operating over western Java. But, just like the RAF, the ML could not distinguish between the Navy O and Army 1. All Japanese fighters with a retractable undercarriage were consistently taken for Navy Os.

Only after the wreckage of a downed Ki-43 had been inspected, did it appear that there were considerable differences between the two types. The Ki-43, for instance, was armed much lighter than the Navy O, with only one 7.7-mm and one 12.7-mm machine gun and no 20-mm guns. The 12.7-mm machine gun fired explosive bullets, though.[5] When the Interceptors were finally committed against the Ki-43s on 24 February 1942 it became clear that the performance of the CW-21B was certainly not inferior to that of the Ki-43 in a turning fight.

All that time the CW-21B had been considered too vulnerable in the turning fight, and consequently the major repairs by the Technical Service at Maospati of several Interceptors that had been seriously damaged (on 3 and 5 February 1942) were not given priority.[6] During the most crucial period in the battle over western Java, from 19 up to and including 25 February 1942, the above circumstances and conviction had caused the withdrawal of ten Hurricanes and, for most of the period, another six Interceptors from the air defence. As for the fighters, therefore, the allied commitment was in fact less than a *maximum effort*.

Commitment of the Hurricanes of 2-Vl.G.IV from Tjisaoek as of 22 February 1942 would certainly have had a positive influence on the balance of strength during the air fights near Batavia on 24 and 25 February. On the former day six RAF Hurricanes entered into combat with 13 Ki-43s. Taking into account the eight aircraft on *Readiness* with 2-Vl.G.IV, this could have been 14 versus 13. A day later eight RAF Hurricanes entered into combat with 13 Navy Os. This could have been 16 versus 13. There is every likelihood that the above situation would have led to greater losses for the Japanese side. However, it would not have tipped the balance of strength to such an extent that it would have become possible to also fight off the Japanese bombers successfully. The Japanese fighters would still have been able to bind the allied fighters effectively. So, it would not have been possible to prevent the large losses of allied bombers as a result of air raids. Taking into account the position of the Japanese Army, which did not want to hear of any (further) postponement of the invasion of Java, higher losses of Ki-43 fighters would probably not have led to a further delay of the invasion, over and above the two days that had been decided upon on 23 February.

Tactics and qualities/performances

The RAF fighters employed hit and run tactics in western Java in their engagements with Japanese fighters. It involved diving onto an opponent from an altitude of at least 7,500 metres, that is, well above the operational ceiling of the Ki-43 Army 1 and A6M Navy O, firing at the enemy plane in the dive and using the speed surplus gathered in the dive to climb out for a second attempt. These were reasonably efficient tactics in case of an enemy air superiority, which prevented the allied fighter being shot down after a successful attack by the wingmen of the enemy fighter pilot under attack. Dogfights with Navy Os were deemed very dangerous anyhow, as the Hurricane could not match the turning circle of this type. This was indeed the case for the Navy O, but it did not apply to the Ki-43 Army 1. The RAF as well as the ML, however, could not distinguish between the two types. The only time (on 25 February 1942) that two pilots of 605 Squadron did venture into a turning fight, the opponents happened to be A6M Navy Os and not Ki-43 Army 1s of the 3rd Hiko Dan.[7]

ML fighter pilots, after having carried out a dive attack from 6,000 metres, if the opportunity presented itself, did enter into a turning fight and showed that the Brewsters (with half to two-thirds filled wing tanks and ammunition bays for the wing machine guns) as well as the Hurricanes Mark IIB (with eight instead of 12 machine guns and without sand filter) and the Interceptors had a turning per-formance that was at least equal to that of a Ki-43.[8] The ML did not encounter any A6M Navy Os over western Java.

As from mid-February all ML fighters were equipped with a modern reflector gunsight, just like the RAF Hurricanes, and from 23 February onwards the Brewsters were allowed, just like the Interceptors much earlier, to use tracer ammunition in their 12.7-mm machine guns. The combination of the new American gunsight and the tracer ammunition gave an enormous increase of firing performance. The Japanese superiority in numbers of one to two or three meant that allied pilots could fire only very briefly at an opponent. So, if possible, the one or two short bursts had better be hits. With the tracers and reflector gunsight this became gradually better. Hitting was not always the same as shooting down and the armament of the ML Brewsters and Interceptors proved to be somewhat too light in practice.

The fighter pilots of the 3rd Hiko Dan operated in standard formations of three fighters, called *shotai*. The ML and RAF, in principle, flew in sections of four fighters, consisting of two *pairs*, at a maximum distance of 200 metres apart. The trailing pair flew 200 hundred metres higher and covered the leading pair. The Japanese did this too, but with one trailing fighter only. Besides, the other trailing plane was further away from its leader than in the ML and RAF *pairs*. Because of this inexperienced opponents could easily miss a trailing plane. Another important difference was that the Japanese larger combat formation was much more echeloned in height than was customary in the ML and RAF. So, in the vertical plane the Japanese fighter pilots flew also further apart, because of which it was easy to miss higher flying *shotais* in the middle of a fight. The Ki-43 pilots did not use oxygen over western Java and therefore operated well below 5,000 metres. The ML used 6,000 metres as the operational cruising altitude and the RAF 7,500 metres.[9]

The qualities of the allied fighter pilots were certainly on a par with those of their Japanese opponents in the period covered in this study. After the first ML losses on 19 February 1942, the ML and RAF losses were of the same order as those of the Japanese Army air force. That they were so severe on 19 February was due to the fact that the ML Brewster pilots entered into combat against superior numbers and that the Japanese fighters (in the battle near Buitenzorg) also had the advantage of height. After the war the Japanese fighter pilots were sometimes depicted as the crème de la crème, but this is not correct. It is true, they were well trained, but the average level of experience was not so high. Thus, the 59th Sentai of the Army air force did indeed have an experienced core of professional NCOs with much combat experience, but it also had many young pilots in its ranks, who had come out of training as late as the summer of 1941 or sometimes even October 1941.[10]

Although they had some successes against the enemy fighters, the allied fighter pilots could not prevent air raids on their own airfields. With every new Japanese attack the damage could be seen to increase. Furthermore, the ML, RAF and RAAF evacuated as much personnel as possible to Australia and Ceylon. This increased the feeling that those who remained were fighting a lost battle and morale suffered somewhat because of it. However, thanks to *esprit de corps* and good leadership the afdelingen and squadrons kept on carrying out their tasks adequately. Until the end of the battle quality was never an issue;

the problem was of a quantitative nature. Among others, the inability to concentrate the fighters and major shortages of anti-aircraft artillery that could not be solved contributed to a situation in which there were quite simply too few fighter planes.

The results of the Counter-air operation

ABDAIR and subsequently JAC threw almost everything they had into the battle. As said above, the offensive of the bombers over southern Sumatra was a *maximum effort offensive*, which in spite of the relatively low number of sorties (due to the small number of available bombers) was a considerable success. Those results, however, were not enough to make an impact on the course of the battle for air superiority over western Java. The allied bombers succeeded in destroying a large part of the fuel supplies that had been captured by the Japanese at Pladjoe. The Japanese Army air force, however, seemed to be less dependent on captured fuel supplies than had been thought, while the provision by ship of the Japanese units at Palembang I could not be degraded enough.[11]

In reality, though, the provision of enough aircraft fuel was in actual fact a true logistic nightmare for the Japanese armed forces. Thus, the supply of aircraft fuel and other aviation materials at Palembang I (the former civilian airfield of Palembang) was barely enough, also because the allied air offensive against the base forced the 3rd Hiko Shudan to order extra standing patrols. The supply of Palembang II, the large military airfield in the jungle south west of the town of Palembang, was even absolutely insufficient for carrying out regular operations from there. The units of the Japanese Navy air force operating from this airfield, therefore, were only able to make a small contribution to the battle over western Java. The logistic problems formed one of the reasons why the Japanese army was so keen on keeping the proposed dates for the invasion of Java. A postponement of a few days was possible, but a greater delay (a longer period of intensive operations prior to the invasion) would put too heavy a burden on the provision of supplies.[12]

In their battle for air superiority over western Java, too, the ML and the RAF did not do so badly. There was no question of any real technical superiority of the Ki-43 Army 1 fighter. The A6M Navy O fighter was superior in a number of respects to the Hawker Hurricanes, Curtiss-Wright CW-21B Interceptors and Brewster B339C and

D 'Brewsters', but this type only carried out one mission over western Java. All the Japanese fighter pilots had combat experience, but this was also the case for the majority of ML and RAF fighter pilots in the period covered.

The outcome of the battle between the fighters was *de facto* undecided and it cost the 3rd Hiko Dan and the Yamada Kokutai seven Ki-43 Army 1s and one A6M Navy O, apart from several reconnaissance planes. The allied assumption that the Japanese air forces had used up their reserves of at least their fighters was correct. If the air battle had lasted longer, this fact would certainly have played a role. As said above, the Japanese air forces did manage to destroy a large number of ML, RAF and RAAF bombers, though, which greatly reduced the possibilities for attacking the Japanese aircraft at Palembang. Nevertheless, the number of Japanese aircraft destroyed by the allied bombers was considerable. The 3rd Hiko Dan lost no Ki-43 fighters on the ground, whereas the total number of Ki-48 bombers eliminated on the ground at Palembang I and over western Java by allied anti-aircraft artillery and the allied fighters amounted to 16 at least.[13]

Air supremacy, in its modern meaning of freedom to operate, was certainly not attained by the Japanese. They did not get beyond local temporary air superiority (in modern terms). During each attack over western Java they encountered enemy fighters. Besides, the allied bombers kept carrying out raids in small groups against targets in southern Sumatra, among which was Palembang I airfield. The allies, however, failed to degrade the Japanese sortie generating capability sufficiently and quickly enough to force the Japanese commanders to consider an extension of the air offensive against western Java with more than two days. It would take quite a lot to make them do that, anyway. Further extension would quickly cause logistic problems for the Japanese army, while it was assumed by the Japanese that the allies would reinforce their defence of Java in the meantime. It can be safely concluded that for this reason the relatively high losses of the Japanese Army air force were acceptable.

PART 1B:
A DESCRIPTION AND ANALYSIS OF THE DEPLOYMENT OF THE BOMBERS

❦

CHAPTER 1B.1

The Reorganisation of the Allied Bomber Fleet after the Evacuation of southern Sumatra

The loss of southern Sumatra

The battle against the Japanese invasion troops advancing from Muntok (the island of Banka) on Palembang via the Banka Strait and the Moesi, Salang and Telang rivers was given up on Sunday, 15 February 1942 at around 15:00 hrs. Palembang I (P I), the former civilian airfield of the town, in use by the Royal Air Force (RAF), had been captured on 14 February around 17:00 hrs by paratroopers that had landed earlier that day. The defenders of the KNIL, anti-aircraft gunners of the British Army and RAF personnel had succeeded in keeping the paratroopers at bay until that moment, but retreated on the order of Lieutenant-Colonel L.N.W. Vogelesang, the southern Sumatra Territorial Commander and *Troepencommandant* (Local Forces Commander), who, subsequently refrained from ordering the Xth Infantry Battalion (Inf. X) of the KNIL to recapture the airfield early the next morning.[1]

This battalion consisting of 850 men had arrived at Praboemoelih from Java on 7 February 1942 as a reinforcement of the territorial troops at Palembang and Djambi (totalling around 1,250 men, but poorly trained, spread over various locations and not very mobile).

One company was immediately stationed at Palembang. An attempt by Inf. X to recapture the airfield would have stood a good chance of success in view of the initial weakness in numbers of the Japanese occupiers. Holding P I after a recapture was a completely different matter, taking into account the Japanese troops advancing over the rivers. Stationing Inf. X in the area had been a temporary measure, awaiting the arrival of Australian and British troops. Of all things, the allied vanguard arrived at Oosthaven in southern Sumatra at the very moment the battle for Palembang broke out. There was little else to do than have these troops re-embark. There was no time to make them combat-ready and much of their materiel and equipment was still underway.[2]

On 14 February 1942 Japanese paratroopers also jumped near the two oil refineries south of the town of Palembang. As with the airfield they were not able not take the two refineries, but they still managed to occupy them in the early hours of 15 February. By that time the refinery of the Nederlandse Koloniale Petrolium Maatschappij (NKPM) at Soengai Gerong had been destroyed, exactly according to plan, after which the demolition team and the troops, who had managed to keep the Japanese away from the complex successfully, withdrew on 15 February around 03:00 hrs. The Japanese paratroopers managed to partially capture the refinery of the Bataafse Petroleum Maatschappij (BPM), but they were driven off in a series of successful counter-attacks by elements of Inf. X and an anti-paratroop squad, consisting of British anti-aircraft gunners.[3]

In the evening of 14 February virtually the entire complex had been cleared of enemy troops and there was only a tiny pocket of about 15 paratroopers holding out in a corner of the yard and several paratroopers who had fled into the marshy wood. They would no doubt have been neutralised the next morning without much difficulty, if not for Vogelesang, who ordered the KNIL troops to retreat to Praboemoelih. At about 06:00 hrs (on 15 February) Pladjoe was given up. Before, Vogelesang had ordered the retreat of all the demolition teams, so the refinery could not be destroyed before it was abandoned. This decision would have far-reaching consequences for the deployment of the allied air forces.[4]

From 15 February onwards fighters and bombers of the RAF and the Royal Australian Air Force (RAAF) flew a great number of sorties from Palembang II (P II), the military airfield in the jungle south-west of the town, targeting the Japanese troops on the rivers and the Japanese ships in the Banka Strait and at Muntok. Due to these raids the Japanese battle group advancing on Palembang along the rivers was

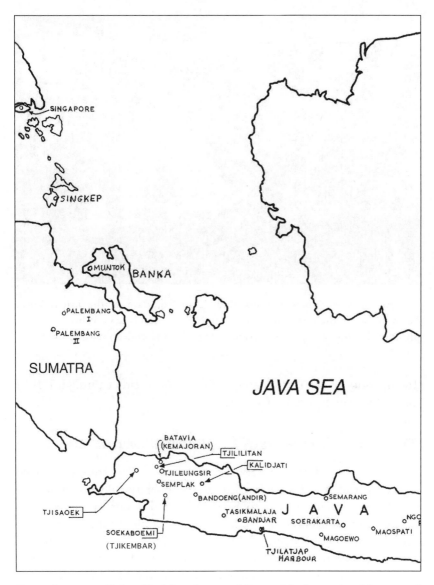

Operating area of the allied bombers and Java with the main airbases and strips

making only slow progress, sustaining considerable losses all the while. In the evening of 15 February only a small vanguard of the main force managed to reach Palembang in landing barges. In the meantime the allies were completing the evacuation of the town of Palembang.

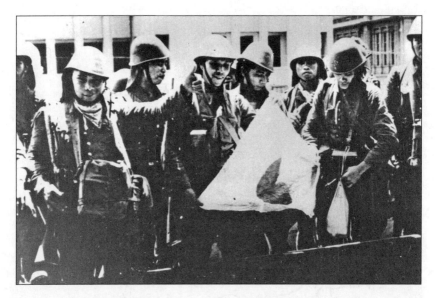

A group of Menadonese soldiers of the 2nd Company of the Xth Infantry Battalion after their return from Palembang at Batavia in February 1942, proudly showing a captured Japanese flag. (Private collection, P.C. Boer)

The majority of the British troops left the town, either through P II or direct, by road and rail for Oosthaven.[5]

The evacuation of the RAF and RAAF to western Java

In the morning of 15 February the evacuation of the troops stationed at the airfield to Oosthaven and of the operationally unserviceable but flyable aircraft at P II to Kemajoran and Andir in western Java began. In the afternoon the exodus of the remaining and still airworthy fighters and bombers started. About 12 Hudson bombers that had been evacuated the previous day to Andir returned to P II in the afternoon to pick up as many men as possible from the squadrons. At sunset the last Hudson left for Kemajoran and the last men were marching down the road towards Praboemoelih. Several small detachments of British ground defence troops, the detachment of the KNIL at P II (two infantry sections reinforced with four machineguns, amounting to about 100 men in all) and some RAF ground crew remained at P II.

In the morning of 16 February the Blenheim bombers of the RAF squadrons at P II departed, as did those of 34 Squadron RAF stationed at Lahat (a small airfield west of P II). At the airfields as much equipment as possible was destroyed, upon which the last remaining pesonnel left for Oosthaven. The various units of the RAF and British Army, destined for the airfields near Palembang and Lahat, which had arrived at Oosthaven in mid-February also evacuated to Java via Oosthaven. Among them were two Batteries of 48 Light Anti-Aircraft Regiment (48 LAA) of the British Army. These units managed to take all but two of their 4-cm Bofor guns back to Java and they arrived at Merak on 17 and 18 February. All their vehicles and the bulk of their ammunition, though, stayed behind at Oosthaven.[6]

To cover the evacuation and to degrade the Japanese as much as possible, the allied air forces carried out as many sorties as they could from Java on 16 and 17 February to P I, Japanese landing vessels on the Moesi river near Palembang and the Japanese ships at Muntok (Banka) and in the Banka Strait. The American squadrons from east and central Java also engaged in these attacks with fighters as well as heavy bombers.[7] In the meantime P II airfield was guarded by Inf. X, which had taken up positions along the road from Palembang to Praboemoelih, to which place the battalion fell back on 16 February after the commander of the KNIL detachment had reported by phone that the air base had been completely evacuated. At Praboemoelih the battalion reorganised, whereby the many loose units of the territorial troops that had joined Inf. X were organised into companies.[8]

Simultaneously with the relocation of Inf. X to southern Sumatra, the IXth Infantry Battalion (Inf. IX, minus a company and machine-gun platoon) had been transferred to Banka, while a company of the XIIth Infantry Battalion (Inf. XII, reinforced with the machine gun platoon of Inf. IX) was sent to Biliton. When the Japanese attack on Palembang and Banka began, these units, however, were ordered not to enter into combat, but to return to western Java. In view of the Japanese superiority in the new area of operations and the great shortage of land forces in Java, the allied command of the land forces, ABDA-ARM, did not want to sacrifice these troops in an attempt to hold on to Banka and Biliton for some time more. During the echeloned retreat to Java the evacuation ships were raided by bombers of the Japanese Navy air force.[9]

The losses of Inf. IX were relatively light, but because of the large number of soldiers who had sustained psychological damage the battalion had to be put on reserve after its return on 21 February 1942. The company of Inf. XII fared much worse and lost about 70 men in

the sinking of the ship *Sloet van de Beele* on 17 February. The Royal
Netherlands Navy (KM) and Dutch Naval Air Service (MLD) (with
flying boats) managed to save many of the passengers and crew, but
of the company only a few dozens of soldiers could be deployed again
after their return. On 23 February 1942 the last soldiers reported back
for duty in the garrison they had set out from.[10]

The planning of the bomber offensive

The tank park of the oil refinery at Pladjoe, which had been abandoned
virtually intact, still contained 250,000 tons of petrochemical products,
that is 250,000,000 litres of shipping and aircraft fuel. The refinery
itself had been almost completely undamaged, too, with the exception
of a few fires that had started during the battle and a few improvised
demolitions. Beside P I, the tank park would become one of the most
important targets for allied bombers in the upcoming bomber offensive. At P I, too, the defenders had been able to carry out only few
demolitions, before they had been forced to retreat. Japanese aircraft
would have little trouble operating from this airfield.[11]

On the evening of 17 February 1942 ABDAIR had finished a
detailed plan for (what is nowadays called) an offensive *Counter-air*
operation, which was to commence the following morning with a
bombing offensive against P I, the tank park at Pladjoe and the Japanese
vessels at Palembang or en route to it, as well as the ships in the Banka
Strait and the roadstead of Muntok in Banka. In the first instance,
attacking the Japanese transport vessels was given a somewhat greater
emphasis, as the plan was to disturb the supply line and reinforcement
of the Japanese troops at Palembang (including the air force) as much
as possible in view of planned counter attacks of the KNIL from
Padang (west coast of central Sumatra). All available bombers of *West
Group* (RAF and RAAF) and *Central Group* (the ML) in western Java,
in addition to as many of the American bombers of *East Group* in
central and eastern Java as could be made available were to take part in
the offensive.

On the evening of 20 February or in the early hours of 21 February
General Wavell ordered the planning and preparation for the counter
attack from Padang to be cancelled. He did not think it would stand
much chance of success and thought that the preparation for it would
take far too much time.[12] As was explained in the introduction chapter,
The Japanese advance: Java given up by the allies, the main objective

of the air campaign was and remained the extension of the period that the Japanese would need to attain air superiority over Java, and through that achieve a postponement of the invasion of Java. For this reason the strategy was directed primarily at making aircraft fuel as scarce a commodity as possible for the Japanese in southern Sumatra and Banka and at lowering the number of (Japanese) operationally serviceable military aircraft as much as possible.

The commitment of *East Group* in the west was limited to one mission only on 18 February 1942, which was not successful, due to the bad weather. As it was, in the night of 18 on 19 February the Japanese landed on Bali, immediately east of Java, which had been barely defended due to a lack of troops. This situation necessitated the execution of two *Counter-air* offensives as of 19 February, one to be carried out by *West Group* and *Central Group* and the other by *East Group*.

The allied navy, ABDA-FLOAT, made an attempt in the night of 18 on 19 February to thwart the Japanese landing operation in Bali, but to that end it had needed first to assemble the dispersed warships of its *Striking Force*. This had cost much time, but now three light cruisers and seven destroyers, augmented by eight Dutch motor torpedo boats, carried out a hit and run-action. Apart from two damaged Japanese destroyers this was not a success, although it was thought at the time that two Japanese cruisers had been damaged heavily and possibly a third enemy cruiser had been sunk. The naval battle, which later became known as the Battle in the Badoeng Strait, cost the KM a destroyer, while a light cruiser was heavily damaged and had be sent to Australia for repairs.[13]

After this, *East Group* took over the offensive, with the result that the number of sorties that ABDAIR could launch against Japanese targets in southern Sumatra and Banka, was drastically reduced. In the first instance the bombing raids to be carried out by *East Group* were directed at obstructing the Japanese landing operation and subsequently neutralising as much as possible the Japanese Navy air force elements stationed in Bali. In the sections below the western and most intensive *Counter-air* campaign, carried out by the ML, the RAF and the RAAF, will be described.[14]

The planning of the allied bomber force

On 12 February 1942, shortly before the Japanese assault on southern Sumatra, the staff of the allied air force headquarters, ABDAIR, issued a new force planning for the short term. As for the bombers, the plan provided in a repositioning of the available units in anticipation of the battle for southern Sumatra and Java, expected to begin soon. The RAF and RAAF squadrons (Singapore had already been given up by that time and was being evacuated) were to be positioned in southern Sumatra, the ML afdelingen were to be concentrated in western Java, and central and eastern Java was to become the exclusive domain for the bombers of the United States Army Air Force (USAAF). The *force requirements*, which specified the minimum strengths, were as follows for the ML, RAF and RAAF (as of 12 February).

a.   Palembang and its satellite airfields: three squadrons medium bombers of the RAF and RAAF (72 assigned aircraft).
b.   Andir, Semplak, Kalidjati and their satellite airfields: four afdelingen medium bombers of the ML (32 assigned aircraft).[15]

The evacuation of southern Sumatra brought about an adjustment of the plans. The evacuated squadrons of the RAF and RAAF were to be deployed operationally at the earliest opportunity from airfields in western Java. It is worth mentioning in this context that the British and Australian Blenheim and Hudson bombers were designated by the RAF planners at ABDAIR as medium bombers, whereas they were in fact light bombers, whose payload was about half that of the Glenn Martin bombers of the ML.

The reorganisation of the RAF/RAAF bomber force

Already before the outbreak of the battle for southern Sumatra several RAF units coming originally from Singapore had been evacuated to western Java. They were 36 and 100 Squadrons, equipped with Vickers Vildebeest and Fairey Albacore torpedo bombers, and the so-called *W-Flight*, which flew Commonwealth Wirraways for *Army Cooperation*. These units had sustained considerable losses and their obsolete fleet made it difficult to find useful employment for them. Consequently, 36 and 100 Squadrons were re-assigned for coastal reconnaissance and later for night bombing missions and together with *W-Flight* took up position at Kalidjati from around 10 February 1942. On 12 February the three units re-located to Pondok Tjabe, a new relatively large shelter airfield northwest of Semplak. After losing two of their aircraft as a result of the marshy terrain, the two squadrons left for Tjikampek, a shelter airfield for Kalidjati on 15 February. *W-Flight* was disbanded.

A British Bristol Blenheim Mark IV bomber, captured by the Japanese. One was later fitted out with Japanese engines at Andir and presented to the Indonesian air force in 1945. (Private collection, P.C. Boer)

The six aircraft of the flight remained at Pondok Tjabe (as unmanned reserves). 36 and 100 Squadrons were combined into one, designated 36 Squadron, at Tjikampek. At this field the units were reunited with the main parties of their ground crews evacuated by ship.[16]

On 16 February 1942 ABDAIR allocated Semplak airfield as the base for the evacuated Hudson bombers and Kalidjati airfield for the Blenheims. As it was, however, these light bombers were for the moment dispersed over Kemajoran, Tjililitan and Andir, and were to be relocated in phases as of 17 February, dependent on serviceability and combat-readiness of their crews. It was the intention to concentrate the two types of bombers in two separate squadrons, eventually.[17]

According to plan, the repositioning of the Hudsons to Semplak and that of the Blenheims to Kalidjati began on 17 February, but only in very modest numbers at first. The squadrons evacuated from Palembang were not ready yet. Most crews had been put on rest, while in the meantime the ground crews were reassembled. In the period between 18 and 21 February 1942, a first preliminary reorganisation of the squadrons was carried through (see the sections below). In total, the following numbers of bombers were present in western Java on 17 February 1942:

29 Bristol Blenheims
26 Lockheed Hudsons
11 Vickers Vildebeestes and two Albacores.[18]

All in all, there were 68 light bombers, a numbers that fell slightly short of the force requirements of 12 February 1942. Most of these aircraft, however, were not operationally serviceable yet. On 17 February the following were "available" (operationally serviceable and available for normal operations): six Hudsons, nine Blenheims (four of which were Mark Is, with operational limitations), nine Vildebeestes and one Albacore (only suitable for night bombing). For operational control of the British/Australian bomber fleet 225 *Bomber Group* was re-established at Bandoeng on 18 February 1942.[19]

The reorganisation of the ML bomber fleet

From the beginning of February 1942 onwards the Glenn Martin afdelingen of the ML were reorganised. This was necessary because of the losses that had been sustained in the battle for eastern Borneo (in which 1-Vl.G.I and 1- and 2-Vl.G.II had been involved) and the fighting in Malaya and British Borneo (the afdelingen of Vl.G.III and 2-Vl.G.I). 1-Vl.G.I, which had become operational again around 2 February 1942 at Andir, was transferred to Kalidjati airfield on 6 February. This base, which had only been used by the ML Vlieg- en Waarnemersschool_Flying and Observer School (VWS), had by now been expanded into a large modern war time base, with such facilities as dispersal areas in the immediate vicinity of the actual airfield and large stores of bombs, ammunition and aircraft fuel. 2-Vl.G.I, initially stationed at Semplak, then re-located to Banjoemas airfield in central Java around 6 February 1942, was now positioned at Kalidjati with its four remaining aircraft on 12 February 1942.[20]

2-Vl.G.II had been disbanded on 15 January 1942 after the battle for eastern Borneo, but 1-Vl.G.II was brought up to strength again and relocated to Maospati in central Java on 2 February 1942. Three days later, as a consequence of Japanese air raids, the afdeling moved to the shelter airfield of Pasirian. On 10 February 1942 the afdeling was stationed at its original home base of Malang (eastern Java), after which it was transferred to Kalidjati two days later. It actually flew over its aircraft on 14 and 15 February 1942.[21]

The original three afdelingen of Vl.G.III were reorganised into two new afdelingen, 2-Vl.G.III en 3-Vl.G.III, at Tjililitan in the beginning of February 1942. Both afdelingen left on 4 February for their new bases in western Java, with 2-Vl.G.III being stationed at the Tjisaoek shelter airfield near Serang, and 3-Vl.G.III at Semplak. Just like the

Glenn Martin WH-3A bombers of the ML, during a visit at Darwin (northern Australia) in May 1941. (AWM, via G.J. Casius)

afdelingen mentioned above, 2- and 3-Vl.G.III were initially mainly employed for seaward reconnaissance missions. On 11 February 3-Vl.G.III was transferred to Andir, with one patrol of three aircraft moving to Tjileungsir shelter airfield near Tjililitan on 26 February to return to Andir two days later.[22]

On 13 February 1942 the strengths of the Glenn Martin units were as follows:

1-Vl.G.I at Kalidjati:	8 Glenn Martins WH-3(A).
2-Vl.G.I at Kalidjati:	3 Glenn Martins WH-3(A) and 1 WH-2.
1-Vl.G.II at Malang:	5 Glenn Martins WH-3(A) and 1 WH-2.
2-Vl.G.III at Tjisaoek:	2 Glenn Martins WH-3(A), 2 WH-2s and 2 WH-1s.
3-Vl.G.III at Andir:	3 Glenn Martins WH-3(A) and 5 WH-2s.

In total there were 32 assigned bombers, exactly in accordance with the force requirements, though only 24 were immediately operationally serviceable (eight at Kalidjati, five at Malang, four at Tjisaoek and seven at Andir). Of this force three aircraft were lost in the battle over southern Sumatra and Banka on 16 February, and they could not be replaced at short notice. On 17 February 1942 the number of operationally serviceable Glenn Martins amounted to 17: seven at Kalidjati, three at Tjisaoek and seven at Andir. On top of that the Glenn Martins of the WH-1 type were strongly antiquated, but assigned nevertheless, due to a shortage of operationally serviceable aircraft.[23]

Allied prospects

Although the numbers of bombers available for the allied *Counter-air* campaign did approximate those of the force requirements of ABDAIR, they were only minimum quantities and there were hardly any replacements. Besides, almost no reinforcements were to be expected on the short term. Only the ML had sent a detachment of 43 men to Archerfield in Australia on 14 and 15 February 1942 to collect new North American B-25C Mitchell bombers. They would be flown across the Pacific for the ML by civilian American and RAF ferry crews. The ML Inspection (the non-operational staff elements of the ML), however, expected the first B-25 afdeling to be operational by the end of March 1942. The RAF and RAAF had no reinforcements whatsoever in the pipeline and it was expected that the squadrons would have to re-equip with B-25s of the ML or Martin B-26 Marauders of the USAAF in the course of March and April 1942. The latter bombers were expected in Australia as reinforcements of *East Group*.[24] It was very doubtful whether the allied bombing campaign would yield enough results, and especially soon enough, in order to allow reinforcements with B-25s and B-26s. However, the units engaged into combat as of 18 February 1942, in the form of a maximum effort campaign. It was all or nothing.

* * *

CHAPTER 1B.2

The Bomber Operations on 18 and 19 February 1942

Introduction

18 February 1942 marked the official start of the bombing campaign of the ML, RAF and RAAF against Japanese targets in southern Sumatra. On the previous day the first six Hudson bombers of the RAF and RAAF and the first seven Blenheims had arrived at Semplak and Kalidjati

airfield, respectively, and they were to be committed for the first time on 18 February 1942. The bombers at Semplak were from 1 Squadron RAAF, 8 Squadron RAAF, including a detachment from 59 Squadron RAF, as well as 62 Squadron RAF. Those at Kalidjati came from 27, 34 and 84 Squadrons RAF. All these squadrons had relocated parts of their flying and ground crews to Semplak and Kalidjati, respectively. In addition, at Andir 211 Squadron RAF was stationed with two operationally serviceable Blenheims. Also on 18 February 1942 many personnel evacuated from southern Sumatra were still arriving at Merak and Batavia and *West Group* did not want to reorganise the RAF and RAAF squadrons before they were fully reassembled again.

All in all, for the time being there were only 15 RAF and RAAF bombers, of which, moreover, four Blenheim Mark Is were only operationally serviceable to a limited extent (and could not be committed over southern Sumatra and Banka). On 18 February 1942 the ML had 13 Glenn Martins available, three at Tjisaoek, three at Andir and seven at Kalidjati.[1] The Americans of *East Group* in central and eastern Java were to fill the capacity hiatus in the west on a temporary basis. In the course of the afternoon, however, it began to emerge that the Japanese were conducting an operation against Bali, which immediately prompted the beginning of a second bombing campaign in the east to degrade the Japanese operation as much as possible.

The first day, a lost day

The weather was bad over large parts of western Java and southern Sumatra, with rain showers and heavy clouds. The two patrols of three Glenn Martin bombers each of 2-Vl.G.I and 1-Vl.G.II, respectively, which had taken off from Kalidjati in the morning, managed to fly over the target, the tank park at Pladjoe, but it was hidden from view under the heavy clouds. The patrols of Tlt G. Cooke and Tlt C.J.H. Samson returned to base without having anything to show for their pains. The same held good for two Blenheim Mark IVs of 34 and 84 Squadrons RAF and two of 211 Squadron RAF, whose targets were the barges on the Moesi river near Palembang. A fifth Blenheim (flown by Sgt G. Dewey of 34 Squadron) had already returned because of a malfunction. Two further patrols of 2-Vl.G.III at Tjisaoek (led by Elt L. Gosma) and 3-Vl.G.III at Andir (commanded by Elt P.J.P. van Erkel), respectively, heading for P I airfield or ships at Palembang, returned as well.[2]

Three Hudsons of 8 Squadron RAAF also carried out a mission to the Pladjoe tank park. As only a few of their own ground crew had arrived, personnel of 2-Vl.G.V at Semplak helped the Australians load their bombs. Showers on their way out forced two aircraft to return to base. Because of the heavy clouds over the target area Flt Lt H.C. Plenty's crew in the third Hudson could do not anything but return to Semplak.[3]

Three Hudsons had been scheduled for carrying out reconnaissance flights. One aircraft, flown by Flt Lt T.P. O'Brien (62 Squadron) flew a reconnaissance mission in the morning over the western part of the Java Sea. This mission, too had to be aborted due to very bad weather, without the crew having observed anything.[4] Another aircraft (pilot unknown) carried out a reconnaissance of Oosthaven (whose harbour was still in friendly hands and whose Koninklijke Marine–Royal Netherlands Navy port commander had stayed on his post) and the road from Oosthaven to Palembang. The crew did not observe any Japanese advance or activities. The third aircraft remained on the ground.[5]

Later that day a few more Hudsons arrived at Semplak. In the meantime some four Hudsons were at Andir with the Technical Service of the ML for major repairs. The RAF and the ML had agreed that the depot of the Technische Dienst–Technical Service (TD) at Andir was going to take care of the major repairs and maintenance of the Hudsons.[6]

Four B-17 bombers of the 7th Bomb. Group at Madioen and six B-17s of the 19th Bomb. Group at Malang also flew a mission to southern Sumatra, their target being the Japanese ships in the mouths of the Moesi and Oepang rivers. Here, too, the bad weather forced them to break off their mission on their flight out and return to base.[7] A renewed attempt later that day was not to take place anymore, because, as mentioned above, in the afternoon of 18 February the allied headquarters began to grasp that the Japanese were staging an operation against Bali. Immediately the bombing offensive was split into two by ABDAIR, where the bombers of *East Group* were given Japanese ships and later also Den Pasar airfield, captured by the Japanese, for targets.[8]

Kalidjati becomes both ML and RAF base

As was said above, the bomber operations of the RAF from Kalidjati started on 18 February 1942. In the meantime the evacuated Blenheim squadrons were gradually being reorganised, with all Blenheim Mark I aircraft assigned to 27 Squadron. 34 and 84 Squadrons and their aircraft were at Kemajoran, Tjililitan and Kalidjati and 211 Squadron at Kemajoran, Tjililitan and Andir. For the time being, the emphasis lay on getting the Blenheims operationally serviceable, and to this end personnel of all the squadrons and several other RAF units were employed.[9]

The Koninklijke Nederlands-Indische Luchtvaartmaatschappij– The Royal Netherlands Indies Airline (KNILM) lent support by providing hangar space and technical assistance. A technical team of the Technical Service depot of the ML from Andir came over to assist in specific repair work on a number of aircraft and the Technical Service and the Magazijndienst–Warehouse Service of the ML provided all kind of materials. In the meantime the RAF collected the evacuated ground equipment, which had been scattered all over the place, and replenished what was missing as best it could from the cargoes of the ships that were unloaded in Tandjong Priok (the harbour of Batavia). Work teams were formed from the ground crews of evacuated squadrons for unloading the ships and sorting out the cargoes in the harbour. Furthermore, all sorts of materials were taken over from the KNIL, which also saw to the accommodation of the RAF personnel.[10]

At Kalidjati the Glenn Martins of 1- and 2-Vl.G.I had been pooled with regard to their operational deployment as of 12 February 1942. A few days later a substantial number of personnel of 2-Vl.G.I were temporarily assigned to 1-Vl.G.I, whereas the remainder was detached to the workshop of the Technical Service at Kalidjati. The result was an extended afdeling, designated as 1/2-Vl.G.I. As of 17 February 1942 the Glenn Martins of all three afdelingen at Kalidjati were pooled for operational deployment, a system copied by the RAF.[11]

The commanding officer of 2-Vl.G.I, Kap R. de Senerpont Domis, was temporarily assigned to Lt Col J.J. Zomer's staff, which had been formed on 16 February 1942.[12] This ML officer, a former liaison officer at Singapore, had been appointed Commandant Luchtstrijdkrachten– local Air Officer Commanding (CL), the operational commander of the Dutch East-Indies units at Kalidjati. He was also Vliegkampcommandant–station commander (VKC) of the air base. With the arrival of the RAF also a staff, called *RAF Station Kalidjati*, was established.[13]

The British had not agreed to a proposal by the ML to make Lt Col Zomer head of a combined command, and appointed Group-Captain G.F. Whistondale as "station commander" and commanding officer of the 'British part' of the air base. Whistondale became local operational commander of the British squadrons and CO of all the other RAF personnel stationed at the airbase in support functions, all assigned to the staff RAF Station Kalidjati. As station commander, Zomer, however, remained responsible for the management of the base (the platform in present days parlour) and kept on arranging quite a lot of things for the British, such as accommodation and food for the personnel and fuel provision for the aircraft and vehicles. Communications also remained in the hands of the Radiodienst–Radio Service of the ML and the Engineers of the KNIL. RAF Station Kalidjati only had a radio truck for communications with BRITAIR (if the circumstances allowed). The consequence of this double command structure was that two command posts were established, with two commanders, who received their orders through two different lines of command (ML Command and *West Group*, respectively).[14]

The available aircraft

The strengths of assigned and operationally serviceable bombers at the beginning of the day on 19 February 1942 were as follows:[15]

Table 7

Unit	Type	Assigned	Operationally serviceable	Remarks
Vl.G.I/II	Glenn M.	16	7	
34/84/211 Sq	Blenheim	?	5	Excl. Mark Is
1/8/62 Sq	Hudson	?	6	
2-III	Glenn M.	6	4	
3-III	Glenn M.	7	3	
Total		?	25	

The weather was fine that day and became gradually better in the course of the morning. Over southern Sumatra and in the vicinity of Banka it was even exceptionally bright, and the absence of cloud cover would hinder the operations.

The operations from Andir

In the early morning of 19 February 1942 three Glenn Martins of 3-Vl.G.III, flown by afdeling commander Elt A.B. Wolff, Tlt J. Coblijn and Tlt H.E. van Thiel carried out a bombing raid on ships in the roadstead of Muntok (Banka). The patrol was not intercepted and made a successful attack through medium-intense anti-aircraft artillery fire from the ships in the roadstead and the shore. One of the six ships in the roadstead received a direct hit from one of a total of nine 300-kilogramme bombs dropped. The Glenn Martins were not hit or intercepted and landed safely at Andir after their mission.[16]

At 09:30 hrs Tlt P.J.P. van Erkel's crew took off in a fourth aircraft of 3-Vl.G.III (the M-533), which had become operationally serviceable in the meantime, for a mission to the BPM refinery tank park at Pladjoe. The seven 100-kilogramme bombs were dropped over a group of tanks filled with aircraft fuel. One of a group of four gigantic tanks with 100 octane aircraft fuel, the westernmost tank in the tank park, containing 4,800 cubic metres, that is 4,800,000 litres of fuel, went up in flames.[17]

To be sure of a good result, Van Erkel, on request of his observer, made up to three runs on the target before dropping his bombs. A big black pillar of smoke proved they had hit the target. On their return flight, however, Ki-27 fighters of the 11th Sentai that had been scrambled from P I in the meantime attacked the Glenn Martin and it was a narrow escape. Air gunner Private J.H. Wetzels and wireless operator Sergeant R. Timmermans together claimed (probably incorrectly) one Japanese fighter, before the Glenn Martin found cover in a cloud. That afternoon Van Erkel landed his undamaged M-533 at Kemajoran and returned at Andir at 17:30 hrs.[18]

The missions from Semplak and Tjisaoek

In the morning of 19 February three Hudsons made reconnaissance flights, one of which was a seaward reconnaissance over the western part of the Java Sea. One of these aircraft, flown by Flg Off H.H. Siddell (59 Squadron) had just returned from a reconnaissance mission to Palembang and the Banka Strait, when Japanese fighters, followed by bombers, attacked Semplak. The Siddell crew had made a low-level reconnaissance of Palembang II, had not seen any aircraft there and had subsequently made photographs of the refinery and the tank park at Pladjoe. They had spotted Japanese fighters flying over Palembang I. They had not observed any Japanese ships in the Banka Strait, nor had the Hudson crew that reconnoitred the Java Sea.[19]

Siddell's aircraft sustained medium to heavy damage from bomb fragments. Two other Hudsons, which had been parked along the edge of the airfield, were lost. A third Hudson was standing on the platform in front of one of the hangars and exploded, also setting fire to one of a pair of KNILM Sikorsky S-43s in the process. Close to or inside the hangar, which had partially collapsed, the second Sikorsky was lost, along with a Ryan STM trainer of Vl.G.V of the ML. There were no casualties.[20]

The raid was carried out by five Ki-48 bombers escorted by 19 Ki-43 fighters. The Japanese were careful during this first raid and the bombers only made one run. A small number of Ki-43s subsequently carried out a strafing of the airfield. Semplak was not defended by anti-aircraft artillery, and it will not have taken the Japanese fighter pilots very long to find out that the wooden dummies there did not fire back at them. The ML fighters of the nearby Tjisaoek shelter base engaged into combat with about 15 of the Ki-43 fighters and sustained severe losses (see Part 1A).

Three Glenn Martins of 2-Vl.G.III, led by afdeling commander Elt F.R. Lettinga, and Sgt M.F. Noorman van der Dussen and Sgt J. Bos flying the trailing aircraft, flew a mission to P I in the morning. This airfield, however, was hidden from view because of low thick clouds. The flight out to Palembang was nerve-racking. Initially, the aircraft were cruising just below a layer of cloud, a fine cover, but the crews suddenly found themselves flying in bright sunshine at about a distance of 70 kilometres from their target. The Moesi river was not visible and a large area around Palembang was covered in extensive unbroken low stratus cloud and ground mist. Above this cumulus clouds were developing. Lettinga decided to try and drop the bombs on the tank park of the BPM refinery, whose position might still be determined by his observer Elt J.M.L. van Roon.[21]

Just about to launch the attack, Lettinga saw a total of 11 Japanese fighters approach. That was a bit much for his liking and he had his bombs dropped. The pilots of the three Glenn Martins increased their relative distances, climbed into the cumulus clouds and made a run for it, the patrol splitting up in the process. When the bombers came back into the sunshine, their pilots dived in order to use the low stratus clouds south of Palembang for cover. As soon as the Japanese fighters were spotted they dived disappeared into the clouds and changed course. The fighters soon gave up and the three ML bombers could return without any further problems to western Java. On their return Lettinga and Van Roon reported that no results had been achieved.[22]

The missions from Kalidjati

Between 09:30 and 10:00 hrs the seven (operationally serviceable) Blenheim Mark IVs, which had become available in the meantime, took off for a raid on P I. Four aircraft had flown to Kalidjati that morning in order to join in the raid. Logistically, the RAF at Kalidjati was not quite ready yet, and the bombers were loaded with 100-kilogramme bombs and .303-inch ammunition from the ML stores. Three Hudsons from Semplak were also to take part in the mission, but shortly before take off two of these aircraft were destroyed in the Japanese attack described above. The third aircraft, flown by Flg Off D. Hughes (1 Squadron) took off after the all clear at Semplak, probably a bit late, and missed the rendezvous with the Blenheims, upon which the pilot returned to Semplak.[23]

The first Blenheim section was led by Wg Cdr R.N. Bateson, the commander of 211 Squadron, with in one of the trailing planes the crew of Plt Off E.P. Coughlan (also 211 Squadron). The second section was led by Ft Lt J.V.C. Wyllie of 84 Squadron. One of the three trailing planes in his section was flown by Sgt G. Dewey of 34 Squadron. Flying personnel of the latter squadron, among whom Dewey and his two crew members, were seconded, temporarily for the time being, to 84 Squadron on 19 February.

The cumulus clouds the crews of 2-Vl.G.III had seen forming, had by now transformed into rather heavy cloud, and as a result of this it was decided to attack individually. One by one the bombers dived through an opening between the cumulus clouds to make a run over the airfield, a few of the crews completely missing it. Soon several Ki-27 fighters made their appearance, forcing Flt Lt Wyllie to seek the cover of the clouds repeatedly before he could go down. Four of the Blenheims escaped, but both Coughlan's and Wyllie's aircraft were intercepted during their climb out for the clouds after the attack.[24]

P I was full of Japanese aircraft and to the left and right of the runway rows of planes were parked. Wyllie's Blenheim appeared from the clouds exactly in line with the runway, upon which his navigator-bombardier Sgt D.C.C. Argent made his pilot go for one side of the rows of planes and threw the four 100-kilogramme bombs on top of them. According to a Japanese source the total damage for the 12th Hiko Dan amounted to one burnt-out Ki-27 fighter, while two other Ki-27s had sustained considerable damage. Undoubtedly several other Japanese planes will have received some lighter damage. However, no damage report of the 3rd Hiko Dan remains, of which unit a number of Ki-48 bombers of the 90th Sentai had arrived at Palembang shortly before the allied attack. The British crews reported direct hits on five twin-engine bombers, which may have been the aircraft that had attacked Semplak earlier that day.[25]

One Ki-27 attacked Wyllie's plane during his climb out for the clouds. Air gunner Sgt R.C.H. Bennet managed to hit this fighter, which made it fall back and disappear out of sight in a cloud, trailing a black plume of smoke. Although one of the Blenheim's engines had been hit and was losing some oil, the crew could fly back to Kalidjati without any problems, thanks to the layer of cloud.[26]

Plt Off Coughlan's crew were having a tougher time of it when they were attacked just south of the town of Palembang by about nine fighters, mainly Ki-27s. These planes had been patrolling just above the clouds and dived for the Blenheim. Coughlan flew from one cumulus cloud to the next, while air gunner Sgt A.P. Richardson managed to hit a Ki-27 over the full length of its fuselage, upon which the fighter went into a sheer dive, trailing a black plume of smoke, and crashed into the ground. The other fighters, however, kept making attacks at the Blenheim, until their fuel and ammunition ran out after some 40 minutes. Coughlan, too, landed safely at Kalidjati. Both Bennet and Richardson got a Ki-27 to their name, though in Bennet's case this might be incorrect. The Japanese claimed (incorrectly) one of the two Blenheims as shot down and a second as a probable.[27]

By this time there were nine Glenn Martins available at Kalidjati and at about 11:00 hrs these aircraft took off in three patrols. The Beckman-patrol of 1-Vl.G.I left for an attack on the oil tanks at Pladjoe and the Samson and Cooke-patrols of 1-Vl.G.II and 2-Vl.G.I, respectively, were to raid the roadstead and airfield at Muntok (Banka). All three patrols, however, returned to base when they flew into bright weather over southern Sumatra. The patrol of Elt J.C. Beckman found itself in a completely bright sky north of Teloekbetoeng, upon which the patrol commander decided to abort the mission. This decision was in line with the instructions he had received from Lieutenant-Colonel Zomer.[28]

Tlt G. Cooke had been given the assignment to drop the seven 100-kilogramme bombs per bomber on the airfield of Muntok if they found enemy aircraft there, or else drop them on the ships in the harbour or roadstead instead. Should there be no enemy activity near Banka, they were to fly on to the Moesi to bomb the vessels in the river. When the patrol approached Banka, they, too, flew into completely bright weather, while the crews spotted fighters flying in the distance.[29]

Tlt C.J.H. Samson's primary target was the roadstead and harbour of Muntok and his patrol had been loaded up with three 300-kilogramme bombs per aircraft. Just like Cooke, Samson took the decision to turn around. The six Glenn Martins flew back to Kalidjati via Tegal. The crews were debriefed at their home base by Kap J.D. de Riemer of the Operations Office of the ML Command, who in rather unfriendly tone asked why they had not carried through their missions. Quite a frustrating experience.[30]

In the afternoon the Van den Broek-patrol of 2-Vl.G.I, led by Elt H. van den Broek, carried out an attack on P I airfield. The trailing aircraft were flown by Sgt L.N. Bieger and Sgt L. Davids. The raid was carried out at around 14:00 hrs, but had to be aborted because of an interception by Japanese fighters. This time the weather was fine for approaching a target undiscovered, but the patrol was attacked by three Ki-27s, just before they were going in for their bombing run. Immediately dropping their bombs, the patrol dived into the clouds and the crews tried to escape by hopping from one cumulus cloud to the next. Their evasive manoeuvring completely disrupted their patrol formation.[31] At one moment the Davids crew was chased by all three Ki-27s which attacked the bomber from behind, below and above. Wireless operator Kpl H.J. Burgers managed to hit one Ki-27 so badly that its pilot had to break off the fight. Shortly after that, Davids crew was the last of the patrol who managed to reach the safety of a cloud, too. On their return at Kalidjati, only Davids' Glenn Martin appeared to have some light damage. The M-568 had bullet holes in the tail section and several bullet holes in the stabiliser, which had been self-inflicted in the heat of battle by Sgt D. Brouwer, the 2nd pilot-airgunner. Burgers got one Army 97 to his name (probably incorrectly).[32]

The ground forces in southern Sumatra

The reinforced Inf. X, more than 1,000 strong, had left Praboemoelih on 17 February and had withdrawn on Martapoera by order of the Territorial Commander Southern Sumatra. The vanguard, commanded by Kap M.U.H.L.E. Ohl, reached this place in the morning of 18 February and subsequently secured the bridge over the Komering river, after which the main force was brought up. The vanguard engaged in battle with Japanese troops from approximately 12:00 hrs until around

16:30 hrs, and sustaining one lightly wounded, managed to stop the Japanese vanguard that was advancing along the road. By order of battalion commander Major B.P. de Vries, Ohl broke off the fight because there was nothing to fight for after the demolition of the bridge, and it would be easy to envelop the battalion.[33]

By this time the unit had received orders from the Territorial Commander to pull back on Oosthaven in order to be evacuated to western Java. The withdrawal was conducted in a professional manner, but there were no further contacts with Japanese troops. From about 15:00 hrs in the afternoon of 19 February the KNIL troops, in the company of other evacuees, left port in three small vessels for Merak in western Java, a six-hour trip. On 20 February 1942 Inf. X was back in Batavia.[34]

Summary

The first two days of the allied bomber offensive yielded relatively few results, because of the weather over the target area, which was either too bad or too good, as well as the Japanese fighter defence. With the help of Ki-27 fighters of the 12th Hiko Dan, sometimes assisted by Ki-43 fighters of the 3rd Hiko Dan, the 3rd Hiko Shudan maintained a fighter permanence south of Palembang. Nevertheless, the bomber force managed to set fire to a first large storage tank filled with aircraft fuel at Pladjoe. Furthermore, the 12th Hiko Dan lost one Ki-27 fighter, while two other Ki-27 fighters were considerably damaged in a raid on P I airfield. In addition, the 3rd Hiko Dan lost several Ki-48 bombers; probably five were destroyed or heavily damaged. At least one Ki-27 was shot down by the gunner of a Blenheim, while several other Ki-27s were damaged in engagements with bombers.

On 18 February B-17 bombers of *East Group* were used for the first and last time in the west. These aircraft, however, had to return because of bad weather, and later were unable to take part in the western campaign because of the Japanese action against Bali. Although the RAF and RAAF squadrons were not fully operational yet, the Hudsons flew (apart from reconnaissance missions) already four sorties in total, two of which had to aborted due to bad weather and one because the rendezvous had been missed. The Glenn Martins of the ML carried out 12 and 19 sorties, respectively, on these two days. Three Hudsons, together with several other aircraft, were lost in a Japanese raid on Semplak on 19 February 1942.

* * *

CHAPTER 1B.3

The Missions of 20 February 1942

Introduction

27 Squadron RAF and 34 Squadron RAF at Kalidjati were de-activated on this day. Most of the personnel of the British and Australian squadrons evacuated from southern Sumatra had by now been re-assigned and on 20 February and on the following days only small groups and individual servicemen came trickling in. The personnel of the squadrons mentioned were partly absorbed by 84 Squadron RAF and 211 Squadron RAF at Kalidjati and Andir, respectively, and the rest were designated for evacuation. The operational serviceability of the bombers was still very low and the bulk of the personnel and air-craft of the Blenheim squadrons were still at Tjililitan and Kemajoran. 211 Squadron was stationed at Andir for the time being, but flew its missions from Kalidjati.[1]

On 20 February 1942 ABDAIR had the following numbers of assigned and operationally serviceable bombers available.[2]

Table 8

Unit	Assigned	Operationally Serviceable	Remarks
Vl.G.I/II	16	7	
84/211 Sq	?	3	Most planes at Kemajoran, excl. Mk Is
1/8/62 Sq	20	4	Several planes still at Kemajoran and Andir (TD)
2-III	6	4	
3-III	7	3	
Total	?	21	

The missions from Andir

In the morning Tlt R.C. Schäftlein carried out a mission with three Glenn Martins against the tank park of the BPM oil refinery. The trailing aircraft were flown by Tlt K. van Gessel and Sgt L.H. van Onselen. There was rather much cloud over the target area, while there were also great black smoke columns rising up from the two refinery complexes. This allowed the patrol to approach unnoticed, without being intercepted. During the attack itself there was intense anti-aircraft fire coming from Japanese ships in the Moesi river near Palembang, as well as anti-aircraft guns positioned at the refinery complexes. The bombers, however, did not sustain any damage. Sgt M. de Mens, 2nd pilot-air gunner, in Schäftlein's crew, took a number of pictures of the target, showing afterwards that four of the bombed large tanks filled with aircraft fuel were indeed in flames.[3]

In the evening two Glenn Martins, flown by Tlt J. Coblijn and Vdg M.P. Bosman, flew another mission against the tank park at Pladjoe. Their target was the remaining tanks filled with 100 octane aircraft fuel there. The attack was carried out in the deep dusk during last light at about 18:45 hrs. The flames of several fires in the tank park were clearly visible. The patrol was intercepted, but too late, by two Mitsubishi F1M float planes of the Japanese Navy. In a shallow dive the bombers quickly outran these fighter-reconnaissance aircraft and disappeared into the darkness, the F1Ms not being able to engage them. The raid had been a successful one and the crews reported several new fires. The Japanese, too, reported that the fire in the tank park was spreading.[4]

The missions from Tjisaoek and Semplak

The patrol led by Elt H.M.E. van Leyden of 2-Vl.G.III (trailing pilots unknown) took off around sunrise from Tjisoek for an attack on the ships in the Moesi river near Palembang. The three Glenn Martins were not intercepted and successfully bombed a freighter. The ship received a direct hit, while a number of cutters and prahns near it were sunk by near misses. The fourth available aircraft of 2-Vl.G.III (crew unknown) was sent on an early morning reconnaissance mission to Oosthaven and Teloekbetoeng and the area around it, as well as the road from Palembang to Oosthaven. No Japanese activity was reported. As it was, the Japanese army was not to reach Tandjoengkarang, just north of these ports, until on 21 February 1942.[5]

The latter mission — a planned repetition of which was cancelled later that day due to bad weather — was meant to support an action of the allied navy and the RAF. The British corvette *Ballarat* and the Dutch gunboat *Soemba* sailed from Batavia to Oosthaven before sunrise with a team of RAF volunteers in order to pick up materiel of 41 Air Stores Park and 81 Repair and Salvage Unit which had been left behind in the harbour. The materiel consisted of spare aircraft parts and replacement engines for Hurricanes. The 50-man strong RAF party salvaged as much materiel as they could and further stashed *Ballarat* to the gunwales with (scarce) Bofor ammunition for the British anti-aircraft artillery units evacuated to Java. It took them 12 hours, during which time they also carried out some demolitions in Oosthaven.[6]

In the morning also four Hudsons from Semplak carried out attacks on Japanese shipping. Two Hudsons of 1 Squadron RAAF (piloted by Flt J.G. Emerton and Flg Off J.M. Sutherland) and an additional two from 62 Squadron RAF (pilots unknown) departed in the early morning for a mission to the Moesi delta and the adjacent sea area of the Banka Strait. The low clouds hid their possible targets from sight, upon which the crews decided to reconnoitre the Moesi river for Japanese shipping. They found them indeed near Palembang, but only one crew managed to drop the four 250-lb bombs on a freighter. Japanese fighters intercepted the Hudsons and forced them into the clouds. All four bombers returned safely, probably without having scored any results.[7]

The missions from Kalidjati

Three Blenheims flown by 84 Squadron crews left in the early morning for a mission against P I, with shipping on the Moesi for alternative targets. P I was hidden under a thick blanket of clouds, but not all the crews managed to attack ships lying at anchor at Palembang. When they were approaching the Moesi river, Japanese fighters appeared. At least one of the bombers, flown by Sgt G.W. Sayer, managed to drop its bombs (probably without results) on a ship lying at anchor at Palembang, only to be attacked immediately after by a Japanese fighter aircraft. Ki-27s went in pursuit of the Blenheims and at about 20 kilometres east of Palembang two Ki-27s again engaged Sayers' Blenheim. One of the fighters was claimed shot down by air gunner Sgt A.H. Ross (possibly incorrectly). By repeatedly diving into the ground mist the bomber escaped.[8]

At about 06:35 hrs in the morning the Samson-patrol of 1-Vl.G.II took off from Kalidjati for a bombing raid on shipping in the Moesi delta. Next to Tlt C.J.H. Samson, the pilots of the three Glenn Martins were, Vdg J.C. Yland and Sgt Th.H.M. Duffels. The weather en route was fine with a layer of clouds at 6,000 metres. After take off the patrol headed straight for the Moesi delta, but over the mouth of the Oepang river no ships were found. The low clouds prevented a clear view of the mouth of the Moesi river, upon which the patrol leader decided to fly on to Muntok (Banka).[9]

Between the mouth of the Moesi river and Muntok a heavy cruiser was spotted, which was attacked from an altitude of 4,500 metres. At 09:00 hrs the patrol observer Elt J. van Loggem and the bomb aimers in the trailing planes dropped their three 300-kilogramme bombs each. There was no anti-aircraft fire from the cruiser, and only a few ships in the roadstead and harbour of Muntok gave off a little, badly aimed anti-aircraft fire. Suddenly, however, the cruiser changed its course 90 degrees, causing all the bombs to miss. After a hasty reconnaissance of Muntok, where five large transport ships, a small war ship (probably a mine sweeper) and a large number of barges and smaller vessels were spotted, the Glenn Martins returned to Kalidjati via the island of Noordwachter and Krawang on the north coast of western Java. There were no enemy fighters up and the return flight went without problems. At 11:00 hrs they were back on the ground once more.[10]

At about 08:00 hrs the (by now) five remaining operationally serviceable Glenn Martins at Kalidjati took off, in one patrol led by Elt F.J.W. den Ouden, for a bombing raid at the BPM tank park at Pladjoe. The patrol, however, was forced to return due to impenetrable cloud. The pilots of the other bombers were Tlt R. Belloni, Sgt J. van Kruiselbergen, SM F. van den Broek and SM D.T. de Bont, as Den Ouden all from 1-Vl.G.I. Near Teloekbetoeng they found that all of southern Sumatra was covered in a close blanket of clouds, which would make it impossible for them to find the target. They turned back to base. In the meantime, the weather over western Java had deteriorated, the heavy clouds causing the formation to break up. Four aircraft managed to make it back to Kalidjati. The M-560 of the Van Kruiselbergen-crew was fired at by friendly anti-aircraft artillery on crossing the northern coast of Java, although it had approached according to the prescribed procedures. Although there were no visible hits, Sgt Van Kruiselbergen thought he had better be safe than sorry, also in view of the heavy clouds and showers, and went along the south coast of Java to Pameungpeuk to make an intermediate landing there. Later that day the crew flew on to their home base Kalidjati.[11]

which, in the meantime, had just received its first raid by the Japanese Army air force, operating from the captured Palembang I.

At about 13:00 hrs the Japanese attacked with ten twin-engine Ki-48s of the 90th Sentai, escorted by 24 Ki-43 fighters of the 59th and 64th Sentais. The alarm came too late, only seconds before the attack began with a first strafing by a group of Ki-43s. Most planes were safely parked in the dispersal areas around the actual flying terrain. But of the Glenn Martins that had been parked in the pens at the southern edge of the airfield for maintenance after their morning missions, two were completely lost. The M-540 and the M-580 of 1/2-Vl.G.I went up in flames. One aircraft of 1-Vl.G.II (the M-592 or the M-5102) sustained medium damage and after being patched up, was flown to the Technical Service at Andir for further repairs a few days later.

Furthermore, one Glenn Martin sustained light damage (the M-545 of 1/2-Vl.G.I) and one Lockheed 212 trainer of the Vlieg-en Waarnemerschool–Flight and Observer School (VWS) of the ML was lost.[12]

The anti-aircraft artillery at the base had not been able to score any results. Kalidjati did not have any anti-aircraft artillery worth mentioning; two 4-cm Bofor guns and six 12.7-mm machine guns of the KNIL, and a number of 7.7-mm machine guns, positioned in a number of small circular concrete rings around the airfield, manned by elderly KNIL personnel. A Battery of ten 4-cm guns of the British Army (49 Battery of 48 LAA), however, was on its way to Kalidjati and became operational at 16:45 hrs. The damage to the airfield itself was not too bad, but by the time that it was operational again it was too late to carry out any daylight missions against targets in southern Sumatra or Banka. On top of that, the weather had deteriorated considerably with heavy cloud and showers over most of western Java and southern Sumatra.[13]

Summary

On 20 February 1942, 24 sorties were sent out, 10 to Pladjoe, 10 to Japanese shipping and 3 to Palembang I airfield. In addition, 2-Vl.G.III carried out a reconnaissance mission for an operation of the allied navy and the RAF to Oosthaven, which had already been evacuated. The allied bombing raids were not successful that day, with most of the bombers either missing their targets, being unable to reach them due to fighter defence or being confronted with low thick cloud over the target areas. Only a patrol of 2-Vl.G.III and two patrols from 3-Vl.G.III were successful, hitting a freighter in the Moesi river near Palembang and storage tanks at Pladjoe, respectively. On this day the Japanese Army air force attacked Kalidjati for the first time, destroying two Glenn Martins and one L-212 trainer completely and putting one Glenn Martin out of action for some time due to medium damage.

* * *

CHAPTER 1B.4

The Events and Operations on 21 February 1942

Introduction

In the early morning of 21 February 1942 the allied bomber offensive was given a somewhat different emphasis. General Wavell ordered all planning and preparation for a counter-attack on Palembang by the KNIL from Padang to be abandoned. The bombers that were to have attacked the shipping in the Banka Strait and near Banka, were given other targets in the early morning. The sorties of the bomber fleet were concentrated on the tank park at Pladjoe and on P I airfield, with the Japanese ships at or en route to Palembang for alternative targets. In the west there were still no signs of a new Japanese operation. Apparently, the Japanese armed forces were still fully occupied with completing the occupation of southern Sumatra, and the activities observed at Muntok seemed to be completely in line with that scenario.

A flying boat of *RecGroup*, which made a reconnaissance flight to the Anambas Islands on 21 February 1942, however, reported it had spotted Japanese cruisers and transport ships near Terempa. This might possibly be the beginnings of the assembly of a new force. In reaction to this discovery ABDA-FLOAT directed two submarines of the Koninklijke Marine–Royal Netherlands Navy (KM) for observation tasks to the Anambas Islands.[1]

In order to hinder the Japanese maritime activities in the Banka Strait and the Moesi river, it was decided on the evening of 20 February to have the flying boats of *RecGroup* lay magnetic mines in the Moesi delta and in the southern approaches of the Banka Strait. These operations were to begin during the night of 21 February, but were postponed for unknown reasons. The missions were subsequently carried out in the night of 22 on 23 February and in the following night, both times by two MLD Catalina flying boats from the Naval air stations at Tandjong Priok and Soerabaja.[2]

The bombing campaign in the west continued with all available aircraft on 21 February 1942, although some bombers had been assigned to carry out seaward reconnaissance missions. This was done with a view to an upcoming operation of ABDA-FLOAT. On 22 and 23 February as many ships as could be managed were to be directed away from the overcrowded harbour of Tandjong Priok (Batavia), which was vulnerable to air raids, via the Soenda Strait.

Shortages of anti-aircraft artillery

A source of worry was the great shortage of anti-aircraft artillery in Java, which exposed the bombers to an increased risk of being destroyed in Japanese attacks on their home bases. Only Tjililitan, Andir and Kalidjati could be armed with extra, British, anti-aircraft artillery in the form of a Battery of 48 LAA, with ten 4-cm Bofor guns for each of them. A detachment of the battery at Tjililitan (with two guns), incidentally, was stationed at Tandjong Priok for the protection of the Naval air station. Besides, a section of two 2-cm guns of A. I Ld. of the KNIL, which was already present at Tjililitan, remained there. In the evening of 20 February 1942 49 *Battery* (48 LAA) at Kalidjati was the last to deploy. Furthermore, a section of 4-cm guns and two sections of 12.7-mm machine guns of A. III Ld. of the KNIL remained stationed at that base, so that the total of anti-aircraft guns amounted to 12 4-cm guns and six 12.7-mm machine guns, not counting the 7.7-mm machine guns that had been positioned along the edge of the flight terrain.[3] That was all the available anti-aircraft artillery and the busy bomber base of Semplak would have to make do without anti-aircraft artillery altogether, except for a number of 7.7-mm machine guns. On top of that, this base, unlike Tjililitan and Kalidjati, did not have any dispersal areas to spread the aircraft out. As it was, the condition of the surrounding terrain was such that they could not easily be constructed and therefore the bombers had to be parked along the edge of the flight terrain and in a limited number of pens at the beginning and end of the main runway. That was the reason why ABDAIR was preparing to relocate the Hudsons. It was a problem, though, that for logistic reasons *West Group* did not want to spread the aircraft over several shelter airfields. Tjisaoek and Tjileungsir, for instance, were shelter airfields that blended in so well with their environment that anti-aircraft fire would have a contrary effect. These airfields were never attacked by the Japanese air forces.[4]

The available bombers

This day saw the completion of the reorganisation of the Hudson squadrons at Semplak. 8 Squadron RAAF and 62 Squadron RAF went "administrative only", and a number of personnel of both squadrons was assigned to 1 Squadron RAAF, that of 62 Squadron RAF being concentrated in a separate detachment consisting of ground personnel and four bomber crews, the administrative transfer of aircraft following the next day.

At daybreak of 21 February 1942 the strengths of assigned and operationally serviceable bombers were as follows:[5]

Table 9

Unit	Assigned	Operationally Serviceable	Remarks
84/211 Sq	?	5	Some planes still at Kemajoran
1/8/62 Sq	20	4	
Vl.G.I/II	14	8	
2-III	6	4	
3-III	7	3	
Total	?	24	

The missions from Andir

In the morning three Glenn Martins of 3-Vl.G.III once again bombed the tank park at Pladjoe. This time the pilots were Tlt P.J.P. van Erkel, Tlt H.E. van Thiel and Vdg L. Kroes. The hit pattern of the seven 100-kilogramme bombs per aircraft was exactly right, but it was difficult to see the result due to all the fires that were already burning and smoke. The crews were convinced they had started at least four new seats of fire.[6]

In the evening 3-Vl.G.III carried out a second attack on the tank park of the BPM refinery. Two aircraft, flown by Tlt K.van Gessel and Sgt L.H. van Onselen, each armed with seven 100-kilogramme bombs, took off from Andir at last light and landed after a successful bombing raid at Kemajoran at about 24:00 hrs. On approaching their target the crews saw several fires already raging in the tank park. Also on the refinery complex itself they noticed a major fire. Although it was difficult to tell, the crews were convinced their raid had been successful. According to one of the tail gunners, they had started one large new fire. Without any problems the crews flew back in the moonlit night. It was so bright during these nights that when the moon had risen in the course of the night, it was possible to read the paper by its light. The next morning the planes were flown back to Andir.[7]

The missions from Semplak and Tjisaoek

In the early morning two Hudsons took off from Semplak to carry out a seaward reconnaissance mission. The Hudson flown by Flg Off P.M. Bonn's crew (62 Squadron RAF) had been assigned to search for and attack several ships that had been reported by a Catalina flying boat near the Riouw Archipelago south-east of Singapore. This, however, was the regular patrol area of Ki-27 fighters of the 12th Hiko Dan stationed at Singapore. After his bomber had been damaged in a fighter attack Bonn managed to fly back to Java, but came to grief fifteen kilometres northwest of Buitenzorg. The pilot died later that day in the Military Hospital at Batavia, his observer, Flt Sgt W.F.F. Perkins passed away two days later. No records of any results of the second reconnaissance mission remain, but it is unlikely that any Japanese ships were discovered.[8]

At 09:00 hrs two Hudsons, flown by Flt Lt J.G. White and Flt Lt K.R. Smith (both 1 Squadron RAAF), took off on a bombing mission against P I and a subsequent reconnaissance of the Moesi river for Japanese shipping. The bombing raid was successful, but on their way to the Moesi river the bombers were intercepted by Japanese fighters and dived into the clouds. Neither Hudson received any damage and they both returned safely.[9]

In the early afternoon 2-Vl.G.III attacked the BPM refinery at Pladjoe with its full strength of four operationally serviceable Glenn

Martins. This time the refinery itself was the target, in particular the cracking unit, the refinery's heart. With seven 100-kilogramme bombs per bomber this installation was completely destroyed. The patrol was led by Elt L.Gosma, his trailing pilots are not known.[10]

The missions from Kalidjati

When by 08:00 hrs the weather had cleared somewhat, the first to take off from Kalidjati were two Glenn Martin patrols. The Samson-patrol (pilots Tlt C.J.H. Samson, Vdg J.C.Yland and Sgt Th.H.M. Duffels) headed for P I, but returned just before they had reached their target due to the weather being too good and enemy fighter defence. Although there was some cloud cover, Samson saw a large number of enemy fighter aircraft, Navy Os he thought, flying over the target area. At the debriefing he was given a good talking to, as Lieutenant-Colonel Zomer, the Commandant Luchtstrijdkrachten (Local AOC), felt his instructions had been interpreted a bit too freely.[11]

The Den Ouden-patrol attacked the tank park of the BPM refinery at Pladjoe, targeting the tanks filled with aircraft fuel. The trailing planes were flown by Tlt R. Belloni and Vdg R. Jacobs. The patrol was intercepted during its attack run by three or four Japanese fighters. The run was carried through, though, in spite of the instructions of the air gunner Private W. Bohre in the command plane, who saw the fighters approach, and who shouted several times, "Into the clouds, Lieutenant". The seven 100-kilogramme bombs per aircraft were dropped by observer Kap R.E. Jessurun and the bomb aimers in the trailing planes, upon which the patrol went for the broken clouds. The crew of the command plane just managed to see the impact of the bombs, which made Jessurun exclaim, "We've got them". The actual results, however, were difficult to ascertain as there were already so many fires raging in the tank park. The bombers flew from one cumulus cloud to the next and got away. One of the two trailing planes had sustained some light damage from a few bullet holes. Their opponent this time had been Ki-43 fighters and not Ki-27s.[12]

At about 10:00 hrs all five operationally serviceable Blenheims of 84 and 211 Squadrons departed for a raid on targets near Palembang. A section of two bombers led by Wg Cdr R.N. Bateson, the commanding officer of 211 Squadron, bombed shipping near Palembang in the Moesi river and another section of two Blenheims, led by Flt Lt J.V.C. Wyllie of 84 Squadron, attacked the tank park of the BPM refinery at Pladjoe. The plane piloted by Sgt J. A. Burrage (211 Squadron) went missing on the way out when the section was flying through a tropical storm. After the war it was found that the pilot and his crew members had perished.[13]

The section led by Bateson found several ships moored at Palembang and raided a larger transport vessel amidst light anti-aircraft fire. The four 250-lbs bombs per aircraft, however, missed their target, although possibly some smaller vessels in the vicinity sank due to a near miss. The section led by Wyllie bombed a number of tanks of the Pladjoe tank park and was convinced they had scored several hits. The four remaining aircraft were not intercepted, thanks to the by now heavy clouds and the smoke coming up from the burning refinery complexes, and returned safely.[14]

Three Glenn Martins of 1/2-Vl.G.I were lost as a result of a Japanese bombing raid on Kalidjati shortly after the Blenheims had left. The aircraft were just being prepared for a seaward reconnaissance mission over the western part of the Java Sea, to be commanded by Tlt P.E. Straatman of 1-Vl.G.II and with crews drawn from 1-Vl.G.II, when the air raid alarm was sounded at about 11:00 hrs. Immediately after the alarm, 15 bombers of the 90th Sentai, escorted by 17 Ki-43 fighters of the 59th and 64th Sentais came in for their attack on Kalidjati. This time, too, the raid began with a strafing by some of the Japanese fighters, while the Ki-48s bombed from a relatively low altitude with light anti-personnel bombs.[15]

SM W.H. Goudswaard and SM K.B.A. Karssen of 1/2-Vl.G.I and their mechanics and assistants had just finished filling up the last two Glenn Martins and loading them with three 300-kilogramme bombs each. The crews were already walking towards their aircraft and together with the ground personnel of 1/2-Vl.G.I managed just in time to seek cover in a trench or nearby ditch before the Ki-43s began their attack. The M-544, M-546 and M-560, parked in their pens along the southern edge of the flight terrain caught fire from the shrapnel and exploded when their own bombs detonated. The explosions were so forceful that some of the engines of the bombers were flung away as far as up to fifty metres. The craters were some ten metres across and four metres deep. One of the servicemen who had dived into the water, Vdg G.A. van Cattenburch of 1-Vl.G.II, fell ill the next day and had to be sent to the Military Hospital at Tjimahi. He had probably caught jaundice from the water in the ditch. He was accompanied to hospital by Tlt P.C. Farret Jenkink of 1-Vl.G.I, who had fallen ill a few days earlier. It was quite a problem, during the wet monsoon period, to keep the service personnel in good health.[16]

The ML also lost two Lodestar transport planes. The anti-aircraft artillery claimed to have hit four of the Japanese bombers and possibly damaged a fifth. Later, however, the wreckage of only two Ki-48s was found. In any case, it was a successful first action of the by now British/Dutch anti-aircraft artillery, though at the cost of two servicemen of 49 Battery killed and five wounded by a bomb.[17]

Summary

On 21 February 1942 the allied bombers flew 24 sorties over western Java, 15 of which were directed against the BPM refinery (one Blenheim went missing on the way out) and five against P I airfield (three returned before reaching their target), while four sorties were directed against Japanese shipping targets. The ABDAIR offensive on 21 February 1942 could not be called an unqualified success. Only the bombing raids on the BPM refinery and the adjacent tank park at Pladjoe had been successful. The cracking installation of the refinery was destroyed by 2-Vl.G. III and several patrols of the ML and RAF attacked the park with success from Andir and Kalidjati. A new Japanese raid on Kalidjati, however, cost the allies three Glenn Martins and two ML transport planes. In addition, one Hudson from Semplak crashed on the way back as a consequence of damage sustained in an aerial combat with Ki-27 fighters south east of Singapore. The anti-aircraft artillery at Kalidjati shot down at least two Ki-48s.

* * *

CHAPTER 1B.5

The Events and Operations on 22 February 1942

Introduction

In the morning of 22 February 1942 ABDAIR (as far as can be ascertained) had available the following numbers of assigned and operationally serviceable bombers.[1]

Table 10

Unit	Assigned	Operationally Serviceable	Remarks
Vl.G.I/II	?	6	
84/211 Sq	?	5	Some planes still at Kemajoran
1/62 Sq	20	5	
2-III	7	4	
3-III	6	3	
Total	?	24	

Part of the bomber fleet was held at readiness during the hours of daylight or part of the day as an element of a *Striking Force* for the protection of allied shipping. Intelligence of ABDACOM had not only warned of a possible air raid on Tandjong Priok, but also of a Japanese fleet action.

Problems at Tandjong Priok

22 February 1942 promised to become a tough day for the allied air command. The weather over a large part of western Java was bad, which made it all the more likely that the aerial surveillance posts would not spot any Japanese formations. The British radar posts on the north and west coasts of western Java were not operational yet. The roadstead of Tandjong Priok and the Bay of Batavia were full of ships. On the one hand, they were ships belonging to a British convoy, originally destined for Singapore, that had been halted at Priok on 3 February 1942, and some ships from several smaller convoys, and, on the other hand, ships that had fled from Singapore or had come from southern Sumatra. All in all, the total amounted to more than 100 ships, including several freighters filled with urgently needed and valuable munitions and spares.[2] In addition, the warships of the *Western Striking Force*, five cruisers and six destroyers, were also stationed at Tandjong Priok.[3]

Batavia harbour was utterly congested. Unloading the ships went painfully slowly and a ship would have to wait for days before its turn came up. If it could be unloaded at last, where a lack of quays with sufficient depth sometimes necessitated transferring the cargo onto smaller ships or lighters, the absence of enough storage capacity and a railway system completely inadequate for transporting the goods caused the loads to be somewhat haphazardly dumped along the roads in the dock area.[4] Already before 22 February 1942 the allied naval command ABDA-FLOAT had therefore unceremoniously begun to send large numbers of ships on their way, usually changing their destinations to Australia or Ceylon. Ships holding urgently needed spares, bombs and ammunition, etc., were directed to Tjilatjap as of 21 February to be unloaded there. In connection with this, 205 Squadron RAF (with three Catalina flying boats) was relocated from Tandjong Priok to Tjilatjap in the early morning of 21 February in order to reinforce the Marineluchtvaartdienst–Dutch Naval Air Service (MLD) there.[5]

Regular reconnaissance of the ABDAIR *Reconnaissance Group* (in western Java consisting of flying boats of the MLD and RAF) showed that the Soenda Strait continued to be "free of enemy", which made the risk of the passage to the Indian Ocean negligible. There was, however, regular Japanese air reconnaissance and any moment a big air raid on the ships at Batavia could follow. Haste, therefore, was of the essence. It was decided to send away as many of the remaining ships as possible on 22 and 23 February and to close the harbour for incoming civilian shipping. ABDACOM's Intelligence section had already warned of a possible Japanese fleet action. However, no trace of any Japanese fleet action was discovered in the night of 21 February and the morning of 22 February 1942.[6]

Because of the great shortage of escort ships in ABDA-FLOAT, the emphasis lay on defence from the air for the ships during their passage of the Soenda Strait, and to this end an *Air Striking Force* had been formed, consisting of a number of ML and RAF fighters and eleven ML and RAF bombers.[7]

The missions from Andir

3-Vl.G.III had been on readiness from the early morning of this day with three Glenn Martins for the protection of the ships mentioned above. Among them was one large troop ship which had left Tandjong Priok in the night of 21 on 22 February and was now sailing out of convoy through the Soenda Strait en route to Ceylon. It was *Orcades*, escorted by only one allied navy vessel some way out into the Indian Ocean, with 2,000 RAF and 700 RAAF personnel on board. The RAF personnel came from, amongst others, 27 and 34 Squadrons and included the bulk of 62 Squadron and 243 Squadron, while the RAAF segment derived from 453 Squadron and 8 Squadron, amongst others.[8]

One Glenn Martin of 3-Vl.G.III carried out a seaward reconnaissance mission from Andir, but without any results.[9] The other three aircraft of the afdeling were not deployed during the entire day, but 3-Vl.G.III was to carry out a raid on Palembang in the evening or night. This was cancelled, however, as the runway at Kemajoran had been damaged during a Japanese raid (see below).

The missions from Tjisaoek

In the morning 2-Vl.G.III, too, was on readiness with three aircraft for the protection of allied ships sailing through the Soenda Strait. One aircraft, flown by Tlt H.M. Franken, carried out a morning reconnaissance of the coast lines of the Soenda Strait. Japanese infiltrations or other activities on or off the shore of western Java were not observed. In the afternoon the afdeling took off for Palembang for a bombing raid of the tank park at Pladjoe with its remaining operationally serviceable four bombers. The weather was so bad, however, that they were forced to return to Tjisaoek.[10]

The Japanese, too, were hindered by the bad weather on this day. The Yamada air group of the Navy air force at Kuching (Navy O fighters and some C5M reconnaissance planes), which had not been operational on 21 February due to the preparations for the transfer to Muntok airfield on the island of Banka, could not take off on 22 February and did not leave for Muntok until the next day. The Navy air force did fly several reconnaissance missions with bombers from Kuching over the Java Sea and a transport plane flew to Palembang in the morning for an inspection of the airfield P II, which had been discovered by the Japanese army the day before.[11]

The missions from Kalidjati

In the morning there were available at Kalidjati five, later six RAF Blenheims and six Glenn Martins, of which all the Blenheims were employed as protection of the ships in the Soenda Strait. Three Blenheims with crews from 211 Squadron were sent up for an attack on four possible enemy submarines. During take off Plt Off E.P. Coughlan's plane had an engine failure, forcing the pilot to return to Kalidjati.

The two other Blenheim crews searched the entrance to the Soenda Strait near St. Nicolaaspunt in vain.[12]

Two patrols of Glenn Martins attacked Palembang in the morning. They were the Van den Broek-patrol of 2-Vl.G.I, which was assigned to raid shipping in the Moesi river near Palembang, and the Den Ouden-patrol of 1-Vl.G.I, which was to target once more the tank park at Pladjoe. This time the aircraft were not intercepted. The patrol led by Elt H. van den Broek, with Sgt L.N. Bieger and Sgt L. Davids piloting the trailing planes, managed to approach the target area without being observed due to the bad weather with heavy clouds. These clouds, however, forced them to release their bombs at a gamble because even the Moesi river was hardly visible. There probably were no results whatsoever. Although there was some incoming anti-aircraft fire, the planes were not damaged.[13]

The patrol led by Elt F.J.W. den Ouden, probably followed by Vdg R. Jacobs and Tlt R. Belloni, could not find their target due to the heavy clouds, released their bombs at a gamble and returned to Kalidjati, probably without having scored any results. All the missions planned for the afternoon were cancelled due to the weather over large parts of western Java and southern Sumatra.[14]

The missions from Semplak

The last morning missions on 22 February 1942 were carried out by three Hudsons. Two Hudsons of 1 Squadron RAAF, flown by Flt Lt J.T. O'Brien and Flg Off P.J. Gibbes, respectively, left around 10:00 hrs to carry out two armed (photo) reconnaissance missions to Oosthaven, P I, P II, shipping in the Moesi river and the BPM refinery at Palembang. The weather over southern Sumatra was bad, but the two Hudsons were nevertheless intercepted by Japanese fighters near Palembang. Both aircraft escaped into the clouds, but an attack on Japanese ships or the tank park at Pladjoe could not be carried out.[15]

The third Hudson left at about the same time for an armed reconnaissance mission to the Banka Strait and Muntok. Plt Off J.F.P. Fitzgerald and his crew (originally from 59 Squadron RAF) carried out their mission and bombed a 10,000-tonnes transport ship in the Banka Strait. They scored two direct hits and a near miss, setting fire to the ship.[16]

The second bombing raid on Semplak

Roughly between 11:30 hrs and 11:50 hrs the Japanese Army air force attacked Semplak and Kemajoran. For half an hour a total of 14 Ki-43s of the 59th and 64th Sentais from Palembang I in two groups machine-gunned the Hudsons parked along the edges of the airfield and in pens (shrapnel defences consisting of a u-shaped earthen wall) at both ends of the runway at Semplak airfield. Six Ki-48 bombers of the 90th Sentai from Palembang I subsequently bombed the flight area. Semplak did not have any anti-aircraft artillery and the allied fighters were occupied with the protection of ships (see Part 1A). The Japanese pilots had a field day. Six Hudsons burned out, three were damaged beyond repair and one was heavily damaged but repairable. In addition, a Lockheed Lodestar transport plane of the D.Vl.A, the transport afdeling of the ML, went up in flames. A Fokker transport plane of the KNILM was heavily damaged and had to be written off.[17]

Nine Ki-48s together with 12 Ki-43 fighters attacked Kemajoran airfield, making the east-west runway unfit for use. The Japanese fighters also carried out strafings at Kemajoran and a number of Blenheims under repair that were parked along the edge of the airfield received damage.[18]

The formation of Java Air Command

The convoy protection, described above, was ABDAIR's last major operation. In the evening of 22 February Air-Marshal Sir Richard Peirse of the RAF transferred command to Major-General L.H. van Oyen, the ML commander, within the framework of the reorganisation of allied staffs and the discontinuance of the coordinating Unified Command. This did not take place in an all too cordial atmosphere. Van Oyen disagreed with Peirse's policy, which in his view came down to "British interests first". Colonel E.T. Kengen, the commanding officer of ML Command, also became acting commander ML.[19]

Unified Command and ABDA-FLOAT rated the operations carried out on this day as a great success. The passage of the Soenda Strait by *Orcades*, amongst others, and the relocation of a number of loaded vessels from Tandjong Priok to Tjilatjap had gone perfectly. With the help of the KNIL and civilian authorities the RAF had stationed a detachment of an *Air Stores Park* at Tjilatjap. Ammunition,

spare engines and other goods for the RAF units in Java were distributed by rail and truck by this unit from warehouses and a storage
area at Tjilatjap.[20] The ML had been doing this for some time now,
and the Inspection ML, the non-operational staff element of the
ML, which directed, amongst others, the Technical Service and the
Warehouse Service, even prepared for the transport of aircraft newly
arrived by ship to Bandoeng by rail. The ML, therefore, could provide
invaluable services to the RAF in setting up this new logistic pipeline,
and it did so wholeheartedly. The large-scale evacuation of RAF and
RAAF personnel did not go down well with Van Oyen and Kengen,
and the former initiated the formation of two light infantry battalions,
consisting of over-complete RAF personnel and British anti-aircraft
gunners that had lost their equipment in southern Sumatra.

Summary

For ABDAIR 22 February 1942 was considerably less successful than
for ABDA-FLOAT. Because of the bad weather the Japanese managed
to approach Kemajoran and Semplak airfields unnoticed. At Semplak
nine Hudson bombers and two transport aircraft were lost, without the
allied fighters being able to interfere. Up to and including 22 February
19 of the original 83 bombers of the ML, RAF and RAAF, had been
lost; that is, 23 per cent. The bombers were badly needed to carry out
attacks on Japanese objectives in southern Sumatra and at Banka and
the loss of so many of them, therefore, was a serious set-back.

   Of the bombers that were on readiness that day for the protection
of the allied ships passing through the Soenda Strait three Blenheims
(one of which was forced to return) were sent on a fruitless search of
enemy submarines that morning. The Glenn Martins that had been
held in readiness were to have been employed against targets near
Palembang in the afternoon (2-Vl.G.III) and evening (3-Vl.G. III),
respectively. The four aircraft of 2-Vl.G. III had indeed taken off,
but had been forced to return due to the bad weather. The attack by
3-Vl.G.III had been thwarted by a Japanese raid on Kemajoran.

   Two Glenn Martins of the afdelingen mentioned above and three
Hudsons of the squadrons at Semplak were sent on individual reconnaissance sorties in the morning. Six Glenn Martins from Kalidjati
attacked targets near Palembang in two patrols, but they did not score
any successes due to the weather.

* * *

CHAPTER 1B.6

The Missions of 23 February 1942

Introduction

On 23 February 1942 JAC had only few operationally serviceable bombers available. The majority of the British and Australian bombers could still not be used and the previous day there had been serious losses at Semplak. The status of the various units, as far as they are known, on 23 February 1942 was as follows:[1]

Table 11

Unit	Assigned	Operationally Serviceable
84/211 Sq	?	6
1/62 Sq	13	2
Vl.G.I/II	?	6
2-III	6	3
3-III	7	3
Total	?	20

The allied bomber offensive against targets in southern Sumatra and Banka was continued with all available means, apart from three Blenheims that were held in readiness for the protection of ships that were sent from Tandjong Priok to other destinations through the Soenda Strait on this day.

Japanese problems at Palembang

The Japanese army and Army air force at Palembang were experiencing major difficulties with the protection of the targets of the allied air forces. In particular, the protection of the BPM refinery was a priority, in view of the long-term need of the Japanese economy and the supplies of oil and fuels in the tank park. Nothing whatsoever came of it, though.

The area around Palembang did not have an air defence system with warning or listening posts, the telephone lines were poor and until 23 February there was not any anti-aircraft artillery at P I. There were enough fighters, but they were unable to intercept all enemy intrusions. On 23 February 1942 an anti-aircraft battery of the Japanese army with two anti-aircraft guns and four anti-aircraft machine guns became operational at P I. However, there were no search lights or other aids. At an earlier stage the Japanese army had already drawn the conclusion that it would all have to come from preventive attacks on allied airfields in western Java.[2]

The missions from Andir

Three Glenn Martins of 3-Vl.G.III carried out a bombing raid on shipping on the Moesi river near Palembang. The pilots of the aircraft were (probably) Tlt J.P.J. van Erkel, Vdg L. Kroes and (certainly) Vdg M.P. Bosman. They managed to score one hit on a transport ship. The aircraft were not intercepted and not hit by Japanese anti-aircraft fire.[3]

Late in the evening Tlt K. van Gessel and Sgt L.H. van Onselen carried out yet another night raid on the tank park of the BPM refinery at Pladjoe. Several fires were already raging there and there was a lot of smoke. The anti-aircraft fire was relatively light so that they could take their time to drop the bombs. The crews were convinced they had started several new fires, but it was not possible to establish this with certainty.[4]

The missions from Tjisaoek and Semplak

In the morning three Glenn Martins of 2-Vl.G.III attacked the tank park of the BPM refinery at Pladjoe. One of the assigned crews was that of Sgt J. Bos, the others are not known. No data remain on any possible results.[5]

The six airworthy and partially operationally serviceable Hudsons that remained after the Japanese air raid of the previous day, left from Semplak in the morning to Kalidjati, which was better defended (with twelve 4-cm Bofor anti-aircraft guns of the British Army and the KNIL apart from machine guns). The two operationally serviceable aircraft were subsequently employed from this airfield (see below).

The missions from Kalidjati

Two patrols of the ML afdelingen at Kalidjati, six Glenn Martins in total, carried out attacks on Palembang and the roadstead of Muntok. One patrol, led by Elt H.J. Otten, the commander of 1-Vl.G. II, left for Muntok (the island of Banka) and (probably) Elt J.C. Beckman's of 1-Vl.G.I bombed P I airfield and subsequently reconnoitred P II. Otten took off from Kalidjati at 06:00 hrs and returned after a four-and-half-hour mission around 10:30 hrs.[6]

The Otten-patrol carried out an offensive reconnaissance mission over the harbour and roadstead of Muntok. One of the trailing aircraft was flown by Sgt J. Bakker with Sgt H. Calf as bombardier, who, after a forced landing in southern Sumatra on 16 February and an eventful journey back to Java, had been reassigned again. The other trailing plane was probably flown by Vdg J.J. Stuurhaan. Over Muntok the crews observed six small transport ships lying side by side in the harbour, while in the roadstead either a cruiser or a destroyer was lying at anchor. The first run failed because the bomb release mechanism in the leading plane malfunctioned. Making a large curve, the planes manoeuvred into position for a second attempt, while observer Elt J. van Loggem in the lead aircraft checked the fuses. During the second run the mechanism again failed to work, upon which the lead aircraft and the trailing aircraft to its left turned away for the return flight. Sgt Bakker, however, took the initiative to drop his bombs nevertheless and made a third run on the transport ships. In the meantime, the Japanese anti-aircraft artillery had begun to find their range and the shells exploded closer and closer to the Glenn Martin. Sgt Calf dropped his three 300-kilogramme bombs at a gamble as the aircraft was not equipped with a bomb sight. Immediately after dropping the bombs Sgt Bakker made a sharp 90 degree turn and from an altitude of 4,000 metres made for the edge of the forest to escape from the heavy anti-aircraft fire. It was impossible to observe any results, and perhaps there were not any. As far as could be ascertained, their aircraft had not been hit and it was not intercepted on its flight home. A lack of fuel forced them to land at Kemajoran, where the crew did find that a piece the size of a finger tip had been shot away from one of the propeller blades. They had been lucky this time. They shrugged their shoulders and flew back to Kalidjati. According to Calf, the least they had achieved was some damage from near misses.[7]

At P I the crews of 1-Vl.G.I observed about 40 dispersed aircraft. Their bomb pattern fell on top of and next to a group of aircraft. The crews saw three planes go up in flames and they had probably damaged some more. They were very likely Ki-48 bombers of the 90th Sentai. There was no activity whatsoever at P II, and the ML Command and JAC concluded (erroneously) that the airfield had probably not been discovered yet by the Japanese.[8]

Three Blenheims, manned by crews of 84 Squadron and commanded by Wg Cdr J.R. Jeudwine, the commanding officer of 84 Squadron, also attacked P I. Theses crews, too, reported about 40 dispersed Japanese aircraft and claimed to have destroyed or damaged several of them. Two aircraft, very likely Ki-48s of the 90th Sentai, were positively seen to go up in flames. The three other operationally serviceable Blenheims were on readiness for the protection of ships and were flying an armed reconnaissance mission in a spread out formation to search and destroy the four (possibly) enemy submarines off the coast of western Java north of St. Nicolaaspunt that had been reported the day before. Flg Off B. Fiheely's (84 Squadron) crew attacked a submarine that had just submerged and were convinced they had sunk it. Afterwards, at JAC, however, the conclusion was drawn that the submarines had probably been sea mammals.[9]

The two operationally serviceable Hudsons coming from Semplak left Kalidjati at 11:00 hrs for an attack on the ships that had been discovered at Muntok by the Otten-patrol. The two bombers, flown by Flg Off P.J. Gibbes and Flg Off J. Lower, attacked individually. They were both intercepted by Navy Os of the Yamada air group that had just arrived in theatre and they were forced to drop their bombs prematurely. They managed, however, to dive away into the clouds in time.[10]

In the afternoon no further missions could be flown from Kalidjati due to bad weather with heavy showers. Only in the evening did it become possible again to fly missions against southern Sumatra and two Glenn Martins of 3-Vl.G.III left for their raid of the tank park at Pladjoe, described above.

Summary

On 23 February 1942 JAC carried out 22 bomber sorties in the morning and evening, during which a ship was hit at Palembang, the tank park at Pladjoe was bombed and at least five Japanese bombers were destroyed and probably several were damaged. Two missions against Muntok were not successful, nor was a mission to search and destroy enemy submarines north of St. Nicolaaspunt. In the afternoon the bad weather prevented any missions. All in all the day had been a reasonably successful one.

***

CHAPTER 1B.7

The Bomber Operations on 24 February 1942

Introduction

At daybreak on 24 February 1942 there were only 18 and later in the morning 21 allied operationally serviceable bombers in western Java. By command of the JAC the ML Command and BRITAIR assigned all their available bombers for attacks on targets near Palembang and Muntok. Bad weather and Japanese raids on Kalidjati airfield, amongst others, frustrated the planning, however. The status of the various units in western Java was as follows:[1]

Table 12

Unit	Assigned	Operationally Serviceable	Remarks
84/211 Sq	21	5	Excl. Mark Is
1 Sq	13	4	
Vl.G.I/II	9	3 (6)	Later 6 operationally serviceable
2-III	6	3	
3-III	7	3	
Total	56	18 (21)	

The missions from Tjisaoek

Like the previous day, 2-Vl.G.III, with all its operationally serviceable, three, Glenn Martins, carried out a bombing raid on the tank park at Pladjoe. Because of the risk of interception the aircraft took off at 03:00 hrs by the light of oil lamps, to be able to make their first run at 05:15 hrs. It was a success and the bombers were safely back on their way home before the Japanese fighters were able to react. They had started a number of major fires at the tank park, and although the Japanese anti-aircraft artillery fired intensely, they were too late and the bombers did not sustain any damage. The refinery complex at Sungai Gerong appeared to have been laid in ashes completely. It is not known who commanded this patrol, but the pilots of the trailing aircraft were Sgt M.F. Noorman van der Dussen and (probably) Sgt J. Bos.[2]

The missions from Andir

Initially, bad weather over the Bandoeng Plateau prevented 3-Vl.G.III from taking off. Between about 08:00 hrs and 08:30 hrs, just before an air raid alarm and the ensuing raid on Andir, however, a patrol consisting of three Glenn Martins, probably led by Elt A.B. Wolff, left for Palembang to attack P I airfield and to reconnoitre P II airfield. The pilots of the trailing aircraft were (probably) Tlt H.E. van Thiel and (certainly) Vdg M.P. Bosman. Heavy clouds made it impossible to observe any possible results of their bombing raid. No planes or activity could be observed at P II.[3]

As it happened, it was precisely on this day that P II airfield was put in use by the Japanese Navy air force and soon after the armed reconnaissance mission of 3-Vl.G.III the aircraft of the Genzai Kokutai began to arrive at P II. They were 29 bombers and one transport aircraft, of which, however, one bomber had to make an emergency landing at P I after having been fired upon by mistake by the airfield anti-aircraft artillery when the formation flew over Palembang at low altitude.[4]

In the evening, at last light around 18:30 hrs, two Glenn Martins of 3-Vl.G.III, flown by Tlt J. Coblijn and Sgt L.H. van Onselen, carried out a second attack on Palembang I airfield. The raid was successful and the crews saw the bombs strike close to a group of more than 18 parked aircraft. Anti-aircraft fire was fairly intense and Van Onselen's plane sustained some damage. After their raid the two Glenn Martins were attacked by six Ki-43 fighters.[5]

Wireless operator Kpl Boedihardjo of Van Onselen's crew managed to hit a Ki-43, upon which the Japanese pilot broke off his attack.

Subsequently, however, their Glenn Martin was set ablaze and Van Onselen gave the order to bail out. All did, except observer Vdg A.B. Hogendorp, who had died in the air battle. Sgt P. van der Zee, a mechanic assigned as air gunner in the co-pilot's position jumped, but was never heard of again. Corporal Boedihardjo also went missing, only to show up after the war, apparently serving in the Indonesian air force. Helped by the local population, Van Onselen finally managed to reach the Bay of Bantam in Java on 19 March 1942. By that time the KNIL had already capitulated and the pilot became a Prisoner of War at Serang.[6]

During the attack of the Glenn Martins six Ki-27s of the 11th Sentai and six Ki-43s of the 59th Sentai were airborne in order to protect P I airfield and the oil refineries. The Japanese fighter pilots claimed to have shot down both bombers, but Coblijn's crew escaped in the dark and made it back in their lightly damaged Glenn Martin without any further problems. According to a Japanese source, the damage inflicted on P I amounted to the following: one K-27 set on fire and severely damaged, one Ki-27 completely destroyed and two Ki-27s lightly damaged.[7]

The missions from Kalidjati

As mentioned above, the weather over large parts of western Java was very bad at first in the morning of 24 February. Five Blenheims, four Hudsons and three Glenn Martins were ready at Kalidjati to fly missions against Palembang and Muntok, but due to the weather they could not take off at first. Just when the first mission had finally been given permission to leave, the air raid alarm sounded shortly before take off time. About half an hour later, around 09:20 hrs, the Japanese Army air force attacked Kalidjati airfield with 16 Ki-48 bombers escorted by 13 Ki-43 fighters.[8]

After the attack the airfield was riddled with craters of bombs. The Ki-48s also dropped light anti-personnel bombs. The main runway was put out of action and the base had to be temporarily closed. Two Hudson bombers of 1 Squadron RAAF were total losses, and one or two others had sustained some minor damage, as had three Glenn Martins. The latter planes had fallen victim to Ki-43 fighters employing their machine guns at low altitude. Because they were well dispersed, the other planes were spared, but the flight terrain itself was heavily damaged and no further missions could be flown from Kalidjati that day. First, the bomb craters in the taxiways and in and right next to the short runway (the emergency strip) in the northern part of the airfield had to be filled. The anti-aircraft artillery claimed to have shot down three Japanese bombers and perhaps a fourth. Later the wreckage of three bombers was found. At Andir, which had been attacked virtually simultaneously by the Japanese Army air force, the Glenn Martin M-545 of 1/2-Vl.G.I, which was in repair at the Technical Service, was lost.[9]

Flt Lt J.V.C. Wyllie (84 Squadron) had been summoned by Air Vice-Marshal P.C. Maltby, the commanding officer of the new BRITAIR headquarters at Bandoeng, to brief him on his experiences over Palembang. He came over in a non-operational Blenheim Mark I to Andir and crash landed when one wheel refused to fold out. After a ground loop the bomber came to a standstill in the middle of the flight terrain. The pilot and his accompanying mechanic were unharmed. When Wyllie returned to his Blenheim after his visit to BRITAIR, the Japanese Army air force was attacking Andir. The bomber did not sustain any further damage and after the landing gear had been mended and some emergency repairs had been carried out at the Technical Service of the ML at Andir, it was flown back to Kalidjati.[10]

In the afternoon a mission was flown from Tandjong Priok to Muntok, after all, by two Dornier flying boats of Groep Vliegtuigen 8 of the MLD. The flying boats attacked individually, but without much success for the crews. Possibly one of the five small transport vessels in the harbour of Muntok received one hit. Both Dorniers were shot down on their return flight, one by probably three Navy O fighters of the Yamada air group that were carrying out a combat air patrol from Muntok and one near the island of Noordwachter by a number of Ki-43s returning from a raid on Batavia. The crew of X-18 managed to reach the lighthouse in Noordwachter and was rescued the next day by the mine sweeper *Djombang* of the KM. Nothing was ever heard of again of the crew of X-17, which was the first to be shot down and was seen to have crashed into the sea in flames.[11]

Summary

The number of missions flown on 24 February 1942 was low due to the bad weather and Japanese counter attacks. Three (successful) sorties were flown against the tank park at Pladjoe and five sorties in two missions against P I airfield, where several Ki-27 fighters were destroyed or damaged. On the last mission, however, one Glenn Martin was lost. At Kalidjati two Hudsons were destroyed in a Japanese air raid, while the airfield had to be closed down due to bomb damage. The anti-aircraft artillery at Kalidjati, however, managed to shoot down three of the attacking Ki-48 bombers. Two Dornier flying boats of the MLD, which carried out a mission against Muntok, were not or barely successful and they were shot down on their return flight.

***

CHAPTER 1B.8

The Missions of 25 February 1942

Introduction

On 25 February JAC again had all operationally serviceable bombers assigned for missions to Palembang and Muntok. The majority of the aircraft were given Palembang for their target in an attempt to destroy the last undamaged tanks at Pladjoe and a substantial number of Japanese combat aircraft at P I by means of a series of concentrated attacks. Little came of the plans, however, due to Japanese air raids and the bad weather. The missions that did go on were partial or total failures because of Japanese combat air patrols near Palembang.

In the morning of 25 February 1942 the following numbers of assigned and operationally serviceable bombers were available in western Java.[1]

Table 13

Unit	Assigned	Operationally Serviceable	Remarks
84/211 Sq	21	6	Excl. Mark Is
1 Sq	11	2	Two still at Semplak, four at TD Andir, one u/s Kemajoran
Vl.G.I/II	9	3	
2-III	6	5	
3-III	6	3	
Total	53	19	

The missions from Tjisaoek

In the morning of 25 February 2-Vl.G.III left with its full strength of five operationally serviceable Glenn Martins for the tank park at Pladjoe. Elt H.M.E. van Leyden led the mission in the lead aircraft of the formation. His trailing pilots were Vdg T. Magnee and (probably) Sgt H.C. Keim. Elt L. Gosma followed him leading a second patrol of two aircraft. The idea was to destroy the remaining undamaged storage tanks in a precision bombardment. Brewster fighters from Andir were to escort them. This support, however, was withdrawn just before take off, as air raids were expected on Batavia and Bandoeng.[2]

The afdeling took off, nevertheless, hoping there would be enough cloud cover over southern Sumatra. This was not the case, however. After crossing the Soenda Strait Gosma's aircraft had to abort the mission due to troubles with one of its propellers. His trailing pilot, Tlt H.M. Franken, joined up with the patrol led by Elt Van Leyden, while Gosma just managed to cross the Soenda Strait again and make an emergency landing in a sawa near Anjer. This landing strip on the coast was full of barriers and could not be landed at. The aircraft was a write off.[3]

The mission was continued in one patrol of four aircraft. At about 135 kilometres south-west of Palembang, near Batoeradja, six Japanese Ki-27 fighters attacked, in a formation led by the Japanese ace Tlt Yutaka Aoyagi of the 11th Sentai. That morning, of all mornings, a detachment of the 11th Sentai had begun to fly *standing patrols* (nowadays called *combat air patrols*) from Tandjoengkarang in order to help intercept allied bombers en route to Palembang. The Glenn Martins released their bombs and dived in an attempt to escape at low altitude, the crews making sharp turns trying to avoid the fire coming from the fighters. Three aircraft made good their escape, while the air gunner in Tlt Franken's aircraft managed to hit a Ki-27 so badly that its pilot had to break off the fight. The aircraft had by now come very close to the Soenda Strait.[4]

Magnee had fallen behind somewhat and his aircraft was fired at by two Ki-27s that were chasing him at low altitude right across Tandjoengkarang until he finally crash-landed in the forest some 1,000 metres south-west of the airfield. The crew survived the crash and made for the fishing village of Kaleander on the south coast, where the villagers, however, refused to ferry them across to the coast of western Java. Vdg Magnee sent air gunner Sld Pengalilah on a mission to find an alternative way of getting across to Java and find help there.

Evolving tropical storm near Kalidjati. These rain clouds could evolve into large Cumulo Nimbus clouds, with dangerous up and down drafts within the cloud, and then combine into lines of clouds, called Squall lines, which could stretch for many kilometres and could not be navigated around. (Private collection, P.C. Boer)

He managed to do so, though he did not arrive in western Java until after the occupation of Batavia by the Japanese. Magnee and the other members of his crew perished on or around 3 March 1942 under circumstances which have never been uncovered.[5]

To his frustration, Elt F.R. Lettinga, the afdeling commander, could not lead the morning mission. In his other position as base commander of Tjisaoek he was busily engaged in a meeting to arrange the final details of the arrival at Tjisaoek of two American squadrons of Curtiss P-40E fighters. The two squadrons, 32 fighters in all, were on their way in the aircraft tender *Langley*. The expansion of the airfield, which involved, among others, the construction of a new dispersal area in a plantation wood, had already been taken up by a working party led by Tlt J.G. Bücker the lieutenant adjutant of 2-Vl.G.III.[6]

The missions from Kalidjati

In the first part of the morning the weather was very bad in and around Batavia with heavy showers. The first patrol despatched, Tlt G.

Cooke's patrol of 2-Vl.G.I, was forced to return to their home base. As of 10:00 hrs air defence sector Batavia had been closed down because of the expected air raids. As a result a patrol of 3-Vl.G.III could not take off from Andir. The air raids were not long in coming. Between 10:30 hrs and 11:00 hrs the Japanese attacked both Tandjong Priok and Tjililitan. In the meantime the weather had deteriorated very much over the Bandoeng Plateau. Kalidjati, in the lowland plane north of the plateau, however, was not much affected by that.[7]

Around 12:00 hrs six Blenheim crews of 84 and 211 Squadrons, after their briefing for an attack on P I airfield, were waiting near the British command post in the north-eastern part of the airfield for clearance to take off. Suddenly, without prior air raid alarm, Japanese bombers attacked the airfield from high altitude. Just before that an aerial combat had developed over the plantation woods around Kalidjati between the escorting Ki-43s and Hurricanes of 2-Vl.G.IV. About an hour later, when the crews were on their way by truck to the dispersal area West, where their aircraft had been parked, there was another attack by bombers. This time the Japanese Army air force carried out a low-altitude bombardment, while Ki-43s were strafing targets on the airfield.[8]

One of the Blenheims standing ready for take off sustained medium to heavy damage from bomb fragments. Two non-operational Blenheim Mark Is went up in flames and a hangar in the north-eastern part of the airfield, in front of which these aircraft had been parked, incurred damage from fire. Two Glenn Martins of 1/2-Vl.G.I received medium to heavy damage from bomb fragments. They belonged to the Cooke-patrol, which had been on the point of making a second attempt to carry out the mission to Palembang I. One of the Glenn Martins needed to have a wing replaced and for this purpose the air-craft was transported to the Technical Service workshop (sub depot) in the north-eastern part of the airfield later that day. Tlt Cooke's M-5105 had received some shrapnel in one of the wings and needed one of its fuel tanks to be removed. Replacement of the tank and further repairs would subsequently have to take place at the depot of the Technical Service at Andir. The remaining aircraft of 1/2-Vl.G.I and 1-Vl.G.II were well dispersed and camouflaged in dispersal area South and did not sustain any damage. The anti-aircraft artillery claimed to have shot down two bombers and to have hit five more. Patrols of the KNIL and police later found the wreckage of two Ki-48s. In addition, I Division and the Air Defence Command Batavia later reported that a Japanese fighter had crossed the coastline near Batavia and made a crash landing at sea.[9]

Not until somewhere between 13:30 hrs and 14:00 hrs could the remaining five Blenheim bombers take off. Sqn Ldr A.K. Passmore of 84 Squadron led the mission and flew the leading plane in a section of three Blenheims. His trailing pilots were Sgt W.N.P. Cosgrove and Flg Off B. Fiheely. The aircraft flown by Cosgrove had to return on its way out because its turret failed to work properly when the armament was test fired over sea. Therefore, the raid was carried out with four bombers.[10]

Passmore's and Fiheely's Blenheims were intercepted south of Palembang by six Ki-27 fighters and their formation was broken up. The individual crews tried to drop their bombs on the nearest alternative target, the tank park of the BPM refinery. There was not much cloud cover, with only the occasional large cumulus cloud here and there. Fiheely's bomber was hit in one of its engines, but escaped from the Ki-27s into the clouds. Leaking oil, the aircraft lost a propeller, though, and had to make a ditching (emergency landing on water) off the coast of south-eastern Sumatra. It was a successful landing, and with a fishing boat bought in a nearby village the crew returned to western Java. After an adventurous journey, involving a few encounters with the Japanese, the crew arrived in the Bay of Bantam in March 1942 and subsequently became Prisoners of War.[11]

The other Blenheims returned safely at Kalidjati. The only crews to have possibly scored any results were Passmore's and Fiheely's, when they dropped their four 250-lbs bombs on the tank park at Pladjoe. The two trailing bombers of 211 Squadron had been forced to release their bombs over the jungle.[12]

The two operationally serviceable Hudsons of 1 Squadron each flew one sortie on 25 February 1942. They were both seaward reconnaissance missions, and they did not yield any results.[13]

Summary

The bad weather and Japanese air raids prevented the Glenn Martin afdelingen at Andir and Kalidjati from completing any missions on 25 February 1942. Three Glenn Martins that had been sent out were forced to return due to the bad weather and when it improved somewhat the Japanese carried out an attack on Kalidjati, which caused two Blenheims to be lost, while two Glenn Martins, which had just returned, and one Blenheim sustained medium to heavy damage. In the morning 2-Vl.G.III left with five aircraft from Tjisaoek to Pladjoe, but lost one plane in an emergency landing and the formation was subsequently intercepted by Ki-27s, upon which the afdeling turned back. In a pursuit by the Ki-27s one Glenn Martin was lost and one Ki-27 was hit.

In the afternoon the five remaining operationally serviceable Blenheims took off after all from Kalidjati for a mission to Palembang. They, too, scored none or only very limited results. One of the planes returned with technical problems on the way out and the others were intercepted near Palembang by Ki-27s. One Blenheim was forced to make an emergency landing at sea during the return flight due to combat damage. Of a total of 13 sorties sent out, only 4 reached their objectives, with some 250-lbs bombs dropped on the tank park at Pladjoe as the only tangible result. In addition, Hudsons carried out two reconnaissance sorties.

***

CHAPTER 1B.9
Crucial Decisions on 25 February 1942

Introduction

From the moment that Dutch officers became fully responsible for the allied command in Java the overall strategy had been directed at keeping Java in allied hands. The General Headquarters (AHK) deemed simultaneous landings in western and eastern Java the most likely scenario. It expected Japanese invasion fleets to approach via the shipping lanes through the Macassar Strait, east of Borneo and via the Karimata Strait and the Gaspar Straits, west of Borneo. Landings in central Java were considered unlikely and in view of the great shortage of troops General Headquarters decided on far-reaching troop relocations in order to reinforce western Java, in particular, as it was here that the main effort of the land battle, should it evolve, was expected. This episode will be described in greater detail in Part 3: The battle of Kalidjati. The overall strategy mentioned above was described in the introduction chapter The Japanese advance: Java given up by the allies.[1]

The allied decisions

In the late morning of 25 February Van Oyen concluded that the race against time had been lost. Earlier that morning *RecGroup* had discovered a Japanese invasion fleet in the roadstead of Balikpapan, doubtlessly bound for eastern Java. Although there was no trace yet of any similar Japanese operation in the west, it was known from intelligence sources that such a fleet was being assembled. The Japanese had hardly postponed their planned invasion and the expected American P-40s and British Hurricane fighters would not arrive in time to fend off an invasion.[2]

As before in eastern Java, the Japanese air forces had also been successful in their battle for air superiority over western Java. Bad weather and the failure to make the British radar stations operational quickly enough had seriously hampered ABDAIR and JAC. The allied fighter aircraft, nevertheless, had been able to put up a respectable fight in the west, but in a week's time about a third of their fighter strength had been lost. Furthermore, the local relative strength had been so disadvantageous for the allies that the Japanese bombers could bomb airfields (and also the harbour at Batavia) almost at will without being disturbed, destroying a great number of the ML, RAF and RAAF bombers in the process. The capabilities for putting pressure on the Japanese in southern Sumatra by bombing Palembang I airfield, in particular, had been greatly reduced because of this. Nevertheless, the allied bombers had been reasonably successful, and the allied anti-aircraft artillery had also been able to shoot down a number of Japanese aircraft over western Java.

In the morning of 25 February 1942, in consultation with Van Oyen and Vice-Admiral Helfrich, the commander of the allied naval forces (ABDA-FLOAT), Lieutenant-General Ter Poorten, the allied Commander-in-Chief *ABDA-Area* decided, in line with the overall strategy the following:

–   The allied fleet, the Combined Striking Force (CSF), is to concentrate at Soerabaja immediately, in order to carry out an attack on the reported invasion fleet from there; to this end as many war ships as possible are to relocate from Tandjong Priok to Soerabaja.
–   The allied air force is to relocate as many fighter aircraft as possible to Ngoro (eastern Java) for the protection of the CSF at Soerabaja.
–   After having carried out its attack, the CSF is to head for western Java in order to carry out a second attack on the Japanese invasion fleet (there was absolute certainty about this, although the fleet had not been discovered yet) heading for western Java. The fighters sent to Ngoro are to relocate for support to western Java.[3]

In spite of all this, the *Counter-Air* offensive was continued. The JAC fighters in western Java, however, were partially employed for the protection of the allied warships in the east. The bomber offensive against Japanese targets in southern Sumatra increasingly lost vigour, as from 26 February onwards more bombers were employed to reconnoitre the expected 'western' invasion fleet.[4]

The Japanese decisions

The Japanese air raids carried out on 25 February were meant to be the last in the context of the operation to attain air superiority over western Java, as a preparation for the invasion of the island. Not until 26 February did the emphasis come to lie on the protection of the ships of the invasion fleet intended for the landings in the western part of Java and for the logistic support of the vitally important bases in the conquered southern Sumatra. The Japanese Army air force was excited about the great successes it had achieved in the battle over western Java.

The Japanese Navy was much more cautious. On its initiative the landings were postponed on 23 February for two days until (the very early hours of) 28 February as the attained air superiority in western as well as eastern Java was deemed inadequate.[5] On 25 February the 3rd Hiko Shudan worked out the results the offensive that had been going on since 19 February over western Java. It was reckoned that up to and including 25 February 33 enemy aircraft had been shot down, 53 destroyed and more than 150 allied aircraft were "supposed to have been damaged".[6]

The liaison officer of the Japanese Navy at Palembang had considerable reservations about the report. Thus, the own losses of the

3rd Hiko Shudan mentioned in the report amounted to a mere three aircraft, but these appeared to be only the direct combat losses of the Ki-43 fighter aircraft that had come into action over western Java, whereas there were also 'operational losses'. Moreover, also other types of aircraft had been lost. If their own losses were presented in such a positive light, what was one to think of the losses inflicted on the enemy? The liaison officer was right; in reality only about 65 (instead of 86) planes had been shot down or destroyed on the ground by the 3rd Hiko Shudan, and this included a number of transport, training and communication airplanes; a hefty over-claim. Nevertheless, the losses inflicted were serious enough.[7]

The commander of the 3rd Hiko Shudan, however, stuck to his analysis, but on 26 February the 3rd Assault Group of the Navy air force (air groups at Kuching and Muntok) presented its own analysis based on the results of reconnaissance missions. It was concluded that there were still strong enemy air forces left in the environment of Batavia. On 27 February the Japanese Navy decided on the basis of this report to augment the force for western Java with the 4th Air Group (consisting of a light aircraft carrier, a destroyer and several auxiliary vessels) from St. Jacques in Indo-China.[8] Further delay of the invasion because of the air situation was no option due to the unbending stance of the Japanese Army in this matter, which had agreed on 23 February to a two-day postponement on condition that it would be the last.[9]

*** * ***

CHAPTER 1B.10

The Events and Missions Carried Out on 26 February 1942

Introduction

As described in the previous chapter, on 25 February 1942 a flying boat of *RecGroup* discovered a Japanese invasion fleet in the roadstead of Balikpapan (eastern Borneo). There was no doubt that its destination was eastern Java. The discovery had prompted the allied headquarters in Bandoeng to take a number of measures. One of them was to intensify the search for a Japanese invasion fleet, which was somewhere in the west. For this purpose *Java Air Command* committed five bombers from Kalidjati in the morning of 26 February 1942 to complement the long-distance reconnaissance missions of the flying boats of *RecGroup*.

JAC had not planned any missions to Palembang I airfield, in spite of its original intention to do so. By now it had been concluded that the only sensible thing to do in order to attain the required precision was to carry out day bombing raids in formation, with a fighter escort to keep the Japanese fighters that were flying combat air patrols south of Palembang occupied. There were no fighters with sufficient range available on 26 February, though, which was due to the fact that a number of the Brewster fighters of the ML at Andir had been sent to Ngoro (eastern Java) for the protection of the allied naval squadron (see Part 2 below).

On the basis of reconnaissance reports and information from the Intelligence section of the General Headquarters (AHK) a concentration of Japanese ships was suspected at Muntok (Banka), and in the morning two missions planned by JAC during the night of 25 on 26 February 1942 were given the roadstead and harbour of Muntok for their destinations. In addition, one final mission against the tank park of the oil refinery at Pladjoe was planned.[1]

The resources available

In the morning the following numbers of aircraft were assigned and operationally serviceable in western Java.[2]

Table 14

Unit	Assigned	Operationally Serviceable	Remarks
84/211 Sq	20	4 (?)	Excl. Blenheim Is
1 Sq	11	2	
Vl.G.I/II	7	4 (?)	
2-III	4	1	
3-III	6	3 (later 6)	
Total	48	14 (later 17)	

This was only a very limited strength, and, on top of that, as explained above, part of the aircraft needed to be committed to seaward reconnaissance purposes.

Reconnaissance by flying boats and bombers

In the early morning first two Hudsons took off, followed by three Glenn Martins, for seaward reconnaissance missions in the sea area south of Banka and Biliton, as well as the entrance to the Karimata Strait, east of Biliton. The Hudsons were committed individually, whereas the Glenn Martins went in patrol formation.[3]

The bomber crews, however, found nothing and around noon and in the early afternoon the aircraft were back on their base. One Catalina flying boat observed some Japanese ship movements in the northern part of the Karimata Strait, but could not report any details due to bad visibility. Then, around 10:30 hrs the crew of a Blenheim, returning from a mission to Muntok (Banka), spotted a Japanese convoy at about 100 miles (180 kilometres) north of St. Nicolaaspunt, the north-eastern entrance to the Soenda Strait. The convoy, however, was sailing a northerly course (345 degrees) and comprised a mere 20 ships, including the escort (see below). This convoy might or might not constitute part of the western invasion fleet. For the time being, the allied headquarters assumed that the acute threat came from the east.[4]

In the late morning of 26 February 1942 a Dornier flying boat of *RecGroup* spotted the eastern Japanese invasion fleet again in the southern part of the Macassar Strait. As a reaction the bomber fleet in western Java was kept on stand-by from 14:00 hrs onward. JAC first wanted to see how the threat would develop, and then, if need be, relocate some of the bombers to central Java in order to support the USAAF squadrons there. The bomber campaign was partially abandoned and the emphasis came to lie on searching for and destroying the ships of the Japanese invasion fleets. JAC's planned attacks on Palembang I airfield and Den Pasar airfield (Bali), in particular, however, were to continue insofar as the capacity allowed.[5]

The last mission to Pladjoe

On 26 February 1942 2-Vl.G.III only had one operationally serviceable Glenn Martin, and Sgt M.F. Noorman van der Dussen and his crew flew the aircraft in the very early hours of the morning to Palembang for an attack on the tank park at Pladjoe. Having taken off shortly after 03:00 hrs by the light of oil lamps, they dropped their bombs in the brief period of twilight just before sunrise at around 05:15 hrs. It was clear from the visible bomb strikes that the attack was a success and the bomber was not intercepted or hit by anti-aircraft fire.[6]

In consultation with the General Headquarters (AHK), JAC decided to stop the missions to Pladjoe. The objectives had largely been attained and the bombers were badly needed for other missions. Photographs taken by Glenn Martins and Hudsons showed that the storage of aircraft fuel in the tanks had been largely destroyed and of the total storage capacity, including shipping fuel, at least 35 per cent and probably more had been lost for the Japanese.[7]

The missions to Muntok

At around 07:30 hrs three Blenheims, flown by 84 Squadron crews from Kalidjati, took off for a first mission to the roadstead and harbour of Muntok (Banka). One of the aircraft was flown by Sgt W.N.P. Cosgrove, the other pilots are not known. They reached their target around 09:45 hrs, but there were only a few freighters there, and the crews went for the largest of them. The raid seemed to be successful and the crews assumed that one of the ships had received a direct hit, although no explosion was observed. There were no fighters up and the bombers that flew back individually after the bombing raid were not intercepted.[8]

As was described above, on their return flight Cosgrove's crew discovered a Japanese convoy around 10:30 hrs. It was sailing a 345-degree course about 80 miles (150 kilometres) south of Toboali on the south-east coast of Banka and rather close to the coast of Sumatra. The low broken clouds made it difficult to see the ships and there was some uncertainty about their numbers.[9] The second mission to Muntok was carried out by 3-Vl.G.III from Andir.

At around 08:00 hrs three Glenn Martins of 3-Vl.G.III took off from Andir for an armed reconnaissance of Muntok. The pilots were Tlt R.C. Schäftlein, Tlt K.van Gessel and Vdg M.P. Bosman. A stop-over was made at Kemajoran to get the latest intelligence and instructions. Engine trouble forced Van Gessel to return to base on his way out, and the mission was continued with two aircraft. In clear weather at around 10:00 hrs the three 300-kilogramme bombs per aircraft were dropped over an 8,000 ton freighter, probably the same one that had been attacked by the RAF earlier. The bombs missed, however, although two landing vessels in her proximity were sunk. When they had begun their return flight, six Navy Os appeared, which had probably been looking for the Blenheims. Three of them attacked the bombers.[10]

Making turns all the while, the two Glenn Martins headed for the low broken clouds hanging over the island of Banka itself. After a short chase the bomber flown by Schäftlein was hit and caught fire, disappearing into a cloud with a trail of smoke. Aircraft commander observer Elt A.F.A.R.Vos de Wael did not manage to bail out anymore, just like two other crew members in the rear of the Glenn Martin. Possibly they had not heard Schäftlein's order to jump because the intercom system had been shot to pieces. Only Tlt Schäftlein jumped from 1,500 metres and during his descent he was fired at by two of the Japanese fighter pilots. He landed in a marsh, wounded in his back and arm, from which he was rescued by a police patrol many hours later. The bodies of the other crew members had been recovered in the wreckage of their aircraft. The Japanese fighter pilots were from the Yamada air group and had been billeted at Muntok with a civil servant of the Postal Services (PTT). They later proudly told him that they had downed a Dutch bomber and then shot the pilot hanging by his parachute to pieces.[11]

The aircraft flown by Bosman also got a rough time of it. In the first attack by the third Navy O it had already received several hits; in the next one the right wing got badly hit. However, the Japanese fighter aircraft also received some hits from fire coming from 2nd pilot-airgunner Corporal R. Haasjes, upon which the Japanese pilot abruptly broke off the fight. Bosman decided to feign his aircraft had become uncontrollable and pulled it into a spin. Once inside a cloud he straightened his aircraft again and headed north, hoping to escape. Because of the hits in his right wing and the risk of a fire breaking out Bosman switched off the right engine, feathering the propeller. The enemy fighters had left the scene and the crew headed for the coast of Sumatra via east Banka and the island of Biliton. Subsequently, Bosman flew along the north coast of Java to Batavia where he made an emergency landing at Kemajoran. This had become necessary as all his manoeuvring had made his aircraft run out of fuel over Tandjong Priok. There was no time anymore for a landing by the book and Bosman simply landed straight in among the 'Friesche ruiters' (movable barbed wire obstructions).[12]

The damage was not too bad and came down to one somewhat damaged wing tip. The combat damage, however, was more serious. Thus, a sizable chunk of the main spar of the right wing had been shot off. Bosman reported Schäftlein's aircraft missing and the results of the mission by phone. There was no convoy near Muntok. The next day he flew his bomber, which had undergone some makeshift repairs, back to Andir together with mechanic Sgt R.E. Lemaire (who had been acting as bomb aimer during the mission), while the rest of the crew followed by road. Bosman got problems first with the right engine, which he had to put into idle, and then with the left one, though, and he had to make an emergency landing at Tjileungsir. He was less fortunate on this occasion. The Glenn Martin lost a wheel in a drainage ditch and finally came to a standstill on its belly, heavily damaged. The Technical Service would write off the bomber a few days later.[13]

The search for the western invasion fleet

The staffs of the allied headquarters in Bandoeng acted quickly on the basis of the reports of the Catalina and the Blenheim flown by the Cosgrove-crew on the ship movements observed in the west. The *Western Striking Force* of the allied navies at Tandjong Priok (several cruisers and destroyers that had stayed behind, so in fact a remnant of the *Western Striking Force*) was ordered to probe in the direction of Banka and Biliton in the evening and night of 26 on 27 February, but it found nothing.[14] Simultaneously, by order of *RecGroup*, a Catalina flying boat of the MLD flew a search mission in and around the Banka Strait looking for Japanese fleet activity in the Strait twice. This was the Y-63 of Groep Vliegtuigen 2 (GVT 2) of the MLD, which took off at 21:00 hrs from Naval air station Tandjong Priok (Batavia). It did indeed find several warships and other vessels in the Banka Strait, but not a large convoy. However, the weather was too hazy for an accurate observation. At 23:00 hrs a telegram mentioning this observation was despatched. At 03:00 hrs (on 27 February) the crew made another attempt and this time they discovered a concentration of ships near Muntok. The report, however, could not be sent because of a protracted exchange of telegrams that was going on between two other naval radio stations.[15]

The order the commander of the Y-63 had received also encompassed a reconnaissance of the south-eastern entrance of the Banka Strait, but it was impossible to see anything there due too very hazy weather. At 06:30 hrs the Strait was empty and the Y-63 flew back to Batavia through or just below the clouds. In a small open space between two cloud formations, however, the aircraft was spotted by six Ki-27 fighters patrolling the area. They lost no time and dived for the Catalina and attacked it. During the attack one of the fighters received a hit from machine gun fire from one of the wireless operators and crashed into the sea. A second Ki-27 got hit and disappeared from the scene of combat. Two out of the seven crew members were wounded during the aerial combat; the 1st pilot seriously with two shots in the head and the aircraft commander lightly.[16]

Because of the combat damage and the ensuing loss of fuel the crew had to make a landing at sea. It was successful and with the help of a rubber boat (though punctured by a bullet hole) the crew finally managed to reach the deserted island Zuidelijke Gebroeders where they found a prahn, with which they sailed to a fishing village on the Sumatran coast. With the help of fishermen they subsequently reached Anjer in western Java. By that time the Japanese had already landed in the Bay of Bantam and at Merak. Three crew members were probably murdered in Bantam by rebellious Indonesians during an attempt to escape, while four others were made Prisoners of War by the Japanese. All this did not come out until 1945 when the war was over; the Y-63, which had sunk shortly after its emergency landing and its crew had been reported missing until that moment.[17]

The Japanese invasion fleet in the east

In the evening of 26 February the Intelligence section of the General Headquarters (AHK) and the Combined Operations and Intelligence Centre (COIC) gave the advice to reckon with the possibility of a Japanese invasion early the next morning. These warnings were probably based on the analysis of tapped Japanese radio traffic and the reported positions of Japanese ships.[18] As was mentioned above, in the late morning a Dornier Do-28 flying boat of Groep Vliegtuigen 6 (GVT 6) had discovered a Japanese convoy in the southern end of the Macassar Strait and had shadowed it for a couple of hours. The convoy amounted to 30 ships with an escort of two cruisers and four destroyers and its position was north-west of the Arends Islands, that is some 200 nautical miles (360 kilometres) north-north-east of Soerabaja. Then, the convoy, which was assumed to be part of the invasion fleet destined for eastern Java, had disappeared for some time. In the evening, however, two Mitsubishi F1M float planes attacked a Catalina of the MLD near Bawean. So, Japanese cruisers and/or aircraft tenders had to be somewhere in the neighbourhood.[19]

Receiving his orders from ABDA-FLOAT, Rear-Admiral K.W.F.M. Doorman put to sea at around 18:30 hrs with the *Combined Striking*

Force (the allied naval squadron at Soerabaja) to try and find the re-ported convoy and attack it. At the same time an American B-17 bomber of *East Group* attacked a convoy of at least 18 ships, with six Navy Os patrolling overhead, some 20 nautical miles (36 kilometres) north-east of Bawean. This was one of the two B-17 bombers that had taken off from Madioen at 17:00 hrs for an armed reconnaissance and attack on ships, should the opportunity present itself. One aircraft did not find any ships and on its return to base dropped its bombs on Den Pasar airfield in Bali. The second aircraft attacked at 18:30 hrs from an altitude of 21,000 feet (about 6,300 metres), but the bombs missed their target.

For unknown reasons, the operations report never reached the Royal Netherlands Navy and Rear-Admiral Doorman. The Staff Room of the Navy Commander Soerabaja first heard about the attack at about 22:30 hrs in a telephone conversation with the Staff IIIrd Division of the KNIL. In the mean time, the allied naval squadron was probing along the northern coast of Madoera all the way to the Sapoedi Strait and back to the west, but found nothing.[20]

Evacuation and departure for British-India of RAF and ML personnel

The bulk of the personnel of 211 Squadron RAF and the remainder of 62 Squadron RAF left for Tjilatjap on this day to be evacuated. Together with personnel of several other RAF units the men left for Ceylon on the evening of 27 February 1942 on board *Kota Gede*, 2,110 RAF and about 350 British Army (mainly anti-aircraft artillery) servicemen in total.[21] Four crews of 2-Vl.G.I of the ML left for Andir in order to pick up new North American B-25C Michell bombers in British India. Three Lodestar transport aircraft took 19 men in total, including some personnel of other units, to Bangalore on 28 February 1942.[22] At Kalidjati this only meant the departure of redundant personnel. Because of the low number of operationally serviceable bombers especially the two Blenheim squadrons had so many crew members that they began to suffer somewhat from a decline of morale due to lack of activity. Twenty complete crews remained with 84 Squadron, while the combined 1/2-Vl.G.I kept a strength of nine complete crews. 84 Squadron was selected to stay because the remainder of its ground personnel had arrived at Batavia from the Middle East a few days earlier.[23]

Summary of the events on 26 February 1942

The measures taken at Bandoeng in answer to the discovery of the first Japanese invasion fleet on 25 February 1942 had great consequences for the employment of the allied bombers. In fact, it meant virtually the end of the bomber offensive. Not only were some of the bombers in western Java needed for seawards reconnaissance missions (five sorties), but also the small capacity that remained was insufficient to keep up the bombing raids on Pladjoe. The latter consequence was not felt to be disastrous in the allied headquarters, as the most important objective, the destruction of the aircraft fuel stores, had been realised to a large extent by now. The last raid (one sortie) was also successful.

Much less so were the two missions (six sorties) to Muntok (possibly one direct hit on a transport ship and two landing vessels sunk), and they cost JAC two Glenn Martins. On their return flight a British crew discovered a Japanese convoy, which was heading north, however. In the east the crew of a Dornier flying boat reconnoitred the 'eastern' Japanese invasion fleet, which was now sailing in the southern end of the Macassar Strait. From about 14:00 hrs the bombers in the west were on stand-by, awaiting any further developments. Catalina flying boats continued their search for the expected 'western' invasion fleet, but they found nothing. Not until the next day, 27 February 1942, would any clarity emerge.

* * *

CHAPTER 1B.11

The Search for the Japanese Invasion Fleets and the Bomber Missions Flown on 27 February 1942

Introduction

In the night of 26 on 27 February 1942 neither the flying boats of JAC's *RecGroup* nor the warships of the *Combined Striking Force* and the remainder of the *Western Striking Force* of ABDA-FLOAT found any trace of the Japanese invasion fleets. The *Operations Staff* of JAC had a busy night with the planning of a number of missions in case the Japanese invasion of Java was going to take place already the coming morning and in western as well as eastern Java the bombers were on readiness to be committed at first light. However, also several missions to Palembang and Den Pasar airfield in Bali were planned as well. In addition, preparations were made for the possible relocation of part of the bomber fleet in the west to central Java.[1]

Around 02:00 hrs it was concluded that there was no Japanese fleet as yet near Banka or Biliton. The Catalina of *RecGroup*, which, amongst others, was reconnoitring the Banka Strait, had sent a reconnaissance report around 23:00 hrs on the evening of 26 February, stating it had spotted several ships but not a convoy. The warships of the remainder of the *Western Striking Force* were searching the sea area south of Banka and Biliton, but according to their first reports they had not seen any ships. Two Catalinas of the RAF, making a reconnaissance flight from Tjilatjap, did not find any trace either of the Japanese naval operation south of Java, of which the *Intelligence* section of the General Headquarters (AHK) had warned on the evening of 26 February.[2]

JAC decided to send out the planned missions to Palembang and to keep the remaining bombers in the west on stand-by for the time being from 05:00 hrs onwards, awaiting any further developments. The exception was five bombers that were given seaward reconnaissance missions, starting at first light, in order to complement the (rather limited) capacity of *RecGroup*. In the west, too, it was vital to get certainty as quickly as possible about whether or not a Japanese invasion fleet was approaching.[3]

In the early morning of 27 February 1942 JAC and the other allied headquarters in Bandoeng concluded that the arrival of the Japanese had apparently been estimated a day too soon. But that they were coming (in any case in the east) was certain. The AHK still deemed simultaneous landings in western and eastern Java the most likely scenario, but a small flicker of hope could be felt there that the Japanese just might first only attack eastern Java and then at a later time western Java. That would perhaps create the opportunity to deploy the *Combined Striking Force* first in the east and then again in the west.[4]

The availability of bombers in western Java

Because several Blenheim bombers had become airworthy again (after lengthy repairs much helped by spare parts brought along from the Middle East by the recently arrived ground party of 84 Squadron), there was an increase in western Java in the number of operationally serviceable bombers from 14 to 20 on 27 February. At Kalidjati the RAF still had three (deployable) dated Blenheim Mark I bombers that were not fully operationally serviceable and for that reason were not included in the strengths, but that could be used for night time bombing. 36 Squadron RAF, too, at Tjikampek, with ten Vildebeest and Albacore light bombers, was not included, but could be deployed in full strength for night time missions against an invasion fleet. In the end no bombers were relocated from western to central Java on 27 February. Not until the morning of 28 February 1942 was it decided (only) to relocate 36 Squadron to Maospati airfield (Madioen, central Java).

The status of the several units in western Java at 05:00 hrs on 27 February 1942 was as follows:[5]

Table 15

Unit	Assigned	Operationally Serviceable	Remarks
84 Sq	16	7	Excl. Blenheim Is
1 Sq	11	2	Three at TD Andir, one still at Semplak
Vl.G.I/II	7	6	
2-III	4	2	
3-III	5	3	
Total	43	20	

Seaward reconnaissance with bombers

Three Glenn Martins and two Hudsons flew seaward reconnaissance missions from Kalidjati over the western part of the Java Sea up to just south of Banka and Biliton, but, with the exception of one Hudson, did not find any enemy activity. The Glenn Martins were flying in a spread-out patrol formation, while the Hudsons were reconnoitring individually. In quite bad weather one of the Hudsons, flown by Flg Off H.H. Siddell, accidentally discovered a small Japanese convoy 50 nautical miles (90 kilometres) south of the south-eastern tip of Banka. As it sailed a north-easterly course, it was difficult to tell whether it did belong to an invasion fleet or not. The bomber was fired at, but escaped into the clouds, lightly damaged.[6]

The mission to Palembang I

In the early morning at around 03:00 hrs three Glenn Martins of 3-Vl.G.III, armed with nine 50-kilogramme fragmentation bombs per aircraft, took off from Andir for a bombing mission against P I. The raid was to take place in the morning twilight, just before sunrise. On approaching the target the patrol was to get a fighter protection from Brewster fighters of Vl.G.V, which would cover their return flight. The pilots were Tlt P.J.P. van Erkel, Vdg L. Kroes and Tlt H.E. van Thiel. The latter two aircraft, however, had to return on their way out with engine trouble, the first trailing plane after half an hour in flight and the second some ten minutes later. By that time the one remaining bomber was in the vicinity of Batavia.[7]

Having arrived at P I, Lieutenant Van Erkel first flew on a bit in northerly direction, as it was still too dark for accurate bombing, but then on his approach of P I he was intercepted by three Ki-27 fighters that did not waste any time and attacked immediately, while the crew of the Glenn Martin could see more fighters taking off from P I. The first attack forced Van Erkel to make a turn, rendering it impossible for observer Elt J.P.G. Sloos in the nose of the plane to drop his bombs. A second attack would have been suicidal and the crew made a run for it. When the Glenn Martin was flying across the Moesi river near the town of Palembang, the aircraft was fired at by anti-aircraft artillery from the shores and the ships on the river. A shell exploded just below the right wing and in the bomb hold holes began to appear. After they had left the anti-aircraft artillery fire behind them, the bomber was again attacked by the three Ki-27 fighters.[8]

Sgt A.H. Erdkamp, a mechanic assigned as air gunner in the position of co-pilot managed to hit one of the attacking fighters in the engine, upon which the aircraft turned away with a smoking engine and disappeared. Van Erkel put his bomber into a dive in order to be able to use the layer of ground mist hanging over Moesi river to make good his escape. This was a hairy affair as the layer was so thin that the tree tops were pointing through it in several places. From time to time Van Erkel dipped into the ground mist and changed course. Each time the two remaining fighters, however, soon picked up the trail again and kept pursuing the bomber until it reached the Soenda Strait. One of its tyres having been blown to pieces, the damaged aircraft subsequently made a belly landing at Kemajoran. The crew left the bomber hurriedly when it was discovered that in the confusion and stress of the air combat no one had remembered to drop the bombs.[9]

The next day the crew made its way back to Andir by road. It appeared that the protection from the Brewsters had been withdrawn, as all fighter aircraft of this type had to be made available for the protection of allied war ships in support of an operation of the *Combined Striking Force* along the northern coast of Java. Elt P.G. Tideman, one of the fighter pilots on duty, was given the order in the middle of the night to be on readiness with all available fighters as of 05:00 hrs in order to protect the war ships. It had been impossible to pass this message on to Van Erkel as he had taken off with one crew member short; the wireless operator had reported in sick and they had not been able to find a replacement at short notice.[10]

The last attacks on shipping near Palembang

2-Vl.G.III had two operational aircraft and in the morning an attack, led by Elt F.R. Lettinga, was carried out on Japanese ships that were suspected to be on the Moesi river near Palembang. This type of mission had a high priority, as in this way the supply of Palembang I airfield could be disrupted. The pilot of the trailing aircraft is not known. Afdeling commander Lettinga was standing in for Elt L. Gosma, who had been grounded for medical reasons after an emergency landing on 25 February 1942.[11]

Lettinga had been woken up by a phone call of his Commandant Luchtstrijdkrachten (Local AOC), Major C.J.J.M. Waltmann, who told him that on the coming mission to Palembang an expected Japanese naval operation south of Java should be reckoned with. On the way out the wireless operator had to listen in continually. In case of a message coming in on the naval action the planes had to return immediately and go to the given location. As there were only three usable headphones observer Elt J.M.L. van Roon gave his to the wireless operator Sgt K.R. Romen.[12]

At around 07:00 hrs the bombers were approaching Palembang. Over the target area (by now) a lot of cloud was hanging, which made an undiscovered approach possible, though at the same time it would be impossible to observe any results. Whether any results were scored at all, is doubtful. The impacts of the three 300-kilogramme bombs per aircraft simply were not visible. Van Roon was an experienced bomb aimer, but he was handicapped somewhat by the fact that he had to make do without any intercom connection with his pilot. With the help of the backup system, a remote-controlled indicator, he gave directions to Lettinga during his run in. The bombers were not intercepted or hit by anti-aircraft fire.[13]

Two Blenheims of 84 Squadron took off for Palembang from Kalidjati almost simultaneously with Lettinga for an attack on the same target, the shipping on the Moesi river. The (unknown) crews of 84 Squadron also managed to get over to target, but they too could not observe any results due to the heavy clouds.[14]

Reconnaissance of the airfields at Palembang

In the first half of the afternoon, by order of JAC, two (unarmed) reconnaissance missions were carried out to P I airfield and P II airfield, respectively. The crew of Flt Lt J.V.C. Wyllie of 84 Squadron discovered some 30 parked bombers at P II, did not see any fighters anywhere and subsequently machine gunned the aircraft that had been lined up on both sides of the runway. One row was targeted with the one machine gun in the wing and the machine gun of the navigator-bomb aimer, the other row was fired at by air gunner Sgt A.W.G. Wakefield with the two .303 inch machine guns in the dorsal turret. The Japanese were taken by surprise and they did not fire back when the Blenheim made its high-speed low-altitude run over P II.[15]

A Glenn Martin of 1-Vl.G.II, flown by Tlt P.E. Straatman, carried out a reconnaissance mission to P I airfield, during which Sgt mechanic J. Stemerdink, assigned as air gunner, made pictures with a camera of the photo section of Kalidjati. This base had a dark room staffed by two aerial photographers of the ML, who were, however, not allowed to fly along on missions because they were too busy developing and printing the photographs the crews of the Hudsons always brought back with them. Over Palembang the Glenn Martin briefly popped below the thick cloud and immediately after taking the pictures went back in. At P I there were many more aircraft than at P II, at least 60, and fighters were flying over the airfield.[16] Although a Japanese invasion fleet had not been discovered as yet in the west, it was clear that the Japanese were concentrating aircraft at Palembang for the coming attack on western Java. At JAC it was (wrongly) assumed that P II had just come into use and this airfield was (rightly) no cause for great worries. It was difficult to supply and it would be many days before the Japanese would be able to fly operations from P II on any regular basis. This was a correct estimation, although the fact that the Japanese Navy air force had taken P II in use already on 24 February had escaped notice. The bombardment of 3-Vl.G.III on Palembang I, which had failed, would have to be repeated.[17]

The bomber fleet on readiness

In the afternoon of 27 February between 14:30 hrs and 15:00 hrs orders were given by JAC to ML Command, BRITAIR and *East Group* to prepare all aircraft immediately for action, on the assumption that the expected invasion of Java would come in the night of 27 on 28 February 1942 or in the early morning of 28 February. *RecGroup* had re-discovered the Japanese invasion fleet sailing for eastern Java near the island of Bawean. From that moment onwards in principle all bombers were on readiness for a deployment against Japanese ships, but at JAC it was decided not to cancel an already planned attack on P I airfield with one Glenn Martin and another attack by a Consolidated LB-30 of *East Group* on Den Pasar airfield in Bali in the night of 27 on 28 February.[18]

In the afternoon of 27 February 1942 the *Combined Striking Force*, commanded by Rear-Admiral K.W.F.M. Doorman, entered the Westervaarwater north of Soerabaja after a search conducted mostly in the dark to refuel in the navy docks. On hearing the news of the invasion fleet, however, Doorman immediately ordered to put about and take to sea again. He did not find the Japanese transport fleet, but ran into Japanese covering squadrons, which he engaged at around 16:15 hrs. The global course of the Battle of the Java Sea, seen from a joint operations perspective, will be described separately in Part 2. Doorman was eventually defeated in the so-called night fight, during which his flagship, the light cruiser *De Ruijter* was struck by a torpedo at around 22:30 hrs upon which it sank. Also the light cruiser *Java* and three allied destroyers were lost in the battle. The Japanese did not lose any ships, but had to withdraw a heavily damaged destroyer from the battle.

The first night mission from Kalidjati to Palembang

At first there was no news about the course of the naval battle at Java
Air Command. The only thing that was known was that the fleet had
taken to sea and during the night some reconnaissance messages were
received through *RecGroup* from two Catalinas that had tracked down
the Japanese transport fleet in the east. In the west *RecGroup* was
still unable to find the Japanese fleet. In the meantime, the already
mentioned night mission to Palembang I airfield by order of JAC was
being carried out. Major-General Van Oyen had at first wanted to
employ the Brewster fighters of the ML in western Java to escort the
Glenn Martin bombers (the heaviest bombers JAC had at its disposal
in the west) to Palembang I airfield.

In order to really degrade the Japanese air forces, precision
bombings in formation were necessary. With an escort there was a
chance that they could be realised. Without one it had proven to be
virtually impossible because of the Japanese combat air patrols. In
contrast to the British Hurricanes the Brewsters had a large enough
range and on top of that they could carry light bombs. The first mission,
as was described above, was to have taken place in the early hours of
27 February, but the protection of the warships was given priority. An
alternative solution was found by letting a small part of the bombers
of the ML carry out night time raids on P I.[19]

Tlt C.J.H. Samson of 1-Vl.G.II at Kalidjati, who had initially
proposed the night time missions, himself carried out the first one
with his crew. The attack took place between around 23:00 hrs and
24:00 hrs (on 27 February) and is considered the last mission flown
in the context of the bombing campaign against targets in southern
Sumatra and Banka. The Samson crew first headed for Palembang and
then looked for P I airfield. That was not easy. Observer Elt J. van
Loggem directed his pilot towards the target up to four times and only
then did he release his bombs. Visible results in the form of explosions or fires could not be observed, nor was there any enemy opposition. Samson landed safely at Kalidjati in the light of oil lamps placed
along the runway. The first test with a bombing mission from Kalidjati,
which did not have any normal runway lighting, was a success. JAC
had planned to have night time missions flown from Andir and
Kemajoran only, as these airfields had runway lighting.[20]

Summary of the events on 27 February 1942

On 27 February 1942 JAC only carried out a small number of bomber missions to southern Sumatra; eight sorties, two of which were aborted due to engine trouble. One Glenn Martin was badly damaged. In addition, the bombers in western Java flew several seaward reconnaissance missions (five sorties), during which a small Japanese convoy was discovered south of the south-easterly tip of Banka. In the first half of the afternoon a Glenn Martin and a Blenheim reconnoitred P I and P II airfield, respectively, and they discovered a large number of Japanese aircraft there. Although the western invasion fleet had not been found yet, it was now clear that the Japanese were concentrating combat aircraft at Palembang for the coming attack on western Java. At the same time a flying boat of *RecGroup* re-discovered the Japanese invasion fleet in the east, upon which the *Combined Striking Force* put to sea in order to engage it. The allied fleet perished after a protracted naval battle, while at the same time a Glenn Martin of JAC carried out a last (night time) mission to P I airfield. With this mission the bombing campaign came to an end.

*** *** ***

CHAPTER 1B.12

The Results Attained, a Concise Analysis and Some Conclusions with Regard to the Struggle for Air Superiority

Introduction

The bombing offensive, which was begun on 18 February 1942 and ended on 27 February 1942, staged by ABDAIR and subsequently

JAC and carried out by the ML, RAF and RAAF from western Java, was directed against Japanese targets in southern Sumatra and Banka. Initially, the primary targets were the tank park of the oil refinery at Pladjoe (filled to the brim with aircraft and shipping fuel), which had fallen into Japanese hands entirely undamaged, and the Japanese ships at Palembang and en route there on the Moesi river, in the Moesi delta, in the Banka Strait and at Muntok. The objective was to degrade as much as possible the Japanese capacity of supplying the troops at Palembang (including the air forces) with a view to a planned counter-attack of the KNIL from Padang. In addition, the Japanese combat aircraft at Palembang I airfield (or P I) were an important target.

The plan for the counter-attack was cancelled late at night on 20 February or in the early hours of 21 February, after which the objective of the bombing campaign came to lie on the disruption of the Japanese supply of Palembang I, in particular (and later also Muntok airfield in Banka), and the destruction of the storage of aircraft fuel in the tank park at Pladjoe, in order to degrade the Japanese air offensive over western Java. It was tried to attain this objective by continuing the attacks on ships near Palembang and en route there and bombing the tank park at Pladjoe. Thus, the offensive was mainly directed at making aircraft fuel as scarce as possible for the Japanese air forces in southern Sumatra and Banka and at taking out as many Japanese aircraft as could be achieved.

From 26 February 1942 onwards, with the discovery of a Japanese invasion fleet in the Macassar Strait, the emphasis came to lie more on searching for and attacking the ships of the expected 'western' invasion fleet. Besides, the attacks on P I and the ships at Palembang were continued. The bombings on Pladjoe could be stopped on 26 February as the raids on the tank park and refinery had yielded enough results.

The efforts and results of the bomber fleet

Below an overview is given of the realised numbers of sorties flown in the context of the bomber offensive (excluding those flown with Blenheim Mark Is), indicating each time the numbers of sorties sent out, followed by the numbers of sorties that actually arrived over the target. When an alternative target was attacked, because of bad weather, for instance, the sorties are stated with the alternative target.

Table 16

	P I	Pladjoe	Ships P'bang	Ships Elsewhere	Sea reconn. (Photo) reconn.	Total
18-02	3/3	9/7	8/7	10/–	2/2	32/19
19-02	14/7	4/1	–/–	9/3	3/3	30/14
20-02	–/–	10/5	10/10	3/3	1/1	24/19
21-02	5/2	15/14	2/2	–/–	2/2	24/20
22-02	–/–	7/3	3/3	4/3	4/2	18/11
23-02	6/6	5/5	3/3	5/3	3/3	22/20
24-02	5/5	3/3	–/–	2/2	–/–	10/10
25-02	6/0	7/2	–/–	–/–	2/2	15/4
26-02	–/–	1/1	–/–	6/6	5/5	12/12
27-02	4/2	–/–	4/4	–/–	7/7	15/14
Total	43/25	61/41	30/29	39/20	29/27	209/142

On average, 20 sorties a day were sent out, 14 of which arrived over the target.[1] In view of the small numbers of available bombers and the weather season (the wet monsoon period), this was not a bad achievement. What is striking is the fact that during the course of the campaign the number of sorties sent out was almost halved, whereas the number of sorties arriving over the target was reasonably constant. This was due to the extremely bad and sometimes extremely good weather during the first days of the bombing campaign. The decline in the total number of sorties was caused by the loss of the support from the American *East Group* after 18 February 1942 and destruction of allied bombers on their bases during Japanese air raids and as a consequence of operations.

On 18 February 1942 ABDAIR had available 24 operationally serviceable bombers suitable for missions over southern Sumatra and Banka; on 27 February this number had fallen to 20. So, this number, too, remained reasonably constant during the campaign, in spite of the losses sustained. This was mainly due to the efforts of the technical personnel at the squadrons and afdelingen and the technicians and specialists of the Technical Service of the ML and 153 MU of the RAF. What were the actual effects of all these efforts? Briefly put, the following results were realised.

Ships: four Japanese ships were hit and probably a fifth.

Aircraft fuel: the cracking plant of the BPM refinery was destroyed and at least 35 per cent of the storage capacity of the tank park at Pladjoe, including the bulk of the storage of aircraft fuel.

Combat aircraft: at least 11 Japanese combat aircraft (eight Ki-48 bombers and three Ki-27 fighters) were destroyed and at least 18 air-craft were damaged at P I and in aerial combat. Apart from that the bomber fleet of JAC made an important contribution to the discovery of the 'western' invasion fleet.

These results of the bomber offensive, too, are not bad at all, given its small scale and short duration. It was far from sufficient, though. The Japanese air actions over western Java simply continued. Although ABDAIR and later JAC realised that the available means were in actual fact inadequate, there was no other way of conducting a sensible air offensive over southern Sumatra and Banka. Keeping the bombers on the ground on their bases was no option. Already as early as 19 February 1942 General Wavell, warned the Combined Chiefs of Staff, that the available combat aircraft were only sufficient for a fortnight at best. Two days later he reduced this period to one week. Wavell also had the planning for a counter-attack of the KNIL on Palembang stopped, as he gave such an attack little chance of success and, moreover, the preparation for it would take too much time.

Major-General Van Oyen, who took over as commander of JAC on 22 February 1942, however, was of the opinion that by employing all available means (bombers, fighters and anti-aircraft artillery) it might be possible to get the Japanese to postpone their invasion of Java for some time. This delay would allow the allies to reinforce their air force, with fighters, in the first instance. It would then become pos-sible to seriously degrade the Japanese effort to attain air superiority, prior to an invasion. In this, Van Oyen got the support from his army commander.

The allied strategy

ABDAIR's and later JAC's strategy was directed at reducing as much as possible the enemy capacity for sending out operational sorties by employing its bombers, fighters and anti-aircraft artillery. To this end on 18 February 1942 a *Counter-air* operation (as it is nowadays called) was begun, with an offensive as well as a defensive component. The bombers in western Java carried out attacks on three primary targets in the occupied part of Sumatra, without fighter escorts and by making use of clouds and smoke of oil fires. They were the tank park of the oil refinery at Pladjoe near Palembang, Japanese shipping on the Moesi river at Palembang and en route there from the roadstead of Muntok (Banka) and Palembang I airfield, where the Japanese Army air force had established itself.

The objective was a maximum disruption of the Japanese supply (especially of aircraft fuel), the destruction of as much as could be achieved of the aircraft fuel stores captured by the Japanese at Pladjoe and the taking out of as many aircraft as possible that could be employed against western Java; in other words, reducing the number of sorties that the Japanese air forces could fly to western Java for the attainment of air superiority there.

The scarce allied fighters were primarily given an air defence task for the defence of the major air bases in western Java, the harbour of Batavia and, as much as possible, the allied fleet. By inflicting as many losses as they could during interceptions, in cooperation with the anti-aircraft artillery, the fighters were also supposed to maximally degrade the enemy capacity for sending out sorties. As a result the Japanese would need more time to attain air superiority; time the allies needed to shore up the defence of Java, in the first instance, with extra fighter aircraft.

The strategy was fine in itself and even today it would stand the test of criticism, if it were related to the principles of modern *Air Power* theory. ABDAIR had identified two centres of gravity, on which it brought a maximum effort offensive to bear. The assessment that the availability of aircraft fuel was the most limiting factor for the Japanese advance, was correct; as was the supposition that the Japanese air forces had used up their reserves, and, in any case with regard to their fighters, would have to make do with the aircraft that had been moved forward to Palembang (for the battle against western Java).[2]

To what extent, however, were the ML and RAF and RAAF's own available means sufficient for attaining the objective aimed at? An air campaign based on attrition takes time to make the enemy clearly feel the effects, and therefore its successful execution requires large reserves of aircraft. The ML and RAF and RAAF had neither the time nor the reserves. One advantage the allied air forces had was that the Japanese could spread the targets for the allied bombers only to a very limited extent. Thus, in the first instance, all Japanese aircraft were concentrated on the relatively small airfield of Palembang I and the bulk of fuel supplies that needed to be destroyed was stored in a part of a tank park of an oil refinery well known to the allies.

There were, however, certain basic problems the allies could not do anything about. The battle took place in the "wet" season, the monsoon period, with often bad weather, heavy clouds and showers. As was already said above, this seriously affected the effectiveness of the sorties flown. Besides, the high humidity caused defects in the electrical systems of the aircraft, such as start up systems and bomb sights. On top of that, there was the general shortage of bomber aircraft, while it was impossible to reinforce the bomber fleet at short notice. There were also great shortages of anti-aircraft artillery and fighter aircraft in Java for, amongst others, the defence of the most important airfields. The shortage of anti-aircraft artillery could not be helped, as there were no units that could be directed to Java. For the fighter aircraft it was different.

American P-40 fighters were standing ready in Australia, but if the allies wanted to get them operational in time, the Japanese would have to be forced to postpone their planned invasion. A delay of one week would suffice. On 22 February 1942 *Langley* and *Sea Witch* left the port of Fremantle with a total of 63 P-40 fighters intended for Java on board. The allies gave their all to make the Japanese postpone their invasion. The combined results the allied bombers, fighters and anti-aircraft artillery achieved, however, were insufficient to reach this objective. The Japanese army could not afford too much delay because it was facing logistic problems, and therefore the extremely positive results reported by the 3rd Hiko Shudan of its own air offensive over western Java were very convenient for the Japanese commanders.

ABDAIR and JAC's results

ABDAIR and later JAC threw everything it had in the way of resources into the battle. As was said above, the bomber offensive over southern Sumatra was a *maximum effort offensive*, which, in spite of the relatively modest number of sorties (as a result of the small number of available bombers) was a considerable success. These results, however, were insufficient to impact the course of the battle for the attainment of air superiority over western Java. The allies managed to destroy a large part of the aircraft fuel that had fallen into Japanese hands at Pladjoe. The Japanese Army air force, however, seemed to be less dependent on captured aircraft fuel for its further offensive than was thought, while the supply by ship of the Japanese units at Palembang I could not be degraded enough.

In actual fact the supply of sufficient aircraft fuel was a logistic nightmare indeed for the Japanese armed forces. Thus, the supply of aircraft fuel and other aviation materials at Palembang I (the former civilian airfield of Palembang) was barely sufficient, also because the allied air offensive against the base forced the 3rd Hiko Shudan to fly extra combat air patrols. The supply of Palembang II, the large military airfield in the jungle south-west of the town of Palembang, was even totally inadequate to allow the Japanese to operate on a regular basis from there. As a consequence, the units of the Japanese Navy air force operating from P II were only able to make a small contribution to the battle over western Java. The logistic problems formed one of the reasons for the Japanese army to want to hold on to the date set for the invasion of Java. A few days' delay could be tolerated, but a longer postponement (a longer period of intensive operations prior to the invasion) would stretch their supply lines to the breaking point.[3]

In the battle for air superiority over western Java itself (described in Part 1A) the ML and RAF did considerably well, too. In reality, the famed technical superiority of the Ki-43 Army 1 fighter, the long-distance fighter of the Japanese Army air force employed over western Java, did not exist. The A6M Navy O fighter of the Japanese Navy air force was superior in a number of ways indeed to the Hawker Hurricanes, the Curtiss-Wright CW-21 Interceptors and the Brewster B 339C and Ds of the RAF and the ML, but this type only carried out one mission over western Java. All Japanese fighter pilots had combat experience, but for the period described in this book, this was also the case for the majority of the fighter pilots of the ML and RAF.

The outcome of the battle between the fighters was in fact un-decided and it cost the 3rd Hiko Dan at Palembang and the Yamada Kokutai at Muntok, apart from at least one reconnaissance aircraft, seven Ki-43 Army 1s and one A6M Navy O. Furthermore, British fighter aircraft shot down one Ki-48 bomber. The allied assumption that the Japanese air forces had exhausted their reserves of, in any case, fighters was correct. Had the air war lasted longer, this fact would certainly have played a role. However, the allied fighters were bound very effectively and, with a few exceptions, were not able to attack the Japanese bombers effectively. This allowed the Japanese air forces to take out a large number of bombers of the ML, RAF and

RAAF on their home bases, which seriously affected the allies' capability of destroying Japanese aircraft at Palembang and Muntok. The number of Japanese aircraft hit by allied bombers, already mentioned above (at least 29), therefore, was relatively low. Moreover, the 3rd Hiko Dan lost no Ki-43 fighters on the ground. Just like the fighters, the allied anti-aircraft artillery in western Java was fairly successful and shot down at least eight Ki-48 bombers and one C5M reconnaissance aircraft.

Of the approximately 167 aircraft flown over to Palembang I by the Japanese Army air force some 35 aircraft of the 3rd and 12th Hiko Dan were lost as a result of air combat or allied bombing raids (21 per cent) in the period of 18 February up to and including 27 February 1942.

The Japanese certainly did not attain air supremacy, in the modern sense of freedom to operate. They did not get far beyond a temporary air superiority (in the modern lingo). Time and again enemy fighters were encountered during attacks on western Java. Moreover, allied bombers kept on carrying out attacks in small groups on targets in southern Sumatra, among which was Palembang I airbase. The ML and RAF and RAAF, however, were not able to degrade the Japanese capacity to send out sorties (quickly) enough to induce the Japanese commanders to extend the air offensive against western Java with more than the two days that had been decided upon on 23 February 1942. It would also take a lot to achieve this. Further extension would immediately cause logistic problems for the Japanese army, while it was assumed that the allies would reinforce the defence of Java in the mean time. It seems that for these reasons the relatively high losses of the Japanese Army air force were acceptable. In fact, in view of the relative strengths, this situation left the allied forces completely without a chance.

Van Oyen's gamble

In retrospect, Van Oyen was wrong in his conviction that there was a small chance of postponement of the Japanese invasion long enough to allow the allies to reinforce Java, with fighter planes, to begin with. That he tried cannot be held against him at all. On 23 February 1942 the Japanese commanders decided on a postponement of two days from 26 February until the (very early hours of) 28 February 1942. Especially the Japanese Navy was cautious and refused to commit its ships for the support of the planned landings of the Japanese army in

Java without air superiority. However, the allies required a postponement of at least a week.

On 25 February the 3rd Hiko Shudan at Palembang analysed the results of the air offensive over western Java from 19 up to and including 25 February. Although some claims of the 3rd Hido Dan were adjusted downwards, the result remained exceedingly favourable. The report of the 3rd Hiko Shudan specified the scores as follows: 33 enemy aircraft shot down, 53 destroyed and more than 150 allied planes supposed to have been damaged. In reality, though, only about 65 instead of 86 aircraft had been shot down or destroyed on the ground, while the over-claim was even greater with regard to the number of damaged aircraft. Own losses were reported to amount to three aircraft, which, however, only related to the direct combat losses of the Ki-43s over western Java. The total number was considerably higher, but this was not explicitly mentioned in the report.

This analysis, however, was crucial to the further course of the battle. Although the Japanese Navy questioned some of the outcomes of the report of the 3rd Hiko Shudan, the commander of the shudan stood by it. On 26 February 1942 the 3rd Assault Group of the Navy air force (Kuching and Muntok) presented its own analysis on the basis of the results of reconnaissance missions and came to the conclusion that there were still strong enemy air forces left in the environment of Batavia. On the basis of this report the Japanese Navy ordered the 4th Air Group at St. Jacques in Indo-China (consisting of a light aircraft carrier, a destroyer and several auxiliary vessels) to join the forces for the invasion of western Java. Further postponement to take out the remaining allied air forces was unacceptable for the Japanese Army, which only wanted to hear good news, as too much delay would bring along logistic problems too difficult to handle.

Van Oyen had lost his gamble and was fully aware of this after the discovery of the first Japanese invasion fleet on 25 February 1942. The P-40s of *Langley* and *Sea Witch* would come too late. Committing the *Combined Striking Force*, the naval squadron of the allied navies, would constitute the last possibility to avert an invasion. On 25 and 26 February JAC transferred as many fighter aircraft as possible to Ngoro in eastern Java in order to maximise the air cover for the naval squadron. On 27 February all the ML Brewster fighter aircraft at Andir were on readiness to give air cover for the allied warships on operations along the north coast of Java. They did not come into action.

The allied naval squadron perished on the night of 27 February 1942 in the Battle of the Java Sea.

The offensive part of the *Counter-air* operation, the bomber offensive directed at targets in southern Sumatra and in Banka, had to be abandoned by JAC on the night of 27 February 1942. The Japanese invasion was imminent and the bombers were held in readiness to carry out attacks on the approaching invasion fleets. Simultaneously, the defensive part of the operation, insofar it concerned the deployment of the fighters, was terminated. The fighter aircraft were needed for attack missions in case of any Japanese landing operations.

The voyage of *Langley* and *Sea Witch* to Tjilatjap was a risky affair after the occupation of Bali and only *Sea Witch* arrived safely on 28 February 1942. The P-40s on board did not make any difference. They were crated and in spite of great efforts, the first three aircraft were ready for flight only on 7 March 1942. The P-40s on *Langley* had been mounted on deck and pilots as well as ground crews were on board. The fighter aircraft were to have flown from an improvised air strip in the dock area of Tjilatjap, via Andir, to Tjisaoek. If *Langley* had not been sunk by Japanese bombers on 27 February, the P-40s might have been able to make a contribution to the air defence of western Java as of the beginning of March; too late to help realise a postponement or even cancellation of the invasion.

Conclusion

Van Oyen's assessment of there being a small chance that the Japanese could perhaps be induced to a postponement of the planned invasion by deploying the allied air forces, has been proven to be only half correct at best. The delay realised was only two days, which was too short by far to realise the required reinforcement of the air defence of Java with fighter aircraft. The allies needed this reinforcement to prevail in the battle for the attainment of air superiority, so that post-ponement would lead to cancellation of the invasion or a situation in which the allies could reinforce their land forces in Java.

JAC did what it could with limited resources, but it was not enough. In part, this was caused by the fact that the Japanese army was prepared to accept relatively heavy losses of the army air force, as logistic problems only allowed a very limited extension of the air offensive before it would have to decide to a temporary abandonment of the invasion of Java. The 3rd Hiko Shudan also had a far too favourable assessment of the results of its air offensive over western Java, as became clear in the period between 26 and 28 February, when Japanese formations kept on being intercepted by allied fighter aircraft and allied bombers, individually or in small groups, kept on attacking Japanese targets in southern Sumatra and Banka. It clearly worried the Japanese commanders, but there was no way back anymore. The allied naval forces ensured a delay of one more day of the Japanese invasion, which eventually took place in the night of 28 February on 1 March with landings in three different locations in the west and one location west of Soerabaja in eastern Java.

The Japanese showed their respect for the air campaign of the ML, the RAF and RAAF after the capitulation of the KNIL and the allied forces and they were clearly surprised that the battle had so tenaciously been fought with so little means. The acting commander of the ML, Colonel E.T. Kengen (by this time titular Major-General, although he did not know this) was even given permission to thank his subordinates in a final daily order for their exceptional efforts. A unique and well-deserved gesture.

PART 2

❦

The Battle of the Java Sea

*Joint action of the allied air and naval forces on
26, 27 and 28 February 1942:
The air support for Doorman prior to and during the
Battle of the Java Sea and the operations after the
battle on 28 February 1942*

CHAPTER 2.1

The Air Support for the *Combined Striking Force* on 26 February and in the Morning of 27 February 1942

Introduction

As was described above in Part 1, ABDAIR and later JAC executed two *Counter-air* operations from 18 February 1942 onwards, consisting of, amongst others, bombing offensives directed against Japanese targets in southern Sumatra and in Banka, from western Java, and against Japanese targets in (mainly) Bali, from central and eastern Java, respectively. These operations were intended to gain some more time during which Java could be reinforced with American and British fighter aircraft. The more time it would cost the Japanese to attain their air superiority over Java, the greater the chance would be to avert the invasion. The allied naval squadron was to be deployed as soon as the Japanese invasion fleets were discovered. This was the case on 25 February 1942, when a flying boat of *RecGroup* spotted the first Japanese invasion fleet in the roadstead of Balikpapan (eastern Borneo). There was no doubt that its destination would be eastern Java. The *Counter-air* operations had failed.[1]

On 25 February 1942 a number of measures were taken at Bandoeng. It was decided to immediately concentrate the allied naval squadron at Soerabaja in order to carry out an attack and to transfer as many fighter aircraft as possible to Ngoro in eastern Java for the protection of the *Combined Striking Force*. At Ngoro, south-east of Blimbing, the American 17 Pursuit Squadron (17 PS) was stationed, which on 25 February, however, had only eight operationally service-able Curtiss P-40 fighter aircraft left. The first reinforcements, three

Brewster fighter aircraft of 1-Vl.G.V of the ML at Andir already left
the same day and arrived at Ngoro in the late afternoon of 25 February,
followed a day later, between 14:00 hrs and 16:00 hrs, by a further
three Brewster fighters from 1- and 2-Vl.G.V and six Hawker Hurricanes from 2-Vl.G.IV of the ML. The Hawker aircraft, however, could
not be used for air defence tasks for the time being. A seventh Hurricane arrived at Ngoro on 27 February.[2]

The air cover for Doorman is taking shape (26 February 1942)

On 26 February 1942 the *Eastern Striking Force* was in the navy docks
during the day in order to take in fuel. The war ships, which had been
sent from western Java to Soerabaja (two cruisers and three destroyers),
arrived in the early afternoon, after which an undivided *Combined
Striking Force* was once more available, consisting of five cruisers and
nine destroyers. The 14 ships of the squadron did not leave Soerabaja
until the early evening of 26 February 1942 for a search operation.

That the squadron in the docks was vulnerable to attacks from
the air had been shown clearly in the morning. At 09:30 hrs nine
American P-40 fighter aircraft together with the three Brewsters of
the ML that had arrived first took off to intercept a Japanese formation approaching Soerabaja. The pilots had been on Readiness since
05:00 hrs and had been waiting beneath the wings of their aircraft for
an order by telephone to take off. The alarm rang for 26 Mitsubishi
G4M bombers escorted by eight Mitsubishi Navy O fighters. They
were flying at an altitude of 9,000 metres, where the allied fighters
could not reach them, the ceiling of the P-40s being about 7,500 meters
and that of the Brewsters around 8,000 metres.

The three ML aircraft were flown by Elt H.H.J. Simons, Vdg B.
Wink and Sgt G. van Haarlem. The patrol (which had been seconded
to 17 PS without its ground personnel) was not fully operational yet,
as extra 7.7 mm ammunition was still underway from Madioen, along
with several other materials needed for maintenance which were not
available at 17 PS.[3]

The Japanese bombers remained at high altitude and dropped
their bombs in a few runs through openings in the clouds. The accuracy was below par and almost all the bombs fell into the water,
missing their targets. The war ships were not hit, although there had
been a few close calls. Lieutenant W.J. Hennon (17 PS) managed to

Curtiss P-40E fighter aircraft of 17 Pursuit Squadron of the United States Army Air Force at Ngoro in eastern Java. (Private collection, P.C. Boer)

take two Japanese fighters by surprise at a somewhat lower altitude and claimed one shot down. At 11:45 hrs the last fighters landed again at Ngoro.[4] The G4M bombers belonged to the Kanoya Kokutai (Kanoya air group), which had only just been transferred from Kendari II (eastern Celebes) to Macassar (south-west Celebes) in order to take part in the air offensive against eastern Java. The eight escorting Navy Os came from Bali.[5]

In the afternoon the Brewsters were deployed again at around 16:45 hrs. By that time a total of six of this type of aircraft had been detached to 17 PS. A patrol consisting of two Brewsters, flown by Elt G.J. de Haas and Sgt G.M. Bruggink, flew a seaward reconnaissance mission north of Soerabaja prior to the *Combined Striking Force* putting to sea. The other four Brewsters were on standby for any other eventualities. Nothing was found during the 90 minutes the mission lasted.[6]

Nightly planning in Bandoeng

In the evening of 26 February 1942 the Intelligence section of the AHK and the COIC, probably acting on tapped Japanese radio traffic and the positions of the discovered Japanese ships, warned of a possible invasion of Java taking place the next morning. At ABDA-FLOAT it was assumed that a naval battle might take place in the night of 26 February. In the morning of 26 February a Dornier flying boat of the Marineluchtvaartdienst–Dutch Naval Air Service (MLD) had discovered a Japanese transport fleet in the southern part of the Macassar Strait, which appeared to be heading for eastern Java. In the west the day's reconnaissance missions had not yielded any reports yet of an invasion fleet, but a Catalina flying boat of the MLD had reported ship movements in the Karimata Strait at 09:25 hrs. No details were available due to bad visibility. Furthermore, the crew of a British Blenheim bomber returning from a raid on Muntok (Banka) had spotted a convoy some 100 miles (180 kilometres) north of St. Nicolaaspunt (the north-eastern entrance to the Soenda Strait) at 10:30 hrs. This convoy, however, was sailing a northerly course (345 degrees) and only amounted to as few as 20 vessels, including the escort. The more immediate threat, it was concluded in Bandoeng, still came from the east.[7]

During the night of 26 on 27 February 1942 neither the flying boats of *RecGroup* nor the war ships of the *Combined Striking Force* and the remainder of the *Western Striking* Force, consisting of three cruisers and two destroyers, which had stayed behind at Batavia, found any trace of the Japanese invasion fleets. The *Operations Staff* of JAC had a busy night of it. The staff, which was mainly British-Dutch (including an officer of the MLD) planned a number of missions in case a Japanese invasion already took place the coming morning and in eastern as well as western Java the bomber fleet was on stand-by for deployment at sunrise. At the same time, however, several missions to Palembang (southern Sumatra) and Den Pasar airfield (Bali) were planned. Moreover, the possible transfer of a part of the western bomber fleet to central Java was prepared.[8]

During the night there was contact between the staff officers of JAC and ABDA-FLOAT in order to coordinate the deployment of their respective forces. In the early evening of 26 February the Soerabaja Naval Base Commander requested air support through ABDA-FLOAT for the *Combined Striking Force* for the following day. In conformity with the standing procedures this request was subsequently worked out and combined with others, after which one overall request went to JAC through the AHK. Planning, however, was difficult due to a lack of results from reconnaissance missions.[9]

At around 02:00 hrs the headquarters at Bandoeng concluded that there was no Japanese fleet as yet near Banka or Biliton. The Catalina of the MLD, which was reconnoitring Banka Strait, had sent a reconnaissance report on the evening of 26 February at 23:00 hrs to the effect that several ships had been spotted, but no convoys. The war ships of the remainder of the *Western Striking Force* were probing the sea area south of Banka and Biliton. According to their first reports no enemy ships had been found. Also two RAF Catalinas, reconnoitring from Tjilatjap, could not find any trace of the Japanese fleet operation south of Java of which the Intelligence department of the AHK had warned in the evening of 26 February.[10]

JAC decided to send out two planned missions to Palembang (which will not be described below), and, for the time being, to keep some of the remaining bombers in the west on stand-by as of 05:00 hrs. With regard to the situation in the east, they were even more cautious. That an invasion fleet was approaching eastern Java was certain, as it had been discovered in the southern part of the Macassar Strait in the late morning of 26 February. In conformity with ABDA-FLOAT's request for air support an order was given to *East Group* to send a heavy bomber on a night reconnaissance mission up to the coast of Borneo. This was done to compensate for the limited capacity of *RecGroup* in the east. The Consolidated LB-30 took off around midnight from Djocjakarta. From sunrise the reconnaissance activities were to be intensified by committing more bombers. In the west this was to be done with a limited number, but in the east all the available American heavy bombers were to carry out armed reconnaissance missions. The bombers in the east were re-tasked for bombing missions, however, when in the early morning hours of 27 February the location data of Japanese shipping became available.[11]

In the early morning of 27 February 1942 JAC and other headquarters at Bandoeng concluded that apparently the arrival of the Japanese had been estimated a day too soon. But that they were closing in (in any case in the east) was certain. On good grounds the AHK deemed simultaneous landings in western as well as eastern Java the most likely, but there was growing some hope that the Japanese might just attack eastern Java first, and then, at a somewhat later time, western Java. That would give the allies the opportunity to commit the *Combined Striking Force* first in the east and then again in the west.[12]

The availability of fighter aircraft

In the very early morning of 27 February 1942 JAC received an order from the Operations section of AHK, on behalf of the army commander, to commit all available fighter aircraft to the protection of the

Combined Striking Force. The protection of the allied naval squadron was given priority over the air defence. This order caused a few raised eyebrows at first at JAC, as only a few hours earlier and in good consultation with ABDA-FLOAT staff officers a mission plan for the coming day had been worked out. These arrangements also encompassed the air support for Rear-Admiral K.W.F.M. Doorman, the commander of the allied naval squadron.

Vice-Admiral C.E.L. Helfrich (commanding flag officer ABDA-FLOAT) knew that Doorman was carrying out a probing mission that night with his naval squadron, but at the moment at which the planning was being finalised he had no idea where exactly Doorman was, nor did he know how far west the *Combined Striking Force* would steam up in carrying out its probing mission. Even if the Japanese fleet was not found, Doorman might sail on to Tandjong Priok. That is why Helfrich requested (still) more support from JAC.

In their consultation AHK and JAC subsequently agreed that all available American P-40s of 17 Pursuit Squadron and the ML Brewster fighter aircraft seconded to this squadron (16 aircraft in all) at Ngoro (eastern Java) and all Brewster fighter aircraft of the afdelingen 1- and 2-Vl.G.V (eight aircraft) at Andir would be available on a permanent basis as of 05:00 hrs for the protection of the war ships during operations off the north coast of Java. So, on top of the deployment of the fighter aircraft at Ngoro, which had already been planned, came that of the fighters at Andir. Taking turns in patrols of two aircraft, the Brewsters at Ngoro, and if necessary those at Andir, would carry out covering flights over the allied naval squadron (the range of the Brewster B-339 fighter was considerably larger than that of the Curtiss P-40). Their main task was to intercept any possible Japanese reconnaissance aircraft.[13]

Incidentally, the total of 14 Brewsters and 10 P-40s indeed constituted the entirety of operationally serviceable fighter aircraft of the ML and the United States Army Air Force (USAAF) in Java. Of the other types of fighters in use, the Hurricanes of the RAF and the ML were unsuitable because of their relatively low range and, on top of that, the ML fighter aircraft of this type were not fully operationally serviceable as yet. Furthermore, the ML had several Curtiss-Wright CW-21B fighter aircraft at its disposal, but they were in maintenance and had too limited a range at that. The Hurricanes of the RAF could take up the protection of Tandjong Priok, should any war ships call there.[14]

Around 06:00 hrs it was clear that there was no Japanese fleet operation to the south of Java, but a tragedy began to evolve in this sea area, nevertheless. A message of the KM stated that the aircraft tender *Langley*, with a cargo of 32 combat-ready Curtiss P-40 fighter aircraft and their crews, would not arrive as planned at Tjilatjap, the port on the south coast of Java, in the course of the morning. These P-40s made up two complete squadrons of the USAAF that were to have been stationed at Tjisaoek (western Java) (see below).[15]

The availability of bombers and flying boats

Due to the fact that several British Blenheim bombers had become available once more (after lengthy repairs) there was an actual increase of the number of operationally serviceable bombers from 14 to 20 in western Java on 27 February. At Kalidjati the RAF still had three (serviceable) obsolete Blenheim Mark I bombers, which were used mainly for coastal reconnaissance missions and for that reason were not incorporated in the operational strength, but which could be deployed for night bombing missions. 36 Squadron RAF at Tjikampek, with ten Vildebeest and Albacore light bombers, was not incorporated in the strength, for the same reason, but the unit could be deployed in its entirety for night missions against an invasion fleet. Nevertheless, these were only small numbers, remnants of previous battles. In the end, no bombers were relocated from western Java to central Java on 27 February. Not until the morning of 28 February 1942 was it decided to relocate (only) 36 Squadron to Madioen (Maospati) in central Java.

The status of the various units in western Java on 27 February 1942 at 05:00 hrs was as follows:[16]

Table 17

Unit	Type	Assigned	Operationally serviceable	Base
84 Sq RAF	Blenheim	16	7	Kalidjati
1 Sq RAAF	Hudson	11	2	Kalidjati
Vl.G.I/II	Glenn Martin	7	6	Kalidjati
Vl.G.III	Glenn Martin	4	2	Tjisaoek
Vl.G.III	Glenn Martin	5	3	Andir
Total		43	20	

In central and eastern Java the American *East Group* at Madioen, Djocjakarta and Malang had only seven operationally serviceable heavy bombers (six Boeing B-17s and one Consolidated LB-30 Liberator) and four Douglas A-24 light (dive) bombers available. What must be taken into account in this respect, though, is the fact that the B-17s and LB-30s constituted a considerably greater capacity than the British, Australian and Netherlands East Indies bombers in the west. Where an American heavy bomber could be armed with eight 300-kilogramme bombs (2,400 kilogrammes per aircraft), a Glenn Martin of the ML could take only three bombs of this type in its bomb hold (900 kilogrammes per aircraft), while the British Bristol Blenheim bombers and the American Lockheed Hudsons of the Australian squadron were light bombers that only had a payload of 450 kilogrammes.

The availability of flying boats was also very limited on 27 February 1942. At Morokrembangan, the Naval Air Station of Soerabaja (eastern Java) and several shelter airfields in the environment of Soerabaja the following units were stationed.

Patrol Wing 10 (U.S. Navy): three assigned Consolidated PBY-4 and PBY-5 Catalinas, two of which were operationally serviceable.

Groep Vliegtuigen 6: three assigned Dornier Do-24Ks, none of which were operationally serviceable (crews on rest).

Groep Vliegtuigen 7: four Dornier Do-24 Ks; the entire unit was not available for operations, as the flying boats were still undergoing major inspection (the flying personnel was temporarely assigned to other duties).

Groep Vliegtuigen 17: three assigned Consolidated PBY-5 Catalinas, two of which were operationally serviceable.

In western Java there were seven operationally serviceable Catalinas (all from the MLD) available, at least five of which were needed for the reconnaissance operations to search for and shadow the expected 'western' Japanese invasion fleet once it had been discovered. This number was needed in order to be able to have a near constant watch of two aircraft up and keep one aircraft on stand-by for eventualities, such as Air-Sea-Rescue. Two of these flying boats, therefore, might be assigned in the east to increase the limited reconnaissance capacity there. Of these seven Catalinas, however, one went missing shortly after sunrise on 27 February 1942.

Reconnaissance by bombers in the west

Flying boats of *RecGroup* did not only fly night missions, but also carried out seaward reconnaissance operations by daylight. One of the flying boats that had been deployed (from Tandjong Priok) in a night mission until sunrise, the Y-36 of Groep Vliegtuigen 2 of the MLD, in a reconnaissance of, amongst others, the Banka Strait, went missing. A second reconnaissance report from the crew was never received.[17] From sunrise onwards a number of bombers in the west had also begun to take part in the reconnaissance effort. A patrol of three Glenn Martins and two individually deployed Hudsons carried out seaward reconnaissance missions from Kalidjati over the western part of the Java Sea as far as just south of Banka and Biliton, but, with the exception of one Hudson, did not find any enemy activity. In extremely bad weather a Hudson, flown by Flg Off H.H. Siddell, accidentally discovered a small Japanese convoy at 50 miles (90 kilometres) off the south-eastern tip of Banka, sailing a north-easterly course. This convoy might or might not be part of an invasion fleet bound for western Java. The bomber was fired at but escaped lightly damaged into the clouds.[18]

During the first half of the afternoon two reconnaissance missions were flown from Kalidjati to P I airfield, the former civilian airfield north of the town of Palembang, and P II, the military airfield in the middle of the jungle, southwest of the town, respectively. Fl Lt J.V.C. Wyllie' crew, flying a Blenheim of 84 Squadron, discovered some 30 parked bombers at P II, and not seeing any enemy fighters machine gunned the aircraft, which had been parked on both sides of the runway. The action took the Japanese by surprise; they did not fire back when the Blenheim made a high-speed low-altitude run over P II.[19]

A Glenn Martin of 1-V.G.II, flown by Tlt P.E. Straatman, carried out a reconnaissance of P I, during which Sgt J. Stemerdink, a mechanic assigned as air gunner, made photographs with a camera of the photo section at Kalidjati. This base had a dark room, staffed with two aerial photographers of the ML, who were not allowed to fly on missions because they were too busy developing the photos the crews of the Hudsons usually brought back. Over P I the Glenn Martin made a quick dip below the thick clouds, and after taking the photographs, hastened back in there. At P I there were many more aircraft than at P II, at least 60, and fighter aircraft were patrolling over the airfield.[20]

It was now evident that the Japanese were concentrating aircraft at Palembang for the coming attack on western Java. At JAC it was

assumed (incorrectly) that P II had just been put into use and there was
little reason to be worried (rightly) about this airfield. It was difficult
to supply the airfield and it would be many days before the Japanese
would be able to carry out regular operations from P II. This assessment
of the situation was correct, although it had escaped attention that the
Japanese Navy air force had begun to use P II already on 24 February.
A bombing mission against P I carried out by 3-Vl.G.III of the ML in
the morning had been unsuccessful, and would have to be repeated.[21]

Langley

On 23 February, in conformity with an order from ABDA-FLOAT,
the aircraft tender *Langley* of the American Navy (*Patrol Wing* 10) left
the convoy in which she had departed from Australia on 22 February
and steamed to Java at full power. Already on 11 February 1942, long
before the Japanese capture of Bali and Timor, the Americans had
had quite a few P-40s flown over to Perth (Australia) in order to have
them shipped to Java by sea. This had become necessary due to the
heavy losses sustained during the ferrying across of P-40 fighters from
Darwin in northern Australia, via Timor and Bali to eastern Java, and
this was a way to spread the risks. Apart from two complete squadrons
of the USAAF on board *Langley*, 27 crated P-40s were shipped on 22
February from Fremantle (the port of Perth) on board *Sea Witch*, a
freighter chartered by the U.S. Navy. This vessel had left Melbourne
with her cargo of fighters on 12 February. After some changes in plans
the freighter had been ordered to Java together with the *Langley* on
orders from ABDACOM.[22]

The cargo of *Sea Witch* and *Langley* was reassigned to India
(Karachi) five days later, but General Wavell (the then *Commander-
in-Chief ABDA Area*) decided on 22 February 1942 and after a Dutch
protest along diplomatic channels that the fighter aircraft had to go
to Java after all. In the Netherlands East Indies Lieutenant Governor-
General Dr. H.J. van Mook got personally involved in this matter to
ensure that the two ships would indeed deliver their cargo in Java. The
captain of *Sea Witch* did not leave the convoy until 25 February from a
position near the Cocos Islands. This was according to plan and meant
to spread the risks, both ships proceeding to Java at their own best speed
and scheduled to make port at Tjilatjap with a difference of a day.[23]

On 26 February two Catalinas of Groep Vliegtuigen 5 (GVT 5)
of the MLD, the Y-65 and Y-71, took off from Tjilatjap, to meet

Langley in order to fly search patterns around the vessel. The minelayer *Willem van der Zaan* of the KM had been ordered the previous day to act as an escort. This vessel had already been operating as an escort ship south of Java and was equipped with a modern and relatively heavy anti-aircraft battery. However, shortly after her rendezvous with *Langley* in the morning of 26 February she began to have problems with her propulsion system, so she could not keep up with *Langley*. This brought down her speed to 10 nautical miles. The problems with the minelayer could not be solved and the captain of *Willem van der Zaan* had a message sent to the KM at Tjilatjap at around 10:00 hrs to the effect that he was forced to refrain from carrying out his escort assignment, upon which the captain of the aircraft tender decided to carry on full steam ahead.[24]

The intention had been to go the last, most dangerous, stretch of the voyage in the evening of 26 February and the night of 26 on 27 February. During the night, however, by order of ABDA-FLOAT, the ship reversed her course for several hours (most probably because of the expected Japanese naval action of which warnings had been issued), until the order was rescinded and course was set again at full speed towards Tjilatjap. As was said above, neither the allied war ships, nor the flying boats of *RecGroup* could find any trace of Japanese operations during that night. Due to the delay caused by *Willem van der Zaan* and the reversal of her course, *Langley*, however, was so far behind her original sailing schedule that she was still hundreds of nautical miles away from Java by dawn on 27 February.[25]

At around 06:00 hrs (on 27 February) the first act of the *Langley* tragedy began to take shape in the KMA (Royal Military Academy) building in Bandoeng. Major-General Van Oyen (the JAC commander) and his subordinate commanders were advised that *Langley* would not arrive according to plan in the roadstead of Tjilatjap. As Vice-Admiral Helfrich (ABDA-FLOAT) could not be reached, Van Oyen personally telephoned the army commander, Ter Poorten (Commander-in-Chief ABDA Area) for information about *Langley* and he asked him whether she might need fighter protection for the last leg to Tjilatjap. It would be possible to re-locate the Brewsters from Andir to Banjoemas to do it. All fighter aircraft, also those at Andir, however, needed to remain available for the protection of the war ships of the *Combined Striking Force* during operations along the north coast of Java. Van Oyen protested, pointing out that the aircraft tender was much more vulnerable to air attacks, but his objections fell on deaf ears. Because of the limited numbers of available fighter aircraft a choice must be made and the protection of the *Combined Striking Force* remained the priority.[26]

The personnel of the ML in the harbour of Tjilatjap was informed through the ML Command that *Langley* would not arrive until the late afternoon. A team of the Technical Depot of the ML from Andir and some American personnel from 17 Squadron from Ngoro were at hand in the harbour to help get the P-40s airworthy and to fly the aircraft off from an improvised runway on the quay. Infantrymen of the KNIL were available to lend a hand with unloading the aircraft tender. At Andir and Tjisaoek there were also service personnel ready to check the P-40's on a stop over respectively to receive the Americans. Also six pilots of 17 PS were to fly along to Tjisaoek.[27]

In the course of the morning of 27 February the inevitable happened: *Langley* was discovered by a bomber of the Japanese Navy air force. By this time the ship was escorted by two American destroyers which had left Tjilatjap the previous night to take over the escort and that had made their rendezvous at around 07:15 hrs the next morning. The two Catalinas of GVT 5, armed with depth charges, again took care of the reconnaissance on 27 February. At around 12:00 hrs, some 75 nautical miles (135 kilometres) south of Tjilatjap, the aircraft tender was successfully attacked by nine Mitsubishi GM4 bombers of the Takao Kokutai from Bali. Japanese fighter aircraft, Navy Os of the 3rd Kokutai as well as the Tainan Kokutai from Bali, also attacked the ships and almost downed one of the two Catalinas. The Y-65 was badly damaged but was able to reach Tjilatjap for an emergency landing.[28]

Langley, ablaze in an inextinguishable fire, had to be abandoned. Almost all her crew and passengers, however, could be rescued by the accompanying destroyers, after which one of them sank the aircraft tender with artillery fire and several torpedoes. The freighter *Sea Witch* did arrive safely at Tjilatjap the next day. As was said above, the ship had 27 crated P-40s on board that were now unloaded with the highest priority and transported by rail to Bandoeng and Tasikmalaja to be assembled.[29]

Air support for Doorman in the morning of 27 February 1942

After a search operation carried out mostly in the dark the *Combined Striking Force* entered the Westervaarwater north of Soerabaja in the

A pre-war photograph of the cruiser *Java* of the Dutch Navy. (Private collection, P.C. Boer)

early afternoon of 27 February 1942 in order to replenish in the Navy docks. The fleet had not been able to detect any Japanese activities (except aircraft) and had reversed its course off Rembang at around 09:30 hrs and had sailed back.[30]

Java Air Command had been searching for the Japanese invasion fleet for Doorman all night of 26 on 27 February 1942 with several flying boats of *RecGroup* and an LB-30 bomber of *East Group*. The latter aircraft returned at Djocjakarta at 06:25 hrs after a six-hour mission. A Catalina of the MLD found one or two Japanese ships in several locations, but no convoy. Due to a broken radio, incidentally, this was not reported until sunrise after the aircraft had landed. In the early morning of 27 February the crew of the LB-30, after long hours of searching by the light of a wan moon and occasionally in heavy clouds with showers, also filed in a negative reconnaissance report.[31]

The *Combined Striking Force* got protection from allied fighters for several hours during the morning. At around 05:15 hrs Elt H.H.J. Simons and Sgt G. van Haarlem took off from Ngoro for a first covering mission. From 05:30 hrs until 07:00 hrs they flew at an altitude of

7,500 metres over the ships when they were relieved by Elt G.J. de Haas and Vdg B. Wink. At 07:00 hrs the allied naval squadron was sailing a westerly course, rather close to the coast of Java and west of the longitude of Soerabaja. On board the ships it could be only be hoped that the planes seen up in the air were indeed the promised fighter cover, for the high altitude made it impossible to identify them. The allied fighter pilots, however, had to fly as high as possible to be in a position for a timely intercept of approaching Japanese planes. Radio communication was technically impossible, as the radios of the ships and the aircraft worked in different frequency bands that did not overlap.[32]

De Haas and Wink had been flying for a little under half an hour at an altitude of 7,500 to 8,000 metres over the allied war ships when a fast two-engine reconnaissance plane approached at still higher altitude. The Japanese aircraft (probably a G4M bomber operating from Balikpapan) was flying at an altitude of some 9,000 metres from east to west over the ships, out of reach of the Brewsters with their ceiling of a little over 8,000 metres, which were nevertheless struggling to gain some height. Radio communication with the Air Defence Command Soerabaja (*Interceptor Control*) had probably broken down because of the large distance or heavy showers in the environment. This made De Haas decide to land as quickly as possible at Ngoro and report by telephone that the naval squadron had been discovered. Besides, the fleet was sailing so far west that the fighter pilots could not remain over the squadron for much longer. The patrol dived back to the base at high speed and landed at about 07:45 hrs.[33]

Around 08:00 hrs the news was announced on the war ships of the naval squadron that allied fighter protection was no longer possible. The *Combined Striking Force* was steaming so far west that it was sailing out of reach of the Brewsters. Moreover, the oxygen for the fighters had been all but exhausted, due to the deployment of the aircraft the day before. A fresh supply was on its way from Madioen, but was not expected until the early afternoon. All that could be done after De Haas and Wink had returned was to have four Brewsters ready for take off at Ngoro. Apparently, Doorman was not informed about these under-lying reasons until he made a request for fighter protection after an aerial attack on one of his ships.[34]

In the morning one of a total of four B-17s that had been sent out from Malang at 06:30 hrs for an attack on warships that had been discovered (probably by a coast watch detachment) found a group of five large ships and several smaller ones, dipped below the clouds and bombed one of the ships in two runs around 09:00 hrs. Only afterwards did Lieutenant P.L. Mathewson's crew find out that the communication had not been optimal and that the ships were in fact the allied naval squadron. The ship attacked, the British destroyer *Jupiter*, had not been hit. The war ships fired back with their anti-aircraft artillery, but the B-17 escaped undamaged into the clouds. The other three B-17s had been forced to return to their base due to engine trouble. At 07:35 JAC informed *East Group* (V *Bomber Command*) by telephone that the location given for the American attacks was probably that of the allied naval squadron. At that time the B-17s had already been sent out and they could not be reached by radio once they were airborne.[35]

Doorman reported the attack by radio, upon which ABDA-FLOAT apparently asked the Navy Commander Soerabaja why the agreed fighter protection was not present over the naval squadron. The staff room at Soerabaja in any case asked the Air Defence Command Soerabaja what exactly was going on. Lieutenant-Colonel H.J. Ente van Gils, the commander of the Command then advised them of the underlying reasons. One problem was that Doorman communicated with two naval authorities at the same time, one of which (ABDA-FLOAT) was not aware of the communication by telephone between the Air Defence Command Soerabaja (*Interceptor Control*) and the staff room of the Navy Commander Soerabaja.[36]

The re-discovery of the Japanese invasion fleet in the east

A second mission of two B-17s sent out from Madioen in the morning at 07:30 hrs also discovered a group of war ships and through some openings in the thick clouds carried out a bombing raid around 10:20 hrs amidst heavy anti-aircraft artillery. That these ships did not belong to the allied naval squadron became quickly clear, when, after the raid a Navy O carried out a failed attack and the B-17s were pursued by several Navy O fighters. The heavy clouds prevented the Japanese Navy pilots from intercepting the bombers. Japanese sources reveal that the cruiser *Jintsu* and escorting destroyers formed the target, but the ships were apparently not hit or seriously damaged by near-misses.[37] The American crews also discovered a convoy consisting of about 35 vessels on a course of 170 degrees. This discovery, however, could not be reported until after they had landed (at 12:30 hrs), after which it still took a considerable period of time for the message to reach Bandoeng, possibly because V *Bomber Command* first carried out an investigation into whether it had not been allied war ships that had been attacked by the B-17s.[38]

At 13:40 hrs the crew of a Catalina of *Patrol Wing* 10 reported a sighting of an enemy fleet at 65 nautical miles north-northwest of Bawean, consisting of 20 transport ships and an unknown number of destroyers.[39] This *RecGroup* aircraft was not intercepted. The weather was terrible on 27 February, making it very hard for the Tainan Kokutai to maintain a fighter presence over the invasion fleet. Three fighters of the fighter group that had taken off from Balikpapan at 12:30 hrs had even gone missing. Their pilots had been surprised by the bad weather, but had managed to make emergency landings, as it appeared later. As of 13:30 hrs there was no longer any fighter cover over the Japanese invasion fleet. A second searching Catalina from Soerabaja did not report any contacts.[40]

The Catalina Y-45 of GVT 18 of the MLD (commanded by LTZ II H. Dorré) took off from the Naval Air Station Tandjong Priok (Batavia) at around 09:30 hrs for a reconnaissance mission for the *Combined Striking Force*. At Soerabaja there were no operationally serviceable flying boats available any more, except for the Y-67. The crew of this flying boat, however, was on stand-by at the Naval Air Station Morokrembangan (Soerabaja) for eventualities, such as Air-Sea-Rescue. The Y-45 was flying along the coast of Java and spotted the allied naval squadron east of Toeban around 11:00 hrs. Near Bawean it carried out a search for submarines, in accordance with its reconnaissance assignment, but nothing was found. In the mean time, the weather had deteriorated badly and the flying boat was flying at low altitude through the rain showers. Just when the Catalina had left the showers behind, the crew discovered an enemy fleet, some 20 nautical miles (36 kilometres) west of Bawean. It was heading south and (insofar as it could be ascertained) consisted of 25 transport vessels, two cruisers, six destroyers and probably a few smaller war ships.

While the crew was making an inventory of the fleet and determining the position, a Japanese cruiser launched a catapult aircraft which came climbing up towards the Catalina for an attack. The commander of the Y-45 gave the order to climb towards a bank of clouds hanging at an altitude of about 3,000 metres over Bawean and from there he sent a reconnaissance report at 13:50 hrs, in 'clear script' because of the urgency and in order to avoid delays in transmitting it, over the so-called "CZM-golf" for aircraft, a Dutch naval command frequency.[41] This frequency was also monitored by war ships, and on top of that messages on the frequency that were received at Soerabaja, were re-transmitted (and repeatedly so) over the "CZM-golf" for ships.

RecGroup only had at its disposal a radio station (coming from an American Catalina) that communicated with the flying boats of the U.S. Navy (on its own frequency). Reconnaissance reports from MLD flying boats were received via a communications bureau of the KM. However, the processing of telegrams (decoding and prioritisation) was frequently lagging far behind, due to overloading at the Signals service of the KM. Stacks of telegrams arrived at the service and every sender often gave his own message (too high) a priority. *RecGroup* immediately distributed the reconnaissance reports on reception, within the city of Bandoeng (all headquarters and the COIC) by dispatch riders, and outside Bandoeng through the Signals service of the KM. For this reason Doorman often received contact reports from the MLD twice; once from ABDA-FLOAT and once via the "CZM-golf", which was monitored by his KM warships. At 14:27 hrs, when he was already sailing again in the Westervaarwater north of Soerabaja, Doorman received the official report of the discovery of the invasion fleet, upon which he immediately had his naval squadron put about.[42]

* * *

CHAPTER 2.2

The Battle of the Java Sea

Introduction

As described above, the allied naval squadron was on its way back to Soerabaja when the Japanese invasion fleet was discovered by *RecGroup*. The ships had been shadowed for a considerable period of time by a Japanese float plane. Shortly after 10:20 hrs the *Combined Striking Force* had been discovered by a float plane from one of the cruisers in the covering squadron of the Japanese invasion fleet.[1]

The official report of the discovery of the Japanese invasion fleet, around 45 transport ships in total, apart from the escort, sailing in a north-south line west of Bawean in two groups, reached Rear-Admiral Doorman through ABDA-FLOAT at 14:27 hrs, when his naval squadron was already sailing in Westervaarwater north of Soerabaja. He immediately had his squadron put about. The float planes of most of the Allied cruisers that had probably already been sent to a shelter in the environment of Soerabaja in the morning of 26 February were not taken on board again. It is known that the plane of *Houston* was sent to Morokrembangan Naval Air Station in the afternoon of 26 February, where it remained on stand-by. This may also have been the case with regard to other cruiser float planes. Only *Exeter* and *Perth*, which had come from Batavia on 26 February, still had their reconnaissance aircraft on board on leaving port. At around 15:00 hrs the naval squadron had already put the mine field north of the Westervaarwater behind them.[2]

Doorman had not waited for the order from ABDA-FLOAT to put to sea for an attack. This order came at 15:00 hrs. At the same time three Douglas A-24 light bombers took off from Malang to carry out a first attack on the Japanese transport fleet (see below). The Japanese Navy also knew that Doorman had put to sea. A float plane of the cruiser *Nachi* reported Doorman's reversal of course and at 15:18 hrs the crew of the plane reported that the allied naval squadron was heading in a north-westerly direction at a speed of 22 knots.[3]

The weather near Soerabaja had improved considerably, but it was still bad over Balikpapan, Bali and Macassar, the home bases of the bombers and fighters of the Japanese Navy air force. For this reason a planned bombing raid on Soerabaja was cancelled. All the bombers and the majority of the escorting fighter aircraft returned on their way out. The few Navy Os that did make it to Soerabaja could not see any targets and returned after all.[4] The only aircraft the crews aboard the allied war ships saw was an occasional Japanese reconnaissance plane. The reconnaissance aircraft of the cruiser *Nachi* shadowed the naval squadron until it had to break off its reconnaissance at 15:30 hrs after having dropped two light bombs, which missed their target. The aircraft appearing over the naval squadron after this were allied fighter aircraft.[5]

In the afternoon of 27 February between 14:30 and 15:00 hrs JAC sent orders to the ML Command, BRITAIR and *East Group* to the effect that all aircraft must be prepared immediately for action, in anticipation of the expected invasion of Java in the night of 27 and 28 February 1942 or in the early hours of 28 February. As described above, *RecGroup* had re-discovered the invasion fleet near the island of Bawean steaming up towards eastern Java, and its course and speed made an invasion during the coming night very likely. From this moment onwards in principle all bombers were put on readiness, but at JAC it was decided not to cancel an already planned attack on P I airfield with one Glenn Martin and an attack by an LB-30 on Den Pasar airfield (Bali) for the night of 27 on 28 February. After all, the Japanese air superiority prior to an invasion of Java needed to be degraded as much as possible.[6]

The final arrangements on air support for Doorman

Almost at the exact moment that Doorman arrived at the entrance to the Westervaarwater north of Soerabaja at around 14:00 hrs, ABDA-FLOAT and JAC were deciding on the arrangements for air support for the allied squadron during the coming attack on the Japanese invasion fleet. This was in fact an update of the previous night's planning. A complete squadron from Ngoro, consisting of 15 fighter aircraft, was to give support to Doorman during his attack on the Japanese transport fleet. Douglas A-24 dive bombers were to first locate the fleet and then carry out the initial attack. *East Group* was given the task to further work out the planned air support mission and initial attack by the A-24s. JAC and ABDA-FLOAT were to coordinate the time of Doorman's taking to sea and the take-off times of the aircraft.[7]

In consultation with Major W.P. Fisher, the USAAF officer in charge of "Interceptor Control" at Air Defence Command Soerabaja and local Air Officer Commanding for fighter operations, *East Group* planned the deployment of the fighters and the A-24s as one mission. The role of the fighter aircraft in this was escorting the A-24s and 'cleansing' the air in the action area just before the arrival of the *Combined Striking Force*. The P-40s and Brewsters were to fly ahead of the allied war ships and give cover to the allied naval squadron against attacks from the air during the naval battle that was expected to evolve. Dependent on the outcome of this naval battle, JAC's heavy bombers were to come into action.[8]

At around 14:30 hrs Elt G.E. Kiser, acting commander of 17 Squadron and Elt De Haas, commander of the Vl.G.V detachment were given their briefing by Fisher. He detailed all the known intelligence on the Japanese ships near Bawean, talked them through the execution of the mission and gave them the take-off time and rendez-vous time for their meet up with the A-24s near Soerabaja. He also told them that the whole set-up of the mission had been talked through with the Royal Netherlands Navy at Soerabaja. Subsequently, the two pilots gave their briefings to their subordinates. Elt J.D. Dale (17 PS) was to lead one of the P-40 patrols, De Haas the Brewster patrol. Kiser would act as overall commander and also lead the other P-40 patrol.[9]

Rear-Admiral Doorman apparently did not know about the arrangements that had been made between ABDA-FLOAT and JAC at Bandoeng regarding his air support, for if he had, it is assumed, he would most probably have waited for the take-off of the aircraft. That would also possibly have given him the time to take the remaining float planes on board again (necessary for observation during artillery duels). Now he requested fighter protection at 16:00 hrs over the radio, while the fighters were already on their way. The Navy Commander Soerabaja advised Doorman that the fighter aircraft had already been deployed to cover an air raid on the Japanese transport fleet, thereby giving the impression that the fighter aircraft were not available for the protection of Doorman's squadron.

Apparently the staff room did not have a clear idea of the set-up of the mission. This may have been caused by language problems. This time Fisher himself had passed on the mission set-up, but the naval officer to whom he had been talking had apparently not quite under-stood him. A colleague of his then checked the story by telephone with Lieutenant-Colonel Ente van Gils, the commander of Air Defence Command Soerabaja. He, too, did not have the full picture and being an anti-aircraft gunner, he had little idea about air operations other than air defence. Within his command staff Major Fisher and a few other Americans formed a separate club of their own (*Interceptor Control*) and he was not allowed to interfere with their activities (operational control of the fighter aircraft other than air defence). Possibly the mistaken interpretation of the set-up of the mission within the staff room of the KM may have been the cause for not taking the initiative to deploy 'from the shore' the (slow and vulnerable) cruiser reconnaissance aircraft that had been left behind. After all, this would only have been possible in case of an expected allied air superiority over the naval squadron.[10]

It seems strange that Doorman did not know about the arrange-ments regarding his air support, but radio communication on 27 February was sometimes very difficult due to the heavy monsoon

showers with much electromagnetic activity, overloading of the network of the Signals service of the Royal Netherlands Navy and the
jamming of frequencies by the Japanese. It is possible that ABDA-
FLOAT did send a telegram containing the arrangements, but that
Doorman never received it. In hindsight, the text of the telegram
Helfrich sent to Doorman with the order to sail looks unprofessional
(unless it was preceded by a more detailed message that did not
survive time) and was certainly not very motivating and inspiring. The
order to put to sea read, "Enemy observed west of Bawean, attack"
and not more than that. No encouragement was given, nor an exact
time in accordance with the arrangements with JAC. The telegram
was simply sent at the agreed time of departure of ships and A-24
dive bombers.[11]

The battle of the Java Sea

In spite of the bad weather at first, JAC also tried to send reconnaissance reports to Rear-Admiral Doorman during the afternoon. In the
early afternoon at least two flying boats were airborne, looking fruitlessly for Japanese ships west and north-east of Bawean and other
locations. Doorman started from the last reported position and course
of the transport fleet, but instead of encountering the transport fleet,
with its transport ships and escorts, he chanced upon a Japanese
screening squadron. In fact, there were two squadrons, one consisting
of the light cruiser *Jintsu* and a number of destroyers coming from
Timor, and one consisting of the heavy cruisers *Nachi* and *Haguro*,
accompanied by two destroyers, that had been trailing the convoy and
had just managed to rendezvous with the convoy in time. On top of
that, Doorman was confronted by a part of the escort of the transport
fleet, the light cruiser *Naka* and a number of destroyers.

All in all, the Japanese had two heavy cruisers, two light cruisers
and 14 destroyers. Around 16:15 hrs Doorman engaged into battle
with his three heavy cruisers, three light cruisers and nine destroyers.[12]

As mentioned above, shortly before doing so, at around 16:00 hrs,
he requested over the radio for fighter cover. The allied fighter aircraft,
however, had already been sent off and, exactly according to plan,
escorted the three (the fourth had technical problems) Douglas A-24
dive bombers of the 27th Bombardment Group (light), led by Captain
H. Galusha, which had left from Malang at 15:00 hrs.[13]

A pre-war photograph of the cruiser *De Ruijter*, Rear-Admiral Doorman's flagship during the battle of the Java Sea. (Private collection, P.C. Boer)

At 15:15 hrs two patrols, consisting altogether of ten Curtiss P-40s of 17 Squadron and one patrol of five Brewster fighter aircraft of 1- and 2-Vl.G.V of the ML took off from Ngoro. The ML aircraft were flown by Elt G.J. de Haas, Elt H.H.J. Simons, Vdg B. Wink, Vdg C.A. Vonck and Sgt G.M. Bruggink. Near Soerabaja they had their rendezvous according to plan with the A-24s, upon which the formation began its search for the Japanese fleet. In the mean time the weather had improved somewhat and the fighter aircraft flew at an altitude of 4,800 metres.[14]

After an hour's flying the invasion fleet was found at some 60 nautical miles (over 100 kilometres) north-west of Bawean, following a southerly course. The pilots counted up to about 45 transport ships, sailing in a closely packed rectangular formation and escorted by a number of smaller war ships, which could not be identified due to the high altitude of flying. First, at about 16:30 hrs, the pilots passed over the *Combined Striking Force*, which was already in combat and a Japanese naval squadron. At roughly ten nautical miles (18 kilometres) south-east of the transport fleet they saw how the Japanese war ships and the allied ships were firing at each other. Galusha took his time searching fruitlessly for an aircraft tender or aircraft carrier, which had been reported earlier by the crews of B-17 bombers, before attacking the transport fleet.

At about 16:45 hrs the pilots of the A-24s dived down from an altitude of 3,000 metres through intensive anti-aircraft artillery, but were not very successful. Each aircraft dropped one 300-kilogramme bomb and two 50-kilogramme bombs. One transport vessel of an estimated 14,000 tons was hit, but kept sailing on. By this time some of the allied fighter aircraft had climbed out and gave cover to the allied war ships.[15]

After the bombardment the A-24s were able to fend for themselves and these aircraft flew back unescorted to Malang. One of the aircraft had been hit by anti-aircraft fire and had received light damage. The fighter aircraft all remained over the battling war fleets in order to give cover to Doorman for as long as possible. From the air it was possible to see how the two naval squadrons kept pounding each other and also that the Japanese had an advantage in the number of ships. In the enemy line there were two whoppers, battle ships, the pilots thought. In fact, they were the two heavy cruisers *Nachi* and *Haguro*. A Japanese ship, a cruiser, the pilots thought, was visibly hit and left the line only to return some time later after the fires had been extinguished. Kiser reported the events by radio to *Interceptor Control*.

It was absolutely impossible for the allied pilots to approach the Japanese squadron. If they as much as headed for this war fleet, the Japanese threw up a dense anti-aircraft barrage at them. What was annoying was that from time to time also the allied ships fired their heavy anti-aircraft guns at the P-40s and Brewsters. Clearly, Doorman did not know that the aircraft flying overhead were his allies, which is also probably the reason why the Supermarine Walrus reconnaissance planes of *Exeter* and *Perth* were not launched. As mentioned above, direct radio contact was technically impossible and the fighter pilots could do little more than report to *Interceptor Control* at Soerabaja, requesting them to pass on the message to the KM. In order to avoid any problems the allied fighter aircraft flew a wide rectangular circuit around the two battling naval squadrons at an altitude of 7,500 to 8,000 metres.[16]

There were no enemy bombers, fighters or reconnaissance aircraft to intercept. Over Balikpapan, Bali and Macassar, the home bases of the assault groups of the Japanese Navy air force, the weather was still very bad. Japanese cruiser float planes did not stand the slightest chance when they were up against the P-40s and the Brewsters, and the five that were airborne were kept far out of reach. So, not only Doorman, but also his Japanese opponent, Vice-Admiral Takeo Takagi, had to fight out the artillery duel without observation from the air.[17] When dusk was approaching the fighter aircraft withdrew at approximately 17:30 hrs in order to be able to land at Ngoro in last light. The fighter pilots were not very optimistic about the outcome of the naval battle. The position of the Japanese transport fleet was west of Bawean and it was now sailing a westerly course. Lieutenant Kiser, the American formation leader, reported the position and change of course around 17:00 hrs to *Interceptor Control* and also requested them to advise the KM that he would have to return within the foreseeable time with his fighter aircraft. Shortly after that he reported the position of the various war ships in relation to the smoke screen that had just been laid. By now it was difficult to tell from an altitude of 7,500 metres which ships belonged to their own and which to the enemy naval squadron. At 17:00 hrs Captain Galusha reported the results of the A-24s and the details about the Japanese transport fleet over the radio. Apart from the transport vessels, he mentioned three cruisers and 12 destroyers. The A-24 pilots thought they had hit three transport vessels, but this was not confirmed later by the fighter pilots. In the end, JAC settled for one direct hit and two near misses.[18]

The last allied fighter aircraft had barely left the skies when the Japanese commander sent his cruiser reconnaissance aircraft up over the *Combined Striking Force*. At around 17:45 hrs, when the allied squadron was re-forming, several planes dropped two light bombs each (without hitting anything, though) over the four American destroyers. After this there were no longer any Japanese reconnaissance planes flying over the allied squadron, *Nachi* and *Haguro* taking their planes on board. A little less than one hour later the battle, which later came to be known as the "day fight" of the battle of the Java Sea, ended.[19]

Doorman had been forced to send one of his best ships, the British heavy cruiser *Exeter*, the only allied war ship equipped with radar, back to Soerabaja, escorted by the destroyer *Witte de With*. At around 17:08 hrs the cruiser had been hit so hard that six of her eight boilers had been put out of action. It was for protection of this ship that the smoke screen observed by the fighter pilots had been laid. Furthermore, the destroyer *Kortenaer* had broken in two after a torpedo hit and sunk at 17:15 hrs. The British destroyer *Electra* sank at around 18:00 hrs. The Japanese had to withdraw the destroyer

Asagumo from the battle with rather heavy damage. Several destroyers received light damage and the heavy cruiser *Haguro* lost a cruiser reconnaissance plane in a fire on board. Measured in terms of ships remaining, Doorman was at a disadvantage, but he had by no means been defeated yet.[20]

The naval battle continued in the evening and night, later called "the night fight", during which several of the remaining allied ships were lost. Doorman did not succeed in closing in on the Japanese transport fleet. Probably at around 18:57 hrs the allied naval squadron commander requested the KM at Soerabaja for the position of the Japanese transport fleet, but this was not precisely known in Soerabaja. Apart from the report from the allied fighter and dive bomber pilots of 17:00 hrs, a flying boat of *RecGroup*, probably a Catalina of GVT 17 of the MLD, had reported 35 ships at 70 nautical miles (125 kilometres) north-west of Bawean and a further cruiser and four destroyers at 60 nautical miles (more than 100 kilometres) west of Bawean at 17:57 hrs.[21]

The Navy Commander at Soerabaja gave the order to telephone Bandoeng and Air Defence Command Soerabaja to verify this information and to check whether there were any more recent contact reports. There were not any, and the information of 17:00 hrs and 17:57 hrs was relayed (again) to Doorman by 19:30 hrs. It is not certain, though, whether he ever received these messages sent to him during the battle. Due to the bad weather radio traffic had been troubled by periods of extremely poor reception all day and sometimes there was no reception at all. At the same time, as mentioned above, the Japanese were jamming certain frequencies, among which there were the CZM frequency for ships and also the so-called "contact golf", a frequency the allied naval squadron used for ship-to-ship contact.[22]

The Navy Commander Soerabaja contacted *RecGroup* at around 19:00 hrs to check if an extra Catalina could be deployed from the west to the east, but none was available. However, Commander F.B. Wagner (U.S. Navy, deputy commander *RecGroup*) sent out Sub-Lieutenant D.A. Campbell's Catalina crew of *Patrol Wing* 10 somewhat earlier than already planned. Taking off at 19:00 hrs was pointless as there was no moon yet. Finding the Japanese ships in moonlight in the vast sea area, however, was not an easy job, either. Furthermore, at around 21:00 hrs Officier-Vlieger 2e klasse G.F. Rijnders, the commander of the stand-by crew at Morokrembangan, was summoned to the staff room, where he was given the assignment to make a reconnaissance sortie with the stand-by aircraft (the Y-67 of GVT 17) to search for the Japanese transport fleet; he took off at about 22:30 hrs.[23]

In aircraft P-5 Campbell found the Japanese transport fleet at 22:22 hrs south-west of Bawean. A contact report was immediately sent to *RecGroup*. From there the message was passed on to ABDA-FLOAT, amongst others, and subsequently to Soerabaja and Doorman via the network of the overloaded KM Signal service, whose radio connections were also disturbed by atmospheric circumstances from time to time. It did not reach the Navy Commander Soerabaja until 23:52 hrs. The crew of the Y-67 found the Japanese transport fleet at around 24:00 hrs.[24]

By that time, the light cruiser *De Ruyter*, Doorman's flagship, had already been hit by a torpedo at 23:34 hrs. Doorman had not been able to find the Japanese transport fleet and had gone into battle with the Japanese screening squadrons with their superior numbers of cruisers and destroyers. The allied fleet lost two light cruisers that night, *Java* and *De Ruyter*, and the British destroyer *Jupiter*, whereas the Japanese did not suffer any losses during the night battle. The role of the allied naval forces in the defence of Java was over. Doorman and more than 1,000 seamen had perished or gone missing. The naval battle and the discovery of the *Western Striking Force* by a Japanese cruiser float plane had won the defenders of Java a respite of one day.[25]

The report on the outcome of the naval battle did not reach the headquarters at Bandoeng until the morning of 28 February 1942. That is why at first the scheduled reconnaissance missions by *RecGroup* went on as planned. Shortly after sunrise the Y-67 and the P-5 returned at Morokrembangan and a shelter in the environment of Soerabaja, respectively. The planned daylight reconnaissance sorties of Dornier flying boats of GVT 6 became search and rescue missions for the survivors of the naval battle.[26]

Summary

The deployment of the allied naval squadron against the Japanese invasion fleet discovered in the Macassar Strait had been thoroughly planned with regard to the cooperation of naval and air forces. JAC provided a daylight fighter cover from Ngoro and an increased number of reconnaissance sorties by flying boats and bombers. The protection of the naval squadron was given the highest priority, which, however, meant that there was no fighter protection for the aircraft tender *Langley* on 27 February 1942, with 32 American P-40 fighter aircraft on board destined for JAC.

Although the day fight of the naval battle did not go all that badly and JAC was able to keep up a local air superiority for almost the entire duration of it, the Battle of the Java Sea continued into the evening and night. This night fight definitely was disastrous for the allies. The *Combined Striking Force* was partly lost with great loss of life.

* * *

CHAPTER 2.3

The Events and Operations in western and eastern Java on 28 February 1942

Introduction

After the discovery of large numbers of Japanese combat aircraft at Palembang by bombers of *Java Air Command* (JAC) on 27 February 1942, the allied headquarters did no longer assume that the Japanese invasion of Java might possibly take place with initial landings in eastern Java only. JAC was aware that the *Combined Striking Force* had fought a battle with a Japanese naval squadron in the afternoon of 27 February, but there was no information on how that clash had developed. JAC did receive, through *RecGroup*, the results of the reconnaissance missions of two Catalina flying boats which had reconnoitred the Japanese invasion fleet approaching eastern Java in the evening and night of 27 February.

Around midnight all available information on the Japanese advance was lined up at the Combined Operations and Intelligence Centre (COIC). The conclusion was that enemy landings in western and eastern Java and even during that same night (the early hours of 28 February 1942) were a distinct possibility. Much, however, would still depend on the naval battle in the east, the outcome of which was still unknown. Besides, the *Western Striking Force* (three cruisers and three destroyers) and two Catalinas of the MLD were still probing for the invasion fleet expected in the west. On the basis of the analysis of COIC JAC gave new orders to the ML Command and BRITAIR, and the American *East Group* in central and eastern Java.[1]

Relocations of bombers in western Java

Between 01:00 hrs and 02:00 hrs the commander of Tjisaoek airfield, Elt F.R. Lettinga (also the commander of the Glenn Martin afdeling 2-Vl.G.III based at this airfield) was alerted. He was given the order by his Commandant Luchtstrijdkrachten–local Air Officer Commanding (CL) to destroy this airfield with its location rather far to the west and close to the expected Japanese landing locations, and to relocate the four bombers of the ML at Tjisaoek to Tasikmalaja. A bit later this was changed into three bombers to Kemajoran and one to Kalidjati. There the crews had to go on readiness for night bombing raids against an invasion fleet that was approaching Java. The order to destroy Tjisaoek was repeated.[2]

Also in the very early hours of 28 February 36 Squadron RAF at Tjikampek, with its ten Vildebeest and Albacore light bombers only suitable for night attacks, was given the order to prepare for a relocation to Madioen (central Java) in order to support the Americans of *East Group* (V *Bomber Command*) from there. In the first instance, the bombers of the ML and the RAF at Kalidjati were to be relocated to Tasikmalaja, just like 2-Vl.G.III, but this order was rescinded after a short time. Subsequently, the crews of the operationally serviceable two Hudsons, ten Blenheims (including a few Mark Is only suitable for night attacks) and six Glenn Martins of the ML, which had been on duty since 19:00 hrs (on 27 February), were kept on stand-by.[3]

Between 04:00 hrs and 05:00 hrs in the morning of 28 February JAC received the news that the *Combined Striking Force* had been defeated. It was assumed that the allied fleet had inflicted considerable damage on the Japanese and *RecGroup* confirmed that the Japanese transport fleet had sailed north during the naval battle. The invasion of eastern Java was now expected in the night of 28 February and 1 March 1942. 36 Squadron could still be relocated in time and was now given the order to move. Nine aircraft arrived at Madioen in the middle of the afternoon of 28 February. *East Group* was given the order to bomb the eastern Japanese invasion fleet, which had been shadowed by a Catalina of the MLD until shortly before sunrise, with all its available bombers.[4]

At 06:40 hrs the three operationally serviceable B-17s took off from Madioen, one of which returned to base because of a malfunctioning of its machine gun turrets. The other two carried out attacks on the 34 transport ships reported by the American crews and 11 war ships. One transport vessel was claimed sunk and a second received a direct hit. Several other B-17s were airworthy but not operationally serviceable and had been used during the night and morning for evacuation of USAAF personnel to Broome in northern Australia. The LB-30s, one of which was operationally serviceable, were used exclusively for night missions from 27 February 1942 onwards.[5]

The *Western Striking Force* and the Catalinas of *RecGroup* in the west still had not found any trace of Japanese ships. This was one of the reasons that it was decided in the morning of 28 February 1942 to repeat the attack on Palembang I airfield which had failed the previous day. This time BRITAIR would execute the mission with a section of Blenheim bombers, while JAC intended to deploy the Glenn Martins, which had shown themselves to be vulnerable in daylight attacks on P I when not escorted, in the evening of 28 February.[6]

The availability of fighter aircraft

Two 'survivors' of the battle of the Java Sea, the cruisers *Houston* and *Perth*, were en route to Tandjong Priok and were expected there in the course of the morning. JAC was given the order to give them fighter protection as soon as they came within range. ABDA-FLOAT was to pass on the necessary information on this.[7] At Soerabaja the cruiser *Exeter*, which had incurred damage in the naval battle, and seven destroyers, among which the American destroyer *Pope*, which had not taken part in the battle, were lying at anchor. The fighter aircraft of JAC at Ngoro were given the task to supply a daytime air cover of the harbour complex, as had been done before on 26 February. The war ships at Soerabaja were to make evasion attempts in the evening of 28 February 1942.[8]

In the morning of 28 February 1942 the strength of JAC of available and operationally serviceable fighter aircraft was as follows:[9]

Table 18

	Type	Assigned	Operationally servicable	Remarks
Western Java				
242/605 Sq	Hurricane	15	13	
1-Vl.G.V	Brewster	5 (+2)	5 (+2)	(+Hawk)
2-Vl.G.V	Brewster	4	3	
2-Vl.G.IV	Interceptor	4	3	
Eastern Java				
17 PS	Warhawk	13	12	
Vl.G.V	Brewster	6	6	
2-Vl.G.IV	Hurricane	7	0	Not operational

The protection of Houston and Perth

The Brewster fighter aircraft of the ML at Andir (Bandoeng) were to be the first to give cover to the two allied cruisers steaming to Tandjong Priok. For this purpose four aircraft had been ready for take-off at Andir as of 05:00 hrs. At Tjililitan (Batavia) five Hurricanes of the RAF were ready to take over from the Brewsters.[10] It was a problem, though, that ABDA-FLOAT had actually only a vague idea of the position of the two cruisers. In the course of the morning the Commandant Luchtstrijdkrachten–local Air Officer Commanding (CL) at Andir was given the order to start looking for the two allied war ships with one of the Brewsters that was on readiness.

To this end an unknown Brewster pilot carried out a seaward reconnaissance as far as 100 kilometres out to sea. It remained a bit like looking for a needle in a haystack and with the clouds forming it was an open question whether he would succeed in finding the cruisers. And he did not.[11]

By the end of the morning, some 90 kilometres from the roadstead of Priok, the captain of the *Perth* reported that the ships had been discovered and he requested fighter cover. From time to time a cruiser float plane was spotted flying at low altitude on the horizon. British Hurricanes immediately took up the protection of the ships and started flying towards them. However, no further enemy aircraft were seen.[12] The patrol at Andir did not come into action.[13]

Three Curtiss-Wright CW-21B Interceptors of the patrol of 2-Vl.G.IV at Andir and the remaining four (later three) Brewsters at Andir formed a readiness flight, commanded by Kap J.H. van Helsdingen, the commanding officer of 2-Vl.G.V. There were no air raids on Andir or Kalidjati (or on Tjililitan) on this day. The Brewster B-3101, the aircraft of Vdg P. R. Jolly of 2-Vl.G.V, was sent to the Technical Service in the course of the day after a serious engine failure during the periodic run up of the engine.[14]

On 28 February the strength in operationally serviceable Hurricanes at Tjililitan was 13 aircraft. Eight fighters were assigned to the air defence and, as mentioned above, five had been assigned as cover for the two cruisers. In the course of the morning the five Hurricanes took off to carry out seaward reconnaissance missions and to fly top cover over *Perth* and *Houston*, which were finally approaching Batavia by this time.[15] They arrived in the roadstead of Tandjong Priok at around 14:00 hrs. Shortly before this the KM destroyer *Evertsen* had arrived in the harbour to take in fuel. This ship had joined the *Western Striking Force* (WSF), which had been in a nightly probing mission into the direction of Banka. When no enemy was found, the four British cruisers and destroyers together with the Australian cruiser *Hobart* of the WSF, in accordance with instructions from ABDA-FLOAT, diverted to Ceylon, via the Soenda Strait making a stop-over at Padang.[16]

Hurricanes kept flying patrols all afternoon as a cover for the war ships. This was no easy task, as by now there were heavy, though broken, cloud formations. At least two British fighter aircraft were airborne at any time.[17] When pilots were guiding the cruisers through the mine fields into the harbour, some crew members saw at a distance a Japanese double-decker float plane firing at a small Dutch patrol boat, without the pilots of the two Hurricanes flying high above the ships noticing this. As was explained in the previous chapter, communication between ships and fighter aircraft was impossible, so that the fighter pilots could not be warned.[18]

In the second half of the afternoon the cruisers, after having carefully negotiated a route among various ship wrecks in the harbour, moored to take in oil and ammunition. When another double-decker appeared, the crew aboard *Houston* thought it was its expected Curtiss SOC-3 reconnaissance float plane that was on its way from Soerabaja. It was not, but this time the aircraft was within range of the allied anti-aircraft artillery at Tandjong Priok and also the ships opened fire, unfortunately enough also on their own two fighter aircraft over the harbour. Twenty minutes later the Curtiss plane of *Houston* landed safely in the roadstead, in spite of a barrage from the anti-aircraft artillery of the harbour front. The Hurricanes, too, remained undamaged.[19]

The protection of the war ships at Soerabaja

For the protection of the harbour complex at Soerabaja 12 P-40s and four Brewsters had been kept on Readiness as of 05:00 hrs when at 09:00 hrs an alert came to intercept enemy aircraft approaching Soerabaja. Nothing was found and at around 11:00 hrs the fighter aircraft returned, having nothing to show for their pains. Furthermore, two Brewsters were assigned to carry out seaward reconnaissance missions or top cover missions for the ships, but it is not known whether these aircraft actually came into action.[20]

At 14:10 hrs there was another scramble; this time ten P-40s and four Brewsters, flown by Elt G.J. de Haas, Elt H.H.J. Simons, Vdg B. Wink and Vdg C.A. Vonck. *Interceptor Control* had reported that 12 enemy bombers, escorted by nine Navy Os were approaching Soerabaja. Two P-40s could not take off because of mechanical failures, while engine trouble forced one P-40 to return on the flight out. The remaining P-40s could not reach the bombers as they were flying at too high an altitude. The Brewsters had a somewhat higher ceiling and struggled their way up.[21]

At an altitude of about 6,500 metres the slowly climbing ML aircraft were surprised by the Navy Os. Diving from a higher altitude and from the cover of a large cumulo-nimbus cloud, they attacked the Brewsters. The battle position was hopeless. Already in the first attack run Simons' aircraft received hits through the fuselage and wing, even before he had had a chance to fire at his opponents. The same happened to Vonck. Somewhat to the south of Soerabaja a turning fight ensued, from which the ML pilots withdrew as soon as they could by diving away. At an altitude of 6,500 metres the Japanese aircraft proved to be somewhat more manoeuvrable than the Brewsters. There were no personal losses, but on the flight back Vonck was forced to bail out because his engine, which possibly had received a hit, seized up. The nine Navy Os were from the Tainan Kokutai and had escorted 12 G4M bombers that had come from Macassar. One of the fighter aircraft pilots was the famous ace Saburo Sakai.[22]

Vonck made it safely back to Ngoro, while Simons flew his aircraft to Madioen for repairs of the damage at the Technical Service workshop there. The next day he transferred to a Brewster which had been delivered by Sgt H. Huys at Ngoro in the afternoon of 28 February. The Japanese bombs fell on the already badly destroyed Naval Air Station of Morokrembangan and the adjacent but abandoned ML airfield at Tandjong Perak.[23]

The escape of the allied war ships was only successful to a certain extent. The four American destroyers that had had taken part in the battle of the Java Sea sneaked through the Madoera Strait and the Bali Strait and made good their escape to Australia. The *Exeter* and two destroyers first sailed east along the northern coast of Madoera and then took a northerly course. They were intercepted by a Japanese naval squadron, were simultaneously attacked from the air, and perished. The Dutch destroyer *Witte de With* stayed behind at Soerabaja with a vibrating propeller shaft and was destroyed by her own crew in the naval docks on 2 March 1942.[24]

The western invasion fleet is finally discovered

Around midday on 28 February 1942 a Catalina of *RecGroup* and Blenheim bombers of BRITAIR discovered the western invasion fleet, which had been predicted by COIC on the basis of reconnaissance reports and information from the *Intelligence* section of the AHK. At approximately 100 nautical miles (180 kilometres) north-east of Batavia 11 transport ships were sailing an easterly course and about 30 nautical miles (50 kilometres) to the south on a parallel course one cruiser and three destroyers. North-west of Batavia and some 85 nautical miles (150 kilometres) north of St. Nicolaaspunt three Blenheim bombers, on their way to raid Palembang I, flew by a much larger convoy, consisting of 50 to 60 transport vessels, escorted by a large number of war ships and a ship that looked like an aircraft carrier. This convoy sailed a more southerly course at a speed of about 15 knots. An invasion in the night of 28 February on 1 March 1942 was now certain. It was clear the Japanese intended to land on both sides of Batavia. In the afternoon several more groups of ships were discovered. JAC relocated four of its Blenheim bombers from Kalidjati to Andir, in order to be able to deploy them from there.[25]

The three Blenheims that attacked PI had left Kalidjati around 10:30 hrs when the bad weather of that morning had improved somewhat. The aircraft flew by a large Japanese invasion fleet, on their way out (at around noon) as well as their return flight (about 14:00 hrs). The heavy clouds made it impossible to indicate the exact size and composition of the convoy and its escort. After the crews had been debriefed, it was assessed that there were about 50 transport vessels (not counting the escort) on a southerly course, spotted during the flight out, and some 30 to 40 transport vessels north of St. Nicolaaspunt, but a bit further to the south and on an easterly course, which had been spotted by the crews that had returned individually after their raid on Palembang. Incidentally, the raid on Palembang I had not been successful due to heavy clouds there.[26]

In hindsight, the destruction of Tjisaoek had been somewhat premature. The abandonment of this airfield, which was located close to the expected landing sites in the west, had cost a Brewster fighter aircraft. A detachment of about 20 ground crew of 2-Vl.G.V was still at the airfield with a Brewster which had just been prepared for flying to Andir for further repairs. However, there was no pilot at Tjisaoek as yet and in the morning, in line with the repeated order to destroy the airfield, Elt Lettinga ordered the mechanics of 2-Vl.G.V to destroy this plane, too.[27]

In the evening of 28 February Java Air Command still had the planned final night raids on Palembang I carried out, in order to degrade the Japanese air superiority over western Java as much as possible prior to the invasion. From then on, all efforts in the west were directed at fighting off the Japanese landing operations. The deployment of the combat aircraft in the west against these operations will be described in the following part (the Battle of Kalidjati). The two allied cruisers at Batavia were not committed by ABDA-FLOAT against the Japanese landing operations, but were ordered to try to escape together with *Evertsen* to Tjilatjap via the Soenda Strait. The ships left port in the evening only to end up right in the midst of the Japanese landing operation in the Bantam Bay to the west of Batavia. Their fate will be briefly described in the following part.

The final bombing raids on P I

The night bombing raids on Palembang I were carried out by a Glenn Martin of 3-Vl.G.III from Kemajoran and a Glenn Martin of 1-Vl.G.I from Kalidjati, flown by Tlt J. Coblijn and Elt F.J.W. den Ouden, respectively. Coblijn was the first to take off from Kemajoran at last

light. Both bombers were armed with nine 50-kilogramme fragmentation bombs for a maximum spread of the bomb pattern. The crews
could drop their bombs over the target without any problems, there
being no enemy resistance. Results could not be observed due to the
bad light, but judging from the visible bomb impacts the bomb patterns
lay within the perimeter of the airfield for both bombers. While this
raid was going on, all remaining operationally serviceable bombers
were taking off from Kalidjati, Andir and Kemajoran to attack the approaching Japanese invasion fleets.[28]

The bomber of the Coblijn crew returned safely at Kemajoran
between 23:00 hrs and 24:00 hrs. The aircraft of the Den Ouden
crew returned at Kalidjati at around 01:00 hrs (on 1 March), only to
be committed again, after refuelling and a short rest for the crew, in
a night mission against a Japanese invasion fleet near Eretan Wetan.
Coblijn flew his aircraft back to Andir by sunrise, and the plane was
also committed against the Japanese invasion fleet at Eretan Wetan with
a fresh crew.[29]

Summary

On 28 February 1942 the JAC fighter aircraft were also largely committed for the protection of war ships. At Ngoro in eastern Java all
12, later ten, operationally serviceable P-40s of 17 Squadron and four
Brewsters of the ML seconded with this unit stood at readiness to
intercept air raids on the naval harbour of Soerabaja. They came into
action two times, one of which actually evolved into aerial combat.
One Brewster was lost and a second was damaged. The four American
destroyers that had fought in the battle of the Java Sea managed to
get away, whereas the escape of the British *Exeter* and two destroyers
escorting was foiled. Four of the Brewsters at Andir and five of the
British Hurricanes at Tjililitan flew seaward reconnaissance sorties
and provided top cover for the cruisers *Houston* and *Perth*, which were
en route to and subsequently lay at anchor in the roadstead and harbour
of Tandjong Priok in western Java.

On 28 February 1942 the bombers of JAC were positioned as
well as possible to withstand the approaching Japanese invasion. In
the early hours of that day still no trace had been found of a 'western'
invasion fleet and at Bandoeng it was still assumed that the main threat
would come from the east. 36 Squadron RAF was ordered to relocate
to Madioen in central Java. All operationally serviceable (three at that

moment) American heavy bombers of *East Group* attacked the 'eastern' invasion fleet in the morning of 28 February. It was the intention to keep up these attacks together with 36 Squadron RAF in the evening and night of 28 February on 1 March 1942. In the west three Blenheims of 84 Squadron RAF carried out a bombing raid against Palembang I airfield in the morning. During their flight out as well as their return flight the aircraft flew by the 'western' invasion fleet. The attack on P I failed due to the heavy clouds. In the evening it was repeated with more success by two Glenn Martins of the ML. In the mean time, all remaining bombers in western Java were committed against the 'western' invasion fleet, which had been discovered around midday.

* * *

CHAPTER 2.4

The Air Support during the Battle of the Java Sea, an Analysis and Some Conclusions

The effectiveness of the allied air support

Rear-Admiral Doorman had depended to a large extent on the recon-naissance reports from the flying boats and bombers of *RecGroup* and *East Group* of JAC, respectively. On 27 February flying boats eventually discovered the Japanese transport fleet with its escort west of Bawean, but they could not find the screening squadron of this invasion fleet. Although there were only few operationally serviceable flying boats and bombers left, these low numbers did not constitute the only problems.

For many hours on end the allied crews searched large expanses of sea, but in the morning and early afternoon of 27 February they were being hindered in their task by extremely bad weather. The weather conditions in the afternoon, however, also made it impossible for the Japanese Navy air force to carry out any operations from Balikpapan, Bali and Macassar over the eastern part of the Java Sea and in the direction of Soerabaja. In the morning some missions did take off from Bali, though, and they were used to make reconnaissance flights and to sink *Langley*.

The deployment of allied flying boats was severely limited by the almost complete lack of reserve crews and maintenance requirements. For this reason each time only two, sometimes three, flying boats were sent up at the same time to support the *Combined Striking Force* operation (also during the night fight), and even a flying boat had to come all the way from Batavia to the east. The American heavy bombers were put on readiness as of around 15:00 hrs on 27 February 1942 to carry out attacks on the Japanese transport fleet (the invasion was expected to take place the coming night) and from then on they were not available anymore for reconnaissance purposes, as the small number of bombers left did not allow simultaneous reconnaissance missions.

The Catalina and Dornier crews flew reconnaissance missions of up to 10 or 12 hours at a time, after which they could not be deployed for a day. In order to retain a certain standard of effectiveness during such protracted missions, two to three extra men were taken along on top of the normal crew. This was done to give the observers some time off during the flight. Because of the long duration of the reconnaissance missions the flying boats also made many flying hours and were quickly up for their scheduled 50-hour and 100-hour maintenance. This meant that, apart from the necessary repairs, one in three flying boats was continually in maintenance. The obligatory and absolutely essential rest periods for the crews brought the effective deployment even further down.[1]

At staff level the cooperation between the air and naval forces was good on 27 February 1942 and well organised, but in its execution there were (technical) limitations. As was explained above, there were only few operationally serviceable flying boats available for long-range reconnaissance missions, but for as long as it was able to JAC made up for this shortage by committing bombers. In the east, even, all operationally serviceable bombers were assigned to armed reconnaissance missions. Unfortunately, one B-17 bomber bombed (without hitting anything, incidentally) a British destroyer of the allied naval squadron, as a result of an error in communication. Although in his memoirs in 1950 Lieutenant-Admiral (ret.) Helfrich wrote regarding the air support for Doorman, "It did not come, nor did it come later that day", this is at odds with what really happened.[2]

On 26 and 27 February 1942 Rear-Admiral Doorman received air support from all operationally serviceable fighter aircraft at Ngoro. These had been kept on readiness all day on 26 February to intercept Japanese air raids on the naval docks, when the allied squadron was taking in fuel, and flew seaward reconnaissance missions in order to ensure that the squadron could put to sea again safely. On 27 February 1942 during the day fight in the Battle of the Java Sea the P-40s and Brewsters provided air cover for the CSF and prevented aerial observation by Japanese cruiser float planes, while three American A-24 dive bombers attacked the Japanese transport vessels.

The air support during the night

Just like the Japanese, the allied fighter aircraft could only be deployed during daylight. However, the availability of air support also played a role during the night fight. The Japanese fleet had a few cruiser float planes suitable for operations at night. Thanks to these nocturnal reconnaissance flights, partially carried out by means of parachute flares, Vice-Admiral Takagi managed to keep his squadron between Doorman's squadron and the Japanese transport fleet and be informed, at least until 22:00 hrs, of the manoeuvre of the allied war ships.

Doorman did not have any cruiser float planes suitable for night missions and, with the exception of *Exeter*'s and *Perth*'s aircraft, did not even have any on board. As he had foreseen a night fight early on, he had sent the other aircraft to a shelter in the environment of Soerabaja (probably as early as 26 February). The allied cruiser float planes could have been deployed on 27 February during daylight from the Naval Air Station or a shelter, but possibly as a result of a wrong perception of the mission of the A-24s and allied fighter aircraft by the Royal Netherlands Navy at Soerabaja, this did not happen.

During night time the Japanese only had a very limited reconnaissance capacity. The two heavy cruisers *Nachi* and *Haguro* had three reconnaissance planes each, two Mitsubishi F1Ms for a crew of two and one Aichi E13A1 for a crew of three, which could, however, only be deployed during the day. Of these six aircraft one was lost during the day fight (on board *Haguro*). The other five were taken back on board again as of 18.57 hrs. After that the only aircraft available were those of the (light) cruisers *Jintsu* and *Naka*. Each cruiser had one reconnaissance plane that could also be employed at night. The aircraft of the former ship reconnoitred first, to be relieved by that of *Naka*. However, contact with the latter plane was lost around 22:00 hrs, while the actual night fight did not begin before 23:00 hrs. In other words, aerial reconnaissance by the Japanese did not play any role in the loss of the cruisers *De Ruyter* and *Java*, both hit by one or more torpedoes around 22:30 hrs.[3]

Neither during the day fight, nor during the most important phase of the night fight, did the Japanese fleet have any effective aerial reconnaissance. In contrast to the allies, the Japanese did not receive any support from their own combat aircraft during the day fight of the naval battle, either.

Allied communication problems

A major problem on the side of the allies was communication. It was technically impossible to maintain radio communication between fighter aircraft or bombers of JAC and allied war ships. For this reason the transmission of messages between, for example, the fighter aircraft of Ngoro and Doorman first went by radio of the aircraft commander to *Interceptor Control*, was then relayed by phone to the staff room of the Navy Commander Soerabaja, and transmitted from there to Doorman. Moreover, radio communication on 27 February was regularly troubled by interference from atmospheric conditions and Japanese jamming of navy frequencies.

In the delays that regularly occurred in the transmission of messages between flying boats, on the one hand, and Doorman and the Navy staff room at Soerabaja, on the other, overloading of the KM Signal service also played a part. In the evening of 27 February 1942 the communication failed at a crucial moment, as a result of which reconnaissance reports from *RecGroup* did not reach Doorman in time. Had he received them, Doorman, in theory at least, might have been able to carry out an attack on the Japanese transport ships after all.

Some conclusions

Absence of direct allied air support was not one of the reasons why Doorman perished with his naval squadron. The allied naval squadron was in fact the only side during the day fight to be supported by its own fighter aircraft, making it impossible for the Japanese cruiser float planes to make aerial observations during the artillery duels. Doorman, in fact, had his own temporary air superiority, though this may have dawned on him only at a very late moment, when he saw the reports of the fighter pilots that had been passed on to him. It is also possible that he never received those and other messages sent to him. Allied air support for most of the day fight (until around 17:30 hrs) was relatively extensive and effective. However, in order to maintain such a relatively extensive air support for the *Combined Striking Force*, choices had to be made, robbing the aircraft tender *Langley* of her fighter protection.

The conclusion of some authors that the *Combined Striking Force* was probably continually shadowed by at least one Japanese aircraft, except perhaps around 19:00 hrs, is not correct.[4] Around 07:30 hrs the allied naval squadron was discovered by a Japanese G4M bomber. This was the first and only reconnaissance by a land aircraft. From shortly after 10:30 hrs a Japanese reconnaissance float plane shadowed the naval squadron and this went on until about 15:30 hrs. During the day fight Vice-Admiral Takagi kept his five airborne reconnaissance aircraft out of the way in view of the cover that was being provided to the allied naval squadron by the 15 American and Netherlands East Indies fighter aircraft. Several of the Japanese float planes briefly ventured once over the naval squadron after the departure of the allied fighter aircraft to drop their light bombs, but then had to return to be tackled back on board their cruisers. Therefore, the Japanese did not have continual information through aerial reconnaissance on the manoeuvre of the allied naval squadron.

During the night fight there was always only one Japanese reconnaissance plane flying over the allied squadron. As of 22:00 hrs contact with this plane was lost. Apart from a brief exchange of hostilities that began around 19:30 hrs with probably no hits on both sides, the actual night fight of the Battle of the Java Sea did not begin until around 23:00 hrs. So, also during this most crucial part of the night fight the Japanese did not have the advantage of aerial reconnaissance.

In the mean time, an American flying boat had re-discovered the Japanese transport fleet, but due to delays in communication this message did not reach Doorman. The fact that Doorman did not succeed in his efforts to engage the Japanese transport fleet had much to do with the small number of deployable flying boats of *RecGroup*. There simply were not enough of them available, while JAC did not have enough bombers to keep on using these aircraft, vital for attacking the Japanese transport fleet and the landing operation, to expand the reconnaissance capacity. JAC could only do this until about 15:00 hrs and no longer. Doorman could not find the transport fleet by himself and in the night of 27 February 1942 he was confronted with superior numbers of Japanese cruisers and destroyers.

PART 3

❧❧

The Battle of Kalidjati

*The battle between the allied and Japanese land
and air forces for possession of Kalidjati airbase
in the period of 28 February up to and including
3 March 1942*

༁༁

CHAPTER 3.1

Introduction

The risky Japanese attack

In the night of 28 February on 1 March 1942, in the middle of the 'wet' monsoon season, the Japanese troops landed in Java and the last phase in the final battle for the Netherlands East Indies began. In western Java, where the centre of gravity of the battle lay and where the bulk of the KNIL and allied troops in Java had been concentrated, landings took place near Merak and in the Bay of Bantam, the western-most part of Java, as well as near Eretan Wetan on the north coast of western Java. The Japanese army did not land in western Java with a great superiority in numbers. In total, it put 23,500 men ashore, while the allied land forces in western Java amounted to more than 27,000 combat-ready troops. It was the air forces in particular that were going to decide which way the balance would go with regard to the outcome of the battle.[1]

The landing at Eretan Wetan was the most dangerous of all the landings as it constituted a direct threat to the defence of Bandoeng, where all important military and civilian headquarters were concentrated. The town was situated on the Bandoeng or Preanger plateau, which, with its many military warehouses and workshops, was the logistic centre of the KNIL. With regard to the positioning of the troops, a landing at Eretan Wetan had not been reckoned with. Especially in the wet season the coastal area near this location with its high surf was less suitable for a landing operation. Forced by a great shortage of troops, the allied land forces had taken a conscious risk.

The threat, however, became already acute on 1 March, when the large air base of Kalidjati, some 50 kilometres inland, fell into the hands of the Japanese Shoji (named after its commander Colonel Toshinari Shoji) detachment. The detachment was, in fact, a regimental battle group. Shoji's main task was cutting the link between the allied troops at Batavia and those at Bandoeng by taking Krawang and the nearby bridge on the Tjitaroem River. The Japanese, too, consciously accepted a risk by landing at Eretan Wetan, as it was here that the important coastal road (part of the advance route) came very close to the beach. From 2 March onwards the remaining available allied air forces assigned to the defence of western Java (which had been deployed as of 28 February against the Japanese invasion fleets and landing operations, especially those at Eretan Wetan) were not only deployed against the Japanese advance from Eretan Wetan to the west, but also against the captured Kalidjati airbase. The KNIL did its utmost on 2 and 3 March 1942 to try and recapture Kalidjati. The series of battles between allied and Japanese air and land forces for possession of the airbase in period between 28 February and 3 March 1942 is known as the Battle of Kalidjati.

The 3rd Hiko Dan at Kalidjati

Already in the late afternoon of 2 March 1942 the 3rd Hiko Dan (air brigade) of the Japanese Army air force, which operated from Palembang in southern Sumatra, transferred the first three fighter aircraft and six assault aircraft to Kalidjati. The 3rd Hiko Dan was a composite force, consisting mainly of Ki-43 fighter aircraft, Ki-48 light bombers, Ki-15 and Ki-46 reconnaissance planes and Ki-51 assault aircraft. On 3 March Kalidjati had been sufficiently supplied to station the main force of the 3rd Hiko Dan there, and in the morning of that day again a number of Japanese aircraft arrived at the base.

The Japanese air forces had a considerable superiority of numbers in combat aircraft, the units of which would be deployed in principle to support the invasion troops in western Java. The vulnerable Shoji detachment (only 3,000-man strong, including the combat train) operated behind the main allied lines at a large distance from the Japanese main force, which had landed much further to the west, and was therefore dependent on air support. In view of the large distance and generally bad weather this could not be provided from southern Sumatra. Possession of Kalidjati, therefore, was essential for the Japanese.

From 19 February 1942 onwards the Japanese Army air force, in cooperation with the Navy air force, had been pounding air fields in western Java, in order to attain air superiority prior to the landings. It was felt that this effort had been successful eventually, even though it had been necessary to postpone the landings by several days. For this reason the Japanese Army air force decided that the risk of positioning the main force of the 3rd Hiko Dan on the captured airfield of Kalidjati was slight.[2] The Japanese had indeed realised an air superiority, but it was no way near as total as was thought, and, on top of that, it could not be maintained on 1 and 2 March 1942 due to the bad weather over southern Sumatra and western Java and the fact that the captured airbase of Kalidjati was not ready for use yet.

Subsequently, the ML and the RAF gave the Japanese air brigade a tough time of it at Kalidjati at a crucial moment (in the evening of 2 March and the morning of 3 March) and in fact there was even a local allied air superiority until around 11:00 hrs on 3 March. Thus, in an allied bombing raid on Kalidjati on 2 March all fighter aircraft that had been flown there by the Japanese Army air force were destroyed or damaged shortly after their arrival. Initially, therefore, allied fighter aircraft and bombers were successful in their air support of the KNIL, which was advancing on Kalidjati on 3 March with a reinforced infantry regiment, supported by a secondary attack carried out by a battalion-size force on the nearby Soebang. The Japanese reinforced battalion (minus) at Kalidjati and Soebang was engaged by greatly superior numbers.[3] On 3 March 1942, at around 11:00 hrs, the tide began to turn for the allies. The Japanese carried out an extremely heavy bombing raid on Andir, from which base all support missions for the advancing KNIL troops were flown. In one fell swoop the allied local air superiority evaporated. In hindsight, it meant the beginning of the end.

✳ ✳ ✳

CHAPTER 3.2

The Allied Organisation, Strategy and Resources

Introduction

The allied command structure which had been established in the middle of January 1942 for the south-western Pacific area (including northern

Australia from 5 February 1942) got Dutch officers in all the top functions. General Wavell's general headquarters at Lembang was vacated
on 23 and 24 February and disbanded administratively on 25 February
1942. Only a few specific sections, such as the allied Combat Operations and Intelligence Centre (COIC), the allied combat intelligence
cell, were left intact and incorporated elsewhere. COIC came to fall
under Java Air Command.[1]

For the rest, the allied command structure still remained as it had
been, but it was down-sized on 22 February 1942. The General Headquarters (AHK) at Bandoeng of the KNIL commander, Lieutenant-
General H. ter Poorten, was assigned the tasks of the deactivated
headquarters of Wavell's. Ter Poorten was already commander of the
allied land forces and he now became Commander-in-Chief ABDA
Area; in the modern lingo, the Joint Forces Commander or Theatre
Commander.

The allied air force headquarters ABDAIR at Bandoeng was
transformed into the considerably smaller Java Air Command (JAC),
with Major-General L.H. van Oyen as Air Officer Commanding, the
present-day joint forces air component commander. Until that moment
Van Oyen had been the ML commander and on the evening of 22
February he assumed his new position. At the same time, Colonel
E.T. Kengen, the commander of the ML Command, also located at
Bandoeng (the staff which controlled the entire operational part of
the ML), became acting commander ML. JAC encompassed three
subordinate staffs, BRITAIR (the logistics and operational head-
quarters of all RAF and RAAF units) and the ML Command in western
Java, and *East Group* (the logistics and operational headquarters of all
USAAF units) in central and eastern Java. Directly under JAC came
the *Reconnaissance Group* (*RecGroup*), a small staff that controlled the
flying boats of the Dutch Naval Air Service (MLD), the RAF and the
United States Navy (disbanded in early March due to the evacuation
of the remaining flying boats), the Air Defence Commands of Batavia,
Bandoeng and Soerabaja, and all anti-aircraft artillery units in Java.

JAC, BRITAIR and COIC were all located in one and the same
building at Bandoeng, the vacated premises of the Royal Netherlands
Military Academy in Houtmanlaan in the eastern part of the town.
This was several kilometres away from the vacated complex of the
Bandoeng Technical University in the northern part of the town, where
the General Headquarters and the headquarters of the Navy commander in the Netherlands East Indies were situated. The so-called Air
support coordination for the ground forces (procedures and regulations

for requesting and granting of air support) had been derived from a routine introduced in the middle of 1941 by the RAF in northern Africa. Within the framework of this coordination an ML liaison officer was assigned to the General Headquarters, as well as *Bandoeng Group* and *West Group* (see below). This organisation was extremely modern at the time. The available resources, however, were very few.[2]

The overall defence plan

On Wavell's departure the General Staff of the KNIL, by order of Ter Poorten, reviewed the defence plans for Java, which in actual fact had been given up by the allies. Except for what was already on its way, there would be no further allied reinforcements to be reckoned with. The promised Australian army corps, was given a different destination, except for those units that had already arrived in Java. In particular two locations qualified especially for the defence against an expected Japanese superiority in numbers. They were the Soerabaja naval base and the Bandoeng 'army base', that is to say, the Bandoeng or Preanger plateau with a large concentration of military installations. Apart from barracks, warehouses and workshops of the KNIL, among which the Artillerie Constructie Werkplaats–Artillery Ordnance Workshop (ACW, a large ammunition factory on the edge of Bandoeng), the plateau was also the location of the large ML airbase Andir. Here were located the warehouses of the Magazijndienst–Warehouse Service and workshops (technical depot) of the Technische Dienst–Technical Service (TD) of the ML. In fact the TD at Andir was actually a large factory for second and third echelon maintenance and repair work of military aircraft and it was the largest of its kind in the whole of south-east Asia.[3]

For military (defence of the naval base) as well as political reasons (support for the maintenance of Dutch rule in eastern Java) it was decided to set up a partial (but relatively heavy) concentration of military resources in western Java. The 6th Infantry Regiment (6-R.I.) was to remain in eastern Java for the defence of the naval base. Central Java, however, was to be emptied as much as possible of troops in order to reinforce western Java. That is where the centre of gravity of the battle was expected, also because at Bandoeng all the important military and civilian headquarters were concentrated. The defence was not only to be limited to the Bandoeng plateau, which could be defended well, but was to encompass the entirety of western Java, including the port of Tjilatjap on the south coast. As for the defence on land, the latter town, however, was to be defended by the troops that were to remain in central Java. The defence plan was based on the principle of a maximum offensive deployment of the KNIL and allied land forces against Japanese landing operations.[4]

West Group and Bandoeng Group

The area of command of the KNIL in western Java was a divided one. In the westernmost part of western Java (with a line some 75 kilometres east of Batavia and Buitenzorg for its eastern boundary) a West Group, under command of Major-General W. Schilling was formed. Apart from commanding the 1st Infantry Regiment (1-R.I.) and a number of artillery and cavalry units of the KNIL (which for administrative purposes were assigned to 1st Division), he was also in charge of the so-called *Blackforce*. This was a motorised brigade, consisting of two Australian infantry battalions, one Australian infantry battalion (minus), one British squadron light tanks, one British signals section (the signals section of the Regimental Headquarters of 48 Light Anti-Aircraft Regiment), two American field artillery batteries and one Australian supply unit. The forming of the Blackforce brigade had not begun until 24 February, but on 1 March the force was operational. Its armament had partially been provided by the KNIL, just like some of the signals equipment (field telephone equipment). The two Australian battalions, which constituted the main force of the Blackforce, had recent combat experience under their belts in northern Africa.[5]

For the defence of the air base of Tjililitan 15 Battery of 6 Heavy Anti-Aircraft Regiment (HAA), originally coming from southern Sumatra, was stationed there, having been reorganised into a(n) (fully mobile) infantry company. This unit of approximately 140 men was relatively well armed and had six Bren carriers and three light armoured vehicles (supplied by the KNIL) and quite a large number of trucks at its disposal. Schilling was only the operational commander of *Blackforce* and 15 Battery. Operational control of the latter unit, though, went through the commander of 6 HAA, Lieutenant-Colonel Hazell, who also commanded two similar units manned with anti-aircraft personnel, which, however, were deployed in the area of command of Bandoeng Group (see below).[6]

Around 27 February 1942 another improvised infantry battalion was stationed in the area of West Group. This was a 450-man strong detachment of the RAF, armed as infantry and under the command of Wing Commander G.H. Alexander. As this unit was only poorly trained, it could only be deployed for guard duties. One of the 'companies' guarded Tjisaoek airfield, the other two went to Semplak and Tjikampek, making the KNIL units, which had up to now guarded these airfields, fully available again for Schilling. Of the security companies 15 Battery was the most useful, as its anti-aircraft gunners were practised in close defence, or had been members of anti-paratrooper squads, etc., and some of them had actually had to bring this training into practice at Palembang. On 1 March Alexander's unit was concentrated at Semplak and surroundings (because of the abandonment of Tjisaoek and Tjikampek airfields on 28 February and 1 March 1942, respectively), and subsequently assigned to *Blackforce*.[7]

Furthermore, on 25 and 26 February the strategic reserve of the allied land forces, consisting of the 2nd Infantry Regiment (2-R.I.) and the Ist Mountain Artillery Battalion (A. I Bg.) of the KNIL was stationed in the area of command of West Group. Including this reserve, West Group had about 21,200 combat-ready mobile troops at the time of the Japanese landings.[8]

In the eastern part of western Java Bandoeng Group was formed for the defence of the Bandoeng plateau and area adjacent to it and on 26 February 1942 Major-General J.J. Pesman assumed command. Apart from the units which had already been stationed at the Bandoeng plateau, at Ceribon and Kadipaten, he got the 4th Infantry Regiment (4-R.I.) and the IInd Mountain Artillery Battalion (A. II Bg.) coming from central Java under his command. These units, however, did not arrive in the Bandoeng area until 25 and 26 February. On 28 February 1942 Bandoeng Group consisted of some 5,900 combat-ready mobile troops.

Besides, Pesman was the operational commander of 78 Battery (originally 35 Light Anti-Aircraft Regiment, but commanded by the CO of 6 HAA) and 12 Battery (6 HAA), which had been reformed into infantry companies and stationed as security units at Andir and Kalidjati on 27 and 28 February 1942, respectively. These, too, were well armed, fully mobile units, which, in contrast to 15 Battery, however, only had a few light armoured vehicles and no Bren carriers. Stationing these British units once again made two companies of the 2nd Infantry Battalion (Inf. II) of the KNIL fully available for Pesman. In his area of command also the so-called Mobiele Eenheid–Mobile Unit (ME) was stationed, belonging to the army general reserve, consisting of, among others, 24 light tanks (armed with machine guns) and an infantry company in light armoured vehicles and trucks.[9]

The instructions for the defence of western Java were officially issued by the General Headquarters in the night of 28 February and 1 March 1942, by which time the repositioning of units within the framework of the formation of the two groups and the relocation of the centre of gravity to western Java had only just been completed.[10]

The Japanese landed in the night of 28 February on 1 March and in the early hours of 1 March 1942. The allied Counter-air operation which had been carried out in the period of 18 February up to and including 27 February, described in Part 1, had only given Java a few days' respite. The action of the Combined Striking Force of the allied navy (the Battle of the Java Sea on 27 February 1942, described in Part 2) had bought the allies one more day. Now it was up to the allied land forces to show their mettle, supported by the remaining air forces. The strength in bombers and fighter aircraft, however, had been considerably reduced due to the losses sustained during air raids on targets in southern Sumatra, which had been conquered by the Japanese, and by Japanese attacks on airfields in Java and during air combat over Java. The latter was the result of a simultaneous Japanese Counter-air operation directed at attaining air superiority prior to the landings.

'Ground-air' cooperation within the KNIL

In the middle of 1941 the ML included the Curtiss-Wright CW-22 *Falcon* tactical reconnaissance plane in its strength, specifically with a view to the cooperation with the ground forces of the KNIL. As of the very early hours of 1 March 1942 the 1e Verkenningsafdeling– 1st Reconnaissance afdeling (Vk.A.1) and the 2e Verkenningsafdeling (Vk.A.2) came under operational control of the army commanders at division level (in western Java, Schilling and Pesman). Vk.A.2 supported the troops in eastern Java and Vk.A.1 those in western Java. Of the latter unit two patrols (sections) of eight CW-22s in total were made available to the commander West Group and one patrol, four CW-22s, to the commander Bandoeng Group. All fighter aircraft and bombers remained under the control of JAC.

Both reconnaissance afdelingen had practised a lot during the second half of 1941 and also in the first few weeks after the war had broken out, often in cooperation with the ground forces. In their tactical support roles the CW-22s replaced the Koolhoven FK-51 double-deckers, trainer aircraft of the Vlieg- en Waarnemersschool– Flight and Observer School (VWS), which were to be mobilised in

A Curtiss-Wright CW-22 Falcon reconnaissance plane of the ML, still unarmed in this factory photograph. (Private collection, P.C. Boer)

times of war. The Falcons, however, were not much more than lightly armed advanced trainers either, whose relatively low speed made them vulnerable to enemy fighters. With a less than full supply of fuel the aircraft could be armed with two 50-kilogramme mine bombs or fragmentation bombs. Apart from that, their statutory armament consisted of a fixed 7.7-mm machine gun in the nose and a movable 7.7-mm machine gun in the rear cockpit for self-protection.

The officer-observers assigned to the afdelingen had all gone through a training programme with the artillery and had had some practice in radio communication (by Morse) with the wireless operators in the radio vehicles on the ground. However, this had been practised from Fokker C-X training aircraft (mainly used as target towing aircraft by Vk.A.1 and Vk.A.2), as the radio in the CW-22 was not suitable for maintaining this kind of communication. Therefore, it was impossible to control artillery fire from the reconnaissance planes in a war situation.

Furthermore, the training of the observers also encompassed the carrying out of tactical reconnaissance (such as road reconnaissance) and tactical photo assignments (such as the photographing of enemy positions), the dropping of 50-kilogramme bombs in cooperation with the pilot and operating as air gunner from the rear cockpit. The

CW-22 crews also practised communication via signalling panels spread out on the ground and dropping message cylinders in response. The first weeks after 8 December 1941 coordination exercises were flown with the infantry with a special emphasis on this kind of assignments and communication practice. In January and February 1942 the ML mainly practised with the infantry using Koolhoven FK-51 trainer aircraft, which belonged to the Flight and Observer School of the ML at Kalidjati.[11]

Apart from reconnaissance planes, ground support to the troops in the field would also be provided by fighter aircraft. The ML considered the bombers as a strategic asset, which could only be used tactically in exceptional circumstances and under strict conditions. For that reason it had already been forbidden to carry out low passes with bombers before the war. (The vision of JAC's was in conformity with that of the RAF, where bombers could be deployed tactically under certain conditions, for example, to block a route of advance or take out a position.) Practice in cooperation between infantry and fighter aircraft had taken place several times in the second half of 1941 within the framework of battalion exercises of the KNIL.

Both the aircraft groups of the ML equipped with fighter aircraft, the IVe Vliegtuiggroep–IVth Aircraft Group (Vl.G.IV) at Madioen and the Vth Aircraft Group (Vl.G.V) at Semplak, were provided with a radio truck with equipment suitable for Morse as well as telephone communication with airborne fighter pilots. An officer-pilot operated the equipment and acted as a sort of *forward air controller*. The on-board radio in the fighters of the ML was (just like that in the CW-22s) a normal commercial radio, which was not suitable for sending and receiving messages in Morse.

For both aircraft groups the training was deplorable due to an almost total lack of cooperation (interest) from the leadership of the battalions concerned. Apart from that, only a few practice sessions could be staged because of the outbreak of the war. In short, the experience of the ground forces of the KNIL in requesting and receiving air support was virtually non-existent, a deficiency that could not be put right anymore once the war had broken out.[12]

Communications

Already before the outbreak of the Pacific war, the KNIL supplied its motorised Cavalry squadrons with a long distance radio and short distance radio's for communications. These units had been given priority, the infantry and artillery coming next. Every infantry battalion had a communications brigade (group) within its staff, which consisted of line teams for the construction of telephone communications, several signal teams for the exchange of light signals with other teams on the ground, dispatch riders and a so-called U-lap (U-panel) team for communication with air crews by means of signalling panels on the ground and by message cylinders to be dropped from the aircraft. In the course of 1941 and also during the first weeks after the outbreak of the war in many battalions the U-panel team was replaced by a radio group. They consisted of several wireless operators with a radio vehicle fitted out with a so-called LARA, a long-distance radio, and several KARAs, short-distance radios. When a radio team was assigned to a battalion it would also act as a U-lap (U-panel) team.

From the radio group, if required, radio teams (usually a wireless operator and a dispatch rider) equipped with a KARA were detached to the subordinate companies. A KARA was a tactical radio suitable for Morse as well as telephony, which could be transported by jeep, on horseback, and if need be, on human back and which in principle was intended for communication with the communication brigade of the battalion.

In January and February 1942 a number of units were eventually provided with a LARA and KARAs. Thus, shortly after its arrival, the Vth Infantry Battalion (Inf.V), which had been relocated from central Java to Bandoeng in February 1942, was given a radio vehicle with a LARA and several wireless operators coming from the ML aviation-radio operator school, discontinued in the meantime. Inf. I, which had also been relocated from central Java, already had a LARA and KARAs for its infantry companies. The Mobile Unit (ME) also got a LARA, at least one KARA and several radio operators from the ML school. In February the light tanks of this unit were fitted out with an American commercial radio transmitter, which, however, worked poorly, and it was forbidden to use it in combat for passing on operational instructions (from tank to tank).

In the artillery all units had a radio vehicle with a LARA, which came under the radio group of the signals unit. Here, too, the personnel of the radio group acted as U-panel team. The subordinate batteries did not have a LARA. However, incorporated in the battalion staff there were so-called artillery reconnaissance patrols (for target tracking), commanded by an artillery observer, which were assigned to the batteries and equipped with a KARA of the signals unit, if required. The artillery observer could use the KARA for communications with the battery.

The LARA was suitable for communications (in Morse) with the higher commanders and for the infantry for requesting fire support from the artillery or (through the staff at divisional level) air support. Because of the frequently poor or even extremely poor radio communications in the wet (monsoon) season, in particular the period between November up to and including April, the infantry as well as artillery units relied to a large extent on telephone lines and dispatch riders. Telephone lines could be laid quickly from specially adapted vehicles or sidecar combinations.[13]

Modernising of 'ground-air' cooperation, Air support coordination

In spite of all good intentions and plans joint operations of land and air forces within the KNIL was still in its infancy. This was partially caused by the fact that the tactical reconnaissance aircraft and the bulk of the fighter aircraft afdelingen were newly established and incorporated in the peace organisation in the course of 1941. Therefore, within the KNIL there was hardly any know-how at the level of company commander and up on the possibilities and impossibilities of the air arm, except with regard to the deployment of reconnaissance aircraft.

Also within the ML, the way in which air forces, in particular bombers and fighter aircraft, would have to be deployed within the framework of the support of the ground troops in Java, had hardly received any attention, either. For example, there did not exist a worked-out doctrine for the deployment of fighter aircraft and it never came during the war days. The ML leadership still perceived fighter aircraft mainly as a means to defend the air bases from which the bombers had to carry out their bombing raids against enemy fleets.[14]

Only with the formation of Java Air Command, with its Dutch-British/Australian Operations Staff, did the deployment of fighter aircraft and bombers become modern. Within the RAF, for example, the various tasks for which fighter aircraft could be committed efficiently had been worked out in depth. Thus, prompted by the experiences of *Fighter Command* of the RAF during operations in France in May and June 1940, the way in which road reconnaissance operations (armed road reconnaissances) should be carried out had been laid down.

As mentioned above, the system employed by JAC for air support coordination, procedures and regulations for requesting and granting of air support, was derived from the one used by the RAF in northern Africa in the second half of 1941.

One of the fixed rules was that commanders of the ground troops did not have air forces at their disposal on a permanent basis. They were too scarce for that and having them available permanently would be detrimental to the flexibility with regard to their deployment. When the troops required air support the commanders had to indicate where (location), when (time) and why (description of target and information on their own manoeuvre) it was needed. Every night the requests would go routinely to the staff of Bandoeng Group or West Group, and from there were passed on at 22:00 hrs to the General Headquarters for approval within the framework of the general plan for the coming day, and subsequently to JAC. Before 24:00 hrs the staff of the group would get a message back with regard to the granted air support. If necessary, this procedure was also followed during combat situations or in case there was an enemy advance in the mean time. JAC integrated the air support in the mission planning for the following day and, if required, in consultation with the liaison officer at the General Headquarters, assigned the resources globally. ML Command and BRITAIR then translated all this into operations orders for the aircraft afdelingen and squadrons and, if necessary, coordinated the execution through the liaison officers at the staff of Bandoeng Group and West Group.[15]

The RAF also had procedures for the execution of *close air support*, that is the carrying out of attacks on enemy troops locked in battle with own troops, so close to the forward line of own troops. Most fighter pilots and crews of the RAF and RAAF in western Java, however, were not actually trained in this. For allied fighter pilots, too, communication with the units on the ground in principle went by signal panels spread out by U-panel teams and message cylinders dropped in response. From Hurricanes of the RAF as well as the Brewsters B 339 fighter aircraft of the ML a pilot could drop a message cylinder. The fighter pilots of the RAF, however, had no experience with the U-panel system. Radio vehicles adapted for telephony were no longer available in March 1942. Incidentally, the fighter pilots of the Hurricanes of the RAF in Java could use their aircraft radio only for mutual communication, as there were no crystals available to tune the radios in the British fighter aircraft in to frequencies used by the KNIL and ML. On top of that, radio communication in the (wet) monsoon season was so poor that it could not be fully relied upon. When the time of attack needed to be accurately coordinated with a manoeuvre of the ground forces, the messaging went as follows: message from the commander involved (for example, a battalion commander) by LARA or dispatch rider to the staff of Bandoeng Group or West Group, order with time of attack by military telephone line via the switch board of Andir or Tjililitan airfield to the operational commander of the ML or RAF. After landing the attack or reconnaissance results were reported directly by telephone to the staff of Bandoeng Group or West Group (and afterwards in writing, by means of a concise operations report that was simultaneously sent to the General Headquarters, JAC, *RecGroup* and COIC).[16]

As was said above, the ground troops of the KNIL were not or at best poorly trained in requesting and receiving close air support. At JAC, therefore, the deployment of fighter aircraft for this kind of direct support to the ground troops was not considered an option, unless there was a forward line of own troops whose position was absolutely clear. On 2 March the execution of the support missions for the allied ground troops began. One of the first missions in the area of Bandoeng Group was a raid by Brewster fighter aircraft of the ML to support an attack of the IVth Infantry Battalion (Inf. IV) of the KNIL on Eretan Wetan, the Japanese landing location on the north coast. The attack was carried out just before Inf. IV began its advance (from positions that had been passed on beforehand by LARA).[17]

The Japanese 'ground-air' cooperation

The Japanese air operation to support the ground troops of Colonel Shoji, which had landed at Eretan Wetan, began on 3 March 1942 and was carried out in its entirety from Kalidjati airfield, captured on 1 March 1942. The support to their own troops consisted of offensive air support and tactical air reconnaissance. Within the framework of the former type of mission Kawasaki Ki-48 light bombers as well as Mitsubishi Ki-51 assault aircraft (tactical support aircraft) were used. The Japanese Army air force flew air support sorties, directed at assisting in the realisation of a break-through of the own troops, as well as battlefield air interdiction sorties, aimed at taking out as many as possible of the enemy units indirectly involved in the battle behind the front line (amongst others, tactical reserves). The tactical reconnaissance missions, flown by assault aircraft, were directed at target acquisition, terrain reconnaissance and surveillance. The bombers, which were vulnerable to attacks by enemy fighter aircraft, were protected in all missions as much as possible by own fighter aircraft, which were supposed to ensure (at least) a local air superiority. Due to a shortage of fighter aircraft as a result of allied air raids, however, they did not manage to do so during the battle.[18]

The whole thing was based on a well worked out doctrine, derived in part from studies of the deployment of the German *Luftwaffe* during the *Blitzkrieg* in 1940 and own recent combat experience from the war in China. In western Java the Japanese worked with a 'forward line of own troops' system. On a daily basis, prior to the commencement of operations, it was indicated on the map of the area of operations to which line the own troops could advance without coming into conflict with the planned air operations. A liaison officer of the Army air force (a captain or major coming from one of the aircraft groups equipped with bombers), together with some signal personnel and a radio, formed a small forward command post that moved along with the battalion commander's command post. The most important task of the liaison officer was to keep a continuous watch on the manoeuvres of the battalion and to report regularly to the air brigade in Kalidjati what had to be the new position of the 'forward line of own troops', given the developments at the frontline on the ground.

Although the deployment of the Japanese forces for the support of their own ground troops could not be called more modern in itself than that of the allied side, the Japanese infantry units deployed in western Java were, without exception, trained in the cooperation with air forces. As was said above, this was the case only to a limited extent within the KNIL. However, also the Japanese had communication problems and they were faced with very much the same sort of difficulties as the KNIL was.[19]

The allied possibilities to provide air support

In February 1942 the ML, RAF and RAAF had suffered severe losses as a result of Japanese raids on airfields in Java and in allied attacks on targets in the conquered southern Sumatra and Banka. As a consequence, the possibilities for providing air support to the land forces after an invasion had been considerably reduced.[20] On 28 February, at the end of the day, Java Air Command had the following numbers of assigned and operationally serviceable combat aircraft available (excluding *RecGroup* and *East Group*). Per assigned aircraft the units had at least one crew or pilot at their disposal.[21]

Table 19

Unit	Base	Assigned	Operationally serviceable	Remarks
Bombers				
1-Vl.G.I/1-Vl.G.II	Kalidjati	7	6	
2-Vl.G.III	Tjisaoek	4	4	
3-Vl.G.III	Andir	4	1	
1 Squadron	Kalidjati	7	2	
84 Squadron	Kalidjati	16	10	
36 Squadron	Tjikampek	10	9	At Madioen
Fighter aircraft				
1-Vl.G.V	Andir	6	5	Excl. Ngoro
2-Vl.G.V	Andir	3	2	Ibid.
2-Vl.G.IV	Andir	3	3	Ibid.
242/605 Squadron	Tjililitan	15	12	
Reconnaissance aircraft (up to 1 March under operational control of AHK)				
Vk.A.1	Tjikembar	12	10	
Total strength		87	64	

On 28 February 1942 the ML still had 16 Brewster B 339 fighter aircraft in total at its disposal in western Java. Of these, however, four heavily damaged aircraft were at Tjililitan, Tjisaoek, Semplak and Kemajoran, respectively, of which two had already received makeshift repairs and were awaiting transfer to Andir for major repairs. One Brewster was in major repair at Andir and nearing completion. Then, there were three further Curtiss-Wright CW-21B Interceptors, which had been assigned to the 2-Vl.G.IV patrol. One (unmanned) replacement CW-21B was at the workshop of the Technical Service (TD) of the ML at Madioen in central Java and was flown over to Andir on 1 March. The Brewster B 339s flew with 1-Vl.G.V and 2-Vl.G.V.[22] On 28 February the RAF had a total of 19 remaining Hurricanes, four of which were in maintenance at 81 Repair and Salvage Unit (81 RSU) or temporarily out of service due to a lack of spare parts. Thus, there were no more spare propellers for the Hurricanes, for instance.[23]

In the afternoon of 1 March 1942 both fighter squadrons of the RAF were amalgamated and designated 242 Squadron.[24] A day later the same happened with 1-Vl.G.V and 2-Vl.G.V of the ML, the latter afdeling being discontinued administratively on 3 March 1942.[25]

The bomber afdelingen of the ML, all equipped with Glenn Martin 139s (B-10s) had an original statutory strength of 11 aircraft (two of which made up the unmanned first-line maintenance reserve). Due to a shortage of aircraft, this strength had been temporarily reduced to six in February 1942, or to eight aircraft in total for some afdelingen. Apart from several damaged aircraft, which had been left behind in central and eastern Java, the ML had 20 Glenn Martins left on 28 February 1942. Three of these, however, were badly damaged and had been left behind at Kalidjati, Tjileungsir and Kemajoran, respectively.[26] The RAF and RAAF still had 25 Bristol Blenheims (nine of which were temporarily out of service due to a shortage of spare parts) and 11 Lockheed Hudsons (four of which were in major repairs or major maintenance).[27] All ten remaining Albacore and Vildebeest light bombers of the RAF (only deployable in night raids) were assigned to 36 Squadron.[28]

The allied bomber fleet was greatly reduced in numbers because of the Japanese capture of Kalidjati on 1 March 1942, when 23 Blenheims and three Hudson light bombers fell into Japanese hands. Four Hudsons of 1 Squadron RAAF managed to escape in the nick of time to Andir. The Blenheim equipped 84 Squadron RAF had been taken out in its entirety (see the chapter below). In the early days of March, however, an all-out effort was made to reorganise the remaining allied air forces and to consolidate them on air bases which were still secure.[29]

Reorganisation of the allied air forces on 1 and 2 March 1942

The 1st Reconnaissance afdeling (Vk.A.1) was stationed at Tjikembar and in the very early hours of 1 March it came under operational command of the commander West Group (eight aircraft, including two first-line reserves), and the commander Bandoeng Group (four aircraft, including one first-line reserve), respectively. There were no further reserve aircraft for this afdeling. All airworthy aircraft of the ML and the RAF that still remained in central and eastern Java after the Japanese landings, were being pulled back on western Java on 1 March 1942. Thus, the 2nd Reconnaissance afdeling (Vk.A.2) flew its remaining four CW-22s over to Andir, but this afdeling was not deployed in the period covered in this part. The flying crews at Andir were given a few days' leave, while the ground crews and other flying crews were on their way to western Java. The four evacuated aircraft were all lost in an air raid on Andir on 3 March 1942.[30]

In central and eastern Java several squadrons of the United States Army Air Force had been active until the beginning of March, but they were evacuated to Australia on 1 and 2 March, when the remaining bombers of the USAAF flew to Broome. The remaining fighter aircraft of the USAAF (together with a number of fighter aircraft of the ML) were all lost on 1 March or heavily damaged in a Japanese air raid on Ngoro airfield. The three remaining non-operational Douglas A-24 dive bombers at Malang were simply abandoned and some time later destroyed by the KNIL. Two A-24s had been flown to Djocjakarta on 1 March and were destroyed there.[31]

2-Vl.G.IV of the ML (Hurricanes, minus the Interceptor patrol at Andir) had been relocated to eastern Java by the end of February 1942, just like a detachment of 1- and 2-Vl.G.V of the ML (Brewster B 339 fighter aircraft). Of the 14 ML fighter aircraft relocated to eastern Java only one Hurricane returned to Andir on 1 March. The next day, after a day's drive, most of the crews of 2-Vl.G.IV and Vl.G.V arrived there. The detachment of Vl.G.V was incorporated into 1-Vl.G.V at Andir. The remaining Hurricane became unserviceable in the early morning of 2 March and was not deployed in the period covered in this Part.

2-Vl.G.IV went "non-ops" on 3 March due to a planned re-equipment with 12 new Curtiss P-40E fighter aircraft. The assemblage of these crated planes under the auspices of the Technical Service (TD) of the ML at Andir (on locations on the edge of Bandoeng) began on 2 March. In the assembly process of these fighter aircraft personnel of various aircraft afdelingen of the ML, as well as personnel of the Naval Air Service (MLD) and the Royal Netherlands Indies Air Line (KNILM) were employed. Twelve other P-40s were assembled for the RAF by the TD at Tasikmalaja, a new airfield south of Andir. These aircraft were designated a few days later to 242 Squadron of the RAF. In the period covered in this Part the allied air forces in western Java did not receive any further reinforcements.[32]

Although the bomber afdelingen of the ML had only few aircraft left, the afdeling structure was left intact. This was done in view of the planned re-equipment with new North American B-25C Mitchell bombers. In early March the first of a total of 60 aircraft destined for

Part of a detachment of Vl.G.III that left for Archerfield in Australia on 14 and 15 February 1942 to pick up new North American B-25C Mitchell bombers. In this picture were some of the first group of pilots and crew members during a stop-over in Darwin. (Private collection, P.C. Boer)

the ML arrived at Archerfield in Australia. American ferry crews had flown the aircraft across the Pacific. Other B-25s were going to be flown to Bangalore in British India. In both locations there were detachments of the ML, Vl.G.III and Vl.G.I, respectively, to take over the bombers and, after a short transition training, fly them on to Java.[33]

If the KNIL succeeded in holding out against the invasion troops for some time, there was a chance that in any case the new P-40s could be deployed in the battle, or this was the conviction at Java Air Command at the time.

The allied anti-aircraft artillery at the time of the invasion

The commanders of the Air Defence Commands were also operational commanders of the anti-aircraft artillery units, KNIL as well as allied, in their area of responsibility. The Air Defence Command Bandoeng encompassed, for example, all anti-aircraft artillery assets at Bandoeng, Andir airfield and Kalidjati airfield. The main force of the IIIrd Battalion Anti-aircraft Artillery (A. III Ld.) of the KNIL was stationed at

Andir in positions designated as Andir North and Andir South. A company (minus) of A. III Ld. manned a position east of the town of Bandoeng, for the protection of the Artillery Constructie Werkplaats–Artillery Ordnance Workshop (ACW) of the KNIL, a large ammunition factory, located there. British batteries had taken up positions, amongst others, near the eastern edge and just north of Andir airfield.

Andir North, consisted of five posts spread out along the northern perimeter of Andir. They accommodated from west to east, two 4-cm guns, four 8-cm guns (in a fixed position called Kapok), two 4-cm guns, two 2-cm guns and a machine gun section with three 12.7-mm machine guns. The latter was positioned in the east near the beginning of the main runway of Andir. A second section of two 2-cm guns and a further 12.7-mm machine gun section had been withdrawn during the abandonment of Madioen airfield in central Java at the beginning of March and were added to 'North'.

Andir South, just south and to the south-west and west of the flight area, consisted of seven posts: three sections with three 12.7-mm machine guns each, two sections of two 2-cm guns each, one battery of four 8-cm guns (in the fixed position Agave) and a further section with two 4-cm guns. The first three sections had their own command post and they were manned by the 1st Anti-Armour and Anti-Aircraft Battalion (Pla. 1) seconded to A. III Ld. The positions of the 2-cm and 4-cm guns consisted of an earthen wall around the gun position and only a trench for shelter, which made the guns mobile in principle. However, the number of vehicles A. III Ld. had at its disposal did in fact not allow a mobile deployment. At the time a position consisting of four guns was designated a battery by the KNIL, while a position of two guns formed a section. All 4-cm and 8-cm guns were Bofors, the 2-cm guns had been built by the German Rheinmetall-Börsig. It must be remarked here that the 8-cm guns at Andir only had improvised fire control equipment, the original equipment having been lost during the transport from Europe to the Netherlands East Indies in a German submarine attack.

The British anti-air artillery consisted of two Batteries of ten and eight 4-cm Bofors guns, respectively, and (as of 3 March) a heavy anti-aircraft Battery of eight 9-cm guns. The light anti-aircraft units were composed of 95 Battery of 48 Light Anti-Aircraft Regiment (LAA) and an improvised unit consisting of two Troops of 69 and 79 Battery of 21 LAA. The heavy anti-aircraft unit consisted of 239 Battery of 77 Heavy Anti-Aircraft Regiment (HAA). This unit of 77 HAA had come under the command of the commander 48 LAA. The organisation of the anti-aircraft artillery units of the Royal Artillery was quite different from what was customary within the KNIL. In the Light Anti-Aircraft Regiments a Battery consisted, apart from a Staff, three Troops with their statutory four guns each, while a Heavy Anti-Aircraft Battery was composed of a Staff and two Troops with four guns each.

The first of the allied units to become operational in the evening of 21 February 1942 was 95 Battery at Andir. The two Troops of 21 Light Anti-Aircraft Regiment were relocated from Maospati airfield (Madioen, central Java) to Andir around 25 February and arrived late in the evening of 1 March 1942. On 3 March 239 Battery, which had been relocated from Tandjong Priok to Bandoeng, followed, but it did not become fully operational until 4 March 1942, with four guns dispersed north of Andir, and two guns at Tjimahi and two at Lembang.

Gunners of the above-mentioned British units also operated at least 12 anti-aircraft machine guns (Brenguns), which had been positioned, amongst others, in the southern sector of Andir air base. In the south-west the hangar complex and buildings of the Technical Service and Warehouse Service of the ML (partially empty now because of a dispersal of these services outside the base) were located, and in the south-east the hangars and buildings of the KNILM (partially in use by now by the ML and RAF). On top of that, the three Pla.1 sections, mentioned above, were positioned along the southern and western perimeter of the flight area.

Near the Artillery Ordnance Workshop (ACW) there were four 8-cm guns, two 4-cm guns and two 2-cm guns of A. III. Ld., plus a section of three 12.7-mm machine guns. At Kalidjati there was a further section of A. III Ld. with two 4-cm Bofors guns, along with six 12.7-mm machine guns. On this latter base also 49 Battery (48 LAA) was stationed with a total of ten 4-cm Bofors guns. The KNIL sections escaped scot-free in the Japanese attack, but 49 Battery suffered heavy casualties and could only bring three guns into safety. The Battery was relocated to Tjikembar in the evening of 1 March 1942 (see the following chapter).[34]

The anti-aircraft artillery at Tjililitan, Batavia and Tandjong Priok and Kemajoran came under the command of Air Defence Command Batavia (Sector Command Batavia). On 28 February 1942 there were two 2-cm guns of the 1st Battalion Anti-Aircraft Artillery (A. I Ld.) and eight 4-cm guns of 242 Battery (minus) of 48 LAA at Tjililitan. On the edge of Batavia and at Tandjong Priok (the coastal front to protect the harbour of the town) there were, apart from eighteen 12.7-mm machine guns, four 8-cm, two 4-cm and four 2-cm guns of A. I Ld.,

plus a section of 242 Battery with two 4-cm guns for the protection
of the Naval air station at Tandjong Priok and the above-mentioned
239 Battery (77 HAA), which had been relocated to Bandoeng on
1 March. Furthermore, the anti-aircraft artillery at Batavia only consisted of three 12.7-mm machine guns at Kemajoran.

The section of 242 Battery was relocated to Tjililitan on 1 March
1942, during which operation one of the two guns was lost when it
slipped from the tackle in a canal crossing. The remaining gun was
positioned as an anti-armour gun near a bridge on the road from
Tjililitan to the main road of Batavia to Buitenzorg. The departure
of the British anti-aircraft artillery from Tandjong Priok was brought
about by the closure of the harbour and the departure of the last navy
ships and flying boats. The allied navy had moved to Tjilatjap on the
south coast and had evacuated as many ships as possible to Ceylon
and Australia. (ABDA-FLOAT disbanded 1 March 1942.) This made
it possible to bring the anti-aircraft artillery defence at Andir up to
the mark.[35]

In a battle on the Bandoeng plateau especially the British light
anti-aircraft units would be of great value. Not only were they fully
mobile, their 4-cm Bofors guns were exceedingly useful as anti-armour
artillery. In fact, there had been some preparations to combine the
LAA Batteries and the three 'infantry companies' of 6 HAA into three
mobile combat groups, if need be.[36]

* * *

CHAPTER 3.3

The Japanese Landing Operation at Eretan Wetan and the First Allied Attacks

Introduction

The concentration of the Japanese troops prior to the attack on western
Java took place in the Cam Rahn Bay in Indo-China and had been

completed on 10 February 1942. With an extremely strong escort of the Japanese fleet the convoys with transport ships put to sea eight days later. For the landings in the westernmost part of Java, in the Bay of Bantam and north and south of the small town of Merak, 47 transport vessels in total were used. For the landing of the so-called Shoji detachment (in fact a regimental battle group) at Eretan Wetan, seven transport ships were employed.[1] The latter landing operation was quite a risky one. The distance between the landing locations in the west, from where the 2nd Division and corps troops of the 16th Army corps were to begin their advance, and Eretan Wetan was around 200 kilometres. This meant that for a certain period of time Shoji could not reckon with any support from the Japanese main force. Besides, air support from southern Sumatra would initially have to be realised over an exceedingly large distance. In other words, there was a chance that Shoji's detachment would be defeated before the 2nd Division or the Army air force could intervene.

In the evening of 28 February, after a day's postponement of the invasion in connection with a reported allied fleet, the convoy conveying Shoji's detachment split itself off from the main convoy. Escorted by three destroyers and a mine sweeper it subsequently headed for a point 100 kilometres north of Eretan Wetan, from which the approach on the landing area would begin. A light cruiser accompanied the vessels and then rejoined the main force with the mine sweeper. The convoy and its escort, however, had been shadowed by Catalina flying boats of the Reconnaissance Group of JAC and the first air raids were not long in coming. At that time the convoy was still 80 kilometres off the coast. During the entire approach and also when the convoy had anchored off Eretan Wetan from around 01:00 hrs (on 1 March 1942), Blenheim, Hudson and Glenn Martin bombers kept on pounding the ships. At around 02:00 hrs the first echelon of the Japanese landing troops came ashore.[2]

The Japanese strength and the advance from Eretan Wetan

The regimental battle group of Colonel Toshinari Shoji was built around a nucleus of the 230th Regiment (minus) of the 38th Division, reinforced with a squadron of light tanks and various artillery, anti-armour artillery, anti-aircraft artillery and engineer units. Two transport companies (minus) had been added as well. All in all, there were some 3,000 men, including the combat train. The battle group had been

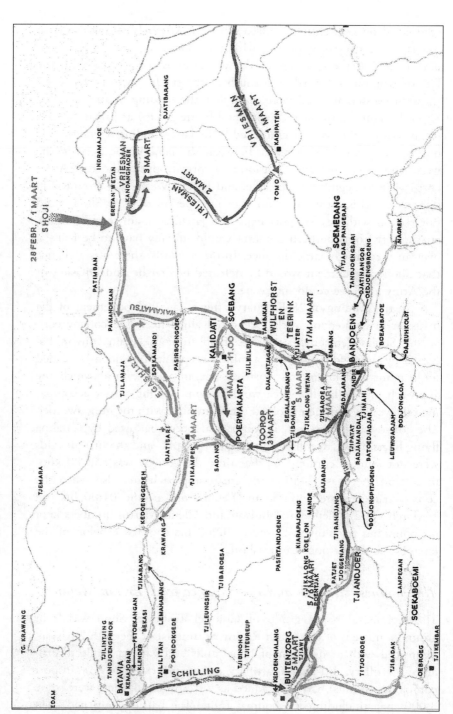

Advances of the Japanese and the Netherlands East-Indies troops

divided into two assault groups and a covering group. The largest assault group was that of Major Shichiro Wakamatsu, with a nucleus of the regiment's 2nd Battalion (minus) and reinforced with, amongst others, a squadron of light tanks (minus) and an engineer company (minus); approximately 1,200 men in total. The second assault group was commanded by Major Masaru Egashira and consisted of the 1st Battalion (minus), which had been reinforced with a battery of mountain artillery and a group of light tanks; around 1,000 men in total. Wakamatsu Group was to capture Kalidjati airbase as quickly as possible, while the Egashira group was to secure a large traffic bridge across the Tjitaroem River near Krawang.[3]

The covering group of Lieutenant-Colonel Takeo Ono was responsible for the defence of the bridgehead at Eretan Wetan and the security of the works there. Ono's group did not amount to much more than a company and a machine gun platoon of the 2nd Battalion, reinforced with some grenade launchers. Inside the bridgehead, however, also Shoji's reserve was located, a company and a machine gun platoon of the 1st Battalion, reinforced with some grenade launchers as well, and an anti-aircraft battery, which was to be positioned at Kalidjati after its capture. Also Colonel Shoji's staff and a Mountain Artillery battalion (minus), the latter destined to be assigned to Wakamatsu Group, initially remained at Eretan Wetan. Furthermore, Major Watanabe commanded the work teams in the bridgehead which came from an independent engineer company (minus).[4]

As was mentioned above, at 02:00 hrs (on 1 March) the first units of both Japanese assault groups landed near Eretan Wetan. At around 04:00 hrs the vanguard of the Egashira group left the bridgehead, followed by the vanguard of Wakamatsu Group around 04:45 hrs. (The reader is advised that all time indications are Central Java Time.) The advance of the latter group was extremely successful. Although they had to deal with some light resistance several times, they managed to break through the defence of the small town of Soebang near Kalidjati airbase on 1 March between 08:00 hrs and 09:00 hrs.[5] The advance of the Egashira group went far less smoothly, which was due to air raids by Hurricane fighter aircraft (see the next chapter).

The Japanese Air power strategy and the air support for Shoji

From 1 March 1942 onwards the cooperation between the ground troops and the air forces became paramount. It was well organised and had been practised thoroughly. For the direct cooperation with the land forces to be deployed in western Java the 3rd Hiko Dan had available two-seater Mitsubishi Ki-51s. These were light single-engine assault/tactical reconnaissance aircraft. The crews of these aircraft had been trained in guiding twin-engine Ki-48 (light) bombers to targets on the ground and they could control artillery fire from the air. If required, they could designate targets for Ki-43 fighter aircraft, but the fighters were in principle only to be committed for the protection of their own bases and bombers. The rather slow but fairly manoeuvrable Ki-51s (given their tasks, the then Japanese counterparts of the modern-day American OA-10A Warthogs) could fend for themselves. Just like the KNIL, the Japanese did not have any close air support, but worked with a 'forward line own troops' system (see the previous chapter).[6]

The Japanese infantry did not have any mobile radio stations and procedures to guide aircraft to their targets from the ground. By means of signal panels short standardised messages could be relayed to the Ki-51 crews, who in their turn could drop signal cylinders. In the Japanese Army the use of radio was by no means commonplace yet and tanks, for example, were not equipped with radio.[7]

The KNIL had a similar communications problem. The so-called U-panel teams in the infantry battalions could lay out messages and the crews of the CW-22 Falcon reconnaissance planes could drop signal cylinders. The observers in the CW-22 crews were able to drop light bombs in support of the ground troops, but they were not trained in guiding fighter aircraft or bombers to their targets.[8]

The Japanese Army air force in southern Sumatra had its head-quarters in Palembang. This was the staff of the 3rd Hiko Shudan (air division), to which two Hiko Dans (air brigades) were assigned apart from a directly subordinate strategic reconnaissance group (81st Sentai). At Palembang I (the former civilian airfield of the town of Palembang) the 3rd Hiko Dan, whose main force was to support the landing operation at Eretan Wetan from Kalidjati, was stationed almost in its entirety. At Palembang I and Tandjoengkarang (the southernmost part of southern Sumatra) was stationed the 12th Hiko Dan, consisting of a part of the 1st Sentai and the 11th Sentai, both equipped with Ki-27 fighter aircraft. These planes had a relatively small range and, together with a part of 3rd Hiko Dan, were designated for the support of the landing operations in the westernmost part of Java. The main force of the 1st Sentai was stationed at Tengah in Singapore.

The order of battle of the 3rd Hiko Shudan (not including the 81st Sentai) was as follows on 28 February 1942:[9]

Table 20

Unit	Type	Assigned	At P I and Tj. karang	Of which operationally serv.	Remarks
3rd Hiko Dan					
75th and 90th SE	Ki-48	61	ca 38	ca 32	
59th and 64th SE	Ki-43	35	35	ca 25	
50th Chutai	Ki-15	ca 2	ca 2	ca 2	
	Ki-46	ca 2	ca 2	ca 2	
27th Sentai	Ki-51	ca 20	16	ca 16	Excl. ca 7 at Singapore
12th Hiko Dan					
1st and 11th SE	Ki-27	ca 34	ca 34	ca 23	Excl. ca 20 at Singapore
Total strength		ca 154	ca 127	ca 100	

A Sentai (SE) or combat unit consisted of a Staff Chutai (staff flight) with several aircraft and three (sometimes four) Chutais (flights or sections) with seven to nine aircraft statutorily. The 50th Chutai was an independent flight equipped with several single-engine Ki-15 and several twin-engine Ki-46 reconnaissance planes.

Initially, there was no air support for the troops that had landed in Eretan Wetan. The distance from Palembang to the landing sites was too large and the weather en route was often bad. The Shoji detachment, however, was relatively small, acting behind the main allied lines against an allied superior force of ground troops (although the Japanese did not have too high an opinion of the combat value of the KNIL) and operating at a large distance from the main Japanese force, which had landed much further to the west. The latter could not provide any support, which made air support for the detachment of crucial importance to be able to survive. Taking Kalidjati airfield quickly, therefore, was absolutely essential. In spite of the fact that the coast near Eretan Wetan was known to be unfavourable in the 'wet' season, the Japanese had nevertheless decided to land in this location, as the important main coastal road, which formed a part of the advance route to Kalidjati, came close to the beach there.

Only over the bridgehead on the coast near Eretan Wetan did some air support become available in the course of the day in the form of four Mitsubishi F1M reconnaissance float planes of the Japanese Navy air force. They were, however, in principle designated to carry out anti-aircraft and anti-submarine patrols in protection of the Japanese ships near Eretan Wetan. In other words, until Kalidjati had been taken, Shoji's regimental battle group would be vulnerable in the extreme.[10]

The units that had been designated for relocation to Kalidjati, however, were standing ready at Palembang I airfield. According to the Japanese plans, the air support for Shoji was to consist of the main forces of the 27th Sentai (Ki-51 assault aircraft), 59th Sentai (Ki-43 fighter aircraft) and the 75th Sentai (Ki-48 light bombers); 50 aircraft in all.[11] The actual numbers and types of aircraft flown over in the period of 2 March up to and including 4 March 1942 will be specified in Chapter 3.6. The total ran up to 69 aircraft, considerably more than had been planned. In order to replace the losses as a result of allied air raids on Kalidjati the Japanese Army air force had been forced to also relocate the 64th and 90th Sentais to this base. In case of an emergency the Japanese Army could also make an appeal on the Navy air force, which had stationed approximately 50 fighter aircraft and bombers at Muntok (the island of Banka) and Palembang II (the military airfield near the town of Palembang). These aircraft, however, were in principle designated to protect Palembang II and the anchorage and fleet facilities at Palembang and Banka, as well as carry out reconnaissance missions over the western part of the Java Sea and attack allied shipping.

Planning of the first missions by JAC

Since the afternoon of 27 February 1942 JAC had kept most of its available bombers at Kalidjati and Tjisaoek on readiness.[12] The next day it became clear that the main landings were not going to take place in eastern Java, but in western Java, simultaneously to the east and west of Batavia. Apparently, the Japanese intended to land on the north coast of Java near Indramajoe in the night of 28 February and 1 March, an extremely dangerous development. If Japanese troops, after landing there, managed in a quick push to capture the large airfield of Kalidjati, which lay close to the coast, the Japanese combat aircraft could be deployed from that base against the allied troops all over western Java already the next day. The coast near Indramajoe was not defended by land forces, on the one hand, because there simply were too few of them, and, on the other, because it was considered dangerous, if not impossible, to disembark enemy units in the usually rough seas there in the 'wet season'.[13]

In the afternoon of 28 February the General Headquarters (AHK) gave priority to fighting off the expected landing in the environment of Indramajoe with air forces, in the first instance. JAC committed the bulk of its bombers against this landing operation. Eleven Glenn Martins (seven at Kalidjati, three at Kemajoran and one at Andir), ten Blenheims (six at Kalidjati and four at Andir) and two Hudsons (at Kalidjati) were operationally serviceable. Two of the Glenn Martins, however, were to carry out a mission to southern Sumatra in order to suppress Japanese activity on Palembang I and four of the Blenheims were kept in reserve for a deployment against an expected landing in the Bay of Bantam in the west of Java.[14] 36 Squadron RAF had left its base Tjikampek in the morning of 28 February with eight Vildebeestes and one Albacore for Madioen (central Java). In the night of 27 on 28 February AHK still assumed that the main threat would materialise in eastern Java and the squadron was earmarked to support the American four-engine bombers of the East Group of JAC.[15]

Between roughly 17:30 hrs and 18:00 hrs (on 28 February) the afdelingen and squadrons received their battle orders from their operational commanders. The Operations Staff of JAC had carefully determined take off times and time slots over the target areas for the units in order to limit the danger of collisions and to prevent the crews from mistaking each other for enemies. The ML Command and BRITAIR, respectively, had further elaborated the global mission planning of JAC. The bombing raids were to be carried out from an altitude of between 1,200 and 1,500 metres and with three 300-kilogramme bombs (the medium heavy Glenn Martins), or four 250-lb bombs (110 kilogrammes) per aircraft (the light bombers of the RAF and RAAF), respectively. The last known position of the Japanese ships was north of Boompjes Eiland, which was located some 40 kilometres on a heading of 015 north of Indramajoe. The Glenn Martins were to attack in a patrol formation; the British bombers were to attack individually. On 28 February 1942, shortly after 18:00 hrs, the first bomber took off from Kalidjati.[16]

The Night Bombing Raids, 28 February–1 March 1942

The attacks by the RAF and RAAF near Eretan Wetan

The first bombers to take off from Kalidjati were the two operationally serviceable Hudsons of 1 Squadron RAAF. The crew of the first plane, piloted by Plt Off A.R. Wilson, left shortly after 18:00 hrs and managed to find the enemy fleet during last light at approximately 80 kilometres north of Eretan Wetan. It was duly attacked by the two Hudson crews at around 18:50 hrs. Flt Lt B.J. Wiley's crew, however, had to drop their bombs without aiming, owing to a defect. Wilson's crew thought they had scored a direct hit on a transport vessel, but according to a Japanese source there was no damage done in the first attack by the two Hudsons.[17]

At around 18:30 hrs, when darkness had just set in, six Blenheims took off one by one from the narrow strip lit by storm lanterns in the northern part of Kalidjati. These bombers, too, were to carry out their attacks individually. Like the Hudsons, the Blenheims were armed with four 250-lb (110 kilogrammes) bombs per aircraft. The remaining four operationally serviceable Blenheims had already left for Andir, in order to carry out attacks from there on the Japanese invasion fleet on its way to the Bay of Bantam.[18]

It was a clear night with broken clouds. In the second half of the night, however, visibility decreased, as, in spite of the fact that an almost full moon had come up, its light dispersed on the clouds. Just below the clouds a trail of foam in the wake of Japanese ships was reasonably visible. The first mission of the Blenheims only resulted in near misses. Gauging the position of a ship by means of the visible part of its wake proved to be a treacherous affair. One of the Blenheims was damaged by the anti-aircraft artillery from the Japanese war ships and was out of service for the rest of the night. A second appeared to be unserviceable on its return, but, just like Wiley's bomber, could be committed once more after repairs.[19]

One Hudson and the four remaining Blenheims took off for a second mission around 21:00 hrs. The seven transport ships of the Japanese convoy were now sailing a southerly course at high speed and were only some 25 kilometres away from Eretan Wetan. Wilson's crew hit a transport vessel, upon which a heavy explosion took place that lit up the sea for miles around.[20] The Blenheim crew of Flt Lt J.V.C. Wyllie also attacked a transport vessel from low altitude, scoring direct hits.[21]

After having been rearmed and refuelled, the Hudson (with its original crew, commanded by Plt Off Wilson) took off for a third mission at 23:30 hrs, followed by the four Blenheims, with, amongst others, Wyllie's crew (on their third and last sortie of the night, like Wilson's). The Japanese transport ships had to be traced anew, but visibility was becoming poor and patches of sea mist and low clouds were hanging over the coast. The crews could not find the Japanese ships anymore. It was assumed that by now they would have anchored near Eretan Wetan, and that the Japanese, under cover of the cloud, had begun to disembark their troops.[22]

Subsequently, at around 03:00 hrs (on 1 March) all operationally serviceable bombers at Kalidjati, two Hudsons and five Blenheims, took off for a last mission. Some of the bombers had got fresh crews, while some of the original crews were flying their third and last sortie. Among the latter were the crew of Wg Cdr J.R. Jeudwine, the commanding officer of 84 Squadron, and Flt Lt M.K. Holland of the same squadron. The two Hudsons of 1 Squadron were now flown by Plt Off P.J. Gibbes and Flg Off R. Richards. By this time the weather had improved somewhat, but visibility over the sea was poor. Amidst heavy anti-aircraft fire the bombs were dropped on the anchored transport ships, without any visible results, however.[23]

At around 05:00 hrs one of the two Hudsons and four of the five Blenheims had returned safely at Kalidjati. One Blenheim, flown by Sgt G.W. Sayer's crew which was committed for the first time that night, had gone missing. The crew arrived back at the airfield in the morning by truck. Thinking he was being pursued by a night fighter, Sayer had used up so much fuel that he had to make an emergency landing in a sawa north of Kalidjati. There were more British crews that reported night fighters, which were supposed to be operating with search lights in the nose. They were, however, disbelieved (rightly so) during their debriefings. With the exception of the odd cruiser reconnaissance plane the Japanese did not operate at night. ML personnel immediately realised what was going on. In the extremely clear tropical night the lights of some planets were so bright that it seemed as if a shining light was hanging in the sky behind the bombers. Once, in December 1941, a Brewster fighter aircraft over western Borneo had been sent after Venus by the ML!

The Hudson, flown by the Richards crew, had been hit by Japanese anti-aircraft artillery in the elevator. The pilot kept flying in circles until sunrise and then crash-landed at Kalidjati.[24]

The missions of the ML near Eretan Wetan

The first mission of the Glenn Martins took place on 28 February 1942 at around 19:30 hrs from Kalidjati. The bombers operated in two patrols, the Straatman patrol of 1-Vl.G.II (Straatman, Stuurhaan and Bakker crews), and the Belloni patrol (Belloni and Van Kruiselbergen crews of 1-Vl.G.I and the Noorman van der Dussen crew of 2-Vl.G. III). The weather had become somewhat hazy again by now, but the foam trails of the Japanese ships were still reasonably visible in the water. After some searching around for the transport vessels, they bombed in patrol formation from an altitude of about 1,000 metres. Both patrols only scored near misses with their three 300-kilogramme bombs per aircraft. On passing their targets the belly gunners fired at them by the light coming from the tracer bullets from the Japanese anti-aircraft artillery. They also fired their machine guns at several other ships emerging from the darkness. Only the Glenn Martin of the Belloni crew sustained any damage from the Japanese anti-aircraft fire and was unserviceable for the rest of the night. At around 21:30 hrs the last bombers landed at Andir. In order to avoid congestion at Kalidjati (with its one narrow strip and the many bomb craters in its immediate proximity), it had been decided to fly the following missions from Andir.[25]

At around 00:30 hrs (on 1 March) the Glenn Martins took off from Andir for their second mission, now in patrols composed as follows. A patrol of three aircraft, led by Tlt P.E. Straatman (Straatman, Van Kruiselbergen and Noorman van der Dussen crews) and a patrol of two aircraft, led by Vdg J.J. Stuurhaan (Stuurhaan and Bakker crews). The Japanese transport vessels were nowhere to be found. They were anchored off the coast near Eretan Wetan by this time, but the low clouds over the coastal area made them invisible to the bomber crews. The Glenn Martins landed at Andir again at around 02:30 hrs,[26] only to take off again at 04:00 hrs for a third and last mission. In the meantime Elt F.J.W. den Ouden had arrived at Andir, after having flown a mission against Palembang I airfield with his crew. The Glenn Martins now operated again in patrols of three aircraft each: the Den Ouden patrol (Den Ouden, Van Kruiselbergen and Noorman van der Dussen crews) and the Straatman patrol (Straatman, Stuurhaan and Bakker crews). They bombed from an altitude of 1,200 metres, and in spite of intensive anti-aircraft fire, the bombers did not receive any hits, the shells exploding far behind them. They did not score any hits themselves. The Den Ouden patrol approached a destroyer or light

Glenn Martin WH-2 Bomber of 2-Vl.G.III of the ML during an exercise at Singkawang II (West-Borneo) circa September 1941. (Private collection, P.C. Boer)

cruiser (they thought it was a cruiser) from the rear and scored several near misses. The Straatman patrol threw their bombs on a transport ship, but without any visible result.[27]

Three aircraft of 2-Vl.G.III, with the Van Leyden, Franken and Groenendijk crews, had been relocated from Tjisaoek to Kemajoran, the civilian airfield of Batavia in the morning of 28 February. The fourth aircraft of the afdeling (the Noorman van der Dussen crew) had been relocated to Kalidjati to reinforce 1-Vl.G.I. The facilities at Kemjoran were minimal. Although the ML had a large supply of bombs and aviation fuel on this civilian and partially militarised airfield, there was only a small ground crew consiting of one mechanic and several assistants of 3-Vl.G.III. For the rest the other air base facilities were taken care of by the KNILM. For this reason the flying crews had to help with loading the bombs. The patrol left at about 22:00 hrs.[28]

The weather over the sea was fine with broken clouds illuminated by a bright moon. As was said above, the abundant moon light in combination with the clouds, however, hampered visibility. For this reason Elt H.M.E. van Leyden dived just below the clouds and flew a northerly course to Boompjes Eiland. On approaching the target area the three Glenn Martins received extremely heavy anti-aircraft fire, upon which the patrol commander decided to carry out the raid from a higher altitude after all. The crews increased their mutual distance and climbed up through the clouds. In doing so, the patrol dispersed and the crews could not find each other above the clouds.[29]

The Franken and Groenendijk crews each dropped their bombs individually and at a gamble (the trailing planes were not equipped with bomb sights) over a transport vessel. The Van Leyden crew dropped theirs over a light cruiser or destroyer. Looking back through his bomb sight the observer Elt J.M.L. van Roon saw an explosion on the aft deck. The anti-aircraft fire was intensive, with quite a lot of tracer and many muzzle flames coming from the guns on the Japanese warships. However, the Glenn Martins were not hit.[30] No Japanese records remain with details on the damage sustained in this air raid, so it is impossible to verify the claim of the Van Leyden crew. When the Franken crew had dropped their bombs, a second Glenn Martin, that of the Groenendijk crew, appeared out of the blue. In formation the two crews flew a southerly course back to the coast and from there in the direction of Batavia, following the coast line. They had come quite close to Tandjong Priok (the harbour of Batavia) when the Glenn Martin of the Groenendijk crew suddenly fell into a spin and disappeared out of sight. It had probably been hit by anti-aircraft fire over the Japanese fleet. The Franken crew could not localise the Glenn Martin, which had probably crashed into the sea. No trace of the plane or its crew was ever found. Franken landed his undamaged Glenn Martin safely on Kemajoran, where his patrol commander had landed about an hour earlier. The Glenn Martin of the latter was also undamaged.[31]

At around 02:00 hrs (on 1 March) the two remaining Glenn Martins took off for a second attack. When the leading plane was airborne, Vdg H.M. Franken took off in the trailing aircraft. His plane, however, got entangled in the 'Friese Ruiters', barbed wire obstacles that were placed on the runway when it was not in use, and which had now been pulled beside the runway. A sudden loss of pressure in the brake system caused the plane to be uncontrollable in its take-off run. The Glenn Martin slid off the runway and hit one of the obstacles with a propeller.[32] Van Leyden continued his mission and attacked the Japanese ships, which were now lying off the shore at Eretan Wetan, on his own. Visibility had decreased very much and the crew did not manage to score any hits. The Glenn Martins of 2-Vl.G.III were not committed again. At Kemajoran an aircraft of 3-Vl.G.III also arrived, flown by the crew of Tlt J. Coblijn, who had carried out a mission against Palembang I airfield.[33]

After a short debriefing the Van Leyden crew left from Kemajoran to Andir at around 04:00 hrs. At the same time the bomber of the Franken crew left for Tjisaoek to pick up ground personnel and as much as possible of their luggage, as it had been decided in the mean time to evacuate Tjisaoek and to withdraw 2-Vl.G.III to Andir. After some makeshift repairs to the propellers and a few hours' rest for the crew, this plane also left for Andir, where it arrived at around 11:00 hrs. The Glenn Martin of 3-Vl.G.III had already relocated from Kemajoran to Andir by sunrise and was to be committed with a 'fresh' crew against Japanese shipping near Eretan Wetan.[34] Due to an unfortunate coincidence the aircraft of the Franken crew made a belly landing (see Chapter 3.4).

The attacks of the RAF in the Bay of Bantam

The four Blenheims of 84 Squadron operating from Andir carried out two missions, in which a total of seven sorties were flown. It took some time before the first missions could be launched because the pilots had to wait for the reconnaissance reports of a Catalina flying boat to come in. When it was clear that the Japanese main landing was going to take place in the Bay of Bantam, the bombers were sent out. At around 23:00 hrs (28 February) just before the Japanese transport vessels with the second echelon landing troops were ready to steam up towards their anchor places, the bombers attacked from low altitude. Four direct hits on the transport vessels were claimed.[35]

Shortly after this the Japanese ships were attacked by two allied cruisers, *Houston* and *Perth* ('survivors' of the Battle of the Java Sea), which were trying to escape through the Soenda Strait to Tjilatjap, and subsequently by the Dutch submarine K-XV. Artillery fire and torpedoes from allied war ships also hit various Japanese transport vessels, among which were probably those already bombed. Japanese war ships fired several torpedoes at the allied cruisers and probably also hit some of their own ships. In the enormous chaos, only made worse by a smoke screen laid by Japanese destroyers, both allied cruisers sank. The K-XV managed to escape safely to Colombo.

The total damage for the Japanese amounted to one transport vessel sunk, and one abandoned and capsizing after listing heavily, two heavily damaged transport vessels beached, one mine sweeper sunk and several war ships damaged. Afterwards the Japanese were unable to tell which ship had been hit by exactly what. The effect of 110-kilogramme aircraft bombs with their delayed fuses, dropped by the British bombers, would fairly often be confused with that of a torpedo and therefore the actual results of the Blenheims cannot be ascertained. The Japanese Navy formally apologised to the Army for the fact that at least one ship had probably been hit by one of its own torpedoes.[36]

The second RAF mission was carried out with three aircraft. These three Blenheims flew back to Kalidjati after the attack, where they arrived at around 05:00 hrs (1 March). The fourth plane remained at Andir awaiting repairs. During the last mission probably no Japanese ships were hit because of the bad weather.[37]

The results of the night raids at Eretan Wetan

The night raids by the Glenn Martins, Blenheims and Hudsons had exacted a heavy toll on the endurance of the crews. In total 46 sorties were flown, 19 by Blenheims (plus seven more to the Bay of Bantam), 6 by Hudsons and 21 by Glenn Martins (plus a further 2 to Palembang I). Most of the crews flew three sorties and made as many as four to six flying hours. All pilots committed were experienced in night flying, but not a single one of them had experience in carrying out night attacks on ships (small moving targets), which made the sorties all the more exhausting. Due to the weather conditions in the area of Eretan Wetan it was impossible to find the Japanese ships during some of the missions, and during the last ones visibility over the target areas had decreased very much. It should therefore not come as a surprise that the results attained, in spite of all the efforts made by the pilots and their crews, could be called meagre at best.

Apart from many near misses, direct hits were claimed on three transport ships (two by 1 Squadron and one by 84 Squadron) and on one cruiser or destroyer (by 2-Vl.G.III). On one of the transport ships, hit by one or more 250-lb bombs from a Hudson, an explosion took place, which lit up the sea brightly for miles around.[38] From the side of the Japanese Navy only a brief summary of the battle remains, which states, "There was some damage done to the transport ships and also the personnel sustained some injuries, but the landing operation was not hampered by this."[39] This seems in accordance with reality. Japanese sources also explicitly state that the ships did not sustain any damage in the first attack by the Hudsons.[40] After daybreak the Japanese would experience much more hinder and damage by allied air raids.

* * *

CHAPTER 3.4

The Operations on 1 March 1942

Introduction

In its nightly planning of the air operations for the daylight hours on 1 March Java Air Command (JAC) committed all its available fighter aircraft against the Japanese landing at Eretan Wetan (west of Indramajoe). The instructions for the defence of western Java had just been approved and issued by General Headquarters (AHK) that night. According to these instructions AHK would determine further where and with which troops the main offensive against the Japanese invasion troops would commence. In the early hours of 1 March it decided not to resort to major troop movements just yet, as there was still no clear indication of the enemy's 'concentration of strength'.[1] Between approximately 02:00 hrs and 03:00 hrs the 2nd Cavalry Squadron (Cav. 2, stationed at Kadipaten) was given orders to move to Djatibarang in order to reconnoitre the enemy bridgehead at Eretan Wetan from there. Besides, the IVth Infantry Battalion (Inf. IV) at Cheribon, with the attached 7th Battery Mountain Artillery, was ordered to counter-attack.[2]

The plans reckoned with a Japanese advance towards the west via Tjikampek to Krawang (in order to cut the connection between Batavia and Bandoeng), an advance in southerly direction, via Soebang to Kalidjati airfield and a possible advance of Japanese troops via Tomo and Tasikmalaja in the direction of Tjilatjap, in order to cut the connection between western Java and this port with its crucial importance for the allied war effort. In spite of Japanese fleet and air actions south of Java, there were still arriving freighters with equipment and supplies and also aircraft for the allied air forces, on a daily basis.[3]

Apparently the Japanese fleet had begun to disembark its troops by means of landing craft somewhere between 01:00 hrs and 03:00 hrs. As an area on the coast needed to be secured first and a rather large number of troops was involved (about 6,000 to 7,000 men, it was thought), the Combined Operations and Intelligence Centre

(COIC) assumed that by daybreak (around 05:30 hrs) a substantial part of the Japanese troops would still have to be ferried ashore.[4] Only in the morning of 2 March was the Japanese strength scaled down to a maximum of 5,000 troops, and probable no more then 4,000, see Chapter 3.5. In reality, there were some 4,000 men involved in the landing at Eretan Wetan, 3,000 of whom belonged to Shoji's regimental battle group, including the combat train. COIC advised directing (keeping on directing) the missions on 1 March exclusively on attacking the landing operation and the Japanese bridgehead on the coast near Eretan Wetan. It was hoped that in the mean time, while these missions were being executed, more clarity would emerge on the Japanese advance.[5]

At around 06:00 hrs Major-General L.H. van Oyen (commanding officer of JAC) was given a situation report based on the scarce information from the land forces and debriefing of the crews of the air forces. During a short conference Van Oyen discussed the report with his subordinate commanders, Air Vice-Marshal P.C. Maltby of BRITAIR and Colonel E.T. Kengen of the ML Command, and then phoned Colonel E.L. Eubank, the commanding officer of the American *East Group* (reinforced with a detachment of fighter aircraft of 1- and 2-Vl.G.V, 2-Vl.G.IV and 36 Squadron RAF) in central and eastern Java. Incidentally, Eubank phoned back an hour later with the proposal to evacuate his American units to Australia. Van Oyen did not agree, apart from non-combat ready bombers, but Eubank was to evacuate nevertheless (himself included), causing a formal complaint through diplomatic channels.[6]

Nothing was known about the Japanese advance in the west, but Van Oyen did not consider that a problem. The land forces in the west were to make a phased withdrawal on a line that could be well defended near Batavia and Buitenzorg, all the while blocking the roads the Japanese would have to use during their advance. The man-made constructions (such as bridges and dams) in those roads would be demolished. The blockades and demolitions had been prepared well. All this would make it possible to leave the Japanese landing troops in the west to their own devices for a day and to direct all the attention on the landing at Eretan Wetan, which was a much greater threat to the defence of western Java. Bandoeng, the place where the most important civilian and military headquarters were concentrated, had come directly in the danger zone.[7]

It was concluded in part from coast guards reports, reconnaissance missions carried out by cavalry squadrons and infantry patrols by Inf. IV that the Japanese were probably advancing on Tjikampek, but not, or in any case not yet, on the south-east (Tomo, Tasikmalaja), nor on the south in the direction of Soebang and Kalidjati airfield. The tired staff officers probably did not realise enough that the situation report was based on only very few hard facts and they concluded that Kalidjati and the road and railway connections between western Java and Tjilatjap were not endangered.[8]

The transmission of messages to the staff of Bandoeng Group and from there to the General Headquarters, the COIC and other staffs was often seriously delayed. It was the monsoon season, with frequent heavy tropical showers, which made telephone and radio communication in the nightly hours impossible. This was also the case in the early morning of 1 March 1942. The cavalry squadrons, mentioned above, did have radios at their disposal but they too were dependent on the civilian telephone network and dispatch riders for their communication. Only JAC had its own operational telephone network, with lines to the General Headquarters, the subordinate staffs and almost all airfields, the so-called ABDAIR lines. JAC also had radio communication with the operational airfields via the radio station of the ML Radio Service near Andir airfield. Furthermore, there were a number of special military lines, such as, for example, the line from the coast guard at Eretan Wetan to Inf. IV at Cheribon.[9]

A possible enemy advance in the direction of Tjilatjap was blocked by the reinforced Inf. IV (about 1,000 men in total), whose main body was on its way to Eretan Wetan via Tomo. Between Eretan Wetan and Soebang, however, there were stationed only a few small warning detachments (due to a shortage of troops) along the stretch of the coastal road going west to Pamanoekan and along the north-south road from Pamanoekan to Soebang near some river crossings and important cross roads. Those detachments were manned by landwachten–country guards (local volunteers, usually planters and personnel from the enterprises, paramilitary forces, much like the British Home Guard) and older conscripts of the so-called Afdeling Landstorm Soebang (Soebang Landstorm detachment), whose commander operated from a command post in Soebang. No reports of any Japanese advance had been received from these warning detachments.[10]

The country guards and the military personnel of the landstorm did not have their own means of communication although they did have sufficient numbers of vehicles. In case they had to give warning, a serviceman drove over in a jeep to the nearest (civilian) telephone or to Soebang. Not until much later would it appear that some of these detachments had been taken out by the Japanese troops, without having been able to pass on their warnings. The Japanese advance remained unnoticed until the troops were close to Soebang.

The Soebang Landstorm Detachment in fact consisted of a landstorm company of about 130 men, who were responsible for the security of the small town of Soebang (where all British and Australian aircrews of the squadrons at Kalidjati were billeted), and several roads leading into Soebang, as well as the security of the bridges and a few important crossroads on those roads. These tasks were executed in cooperation with the local country guards and the local (rural) police. Some of the objectives the company secured were the road and the bridges from Sadang to Soebang. For reconnaissance and patrol purposes the company had jeeps and several assault vehicles (light armoured cars with an open platform) at their disposal, but with the exception of a few machine guns they had not been issued with heavier armament.

The company was part of a landstorm battalion stationed at Bandoeng, one of two such units that together took care of the security of a large number of objects and roads on the Bandoeng plateau and the terrain adjacent to the Bandoeng plateau. The two battalions were so-called garrison-bound units without a full combat and supply train and for that reason they were considerably smaller than regular battalions. Their combined strength was around 1,000 men, who together had 12 assault vehicles. The plan was to reinforce the troops at Soebang as soon as possible in case of a landing on the coast from the battalions stationed at Bandoeng. That was not to be anymore, however.[11]

The ML fighter operations in the morning of 1 March 1942

In the morning of 1 March 1942 the allied fighter aircraft took care of the principal part of the actions against the Japanese invasion fleet near Eretan Wetan. The first to attack were the Brewsters of 1-Vl.G.V and 2-Vl.G.V. The fighter pilots assigned for duty of these afdelingen were woken up at 04:00 hrs and reported for duty with their afdeling commanders in the North Hangar, a hangar standing on its own in the northern part of Andir airfield, about an hour later. Both commanders had received their instructions from ML Command shortly before that. The available information was scanty. Near Eretan Wetan, somewhat to the west of Cheribon, seven Japanese transport vessels and five warships had anchored, and troops were disembarking there by means of landing craft. The two operationally serviceable Interceptors of 2-Vl.G. IV were to take care of the protection of Andir during daylight.[12]

Captain J.H. van Helsdingen, the most senior afdeling commander, was to lead that day's missions of 1- and 2-Vl.G.V in person, which is why he gave the briefing for the other pilots. It did not amount to much more than the following announcement, "First we drop our two bombs over the Japanese invasion fleet. You can pick a ship yourself. Next, you fire your four machine guns almost empty on the landing troops. Keep some ammunition in case you are attacked yourself on your way back."[13] In the meantime the Brewsters were armed with two 50-kilogramme fragmentation bombs, while the ammunition bays were filled to the brim; those of the 12.7-mm machine guns partly with 'tracers', which meant one tracer bullet in every five to eight normal bullets.[14]

At around 05:15 hrs the seven operationally serviceable fighter aircraft took off, five of 1-Vl.G.V and two of 2-Vl.G.V. The eighth plane assigned to the mission could not leave because it was still in repair at the Technical Service. This was aircraft B-3101 of Vdg P.R. Jolly, a plane with a notorious troublesome engine. The fighters formed up in two patrols. Kap Van Helsdingen led Sgt A.E. Stoové of 2-Vl.G.V and Sgt A.E. van Kempen and Sgt J.P. Adam of 1-Vl.G.V. Kap A.A.M. van Rest, the commander of 1-Vl.G.V, formed a patrol with Elt P.G. Tideman and Elt P.A.C. Benjamins of his own afdeling.[15]

On their way out to the coast the pilots test fired their machine guns and Van Helsdingen gave his final instructions. "When we get there, get your plane in a sheer dive, while you aim for one of the ships. Let go of your bombs. Get out of there and machinegun the landing craft. Watch out for any enemy fighter aircraft protection up there." Soon after this, the fighters were approaching the coast. The first sunrays were sparkling in the water. From an altitude of 2,000 to 2,500 metres the Japanese ships were clearly visible. There were indeed seven transport ships anchored off the coast, protected by three destroyers, as far as could be ascertained. Two destroyers were lying off shore, while a third was patrolling further out. Several dozens of launches and a few larger landing craft were moving to and fro between the transport ships and the beach. With the calm sea and the clear sky it was almost a peaceful sight; a picture only to be torn to shreds within a few minutes by the Japanese, when all the ships began giving off fire. In particular the destroyers put up an impressive screen of fire. The fighter pilots could clearly see the flames and smoke coming from the muzzles of the anti-aircraft guns and already before they had passed the coast line were flying among little puffs of white smoke of the exploding shells. The intensive gun fire sounded like a continuous roar of thunder.[16]

The Brewster fighter pilots were flying relatively far apart and, flying a zigzag course, each picked its own target. In a steep dive they dropped their bombs from an altitude of 1,000 to 1,500 metres, most of them over a transport vessel, some over a larger landing craft or on the beach with the landing pier. They were not hugely successful. Subsequently, the pilots fired their machine guns from a low altitude at the lauches and the troops that had already landed on the coast. The anti-aircraft fire was intensive and the Brewsters were fired at from the Japanese ships as well as from the coast.[17]

Most of their ammunition was spent in two or three runs, the pilots each time diving for the one rain cloud that was lying low over the water after completing one. It was the only protection from the withering anti-aircraft fire. Continuous manoeuvring prevented the Japanese gunners from finding their range, while the Brewsters were roaring at high speed over the landing craft in a shallow dive. The tracer ammunition told them were their fire struck, which made it possible to fire accurately. The pilots saw their bullets strike in the square launches packed to the brim with men on their way to the coast. In front of their eyes the fighter pilots saw Japanese soldiers jump over board fully packed.[18]

The fighter pilots flew back to Andir individually, where in the meantime Captain Van Rest had already landed. After a failed dive bombing attack on a transport vessel his Brewster had been hit in one of the wings, starting a fire in the wing tank, which was extinguished quickly. Van Rest made it back safely to Andir, where his plane was sent to the Technical Service for repairs.[19]

The other six Brewsters landed without any damage and, after having been refuelled and rearmed, were committed again with mostly the same pilots at around 07:45 hrs. Sgt Van Kempen was replaced in this second mission by replacement pilot, Sgt P. Compaan of 1-Vl.G.V. Lt Tideman had proposed to have the replacement pilot take operational turns, so that one by one the pilots would get some rest. The second mission was carried out in the same manner as the first one. The planes did not incur any damage worth mentioning, the odd bullet hole quickly being taped over. Sgt Stoové, however, got engine trouble on his way back. After having been repaired, his plane (B-3114) was test flown by Elt Th. G.J. van der Schroeff of the Technical Service.[20]

After a successful test flight he was landing at Andir at a short distance behind a Glenn Martin, when he thought he saw a Navy O on his tail. Looking backwards he was suddenly fired at from the front. Startled, the test pilot instinctively landed his plane on its belly. The crew of the bomber, led by Vdg H.M. Franken of 2-Vl.G.III had taken the Brewster for a Navy O and had fired at the fighter aircraft from the rear cockpit. As the bomber's landing gear had not been secured properly, it, too, landed on its belly. Both aircraft were sent to the Technical Service, where the B-3114 was declared unfit due to irreparable damage to the wing. Spare wings were no longer available and the fighter aircraft was already partially cannibalised in the evening and night of 1 March. The repair of the Glenn Martin M-523 would later be finished by the Japanese, employing Dutch POWs.[21]

The results of the two raids by 1-Vl.G.V and 2-Vl.G.V are difficult to ascertain. Several dozen landing craft were machine gunned. One direct hit on a larger landing craft was by Kap Van Heldsdingen. Four launches were stopped on the water, but they did not sink. The (only) jetty at Eretan Wetan, with an anti-aircraft machine gun positioned at its end by the Japanese, received a direct hit from one of the 50-kilogramme bombs of Elt Benjamins, which took out the anti-aircraft position. On land, troop formations were machine gunned by Benjamins and Stoové, amongst others. All the bombs dropped over the transport vessels missed their targets. This was partially due to a lack of training of the pilots coming from the former 3-Vl.G.V (disbanded in February 1942): Tideman, Adam, Van Kempen and Compaan. These pilots had no experience whatsoever in bombing, as, with the exception of one training flight, there been no time for training.[22]

Immediately after the first mission of the Brewsters three Glenn Martins attacked. After the first and second attack by the ML the Hawker Hurricanes of the RAF at Tjililitan carried out strafings (attacks in a low pass employing the guns) against the Japanese landing on the shore (see below). From the early hours of the morning onwards the two, later three Curtiss-Wright Interceptors of the ML (afdeling 2-Vl.G.IV) had been on Readiness, but they did not come into action. There were no attacks on Andir or any allied aircraft near Eretan Wetan by enemy fighter aircraft. After their second attack the Brewsters at Andir also went on Readiness.

At Andir, in the meantime, there was no information available on the land battle, other than the shocking news brought around 11:00 hrs by several Australian crews of Hudson bombers, that Japanese troops were attacking Kalidjati airfield. Two of the Hudsons that had arrived at Andir had managed to escape from there in the nick of time and had been fired at during take off.[23]

The fighter missions of the RAF in the morning of 1 March 1942

After the first raid by the Brewsters and the Glenn Martins of the ML, the Hurricanes of 242 and 605 Squadrons attacked the Japanese landing operation near Eretan Wetan from Tjililitan. The take off times of the various missions had been determined by JAC and planned carefully by the Operations Staff of JAC in order to avoid congestion and misunderstandings over the target. At around 05:30 hrs, at daybreak, three Hurricanes of 242 Squadron, led by Flt Lt I. Julian, were the first to take off, followed by five fighter aircraft under Sqn Ldr R.E.P. Brooker of 242 Squadron (two of these Hurricanes were flown by pilots of 605 Squadron) and a section of four fighter aircraft of 605 Squadron commanded by Flt Lt F.W.J. Oakden.[24]

The British fighter aircraft fired at Japanese troops on the coast and the beach and subsequently at the many landing craft that were going to and fro between the transport ships anchored off the coast and the beach. Flg Off N.S. Sharp's aircraft (605 Squadron) was hit by the intensive anti-aircraft fire. He made a successful emergency landing a few miles inland in a sawa, but he was never heard of again. Sgt W.J.N. MacIntosh's fighter aircraft (605 Squadron) was hit in several places, among which the air bottle in the fuselage, which put the armament and the brakes out of use. He managed to reach his home base, but his plane was out of action for the rest of the day. The other assigned pilots of 242 Squadron were: Plt Off W.M. Lockwood, Sgt J. Sandeman Allen, Sgt T.W. Young and Sgt I.D. Newlands.[25] Besides the already mentioned pilots, the six aircraft of 605 Squadron were flown by Plt Off G.P. White, Plt Off H.S. Pettit and Sgt E.E.G. Kuhn.[26]

At around 10:00 hrs the first of the ten still operationally service-able Hurricanes of both squadrons took off for a second mission against Eretan Wetan. The attack was carried out in the same fashion as the first one. The anti-aircraft fire was still very intensive. Two aircraft of 242 Squadron incurred some damage from fragments of anti-aircraft shells.[27] This time Sqn Ldr Wright of 605 Squadron led three pilots of the other flight (B Flight) of his squadron, Sgt A. Lambert, Sgt P.M.T. Healy and Sgt T. Kelly, plus a Hurricane of 242 Squadron flown by Sgt Young. The pilots of 242 Squadron had not been replaced and the other five pilots of this squadron were led by Sqn Ldr Brooker this time.

Arriving at Eretan Wetan, Wright's section encountered a patrolling Mitsubishi F1M fighter reconnaissance float plane, but in spite of many attempts the pilots did not succeed in shooting the highly manoeuvrable double-decker down. Worse still, the pilots had to take care not to be shot down by the gunner in the rear cockpit of the F1M.[28] The crew of the Mitsubishi, coming from the aircraft tender *Kamikawa maru* (belonging to the 1st Air Group of the Japanese Navy), was even convinced they had shot down three of their five opponents.[29] In actual fact, three fighter aircraft returned to Tjililitan, their pilots having used up all their ammunition. Subsequently, Sgt Young mistakenly thought he had shot the F1M down.[30] Sgt Kelly was the only one who still have plenty of ammunition left and, after having carried out several attacks on landing craft and an anti-aircraft gun spotted a few camouflaged float planes (F1Ms of the 1st Air Group) on the coast. He managed to set one of them ablaze. According to a Japanese source the aircraft had been taken by surprise during refuelling and one had become a total loss and a second F1M had been damaged.[31]

Just as was the case with those of 1- and 2-Vl.G.V, it was difficult to assess the results of the British squadrons. The landing boats that had been fired upon did not sink, but in at least six of the launches fires seemed to have started. On the coast three vehicles had been set on fire and on the beach one Mitsubishi F1M float plane had undergone the same fate.[32] However, the RAF lost one Hurricane and a pilot, while three other fighter aircraft incurred damage during their first or second missions and could not be used anymore during the rest of the day.

The bomber and reconnaissance operations in the morning of 1 March 1942

After the exhausting night operations a stand down had been planned for the afdelingen and squadrons at Kalidjati. The British and Dutch bombers were not going to come into action until the late afternoon. After the night bombardments 2-Vl.G.III had to evacuate Tjisaoek

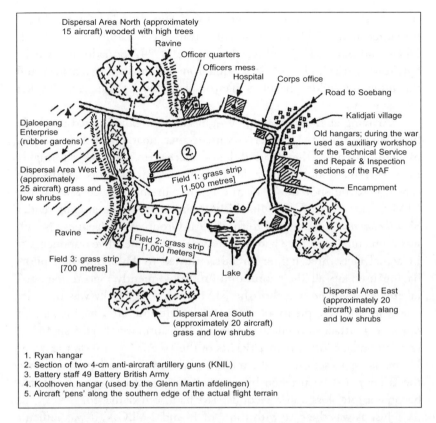

Sketch (not to scale) of Kalidjati Airbase. (Drawn by A.D.M. Moorrees and J. Staal)

On the so-called Field 1 the main runway had been laid out (1,100 metres in length). Not indicated is the (emergency) strip, which ran roughly from the middle of Field 1 in the direction of the Corps Office, and a taxi track somewhat west of this with shrapnel pens, running in front of the anti-aircraft artillery position of the KNIL (2) in the direction of the officer quarters. British 4-cm anti-aircraft guns were dispersed along the eastern, southern and western edge of the flight terrain, with one gun somewhat to the north of the battery staff (3).

airfield relatively far out to the west and help to destroy it, and then withdrew to Andir. 36 Squadron RAF, deployed in eastern Java from Maospati (Madioen, central Java), was on its way back to Tjikampek. Therefore, 3-Vl.G.III at Andir was the only unit of the entire JAC bomber fleet that could be committed.

In the early morning of 1 March 3-Vl.G.III had three Glenn Martins available, one of which had just returned from a night mission against Palembang. All day on 28 February the two other aircraft had been worked on and only in the course of the night did both planes come out of repair.[33] Shortly after sunrise the two repaired Glenn Martins attacked the transport vessels lying at anchor in patrol formation. They were flown by the Van Thiel crew and the Kroes crew, with Tlt H.E. van Thiel acting as the patrol leader. The Glenn Martins bombed immediately after the attack by the Brewsters of 1- and 2-Vl.G.V, described above. Two of the seven transport ships lying at anchor received direct or near hits from 300-kilogramme bombs. From one of the ships a column of smoke came rising up, the second disappeared in a column of water. Both ships did not sink.[34]

Some 20 minutes later the bomber that had returned from Palembang, flown by the Van Erkel crew, attacked the same target on its own, also hitting a transport vessel, but not sinking it either. The three aircraft of 3-Vl.G.III were not or only lightly damaged and returned safely at Andir.[35] Besides the Glenn Martin flown by Tlt P.J.P. van Erkel, also the four Curtiss-Wright CW 22 Falcon reconnaissance planes of the 1st Reconnaissance afdeling (Vk.A.1), each armed with two 50-kilogramme bombs, were to carry out an attack on the Japanese transport vessels. Nothing came of this, however.

The patrol of Vk.A.1 had been relocated from Tjikembar to Andir to support Bandoeng Group of the KNIL with reconnaissance missions and left for its new home base at sunrise, flying via Eretan Wetan. When approaching Eretan Wetan, patrol leader Tlt W. Jessurun was confronted with such intensive anti-aircraft fire, that he did not want to risk his slow and vulnerable reconnaissance planes. The patrol came under operational control of Group Bandoeng. The two patrols of Vk.A.1 that stayed at Tjikembar, flew intensively in support of West Group (see Chapter 3.6).[36]

The fall of Kalidjati

As early as 28 February JAC started to make preparations for the evacuation and destruction of Kalidjati, following enemy ship movement north-west of Pamanoekan. The airfield, which was weakly defended by one company of the KNIL, consisting of about 180 men, was only 50 kilometres away from the north coast and 75 kilometres from Eretan Wetan as the crow flies. The events developed at a quicker pace than JAC had foreseen and could follow from its Bandoeng headquarters.

The duty NCO of the ML in the command post of the Commandant Luchtstrijdkrachten–local Air Officer Commanding (CL, the operational commander of the ML afdelingen) in the Kalidjati kampong received a telephone call at around 02:00 hrs in the morning of 1 March from the assistant Wedana (village chief) of Eretan Wetan. He told him that right in front of his house the Japanese were making a landing with, amongst others, tanks. Led by the picket officer, several functionaries on duty of the ML, the RAF and British light anti-aircraft artillery and the KNIL were subsequently alerted. At around 03:00 hrs the CL, Lieutenant-Colonel J.J. Zomer, who had been on a duty trip to Bandoeng, arrived in the command post.[37] Zomer immediately ordered the only present but not operationally serviceable Glenn Martin to be flown over to Andir. A crew, led by Tlt C.J.H. Samson, flew the plane over shortly after 03:00 hrs.[38]

The ML Command at Bandoeng could not be reached, as the telephone lines were out of order due to the heavy tropical showers and radio communication was also impossible. So, it was out of the question to ask for instructions and Zomer's personnel would only manage to make contact with Bandoeng in the morning after many hours of fruitless trying. In the mean time, the British Station Commander, Group Captain G.F. Whistondale (operational commander of the British and Australian squadrons and commanding officer of the British RAF Station Kalidjati staff), had also arrived at Kalidjati, but he could not make contact with BRITAIR from his command post near the north-east entrance of the airfield either. Zomer did not want to keep on waiting for instructions. An officer of the rural police at Soekamandi had also reported by telephone that the Japanese had landed and that the enemy was advancing on Soebang. Therefore, Zomer (who was also ML base commander, in modern parlour, the platform commander), decided on his own initiative to carry out the ML part of the demolition plan for Kalidjati airbase and ordered the Glenn Martin afdelingen to collect their personnel at the airfield. This took place at around 05:00 hrs. Whistondale decided to keep on waiting for instructions from BRITAIR. Annoyed by the latter's inflexible attitude, Zomer had the British and Australian unit commanders informed that the Japanese had landed and that an attack on the airfield could be expected at short notice. He informed the commander of 49 Battery, Major R. Earle, who had been charged by Whistondale with the entire ground defence of Kalidjati, in person.[39] The majority of 1-Vl.G.I had been on leave for the weekend since the afternoon of Friday 27 February (after an exhausting series of operations over southern Sumatra), but those of 1-Vl.G.II were 'in'. It was this afdeling that supplied the bulk of the men for the demolition teams. Their first task was to set fire to the approximately five large depots of piled up drums of aircraft fuel in the woods near Soebang.[40]

At around 05:30 hrs the Glenn Martins returned from their last night raid, and their crews were informed that after their debriefing and preparation of their aircraft they would have to go to Andir. The remaining flying personnel of 1-Vl.G.I and 1-Vl.G.II would have to go to Andir by bus and train. The Glenn Martins left between 07:00 hrs and 07:30 hrs. After three missions the crews were exhausted, but they were not replaced. Only Elt F.J.W. den Ouden, who had done the most hours as he had flown a mission to Palembang, had himself replaced by Sergeant-Major D.T. de Bont.[41] The remaining flying personnel left by bus to the small railway station of Pasir Boengoer north of Kalidjati. The road there, however, was obstructed by fallen trees (an action of the KNIL which had not been reported to the airfield), so that they had to make a detour to reach Andir. Both the group of six Glenn Martins and the bus arrived safely.[42]

At around 07:00 hrs the lines of communication with Bandoeng had been restored and Zomer and Whistondale finally received instructions from their respective headquarters. The operational telephone line, the so-called ABDAIR line, was working again, but the civilian PTT line with Bandoeng was still out of order. BRITAIR as well as the ML Command stated that Kalidjati was not facing any direct threat. A cavalry squadron of the KNIL had been told to make a 'reconnaissance push' and by now an infantry battalion at Cheribon had been ordered to carry out a counter-attack on Eretan Wetan, both officers were advised. This did not reassure Zomer, because he knew that it involved a reconnaissance squadron which was equipped with only a few armoured vehicles and that the IVth Infantry Battalion (Inf.IV) was at a relatively large distance and would never be able to carry out a counter-attack at short notice.[43]

Apart from its many jeeps, 2nd Cavalry Squadron (Cav. 2) had actually only five armoured vehicles. Besides Cav. 2 was some 75 kilometres as the crow flies away from the landing location. Inf. IV was even further away, some 100 kilometres as the crow flies from Eretan Wetan, and had to move along secondary roads via Tomo (a movement in westerly direction, of almost 100 kilometres by road), from where it was still a 100-kilometre drive to the landing area.[44]

Whistondale was given the order to disperse his Blenheims and Hudsons as much as possible and to hide them from view (which had already been done after the last night mission) and to have them prepared for a renewed deployment in the late afternoon. Zomer pointed out that he had already sent his ML bombers away and was given orders to stop the demolitions immediately. The CL had the demolition teams pulled back. So far they had only set fire to only a small part of the fuel dumps of the ML. Zomer ordered the commanders of 1-Vl.G.I and 1-Vl.G.II to gather their personnel together and to prepare an evacuation by road to Andir with their own vehicles, pending further orders.[45]

To his utter surprise Group Captain Whistondale saw the first ML bombers leave shortly after 07:00 hrs, by order of Zomer, he later found out. The latter tried to convince Whistondale, without any success, that own initiative was of the essence now and that the evacuation of Kalidjati could become a reality at any moment. Whistondale first consulted with Major Earle in his battery staff, located in one of the evacuated officers' houses just north of the airfield, and drove back to his own headquarters at around 08:00 hrs. Zomer finally managed to convince the British colonel to some extent by 09:30 hrs, when it became clear that there was fighting going on in Soebang.[46] Then, Whistondale, too, ordered the commanders of his RAF and RAAF squadrons and the commander of the ground defences, Major Earle, to prepare an evacuation to Andir of aircraft, guns and as much other materiel as could be managed. Also the anti-aircraft sections of the KNIL (two Bofors guns and six 12.7-mm machine guns), stationed at Kalidjati, which had already been alerted by order of Zomer, were given their warning orders. Whistondale, however, refused to give the order to fly the ready Blenheims and Hudsons over to Andir just yet. Instead he decided to go to Soebang to see for himself, which, incidentally, would give him the opportunity to pick up his luggage in the process, he explained to the people standing around when he took his leave.[47]

Also present in Lieutenant-Colonel Zomer's command post was Captain L.J. Prummel, the commanding officer of 3-Inf. II, who had transferred command of the airfield defences to Earle shortly after midnight and who was waiting for orders to take his company to a location to be specified further. As the telephone lines with Bandoeng were down, Prummel did not know where to go and decided to stay at Kalidjati for the time being. After consultation with Zomer he dispatched a section (a platoon of about 45 men), led by Sergeant-Major H.J. Heijligers, in the direction of Soebang at first light, in order to take up a position some ten kilometres east of the airfield. A section led by reserve 1st Lieutenant J. van den Berkhof was sent to Pasir Boengoer, directly north of the airfield, in order to block the road coming from Soekamandi. Prummel had a part of his third section, led by Vdg J.R.J. Rugebregt, take up positions on the edge of the Kalidjati kampong, and he held the remainder of his company in reserve in the southern part of the airfield, where also the vehicles of the company were located. Later in the morning Van den Berkhof's section took up positions along the road from Soebang to Poerwakarta, at some ten kilometres west of the airfield.[48]

The company of the British Army that took over the airfield defences consisted of around 140 men. Apart from that, there was also the defence section of 84 Squadron RAF of around 30 men. The company in fact was manned by gunners equipped as infantry of 12 Battery of 6 Heavy Anti-Aircraft Regiment that had lost their materiel in southern Sumatra. The company, which was reasonably well armed (rifles, Tommy guns and Bren guns) and trained in security and defensive operations, was commanded by Major N. Coulson, who deployed his unit in consultation with Earle. For the time being, that was on and around the airfield, as the unit was completely unfamiliar with the surroundings and had arrived at late as 28 February around 20:00 hrs in darkness.[49]

Coulson committed just over 100 men, ten of whom were RAF personnel, who occupied the four pill boxes (each armed with one 7.7-mm or 12.7-mm machine gun) in the south-eastern corner of the terrain and the north-western corner of the so-called Field 1, an enormous stretch of grass on which the take off and landing runway had been plotted. These pill boxes, which were surrounded by barbed wire, only had a limited usefulness, as their embrasures only allowed the application of fire on the flight terrain itself. Furthermore, eight RAF personnel manned several fake pill boxes made of canvas over a dug-in concrete ring with a 7.7-mm machine gun inside. In the mean time, Earle and Coulson were making plans for the commitment of the platoons of 12 Battery and at around 09:45 hrs Earle ordered a combined deployment in two detachments of two Bofors guns of his own battery and two 'infantry' platoons of Coulson's. These two detachments were to guard two roads leading to Kalidjati.

The remaining personnel of 12 Battery were in part given some patrol tasks. Prummel transferred several jeeps and three assault vehicles (light four-wheeled armoured cars with open platforms) for carrying out reconnaissance and patrol tasks. Coulson's staff took over the location of 3-Inf. II in the southern part of the airfield, where, just like 3-Inf. II before, 12 Battery (fully mobile) parked the bulk of its vehicles.[50]

Shortly before 08:00 hrs the Japanese advance guard was approaching Soebang along the road from Pamanoekan leading south. A patrol of several country guards came racing ahead of the Japanese, alerting the landstorm detachment, which had already been warned, however, and part of the detachment stationed at Soebang itself had by now taken up positions around the northern entrance of the small town.[51] It was not long before the first shots were fired. The hastily warned Wing Commander J.R. Jeudwine, the commander of 84 Squadron (and at that moment the most senior officer on the spot), who had gone to Soebang after the departure of the ML bombers to direct his personnel there to Kalidjati, immediately ordered the RAF and RAAF personnel to drive to Kalidjati with all the available vehicles. Most of the crews that had taken part in the exhausting night missions were fast asleep by now, and in spite of the already climbing temperatures had to be woken up. At Kalidjati everyone was to report at the command post of the Station Commander. For some personnel, however, there was no transport directly available. They would have to wait for the return of the trucks from Kalidjati.[52]

The Japanese advance guard of Wakamatsu Group consisted of an infantry company (150 to 200 men) in trucks, on one of which a light cannon had been mounted, and six light tanks. The latter and some infantry were still on their way.[53] The infantry on the two lead trucks (about 40 men) attacked the Dutch troops near the northern edge of Soebang at around 08:00 hrs and the landstorm troops could not hold out against the Japanese for long with their relatively light armament.

It had been impossible to request reinforcements in Bandoeng because the (civilian) telephone lines were still down. Reports on the Japanese advance from other places did come in, though, by telephone and country guards, to the effect that Japanese tanks were approaching. After an hour or so the remaining defenders used a lull in the fighting to fall back on the western part of the small town. The European population of Soebang, insofar as they had wished to leave, had been evacuated by now, as had the nursing staff and patients of the small

Armoured personnel vehicles of the KNIL. Lightly armoured trucks with an open platform for the transport of seven to ten infantrymen, used, among others, by the Afdeling Landstorm Soebang during the war. (Private collection, P.C. Boer)

hospital in the town, which was also used by Kalidjati. About 20 patients (almost exclusively RAF and RAAF personnel) that could not be moved and several nursing staff stayed behind. In the mean time, the RAF and RAAF personnel had made good their escape in the trucks. A number of landstorm troops died in the fight and only part of those manning the positions in Soebang managed to get away along with the personnel of the command post in several assault vehicles and other vehicles. A small number of KNIL personnel and the above-mentioned patients, along with several European inhabitants that had remained behind and some nursing staff, fell into Japanese hands. All were later murdered or executed by Japanese soldiers. Two country guard members had been asked to go and alert Kalidjati, while the troops of the landstorm company retreated using the road that ran along the airbase to Bandoeng via Sadang. Their retreat was covered by the infantry section that Captain Prummel had sent from Kalidjati.[54]

When Soebang had been captured, this section, under the command of Sergeant-Major Heijligers, which had taken up positions several kilometres west of Soebang in a rubber plantation, engaged in combat with elements of the Japanese vanguard at around 09:15 hrs. After having opened up fire on the Japanese infantrymen on the road to Kalidjati, who had halted at a distance of about 150 metres from this section, a brief exchange of fire ensued. The Japanese subsequently carried out a flanking attack on the position of the section. Firing all the time, Heijligers retreated in southerly direction. During this retreat, a number of Brewsters of the ML, on their way back from an attack on Eretan Wetan, happened to be passing. This caused some panic and the section broke up.[55] At around 09:15 hrs the rest of the Japanese vanguard with the tanks arrived at Soebang (while the fight with Heijliger's section was still in progress), but they were not needed anymore for the mopping up operation of the resistance. For the moment the Japanese did not advance any further, as they had to wait for the main force of the infantry on its way from Eretan Wetan in two columns and mostly by bike, to catch up.[56]

As was stated above, the flying personnel of 1-Vl.G.I and 1-Vl.G.II had already left for Andir earlier, by Glenn Martin and bus, and some in their own cars. On hearing the report of the Japanese landings on the radio, many personnel of 1-Vl.G.I who had been on leave tried to return to Kalidjati. But this proved to be impossible. Virtually everyone on their way to the base was sent back at the KNIL roadblocks or at the station. Only Elt J.C. Beckman and Vdg P.A. Cramerus were trapped. On their way to Soebang in their car they encountered Elt J. van Loggem of 1-Vl.G.II, who advised them that Kalidjati was being evacuated and that he was on his way tot Andir because of that. Nevertheless, the two officers drove on, only to be duly taken prisoner by Japanese infantry near Soebang. Cramerus managed to escape later that day and reach Bandoeng. Beckman was found after the capitulation of the KNIL at Kalidjati, decapitated.[57]

At around 09:00 hrs the two country force members who had come from Soebang by jeep arrived at Zomer's command post. They reported that Soebang had already been occupied by the Japanese and that Japanese tanks were on their way. Hardly had the two left when remote but clearly audible firing could be heard. Just at that moment, around 10:00 hrs, ML Command called. An unidentified officer (probably Colonel Kengen) tried to explain to Zomer that Kalidjati was not facing any direct danger. Zomer exploded in anger, held the receiver outside the window and then shouted in the mouthpiece, "That's the Japs, damn it, we are not firing ourselves, for heaven's sake, listen." The firing that could be heard was probably Japanese gun fire directed at Group Captain Whistondale's car, whose was leaving Kalidjati on his way to Soebang at around 10:00 hrs. He was captured and subsequently killed by Japanese soldiers.[58]

Around 10:15 hrs, after Zomer's telephone call, Prummel sent out another group of some ten men, led by Rugebregt, in an assault vehicle which he had retrieved from the British for this occasion. Their orders were to reconnoitre the approach road to Kalidjati from the direction of Soebang and to make contact with the section that had been sent out earlier. They did not get very far, and afterwards it appeared that their assault vehicle had been blown off the road by a Japanese tank. Rugebregt and the other servicemen, some of whom had been wounded, were captured and experienced the capture of Kalidjati as POWs.[59]

At around 10:00 hrs the ground personnel of 1-Vl.G.I remaining at Kalidjati had left for Andir, via Poerwakarta, by truck, where they arrived safely. The personnel of 1-Vl.G.II were standing ready to leave in the southern part of the base. Elt H.J. Otten, the afdeling commander, checked out by 10:30 hrs in a temporary command post which Zomer had had established in the officers' mess (just north of the airfield and several kilometres to the west of Kalidjati kampong).[60] The Australians and British of 1 Squadron, too, were gathered, ready to leave, in the southern part of the airfield and awaiting instructions from their Station Commander. The last remaining group of flying personnel of 84 Squadron had arrived from Soebang by truck at around 09:15 hrs. The ground crews of this squadron (billeted in Kalidjati village) had gathered almost completely in the Dispersal Area West ('West') of the airfield. Trucks were waiting for them there, ready to take them to Andir. A group of armed volunteers was standing ready to destroy the Blenheims, both unserviceable and not airworthy, that had been parked in 'North'. Crews were ready to fly the eight airworthy Blenheims in 'West' to Andir.[61]

Wing Commander Jeudwine was waiting in the command post for the return of Whistondale, while in the distance occasional rifle fire and fire of automatic weapons could be heard. When Lieutenant Moundson of 49 Battery arrived on his motorbike and warned that the Japanese were coming along the road from Soebang, Jeudwine gave to order to evacuate to Andir in accordance with a plan which had been drawn up earlier that morning by Whistondale and his subordinate commanders. The personnel of the light anti-aircraft artillery and the ground defence were to evacuate to Tjimahi simultaneously and immediately after the flying squadrons. Major Earle, incidentally, did not receive any orders anymore. Jeudwine and the officers of 84 and 1 Squadrons with whom he was waiting in the Headquarters RAF Station Kalidjati were just about to leave when the building came under fire. The men raced in several cars along the runway in the direction of 'West', but before they had got half way, Japanese light tanks arrived at the airfield at around 10:30 hrs firing their guns.[62]

The 1-Vl.G.II column immediately left and drove towards Tjikampek, west of Kalidjati, via various kampongs. As, according to the KNIL, the road could not be used anymore, they left from there for Bandoeng by train, where they arrived in the middle of the night. During the journey to Tjikampek an infantry section had joined 1-Vl.G.II. This was Lieutenant Van den Berkhof's section, which had initially secured the road from Soekamandi to Pasir Boengoer. The section had taken up position along the road to Poerwakarta, just west of the point where the columns of vehicles that were retreating through the rubber plantation west of the base were directed back to the main road again. The journey to Bandoeng took place without any further contacts with the enemy, although on arrival two crew members of 1-Vl.G.II appeared to be missing.[63]

The personnel of 1 Squadron that were in Whistondale's command post until shortly before the Japanese tanks entered the airfield through the north-eastern entrance close by, were on their way to Disperal Area West, where the operationally serviceable aircraft of the unit were parked, or the southern part of the airfield. The ground personnel and a part of the flying personnel of 1 Squadron arrived at Bandoeng in a similar fashion to that of 1-Vl.G.II, without making contact with the enemy.[64] A large section of the personnel of 84 Squadron, too, managed to escape via the southern end of the airfield with the trucks that were available in 'West'. It was in the nick of time and thanks to Wing Commander Jeudwine and several officers of the squadron, who acted as a decoy, racing ahead of the onrushing Japanese, all the while firing their Tommy guns at them from Jeudwine's civilian car. Some personnel of the defence section of 84 Squadron and of 12 Battery also evacuated by truck via the southern part of Kalidjati.[65]

Four Hudsons, three of which were airworthy but not operationally serviceable, managed to escape just in time. Two had only just left when the Japanese attack began, two others (one with only Flg Off P.J. Gibbes on board, who had had crept into his plane while under fire) were taking off when the Japanese tanks came racing onto and firing at the airfield. Although fired upon and hit several times during take-off, both aircraft reached Andir safely.[66] Personnel of 84 Squadron still tried to taxi several Blenheims from the Dispersal Area West to the flight terrain, but the first got stuck in a filled up bomb crater with one wheel. Then, the Japanese began to fire at the dispersal area and all manned aircraft had to be deserted in a hurry. During the attempt to escape several pilots and crew members and ground personnel were killed.[67]

Somewhat earlier, the Japanese tanks had driven through Kalidjati kampong, firing. The command post of the ML there had already been largely abandoned. Zomer was looking down the road when suddenly projectiles impacted right in front of him. He could not get to his car anymore and ran into the terrain. After a two days' walk, around the Goenoeng Boerangrang mountain the CL arrived at Bandoeng.[68] Sgt F. Stapel, the NCO on duty, had parked his private car nearby and when he raced onto the airfield he saw the Japanese tanks approaching in his rear view mirror. Stapel escaped, as did the service personnel in the new command post.[69] Captain Prummel ran towards the edge of the wood to gather his remaining men on the edge of Kalidjati kampong. He did not succeed. The men were already engaged in combat and some of them would be killed in the battle. With his men along the southern edge of the airfield, however, Prummel made himself useful by taking care of fleeing RAF personnel (mostly RAF station staff), British ground defence personnel and ML personnel (of the air base staff, the Technical Service and Flying School and 2-Vl.G.I personnel detached with the Technical Service) and later guiding them through the woods south of the base in the direction of Segalaherang.[70]

The personnel of the workshop (sub depot) of the Technical Service of the ML at Kalidjati, where people had still been working as if nothing had happened (the CL had no authority over this personnel) left their workshops and hangars running along the north-eastern perimeter of the airfield towards the tracks leading into the terrain. The chief of the workshop, 2nd Lieutenant H.J. van Pesch, died with a number of his subordinates in the attack.[71]

As it was a while before the Japanese vanguard with its tanks was followed up by the infantry of the main force, most of the ML personnel and the RAF and RAAF personnel managed to escape. Apart from Prummel and his infantrymen (south of the airfield), personnel of the Djaloepang rubber enterprise near Kalidjati (west of the airfield) played an extremely commendable role in this. Vehicles with personnel of, amongst others, 1 Squadron, 84 Squadron and 1-Vl.G.II were led through the rubber plantation via 'garden paths' to a point on the main road of Soebang to Poerwakarta some ten kilometres from the airfield. In the middle of the night the first groups of personnel that had been gathered in the south set out on a journey on foot towards the Tjiater position.[72] 84 Squadron lost approximately 26 men, including 14 of the defence section, while 1 Squadron suffered no personnel losses in the evacuation at all, apart from one officer who had gone to Soebang with Whistondale earlier. Two other members of this squadron that had gone missing showed up again later.[73] Several wounded of the British ground defence were left behind in the small Djaloepang company hospital, which was also used by Kalidjati. On the advice of one of the British wounded the armourer of the Bofors anti-aircraft section of the KNIL, Corporal J. Tap, made his escape still wearing his pyjamas and went straight for the Tjiater position through the terrain.[74]

In the meantime the Japanese infantry took the positions of the anti-aircraft artillery and the ground defence on the airbase in a quick and efficient fashion. The Japanese tanks and the trucks with infantry of the vanguard had been the first to enter the airfield. The preparatory bombardment had been carried out by the six light tanks and the light cannon of the vanguard, which fired on the pill boxes in the corners of the field and the gun pits. After that the infantry stormed the positions, which were taken without any losses worth mentioning. The British defenders, insofar as they had not been killed, quickly left their positions holding up their hands. They did not have any anti-armour guns.[75] As was said above, Major Coulson had been ordered to take up positions along two roads together with a few gun detachments of 49 Battery and two of his platoons were packing their gear and loading their trucks when the Japanese attack began. The two 4-cm anti-aircraft guns had just been taken from their emplacements, but it was too late to use them as anti-armour guns anymore.[76]

The anti-aircraft artillery of the KNIL, two 4-cm Bofors guns, commanded by Sergeant-Major J. Hendriks and two sections with six 12.7-mm machine guns in total escaped in time. Contrary to what has been stated elsewhere, the crews of the British anti-aircraft artillery (ten 4-cm guns in total) did not take part either in the battle. Around 10:30 hrs Earle, who had seen a Japanese light tank approaching during a reconnaissance of the road leading to Soebang, ordered the personnel of 49 Battery to evacuate to Tjimahi, with their guns and as much other materiel as possible. While the crews of the guns, dispersed along the perimeter of the airfield, were being informed of this and the first gun teams were beginning to couple their Bofor guns to the trucks, the Japanese came racing onto the airfield, all the while firing their guns. Almost all the British guns were still standing with their barrels pointed up and in the end only three could be evacuated. The Battery arrived at Tjimahi with its three guns, about 20 vehicles and 155 officers and men at around 17:30 hrs. Initially, about 70 anti-aircraft gunners were missing, but later this figure dropped to 55. After the war it appeared they had all been killed in action or remained missing, probably having been murdered or executed by Japanese soldiers at Kalidjati or Soebang. Shortly before midnight on 1 March 49 Battery received new orders and the unit was transferred to Tjikembar. The anti-aircraft artillery sections of the KNIL went to Andir.[77]

Major Coulson and a number of his men of 12 Battery were killed in the battle, while several others were made Prisoners of War. In the afternoon and evening of 1 March the platoons of the battery came trickling in at Tjimahi. On 2 March 1942 79 men were still missing out of a total of about 140, some 30 of whom showed up later. After the war the number of those killed in action and gone missing on 1 March 1942 was determined at 35. A majority of these servicemen, too, were murdered or executed by the Japanese at Kalidjati or Soebang. On 2 March still many more men of the British Army and the RAF and RAAF, who had managed to get away, arrived at Bandoeng. Of the approximately 350 men of the British Army (about 140 ground defence and 210 of the light anti-aircraft artillery) at Kalidjati, however, 105 to 110 remained missing. Only a few of these soldiers had been killed in action during the Japanese attack, according to eye witness reports; after the capitulation a small number appeared to have been made Prisoners of War. The fates of the others did not become clear until after the war.[78]

Although Zomer's personal initiative had ensured that many personnel and much materiel could be evacuated in time, the Japanese managed to capture much of the latter and especially the British Army had suffered severe personnel losses. The RAF and RAAF had had to leave behind 23 Blenheims and three Hudsons (one of which had made a crash landing) at Kalidjati. The ML had lost 30 Ryan STM-2 training aircraft of the Flying School, most of which were in the

Dispersal Area East of the airfield, awaiting crating at the Sub Depot of the Technical Service and transport to the harbour of Tjilatjap. Also ten Curtiss-Wright CW-22 and one Lockheed L212 advanced trainers were lost at Kalidjati. Furthermore, two old Glenn Martin WH-1s of the Airworthy Reserve Bombers afdeling from Andir had had to be left behind. The ML had also left behind one Glenn Martin of 1-Vl.G.I.[79] Several mechanics and their assistants who were busy replacing a wing of this bomber had been killed in the Japanese attack.[80] It had been impossible to demolish most of the large supplies of aircraft fuel and all aircraft bombs that were stored in dumps around the airfield and they had had to be left behind.[81] The worst of it all was that the Japanese had captured a large airfield in the direct vicinity of Bandoeng.

The afternoon mission of 242 and 605 Squadrons on 1 March 1942

In the first part of the afternoon on 1 March the British fighter pilots of 242 and 605 Squadrons carried out two missions to Eretan Wetan. The first one was flown in the beginning of the afternoon. At that time there were eight operationally serviceable Hurricanes (four per squadron) available. Some of the fighter pilots of 242 Squadron now carried out their third and last mission. Sqn Ldr Wright again led the three pilots of B Flight, who had been up already once before. The landing of the troops had been completed by now and after a strafing of targets on the coast and a few landing craft off shore, the British fighter pilots attacked a Japanese column on the road from Eretan Wetan to Pamanoekan at around 12:30 hrs. The column, which had the strength of several companies of soldiers on bikes, was brought to a complete standstill.[82] According to a Japanese source, these were elements of the infantry battalion of the Egashira Group, the first echelon of which had left the bridgehead at around 04:00 hrs to advance on their final destination Krawang via Pamanoekan.[83]

Sgt Young's aircraft received a hit in the wing over Eretan Wetan, but that did not seem to cause any problems at first. During his approach of Tjililitan airfield, his engine had shut down, however, and Young made a successful belly landing in a swamp.[84]

Between approximately 14:00 hrs and 15:00 hrs 242 and 605 Squadrons carried out a final mission to Eretan Wetan with their six remaining operationally serviceable fighter aircraft. The Hurricanes

The Hurricane of Sgt Dunn, 242 Squadron, as it was found by the Japanese at Kemajoran. (Private collection, William H. Bartsch)

were now flown in part by 'fresh' pilots. In conformity with an instruction from JAC, ML and RAF crews were allowed to fly a maximum of three sorties per day. For this reason the three remaining Hurricanes of 242 Squadron were flown by pilots of A Flight which had 'come on duty' at 12:00 hrs, Flt Lt B.J. Parker, Plt Off M.C. Fitzherbert and Sgt G.J. Dunn. Flt Lt Oakden, Sgt Kuhn and Plt Off Pettit (A Flight 605 Squadron) flew their second mission of the day in the three remaining operationally serviceable aircraft of 605 Squadron.

Parker's section was the first to attack and fired at three landing craft that were sailing off shore and Japanese troops inside the bridgehead, who had positioned themselves in dispersed groups and fired their rifles at the Hurricanes that were flying over at an extremely low altitude. Fitzherbert spotted some Mitsubishi F1M reconnaissance float planes on the beach, and attacked them several times. On his return he claimed two flying boats. In fact he had been firing at the two F1M fighter reconnaissance float planes of the *Kamikawa maru* which had earlier been attacked by Sgt Kelly, and which were both total losses now. Having sustained some damage from anti-aircraft fire,

Sgt Dunn made an emergency landing on Kemajoran, during which he damaged a wing and a wheel suspension.[85]

Flt Lt Oakden's section attacked shortly after Parker's return, but during a quick reconnaissance of the beach and the bridgehead they could not find any suitable targets, upon which the three pilots carried out the second part of their mission, an armed reconnaissance of the coastal road from Eretan Wetan to Pamanoekan. The Japanese column which had been attacked in the previous mission had hardly made any progress since then and was quickly discovered. When the section of 605 Squadron attacked, a Japanese F1M float plane appeared that tried to engage one of the Hurricanes. Sgt Kuhn prevented this and was convinced he had shot the plane down.[86] According to Japanese sources, however, the F1M crew (coming from the aircraft tender *Sanyo maru*, which belonged to the 1st Air Group) escaped, without their plane even being damaged.[87]

The two attacks on the Egashira Group must have caused many casualties among the Japanese infantrymen. After all, it was a column on a long straight road amid sawas, so with virtually no possibilities for cover whatsoever. Here, too, Japanese infantrymen showed great discipline and, standing up, fired their rifles at the fighter aircraft. These were flying at high speed, though, and at an extremely low altitude, so the chances of receiving a hit were minimal. The Japanese reported that their advance was hindered severely by attacks from British fighter aircraft and it was not until the evening that the Egashira Group had assembled in its entirety at Pamanoekan at a mere 40 kilometres from their landing point.[88]

The afternoon missions differed from the morning ones, as the disembarkation of the landing troops had been completed. After an attack on targets of opportunity on and near the coast some British fighter pilots carried out armed reconnaissance missions of the road that ran west from Eretan Wetan via Pamanoekan. The ML was to cover the road from there to Soebang (see below). The Japanese activities in the bridgehead and the ferrying with small craft between the coast and the transport ships appeared to be very limited during the afternoon of 1 March. Apparently, the Japanese had begun to transport and unload their supplies at night because of the danger of air raids.

At the end of the afternoon 242 and 605 Squadrons were merged due to a lack of aircraft, a decision which had already been taken as early as 28 February. The latter squadron transferred its four aircraft to 242 Squadron, which now incorporated all 12 remaining Hurricanes of the RAF. There were also a number of personnel transferred to fill up vacancies, upon which 605 Squadron left for Tjilatjap on its way to its final destination in Australia. The evacuation was only to be successful in part. Thus, a number of pilots only arrived in the harbour after it had been closed due to Japanese air raids and a naval blockade.[89]

The third fighter mission of 1- and 2-Vl.G.V and the advance of Inf. IV on Eretan Wetan

When the British squadrons had carried out their third and fourth missions to Eretan Wetan and surroundings in the first part of the afternoon, 1-Vl.G.V and 2-Vl.G.V took over the battle. At around 15:00 hrs the five remaining operationally serviceable Brewsters took off from Andir, flown by Van Helsdingen, Tideman, Benjamins, Van Kempen and Compaan, who replaced Adam on this occasion. The attack was carried out in a similar fashion to the two morning attacks. The pilots dropped their two 50-kilogramme fragmentation bombs over transport ships or targets inside the Japanese bridgehead. Subsequently, enemy troops and anti-aircraft artillery on the coast and near the coastal road were attacked. After a few runs van Helsdingen gave orders to break off the attack, as the anti-aircraft fire was much more intensive compared to that during the morning missions of the ML. Besides, the Japanese had now also put into position a substantial number of anti-aircraft machine guns on land.[90]

After this, the pilots carried out the second part of their mission, which was a reconnaissance of the coastal road from Eretan Wetan to Pamanoekan and the north-south road from there to Soebang. On this latter road Japanese troops on bikes had been spotted and attacked by the crew of a Falcon reconnaissance plane, consisting of Sgt M. Cox (pilot) and Tlt W.A.N. Eduard (observer). The fighter pilots roamed the roads individually or in pairs, but nothing was found. All Brewsters returned safely at Andir, some with light damage.[91]

JAC kept the fighter aircraft on standby after this mission to clear the way for an attack on Eretan Wetan by Inf. IV of the KNIL. This unit was to take the Japanese bridgehead, making further supply of the Japanese landing troops impossible. The mission of 1-Vl.G.V had in part been intended to lend support to the infantry battalion, which was to mount an attack in the second part of the afternoon.[92] In the morning only the Cav. 2 reconnaissance squadron had operated in the environment of Eretan Wetan.

Operating from Kadanghaoer (south-east of Eretan Wetan) the armoured vehicle platoon of Cav. 2 had twice sought and got contact with enemy troops, during which two armoured vehicles conducted an exchange of fire with a Japanese infantry unit that was moving in southerly direction across the coastal road. The armoured vehicles had been forced to withdraw when, next to machine guns, the Japanese began using anti-armour guns as well. One of the two jeep platoons of the reconnaissance squadron also carried out a recce of the Japanese bridgehead. If the situation had allowed, Cav. 2 was to have advanced on Pamanoekan, but that proved to be impossible. The Ono Group (a reinforced infantry company) held positions around the village of Eretan Wetan, both north and south of the coastal road leading from this village in the direction of Patrol and Pamanoekan. At around 15:00 hrs, however, the advance guard of Inf. IV arrived in the area of Kadanghaoer.[93]

This battalion, reinforced with the 7th Mountain Artillery Battery (four 7.5-cm guns) had been alerted in the early morning of 1 March, upon which it made preparations according to the standing order for a movement to Tomo, where there was a prepared position of the KNIL which the unit was to take up to secure the route to Tasikmalaja and Tjilatjap. Even before they had taken off, an order was received for an attack on Eretan Wetan. One of the infantry companies first had to be assembled again, as it had been deployed to close off several roads near Cheribon. A second company, reinforced with a machine gun platoon, occupied a position of the KNIL at Koeningan and did not come along to Eretan Wetan.[94]

Of necessity, the movement took place along back roads and there was a short rest period at Tomo. The distance by road from Cheribon via Tomo to Eretan Wetan was some 200 kilometres and the movement of the three companies and the mountain battery took about nine hours. Most of this took place in the moist heat of the lowland plain, with a logistic train that could not immediately keep up with the advance. As a result, the troops had not been fed anymore after an early breakfast and morale among the infantrymen had dropped considerably when they arrived at the starting point for the attack, Kadanghaoer, about a kilometre from Eretan Wetan. The battalion commander, Lieutenant Colonel L. Vriesman consulted with his subordinate commanders and subsequently concluded rightly that before an attack could be launched, the men must be fed and rested for a few hours. Besides, the advance guard had only arrived at around

15:00 hrs and it would take some time before all troops (about 750 men) would have assembled for an attack. Vriesman postponed the attack until the following morning and had his battalion fall back some ten kilometres and set up camp near Losarang. In the mean time, contact had been made with Cav. 2, which was going to act as a reconnaissance unit for Inf. IV. Most of this unit fell back on Losarang in the evening of 1 March and played a role in securing the KNIL troops during the night.[95]

Order in the chaos, the reorganisation of the allied bomber units at Andir

The Glenn Martin afdelingen which had fallen back from Kalidjati on Andir were in some sort of order only in the morning of 2 March. The bombers had arrived there in the morning of 1 March, but had been sent on to Pameungpeuk around 08:00 hrs to 'shelter' there because of the danger of air raids and had not returned to Andir until around 17:30 hrs. The remaining flying and ground personnel of 1-Vl.G.I arrived at Andir in the afternoon of 1 March, while those who had been on leave came trickling in in the course of the afternoon. In the first instance, the afdeling was assembled in the Noordhangaar (North hangar), after which personnel of 1-Vl.G.I was accommodated in a hotel at Bandoeng. On their return, the Glenn Martins were parked in pens (shrapnel defences in the form of a U-shaped earthen wall) in the southern part of Andir, while some room was created for the evacuated afdelingen in nearby buildings and hangars.[96]

There was great confusion at Andir. Nobody knew anything, let alone have an idea how the battle was developing. It was not until well into the night before Captain W.F.H. van Rantwijk (commander of 1-Vl.G.I) had organised his afdeling to some extent. 1-Vl.G.II was also accommodated in a commandeered hotel in the town. The ground echelon of this afdeling only arrived at Bandoeng in the course of the night. The pilots and other crew members who had carried out the night operations were exhausted and many slept for 24 hours at a stretch once they had found a bed.[97]

36 Squadron RAF returned to its base at Tjikampek after having been deployed in eastern Java in the morning of 1 March. This air-field, however, was located on the Japanese advance route from Eretan Wetan to the west and had to be evacuated in a hurry. Not only did 36 Squadron have to go to Andir. On top of that Tjikampek was used as

a 'shelter terrain' for transport aircraft of the Koninklijke Nederlands-Indische Luchtvaart Maatschappij–Royal Netherlands Indies Airline (KNILM) which operated from Andir. In the morning of 1 March eight KNILM aircraft were parked at Tjikampek.[98]

In the morning the extremely tired pilots of 36 Squadron flew the five still flyable Vildebeest light bombers to Andir, where also the ground echelon of the squadron went. In the more than 24 hours since their departure for Madioen the crews had made more than 15 flying hours in open cockpits and they were close to exhaustion. In the battle over eastern Java the unit had lost three aircraft and two crews, among them their squadron commander Sqn Ldr J.T. Wilkins, who had been killed in action. One Vildebeest and one Albacore were left behind at Tjikampek and set on fire. Also some personnel of 81 RSU that had been working on a stranded Hurricane had to leave Tjikampek. The Hurricane which was not airworthy yet was set on fire.[99] The three Douglas DC-5s, two Douglas DC-2s, two Grumman G-21A amphibious planes and one Lockheed 14 of the KNILM almost faced the same fate. Their crews had to come from Andir, but there was no transport. In the end, one of the Hudsons which had escaped from Kalidjati was employed to fly the KNILM crews in. It was all just in time, for at 12:00 hrs Tjikampek airfield had to be completely abandoned, as a demolition team was ready to go in then. It worked, but only in the nick of time.[100]

1 Squadron RAAF was also reorganised at Andir. Although only four Hudsons had escaped from Kalidjati, two of which had received quite substantial damage while doing so and one had been flown over with a damaged fuel tank, there were still three Hudsons at the depot of the Technical Service of the ML for major repairs or maintenance. Moreover, at Semplak the squadron tried to get an eighth heavily damaged Hudson airworthy, so that the plane could be flown to Andir. The personnel of 1 Squadron who had stayed behind at Semplak (some 140 men) had finished cannibalising written-off Hudsons for usable parts and were to leave for Kalidjati on the morning of 1 March. However, when Wing Commander R.H. Davis heard about the tenuous situation at Kalidjati, he left with his men for Bandoeng, leaving behind a team of 11 men which was to attempt to get the damaged Hudson airworthy before Semplak would have to be given up. This was not to be, however, and the aircraft was demolished several days later together with the rest of the base.[101]

84 Squadron RAF had been put out of the battle completely. The personnel, who had escaped by truck, arrived at Bandoeng on 1 March, but they had had to leave 23 Blenheim bombers behind. Among them there had been eight operationally serviceable aircraft (including a Mark I), some of which had probably been damaged during the battle for the airfield. One was fired at by Sqn Ldr A.K. Passmore of 84 Squadron with a Tommy gun when it had got stuck with a main wheel in a filled-up bomb crater.[102] When this news reached JAC in the evening, and it appeared that also most of the British Bofors anti-aircraft guns had fallen into Japanese hands intact, missions were planned to take out as many of the Blenheims and anti-aircraft guns as possible. Those missions, however, would not be carried out until 3 March.[103]

Bomber operations in the late afternoon and evening of 1 March 1942

In accordance with instructions from JAC the bomber operations were resumed at around 17:00 hrs. As long as the Japanese operated from Palembang, the danger of interception by Japanese fighter aircraft from this time of the day onwards would be small. Should they still be up by then, there would always be enough cover of clouds in the late afternoon. Besides, it would still be possible to bomb with precision until sunset (at around18:30 hrs). The first to take off to Eretan Wetan was the Van Erkel patrol of 3-Vl.G.III, consisting of the Van Erkel, Bosman and Kroes crews. The weather was good with broken clouds. The three 300-kilogramme bombs per aircraft were dropped over the transport ships. The bombing raid missed the selected target, but there were several near misses. They were so close to the transport ship in question that damage was thought likely. The three aircraft incurred no or only little damage. After his landing Vdg L. Kroes found fragments of anti-aircraft shells in the sandbag which protected his back.[104]

A patrol which took off about an hour later, the Samson patrol of 1-Vl.G.II (Samson, Yland and Duffels crews) had to return without having been able to do anything. The broken clouds over Eretan Wetan had now become a closed deck, hiding the Japanese ships completely from view. They kept cruising around for a bit, looking for an opening in the clouds, but then the patrol flew back in last light.[105] Later that evening heavy rainfall made the weather too bad for any further operations. The planned night operations were cancelled and the operationally serviceable aircraft of the Glenn Martin afdelingen of the ML were not sent out again.[106]

The first attempt at recapturing Kalidjati and the first air reconnaissance on 1 March 1942

In the late afternoon 1-Vl.G.V had two operationally serviceable aircraft available again and 2-Vl.G.V had one serviceable Brewster. 1-Vl.G.V was given the order to fly an armed reconnaissance to Kalidjati with two Brewsters.[107] It was completely unknown what the situation was there. The Australian crews of 1 Squadron that had arrived at Andir had only seen an attack with light tanks, supported by mortars or light guns, but had spotted few Japanese infantry. In the afternoon JAC and the General Headquarters (AHK), however, deemed it impossible that the British airfield defence had been able to drive the Japanese off Kalidjati. If this had been the case, they would have received reports to that effect by then. So, there was a chance that the Japanese air forces had established themselves at the airfield already.[108]

At around 13:00 hrs AHK made the Mobile Unit (ME, part of the general army reserve) available to Major-General J.J. Pesman, the commander of Bandoeng Group. Apart from staff and trains, this unit consisted of 24 light tanks, 4 armoured vehicles, a section of 3 anti-armour guns and an infantry company (of about 150 men) in 16 assault vehicles and several trucks. Shortly before this, Pesman had given the patrol of Vk.A.1 the assignment to carry out a reconnaissance of the route from Eretan Wetan to Kalidjati in order to find out whether the Japanese were advancing from Kalidjati or Soebang, or were bringing up reinforcements. As was already described elsewhere, Cox and Eduard did indeed find a (rather small) column of Japanese troops on bikes on the road to Soebang.[109] The ML was given orders to take them out, but was unable to find the column again, as probably too much time had gone by in the mean time. At around 14:00 hrs Pesman ordered the ME to recapture Kalidjati and subsequently hold it. When the ME left at 14:30 hrs a mountain artillery battery was assigned to join them as quickly as possible.[110]

The advance of the ME was to go via Lembang, the Tjiater pass, Segalaherang and Soebang, because Pesman's staff mistakenly assumed (on the basis of an erroneous report) that the road via Sadang, through the lowland plain, was blocked. AHK remained adamant that the road could not be used, until the opposite proved to be the case in the evening of 1 March. Because of this the ME, which had been encamped in several locations in the environment of Bandoeng, had to advance along narrow mountain roads. This did not only take much time, but it also cost them an armoured vehicle, two assault vehicles and two trucks in road accidents. Furthermore, the advance route ran straight through Soebang, where they would first have to drive out the Japanese. In the evening of 1 March the ME had progressed no further than some ten kilometres south of Soebang. Around 21:00 hrs the men were encamped on a tea enterprise near Tambakan. This meant that an attack could not take place until the next morning.[111]

The ML Command and JAC were aware of the attack, but there was no information on the progress the ME was making. The problem was that the long-distance radio (LARA) of the ME had broken down. The chief of the mobile radio station of the ME was Corporal M.J.M. Verkaar, coming from the recently disbanded aviation radio operator training of the ML at Andir. Private wireless operator A.H. Holslag, coming from the same training, had also been assigned to the ME. After having passed the Tjiater position, Captain G.J. Wulfhorst, the commander of the ME, became mainly dependent on dispatch riders. Here and there, at an enterprise or hotel along the advance route they could use a telephone, but out of security considerations this could only be done sparingly. On top of that, heavy showers over the Bandoeng plain disrupted the telephone lines for part of the evening. At around 20:00 hrs Wulfhorst sent a dispatch rider with a situation report to the staff of Bandoeng Group. It took him hours to get there, riding in the pitch dark and along narrow twisting mountain roads.[112]

By 18:00 hrs a Japanese reconnaissance plane briefly dipped below the clouds over Andir, dropping two light bombs, which did not do any damage. The plane might have come from Palembang as well as Kalidjati. Only in the evening of 1 March would the General Headquarters conclude, on the basis of reports from KNIL units and information from British and Australian servicemen who had escaped from there, that Kalidjati (still) was firmly in Japanese hands.[113]

Vdg C.H. Weijnschenk (who had been shot down near Tjililitan on 9 February and only just reassigned) and Sgt Van Kempen of 1-Vl.G.V had better go and see what was going on at Kalidjati. The briefing by Lieutenant Tideman was vague, but he, too, lacked any information. When asked, however, he gave permission to attack any possible Japanese aircraft at Kalidjati. They took off from Andir by 18:30 hrs, but after some time in flight Weijnschenk reported over the radio to his colleague that he was having trouble with the oil pressure in the engine of his aircraft. Van Kempen continued on his own and arrived over Kalidjati in deep twilight. Cutting back the engine, the pilot descended towards the base, which seemed to be deserted and no Japanese aircraft were to be seen. Van Kempen made another low run over the field and made a half turn. He noticed not a single suspect activity, and the only thing which struck him was a plume of smoke coming from a guard house near the encampment. He briefly fired the machine guns of his fighter aircraft at it, before flying back through one of the passes to Andir, where he made a successful night landing.[114]

Results of the day attacks on the Japanese landing operation on 1 March 1942

The fighter aircraft of JAC carried out 56 sorties on 1 March, 36 of which were flown by 242 and 605 Squadrons and 20 by 1- and 2-Vl.G.V. Except for two sorties by 1-Vl.G.V to Kalidjati, one of which was aborted because of engine trouble, all sorties were targeted at the environment of Eretan Wetan and the roads leading to Pamanoekan and from there to Soebang. The RAF lost two Hurricanes and one pilot, the ML lost one Brewster during a test flight after repairs by the Technical Service. During the attacks on the Japanese landing launches and larger landing craft the Japanese troops suffered losses. Inside the bridgehead several anti-aircraft machine guns were taken out and three Japanese trucks were set on fire. Two Mitsubishi F1M reconnaissance float planes (at the time it was mistakenly thought there were three) were destroyed on the beach by strafing. The most important result of the fighter attacks was probably the severe delay caused to the advance of Egashira Group, which was made to suffer losses on the coastal road from Eretan Wetan to Pamanoekan.

The Glenn Martin bombers of the ML flew nine sorties on 1 March from sunrise onwards, during which two direct hits and one near miss on transport ships were claimed. During the last mission (three sorties) in the late afternoon the target could not be localised due to heavy cloud. After sunset all planned missions had to be cancelled because the weather had become too bad with heavy showers. This was a set-back, but at JAC there was a conviction that the Japanese had never-theless been made to suffer heavy losses and that the day missions of 1 March had been a success. The Japanese admit to losses during the landing operation and the advance of Egashira Group. On one of the transport ships a direct hit had caused a visible fire. Japanese documents describing the damage inflicted or numbers of casualties, however, have not survived.

The day attacks did not have an influence on the Japanese advance on Kalidjati airfield, which went unnoticed. Only in the afternoon of 1 March was Bandoeng Group able to respond to the fall of the base and was the Mobile Unit of the KNIL ordered to recapture Kalidjati. This order, however, could not be carried out on 1 March anymore. The afternoon attacks by the fighter aircraft had been intended in part to support an attack of the reinforced Inf. IV (minus) on Eretan Wetan. This attack, too, could not be realized anymore on 1 March.

***

CHAPTER 3.5
The Operations on 2 March 1942

Introduction

The Japanese capture of Kalidjati was an enormous setback and completely unsettled the entire defence of western Java. A large action directed at recapturing Soebang and Kalidjati, which the General Headquarters had decided upon in the evening of 1 March, however, commenced on 2 March 1942.[1] Apart from the Mobile Unit (ME, see the above chapter), which had already been deployed for this purpose by Major-General J.J. Pesman (commander of Bandoeng Group), the so-called Teerink Group was committed on 2 March. This group was the equivalent of a battalion reinforced with an artillery battery, altogether some 1,000 men (see below). On 3 March 1942 a big attack was to follow, carried out by troops of the 2nd Infantry Regiment (2-R.I.), who had been called away from the vicinity of Buitenzorg, reinforced with as much artillery as could be mustered and some anti-aircraft artillery. The ML and the RAF were to support the attacks of the KNIL to a maximum.[2]

At the request of the commander of West Group of the KNIL (Major-General W. Schilling) the Japanese in the extreme west of Java were attacked by fighter aircraft in the morning of 2 March 1942. Java Air Command (JAC) committed seven of its 18 operationally service-able fighters to armed road reconnaissance missions. The Japanese landing operation in the west was now being attacked again for the first time since the bombing raids carried out by several Blenheims of 84 Squadron in the night of 28 February on 1 March 1942 and a number of attacks by CW-22 Falcon reconnaissance planes of Vk.A.1 on 1 March, ordered by West Group itself. The CW-22s had carried out reconnaissance missions on 1 March from the early morning onwards, the first aircraft taking off at 03:00 hrs, and they had flown eight sorties in total that day to map out the Japanese advance and count the number of Japanese ships in the Bay of Bantam. During several of these sorties 50-kilogramme bombs had been dropped on transport vessels and Japanese columns. Missions to Eretan Wetan had been given priority the previous day with a view to the threat to the nearby Kalidjati. By midnight on 1 March Schilling was informed by his ML liaison officer (Lieutenant Raden S. Soeriadarma) that JAC would not be able to give any air support to West Group on 2 March either, due to actions against Kalidjati, which had been captured by the Japanese. The general did not accept this and he personally phoned General Headquarters. He got what he wanted and in the process ordered Vk.A.1 at Tjikembar (under operational command of West Group) to carry out armed road reconnaissance missions the next day.[3]

In the morning of 2 March the allied fighters and bombers, how-ever, were mainly assigned for missions to Eretan Wetan and its vici-nity. The bombers flew interdiction missions in order to disrupt the Japanese supply lines from Eretan Wetan to a maximum. A compli-cation was that the Japanese had begun to unload their transport ships and carry out the resupply of their troops between sunset and sunrise. Night attacks on road convoys was no option for JAC, as this was unfeasible with the means available at the time, so it came down to keeping up the bombing raids on the transport ships. Fighters of the ML and RAF were committed to degrade the occupation of the Japanese bridgehead as much as possible, with a view to the planned attacks of the KNIL on Pamanoekan and Eretan Wetan. Simultaneously, the aircraft carried out armed reconnaissance activities of the road leading west from Eretan Wetan and the roads from Pamanoekan leading south. Two fighter aircraft were committed to secure Teerink Group in its passage of the Tjiater pass.[4]

In the evening of the previous day no Japanese activities had been observed at Kalidjati by the ML and JAC rightly assumed that no air forces had established themselves there as yet. Bombing the extensive airfield was deemed rather pointless. Just like the ML and the RAF had been able to keep on using Kalidjati after heavy Japanese bombing raids, so would the Japanese armed forces be able to keep the airfield operational after allied raids. Attacking Japanese aircraft at Kalidjati in due course was a different matter.

The development of the allied strategy

The vulnerability of the Japanese battle group which had landed at Eretan Wetan had not escaped notice of the staff officers of the allied headquarters at Bandoeng. On the basis of the relatively small number of transport vessels a preliminary estimate of the size of the battle group that had come ashore had already been made on 1 March and in the course of that day it became increasingly clear that here was a chance for the allied land and air forces. The initial strategy came down to a maximum degradation of the Japanese landing operation by means of air raids, committing virtually all available means against the landing at Eretan Wetan. In the first instance, the land forces limited themselves to reconnaissance activities in order to establish the Japanese axis or axes of advance and to get a better idea of numbers and equipment of the landed troops. Only the IVth Infantry Battalion (Inf. IV) was given orders already in the very early hours of 1 March to stage a counter attack on Eretan Wetan.[5]

When it became clear in the afternoon of 1 March that the Japanese had captured Kalidjati airfield after a swift push, the strategy with regard to the deployment of the air forces was not immediately adjusted to this situation. Initially, Bandoeng Group assumed (erroneously) that the Japanese occupation of Kalidjati involved a relatively small vanguard and that the Mobile Unit (ME) would be able to recapture the base. The reserves of the group would be committed to secure the area once the ME had recaptured it. However, it was not possible to execute the ME attack anymore on 1 March.[6]

The only chance of success against the Japanese landing troops in western Java came down to quickly taking out the Shoji detachment and then attacking with all available strength the Japanese troops that had landed further west. Possession of Kalidjati was essential in this. As mentioned above, the General Headquarters took the decision in the evening of 1 March 1942 to recapture Kalidjati. It was assumed at the General Headquarters (mistakenly) that the Japanese had considerably reinforced their troops at Soebang and Kalaidjati by now and that this would require a far greater effort than solely deploying the ME.

On 2 March several actions of the land forces were planned in preparation of a major attack, which, as was said above, was to be carried out by the reinforced 2nd Infantry Regiment (2-R.I.) on 3 March. The secondary actions consisted of an attack on Pamanoekan from Tjikampek by elements of the Xth Infantry Battalion (Inf. X minus), reinforced with a battery of the 1st Battalion Howitzers (A. I Hw.) and the 1st Cavalry Squadron (Cav. 1), an attack on Eretan Wetan from Losarang by Inf. IV (minus), reinforced by a mountain artillery battery and Cav. 2, and an attack by the Mobile Unit and Teerink Group on Soebang and Kalidjati (see below).

The strategy of the allied air forces was adjusted accordingly. In the early morning of 2 March, around sunrise, there was to be a final all out attack with all available bombers on the Japanese transport ships. After this, the air forces were to resort to smaller-scale harassing attacks, because it was (rightly) assumed that the Japanese ships would have mostly been unloaded. The deployment of the combat aircraft, particularly the fighters, from 2 March onwards was to be as much as possible in support of (planned) attacks by the KNIL.[7]

In the course of the morning of 2 March a reasonably clear idea of the Japanese advance from Eretan Wetan began to emerge at JAC and the other headquarters at Bandoeng. The Combined Operations and Intelligence Centre (COIC) had mapped out the enemy advance with the help of a calculation of the Japanese strength by Captain C.G. van Houten of the ML Command and information gleaned from the debriefings of the aircraft crews and the results of reconnaissance missions by the Falcons of the Vk.A.1 patrol at Andir (under operational command of Bandoeng Group). A Japanese battle group with a strength of one to two battalions was advancing from Pamanoekan to Tjikampek, with Krawang as its probable final destination, but it had suffered losses and had been slowed down due to the air raids. A second battle group, of similar size, it was assumed, had occupied Kalidjati and Soebang but had not advanced any further from there.[8]

The calculation by Captain van Houten, on the basis of the tonnages of the seven transport vessels at Eretan Wetan, of which a

Glenn Martin crew had made several photographs, showed that the Japanese had landed with a maximum of 5,000 men, but 4,000, more likely. These would certainly also include engineer troops for the reconstruction work at Kalidjati, work teams to load and unload at Eretan Wetan and air force personnel for Kalidjati. Not counting the Japanese infantry occupation of the bridgehead and the Japanese anti-aircraft artillery at Eretan Wetan, the two Japanese battle groups, which were operating geographically separately, could be assumed to consist of a maximum of 1,500 men each. In other words, it should be possible to defeat both Japanese battle groups with the available troops and air forces.[9]

Van Houten's estimates (he was an intelligence and operations officer) came very close to the actual situation. Colonel Shoji's regimental battle group consisted of about 3,000 men, including the combat train, and in total some 4,000 troops had landed. The assault groups, the Egashira Group and Wakamatsu Group, each consisted of a reinforced battalion (minus) of 1,000 to 1,200 men. The much smaller Ono Group, including Shoji's reserve only some 500 troops (excluding the work parties), secured the bridgehead at Eretan Wetan.[10]

From the evening of 2 March onwards the air forces were mainly deployed against Kalidjati, which had been brought into use by the 3rd Hiko Dan by now. A reconnaissance by a Brewster fighter late in the morning had shown that the base was still firmly in enemy hands. Subsequently, in the afternoon several Glenn Martins were tasked to destroy the runway, pending the expected recapture by the KNIL. The allies had not been able to push back the moment at which the Japanese air forces had brought Kalidjati into use. At around 17:00 hrs the men at the Tjiater position (who looked down at the air base on the lowland plain at the foot of the Bandoeng plateau) reported that by then some ten single-engine aircraft had landed. At night as well as by day the fighters and bombers of the ML of the KNIL and the RAF now carried out raids to suppress Japanese activities from Kalidjati as much as possible, and, by doing so, enable a successful attack by the reinforced 2-R.I.

The bomber operations in the morning of 2 March

In the early morning, around sunrise, all available bombers of JAC attacked the Japanese transport vessels near Eretan Wetan. This came down to ten Glenn Martins, as the remaining Hudsons were not operationally serviceable and the remaining Vildebeest light bombers could only be used for the carrying out of night raids because of their vulnerability. They took off in the dark at around 05:00 hrs. In total there were four patrols involved in the raid: the Den Ouden patrol of 1-Vl.G.I (Den Ouden and De Bont crews), the Gosma patrol of 2-Vl.G.III (Gosma and Keim crews), the Van Gessel patrol of 3-Vl.G.III (Van Gessel, Van Thiel and Zoetemeyer crews) and the Straatman patrol of 1-Vl.G.II (Straatman, Bakker and Stuurhaan crews). While Hurricane fighter aircraft were attacking targets in the Japanese bridgehead and on the beach, the patrols bombed the transport ships anchored in line astern with short intervals.[11]

The anti-aircraft fire was intensive, but there were no enemy fighters up. With three 300-kilogramme bombs per aircraft there were direct hits or near misses on five ships, according to the crews. Two ships lay exactly in a hit pattern, so that it was likely they would sink soon. A later reconnaissance showed that none of the ships had actually sunk, but that they had certainly sustained considerable damage. Several allied bombers had incurred some light damage from anti-aircraft fire.[12]

The fighter operations in the early morning of 2 March 1942

At around 05:00 hrs four Hurricanes of 242 Squadron took off from Tjililitan, led by Sqn Ldr R.E.P. Brooker, for a first mission to Eretan Wetan and environment. After a brief strafing of several targets of opportunity in the bridgehead, Brooker and the three pilots under his command carried out a road reconnaissance of the coastal road leading west from Pamanoekan. Near Tjiasem (west of Pamanoekan) the section discovered a motorised Japanese column, which was fired at several times from a low altitude. A large number of the vehicles of the Japanese unit, which was in fact a part of the Egashira Group advancing along the road from Pamanoekan on Krawang, were set ablaze.[13]

Shortly after this raid the ML attacked. Around 06:00 hrs the four remaining operationally serviceable fighter aircraft of 1-Vl.G.V, flown by Elt P.G. Tideman, Elt P.A.C. Benajmins, Sgt A.E. van Kempen and Sgt A. Bergamin took off from Andir, followed by the two Brewsters of 2-Vl.G.V with Elt G.J. de Haas and Vdg P.R. Jolly. Lieutenant De

Haas had flown over an Interceptor from Madioen the previous day and had been temporarily assigned as second-in-command to 2-Vl.G.V. Captain J.H. van Helsdingen and Captain A.A.M. van der Rest, the commanders of 2-Vl.G.V and 1-Vl.G.V, respectively, had been forbidden by ML Command to fly operationally due to the risk of operational missions and the shortage of experienced afdeling commanders. The fighters flew in pairs in a loose formation. Like that of the section of 242 Squadron the attack of the ML was intended as support for the actions of the KNIL against Pamanoekan and Eretan Wetan.[14]

First, the Brewster pilots carried out a dive bombing raid, each picking a target inside the Japanese bridgehead. Next, Japanese positions and anti-aircraft artillery inside the bridgehead were attacked from low altitude. Tideman had mentioned during his briefing that the RAF had encountered Japanese reconnaissance float planes the previous day. Because of this danger and the fact that the dive bombing raid was paramount he did not allow lengthy low-altitude manoeuvring to engage ground targets or landing craft. In a shallow dive the pilots each carried out one strafing run and subsequently left the target area immediately. They flew back in a loose formation and within the hour everyone had returned at Andir individually, without spotting any enemy aircraft. The fighters incurred no or only very light damage. Reconnaissance of the roads was to be carried out by the Falcons of the Vk.A.1 patrol at Andir.[15]

The two operationally serviceable Interceptors of 2-Vl.G.IV carried out a covering mission over the Tjiater pass, through which a column of the KNIL was passing on its way to Soebang and Kalidjati. This was the above-mentioned Teerink Group (see below). The pilots were Elt W. Boxman and Sgt H.M. Haye. There was no enemy air activity. On their way back to Andir the two pilots reconnoitred the roads from the Tjiater pass to Soebang, but they did not observe any enemy activity there, either.[16]

Air actions in the West Group area

Mainly on the basis of the number of Japanese transport ships ('recounted' on 1 March by Vk.A.1 because of some uncertainty) the strength of the Japanese main force which had landed in the west had been established at a maximum of 30,000 men. COIC thought that West Group was facing two divisions totalling more than 20,000 troops, not counting staffs, supply units, etc. In actual fact one division and army corps troops were involved, over 19,000 men, altogether. The British fighter aircraft (10, later 11 operationally serviceable aircraft) were still operating from Tjililitan on 2 March. Apart from the mission of four Hurricanes to Eretan Wetan and Pamanoekan, described above, 242 Squadron was deployed in the early morning against the Japanese landing operations in the extreme west of Java. The first four Hurricanes took off at 05:00 hrs. This section, led by Flt Lt I. Julian, and with pilots Plt Off E.C. Gartrell, Flt Lt B.J. Parker and Plt Off M.C. Fitzherbert, carried out an armed reconnaissance of the roads from Merak (Soenda Strait) to Serang. They discovered a long horse-drawn column of carts, which the four pilots attacked several times from a low altitude. Afterwards the road was strewn with dead horses and upturned carts and seemed completely blocked.[17]

Three Hurricanes, led by Plt Off T.W. Watson, followed suit somewhat later that morning, carrying out a similar assignment, an armed reconnaissance of the roads leading from the Bay of Bantam to Serang. One aircraft, flown by Sgt I.D. Newlands, was forced to return on the way out to the target with engine trouble. During the machine gunning of Japanese troops near Serang, infantry columns and a number of vehicles, Watson's Hurricane incurred so much damage that the pilot had to make an emergency landing in a sawa. Sgt Sandeman Allen, the third pilot in the section, returned on his own. After an adventurous journey Watson returned with his unit on 6 March.[18]

The British attacks in the west were carried out at the request of the commander of West Group, partially in response to reconnaissance missions carried out by two patrols of Vk.A.1 at Tjikembar. These patrols were also fairly active on 2 March and carried out several road reconnaissance missions for West Group, each time with one Falcon. There were two sorties around sunrise, two sorties between 10:00 hrs and 12:00 hrs, two sorties in the late afternoon, and one sortie in the night of 2 on 3 March. The crews reported several columns of motor vehicles and a few groups of motor cyclists, which were fired upon each time, in accordance with a specific order from West Group.

During one of the morning sorties the aircraft flown by Sgt R. ten Cate, with mechanic Sgt C.W. Bilderbeek as air gunner, was damaged by anti-aircraft fire. The pilot got a bullet in his behind and made an emergency landing at Kemjoran. Ten Cate was taken to the military hospital in Batavia by ambulance, while Bilderbeek was picked up around 16:00 hrs with another CW-22 from Tjikembar.[19]

A second CW-22 was (lightly) damaged during one of the afternoon sorties. Tlt A. van Hessen and observer Elt A. Eman reconnoitred the landing locations near Merak and subsequently the main road from Serang to Batavia. They spotted a military column near Serang that was fired at successfully. During the second run their aircraft was hit by anti-aircraft fire, Lieutenant Eman receiving a bullet wound in his leg. He was dropped off at Tjililitan and was taken to the military hospital, while Van Hessen went on to report on his mission at the staff of West Group.[20]

Together with observer Elt O. Cramer, who, in the mean time, had arrived from Tjikembar, Van Hessen made a night reconnaissance from Tjililitan to Pamajaran and Serang to see how far the Japanese advance had progressed. By sunrise the crew discovered, as we now know, the Fukushima Battle Group. They attacked it three times, but without any apparent results. They were not carrying any bombs, because there were none available anymore at Tjililitan, due to the fact that that base was being dismantled.[21]

No further JAC combat aircraft were deployed in the west, as all capacity was needed for the area of command of Bandoeng Group. It was in part because of this that the Japanese advance in the west went fast. The KNIL units that were to have carried out a withdrawal in the direction of Batavia and Buitenzorg, all the while offering as stiff a resistance as possible, often could not come up with more than a chaotic retreat. Only the Japanese units which had landed in the Bay of Bantam were having a difficult time of it, but this was mainly due to demolitions and knocked down trees blocking their progress. The so-called Sato Battle Group left Bantam before sunrise on 2 March and advanced along the northerly main road to Batavia. It did not get beyond Kragilan (60 kilometres as the crow flies from Batavia) and the main force encamped 5 kilometres west of that town. The Japanese main effort of the advance, however, lay in the south.

Two Japanese battle groups advanced on Buitenzorg via Rankasbitoeng, in order to launch an attack on Batavia from there. In the morning of 2 March the vanguard of the 2nd Reconnaissance Regiment reached the west bank of the Tjianten River (extremely swollen due to the heavy rainfall), opposite the Leuwiliang position, manned by the Blackfore brigade. On 2 and 3 March, however, Blackforce managed to withstand all Japanese attacks and carried out several successful counter-attacks.[22]

New fighter attacks in the area of command of Bandoeng Group

From around 07:00 hrs onwards the Hurricanes were committed a second time. This time the British fighter pilots carried out road reconnaissance missions along the roads from Eretan Wetan in the direction of Tjikampek and the north-south road in the direction of Soebang. In the mean time, the patrol of Vk.A.1 at Andir had carried out two reconnaissance flights. Tlt W. Jessurun and Sergeant-Major R.E. Nobbe with their observers had spotted enemy columns in various locations, which (in conformity with an earlier request from Bandoeng Group) were now going to be attacked.[23]

Four Hurricanes were put on Readiness at Tjililitan to meet with any air raids against the base. The remaining six operationally serviceable British fighter aircraft were committed in patrols of two aircraft to carry out armed reconnaissance missions. The patrol consisting of Flt Lt Parker and Plt Off Fitzherbert fired at an anti-aircraft machine gun inside the bridgehead at Eretan Wetan and then spotted a column of Japanese soldiers on bikes on the coastal road near Pamanoekan, which they fired at several times from a low altitude.[24]

Near Losarang (west of Djatibarang) another Hurricane patrol (pilots unknown) machine gunned an enemy infantry unit consisting of about 600 men. These British fighter pilots, however, had accidentally fired at the reinforced Inf. IV (minus), instead of clearing the road for them. Lieutenant-Colonel L. Vriesman had been advancing with his unit on the nearby village of Kandanghaoer to mount an attack on Eretan Wetan (see below). The British fighter pilots, however, were not aware of Vriesman's advance. His unit suffered some damage to its equipment but no personal losses, although morale was shaken a bit.[25]

Within Major-General Pesman's staff the synchronizing with operations of the land forces in case of support from air forces was the responsibility of Elt H.F. Zeylemaker of the ML. In the Operations section this energetic regular officer took care of the communication (mainly by telephone) with the ML Command, BRITAIR, the ML and JAC liaison officer with the Operations section of the General Headquarters and the Operations Staff of JAC, in an effort to coordinate all this in the best possible manner. Initially, he did not have any direct contacts with operational commanders at Tjililitan, but this omission was quickly put right.[26]

The third patrol of 242 Squadron (pilots unknown) did not find any targets on the roads to Soebang, but in the town itself they did. The Japanese troops the fighter pilots found there consisted of the Staff of Shoji's detachment and some reserves the size of a company, which had arrived in the small town in the night of 1 on 2 March and in the early morning of 2 March. According to Japanese sources the attack took place around 07:30 hrs (local time) and did not cause any damage or casualties.[27]

During the actions described above, the four fighter aircraft at Tjililitan were sent up to intercept enemy aircraft approaching Batavia. Near Tjililitan, at an altitude of 3,500 metres, they engaged probably nine Japanese Ki-43 fighter aircraft. Sgt G.J. King claimed to have shot one of the fighters down during the brief encounter, but his claim was not confirmed by others and no wreckage was found afterwards. In the meantime Tjililitan was unexpectedly bombed at around 09:00 hrs by nine Ki-48s and less than an hour later again by nine Ki-48s. During the first attack the anti-aircraft artillery was hardly able to fire, but 242 Battery shot down a Ki-48, nevertheless. One of the returning fighter pilots saw the bomber crash. During the second attack the anti-aircraft artillery was ready for them and again a Ki-48 was hit. A piece of the aircraft broke off, but the bomber stayed airborne. 242 Battery suffered four fatalities and one seriously wounded in a chance hit on Battery HQ. The airfield was strewn with bomb craters, but no aircraft were lost and the base remained operational.[28]

The combat aircraft of JAC on readiness

From 08:00 hrs onwards all operationally serviceable combat aircraft at Andir, and later also at Tjililitan, were on readiness to give air support to the KNIL units. Among them was the Mobile Unit (ME), mentioned in the previous chapter. This unit continued its advance from Tambakan on Soebang at 06:30 hrs. There were, however, no assignments for air support coming in at the ML Command and BRITAIR and this was not only due to poor lines of communication.

As mentioned above, in the early morning Bandoeng Group had the patrol of Vk.A.1 at Andir fly several road reconnaissance missions. The main purpose of this was to find out whether the Japanese troops that had captured Soebang and Kalidjati had continued their advance. This did not appear to be the case. Furthermore, in conformity with an earlier request from the Group, JAC had 242 Squadron carry out armed road reconnaissance missions in response to reconnaissance results of the Falcon crews.

For direct support of land forces close to the forward line of own troops (close air support in the modern lingo) the air units lacked the means of communication and, moreover, the training and procedures. Only in case the position of the forward line was known and the time slots of the infantry manoeuvre and the attack of the combat aircraft could be coordinated in advance, could direct support from the air be given safely. It was impossible to communicate with the radios in the allied fighter aircraft and those used in the Falcons of the ML with the radio trucks employed by the infantry and artillery. The Hurricanes of the RAF were even more difficult to use for ground support, as they even lacked the crystals to tune in their aircraft radios with the frequencies used by the ML. For this reason it was also impossible to communicate with ML aircraft from the Hurricanes.

There were good procedures in place for requesting air support by the land forces, though. Many infantry battalions and all artillery battalions of the KNIL, too, were practised in cooperating with reconnaissance aircraft to carry out reconnaissance missions and the pick up or drop off of messages, and also for observation or fire control purposes. Thus, Inf. IV, for instance, had held intensive exercises at Cheribon as recently as February 1942 in working together with reconnaissance aircraft of the ML, during which from Tjikampek Koolhoven FK-51 double-deckers of the Flying School had been employed as training aircraft near the north coast west of Cheribon.[29]

The Mobile Unit did not have any radio communications as its own long-distance radio (LARA) had been out of order since 1 March. The mountain artillery battery which had been assigned to the Mobile Unit did not have a LARA radio truck, either, and only had a communications truck with telephone equipment. Teerink Group did have a radio truck which was handed over to the Staff of Inf. V shortly after its arrival at Bandoeng, complete with several wireless operators coming from the ML. Teerink Group therefore had a usable LARA, but atmospheric interference caused radio communication to be very poor. Thus, on 1 and 2 March for most of the day there was no radio communication possible, a problem which also Shoji's troops were facing. Out of necessity communication on the allied side had to rely on an overburdened (civilian) telephone network often suffering from interference, and especially on dispatch riders. The latter, needless to say, caused large delays. From the late morning onwards, however, Teerink had a usable radio connection again (for several hours).[30]

The situation at Kalidjati in the morning of 2 March 1942

As mentioned above, the Japanese regimental battle group of Colonel Shoji was also hindered by very poor communications and for that reason it could not report that Kalidjati had been captured. However, Shoji still managed in the late morning of 2 March to send word through Navy channels to the staff of the Japanese 16th Army at Palembang that he had captured Kalidjati the previous day. Immediately the 3rd Hiko Dan began preparations for the transfer of units from Palembang to Kalidjati. The first to fly there, however, was a Chutai of the 81st Sentai, commanded by Captain Minami, with three recon- naissance aircraft (Ki-15s and/or Ki-46s). One of the passengers to fly along was Major Kuboki, liaison officer with the 3rd Hiko Shudan, who had been seconded to Colonel Shoji's staff.[31]

Subsequently, Major Kiyoshi Kanzaki of the staff of the 3rd Hiko Dan left for Kalidjati with four staff personnel in a Ki-48 light bomber of the 75th Sentai to make preparations for the transfer of the air brigade. At around 13:15 hrs, the Ki-48 had landed safely at Kalidjati at 12:30 hrs, a Glenn Martin patrol bombed the air base. The Ki-48 bomber escaped and returned to Palembang with a report from Major Kanzaki to the effect that at Kalidjati he had made contact with two companies of Wakamatsu Group and a part of the so-called Sigumura Butai, named after its commander Lieutenant-Colonel Takayoshi Sigumura. This was in fact the 4th Regional Aviation unit, assigned to the Japanese 16th Army, part of which had landed with the Japanese main force in the western part of western Java. The 24th Airfield Battalion and part of the 28th Airfield Battalion of this unit, were to take care of airfield security and supply of Kalidjati, as well as con- struction works on this airfield. Small units and detachments had been added to these battalions, consisting of signals, meteorological, trans- port and loading and unloading personnel of the Army air force. Until a few days after the capitulation of the KNIL the entire group was under the command of Colonel Shoji, and only then came to fall under the 3rd Hiko Dan. On 2 March hardly any ammunition and aircraft fuel had been supplied or captured by the airfield battalions.[32]

On 1 March at around 17:30 hrs some of the landed personnel and materiel of the regional aviation unit arrived at Kalidjati. This was late, as these units and detachments had run up some considerable delays due to air raids and the reconnaissance activities of Cav. 2 in the neighbourhood of Eretan Wetan, and a subsequent blockage on the road to Soebang. In the evening of 1 March an all out campaign was started to ship over as much as possible of the materiel destined for Kalidjati. But in the evening of 1 March and the early morning of 2 March the transfer of ammunition, bombs, fuel and other stores to the air base suffered serious delays. The route appeared to be unsafe due to (reconnaissance) activities of the KNIL. During at least one of the transports a group of KNIL soldiers, probably a team of country guards, commanded by Sergeant-Major P.G. de Vries, carried out an attack. On 1 March 1942 the KNIL had been forced to let the Japanese troops go through on their way to Kalidjati, but already in the afternoon of that day it began to stage actions against the Japanese supply lines.

On 2 March at around 06:00 hrs the Japanese had managed to make available sufficient ammunition and bombs to carry out a limited number of sorties for fighters as well as assault aircraft. There was, however, only very little aircraft fuel. More supplies were not to be shipped to the airbase until the evening of 2 March and the early morning of 3 March. Nevertheless it was decided to begin with the transfer of the vanguard of the 3rd Hiko Dan from Palembang to Kalidjati.[33] By this time Colonel Shoji was badly in need of support from the air due to the unexpectedly intensive attacks from the allied air forces.

At around 10:30 hrs on the morning of 2 March the allied Commandant Luchtstrijdkrachten–local Air Officer Commanding (CL) of the ML at Andir was given the mistaken report that Kalidjati had been recaptured by the KNIL. At the same time an order was given to have a Glenn Martin carry out a reconnaissance mission to assess the condition of the airfield. The Belloni crew of 1-Vl.G.I was sent out, and it was given the additional task to land, if possible, and gather as much luggage of the personnel of 1-Vl.G.I as it could take back to Andir. The plane, however, went missing. 48 LAA also received a message to the same effect around 10:30 hrs, which prompted the plan to go and collect, with the help of the 'infantrymen' of 6 HAA, the anti-aircraft guns which 49 Battery had been forced to leave behind and to re-occupy the air base if possible. In the afternoon a reconnaissance patrol of 6 HAA ran into troops of Teerink Group on the road to Soebang via the Tjiater pass, and then it appeared that the fight for Soebang was still going on.[34]

The fighter missions in the late morning of 2 March 1942

Between 09:30 hrs and 10:00 hrs four Brewsters of 1- and 2-Vl.G.V took off for a raid against the Japanese bridgehead at Eretan Wetan, in support of an attack mounted by the KNIL. The unit concerned was the reinforced Inf. IV (minus) (see below). The pilots this time were Elt Tideman, Elt De Haas, Sgt P. Compaan and Sgt Bergamin. Shortly after the Brewsters, the two operationally serviceable Interceptors of 2-Vl.G.IV left with the same assignment. They were flown by Elt Boxman and Sgt O.B. Roumimper. Due to a shortage of available fighter aircraft and, in spite of their not really being suitable for it, the Interceptors were nevertheless, and for the first time, committed in a strafing of ground troops. Necessity, however, knew no law. It was not possible to wait for the British Hurricanes of Tjililitan (which had only just been bombed by the Japanese). It was paramount that as many fighters as possible would get up as quickly as possible because the KNIL was on the point of launching its attack on Eretan Wetan. The second Brewster of 2-Vl.G.V was not yet operationally serviceable. Elt Benjamins was confronted with a failing engine during the run up and could not take off. Compaan got engine trouble halfway on the flight out to the target and was forced to return, landing safely at Andir. Thus, the attack was only carried out by three Brewsters and two Interceptors.[35]

After the Brewsters had dropped their bombs, the pilots of 1- and 2-Vl.G.V, led the Interceptor pilots in an attack against targets inside the bridgehead at Eretan Wetan and then at Japanese soldiers on bikes in the environment. On their way back the ML pilots reconnoitred the north-south roads in the direction of Soebang. No enemy activity was found there, however. Because of the frequent allied air raids the Japanese had resorted to moving their personnel and supplies between sunset and sunrise. Soebang and Kalidjati were deliberately avoided by the fighter pilots, as the small town and the airfield were reported to have been recaptured by the KNIL by now.[36]

By the end of the morning two fighter aircraft were assigned to fly an armed reconnaissance; one to map out the Japanese advance from Rankasbitoeng in the west of Java in the direction of Buitenzorg, with a view to supporting Blackforce, and the other to assess the situation at Kalidjati airfield, assumed recaptured. In his Hurricane Plt Off Lockwood carried out the armed reconnaissance of the enemy advance on Buitenzorg. He dropped a sketch detailing the positions of the Japanese column near Leuwilang over a golf course in the north-eastern part of Buitenzorg and returned to Tjililitan without any problems.[37] Elt Benjamins (in Captain Van Rest's plane, having just returned from the Technical Service after repairs) took off for Kalidjati around 11:45 hrs.[38]

So far, there had still been no news from the Belloni crew and only after the capitulation did it appear that their Glenn Martin had been shot down on landing at Kalidjati, the entire crew perishing. At first Tlt R. Belloni, Sld A.A. Maaskamp, Sgt A.H. Cannoo and Kpl W.M.D. van Dijk were reported missing. It was decided to have a fighter carry out a second mission. By this time communication with the KNIL troops which were carrying out the assault to recapture Kalidjati had completely broken down for a considerable period of time. The report of the recapturing of the airfield came from the staff of Bandoeng Group, which had got a message to this effect from the troops manning the Tjiater position, but afterwards the original text of the message appeared to have been roughly as follows, "The ME is in Soebang, no further details."[39]

Benjamins circled over a deathly quiet Kalidjati, without noticing any activity whatsoever. Also at low and extremely low altitude the airfield seemed deserted. There was no movement. Blenheims were parked criss-cross and anti-aircraft guns were standing completely deserted in their positions. There was not a single sign of life and according to the pilot there was "an eerie silence". When Benjamins finally landed, however, he was fired at by machine guns, and he received various hits in the fuselage of his aircraft. He accelerated and escaped. Suddenly the whole place was swarming with Japanese, coming from everywhere and nowhere. When the Brewster buzzed over the buildings in the north-east of the base, scores of Japanese were standing on the platforms in front of the hangars firing their rifles at the fighter aircraft. Over the radio Benjamins sent the sad message that Kalidjati was still occupied.[40]

The ground post of the Air Defence Command Bandoeng tried to tempt the pilot into making a second reconnaissance on his way back, but Benjamin wisely declined, not knowing exactly what the damage to his aircraft was. In his stead Vdg Jolly was assigned to carry out a seaward reconnaissance north of Indramajoe, some 200 kilometres off the coast. Jolly took off in his B-3101 (which had been repaired in the mean time) at around 12:15 hrs and returned safely at approximately 14:00 hrs. He had not been able to discover any new Japanese convoys or any Japanese activity in the air. The other allied fighter aircraft were kept on Readiness, but no new assignments came for support of ground troops.[41]

Air raids on Kalidjati in the afternoon of 2 March 1942

When it had been firmly established that Kalidjati was still in Japanese hands, JAC sent out a patrol of Glenn Martins to bomb the runway of the airfield. This was the Samson patrol of 1-Vl.G.II, consisting of the Samson, Yland and Duffels crews, which attacked at around 13:15 hrs,[42] followed by one Glenn Martin, flown by Sgt L.N. Bieger of 1-Vl.G.I, at around 14:30 hrs. The Bieger crew dropped nine 50-kilogramme fragmentation bombs in an attempt to disrupt Japanese repair works. The runway (emergency strip) in the northern part of Kalidjati was successfully bombed and for the time being Japanese fighter aircraft would not be able to operate from the airfield or so it was (incorrectly) assumed.[43]

At around 15:15 hrs 242 Squadron arrived at Andir with seven Hurricanes. The squadron (minus four aircraft left behind at Tjililitan for the protection of this base) was to be committed in a third attack on Kalidjati in cooperation with the ML fighters. On being informed of incoming reports of an enemy advance from Eretan Wetan on Poerwakarta and Krawang, the commander BRITAIR, Air Vice-Marshal P.C. Maltby, who was visiting Tjililitan that day, feared a repetition of the Kalidjati debacle and immediately decided to relocate the squadron.[44] Only in the evening of 2 March did it become clear that, for the time being, the Japanese advance from Pamanoekan was not a threat. The ground echelon of 242 Squadron, which was to be relocated the next day, therefore, remained at Tjilitan after all. On their arrival at Andir, the Hurricanes, incidentally, were fired upon by their own anti-aircraft artillery, causing light damage to Flt Lt B.J. Parker's aircraft.[45]

After Lieutenant Benjamin's return it was certain that Kalidjati was still in Japanese hands. What was not known, however, was how far the bid for its recapture by the KNIL had fared. Communication lines were so poor that only in the afternoon some clarity on this was obtained. The attack of the Mobile Unit (ME) on Soebang appeared to have failed. Teerink Group, however, was still advancing and was to carry out a "reconnaissance probe" in the direction of Soebang and Kalidjati in order to keep up the pressure until the next day 2-R.I.

would launch its major attack to retake Kalidjati. Hurriedly, JAC planned an attack to support Teerink Group, to be carried out by the Brewsters of the ML and the Hurricanes of the RAF which had been kept on Readiness at Andir and Tjililitan until now.[46] The mission, however, was much delayed due to a Japanese raid on Andir (see below).

The Land Battle on 2 March 1942

The action of the ME

On 2 March at around 08:15 hrs the ME launched its attack on Soebang. Firing continuously, the tanks made a run through the village. Mainly due to the conditions of the terrain, however, the infantry could not advance quickly enough to exploit this success. About an hour later the tanks carried out a second attack, which allowed the infantry to advance further. They were, however, unable to drive the Japanese out of Soebang. The southern part this village consisted of two expanses of built-up areas along a road, on one side bounded by a ridge and on the other by a ravine. The ME infantry company engaged a Japanese infantry unit occupying positions in the densely wooded terrain just south of Soebang, in the houses and in a trench running parallel to the road. The sloping terrain on one side of the road allowed the Japanese to fire into the open platforms of the assault vehicles, forcing the two lead infantry sections (about 85 men in total) to dismount. Fierce fire fights followed in the southern part of the small town, during which the infantrymen made only little progress.[47]

After the second tank attack, which caused some losses among the tank crews, as it lacked the element of surprise, two tanks supported the infantry in their attempt to drive the Japanese from several houses, while some terrain was gained by committing the reserve section. The Japanese, however counter-attacked, causing the advance to bog down. The commander of the ME, Captain G.J. Wulfhorst, decided to break off the fight in order to prevent the destruction of his infantry. Under cover of a third run of the remaining tanks, which began around 10:30 hrs, the infantry managed to disengage successfully from the battle and withdrew from the occupied southern part of the town. The battle ended around 12:00 hrs. The third tank attack was not without casualties, either. In total, the battle had cost the infantry 14 killed in action, 13 wounded and 36 missing, who, except for two (probably both killed in action) reported back later. Two soldiers were taken

A platoon of Vickers Carden Lloyd light tanks. Armed with a 7.7-mm machine gun, these light tanks with their two-men crews, served in the Mobile Unit of the KNIL during the war. (Private collection, P.C. Boer)

Prisoner of War. Including the losses due to accidents on 1 March, 13 tanks, one armoured vehicle, five assault vehicles and one anti-armour gun had been badly damaged or lost. The anti-armour gun had to be destroyed because the vehicle on which it was transported broke down in the retreat. Five heavily damaged tanks could be towed away from Soebang.[48]

The Japanese suffered 20 killed in action and an unknown number of wounded. This was relatively much and later they admitted that they had barely been able to fend off the attack. The ME had failed by a hair's breadth.[49] The battle had been conducted with fervour, also by the infantry. The Indonesian regular troops and the short-term contract volunteers performed with excellence during the battle, clearing a trench and shooting several Japanese infantrymen from roofs and out of trees, slowly gaining terrain until the Japanese brought in an excess of reinforcements. The own infantry strength had been too small, while the conditions of the terrain made it difficult to give them fire support. Being bound to the road, the tanks could only help to a limited extent and the mountain artillery battery could not fire at all, as they could not go into the side terrain with their vehicles and guns and lacked observation points overlooking the battle field.[50]

During the battle there was no connection with Bandoeng, as the mobile radio station (with the long-distance radio) of the signals platoon of the ME was still out of order. Messages had to be sent by dispatch rider to the Tjiater position and from there by radio or telephone to the staff of Bandoeng Group. There was a radio connection, though, between the tank platoons and the infantry. Private A.H. Holslag, a wireless operator, had been detached to the infantry section of Lieutenant J.L.W. Rhaesa. From a jeep fitted with a (short-range) radio he took care of the communication between the tanks, the infantry sections and Captain Wulfhorst's command post. The assault vehicles did not have radios and Holslag usually received messages coming from the dismounted infantry sections orally. He passed on requests for support via his radio to the fighting vehicles (tanks) or Captain Wulfhorst's command post. For other addressees he wrote out the message on a message form and had it dispatched there.

The wounded were evacuated by ambulance jeeps or "casualty sidecars" to Bandoeng via the Tjiater position. The first reports from the drivers of these vehicles were the source of the incorrect message to the CL at Andir that Kalidjati had been recaptured. Among those killed in action were three Javanese hospital orderlies who had perished doing their duty in the front lines.[51]

The action of Teerink Group

Teerink Group, so named after the commanding officer of Inf. V, Major C.G.J. Teerink, was a reinforced battalion of about 1,000 men in total, with at its core the main force of the Vth Infantry Battalion (staff, 1-Inf. V and 10-4 R.I. and elements of the machine gun company 4-Inf. V). The augmentations consisted of elements of the IInd Infantry Battalion (2-Inf. II and a part of the machine gun company 4-Inf. II), the 1st Battery of the IInd Battalion Mountain Artillery (1-A. II Bg.) and a section of anti-armour guns of the 4th Anti-armour and anti-aircraft Battalion (Pla. 4). Most of the troops came from central Java, having arrived at Bandoeng as late as 24 or 25 February, and were still unfamiliar with the area of operations on 1 March.[52]

Having been relocated and their orders changed several times in the days after arrival at Bandoeng, the infantrymen were tired and insufficiently and irregularly fed. The men of Inf. II and Inf. V (belonging to 4-R.I.) were well motivated though and, except for the company

10-4 R.I. (brought up to strength just before the war broke out), well trained. The percentage of regular soldiers that had been serving for a longer time was relatively high. This was also the case for the battery of A. II Bg. The company 10-4 R.I. had originally been intended for reconnaissance tasks and came directly under the staff of 4-R.I. In 1941, however, the unit became a normal (motorised) infantry company, which came under command of the commander Inf. V on their arrival at Bandoeng.[53]

On 1 March Teerink learned how his group (in fact the reserve of Bandoeng Group) was to be composed and he was given the order to be ready for action. The troops arrived in the assembly area near the location of Inf. V staff in the afternoon of 1 March. With several other battalion commanders Major Teerink reported at the staff of Major-General Pesman only at around 23:00 hrs for receiving further instructions. Apparently Pesman at first kept his reserve at Bandoeng, pending news from the ME. However, they could not wait for this forever and besides the army commander decided that night that all reserves had to be committed for the recapture of Kalidjati. Teerink informed his subordinate commanders around midnight. By the time they had briefed their officers and cadre it was 01:00 hrs on 2 March. The troops were woken up at 02:00 hrs and given their orders and supplied with extra combat rations and ammunition.

Teerink had been given the assignment to carry out a "reconnaissance probe" in the direction of Soebang and Kalidjati at day break, via the (mountain) route across Lembang and the Tjiater pass. When he received his orders he was told about the coming main attack by 2-R.I. on Kalidjati airfield (on 3 March) via Poerwakarta (through the lowland plain), but not about the assignment and situation of the Mobile Unit. He only received the oral message that the ME had been directed towards Kalidjati (on 1 March), but he was not told via which route and much less what its position was. Later it appeared that Teerink had concluded that the ME had been deployed via Poerwakarta and had not asked any further questions.[54]

On 1 March around 20:00 hrs the Mobile Unit commander had sent a dispatch rider to Bandoeng with a situation report. This message arrived at the staff of Bandoeng Group at around 22:00 hrs. Lieutenant-Colonel H.A. Reemer, head of operations of the staff, gave Teerink his (oral) instructions, but apparently he had not seen the situation report of the ME yet. The news on the situation of the ME, however, was not sent after Teerink, a mistake of Major-General Pesman's staff. Nor was the ME informed about the advance of Teerink Group. To do this quickly, the radio of the ME having broken down, for instance a CW-22 reconnaissance plane of the Vk.A.1 patrol could have dropped a message in the early morning.[55]

Shortly after 04:00 hrs Teerink Group left Bandoeng in the direction of Soebang. As was described above, during their passage of the Tjiater pass two Interceptors flew as cover over the columns. On the narrow mountain road leading towards the lowland plain the columns, consisting of dozens of trucks, were extremely vulnerable to air raids. For half an hour the two fighter aircraft flew circles over the various columns of vehicles, but there was no enemy air activity. When Teerink Group had left the mountains safely behind them the fighters reconnoitred the route of advance. They did not observe any Mobile Unit activity from the air at that time.[56] The patrol leader was to drop a message if the enemy was seen to advance or was spotted on the roads from Soebang, but he only made one fly by as a goodbye without dropping any message. This did not tell Teerink very much. The fact that no enemy had been seen on his advance route at 06:30 hrs did by no means mean that this would still be the case an hour later. In part because there was no information on the conditions of the roads, it was decided to advance slowly after having passed the Tjiater pass.[57]

Around 08:00 hrs 10-4 R.I. was given the order to establish a secured position on the three-forked road near Djalantjagak. Subsequently, 1-Inf. V was sent ahead in the direction of Soebang. When this unit was busy taking up positions near the hydro-electric plant at Tjileuleuj (some eight kilometres from Soebang), a column unexpectedly came driving down the road from Soebang. The ME soldiers told their sad story. In the afternoon the company, which had taken up positions left and right of the road (with several forward positions in the terrain) made contact with the Japanese. One of the forward positions was fired at by a Japanese light tank, upon which it returned to Soebang.

One of the reconnaissance patrols sent out by 1-Inf. V made contact with the enemy close to Soebang. In a bend in the road the patrol suddenly encountered a group of about 90 Japanese, upon which the men fell back into the terrain to continue their reconnaissance from there. One of the *brigades* (a group of about 15 men) in the forward terrain made a reconnaissance with two men of the southern edge of Soebang in the first part of the afternoon. To this end Sergeant Snijtsheuvel and Private Vodegel donned "indigenous" garments. They were not discovered and returned to the position of their company over the road. By order of the staff of Inf. V various reconnaissance patrols were carried out between 15:00 hrs and 18:00 hrs. The area between 1-Inf. V and Soebang appeared to be free of enemy units, but the southern edge of Soebang had been considerably reinforced by the Japanese.[58]

From around 10:00 hrs onwards "casualty sidecars" and ambulance jeeps of the ME had begun passing Teerink Group positions. Initially it was thought (in 10-4 R.I. and further back) that they were casualties of 1-Inf. V, with which there was no contact via dispatch riders or a rolled out telephone line. As a result of this mistaken assumption, by the end of the morning the entire Group had deployed and taken up positions or were busy doing so by order of Teerink: 1-Inf. V at Tjileuleuj, 10-4 R.I. some kilometres to the south near the Tambakan tea enterprise, also left and right of the road, and the other elements several kilometres back in the environment of the kampong of Djalantjagak. There, beside the road to Segalaherang, was Major Teerink's command post. By this time he had talked to the men of ME (who could give only little information) and he had learned to his utter surprise that the ME was "acting" along his advance route and was fighting in Soebang. Teerink then informed his subordinate commanders about this.[59]

In the beginning of the afternoon information from the staff of Bandoeng Group was received over the radio, possibly the results of earlier road reconnaissance missions by the ML and RAF. Teerink reported over the radio to Bandoeng Group that he was going to lend assistance to the ME, but the battle in Soebang was over before he could come into action. He subsequently ordered a number of reconnaissance patrols.[60]

By this time officers of the companies 2-Inf. II and 10-4 R.I. had already heard from Captain P.E. Hendriksz, commanding officer of A. II Bg. what the real situation was. The men of the above-mentioned companies had seen the traces of tracks on the road, but had not realised that they might have been caused by the ME. Hendriksz did not have his batteries under his direct command any more, but he came by to encourage his men and to see if he could be of any use. On his way to the 2nd Battery, assigned to the ME, he passed his 1st Battery detached to Teerink Group (whose commander had been ordered to take up positions shortly before), at around 11:15 hrs, and subsequently passed positions of the two companies mentioned above.

Shortly after midday he met the retreating 2nd Battery several kilometres north of the positions of 10-4 R.I. on the road to Soebang. It
appeared the ME had been defeated.[61]

Hendriksz and Captain Wulfhorst, commanding officer of the
ME, reported between 14:00 hrs and 15:00 hrs at Teerink's command
post, where shortly before that, Captain L.J. Prummel with a part of
his company had arrived from Kalidjati (see the previous chapter).
Prummel had guided a large number of ML and (especially) fleeing
RAF and British Army personnel through the bush south of the airbase
to Segalaherang and Djalantjagak. They were sent along the road in
the direction of the Tjiater fortification for further shelter. Prummel
gave Teerink a sketch of the situation and the possibilities of approaching Kalidjati from the south through the bush.

On the basis of this information, the results of his own reconnaissance patrols and data from the ME, Teerink, completely unfamiliar with the local circumstances himself, decided to advance on the
wooded area south of Kalidjati in the evening along an enterprise road
which led to a location just west of Segalaherang. A reconnaissance
showed that this enterprise road was reasonably negotiable for heavy
motor vehicles. After that Teerink intended to launch a surprise attack
on Soebang from Kalidjati, coming from the west. In view of the
experiences of the ME, he was convinced that an attack from the
south was not feasible. That meant he would have to force his troops
through the bottle neck that was formed by the ridge and the ravine in
the southern part of Soebang. In his judgment the Japanese, who had
now been warned, would make "minced meat" of his troops.[62]

Teerink discussed this plan with his subordinate commanders in
the second half of the afternoon, in the presence of Wulfhorst and
Hendirksz. The battered ME was to stay behind and act as a cover in
the back. This was necessary, for otherwise the road from Soebang to
the Tjiater fortification would be open to the Japanese troops. The 2nd
Battery of A. II Bg., however, would advance together with Teerink,
with the guns of both mountain batteries operating in an anti-tank role,
if necessary. Wulfhorst and Hendriksz were among those who offered
objections. Teerink, however, felt the two officers were too careful and
pushed his plan through, although he did agree to Captain Hendriksz
going to inform Major-General Pesman's staff, the radio communications with the staff having broken down again in the meantime.[63]

Hendriksz left for Bandoeng at around 17:00 hrs. At the same
time 10-4 R.I. and 1-Inf. V were pulled back. 1-Inf. V left behind a

group of 15 to guard the road (until 24:00 hrs) and was the last to arrive at the three-forked road near Djalantjagak in the early evening. By the late evening the entire Teerink Group had concentrated near Segalaherang and was ready to advance. As there was no word from Hendriksz, the advance was actually commenced just before midnight, in order to attack Kalidjati in the early morning.[64]

Pesman's staff, however, did not agree. Teerink Group was to launch an attack on Soebang in support of the reinforced 2-R.I. which was to attack Kalidjati via Poerwakarta on 3 March. Due to a lack of means of communication the orders to this effect had to be sent back by road and did not reach Teerink until around midnight, because of road blockages as a result of the retreat of the ME (on positions near Djalantjagak and, as for part of the trains, to the Tankoeban Prahoe hotel behind the Tjiater fortification, by order of the staff of Bandoeng Group). Angry, Major Teerink had his vanguard, which had already left, called back and ordered a general reassembly in the environment of Segalaherang. There the men spent the rest of night shivering with cold.[65]

The actions of the KNIL against Pamanoekan and Eretan Wetan

The planned "reconnaissance probe" from Tjikampek by Inf. X (minus), reinforced with a battery of A. I Hw. and Cav. 1 (a cavalry reconnaissance squadron) against the Japanese assault group at Pamanoekan could not be carried out. At around 08:00 hrs elements of the infantry battalion and the artillery battery left Krawang for Djatisari, near Tjikampek. The bridge in the road to Pamanoekan near Djatisari, however, had already been demolished by Cav. 1 on 1 March by order of the commander of West Group. This made it impossible for the KNIL to advance and also the Japanese Egashira Group would eventually founder at this destroyed bridge. This Japanese assault group fell back on Pamanoekan on 3 March and did not take part anymore in the battle for Kalidjati. The elements of Inf. X and Cav. 1 mentioned above were later added to 2-R.I. to take part in the main attack on Kalidjati (see the following chapter).[66]

A second similar action in preparation of the main attack by 2-R.I., planned the following day, did take place. This, too, was a "reconnaissance probe" to be carried out by Inf. IV (minus) reinforced with Cav. 2 and the 7th Mountain Artillery Battery, altogether some 850 men. If the situation allowed Lieutenant-Colonel Vriesman was to push through to Pamanoekan in order to attack the enemy battle group in the back in the environment of Pamanoekan.[67]

The reinforced Inf. IV (minus) had arrived at Kadanghaoer in the afternoon of 1 March, too late to carry out an attack. It was decided to pull back some ten kilometres to Losarang (west of Djatibarang) to give the men the rest they needed. However, several alarms, during which nervous men started firing their weapons, made sleep almost impossible. The next morning Inf. IV had to suffer an attack from two British Hurricanes (described earlier) at around 07:15 hrs. While Cav. 2 was carrying out reconnaissance patrols, Inf. IV advanced on Eretan Wetan in the morning of 2 March.[68]

The unit took up positions at approximately one kilometre from the enemy bridgehead in and near the village of Kadanghaoer. The forward terrain consisted of little else than wet sawas and the asphalt road from Kadanghaoer to Eretan Wetan. With the exception of the buildings in the village there was no cover. From their starting positions the men of Inf. IV could see the Japanese ships lying offshore. They also saw the Japanese troops digging in on the beach. For infantrymen this was nightmare terrain. Just before the attack was launched, fighter aircraft attacked the Japanese inside the bridgehead (the attack by Vl.G.V and 2-Vl.G.IV, described above). The four guns of the mountain artillery were positioned left and right of the position of the machine gun company of Inf. IV. In the centre of that position were the mortars of this company.

Between 10:30 hrs and 11:00 hrs the guns opened fire, upon which the 3rd Infantry Company, reinforced with elements of the machine gun company advanced, first by the side of the road and then spread out across the sawas for the actual "reconnaissance probe". The mortars positioned on the edge of Kadanghaoer successfully fired on the enemy digging in, who subsequently opened fire on the approaching infantry, using heavy machine guns. This caused the advance to bog down some 250 metres from the bridgehead. The Japanese directed their artillery on Kadanghaoer, killing and wounding several men. Vriesman ordered the retreat, the machine gun company covering the infantry during their crossing of the open sawas. The units returned to Losarang, where Cav. 2 was the last to arrive in the evening.[69] Early the next morning a patrol, consisting of the armoured vehicles of Cav. 2 and an infantry section on a truck, was sent out to Kadanghaoer to recover missing men left behind in the terrain during the retreat. None were found, however.[70]

A Japanese air raid on Andir throws a spanner in the works

The Hurricanes of 242 Squadron, which had been sent to Andir for the planned attack on Kalidjati, had all just been parked ready to be topped up with fuel, when an air alert was given at Andir. In response, all available still operationally serviceable ML fighter aircraft, five Brewsters and two Interceptors took off at around 15:30 hrs to intercept an enemy formation which was reported to approach from the direction of Poerwakarta. Shortly before this the four Hurricanes on Readiness at Tjililitan had been sent up, but the British pilots could not find the reported enemy formation amidst the heavy clouds. The ML fighter aircraft were led by Elt Tideman, who formed a patrol with Sgt Van Kempen and Sgt Compaan of 1-Vl.G.V. The other two Brewsters, flown by Elt De Haas and Vdg Jolly of 2-Vl.G.V, acted as a pair. The two Interceptors of 2-Vl.G.IV were piloted by Elt Boxman and Sgt Haye.[71]

The fighter aircraft had been circling for half an hour over Poerwakarta when the all clear signal from the ground post came, upon which the two patrols returned to Andir. The Brewsters of 1-Vl.G.V were the first to approach their home base and the pilots were already getting ready to land when the ground post of the Air Defence Command reported three enemy fighters. The ML fighter aircraft chose their positions over Lembang. Almost immediately Tideman spotted (what he thought to be) a Navy O at the same altitude over Andir. He accelerated and simultaneously gave the order to attack over the radio. Among the enormous cumulus clouds a confused turning fight ensued.[72]

While Tideman spurted away at full throttle, Van Kempen and Compaan were attacked by two or three Ki-43s. Van Kempen got one on his tail, and with his first burst the Japanese fighter pilot managed to shoot the radio mast of the Brewster in two. The ML pilot felt several strikes in his aircraft and, in part because of the low altitude (above ground level) the patrol had been flying, dived into a cloud. Compaan followed suit. In the meantime Tideman had engaged the Ki-43 he had seen flying over Andir. The two other patrols did not see combat.[73]

Amid the heavy clouds De Haas and Boxman had lost the Tideman patrol out of sight, but suddenly spotted 12 Navy Os. In conformity with their instruction to avoid a fight against a numerical superiority they dived away with their patrols. None of the pilots heard Tideman over the radio. Such a communication breakdown was not exceptional: radio communication among the heavy clouds that would hang over the Bandoeng plateau in the afternoon, was usually a difficult affair with reception being poor or even extremely bad.[74]

Tideman called the fight with his opponent "sheer pleasure". Twice, both pilots used all the skills they had to the extreme in a classic turning fight among the cumulus clouds. Tideman managed to hit his opponent a few times, while his Brewster received a few hits through the tail section and the rudder fabric. Finally, Tideman dived into a ravine, hoping that his familiarity with the terrain could make his opponent fly into a hill. The (unknown) Japanese pilot, however, made good his escape. The aerial combat near Andir and over the hills around Lembang lasted some six minutes and was watched in breathless silence by many troops from their trenches and anti-aircraft positions. Groups of anti-aircraft gunners of the KNIL and the British Army applauded when Tideman landed.[75]

The damaged fighter aircraft of the 59th Sentai went missing on its return flight to Palembang.[76] Tideman crash landed at Andir, because the fabric cover of the rudder panelling of his fighter aircraft had been partly shot away. His fighter got into a ground loop, went off the runway and ended up with one wheel in the still soft earth of a filled up bomb crater. The aircraft was badly damaged and was sent for major repairs to the Technical Service for the second time (the first had been on 19 February 1942). The damage to Van Kempen's aircraft was light and the Brewster Compaan had flown had not sustained any damage, although on their return their opponents claimed to have shot both aircraft down.[77]

At around 14:30 hrs a formation of Japanese bombers of the 75th and 90th Sentais, escorted by Ki-43 fighter aircraft of the 59th and 64th Sentais, took off from Palembang I (the former civilian airfield of the town of Palembang) for a raid on Andir. The bad weather on the way out forced the bombers to return and the fighter aircraft of the 64th Sentai did not manage to reach Andir either, nor did they make any contact with their enemy.[78] The 12 Japanese fighters that did make it to Andir were aircraft from the 59th Sentai. Nine of these fighters came directly from Palembang I, while the other three had first escorted six single-engine Ki-51 assault aircraft (Army Co-operation aircraft) of the 27th Sentai from Palembang I to the captured Kalidjati. These three fighters subsequently flew to Andir and carried out an attack on the base at around 16:30 hrs. From a very low altitude they attacked targets such as anti-aircraft positions around the base. They met with intensive fire, but insofar as could be established none were hit. Almost immediately after this the nine fighter pilots of the 59th Sentai from Palembang engaged the Tideman patrol near Andir. The group claimed to have shot down two "Buffaloes" (the British version of the Brewster B-339 fighter aircraft) and reported the loss of one fighter of their own.[79]

Various planes parked at Andir sustained damage during the strafings before and after this fight. The ML lost one Koolhoven FK-51 trainer, the plane going up in flames. Two Glenn Martins of 2-Vl.G.III and two of 3-Vl.G.III sustained hits in their pens, and so did two Hudsons of 1 Squadron. At the Technical Service a few American bombers in repair received some damage. The Japanese fighter pilots concentrated on the bombers, which had been parked in pens, and the aircraft dispersed near the depot of the Technical Service in the south-western part of the airfield. They failed to spot the parked Hurricanes of 242 Squadron.[80]

After the all-clear signal had sounded the ML fighters landed at Andir. Because of this, it was not until around 17:15 hrs that the preparation of the planes for the planned attack on Kalidjati could begin. It became a race against the clock. To be able to attack by last light, they would have to take off by 18:00 hrs. There was no time anymore for a good preparatory briefing, although this was necessary as crews unaccustomed to working with each other in different types of fighter aircraft were to be committed, without there being any radio contact between the ML and RAF fighters. At the last possible moment it was also decided to commit the Interceptors. Finally, at 18:15 hrs, too late actually, they could take off. Their assignment was to attack the anti-aircraft artillery and the parked Japanese aircraft at Kalidjati.[81]

The first allied fighter attack on Kalidjati in the evening of 2 March 1942

The formation for the attack on Kalidjati consisted of four Brewsters of 1- and 2-Vl.G.V, two Interceptors of 2-Vl.G.IV and six Hurricanes of 242 Squadron, led by Sqn Ldr Brooker. Elt De Haas had general command (due to his local terrain knowledge) and flew the lead pair with Vdg Jolly. The other two assigned Brewsters were flown by Vdg Weijnschenk and Sgt Compaan of 1-Vl.G.V. The Interceptors of 2-Vl.G.IV were flown by Elt Boxman and Sgt Roumimper.[82]

When the formation was approaching its target, the pilots test fired their guns. It appeared that the firing system of the De Haas' B-3110 had not been connected, upon which De Haas transferred command of the (loose) formation to Lieutenant Boxman. Brooker did not understand what was going on and flew on with his two sections.[83]

Sqn Ldr Brooker, Plt Off Gartrell, Sgt G.J. Dunn, Sgt R.L. Dovell and two unknown pilots arrived over Kalidjati at dusk and were intercepted there by a lone Ki-43 flying over the airfield. The Japanese fighter pilot managed to hit Dovell's Hurricane in the wing, but he disappeared so quickly in the darkness that only a few shots could be fired back at him. Nevertheless, on his return, Dovell claimed a probable, just like the Japanese fighter pilot of the 59th Sentai. By this time only vague shadows could be seen at the airfield, so the British flew back to Andir. This was no easy thing as not all pilots had maps or had jotted down their course to Andir. Dovell managed to land his plane safely, but a wing tank had been perforated and for the time being it was unserviceable.[84]

Led by Boxman, the ML fighter aircraft arrived over Kalidjati at last light. In a spread out formation they made one run at low altitude over the airfield. No aircraft could be seen. De Haas was flying at a somewhat higher altitude over the base, when quite unexpectedly he was fired upon. His Brewster received a hit through a wing tank. In the dark the Japanese fighter pilot of the Ki-43 had thought he had fired at a Glenn Martin and also claimed this as a probable. The ML pilots also returned to Andir with nothing to show for their pains. Only De Haas' aircraft had sustained some damage and was out of action for a couple of days for repairs at the Technical Service.[85]

On this afternoon 1- and 2-Vl.G.V were amalgamated into one afdeling, with the designation 1-Vl.G.V and Captain Van Helsdingen as commanding officer. Tideman remained second-in-command. 2-Vl.G.V was disbanded administratively the following day and Captain Van Rest was transferred to the Flight School, which had been evacuated to Australia in the meantime.[86]

The bomber missions in the afternoon and evening of 2 March 1942

Partly as a result of the Japanese raid on Andir there were only few remaining operationally serviceable aircraft in the squadrons and afdelingen in the late afternoon. At Andir and Tjikembar (a part of 36 Squadron RAF) the following number of bombers was available.[87]

Table 21

Unit	Assigned	Operationally serviceable	Remarks
1-Vl.G.I	2	1	
1-Vl.G.II	4	2	
2-Vl.G.III	2	Nil	
3-Vl.G.III	3	1	
1 Squadron	3	Nil	Excl. 4 Hudsons at the TD
36 Squadron	5	2	Three planes at Tjikembar

JAC committed the aircraft first and foremost to conducting reconnaissance missions towards the coast (by order of the General Headquarters) and to carry out attacks on any remaining or newly arrived Japanese transport vessels. JAC's RecGroup evacuated its remaining flying boats and did not function anymore, while the slow and vulnerable Curtiss-Wright CW-22 Falcon reconnaissance planes of the ML (in fact little more than armed trainer aircraft) were barred from action over the Japanese landing area. This was in response to reports of the presence of Japanese float fighters at Eretan Wetan. (Two CW-22s of Vk.A.2 had been shot down by Mitsubishi F1M float planes over eastern Java on 1 March.) Mapping the positions of the Japanese ships would have to be done by the crews of Glenn Martins and Hudson bombers.[88]

The first to take off at around 17:00 hrs was the Bosman crew of 3-Vl.G.III. Their aircraft was intercepted south of Indramajoe by two Mitsubishi F1M fighter reconnaissance float planes, upon which Vdg M.P. Bosman decided to abort the mission. The ML had already lost one Glenn Martin over western Borneo in December 1941 in an attack from this type of fighter reconnaissance plane. The F1Ms belonged to the 1st Air Group (aircraft tenders *Kamikawa-maru* and *Sanyo-maru* with their auxiliary vessels), flying anti-aircraft and anti-submarine patrols from a base on the coast near Eretan Wetan. Bosman dived to a lower altitude and quickly left the float planes behind. The crew returned to Andir.[89] Allied fighter aircraft to escort the bombers were not available, as all operationally serviceable aircraft were standing ready or were being prepared for carrying out the attack on Kalidjati, described above.

For the Japanese F1M crews (who reported a 'twin-engine Boeing' that could not be intercepted) these were probably their last patrols.

The next day the remaining float planes left for the Bay of Bantam, in part because their base near Eretan Wetan was not adequate due to the high surf there. A number of fighter aircraft of the Japanese Navy air force from Palembang were to be stationed at Kalidjati as replacements, but these aircraft did not arrive until 4 March.[90]

In the evening the Bieger crew of 1-Vl.G.I, followed by the Samson crew of 1-Vl.G.II, took off for a reconnaissance of Eretan Wetan.[91] The Haye crew of 1-Vl.G.II, finally, was the last to leave at around 21:00 hrs. These reconnaissance flights did not yield any results as nothing could be observed. The night over the Bandoeng plateau was a splendidly clear one, but over the coast and sea a low cloud overcast had developed.[92]

Night raids on Kalidjati (2 on 3 March 1942)

After this, JAC directed its efforts at Kalidjati. The fighter attack around dusk had been a big failure. Suppression of Japanese air activity from Kalidjati, however, was essential, if the nearby Andir (a ten-minute flight) was to keep on functioning as a base. From around 22:30 hrs onwards two Glenn Martins of the ML took off at an hour's interval to carry out night raids. The first to attack was the Van Thiel crew of 3-Vl.G.III, who managed to take the Japanese by surprise and drop their bombs amidst medium anti-aircraft fire. The only operationally serviceable aircraft of 1-Vl.G.I, with the Van den Broek crew, followed suit.[93]

By now a low cover of cloud was hanging over the Bandoeng Plateau, but the sky was completely clear over Kalidjati, with plenty of light coming from an almost full moon. The crews attacked in a low pass from an altitude of 100 to 150 metres and dropped their 50-kilogramme fragmentation bombs on the hangars in the north-eastern part of Kalidjati or on the planes that had been parked in front of them. The hit pattern of the first Glenn Martin flown by the Van Thiel crew was exactly right and some of the bombs fell among some ten (as the crew thought) Navy Os parked there. The crew saw how several of the aircraft were blown over by the force of the explosions and how one "Navy O" was set ablaze as a result of a direct hit. In fact, they were three Ki-43s of the 59th Sentai and six Ki-51s of the 27th Sentai, while possibly a few reconnaissance planes of the 81st Sentai might have been left behind at Kalidjati. In view of the experiences of the allied crews, the Ki-43s were not operationally serviceable the following morning (see the next chapter). Probably only one Ki-43 became available again in the course of the morning of 3 March, and it seems likely that two Ki-43s had at least been damaged considerably.[94]

When the second attack came the Japanese were better on their guard and the anti-aircraft fire was intensive. This time the Japanese also fired some of the captured Bofors guns. Sgt F. van den Broek's aircraft sustained medium damage from a 4-cm projectile that went clean through one of its wings. The detonation altitude, however, far exceeded that of the bomber and the shell that penetrated the wing did not explode. The Van den Broek crew flew in an aircraft whose intercom system broke down as soon as it became airborne. Observer Captain R.E. Jessurun therefore had to guide the pilot to the target by means of the backup system (a dial by which left or right direction could be indicated from the bomb aimer position in the nose). This worked out fine and a glow of a fire was already rising up from the bombed hangar. That night the Japanese lost one transport plane, which had probably gone up in flames inside or in front of the hangar.[95]

On their approach of Andir the Van den Broek crew suddenly saw a transport plane emerge from the low-lying clouds. It was just as well that it was a near miss. The transport plane was the civilian PK-ALO, a civilian DC-3 of the Koninklijke Nederlands-Indische Luchtvaartmaatschappij–The Royal Netherlands-Indies Airline (KNILM), commanded by E.E. Hulsebos, who left for a flight to Australia at 00:30 hrs. Van den Broek parked his damaged Glenn Martin in front of one of the hangars of the Technical Service, where ground personnel were working on an American four-engine B-17 bomber.[96]

After Van den Broek's landing the weather quickly deteriorated and the thickening cloud and thunderstorms with fierce gusts of wind and heavy rainfall made it impossible to send out the other bombers. The two Vildebeest light bombers of 36 Squadron RAF had been standing ready, armed with 50-kilogramme bombs from the ML stocks, but had already almost been blown over by gusts of wind during the first thunderstorm around midnight. Shortly after sunrise the RAF crews flew their aircraft over to Tjikembar.[97]

Results of the operations on 2 March 1942

The combat aircraft of JAC carried out a large number of sorties on 2 March. In the morning Glenn Martin bombers flew ten sorties to Eretan Wetan and in all probability damaged two of the Japanese transport vessels. Later that morning a Glenn Martin and its entire crew were lost near Kalidjati as a direct consequence of the erroneous report that the KNIL had recaptured the base. Fighter aircraft flew 22 sorties in the morning in support of Bandoeng Group (planned attacks of the KNIL on Pamanoekan, Eretan Wetan and Soebang, one of which had to be aborted due to engine trouble), a reconnaissance mission to Kalidjati (one sortie) and eight sorties in support of West Group (armed reconnaissance sorties, one of which had to be aborted also to engine trouble). Furthermore, in the morning four sorties were flown from Tjililitan in an attempt to intercept an enemy bomber and fighter formation, during which action probably one Ki-43 was damaged.

Near Pamanoekan Japanese troops on bikes were fired at and to the west of this town a number of motor vehicles were set ablaze by Hurricanes. Brewsters and CW-21s bombed and fired at Japanese positions inside the bridgehead at Eretan Wetan and Japanese soldiers on bikes to the west of the bridgehead. On the roads to Serang and in the environment of this town Hurricanes fired at a column of horse-drawn wagons, a number of motor vehicles and Japanese infantry columns. One of the British fighter aircraft was forced to make an emergency landing in the terrain due to hits from anti-aircraft fire, but the pilot managed to make it back to his own troops a few days later. During a reconnaissance mission of Kalidjati a Brewster was damaged.

In the afternoon again a number of sorties were flown by the fighter aircraft. One sortie was a seaward reconnaissance flight around Eretan Wetan by a Brewster by order of the General Headquarters. An alarm take off (four sorties) carried out by Hurricanes from Tjililitan was not successful, but another (seven sorties) by Brewsters and CW-21s from Andir resulted in aerial combat, during which one Ki-43 was shot down, but also one Brewster was badly damaged on landing. In the late afternoon a mission to Kalidjati was carried out by Brewsters, CW-21s and Hurricanes (12 sorties) in support of an attack by the KNIL on Soebang, but because of the late hour this was not successful. A Brewster and a Hurricane sustained damage. Incidentally, the attack of the KNIL on Soebang was cancelled.

In the early afternoon Glenn Martins flew four sorties to the occupied Kalidjati and successfully bombed the landing strip. In spite of this, the Japanese 3rd Hiko Dan was able to take the base into use in the late afternoon. Late that afternoon and in the evening the bombers were again sent out. The four sorties by Glenn Martins to Eretan Wetan remained without any results due to an interception by Japanese F1M fighter reconnaissance float planes and, subsequently, a low cloud overcast over the coast. Later that evening, however, two Glenn Martins flew two very successful sorties against Kalidjati. Of the three Ki-43 fighters and six Ki-51 assault aircraft that landed there in the afternoon a number of planes, among which probably two Ki-43s, were put out of action for a longer period of time. Furthermore, although this was not known at the time, a Japanese transport plane was lost. Shortly after midnight the weather deteriorated too much to commit the bombers any further.

***

CHAPTER 3.6

The Operations on 3 March 1942

Introduction

On 3 March 1942 at the beginning of the day Java Air Command (JAC) had available the following number of bombers and fighter aircraft for direct and indirect support of the land forces.[1]

Table 22

Unit	Assigned	Operationally serviceable	Remarks
Bombers			
1-Vl.G.I	2	0	Incl. one plane at the TD
1-Vl.G.II	4	2	Incl. one plane at the TD
2-Vl.G.III	2	2	
3-Vl.G.III	3	3	
1 Squadron	7	3	Incl. four Hudsons at the TD
36 Squadron	5	4	
Fighters			
1-Vl.G.V	7	5	Incl. one plane at the TD
2-Vl.G.IV	4	2	Incl. two planes at the TD
242 Squadron	11	10	
Total	45	31	

With the help of these 31 operationally serviceable aircraft in total (on 28 February 1942 there had still been 54) JAC mainly carried out missions against the occupied Kalidjati on 3 March. Also several reconnaissance missions were flown by order of the General Head-quarters (AHK). Initially, the missions against Kalidjati were intended to destroy the British anti-aircraft guns and Blenheim bombers that had been left behind, and as much of the infrastructure that could be used by the Japanese as possible. The latter, in particular, involved the hangars in the north-eastern part of the air base and the encampment. At the same moment that the KNIL launched its attack on Kalidjati at around 09:30 hrs, the first mission in support of the committed (reinforced) 2nd Infantry Regiment (2-R.I.) was taking off. After a very successful operation carried out by 242 Squadron RAF, however, further missions had to be cancelled as a consequence of a very heavy air raid on Andir.

Early morning reconnaissance missions in support of 2-R.I.

Around sunrise a CW-22 Falcon of the patrol of Vk.A.1 at Andir (crew unknown) by order of Bandoeng Group reconnoitred the advance route of 2-R.I. (Sadang-Kalidjati) and the roads from Poerwakarta via Sadang to Tjikampek. The weather was bad over the Bandoeng plateau and immediately after take off the aircraft disappeared into the mist. The mist and low clouds, however, were only hanging over the plateau and did not pose any problems during the actual reconnaissance. There was no Japanese activity to be seen anywhere, not on the ground, not in the air. Incidentally, by order of ML Command all activity during daylight of the entire Vk.A.1 had been limited to the early morning around sunrise and the late afternoon, when there was enough cover of cloud. This was in response to an injudicious manner of deploying the CW-22s by the staff of West Group. The head of operations of this staff had not heeded the advice of his ML liaison officer, which had resulted in two wounded in Vk.A.1 the previous day.[2]

Furthermore, by sunrise JAC committed a Glenn Martin for a reconnaissance of the Japanese fleet at the request of the General Head-quarters. The Bosman crew was given the assignment to reconnoitre a section of the coast near Indramajoe and then bomb the Japanese transport ships off the coast with three 300-kilogramme bombs. The weather was also clear over the coast and at dawn (around 05:30 hrs) bombardier Sgt G. Paalman dropped the bombs over one of the ships anchored there. They had a direct hit. The Glenn Martin was not hit by anti-aircraft fire and there were no Japanese fighter aircraft up.[3]

After having their aircraft rearmed, Vdg M.P. Bosman and his crew took off for Indramajoe at 06:30 hrs for a second time. The weather was still good there and there were no Japanese fighters. The ship that had been attacked during the first run was still smoking. Again Paalman managed to place a direct hit on a transport ship, and the bomber only sustained a few holes from fragments of Japanese anti-aircraft shells that exploded nearby.

There was little Japanese activity to be seen on the coast and there was little traffic of smaller vessels ferrying between the transport ships and the coast. Apparently the seven Japanese transport ships were still the original ones and that was what General Headquarters wanted to see firmly established now that the reinforced 2-R.I., Teerink Group and the reinforced Inf. IV (minus) were on the brink of launching their attack (see the previous chapter). The Japanese troops in the area of Bandoeng Group had not had any reinforcements in the meantime.[4]

The first bomber and fighter aircraft raids on Kalidjati

As was said above, the first missions against Kalidjati had been intended to deny the Japanese the use of Kalidjati as much as possible. This involved, in particular, the hangars in the north-eastern part of the airfield (containing equipment and provisions of a sub depot, a workshop of the Technical Service of the ML) and the British anti-aircraft guns and bombers which had been left behind. The first to take off in the dark at around 05:00 hrs was a patrol of Glenn Martins and the two operationally serviceable Interceptors of 2-Vl.G.IV for an attack on the anti-aircraft guns and the hangars.

Because of the morning mist the fighter pilots lost sight of each other and the two bombers of 2-Vl.G.III. Of the fighter pilots the only one to reach the target was Elt W. Boxman. He fired at a hangar and Japanese personnel on the ground. On his flight back (some 30 minutes later) he met his colleague Sgt H.M. Haye near Andir, who was still circling around to find Boxman and the Glenn Martins. Haye had a terrible fright because at first he took Boxman's Interceptor that suddenly appeared alongside him for a Navy O. Together the two pilots flew back to Andir.[5]

Two of the four Interceptors of the patrol of 2-Vl.G.IV were with the Technical Service for a repair of its engine and that is where later in the day also Haye's CW-360 ended up. When the engine of this aircraft was tested by the mechanic it proved to be unserviceable. There were no more spare engines for the CW-21Bs and the engines had to be taken apart bit by bit in the engine department of the Technical Service, to be put together again after a partial revision; a matter of days. As it was, ML personnel were to finish the job under Japanese supervision.[6]

The two Glenn Martins of the Gosma and Keim crews flew above the clouds and mist to Kalidjati and dropped eighteen 50-kilogramme bombs in total through the broken clouds. One of the British anti-aircraft positions along the edge of the flight terrain (probably three 4-cm Bofors guns) was destroyed with seven hits. The aircraft were fired at extremely intensively, but apart from some small fragments of shells having exploded nearby, they did not receive any hits. The bombers were not intercepted and returned safely at Andir.[7]

Five Brewsters of 1-Vl.G.V, led by Elt P.G. Tideman, followed by six Hurricanes of 242 Squadron led by Sqn Ldr R.E.P. Brooker, took off from Andir between around 05:45 hrs and 06:00 hrs for a second raid on Kalidjati. Sgt R.L. Dovell's Hurricane was out of action due to a partly blown away wing tank, but Flt Lt B.J. Parker's fighter had been repaired in the evening of 2 March with parts coming from the former plane. Their assignment was the destruction of the 23 RAF Blenheim bombers which had been left behind on this airfield. The debriefings of the fighter pilots and bomber crews who had carried out attacks on Kalidjati the previous evening and night had shown that there were still only few Japanese aircraft on the airfield. Some ten parked 'fighter aircraft' had been successfully bombed by one of the Glenn Martin bombers. Therefore, much resistance, other than coming anti-aircraft artillery, was not expected.[8]

The raid was well prepared, but the weather conditions spoiled it. Visibility had become very poor because the morning mist had changed into a low-hanging fog. The fighter pilots took off alone or in pairs. Tideman and his wingman Sgt J.P. Adam were the first to return, followed by Sgt A.E. Stoové (left trailing pilot of the second patrol) in a third Brewster with engine trouble. Tideman had considerable communication problems with Adam, who was concentrating so hard on keeping in formation that he had forgotten to retract the wheels of his Brewster. Tideman did not manage to signal the problem to him by making gestures (the radio was not working) and returned, also because of the weather.[9] When the remaining fighter aircraft climbed through the layer of fog, it appeared that it was so thick and dense that also most other fighter pilots decided to return to base. Only Elt G.J. de Haas, with his right trailing pilot Elt P.A.C. Benjamins and one Hurricane pilot (probably Plt Off E.C. Gartrell) went on and climbed through the fog and low clouds.[10]

When De Haas and Benjamins had left the clouds, they kept circling for a bit, but did not see any other fighter aircraft and went on together. The weather over Kalidjati was a whole lot better and without problems both pilots dropped their 50-kilogramme fragmentation bombs over the hangars and the encampment. All their bombs hit their targets. The anti-aircraft fire was intensive and from time to time formed a veritable curtain of tracers. After dropping their bombs they carried out strafings from an altitude of about ten metres, both pilots making two runs, hitting several Blenheims and also a parked Japanese Mitsubishi Ki-21 (heavy) bomber. This plane (probably a transport version of the Ki-21) went up in flames. After his second run Benjamins suddenly spotted a third fighter aircraft firing tracer ammunition at ground targets in the north-eastern part of the flight terrain and he turned to identify it. It appeared to be a Hurricane, which, however, turned away and disappeared. When the Brewster fighter pilots were on the brink of commencing their third run, they had to abort it as precisely at that moment a Glenn Martin patrol was attacking. No Japanese fighter aircraft were up and the two fighter pilots returned to Andir.[11]

At around 06:00 hrs two Glenn Martins of 3-Vl.G.III, flown by the Van Erkel and Coblijn crews, took off from Andir. There was no escort this time, but the bombers were to attack immediately after the fighter aircraft of the RAF and ML. The patrol was able to carry out a normal altitude bombardment and the bombers were neither intercepted nor hit by the intensive anti-aircraft fire. The two Brewsters and the Hurricane were not spotted by the crews. Amid a curtain of tracer ammunition the nine 50-kilogramme bombs per aircraft were dropped, which hit several hangars the Japanese had begun to use. The patrol returned safely at Andir.[12]

Shortly after the Van Erkel patrol a third and last patrol of Glenn Martins left, this time two aircraft of 1-Vl.G.II with the Samson and Haye crews. Their primary assignment was a reconnaissance for General Headquarters of the towns of Pamanoekan, Krawang and Soebang. If the situation allowed, they were then to carry out a raid on Kalidjati. Near Pamanoekan the Japanese invasion fleet was observed, but nothing worth mentioning was seen near Krawang and Soebang, though. There was no Japanese advance from Pamanoekan on Tjikampek and Krawang, nor was there any advance from Soebang. The crews did spot some military traffic on the road between Kalidjati and Soebang. They approached Kalidjati around 07:30 hrs. There was little doubt that the enemy would be on his guard there after previous attacks and Tlt Samson braced himself for some very intensive anti-aircraft fire. In the patrol leader's estimate the two Glenn Martins dropped their nine 50-kilogramme fragmentation bombs per aircraft from an altitude of 150 metres. The bombers made a low pass attack in which they dived for the target, gathering as much speed as possible in an attempt to confuse the Japanese anti-aircraft artillery and to prevent an interception by fighters. Their plan, however, failed.[13]

There were no Japanese fighter aircraft, but the anti-aircraft artillery was so intensive that both bombers were hit. Not only was the M-5108 of the Hayes crew shot down, the M-585 of the patrol leader also received several hits. The damage to the leading bomber was light and there were no casualties on board. With the exception of wireless operator/air gunner Corporal J.F. Samola, however, the entire Haye crew perished. The bombing raid had been reasonably successful. Almost all bombs fell within the Kalidjati encampment, in use by the Japanese by now. Samola landed by parachute near the village Kalidjati and went through some hairy moments, during which he had to shoot a Japanese soldier to escape. Largely on foot and through the terrain, he managed to reach Bandoeng via Boerangrang mountain. Tlt Samson reported the M-5108 missing at 07:50 hrs.[14]

In the mean time, 1-Vl.G.I had managed to get the M-542 airworthy, and at around 07:00 hrs SM D. T. de Bont was sent out for an attack on Kalidjati, with the motto "see what you can do", without a fighter escort. Over Kalidjati the crew saw three 'fighters' circling and on the airfield, near the Corps bureau, approximately 20 single-engine aircraft (probably mainly Ki-51 assault aircraft of the 27th Sentai) were parked. On its approach of the target the Glenn Martin was attacked near Poerwakarta by one Ki-43 Army-1 fighter, which forced the crew to drop their bombs over the airfield without aiming.[15]

An aerial battle ensued which mainly took place close to the ground. Both air gunners in the M-542 were wounded but kept on firing until the Japanese fighter pilot, possibly because of a lack of fuel or the hits the air gunners had managed to inflict on his aircraft, broke off the fight. There were no other Japanese fighter aircraft up and, flying at low altitude and making a detour via Pameungpeuk, the De Bont crew reached Andir. Their plane landed safely, but its tail and one of the wings had received quite some hits. The M-542 would not be operational for the time being and that meant that 1-Vl.G.I was out of business. Repairs on the M-542 went on until the capitulation. The Japanese would finish the job, employing Dutch Prisoners of War (militarised personnel of the KNILM).[16]

In the evening of 2 March General Headquarters had made all operationally serviceable aircraft available to Bandoeng Group in support of the attack on Kalidjati by the reinforced 2-R.I. In a consultation between General Headquarters and JAC a time slot had subsequently been established, starting at 08:00 hrs, probably after Colonel Toorop had reported in the morning of 3 March that the advance of his units had been delayed. For the time being, JAC had planned three missions, for which the aircraft would be ready to take off as of 08:00 hrs. The actual take off time would be given by the staff of Bandoeng Group and passed directly to the operational commanders at Tjililitan and Andir. Elt H.F. Zeylemaker, the ML liaison officer at the staff of Major-General J.J. Pesman, was responsible for the contact by telephone between the operations section of the staff (led by Lieutenant-Colonel H.A. Reemer), the Operations Staff of JAC and BRITAIR and the ML Command. On Toorop's instruction he was to pass on the orders to take off by phone.[17]

The second fighter attack on Kalidjati

The six remaining operationally serviceable Hurricanes of 242 Squadron at Andir returned to Tjililitan at around 07:00 hrs by order of Java Air Command, where the entire squadron was kept on readiness for the support of the KNIL in its attack on Kalidjati. The damaged aircraft of Sgt R.L. Dovell stayed at Andir for repairs. Four Hurricanes which had been on readiness at Tjililitan were sent up earlier that morning (at around 06:30 hrs) when there was a report of several Japanese aircraft flying in the direction of Batavia via the Duizend Eilanden. The aircraft, however, kept flying at a considerable distance from the coast and seemed to be heading in the direction of Indramajoe. The British fighter aircraft patrolling over Tjililitan returned to their base without having come into action. The aircraft reported by Batavia Air Defence Command were probably some of the Ki-51s of the 27th Sentai arriving at Kalidjati at around 07:15 hrs.[18]

At around 09:30 hrs all ten operationally serviceable Hurricanes, led by Sqn Ldr Brooker, took off from Tjililitan for an attack on Kalidjati. Among the pilots were Flt Lt B.J. Parker, Plt Off A.R. Mendizabal, Plt Off M.C. Fitzherbert, Plt Off E.C. Gartrell and Sgt G.J. King. Some of the fighter aircraft were flown by pilots who had just returned from Andir. Their assignment was to take out as many Japanese aircraft as they could. They were to land again at Andir in order to escort the allied bombers from there during a next attack on Kalidjati. This was the first mission flown by JAC units by order of Bandoeng Group of the KNIL. It was to remain the only one.[19]

Kalidjati was now packed with aircraft all nicely parked in rows. The anti-aircraft artillery was light and the Japanese were clearly taken off guard. The Hurricanes fired at a large number of mainly twin-engine aircraft. They were transport aircraft, which had flown in personnel of the 27th, 59th, and 75th Sentais and the staff of the 3rd Hiko Dan, ten Ki-48 light bombers of the 75th Sentai and two Ki-46 reconnaissance planes of the 50th Chutai. Eight more Ki-43s of the 59th Sentai had arrived as well, along with a number of Ki-51 assault aircraft and Ki-15 reconnaissance planes (see below). Parker and Mendizabal were flying top cover, but as there were no enemy aircraft up, they subsequently dived down. Just when they were carrying out their first strafing, they were engaged by four of five Ki-43s. The other Hurricane pilots had broken off the attack after several strafings and were on their way back to Andir.[20]

Parker managed to escape, but Mendizabal's aircraft was badly hit. The pilot tried to make it to the alternate base of Pameungpeuk on the south coast, but had to bail out by parachute before reaching this field. The Ki-43s pursued the Hurricanes to Andir and an aerial battle ensued, which the British had to break off after some time because of their fuel position.

The British fighter pilots claimed to have shot down three Navy Os, but this success was offset by the loss of Mendizabal's Hurricane and damage to almost all other fighters, though mostly light or very light. Plt Off Gartrell was lightly wounded and his aircraft was the only one to have sustained heavy damage. In fact, the Japanese lost only one Ki-43 (at least in the aerial battle). The two other Ki-43s claimed shot down by the British were surely damaged, and probably managed to make emergency landings on Kalidjati. The Japanese losses on the ground were considerably.[21]

The Ki-48s, Ki-46s and transport aircraft, which had been lined up in neat rows, were an easy prey. Many aircraft were damaged and four or five twin-engine aircraft (probably mostly transport aircraft) sustained serious (fire) damage. Brooker reported that his squadron had taken out at least 12 Japanese bombers and a few transport planes.[22]

The Japanese raid on Andir on 3 March 1942

At around 10:30 hrs Andir was attacked by nine Ki-43 fighter aircraft of the 64th Sentai from Palembang I. These fighters had escorted nine Ki-48s of the 90th Sentai and 25 G4M bombers of the Japanese Navy air force. In the meantime six of the G4Ms were carrying out a bombing raid on Tjimahi. Near this small garrison town there was a landing strip and an important crossroads and railway junction. The KNIL had workshops and warehouses there, but they were not attacked. The large barracks complex at Tjimahi, which accommodated, among others, the Depot Mobiele Artillerie (Mobile Artillery Depot) and Tjimahi military hospital was also the location of the Regimental Headquarters of 48 LAA. The other 19 G4M bombers (of the Kanoya Kokutai from Palembang) and the nine Ki-48s attacked Andir some time after the Ki-43s.[23]

The Air Defence Command had almost completely lost its value for warning purposes. Since 1 March the bulk of the warning posts had been withdrawn or communication with them had been severed. When an alarm was given at Andir, it was often possible to see the enemy aircraft already approach with the naked eye. In fact, the standing order which specified that in case of an air raid alert the flyable bombers were to take off and circle around south of Bandoeng until the all clear was given, could not be followed up. This time, too, the crews of Glenn Martins and Hudsons were still rushing for their aircraft when the Army 1s began their strafing. None of the bombers could be manned in time.

The Japanese fighter aircraft quickly disappeared, but were almost immediately followed by bombers. The two formations from Palembang were flying via Tjimahi and downwind of the main runway (runway 29) of Andir to a position east of the town of Bandoeng, where almost at the same time Japanese bombers coming from Bali with their fighter escort arrived. The G4Ms and the Ki-48s from Palembang queued up behind the formations from Bali. Around

The barracks complex of the KNIL at Tjimahi, a very large complex which, among others, accommodated the Depot Mobiele Artillerie (Mobile Artillery Depot) and a military hospital. The parade square, bottom right hand, was also used as a landing strip for reconnaissance aircraft. (Private collection, P.C. Boer)

11:00 hrs the first bombers appeared over Andir, closely packed formations of 17 and seven G4M bombers of the Takao Kokutai from Bali, respectively. The escort of 24 Japanese fighter aircraft were from the Tainan Kokutai and the 3rd Kokutai, also stationed in Bali. The Takao Kokutai attacked the southern part of Andir, whereas the aircraft from Palembang, first the 19 G4Ms and then the nine Ki-48s, bombed the northern section of the air base.

Within half an hour in total 52 G4Ms and Ki-48s dropped their bombs, creating an enormous rumble from the dull booms of bombs impacting at short intervals, the mountains surrounding the Bandoeng plateau resounding with the noise of countless echoes of the the explosions. Given the altitude at which the Japanese bombers were flying, the 2- and 4-cm anti-aircraft guns were doomed to powerlessness. The heavy anti-aircraft artillery, however, fired fanatically at the approaching aircraft, without any visible result, until they had one direct hit on what was (incorrectly) assumed to be a Navy O.[24]

The last fighter operation of the ML on 3 March 1942

Shortly before the air raids on Andir began, the Hurricanes of 242 Squadron returning from Kalidjati had landed there. The aircraft were dispersed along the southern edge of the airfield, but had not yet been refuelled or rearmed. The RAF pilots saw four Brewsters take off and shortly after this, with the air raid alert sounding, an Interceptor. From their trenches they saw these fighter aircraft climb out directly after the first air raid, while a number of Navy Os were diving for them.[25]

The Brewster patrol, led by Elt H.H.J. Simons, had taken off at around 10:15 hrs to escort a Glenn Martin for a reconnaissance flight to the Wijnskoopbaai. This mission was an assignment from General Headquarters, which expected a Japanese secondary operation there. Apparently, there were fears at General Headquarters that the Japanese would attempt to carry out a landing in the back of Blackforce (see the previous chapter). In spite of what had been agreed on with regard to the support for 2-R.I., JAC was ordered to carry out this armed reconnaissance. For this purpose the Brewsters on readiness and one Glenn Martin were committed. Simons flew with Vdg P.R. Jolly in one pair; the other pilots were Vdg C.H. Weynschenk and Sgt P. Compaan. Instead of a Glenn Martin an Interceptor came alongside, whose pilot gave the "follow me" signal with his wing tips. Lieutenant Boxman had been ordered to pick up the Brewsters and to intercept the approaching Japanese bombers together. His Interceptor was the only aircraft of the patrol of 2-Vl.G.IV that was still operationally serviceable, albeit barely. His engine also did not make the normal revolutions during the run up.[26]

While the five fighter aircraft were climbing up through the broken clouds to a position over the Boerangrang mountain, to the north-north-west of Andir, Boxman forgot that his fighter aircraft had a higher climbing speed than the Brewsters, which he only realised when, having reached an altitude of 4,000 metres, he suddenly saw a group of Navy Os diving for him from his left. When Boxman looked behind him he saw that the Brewsters were still some 300 to 400 metres below him. Simons and his pilots also spotted the Navy Os, and, vulnerable as their aircraft were during a climb and in conformity with the standing instruction to avoid confrontations with a numerical superiority, they immediately dived away. The patrol made an evasive landing on Pameungpeuk.[27]

Boxman was trapped. The leading three Navy Os were already very close, and in a desperate move he decided to climb headlong into the enemy formation, hoping to dive away after that. His surprise tactic seemed to work. One of the Navy Os fired at him, but missed. The Japanese fighters shot passed him. At that moment, however, own anti-aircraft artillery opened fire. One of the first shots hit the Interceptor in its left wing tank and set the aircraft ablaze. Boxman bailed out from an altitude of about 4,500 metres over Tjisaroea. Burning fuel was blown into the cockpit and set his clothes on fire when he opened the canopy, but the pilot had the presence of mind to make a free fall to extinguish the flames and only opened his parachute at a low altitude. Badly burned, Boxman was found by an infantry patrol and taken to the military hospital at Tjimahi.[28] Navy pilot Kazuo Yokokawa of the Tainan Kokutai (incorrectly) claimed a probable.[29]

The Simons patrol had landed on Pameungpeuk, but was not safe there either. After the attack on Andir the escort of the bombers from Palembang had flown on to Pameungpeuk. Just when the Brewsters had been parked in their pens, the nine Ki-43 fighters attacked the aircraft parked on the airfield. One of the Brewsters caught fire and became a total loss; a second sustained bullet and fragmentation damage and lost the top of its tail after the attack. A non-operational Blenheim of the RAF, which had arrived from Andir on 1 March for 'shelter', the only remaining one after the fall of Kalidjati, also went up in flames.[30]

The Japanese fighter pilots returned via Bandoeng. Near Andir the Ki-43 flown by Major Tateo Kato, commanding officer of the 64th Sentai, found a Navy O of the 3rd Kokutai from Bali on his tail. He did not manage to shake this pilot off and his Ki-43 received so much damage that he had to make an emergency landing on Kalidjati. The badly damaged Ki-43 was out of action for the remainder of the battle. The fact that a Navy pilot had almost downed the great Army air force ace Kato (a celebrity from the China campaign with more than ten victories to his name), will have spread like wildfire over Bali and will undoubtedly have been the talk of the town.[31]

The damage and the casualties

At the request of the Army air force and in connection with the reloca-tion to Kalidjati of elements of the 3rd Hiko Dan, the Japanese Navy air force had taken on most of the task of breaking the last resistance at Andir. This was a difficult job, which for most of the crews meant a 900-kilometre journey and some three hours of flying over eastern and central Java, in rather bad weather from Bali to Bandoeng. And then, the same journey back, sometimes in a damaged aircraft. The result, however, was something to be proud of.

The bombing raids on Andir had strewn the airfield and its immediate surroundings with craters and had caused heavy material damage. The Takao Kokutai dropped its bombs in a carpet over the southern part of Andir. An ammunition dump and various parked aircraft went up in flames. Several buildings, hangars and warehouses were hit and partly burned down and just south of the base the railway track was destroyed. The bombs also fell around a number of anti-aircraft positions of the KNIL (Andir South of A. III Ld.) and the British Army (95 Battery and two Troops of 21 LAA), but the anti-aircraft artillery did not receive any direct hits.

Subsequently, some ten Navy Os fired from a low altitude at the anti-aircraft positions around the flight terrain, after which bombers from Palembang did their destructive work in the northern part of the base. Here, too, several aircraft were hit. Furthermore, the anti-aircraft artillery positions along the north-eastern edge of the airfield (Andir-North of A. III Ld.) had been targeted. With the 8-cm Bofors battery (the 'Kapok' post) only two guns had been somewhat displaced by near misses, but one of the two 4-cm Bofors sections (the 'Rubber' post) had to be relocated due to bomb damage. After this, Navy Os attacked again. The anti-aircraft artillery fired at the fighter aircraft with all they had got and they even fired their 4-cm guns regularly. Hitting the fast and manoeuvrable fighter aircraft was difficult enough under normal circumstances, but the Japanese aircraft were now benefiting from the large smoke and dust clouds hanging over the air base and, in spite of several claims to the contrary, were not hit or only lightly damaged.

The number of dead and wounded among the ML and anti-aircraft gunners of the KNIL and the British Army was relatively low. A shelter received a direct hit, causing two dead and several wounded among the ML personnel. There were several light and heavily wounded among the anti-aircraft gunners due to near misses, while three men of the 95 Battery Headquarters (48 LAA) were killed by a chance hit next to a dug out.[32]

Disruption of the allied air operations

Fifteen minutes after the last air raid six Wirraway Army Co-operation aircraft of the RAAF landed, whose pilots were not aware that Andir had been closed down. The aircraft had been picked up at Pondjok Tjabe, where they had been held in reserve. During landing two hit bomb craters and were lost, the pilots being unharmed.

From the end of the morning onwards the main runway at Andir could be used again, albeit for only a short period. Work parties immediately started filling up the craters that were most in the way, in and next to the runway and the taxi routes. Female drivers, volunteers of the so-called Vrouwen Auto Corps–Women's Automobile Corps (VAC), trucked in the sand and gravel for the men to fill up the holes with. In doing so, they found many duds. During the entire afternoon there were continuous air raid alerts interrupting the work. The Japanese aircraft that had been reported were attacking KNIL units advancing on the occupied Kalidjati. This situation resulted in the air base being closed during the entire afternoon. As a result the remaining Brewsters at Pameungpeuk could not return to Andir. In the evening repair teams began the repair work on the buildings and facilities of the air base.[33]

A team of the Technical Service inspected the damaged aircraft. The Japanese had partly concentrated on the bombers parked in their pens and the aircraft parked (although camouflaged and with cover from palm trees) in a dispersal area used by the Technical Service in the south-western part of the airfield. Of the Glenn Martins and Hudsons alone two aircraft in total were total losses and 11 bombers had incurred damage to a varying extent. A Glenn Martin of 1-Vl.G.I (the damaged aircraft of the Van den Broek crew) was the first to have been set ablaze by a Ki-43 and was a total loss. In a piece of bravado Major Kato had flown a circuit, fired at the Glenn Martin and had climbed out at full throttle before the anti-aircraft artillery had been able to fire a single shot at him.

The damage in the vicinity of the Noordhangaar (North hangar) came from bombs as well as fighter fire. There had been two Curtiss H-75A Hawk fighter aircraft of 1-Vl.G.V (both out of use) parked near the Noordhangaar, along with four Brewster Buffalo fighters, which had been transferred to the ML around 26 February 1942 by the RAF, but were not operationally serviceable yet. One of the H-75As was a total loss. Of the four Glenn Martins of 3-Vl.G.III in the pens along the north-eastern edge of the flight terrain right in front of the Andir-North position, including the aircraft of the Bosman crew, three sustained light and one heavy damage from bullets and fragmentation. The former three had their electric systems destroyed, amongst other damage. With the help of the Technical Service it would be possible to repair these bombers in a couple of days.[34]

In the southern part of Andir the damage was much more extensive. Apart from the Glenn Martin of 1-Vl.G.I, mentioned above, the M-585 of 1-Vl.G.II received a row of bullet holes in the fuselage and bomb fragments in both wings and engines. The Glenn Martin was taken to the Technical Service for repairs of the fragmentation damage and replacement of the engines. Two Glenn Martins of 2-Vl.G.III had received light to medium damage in strafings and could be repaired at the afdeling itself.[35] A Hudson bomber of 1 Squadron RAAF had been hit by a bomb and had completely gone up in flames. A second Hudson had its fuel tank damaged by machine gun bullets and was sent to the Technical Service for repairs. Four CW-22 reconnaissance planes of Vk.A.2, which had been withdrawn from eastern Java on 1 March and which were not fully operational yet, were total losses due to direct hits or near misses. A few four-engine B-17s and one twin-engine B-18 bomber of the USAAF, parked at the Technical Service, in the dispersal area used by the Service, sustained bullet and fragmentation damage. A CW-21B of 2-Vl.G.IV at the Technical Service was a total loss. Furthermore, in the south-eastern part of the airfield a Douglas DC-5 and a Grumman G-21 amphibious aircraft of the KNILM received fragmentation damage.[36]

After the bombing raids there only remained one bomber operationally serviceable at Andir, a Glenn Martin of 1-Vl.G.II. This was the M-598, which could not be committed in the early hours of the morning due to engine trouble, but had been repaired in the course of the morning. This aircraft arrived at Tasikmalaja by the end of the morning. As soon as possible the other bombers would be flown over to this airfield, which was assumed to be less vulnerable. The remaining fighter aircraft of the ML were at Pameungpeuk and were to return as soon as possible to Andir. (This happened in the morning of 4 March.) Almost immediately after the departure of the M-598 Andir had to be closed again. The bomber, incidentally, was not operationally serviceable at Tasikmalaja. The improvised crew, led by Sgt W.J. Hofmyster, lacked an observer or bombardier, and M-598 did not have a bombsight, making it suitable only as a trailing aircraft.[37]

Apart from one or two, the fighter aircraft of 242 Squadron had all been damaged (albeit mostly lightly to very lightly) and they were all operationally serviceable again the next morning, with the exception of one aircraft. In the early morning of 4 March the Hurricanes returned to Tjililitan by order of JAC. Sgt Dovell's damaged aircraft, which had already been left behind on 2 March at Andir, was probably still being repaired. Furthermore, Plt Off E.C. Gartrell's badly damaged aircraft stayed behind. Later, on 4 March, the squadron was to be re-located for good to Andir and the Tjililitan base was to be dismantled. The RAF withdrew to Andir. Already on 2 March the KNIL had begun to ship out supplies of bombs and ammunition, but at first the ML still left a small detachment of ground personnel behind. Vk.A.1 still carried out a reconnaissance mission from Tjililitan in the nights of 2 on 3 March and 3 on 4 March for West Group. On 3 and 4 March the RAF also dismantled both radar stations on the eastern and western edge of Batavia, respectively, in order to prevent this top secret equipment from falling into enemy hands. The equipment was destroyed and the personnel were evacuated to Bandoeng. The two Batteries of 48 LAA at Tjililitan and Tjikembar, respectively, and the infantry of 15 Battery (6 HAA) at Tjililitan were ordered to fall back on Tjimahi in the evening of 3 March and arrived there in the evening of the following day.[38]

A recently repaired Brewster of the ML was still waiting at Tjililitan for a pilot. Collecting this aircraft (for further repairs at the Technical Service at Andir), however, would prove to be impossible. Tjililitan airfield was thoroughly demolished by the KNIL in the afternoon of 4 March 1942, whereby all remaining aircraft including the Brewster were set on fire. Vdg B. Wink only received his order to go and collect the Brewster in the evening of 4 March and imme-diately left by military car and driver. He got stuck in the columns of retreating KNIL units and was unable to reach Tjililitan.[39]

The 'big' attack of the KNIL on 3 March 1942

In the mean time, the KNIL had launched its attack on Kalidjati and Soebang. The main force of 2-R.I. had arrived at Bandoeng and Padalarang in the course of 2 March after an exhausting movement. They had been joined by the necessary reinforcements on the Bandoeng plateau and this brought the reinforced regiment up to some 3,500 men in the end, only a small minority of whom had seen any previous action. Inf. X (belonging to 1-R.I. and coming under the command of the commander of 2-R.I. especially for this attack) and a company of Inf. XIV (this battalion originally belonged to 1-R.I. and had been assigned to 2-R.I. in the formation of West Group) had taken part in the battles around Palembang. In these battles Inf. X had been very successful in fighting off the Japanese paratroopers. The main force, however, consisted of well-trained battalions, with relatively many regular personnel having served in them for a longer period of time. Especially Inf. XV and Inf. X were known as 'good'.[40] After the additions the reinforced regiment consisted of the following units:

Staff 2-R.I.

Inf. XIV, XV and X (minus) battalions, all motorised

1st Cavalry Squadron (Cav. 1)

A. II Vd. (minus, that is, one battery and one section only)

A. I Bg. (one battery, but reinforced with the 3rd battery of A. I Hw. and a section Hw.)

2nd Anti-armour and anti-aircraft Battalion (Pla. 2)

Pioneer Troop (engineers for mining and demining and demolitions)

3rd Field Dressing Station (3 V.P.A.)

Elements of the Division vehicle train[41]

Major-General Pesman had been given operational command of the offensive against Kalidjati by General Headquarters. The commander of 2-R.I., Colonel Toorop, received his instructions for the attack in the late afternoon of 2 March at the staff of Bandoeng Group and subsequently worked out a plan of attack with the Operations section of the staff. By now the most recent information on the Japanese advance and assessment of the further Japanese plans had been received from General Headquarters, while Elt Zeylemaker gave a briefing on the possibilities of air support for Toorop and the Operations section. Incidentally, Zeylemaker was not involved in the further planning of the advance and had to find out for himself afterwards how things had been arranged. He got the assignment to pass on Toorop's requests for air support (which were to be sent by radio to the staff). When all movements had been completed and the men of 2-R.I. had been encamped for their well-deserved rest, Toorop's subordinate commanders were called to the staff of Bandoeng Group in the evening of 2 March.[42]

Around 22:30 hrs (on 2 March) the marching order was issued and deployment of 2-R.I. took effect. The movements were conducted

A 4.7-cm anti-armour gun of an anti-armour and anti-aircraft battalion of the KNIL during an exercise in 1940. (Private collection, P.C. Boer)

in a somewhat chaotic manner and with great delay, caused by a road-block of the so-called Tjisomang fortification of the KNIL, the exhaustion and lack of practice of the drivers in night movement and also by the leading battalion taking the wrong road just outside Poerwakarta. At 06:00 hrs on 3 March the leading units reached Sadang.[43]

With a delay of four hours the actual advance began, around 10:00 hrs. By this time Toorop had received several reconnaissance reports from Cav. 1 and the staff of Bandoeng Group. Reports from the air reconnaissance showed that there was no enemy advance towards Tjikampek, so that Toorop's rear guard at Sadang did not run the risk of being attacked from the north.[44] Cav. 1 reported that the road to Kalidjati was not blocked and that all bridges were intact, but requested support from anti-armour artillery as it expected an enemy tank attack over the road after the loss of an armoured vehicle. Inf. XIV dismounted at Tjikoempaj, in a rubber plantation several kilometres north-east of Sadang, and Inf. XV did the same at Tjibatoe, about seven kilometres east of Sadang. The latter battalion advanced through the terrain along the road towards the Tji Lamaja River, where it secured the bridge in the road to Kalidjati.[45] In the mean time, fighter aircraft of JAC carried out their supporting attack on Kalidjati airfield, which was described above.

The Japanese Army air force was hard pressed in this attack by the Hurricane fighter aircraft of 242 Squadron. After Toorop had sent a radio message to the staff of Bandoeng Group at around 09:30 hrs that he was about to issue his marching orders, these aircraft had been immediately dispatched to take out as many Japanese aircraft as they could.[46] Some 20 minutes later the fighters carried out their attack on Kalidjati. It was quite successful, but when it was all over there were still enough operationally serviceable assault and bomber aircraft available in the 3rd Hiko Dan. It was all JAC would be able to do for Toorop.

Around 10:30 hrs the Japanese attacks to crush the last resistance from Andir began. The base had to be closed. The moment of the Japanese attacks was a coincidence, as the air raids on Andir had been pre-planned. Coordinating and preparing them had cost quite a lot of time as this was a large-scale affair, involving Navy air force contributions from Palembang and Bali. After the air raids on Andir the staff of Bandoeng Group had no other option than to inform Toorop that for the next few hours he could not count on air support from JAC. Moreover, he was told that he had to reckon with enemy air raids on his troops, upon which the colonel dropped the idea (if all went well) to carry out a motorised attack over the road, with a battalion preceded by armoured vehicles of Cav. 1 and supported by artillery.[47] The Japanese attack on Andir came too early and Toorop's attack began too late.

At 12:00 hrs Inf. XV, reinforced with an anti-armour section (three 4.7-cm guns) and an anti-aircraft section (three 12.7-mm machine guns) began to cross the river to launch its attack on Kalidjati. The infantry subsequently advanced through the terrain next to the road, while both Pla. 2 sections followed the advance over the road. Inf. XIV marched over the road to Tjibatoe and then to Bongas (the twin kampongs of Bongas Kalis and Bongas Kidoel). From there they advanced in battle formation through the terrain in easterly direction from 12:00 hrs onwards. In doing so, Inf. XIV advanced behind and on the right of Inf. XV at a distance of a few kilometres. It was the intention that Inf. XIV would attack Kalidjati from the south.

The infantry was followed by artillery units, which moved along the road to Tjibatoe and Tjipeundeuj from 12:00 hrs onwards. A. II

Vd. supported Inf. XV and A. I Bg. (the mountain artillery battery and the howitzer section) supported Inf. XIV. In the mean time, Cav. 1, reinforced with an anti-armour section, carried out several reconnaissance patrols and closed the road to the airfield off, while Inf. X (Toorop's reserve, which had just been brought forward from Sadang to Tjibatoe) got orders at 12:00 hrs to move to Bongas. The 3rd Battery of A. I Hw. remained in position near Sadang. Shortly after 12:00 hrs the Japanese Army air force attacked from Kalidjati with seven Ki-51s and six Ki-48 bombers. It was the beginning of the end.[48]

Two Ki-51 assault aircraft, returning after a reconnaissance to Batavia and the area west of Buitenzorg, spotted several columns of vehicles on the road from Poerwakarta to Kalidjati. This was at around 09:00 hrs, when the spearhead of the column was some 20 kilometres from Kalidjati airfield near Sadang and it probably consisted of the trucks of Inf. XIV and Inf. XV, which battalions were on their way to their starting positions. The air reconnaissance was not noticed by the KNIL units. The crews of the Ki-51s dropped a message cylinder over Kalidjati containing particulars on the enemy advance (apparently they had no radio communication) and continued their reconnaissance. On the road from Bandoeng to Soebang they discovered Teerink Group near the village of Tjileuleuj (see below).[49]

In response to the information which had been dropped by the Ki-51s and its very alarming content, all available Ki-51s of the 27th Sentai were immediately made ready. The Ki-48 bombers of the 75th Sentai had arrived at Kalidjati around 08:30 hrs, and the first echelon of this unit was immediately prepared for action, which took quite some time, though. Because of an air raid on Kalidjati (the attack of the British fighter aircraft, described above) and heavy rainfall it was not until 12:00 hrs that they could take off. Besides, the number of operationally serviceable Ki-48s had been reduced to six, as quite a few planes had sustained damage from the low level attacks of the Hurricanes.[50]

For the Japanese, too, it was sink or swim, with the battalion at Kalidjati being too weak to withstand the approaching enemy force without air support. The two Sentai commanders flew along in person to be able to lead the operation. First, one Ki-48 bombed the bridge nearest to Kalidjati in the road from Sadang to Kalidjati near Tjidjoged, some seven kilometres from the airfield. Subsequently, around 12:30 hrs five Ki-48s and seven Ki-51s of the two Sentais attacked first the lead and then the trailing vehicles of the columns near Tjibatoe (approximately 13 kilometres from Kalidjati). The result was that the two columns were completely trapped on an open road with rice fields on both sides of the roads over a distance of some five kilometres. Then, the columns themselves were attacked. Within minutes the road was strewn with bomb craters and dozens of trucks on fire, ammunition containers exploding with a thundering roar.[51]

The Inf. X (minus) troops, a rifle company and a machine gun company, were just dismounting their vehicles and buses when they were being raided. The men fled into the terrain next to the road, where they were machine gunned by several Japanese assault aircraft. The number of dead was limited but there were many wounded. Due to bomb blast dozens of wounded were left in nothing but rags of uniforms. Many men crawled away from the road into the sawas trying to find cover as best they could. With the trucks also the bulk of the equipment and weapons of the machine gun company of Inf. X was lost. The forward elements of the combat trains with the ammunition vehicles were also bombed and machine gunned. Eventually, almost all vehicles containing ammunition, including the ammunition containers of the artillery, blew up. The result was an enormous mayhem on the road.[52]

Most artillery guns were lost in Japanese raids or became useless. Also Toorop's regimental command post, which had recently been moved to the rubber plantation near Tjibatoe, was discovered and machine gunned and subsequently bombed. In this action the radio vehicle (with the LARA) for the communication with the staff at Bandoeng was lost. The Japanese assault aircraft and bombers kept up the attack on the columns near Tjibatoe, Tjikoempaj and also in the environment of Sadang, where, amongst others, the battery of A. I Hw. (assigned to the reserve) was bombed and machine gunned until around 12:30 hrs.[53]

According to Japanese counts 179 vehicles were destroyed and at least 50 fell into Japanese hands intact or damaged, but which could still be repaired.[54] In the beginning of the afternoon Toorop reported by telephone to Major-General Pesman that in the first Japanese air raid about 100 men had been killed or wounded and that quite substantial damage had been inflicted on vehicles, artillery and ammunition tenders, causing the advance route be completely blocked on top of that.[55]

From around 12:45 hrs and 13:00 hrs the assault aircraft and bombers, respectively, kept up a continuous attack on the advancing

A section of 12.7-mm machine guns (Colt Browning) of an anti-armour and anti-aircraft battalion of the KNIL during an exercise in 1940. The machine guns, which were mounted on light trucks, appeared to be extremely vulnerable in combat. (Private collection, P.C. Boer)

Inf. XIV and Inf. XV and they did not stop until about 17:30 hrs. The Ki-51s now operated in two pairs and the Ki-48s in patrols of three or five aircraft, so that at any time there were at least seven aircraft in the target area.[56] Inf. XV, which in the meantime had passed Tjipeundeuj, was to first to be attacked by the Army air force. Inf. XIV, which had by now progressed beyond Bongas, was next. Ki-51 assault aircraft carried out attacks with light bombs and machine gunned the troops, while a Ki-48 patrol bombed them intermittently. The majority of the attacks, however, were strafings by Ki-51s. Against this the KNIL infantry brought to bear their 6.5-mm machine guns of the battalion machine gun companies. The three 12.7-mm machine guns mounted on light trucks of the Pla. 2 section, which was advancing along with Inf. XV and one other of these sections which was defending the position of A. II Vd. near a bosket along the road, were soon taken out by strafings of the Ki-51s. Pla. 2 suffered several dead and wounded, as one machine gunner after another was shot behind his weapon. The 6.5-mm machine guns of the Infantry kept the

Ki-51s at a somewhat higher altitude and thus limited the number of casualties of the strafings to some extent.[57]

The weather was fine in the afternoon of 3 March and the Japanese aircraft were operating on a five-minute flight from Kalidjati. This meant that they could take off with a maximum bomb load and the Ki-51s and Ki-48s could stay over the target area for one or several hours, respectively. This allowed an almost uninterrupted attack on the troops of Inf. XIV and Inf. XV, which quickly put an end to any sort of forward movement. On top of that, it was impossible to make contact with Toorop's command post, as dispatch riders did not stand the slightest chance against the Ki-51s, and rolling out telephone lines for a field telephone connection was completely out of the question. Orders and requests for information from Toorop did not reach the battalions. The only information he received came from Cav. 1, as this unit could clearly follow the air raids on the battalion sectors from the roads along which the squadron was operating.[58]

The infantry of 2-R.I. was machine gunned and bombed almost incessantly for almost five hours (the Ki-51s and Ki-48s being regularly relieved). Everyone tried to find cover as best they could and stay there. There were no means to put up an effective resistance. Apart from the lighter anti-personnel bombs the Japanese also used heavier ones. The reason for this may have been that the bombers of the 75th Sentai had a shortage of anti-personnel bombs. The enormous explosions, however, had a great psychological impact. The losses remained relatively light, but when the air raids stopped the officers and NCOs could not reassemble their men or get them to move. Entire sections (platoons) of the different companies of Inf. XV were missing, as the men had spread out over a large area during the first air raids. Of 3-Inf. XIV, the only company of Inf. XIV with combat experience, the commanding officer, of all people, was killed in action. Captain J.H. Scheffer died with several of his men in a raid. A part of Inf. XIV moved away to the south to get away from the area in which the Japanese were carrying out their air raids. By 18:00 hrs both battalions began their retreat towards Sadang.[59]

Colonel Toorop intended to regroup behind the Tji Lamaja River and to make a renewed attack under cover of darkness. Cav. 1 received the returning men, at least, tried to do so. The majority of the men of Inf. XIV and Inf. XV they saw come by were visibly shocked, deadly tired and very nervous. They did not listen to orders or simply ignored them, not grasping what was required of them. Hundreds of soldiers did not stop at the river, but walked on to Sadang where the rear-guard of 2-R.I. with the field dressing station was located. Some did not even stop there and walked all the way to Poerwakarta. It was a chaotic retreat, which the officers of the battalions and the Staff of 2-R.I. were unable to stop.[60]

The stress which the men had already built up in the chaotic circumstances of their departure from Buitenzorg, the exhausting movement to Bandoeng, insufficient rest, bad and irregular nourishment and the exhaustion caused by the advance through the terrain in the sweltering heat, had been augmented by the Japanese air raids to such an extent that many men were suffering serious combat stress.[61]

The troops fleeing over the road mainly consisted of men of the European rifle companies and machine gun companies of Inf. XIV and Inf. XV. At first, the majority of the soldiers of the indigenous companies of both battalions and also the Menadonese company of Inf. X were missing. Also exhausted and nervous, the Indonesian infantrymen, who had missed out on the retreat due to the very wide dispersion of the units, or who had at first not dared to leave their cover for fear of new air raids, were sent on to Sadang. While Cav. 1, reinforced with Inf. XV personnel who had stopped at the Tji Lamaja River (about 50 men) were covering the retreat, Major H.J.M. Klaar, the commanding officer of Pla. 2, who was acting as Toorop's second in command, tried to stop the fleeing troops at Sadang and to transport them as much as possible in their organic entities to Bandoeng in trucks of the combat trains. In the mean time, Colonel Toorop reported to Major-General Pesman. The Japanese air forces had defeated his reinforced regiment, without even making use of land forces.[62]

Colonel Toorop had intended to augment the first battalion to fall back on the Tji Lamaja River, Inf. XV, with still available elements of Inf. X (minus). When darkness fell at around 18:30 hrs, the disastrous state of affairs really began to dawn on him. Of Inf. XV only 50 men could be deployed and of Inf. X (minus) only 30. Subsequently, Toorop's hope was placed on Inf. XIV, but this battalion appeared to have dissolved completely. Unknown to Toorop, elements of this battalion had walked on towards the rear, and a few companies could not be found anywhere. Afterwards, it became clear that some sections of these companies had fled in southerly direction in an attempt to escape from the air raids. The bulk of Inf. XIV seemed simply to have disappeared, whereas it was unthinkable that Inf. X (minus) and Inf. XV could be committed again without a rest and regroup period.[63]

Partly on the advice of some of his battalion doctors, Toorop decided to refrain from further action and ordered the men who had reassembled on the Tji Lamaja to fall back on Bandoeng via Sadang in the evening and night of 3 March. The European company of Inf. XV, which had reassembled and reformed at Sadang, covered the retreat via Poerwakarta to the positions of the KNIL near Padalarang. Many dozens of stragglers were subsequently sent on to Sadang by Cav. 1 until the squadron was forced to give up its position by midnight after having been engaged by Japanese troops. Even shortly after the capitulation of the KNIL Japanese units still found wandering KNIL soldiers in the battle area. They were sent to Bandoeng. A KNIL inventory resulted in approximately 300 dead, wounded and missing.[64]

The secondary attack by Teerink Group

In support of the main attack of the reinforced 2-R.I. Teerink Group attacked Soebang from the south. The intention was to bind as many Japanese troops as possible and, if the situation allowed, occupy Soebang. At last, in the morning of 3 March, the Group was to attack, albeit with men who had only slept for a few hours on two consecutive nights and had only been fed bread and tinned rations. As every Cadet at the Royal Netherlands Military Academy nowadays knows, but what was hardly known at the time, this was a fine breeding ground for combat stress. Nevertheless, there was great enthusiasm at first.[65]

By dawn the Group once more passed Djalantjagak kampong, where 2-Inf. II was left behind as a security guard. Near the Tambakan enterprise the vehicles were left behind and the troops marched towards their starting point, the hydro-electric plant near the village Tjileuleuj, some seven kilometres from Soebang as the crow flies. From here the advance began at around 09:00 hrs, through the terrain to the left and right of the road to Soebang. On the right was 1-Inf. V (Europeans), reinforced with a machine gun platoon. To the left was 10-4 R.I. Company (Ambonese), also reinforced with a machine gun platoon, followed by a mortar platoon. Teerink kept the rest of his unit in reserve for the time being. At around 11:00 hrs, however, he had 2-Inf. II (Javanese), reinforced with a machine gun platoon, moved forward on trucks. This company followed both spearhead companies left and right of the road. The 1st Battery of A. II Bg. followed the troops over the road, while the 2nd Battery stayed behind as a reserve at the three-forked road at Djalantjagak.[66]

Shortly after 09:00 hrs the troops were reconnoitred by two Japanese Ki-51s, keeping an eye on the advancing companies and machine gunning them from time to time, especially when they were crossing stretches of open terrain. This did not harass the troops very much, although there were a few casualties, and one or two packhorses were killed. With their anti-aircraft fire the machine gun platoons kept the assault aircraft at an altitude of about 300 metres. The terrain, however, proved to be a much bigger obstacle for the advance. Teerink had no clue where the enemy ground forces were located and at the same time he had to reckon with air raids on his troops. He had no communication with the staff in Bandoeng and had received no further information from there. For this reason he had the advance commence in battle formation at some seven kilometres as the crow flies from the objective.

The terrain was extremely difficult and unfamiliar for the men, and, on top of that, often rocky, hilly and wooded, with an occasional stretch of open terrain with wet sawas. The packhorses of the machine gun platoons and the mortar platoon had to be left behind after some time. When the Japanese aircraft disappeared by 10:30 hrs, it began to pour, soaking the troops. The conditions of the terrain made the advance ponderously slow, causing the troops to spread out over a large area. Regularly there were reports on enemy patrols that needed to be looked into. The companies repeatedly had to stop in order to be reassembled, not always with success. Especially 10-4 R.I. began to lag behind.[67]

In the course of the afternoon, when the rain had stopped, the Japanese assault aircraft resumed their shadowing. Constantly, two Ki-51s were flying over the battle field, being relieved after an hour or so. There was little to be done against this. Already during the morning Teerink had failed to establish radio contact with the staff at Bandoeng, which was probably due to atmospheric interference caused by the heavy showers in the environment. In the afternoon his wireless operators with the help of the LARA again repeatedly tried to request air support, to no avail, and it was not until in the evening that Teerink learned that the heavy bombardment of Andir would have made it impossible to provide air support, anyway.[68]

Around 17:00 hrs the front units (of 1-Inf. V) had progressed to about one kilometre from Soebang. The 1st Battery of A. II Bg., which had advanced along over the road, was just behind them at about one and a half kilometre from the small town. At that moment

Teerink issued his orders for the actual attack, which was mounted at 17:30 hrs. A few minutes later six Japanese Ki-48 bombers attacked, together with two Ki-51 assault aircraft, which had been up already. The bombings and strafings went on until around 18:30 hrs and brought the advance to an almost complete standstill. Initially, the sections had spread out in panic, but most of them could be reassembled again. The Japanese air raids by the Ki-51s assault aircraft and Ki-48 bombers, however, were so intensive that the majority of the men were pinned down in their covers. On the road an anti-armour gun was lost and the 1st Battery lost several vehicles. Teerink's command post near Tjileuleuj was also raided from the air.[69]

Only a section of 1-Inf. V, accompanied by a machine gun section of 4-Inf. V (altogether some 50 men with two 6.5-mm machine guns), which had lost contact with the rest of 1-Inf. V because of the harsh conditions of the terrain, escaped the air raids. At around 18:00 hrs these men reached the small river at the southern edge of the small town of Soebang. Several reconnaissance patrols that were sent out reported that the Japanese had taken up positions all over a rubber plantation on the other side of the 'kali'. At around 19:00 hrs the isolated group retreated under cover of darkness, which was no easy task, since the cadre at first could not get the totally exhausted men to move. The only thing that got them on their feet again was the explanation that waiting until sunrise would bring along great risks for their safety, in view of the close proximity of a large Japanese numerical superiority.[70]

The exceedingly tired and very nervous troops were sent several kilometres back in the evening by Teerink. Although the losses incurred during the air raids were small, morale had suffered a considerably blow in the intensive firing from the Ki-51s and the bombardment of the Ki-48s. Many men were very nervous and showed signs of what nowadays would undoubtedly be qualified as combat stress. The company commanders tried to reassemble their units and established makeshift close defences here and there along the road to Soebang. Company 2-Inf. II relieved 1-Inf. V as advance guard and occupied a chain of outposts. Teerink established his command post some five kilometres south of Soebang. 1-Inf. V took up positions in the direct environment of the command post and somewhat further back was 10-4 R.I. The chaos in the dark night, however, was great.

At the beginning of the evening a number of Ambonese soldiers of 10-4 R.I. came running straight through the position that 1-Inf. V was at that moment taking up, shouting that the enemy was coming. In order to stop the panic, Lieutenant J.C.A. Faber, the company commander, even shot two Ambonese men. Later that night, Faber was suddenly fired at by an Ambonese soldier with a carbine machine gun (light machine gun). He managed to disarm the man, who had gone totally berserk, but the firing was answered here and there by panicky soldiers of his company who began to discharge their arms indiscriminately.[71]

It was not until 22:00 hrs that peace and quiet had returned to some extent. Bivouacs had been improvised in deserted village shacks along the roads. In the forward and side terrain regular patrols were carried out. There was no enemy activity whatsoever, and only when the patrols returned there was some danger, as nervous men would now and then fire at them. It was a problem that Teerink Group did not have a forward supply train, which meant that there was little food (some bread in the morning of 3 March) apart from the combat rations the men had brought themselves. And some men did not even have these. When they marched out from Bandoeng the baggage train of 4-Inf. V had not arrived yet in the assembly area, so that the men did not receive any (extra) combat rations. Fortunately, a truck from the Staff Inf. V arrived from Bandoeng that night, bringing bread, tins of combat rations and cigarettes for the men.[72]

Major Teerink had wanted to resume the attack in the early morning, but he refrained from doing so on the advice of his battalion doctor, medical officer F.H. Wolthuis. Morale was so low, as a result of physical exhaustion, the psychological stress from the air raids and bad nutrition, that Wolthuis deemed it irresponsible to commit these men again without giving them proper rest and good food. Initially, Teerink was ordered to hold out where he was, but, after a consultation with Lieutenant T.H. Bakker of the staff of Bandoeng Group (who visited him during the night), retreated — much against his will — to Segalaherang and (by order of Bandoeng Group) later to Lembang. Now that the attack of the reinforced 2-R.I. had failed, continuing the action of Teerink Group was rather pointless. The retreat on 4 March mostly went in an orderly and professional manner, and, in spite of repeated attacks of Ki-51s and Ki-48s, with a minimum of casualties. Apart from the Ambonese company 10-4 R.I., which had been temporarily taken out of the front line, due to morale having dropped too far, Teerink Group would perform fine during the later battle of the Tjiater pass.[73]

The secondary attack by the Vriesman detachment

On the evening of 2 March Lieutenant-Colonel L. Vriesman received the assignment to carry out an attack on Eretan Wetan the next day. The reinforced Inf. IV (minus) began its advance in the morning of 3 March from its encampment near Losarang and once again moved towards Kadanghaoer close to Eretan Wetan. Vriesman had been ordered to capture the Japanese bridgehead if possible and in any case to bind the Japanese troops there. Towards the end of the morning there was quite some activity of overflying Japanese aircraft, probably fighters and bombers of the Japanese Navy air force en route to Andir, or on their way back after their raids there via Cheribon and Semarang to Bali. This delayed the advance considerably. In the afternoon the troops took up positions at about a kilometre from the bridgehead, with the infantry on the edge of Kadanghaoer and the guns of the mountain artillery and the mortars of the machine gun company of Inf. IV somewhat further back.[74]

In the afternoon the 1st Company, supported by elements of the machine gun company (probably one machine gun platoon and a machine gun section with six machine guns in total), advanced across the sawas towards the eastern perimeter of the Japanese bridgehead. During the advance the mortars of the mortar platoon and the mountain artillery fired at a Japanese position near the target, a cemetery at some 200 metres from Eretan Wetan. This fire was well aimed, thanks to the artillery observer who had advanced along in the attack. The 3rd Company and the remainder of the machine gun company of Inf. IV had taken up positions in the western part of Kadanghaoer and next to the road to Eretan Wetan, and were to advance from there.[75]

The terrain was not really suitable for an infantry attack. The men of the 1st Company had to advance through wet, muddy sawas, with only the low earthen dikes for cover. Supported by the fire from the mountain artillery and the mortars, however, the spread out company, led by Captain L.H. Mulder, managed to advance very close to the enemy. A fierce fire fight ensued. The Japanese spotting the approach early on had reacted instantly. The shipboard ordnance of the destroyers lying at anchor off the coast was employed as artillery. The fire was well aimed. The first objective was Kadanghaoer, which pinned down the troops there, but also forced the mountain artillery to retreat. The four guns had been positioned on a stretch of road, there being no other way to take up a position. There were several dead and injured.

The 3rd Company, which had just started its advance through the rice fields, also became pinned down as there was almost no cover other than that created by the fire support. The 1st Company had taken its objective but it became isolated and began to receive increasingly heavy fire from the Japanese, the number of casualties among the Ambonese and Menadonese soldiers rising rapidly.[76]

Not having the means at his disposal to take out the Japanese guns and with the 3rd Company unable to advance, Vriesman ordered his 1st Company to retreat under cover of mortar fire. He could not expect to get air support, as the scarce resources needed to be concentrated against Kalidjati in support of the main attack of 2-R.I. Anyway, air support would not have been possible, due to the air raids on Andir.[77] Cav. 2 covered the retreat along the road to Djatibarang, where the entire unit reassembled again (probably by order of the Bandoeng Group, with which they were in touch through a LARA), to fall back on Tomo on 4 March. From there the unit left for Soemedang the next day, less some 30 dead, missing and wounded infantrymen, mostly Indonesian. In the evening of 3 March the Ono Group occupied the village of Kadanghaoer, which was fully in Japanese hands by 22:30 hrs.[78]

The deployment of the 3rd Hiko Dan

As was described above, the first aircraft of the 3rd Hiko Dan of the Japanese Army air force arrived at Kalidjati in the late afternoon of 2 March. In the period from 2 March up to and including 4 March more followed:

2 March: in the afternoon, three Ki-43 fighters of the 59th Sentai and (probably) six Ki-51 assault aircraft of the 27th Sentai.

3 March: in the morning at around 07:15 hrs (probably) ten Ki-51 assault aircraft and between around 08:30 hrs and 09:30 hrs eight Ki-43s of the 59th Sentai and ten Ki-48 bombers of the 75th Sentai. In one of two Ki-15 reconnaissance planes of the 50th Chutai Major-General Endo, the commanding officer of the 3rd Hiko Dan, arrived at Kalidjati at around 10:00 hrs. Also two Ki-46 reconnaissance planes of the 50th Chutai arrived.

4 March: in the morning eight Ki-43s of the 64th Sentai, 20 Ki-48 bombers of the 75th and 90th Sentais and three A5M Navy-96 fighter aircraft of the Navy air force (for the protection of the anchorage

at Eretan Wetan) arrived. The above does not include the aircraft flown back to Palembang on 3 March and returning to Kalidjati the next day.[79]

Initially, the Japanese Army air force got into quite some trouble at Kalidjati and was forced to send half of the aircraft back to Palembang I in the late afternoon of 3 March. These aircraft returned in the morning of 4 March. Probably 5 of the 11 fighter aircraft of the 59th Sentai had been lost or put out of action for the time being as a result of allied air raids on Kalidjati and an aerial combat with Hurricanes in the morning of 3 March 1942. Most of the ten Ki-48 bombers of the 75th Sentai that were the first to fly over were damaged in the morning of 3 March, due to strafing. In spite of this and thanks to Andir having been taken out of action by the Japanese Army and Navy air forces, the 3rd Hiko Dan achieved a major feat on 3 March, which was to change to further course of events in the most favourable manner for the Japanese army. For the allies, the defeat of the reinforced 2-R.I. by the Japanese air forces, without involvement of Japanese land forces, was the beginning of the end. Nevertheless, there were in fact too few air forces available to continue to support Colonel Shoji and protect Kalidjati. For this reason the commander of the 3rd Hiko Dan was forced to also transfer the 64th and 90th Sentais from Palembang to Kalidjati.

The 27th Sentai carried out six missions against 2-R.I. on 3 March, during which a total of 27 sorties were flown, several assault aircraft receiving damage from machine gun fire. The 75th Sentai only arrived at Kalidjati on 3 March between 08:30 hrs and 09:30 hrs and saw its aircraft fired at by British Hurricanes. It would take quite a while before this unit could be deployed once more. Probably with six remaining operationally serviceable aircraft the Sentai took part in the attacks against 2-R.I. and they also bombed the bridge west of Kalidjati. The 75th Sentai carried out four missions, with a total of 19 sorties, while the 3rd Hiko Dan tried to protect Kalidjati with the (probably) six remaining fighter aircraft of the 59th Sentai.[80]

The air raids against Teerink Group were less comprehensive. The 27th Sentai and the 75th Sentai carried out a total of 24 sorties. Pairs of Ki-51s shadowed the Group until the raids on 2-R.I. had been completed and the Japanese Army air force had its hands free to deal with Teeerink. From around 17:00 hrs two Ki-51s and six Ki-48s pummelled Teerink's men for an hour. Teerink Group retreated, but unlike 2-R.I. was not taken out as a fighting force. Nor was the

3rd Hiko Dan able to inflict a definitive defeat on Teerink Group the next morning.[81]

The psychological effects of the deployment of the air arm

Although *Air Power* has been used from time to time, since at least as early as 1939, with great success because of its psychological effects, analyses of such deployments are scarce. Analyses and studies all date from the post Gulf War (1991) period and are almost without exception of American or British origin. Still, already during World War II the air arm replaced the artillery as the major cause of casualties among the land forces.[82] Wherever air superiority could be attained, the air arm was employed to attack enemy ground forces by means of bombardments and strafing. A local and/or temporary air superiority in the modern lingo, proved to be an essential pre-requisite each time. Subsequently, the effect of the attacks on the ground troops was strongly dependent on morale and the cohesion of these units. During the Korean War it was found for the first time that air raids have a great impact on the incidence of symptoms of combat stress. Air raids proved to increase (already present) stress levels to such an extent that the morale of the troops under attack could break. What should be borne in mind here is that the consequences of stress, derived from different causes, tend to be cumulative.[83]

In fact, there is an uninterrupted series of examples from the history of warfare showing that, in certain circumstances, air forces can completely crush the morale of ground troops. In May 1940, for instance, this happened during the battle for France near the so-called Marfee heights in the environment of Sedan on the Meuse River. Unrelenting air raids by the *Luftwaffe* caused widespread panic and flight of the French troops, which, until that moment had hardly suffered any losses. Subsequently, a German army corps crossed the river and penetrated France's defence.[84] In the autumn of 1950 United Nations troops broke through the North Korean lines at Pusan. After large-scale air attacks by the American air force the North Korean front completely collapsed, with thousands of troops taking flight or surrendering.[85] Examples such as these can be found up to and in-cluding the Gulf War of 1991. Continuous air raids by B-52 bombers on Iraqi divisions at the front in Kuwait caused shortages of water and food and, most importantly, sleep deprivation among the soldiers under attack, in addition to feelings of isolation and disorientation. As soon as they got the chance, the Iraqi soldiers deserted in increasingly large numbers. Nevertheless, the morale of the Iraqi divisions had been good at the outset of the war.[86] The Dutch experience during the defence of western Java is not widely known, but it is also a case in point.

On the basis of historic cases including the concisely rendered historical examples above, the following can be concluded.

– Air superiority is a necessary condition for an effective deployment of air forces against ground forces.
– Given air superiority, offensive air support can bring about such an increase to the levels of stress among ground forces, that the ensuing combat stress can break morale completely.
– The numbers of sorties that need to be flown is relatively high, but dependent on stress already present, in other words, dependent on the sensitiveness among the grounds troops under attack for the symptoms of combat stress originating.[87]

The sensitiveness for combat stress originating was relatively high among the men of the reinforced 2-R.I. and Teerink Group. In most of the companies cohesion was good and so was morale at the time of the Japanese landings. The latter, however, suffered quite considerably, due to the many movements, insufficient and irregular nourishment, and most of all lack of sleep. The main force of 2-R.I. consisted of men who had hardly had any sleep for two consecutive nights and, on top of that, had had to undergo an exhausting trip by truck or bus from Buitenzorg to Bandoeng and from there to Poerwakarta, before they were finally committed. The subsequent advance took place through the terrain, which was physically tough (in the sweltering heat of the 'wet' season). Then, after the Japanese air raids a chaotic rout followed, with no distinction between European and Indonesian troops. The retreat of Teerink Group, which had been exposed for a much shorter time to the Japanese air raids, did not have the character of a flight, with only one of the companies being withdrawn from the first line the following day.

The allied results on 3 March 1942

The results the allies achieved on 3 March were in fact entirely due to the air forces. The fighter aircraft of JAC had been deployed rather successfully in the morning of 3 March. There had been nine Glenn Martin sorties (three of which had been flown for reconnaissance purposes at the request of the General Headquarters, one for a bombing raid on the transport ships at Eretan Wetan, and five for what is nowadays called *airbase denial* to Kalidjati), and 28 fighter sorties. Of the latter, ten had been aborted due to weather conditions. Ten sorties were flown in support of the attack of 2-R.I. and four were armed reconnaissance sorties to Wijnskoopbaai by order of the General Headquarters. This reconnaissance mission had to be aborted because of a Japanese attack on Andir. Furthermore, four sorties were flown from Tjililitan as an alert take off.

Two direct hits were claimed on as many Japanese transport vessels (one of which was confirmed in a later observation) and during missions to Kalidjati to take out British anti-aircraft artillery and bombers that had been left behind and the most vital parts of the airfield infrastructure, several Blenheims were hit, one Japanese Ki-21 bomber was set ablaze, several anti-aircraft guns were hit as well as various hangars and parts of the Kalidjati encampment. One Glenn Martin was shot down. The mission in support of the attack of 2-R.I., carried out by 242 Squadron, resulted in the taking out of a number of transport aircraft and some four out of ten Ki-48 bombers which had just been flown over from Palembang, the shooting down of one Ki-43 fighter aircraft and the damaging and putting out of action of two, for the time being. The British lost one Hurricane and during the Japanese air raids on Andir and Pameungpeuk one Interceptor was lost, apart from the losses on the ground.

The Japanese air raids on Andir were so successful that no missions could be flown from it for the rest of the day, and that at a moment when the 3rd Hiko Dan at Kalidjati found itself in an extremely vulnerable position, with hardly any operationally serviceable Ki-43 fighter aircraft left. Renewed allied air raids on Kalidjati would undoubtedly have been disastrous.

As it was, the 3rd Hiko Dan, without being able to maintain local air superiority, had its hands free to attack the reinforced 2-R.I. and Teerink Group. The main force of the KNIL had successfully been beaten back without the Japanese ground forces having to come into action. The attack of the reinforced Inf. IV (minus) on Eretan Wetan had been repelled by the Ono Group, with the support of the naval guns of the Japanese destroyers lying at anchor off the coast. If the allies had wanted to take out the Japanese artillery they would have needed the support from the combat aircraft of JAC, but already in the evening of 2 March Lieutenant-Colonel Vriesman was told that these would not become available for the time being, as priority was given to the support of the main attack by 2-R.I. Vriesman's unit, like Teerink Group, was not put out of action by the Japanese.

* * *

CHAPTER 3.7

Analysis and Conclusions

Introduction

The attempts by Java Air Command to thwart the landings at Eretan Wetan by bombing the Japanese invasion fleet were a failure. In the early morning of 1 March 1942 Kalidjati airfield fell into Japanese arms. In fact, from 1 March 1942 onwards the battle in the area of operations of Bandoeng Group of the KNIL against Colonel Shoji's landed troops was for possession of this large air base. Being able to use Kalidjati was crucial for both parties. For the Japanese, because Shoji's relatively small battle group (about 3,000 men, including the combat train) would not be able to hold out behind the main allied lines and against an enemy superiority of numbers (Bandoeng Group consisted of about 5,900 mobile troops) without air support. In view of the large distance and the prevailing weather conditions this air support could not come from Palembang. For the allied armed forces a Kalidjati in enemy hands meant a direct threat to the Bandoeng plateau (the logistic centre of the KNIL and ML).

Supported by fighter aircraft and bombers operating from Kalidjati, the troops landed at Eretan Wetan could be deemed capable of forcing their way into the Bandoeng plateau via one of the passes. The city of Bandoeng, where all major civilian and military head-quarters were located, was in danger of coming under threat already in the early stages of the battle, whereas the scenario envisaged a final battle for the easily defendable Bandoeng plateau. The KNIL would do all it could to recapture the base and to this end relocated the bulk of its strategic reserve of the land forces, consisting of the 2nd Infantry Regiment (2-R.I.) and the Ist Battalion Mountain Artillery (A. I Bg.) of the KNIL from the area of West Group to the area of operations of Bandoeng Group. In support of this, Java Air Command (JAC) first of all tried to delay the Japanese putting into use of Kalidjati with several air raids and, subsequently, when these failed, to suppress the activities of the Japanese air forces on the base to a maximum.

The first attempt to recapture Kalidjati in the morning of 2 March failed, but a large attack by 2-R.I., reinforced with as much artillery as possible and some anti-aircraft capacity, supported by several secondary attacks, was to follow on 3 March and stood a good chance of success. Although in the late afternoon of 2 March the 3rd Hiko Dan of the Japanese Army air force had occupied Kalidjati, the ML and RAF carried out several very successful air raids in the evening of 2 March and the morning of 3 March 1942 to deny the Japanese the use of the air base as much as possible and in order to take out as many Japanese aircraft as could be managed.

The strategy of Java Air Command

The strategy behind the deployment of the allied combat aircraft was clear and logical. As the available resources were few, they were concentrated as much as possible against the Japanese landing operation at Eretan Wetan. This was the most dangerous development due to the direct threat it constituted to Kalidjati air base and Bandoeng. On top of that, the enemy force landed at Eretan Wetan proved to be relatively small and, in principle, it should be possible to take it out with the available land and air forces. Subsequently, the much larger Japanese landing operation in the westernmost part Java could be tackled with all available means.

On 1 March all effort was directed at fending off the Japanese landing operation at Eretan Wetan itself. All available bombers raided the transport vessels in the early morning and fighter aircraft of the ML and RAF kept on attacking ships, landing vessels and targets inside the bridgehead throughout the day. The capture on 1 March of Kalidjati air base so close to Bandoeng was a major setback. It was sheer bad luck and weak leadership of the British Station Commander that the base was captured so quickly and intact.

Due to a pressing shortage of troops, there were no KNIL units stationed near Eretan Wetan, as the chances of the Japanese landing there were deemed to be slight because of the usually heavy seas in this period of the year. Nevertheless, the Japanese army had chosen Eretan Wetan as its landing location, as an important road, which formed part of the advance route towards Kalidjati, ran close to the coast there. The landing operation at Eretan Wetan went smoothly, but the Mitsubishi F1M fighter reconnaissance float planes of the Japanese Navy air force, which had been stationed near this small village on 1 March, had to be withdrawn to the Bay of Bantam, due to problems with the heavy swell there.

The message of an imminent attack on Kalidjati could not be passed on to the staffs at Bandoeng until around 07:00 hrs on 1 March, due to heavy rainfall which caused communication to break down. It was disbelieved at first. There were no reports from the 'warning detachments' of the Soebang Landstorm Afdeling and at JAC, amongst others, it was wrongly believed that Kalidjati was not in any direct danger. When the enemy was advancing on Soebang, this could not be communicated back to the staff of Bandoeng Group either, because the telephone system had broken down and requests for reinforcements could not be made. Subsequently, Kalidjati was attacked while the evacuation of the air base was still in progress, and a part of the air base ground defence of the British Army was about to go and close off two roads leading to Kalidjati. Large stores of aircraft fuel, aircraft bombs and, a number of aircraft, amongst others, 23 Blenheim bombers and 30 Ryan STM-2 trainer aircraft fell into Japanese hands.

The fall of Kalidjati forced JAC to commit part of its resources against this base from the afternoon of 1 March onwards, in an attempt to delay the use of it by the Japanese air forces. These harassing attacks with Glenn Martin bombers were not very successful in achieving this objective. In hindsight it is clear that the resources committed had been too few, and the capacity of the Japanese to carry out repair works quickly had been underestimated. The gamble of a quick recapture of the base by the KNIL had not worked out. As was mentioned above, in the late afternoon of 2 March the 3rd Hiko Dan brought Kalidjati into use. In the evening of 2 March the allies were successful, though, in taking out the Ki-43 fighter aircraft and a Japanese transport plane that had flown over to Kalidjati.

All available allied bombers were committed again in the early hours of 2 March against the Japanese transport vessels at Eretan

Wetan with the intention of degrading the Japanese supplies. Planned missions to Eretan Wetan had had to be cancelled in the late afternoon and evening of 1 March due to the weather conditions. On 2 March 1942 JAC changed over to a strategy in which support of counter-attacks by the KNIL was given priority. It was assumed (correctly) that the Japanese transport vessels would be mostly 'empty' by now, and, apart from some small-scale harassing attacks, the bombers were committed against Kalidjati to destroy the infrastructure and Japanese aircraft to a maximum. The more direct support of the KNIL was to be executed with fighter aircraft.

JAC did not realize that the local air superiority was (still) lying with the allies, and that is the reason why it stuck by its policy of only committing bombers, vulnerable to fighter aircraft, in the early morning and in the second half of the afternoon when there would be cover of clouds. Because of this the opportunity to destroy the Egashira Group (advancing from Pamanoekan in the direction of Tjikampek along an open road amid the sawas) was lost. This Japanese assault group was only attacked by allied fighter aircraft, which, incidentally, caused quite some delay and considerable losses to it.

The coordination between land and air forces was reasonably smooth and quick. Requests for air support of West Group and Bandoeng Group commanders were considered at the Operations section of the General Headquarters in the light of the general operations plan for the coming day, and then approved or rejected. On the basis of the approved requests the Operations staff of JAC made a global plan for the missions and assigned the necessary resources. This mission planning was then worked out in detail and transformed into operational orders for the afdelingen and squadrons by BRITAIR and the ML Command. If required, specific arrangements were made to coordinate take off times and actual start times of ground operations. The commanders of Bandoeng Group and West Group and their respective heads of operations were quite unaccustomed to working with an ML liaison officer inside the staff of their group, a novelty derived from the recent RAF experiences in northern Africa (second half of 1941). The cooperation with the assigned ML officers gradually improved, however. The operations of the CW-22 Falcon reconnaissance planes of Vk.A.1 were planned by the Operations sections of the group staffs themselves.

The Falcons flew fairly intensive reconnaissance flights to help map the Japanese advance and also carried out a number of light bombardments in the area of operations of West Group. The four aircraft under operational command of Bandoeng Group flew five sorties on 1 March, four sorties on 2 March and one on 3 March. Further sorties planned on the latter date had to be cancelled as a result of the raids on Andir. The reconnaissance planes proved to be a vital means for collecting combat intelligence. On 3 March, however, their deployment was limited by ML Command, which was due to an injudicious use of the aircraft by West Group. The head of operations of this staff had not heeded the advice of the ML liaison officer, which resulted in two casualties. The two patrols of Vk.A.1 under operational command of West Group flew 20 sorties in total in the period between 1 and 3 March.

The deployment of the allied air forces

In the period between 28 February 1942 and 3 March 1942 the crews of the combat aircraft of the ML, RAF, and RAAF put up a great performance. With an extremely limited and ever-shrinking number of fighter aircraft and bombers, 37 assigned bombers (23 operationally serviceable) and 27 assigned fighters (22 operationally serviceable) at the end of the day on 28 February, a great many sorties were flown. In the evening of 28 February and the night of 28 February and 1 March 1942 these were bombers sorties, which, apart from a few, were directed against the Japanese invasion fleet en route to and near Eretan Wetan. The days of 1 and 2 March, when the landed troops of Colonel Shoji had to go without air support, were used efficiently by flying as many sorties as possible with the available fighter aircraft and bombers. Most of these sorties were flown in the operational area of Bandoeg Group. Nevertheless, they could not prevent the putting to use of Kalidjati air base, captured on 1 March by Japanese troops. From 3 March onwards Shoji had air support, even though it had been considerably reduced by a successful air raid on Kalidjati in the evening of 2 March and a successful fighter sweep by allied fighter aircraft in the morning of 3 March 1942.

By the end of the day on 3 March Java Air Command had only 21 assigned bombers (nine of which were operationally serviceable) and 15 assigned fighter aircraft (11 operationally serviceable) left. By the end of the morning of this day operations had to be abandoned as a result of heavy bombardments carried out by the Japanese Army and Navy air forces on Andir airfield, where at that moment almost all operationally serviceable combat aircraft had been concentrated, including the British fighter aircraft from Tjililitan, for planned missions in support of the KNIL.

The real extent of the achievement of the average 50 bombers and fighter aircraft can be shown by the survey of sorties presented below. The numbers of actual take-offs are given.

Table 23

28 February after sunset and night until sunrise	
Bombers:	23 ML + 32 RAF/RAAF

1 March sunrise up to and including sunset	
Fighter aircraft:	20 ML + 36 RAF
Bombers:	9 ML + nil RAF/RAAF

1 March after sunset and night until sunrise	
Bombers:	Nil

2 March sunrise up to and including sunset	
Fighter aircraft	29 ML + 32 RAF
Bombers:	16 ML + nil RAF/RAAF

2 March after sunset and night until sunrise	
Bombers:	5 ML + nil RAF/RAAF

3 March sunrise up to and including sunset	
Fighter aircraft	12 ML + 20 RAF
Bombers:	9 ML + nil RAF/RAAF

Total number of sorties flown by combat aircraft JAC	
– fighters ML:	61
– fighters RAF:	88
– bombers ML:	62
– bombers RAF/RAAF:	33
– ML/RAF/RAAF:	243

Of these sorties, 20 fighter and seven bomber sorties were flown in the area of West Group and 216 in the area of Bandoeng Group. Per assigned aircraft the number of sorties in the period of three days covered (in spite of being unable to fly missions in the evening of 1 March due to bad weather and in the afternoon and evening of

3 March 1942 as a result of the air raids on Andir) is five on average. Per assigned fighter aircraft seven sorties were flown, and per assigned bomber, three. Given the level of operational serviceability and the deployment of bombers during only a limited part of the day, the outcome may be called high. However, was this sufficient to support the KNIL?

Support of KNIL

Thanks to an intensive deployment of allied fighter aircraft carrying out fighter sweeps, in particular, it became possible on 2 and 3 March to support the KNIL as requested in its execution of the (planned) counter-attacks directed at recapturing Kalidjati and Soebang, as well as the Japanese bridgehead at Eretan Wetan. An attack of the reinforced Inf. X on Egashira Group near Pamanoekan (which had incurred losses in frequent attacks by allied fighter aircraft on 1 and 2 March) was cancelled due to a prematurely demolished bridge. This, incidentally, also kept the Japanese from carrying out a further advance in the direction of Krawang. Inside the Japanese bridgehead at Eretan Wetan the number of targets was small after 1 March, which made flying more sorties than the fighter sweeps that had already taken place to this area to be attacked by the reinforced Inf. IV (minus) pointless. On 2 March Inf. IV carried out a first 'reconnaissance probe', immediately after an allied air raid.

The weak Japanese defence (Ono Group) of the bridgehead relied heavily on artillery support of two destroyers lying at anchor off the coast. This support would have to be neutralised (temporarily) by means of air raids. The four guns of the mountain artillery of the reinforced Inf. IV (minus) were insufficient to support an infantry attack and simultaneously force these war ships to break off their artillery support. Carrying out air raids during the attack of Inf. IV to recapture the bridgehead, planned for 3 March, however, was impossible, as all JAC capacity was needed to carry out strafings and bombardments on Kalidjati, in support of the attack by 2-R.I. on this base and the secondary attack on the nearby Soebang by the Teerink Group. Within Bandoeng Group this was not felt to be a big problem, as binding the Japanese troops in the bridgehead was enough and Inf. IV could achieve that without air support.

Of a total of 73 fighter sorties flown in the area of Bandoeng Group on 2 and 3 March, 37 (50 per cent) were intended to support the KNIL attacks. These air raids served to clear the way for the ground troops, but the recapturing of the objectives failed.

On 2 March allied fighters carried out the following four fighter sweeps.

Eretan Wetan, Pamanoekan and surroundings

1. Four Hurricanes (support for planned attacks by Inf. IV and Inf. X at Eretan Wetan and Pamanoekan, the attack of Inf. X at Pamanoekan was cancelled, however).
2. Six Brewsters (ibid.).
3. Four Brewsters (one of which returned with engine trouble) plus two Interceptors (direct support of Inf. IV preceding an attack on Eretan Wetan).

    Remark: six Hurricanes further flew armed road reconnaissances in the above mentioned area in sections of two aircraft.

Kalidjati and Soebang

4. Four Brewsters, two Interceptors and six Hurricanes (direct support for an attack by Teerink Group at Soebang. This mission failed by a too late moment of execution, but the attack of Teerink Group was cancelled).

    Remark: two Interceptors further covered Teerink Group during passing of the Tjiater pass.

After a very successful first fighter sweep with ten Hurricanes to Kalidjati, in direct support of the large push by the reinforced 2-R.I. in the morning of 3 March, the Japanese Army and Navy air forces put out of action Andir air base, including the allied bombers that were waiting there to carry out their next mission. Not until the evening did the base become operational again, and because of this the KNIL troops were made to feel the full force of the 3rd Hiko Dan and the ensuing psychological effects of the use of the air arm under conditions of enemy air superiority.

The psychological effects of the use of the air arm

The psychological effects of an intensive use of air forces against ground troops are often more important that the direct effects measured in numbers of dead and wounded soldiers and destroyed hardware.

Although on a much smaller scale, the effects of the Japanese air raids on Colonel Toorop's and Major Teerink's troops are comparable to the attacks of the coalition forces on the Iraqi troops at the front in Kuwait during the Gulf War of 1991. Stress, already originating from different causes, was increased by means of continuous enemy air raids to such an extent that many Iraqi servicemen began to suffer severe symptoms of combat stress and entire divisions began to disintegrate. What must be borne in mind here is that the building-up of stress is a cumulative process.

In the case of Teerink's and Toorop's troops the causes of the stress came immediately prior to their operational deployment, in particular a deteriorated physical condition due to insufficient sleep and nourishment. On top of that came the physically exhausting advance through the terrain in the humid clammy heat of the 'wet' (monsoon) season and the fact that (with the exception of Inf. X minus and a company of Inf. XIV) the troops had to operate under combat circumstances for the first time. In other words, the men had already been more or less at the end of their tether before they had gone into actual combat. And it did not come to the expected ground battle. There were only attacks from the air, while there were hardly any means to fight back. In the process it became clear to the men that the Japanese aircraft had no longer anything to fear from their own air forces. The 3rd Hiko Dan flew a total of 46 sorties against the advance of the reinforced 2-R.I. and 24 sorties against the advance of Teerink's group. During the air raids, which kept going on for hours, morale in most of the deployed companies broke.

Conclusions

Air Power played a crucial role in the fight against the Japanese troops of the Shoji detachment (regimental battle group) which had landed at Eretan Wetan. In the evening and night of 28 February and 1 March 1942 it fell to the ML, the RAF and the RAAF to bear the main load of the allied counter actions, during which they tried in the first instance to degrade to a maximum the landing operation itself. There were some successes here, while in the afternoon of 1 March the advance of the so-called Egashira Group on Pamanaoekan was seriously hindered. The advance of Wakamatsu Group, however, went almost entirely unnoticed and no air forces could be brought to bear against it.

When KNIL units began carrying out counter-attacks on 2 March, the ML and RAF supported the (planned) operations against Eretan Wetan, Soebang and Kalidjati with fighter aircraft. For Java Air Command this meant a continuous utilisation of scarce resources, but the requested support could be given. When the 3rd Hiko Dan stationed its first combat aircraft at Kalidjati in the late afternoon of 2 March, the fighter aircraft that had come along were put out of action, mostly for a longer period of time, during an allied air raid in the late evening of 2 March. This allowed an uninterrupted attack on Kalidjati in the morning of 3 March until about 07:15 hrs, after which the 3rd Hiko Dan had again one Ki-43 fighter up in the air. This defensive capacity was only extended to nine with the arrival of the main force of the 59th Sentai from Palembang between 08:30 hrs and 09:30 hrs. The number of fighters, however, remained too low for local air superiority.

At around 10:00 hrs ten Hurricanes attacked, taking out a large part of the newly-arrived bombers of the 75th Sentai and shooting down one Ki-43 fighter aircraft and damaging several other Ki-43s. Then, things began to go wrong. Planned follow-up attacks with Hudsons and Glenn Martins, amongst others, could not take place because the Japanese Army and Navy air forces put Andir air base out of action with an extremely heavy bombing raid. It was here that at this moment all remaining operationally serviceable allied combat aircraft were concentrated due to a lack of other usable air bases. The allied aircraft could not take off anymore during the rest of the day and the own local air superiority had evaporated in one blow. This was not a moment too soon for the Japanese troops of Colonel Shoji, for the reinforced battalion at Kalidjati and Soebang was too weak to hold out against the approaching triple numerical superiority without air support. The 3rd Hiko Dan had hardly any operationally serviceable fighter aircraft left, but it now had its hands free for attacks with assault aircraft and bombers on the advancing 2-R.I. and Teerink Group of the KNIL.

Those units were attacked with such intensity, that, mostly because of the psychological effects of the use of Air Power, many men began to suffer of severe symptoms of combat stress and morale began to break down in several companies. The strategic reserve of the allied land forces and one of the companies in Teerink Group (the reserve of Bandoeng Group) were defeated by the air forces, without the help even of enemy ground forces. The chances of recapturing Kalidjati had been lost. In hindsight, it was the beginning of the end.

PART 4

❧❧

The Battle of the Tjiater Pass

The battle between the allied and Japanese land and air forces for access to the Bandoeng plateau from 4 March up to and including 7 March 1942

※ ※

CHAPTER 4.1

Introduction

The failed attempt to recapture Kalidjati[1]

As was described in the previous part, on 2 and 3 March 1942 the KNIL made several attempts at recapturing Kalidjati from Colonel Shoji's detachment (regimental battle group), which had landed at Eretan Wetan. On 2 March the KNIL deployed the so-called Mobile Unit (ME), a unit consisting, amongst others, of 24 light tanks and an infantry company of some 150 men in armoured vehicles. In their own words, the Japanese stated that they were barely able to repel the attack of the ME on the small town of Soebang near Kalidjati. On 3 March new attacks followed, this time from the south in the direction of Soebang, by the so-called Teerink Group, and from the west, over the road of Poerwakarta to Kalidjati by the reinforced 2e Regiment Infanterie–2nd Infantry Regiment (2-R.I.). The allied supreme command first wanted to take out the Japanese troops that had landed at Eretan Wetan and subsequently taken Kalidjati, and then, with all available means attack the much bigger Japanese main force, which had landed farther to the west. In the mean time, West Group was to make a phased withdrawal on a line that could be well defended, with several prepared positions, west of Batavia and Buitenzorg.

Teerink Group (the reserve of Bandoeng Group) consisted of a mixed bag of units, of battalion size altogether. Its core consisted of the staff and three companies of the Ve Bataljon Infanterie–Vth Infantry Battalion (Inf. V), whose 4th Company (machine guns and mortars) was incomplete, however. Two infantry companies, one incomplete, and a mountain artillery battery had been added to this core. In total the entire Group amounted to some 1,000 men, commanded by Major C.G.J. Teerink. The 2nd Infantry Regiment, commanded by Colonel C.G. Toorop, to which as many artillery as possible and some anti-armour and anti-aircraft artillery had been added, consisted of about 3,500 men, including the reinforcements. Relocated for the attack from the environment of Buitenzorg, the regiment had already had to stomach a tiring movement.

Toorop's big attack on Kalidjati, supported from the south by Teerink, completely bogged down in the afternoon of 3 March, due to unrelenting Japanese air raids and a complete lack of allied air support as a result of a bombing raid on Andir. By the end of the afternoon the retreat of the infantry battalions of 2-R.I. turned into chaotic flight. For five hours on end twin-engine Mitsubishi Ki-48 light bombers and single-engine Mitsubishi Ki-51 assault aircraft of the 3rd Hiko Dan, coming from the captured Kalidjati, kept on attacking the vehicles, artillery pieces and the advancing infantry battalions. At the end of it, most of the vehicles and heavy weaponry had been lost, there had been dozens of wounded and dead soldiers and the morale of the infantrymen had been completely crushed. After this, the 3rd Hiko Dan had its hands free for an attack on Teerink Group, whose advance was brought to a standstill. The unit, however, was not put out of action and could be withdrawn on Lembang on 4 March with minimal losses, to be subsequently deployed for the reinforcement of the troops in the Tjiater pass.

After one single successful fighter sweep the allied air forces had not been able to support Toorop anymore, as his attack was delayed and the Japanese carried out a heavy air raid on Andir air base with some 50 bombers, escorted by fighter aircraft at the end of the morning (the moment was purely coincidental, as the attack had already been planned before). The raid forced Andir to close down, the base being strewn with bomb craters and heavily damaged. Continuous new air alerts caused the clearing of unexploded ordnance and wreckage to go painfully slowly. Several aircraft were lost or damaged.

Putting Andir out of action meant a heavy blow, for from this base all support missions for the KNIL troops advancing on Kalidjati were flown. The allied local air superiority had evaporated in one fell swoop. Not hindered by the risk of allied interventions, the Japanese Army air force subsequently carried out a large number of sorties directed against the KNIL troops advancing on Kalidjati. They caused relatively few casualties, but the psychological effects eventually destroyed the morale of most of the advancing KNIL troops, without the Japanese ground troops even coming into action. As was said above, the retreat of the reinforced 2-R.I. turned into a rout, and also one of the companies of Teerink Group would have to be taken out of the first line a few days later. The battle for possession of Kalidjati air base had been lost. In hindsight, this was the beginning of the end of the defence of western Java.

At that moment this was by no means obvious for Colonel Shoji. On 4 March he again lost part of his air support at Kalidjati due to a successful allied fighter sweep by 242 Squadron RAF. A few more of these allied air raids and the air support from the 3rd Hiko Dan might be reduced to almost nothing. Besides, there was a relatively large enemy motorised unit (Teerink Group and the Mobile Unit) positioned south of Soebang and Shoji's troops were in danger of being surrounded. The action to take the large road bridge near Krawang across the Tjitaroem River, in order to control the connection between Batavia and Kalidjati, failed on 4 March, when the bridge was blown up in front of the eyes of the Japanese advance guard. Because of the danger of renewed attacks on Soebang and Kalidjati and the weakness of his detachment, Shoji immediately withdrew his battle group at Krawang. Attack seemed the best defence and, in close consultation with Major-General Endo, commanding the army air forces at Kalidjati, Colonel Shoji decided to launch an attack on Bandoeng. The route which was the least risky was that from Soebang via the Tjiater pass.

The balance of strength on 4 March 1942

The option of organising a renewed major attack on Kalidjati was considered by General Headquarters (AHK), but was deemed to be infeasible. The shortage of troops after the annihilation of 2-R.I. in the attack on Kalidjati was so pressing that there was only one solution left: a concentration of all available troops which could still be moved safely on the Bandoeng plateau. There, one battle group would be formed from West Group and Bandoeng Group which was felt to be strong enough to defend the plateau and to execute sallies to take out the Japanese units. The withdrawal of West Group, however, was a complex logistical operation that would take several days to complete. In the mean time, Bandoeng Group was to deny the Japanese access to the plateau. In all passes that could be used by motorised traffic the KNIL had established fortified positions, such as the Tjiater forti-fication in the pass of the same name north of Lembang and the Tjisomang fortification south of Poerwakarta.[2]

Major-General Pesman, the commander of Bandoeng Group of the KNIL, was responsible for the defence of the plateau and the area adjacent to it. On 1 March he was in command of some 5,900 combat-ready men. As a result of the transfer of 2-R.I. and an infantry battalion from Central Java this number rose to about 9,000 men. A considerable number of them, however, in particular 2-R.I., with its attached artillery and anti-armour and anti-aircraft units and one company of Teerink Group, constituted little combat value anymore on 4 March. Nevertheless, Pesman had a superiority of numbers. As he had to defend several passes, however, he could not commit his troops in a concentrated fashion (unlike Colonel Shoji). Besides, all his companies with some battle experience (acquired in the battle for Palembang in southern Sumatra) had been put out of action with 2-R.I.[3]

Shoji's regimental battle group consisted of a mere 3,000 men, including the combat train, of whose strength, incidentally, the allies had a fairly precise idea. Of this force, the reinforced infantry battalions (minus) of Major Wakamatsu (Wakamatsu Group) and Major Egashira (Egashira Group), each with a strength of 1,000 to 1,200 men, were deployed in the battle for Bandoeng. Shoji's men, however, were somewhat better trained than those of the KNIL units that could still be deployed and had battle experience to some extent. They were also trained in joined operations, including cooperation with their own air forces. As was described in the previous part, this was hardly the case in the KNIL, although the air support coordination was regulated well and according to modern standards.[4]

On the morning of 4 March (see the following chapter for the order of battle) the allied air forces had the following numbers of operationally serviceable combat aircraft available for the defence of the Bandoeng plateau: 12 bombers, 11 fighter aircraft and four reconnaissance planes. In the period of 2 March up to and including 4 March the Japanese moved the main force of the 3rd Hiko Dan (air brigade) of the Army air force to Kalidjati, with 19 fighter aircraft, 30 light bombers, 16 assault aircraft and four reconnaissance aircraft, all in support of Shoji. After a final fighter sweep against Kalidjati in the morning of 4 March the number of operationally serviceable Japanese combat aircraft on this base had been reduced to 10 fighter aircraft, 14 bombers, 14 assault aircraft and one reconnaissance aircraft (approximate numbers). With the 3rd Hiko Dan as force multiplier and given the assessed combat value of the KNIL, which was deemed to be weak, Shoji should be able to maintain his presence at the very least until backup would come from the Japanese main force to the west advancing on the Bandoeng plateau, according to his superiors.[5]

Shoji's gamble

On 5 March Shoji attacked with all the air support he could get from Endo. In doing so, the Japanese troops were taking considerable risks. If the enemy succeeded in consolidating his troops in time, the Japanese troops might bog down in the Tjiater pass. On top of that, it was by no means certain that the 3rd Hiko Dan had been able to put the last allied aircraft out of action with its renewed air raids on Andir on 4 and 5 March. Shoji's gamble paid off for the Japanese. In the early hours of 7 March the battle of the Tjiater pass, described in this part, was over and the last KNIL troops were withdrawn to the vicinity of Lembang. With this, the capitulation of the allied armed forces had become unavoidable.

* * *

CHAPTER 4.2
The Battle on 4 March 1942

Introduction

The failure on 3 March 1942 of the 'big attack' on Kalidjati by the reinforced 2nd Infantry Regiment (2-R.I.) and Teerink Group, had serious consequences and it forced the Algemeen Hoofdkwartier– General Headquarters (AHK) to take a number of far-reaching measures. The strategic reserve of the allied armed forces had been almost completely lost, while Bandoeng and the area around it, of such strategic importance, was still under threat from the Japanese combat troops of the Shoji detachment that had landed at Eretan Wetan. General Headquarters wanted to launch a new offensive against Colonel Shoji's units, but Bandoeng Group was now facing a great shortage of troops and would have to be reinforced substantially. Apart from the 6th Infantry Regiment (6-R.I.) at Soerabaja, only units of West Group (1-R.I. and the *Blackforce* Brigade) could be considered for this. General Headquarters decided not to move 6-R.I., as the battalions of this unit could probably not be moved in safety from eastern to western Java, due to the rapid Japanese advance in the east and the Japanese air superiority. Besides, if 6-R.I were to leave eastern Java, there would hardly be any troops left to bind the Japanese troops there. This left General Headquarters only with the troops of Major-General W. Schilling, the commander of West Group at Batavia.[1]

Schilling got the first reports of the failed attack by 2-R.I. on 3 March at around 18:00 hrs and as a direct outcome of this failure he received a late-night visit from Major J.M.R. Sandberg, Esq. of the AHK. Together, Sandberg and Schilling made up the balance of the fight up to that moment and, when asked, the latter shared his views with regard to the possible evacuation of Batavia and Buitenzorg and the retreat on the Preanger (Bandoeng) plateau. The commander of West Group needed to take the latter into serious account. Schilling saw three possibilities: defence only of the towns of Batavia and Buitenzorg from the positions to the west of these places (with a probable loss of the troops involved), a delaying retreat with the entire West Group on the plateau, or a full retreat with the entire force on the Preanger plateau. Promptly, the next day he received orders to withdraw all his troops as soon as possible (so at once) on the plateau.[2]

The retreat necessitated elaborate logistic measures, in particular, and could not be organised instantly. In the evening of 4 March Major Sandberg returned to assist Schilling in the planning of it all. The failure of the attack on Kalidjati had made the route via Tjikampek and Poerwakarta impossible, which left them with only one route of retreat via Buitenzorg and Tjiandjoer. On top of that, all sorts of demolitions would have to be carried out on leaving Batavia and Buitenzorg, and this would take a lot of time. In the afternoon of 4 March the retreat of the units from Batavia began by train and road. The first units of West Group were expected in the environment of Bandoeng on 6 March, among them also the Australian/British/American *Blackforce* Brigade, but these troops would not be deployable for at least four days.[3]

In the mean time, Major-General J.J. Pesman did all he could to reinforce the positions protecting the access points to the Bandoeng plateau. The troops in the Tjisomang fortification south of Poerwakarta were reinforced in the night of 3 on 4 March and the following morning. This position had been manned since the end of February by the 2nd Company of the Vth Infantry Battalion (2-Inf. V), a battery of the Ist Battalion Mountain Artillery (A. I Bg.) and a section of anti-armour guns. The reinforcements consisted of a second battery of A. I Bg., the complete IXth Infantry Battalion (Inf. IX) and a platoon commanded by Lieutenant C.A. Heshusius with three Marmon Herrington (so-called South-African) armoured vehicles. The platoon belonged to the Van Dongen Squadron (named after the commander of this reconnaissance squadron, Captain E. van Dongen).[4]

The reinforcement of the Tjisomang position was given priority on the basis of information on earlier Japanese movements from Eretan Wetan in a westerly direction and the reports of the reconnaissance missions by the air forces. In the morning of 4 March this still fed AHK's assumption that a Japanese attack on Bandoeng via Poerwakarta and the Tjisomang fortification was a very strong probability. Japanese air reconnaissance missions in the area and a light bombing raid in the morning of 4 March only strengthened the AHK's initial conviction.[5]

The Japanese indeed occupied Poerwakarta around sunrise on 4 March. Some of the troop movements in the direction of this town were reconnoitred by a Falcon of the ML, but at first it was entirely missed that the Japanese battle group responsible for this was largely drawn back to Kalidjati some hours later. In the first part of the afternoon a reconnaissance of the southern edge of Poerwakarta by the Heshusius platoon firmly established the presence of Japanese troops there.[6]

Already on 3 March Colonel Shoji had decided to take Poerwakarta and Tjikampek as soon as possible, and on 4 March at around 04:00 hrs a telephone operator of the PTT (the civilian postal, telephone and telegraph service) reported the presence of the advance guard of Wakamatsu Group (a reinforced infantry battalion minus) in Poerwakarta. The occupation of this town was meant as a security for the advance of Egashira Group (also a reinforced infantry battalion minus), which had been called back from Pamanoekan, via Soebang and Sadang to Tjikampek. Major Egashira's final objective was Krawang and his battle group was to cut the connection between Batavia and Bandoeng. This was Colonel Shoji's primary assignment. When Wakamatsu got word of the successful occupation of Tjikampek, which had been evacuated by the KNIL, he withdrew to Kalidjati at around 12:30 hrs. There was an enemy motorised unit south of Soebang

(Teerink Group and the Mobile Unit of the KNIL) and the battle group could not be missed in the Kalidjati-Soebang area.[7]

For a possible reinforcement of the Tjiater fortification south of Soebang Pesman had available the Inf. L.H. XXI infantry battalion, which had arrived in the Bandoeng area from central Java on 3 and (mostly) 4 March, and six 'South-African' armoured vehicles of the squadron of Captain Van Dongen, which was located at Lembang. Three armoured vehicles of this unit closed off the road between Tjimahi and Bandoeng in the morning of 4 March, to prevent the demoralised troops of the beaten 2-R.I. from walking on all the way to Bandoeng. Subsequently, at around 13:00 hrs, the platoon, already mentioned above, commanded by Lieutenant Heshusius, became available for carrying out reconnaissance patrols to the commander of the troops in and near the Tjisomang fortification (Major J.W.G.A. Hoedt, commander of Inf. IX). Van Dongen's one remaining armoured vehicle was assigned to a position somewhere else on the plateau. In consultation with General Headquarters, Pesman further moved the IVth Infantry Battalion from the Tomo position to Soemedang to reinforce the troops in the nearby Tjadas Pangeran fortification, which guarded the easternmost access to the plateau.[8]

There were only few resources left for any possible air support for Pesman's troops. At the beginning of the day on 4 March 1942 JAC had the following assigned and operationally serviceable aircraft.[9]

Table 24

Unit	Assigned	Operationally Serviceable	Remarks
1-Vl.G.I	1	0	
1-Vl.G.II	3	3	
2-Vl.G.III	2 (3)	2 (3)	One plane assigned ex TD
3-Vl.G.III	3	0	All three planes at TD
36 Squadron	5	4	
1 Squadron	7	3	Incl. three planes at TD
			One plane in rep. at Semplak
1-Vl.G.V	5 (6)	3 (4)	One plane assigned ex TD
			One plane in rep. at Pameungpeuk
242 Squadron	10	8	
2-Vl.G.IV	2	0	Both planes at the TD
Total	38 (40)	23 (25)	

The (very) early morning missions of JAC (4 March)

For the time being, JAC held on to the policy adopted on 2 March of flying bombing raids on Kalidjati air base between sunset and sunrise, while during the day the emphasis lay on providing air support to the ground forces and carrying out fighter sweeps to Kalidjati (see the previous part: The battle of Kalidjati). In the night of 3 on 4 March 36 Squadron RAF at Tjikembar was the first to carry out a night attack on Kalidjati with four Vickers Vildebeest torpedo bombers from Andir.

It was possible to take off safely in the dark at Tjikembar, but landing safely was impossible. The night lighting of the airfield consisted of little more than a number of oil lamps and a lamp on a stick marking the end of the runway. Besides, the stores of bombs were limited there. The Vildbeestes, slow double-deckers and already obsolete at the time, could also be committed as light bombers with a maximum payload of 450 kilogrammes. The aircraft were to be 'bombed up' with 50-kilogramme fragmentation bombs from the ML supplies.

From sunset on 3 March work parties had been repairing the damage caused by the bombing raids at Andir in the morning of that day. They had already begun to fill up the bomb craters in the afternoon of 3 March. Mostly female drivers, volunteers of the so-called Vrouwen Auto Corps–Women's Automobile Corps (VAC) also shipped in sand and gravel in trucks all night. Working parties consisting of ML, RAF and RAAF personnel filled the many dozens of bomb craters that were most in the way of the air operations.

In the late evening of 3 March, at around 23:15 hrs, the four Vildebeestes were coming in, during which Sgt B. Appleby's crew missed the marking in the dark and taxied into one of the bomb craters which had not been filled up yet. Their aircraft was a total loss. The three remaining Vildebeestes took off around midnight of 3 on 4 March with a ten-minute interval. Poor visibility and rain did not make things easier for the crews and it took hours of circling around before they could find Kalidjati. Plt Off T.R. Lamb's crew even did not manage to find the air base at all. Flg Off B.B. Callick and his crew had been flying around for about three and a half hours before they could make an attack, which did not cause any visble damage.

Flt Lt I.W. Hutcheson was the first to attack after a two-hour search and dropped his bombs on several vague shadows, possibly parked aircraft, and on an anti-aircraft machine gun. This gun stopped firing and was possibly destroyed. Hutcheson was the only pilot to fly a second sortie to Kalidjati. He attacked again between 04:00 hrs and 05:00 hrs, without any visible results. By this time visibility had become exceedingly bad. Hutcheson, acting commander of 36 Squadron, subsequently landed shortly after sunrise at Tasikmalaja, a new large air base south-east of Andir, where his squadron had been transferred the previous day.[10]

In conformity with an order of General Headquarters to JAC, Callick and Lamb flew a reconnaissance mission together along the south-west coast of western Java. They took off at 05:00 hrs and after a fruitless search for any possible new Japanese landings, the aircraft landed at Tasikmalaja at around 06:30 hrs, where a fourth Vildebeest arrived from Tjikembar. The ground echelon of 36 Squadron left Tjikembar for the new base in convoy at around 08:00 hrs.[11]

The ML had five operationally serviceable Glenn Martins available, three of which were of 1-Vl.G.II. One of these aircraft had been flown over from Andir to Tasikmalaja on 3 March by a crew led by Sgt W.J. Hofmeyster. This aircraft, however, did not have a bomb sight and bombardier among its crew and therefore could not be committed at first.

Two aircraft of 1-Vl.G.II, flown by Tlt C.J.H. Samson and Tlt P.E. Straatman, which had been prepared at Andir in the night of 3 on 4 March, and which were both fitted out with bomb sights, attacked Kalidjati individually between 03:00 hrs and 04:00 hrs with nine 50-kilogramme fragmentation bombs each. The Samson crew were the first to leave, seen off by Captain J.D. de Riemer, head of the Operations Office of the ML Command. The Glenn Martins subsequently landed at Tasikmalaja. Visibility was still poor and there were no explosions or fires, so that there were probably no results for the ML.[12]

The airfield of Tasikmalaja, the new operational base for 36 Squadron and 1-Vl.G.II, had many possibilities for cover for parked aircraft and was not threatened by an enemy advance over land. For this reason all remaining bombers of the RAF and the RAAF and some of the ML were to be transferred to Tasikmalaja. A disadvantage of this base, which was still partially under construction, was that it was situated in an area with quite a lot of rainfall in the wet season. The airfield lacked sufficient natural drainage and this meant that its surface was very soft, causing parked and heavily loaded taxiing aircraft to easily sink away in the mud. The engineers did all they could to finish the construction works, while the RAF and the ML were bringing their stocks of ammunition and bombs up to standard. There were already large supplies of aircraft fuel (mostly 80 octane for the bombers and 91 octane for the fighter aircraft of the ML), and only 100 octane fuel for the fighter aircraft of the RAF and modern bombers such as the Boeing B-17 Flying Fortress and the Consolidated B-24 Liberator needed to be moved up. It was also the intention to position some anti-aircraft artillery capacity at Tasikmalaja. In the afternoon of 5 March 1942 a detachment of 21 LAA (two Troops with a total of eight 4-cm guns) left Andir for its new location. Incidentally, 48 Battery of 21 LAA was at Tjilatjap. One Troop of this unit (four 4-cm Bofors guns) left for Tasikmalaja on 6 March 1942.

One part of the air base which still needed to be finished was the extension of the main runway in order to make it suitable for operations of American B-17s and B-24s. They had been evacuated from eastern Java to Australia in the early days of March and it was not until 6 March that the Radio Service of the ML received a telegram from an American commander with a request to inform him at what times and on which airfield the B-17s could refuel for carrying out missions to be specified by JAC. The offer was not taken up anymore, and the B-17s and B-24s never landed on Tasikmalaja.[13]

The two other operationally serviceable Glenn Martins were of 2-Vl.G.III. These aircraft had incurred light damage during the Japanese air raid on Andir on 3 March and they were repaired in the evening of that day. The crews of Elt L. Gosma and Sgt J. Bos were to take off at 05:00 hrs, in order to be able to carry out an altitude bombardment in formation on Kalidjati. However, the aircraft of the Bos crew got engine trouble during the run up prior to the take-off and did not leave. Gosma went on his own and set course to Kalidjati in the twilight. Near the airfield the crew spotted Japanese fighter aircraft circling round, and Gosma did not take any risk and turned around. The crew had all the luck in the world, in that they narrowly missed six Ki-43 fighter aircraft of the 3rd Hiko Dan that were attacking Andir (see below). In the morning of 4 March 2-Vl.G.III received an aircraft which had been prepared by the Technical Service, bringing the total strength up to three Glenn Martins.[14]

The Lockheed Hudson light bombers of 1 Squadron RAAF were not committed this night. After the raid on Andir of 3 March 1 Squadron had six aircraft left on this base, three of which were operationally serviceable again at 05:00 hrs on 4 March. There were three Hudsons for major repairs with the Technical Service of the ML. The operational value of the aircraft that were made ready for flight at the squadron was somewhat questionable with regard to their technical condition. Given their flying hours, they had already been up for major maintenance for some time. The operationally service-able aircraft were not committed anymore against Kalidjati, possibly because of the bad weather and the delays that had been incurred in the flying of missions. They may also have been kept on readiness in case the two Vildebeestes discovered a new Japanese landing operation after all.[15]

The planned transfer of the unit to Tasikmalaja did not take place. Instead, in the evening of 4 March the JAC commander, Major-General L.H. van Oyen, gave the squadron permission to fly the aircraft that could be made ready to Australia for major maintenance and to evacuate the redundant personnel. The ferrying across took place in the nights of 4 on 5, 5 on 6 and 6 on 7 March. The three aircraft all made it safely to the north coast of Australia, where they managed to make successful landings on flat terrain and on a saltpan, in one case. Five crews and part of the ground echelon stayed behind in Andir, awaiting the repair of the remaining Hudsons. The evacua-tion of the remainder of the ground personnel and 54 men flying personnel via Tjilatjap failed, however, as the port was heavily bombed on 5 March. A Hudson that had been left behind badly damaged at Semplak had to be destroyed on 4 March. It had been impossible to get the aircraft ready for flight in time. A Brewster fighter aircraft of the ML (only lightly damaged but not flyable yet) shared the same fate. Semplak airfield was evacuated and subsequently destroyed.[16]

Allied air reconnaissance and a Japanese air raid in the early morning (4 March)

In the evening of 3 March the staff of Bandoeng Group had requested two armed (air) reconnaissance missions. 1-Vl.G.V, subsequently, got the assignment to reconnoitre the possible Japanese route of advance from Eretan Wetan to Tomo and 242 Squadron for a reconnaissance of part of the road from Soebang to Bandoeng, south of Soebang, the road from Soebang to Kalidjati and Kalidjati airfield. The first recon-naissance sortie that was flown on this day, however, was that of a CW-22 of Vk.A.1, by order of Bandoeng Group itself. The (unknown) crew took off from Andir at around 05:00 hrs in semi-darkness and in the twilight around sunrise reconnoitred the roads from the Preanger plateau to Poerwakarta and from Poerwakarta in the direction of Kalidjati, as far as several kilometres east of Sadang. Near Sadang it spotted a column of Japanese infantrymen on bikes.[17]

In the mean time, at around 05:15 hrs and still in the half dark, six Ki-43 fighter aircraft made a low-level attack on Andir. The Japanese suddenly attacked from low altitude and for about half an hour they kept on pounding the airfield in low passes. Their targets were, amongst others, the Hudsons of 1 Squadron and the Glenn Martins of 2-Vl.G.III, which were standing in their pens near the buildings and hangars in the south-western part of the airfield, fighter aircraft parked near the Noordhangaar (North hangar) and the anti-aircraft positions around the flight terrain.[18]

The three Hudsons and the two Glenn Martins all received some damage. Both Brewsters of 1-Vl.G.V, which had been standing ready for take off at the beginning of the short (north-south) runway, were hit, as well as most of the fighter aircraft that were not actually being used and had been parked near the Noordhangaar. They were four Brewster Buffaloes of the RAF, which had been transferred to the ML, and one Curtiss H-75A Hawk of 1-Vl.G.V. The damage ranged from a single bullet hole to medium damage. The Ki-43s also targeted the camouflaged aircraft that were parked in a dispersal area used by the Technical Service just outside the airfield perimeter in the south-west, among which there was an American B-17 that was just being prepared (by ML personnel) for an escape attempt to Australia. The B-17 and a few other aircraft with the TD incurred light to medium damage. The bombardment, expected after the strafing, however, did not come, possibly as a result of an attack of three Hurricanes of 242 Squadron on Kalidjati (see below). There were two false air alerts in the course of the morning, though, which were probably due to reported Japanese formations landing at Kalidjati.[19]

The 3rd Hiko Dan at Kalidjati did not take any risks. A fighter sweep carried out by JAC on 3 March had caused much damage to aircraft (see the previous part: The battle of Kalidjati). In all probability, all still operationally serviceable fighter aircraft of the 59th Sentai had taken to the air while it was still dark to beat the allied air forces to it this time. The attack was mainly intended to secure the expected arrival of the 64th and 90th Sentais. JAC, however, had sent the fighter aircraft of 242 Squadron from Andir to Tjililitan in the early morning of 4 March and the allied fighter sweep came after all. The consequences were serious, and, in spite of the arrival of the 64th Sentai (Ki-43 fighter aircraft) to Kalidjati, caused a pressing shortage of fighter aircraft for the 3rd Hiko Dan. Shortly after the air raid Elt H.H.J. Simons of 1-Vl.G.V returned with two Brewsters from Pameungpeuk. A third fighter stayed behind with engine trouble and was to follow in the morning of 6 March. Simons had diverted with his patrol of four fighters to Pameunpeuk during the Japanese air raid on Andir of 3 March. Nine Ki-43s, which had escorted bombers to Andir, however, flew on to Pameungpeuk and set fire there to one of the Brewsters and a British Blenheim (the only one left after the occupation of Kalidjati).[20]

The Brewster, flown by Ens C. H. Weynschenk, damaged at Pameungpeuk on 3 March and subsequently patched up, went directly to the Technical Service. Simons (in aircraft B-3120) first flew a road reconnaissance north-west of Tomo for Bandoeng Group, before he landed as second on Andir. There was no question of any enemy advance from the direction of Eretan Wetan and the road to Tomo was completely empty.[21]

Elt G.J. de Haas (in the B-3120 flown back by Simons) and Sgt H. Huys (in the B-3110, which had just been picked up after having been repaired at the Technical Service) took off after all between 07:00 hrs and 08:00 hrs in response to a new request from Bandoeng Group. The last two operationally serviceable fighter aircraft of 1-Vl.G.V were to attack the Japanese unit discovered by the crew of the CW-22 near Sadang. They could not find it, however. They did spot a Japanese truck on the return fllight, though, which they set fire to.[22]

Three Hurricanes of 242 Squadron, flown by Flt Lt I. Julian, Sgt G. Hardie and Sgt J.P. Fleming, had already taken off earlier (at around 05:45 hrs) from Tjililitan for a road reconnaissance of the roads south of Soebang and the road leading from Soebang to Kalidjati within the framework of the support for Teerink Group of the KNIL (see below). They did not observe any enemy activity. After this the pilots reconnoitred Kalidjati at around 06:50 hrs. This airfield was full of Japanese aircraft and Japanese fighter aircraft were up for protection.

The Hurricanes pilots dived down from the sun for a quick hit-and-run attack. Julian flew across the airfield, while Sgt Hardie flew at high speed along one edge of the airfield and Sgt Fleming along the other. Suddenly, Fleming spotted three twin-engine aircraft with running engines and he managed to hit them all, setting them ablaze. When he turned away after his attack, he found three Ki-43s on his tail.

Fleming tried to escape to the west, but had to use his parachute when the engine of his Hurricane gave up on him after several hits. He came down in a sawa and was wounded when the pilot of one of the chasing Ki-43s fired at him on the ground. He arrived in Batavia per ambulance in the early evening, where he became a Prisoner of War the following day.[23]

A new fighter sweep to Kalidjati

Flt Lt Julian and Sgt Hardie returned on Tjililitan without any problems after an aerial combat with a few other Ki-43s. Julian thought, but possibly incorrectly, that he had shot down a 'Navy O' and reported Fleming as missing. On the basis of Julian's report 242 Squadron was immediately readied for a strafing attack with all available Hurricanes. The unit had just been transferred to Andir and the two airworthy but not operationally serviceable fighter aircraft left for this airfield. Seven fighter aircraft, flown by squadron commander Sqn Ldr R.E.P. Brooker, Plt Off W.M. Lockwood, Plt Off M.C. Fitzherbert, 2 Lt N. Anderson, Sgt G.J. King, Sgt J.A. Sandeman Allen and Sgt I.D. Newlands, first attacked Kalidjati at around 09:00 hrs. This airfield was indeed full of Japanese aircraft.[24]

Apart from the 27th, 59th and 75th Sentais, which had already been transferred on 2 and 3 March (see the previous part: The Battle of Kalidjati), the following aircraft arrived at Kalidjati from Palembang on 4 March 1942: eight Ki-43 fighter aircraft of the 64th Sentai, 20 Ki-48 light bombers of the 75th and 90th Sentais and three A5M Navy 96 fighter aircraft of the Japanese Navy air force for the protection of the anchorage at Eretan Wetan. The latter aircraft arrived after the attack of 242 Squadron.[25]

The fighter aircraft of the 64th Sentai had probably only just touched down and a transport plane was in the process of landing when 242 Squadron appeared over the airfield. Three of the British fighters were flying top cover, while Brooker led the rest of his squadron down a little distance from the airfield for their first strafing run at an altitude of about 10 metres over the field.

As no enemy aircraft were in sight, Lockwood, Anderson and Sandeman Allen, who were flying top cover, dived down. At an altitude of about 2,000 metres they encountered two fighter aircraft (they thought Navy Os) in their climb-out. A number of Ki-43s were taking off when the four Hurricanes led by Brooker attacked and for this reason the British could only make one run over the airfield.[26]

An aerial combat ensued which seemed to go in favour of the British. KNIL service personnel which were looking down on Kalidjati from their elevated Tjiater fortification saw six more fighter aircraft appear shortly after the aerial combat began. Eventually, 17 fighter aircraft were involved in the battle. The British fighter pilots had taken the Japanese completely by surprise and had not been noticed by the six Ki-43s of the 59th Sentai, which had been sent up for protection of Kalidjati. They were convinced they had shot down three 'Navy O's, apart from several probables. On balance, though, 2 Lt Anderson went missing and Sgt Sandeman Allen was lightly wounded in the legs and head, landing at Andir in a Hurricane riddled with dozens of bullets and fragmentation holes.[27]

The British pilots were convinced they had shot down four 'Navy O's [Ki-43s], including the aircraft claimed by Julian, and damaged several enemy planes on the ground. Fleming's results were not known. One of the three Ki-48s which he had attacked, however, had completely gone up in flames, and the two others had received severe (fire) damage. According to a Japanese source, during the two strafing attacks in the morning of 4 March one Ki-48 bomber and a Ki-15 or Ki-46 reconnaissance plane were completely lost. Two Ki-48s received severe damage and one Ki-43, one Ki-15 or Ki-46 reconnaissance plane and one Ki-48 bomber were damaged considerably. It is likely that several Ki-48s will have incurred light damage.[28]

In the aerial combat or as a direct result of it (probably), only one Ki-43 was lost. Observers in the Tjiater fortification saw a further Ki-43 land rather early on in the fight at Kalidjati, possibly because of battle damage. In view of the number of British claims, there were probably more Ki-43s that incurred damage. The Japanese fighter pilots thought they had shot down five Hurricanes in the two aerial battles, where in actual fact two had been lost. A third British fighter aircraft, however, landed badly damaged at Andir and several other Hurricanes sustained lighter damage.[29]

The allied fighter aircraft on readiness

After their raid the Hurricanes landed at Andir, where they were dispersed along the southern edge of the airfield. Together with the two still operationally serviceable Brewsters of 1-Vl.G.V the three undamaged fighter aircraft of 242 Squadron were subsequently put on readiness, for carrying out any possible assignments for the support of the ground forces.[30] It was impossible, though, to give the Hurricanes orders from the ground once they were airborne, as there were no crystals to tune the radios of these fighters in to the frequencies used by the KNIL and the ML. Because of this, lending support to ground troops in a moving front line was problematical.

It had already happened once before that Hurricanes had attacked a KNIL unit by mistake (Inf. IV, see the previous part: The Battle of Kalidjati). It was mostly for this reason that JAC wanted the actual support to the ground troops as much as possible carried out by the Brewsters of 1-Vl.G.V and to use the Hurricanes as cover for the ML fighters or as bomber escorts. The Brewsters were deemed to be a bit more suitable for carrying out attacks on ground targets, as they could be armed with two 50-kilogramme bombs per aircraft, and, in contrast to the Hurricanes with their fluid-cooled engines, had air-cooled engines, which made them somewhat less vulnerable to ground fire. Such a policy, however, could not be sustained with the strongly decreased numbers of available fighter aircraft.[31]

The few remaining air forces were originally meant to support Teerink Group (a reinforced battalion equivalent of some 1,000 men, commanded by Major C.G.J. Teerink) during their advance from positions some five kilometres south of Soebang, to Soebang (see below). The mission of 242 Squadron, described above, was the first in the context of support for Teerink, who was to commence his advance at around 07:00 hrs. However, no further orders for ground support came in at ML Command and BRITAIR in the course of the morning. Afterwards, it appeared that this was due to the advance having been cancelled.[32]

In the early afternoon the Operations section of the staff of Bandoeng Group first requested an armed reconnaissance of the roads south of Poerwakarta, via Poerwakarta and Sadang to Tjikampek. The two assigned pilots of 1-Vl.G.V, however, were unable to take off due to bad weather with heavy rainfall, upon which the mission was cancelled. Subsequently, a reconnaissance to Poerwakarta was carried out by armoured vehicles from the Tjisomang fortification. The platoon of Lieutenant Heshusius, for this occasion reinforced with an infantry group with one anti-armour gun transported on a light truck, drove around in a sort of no-man's land. From time to time an occasional Ki-51 flew over and the patrol had to seek cover. There was no Japanese advance, although groups of Japanese soldiers were spotted from positions somewhat south of the town.[33]

Later there was a request for an armed reconnaissance of the road from Soebang in the direction of Tjiater, taking into account the presence of own troops near Tjileuleuj and further to the south. The two pilots of 242 Squadron were also unable to take off, this time due to a Japanese attack on Andir (see below).

In the mean time, the number of operationally serviceable fighter aircraft had fallen so drastically that Major-General Van Oyen proposed at General Headquarters to terminate the practice of supporting the ground troops during daylight by means of the existing system of Air support coordination on request. JAC wanted to commit the few available aircraft in a concentrated manner for attacks against the Japanese aircraft at Kalidjati. In JAC's view this was the most efficient and best way to support the ground troops, albeit indirectly. As soon as the Japanese troops in the area of Bandoeng Group commenced their advance or concentrated prior to an advance, JAC would divert its efforts to the Japanese ground forces. In this way attacks on Kalidjati could be combined with (road) reconnaissances, to complement the reconnaissance missions of the CW-22s. General Headquarters accepted his views, but Major-General Pesman of Bandoeng Group reacted furiously and subsequently complained to the armed forces commander.[34]

The withdrawal of the Mobile Unit (ME) and Teerink Group (4 March)

Instead of the initially planned advance, in the morning of 4 March 1942 at about 07:00 hrs, Teerink Group commenced a phased withdrawal from positions some five kilometres south of Soebang, to the twin villages of Djalantjagak and Segalaherang. Very early in the morning, after consulting Lieutentant T.H. Bakker of the staff of Bandoeng Group, Teerink had decided, much against his will, to withdraw to the vicinity of these two villages, and to abandon the idea of a(n) (second) attack. According to Bakker, there were only a few own aircraft left in case air support was required. Besides, Teerink's battalion physician advised against an advance of the exhausted troops and deemed a rest period of several days necessary.

The staff of Bandoeng Group had ordered Teerink to hold out south of Soebang at all cost, and the environment of Djalantjagak and Segalaherang offered good possibilities for this. Djalantjagak was also the area to which the Mobile Unit had retreated after their failed attack on Soebang on 2 March (see the previous part: The Battle of Kalidjati). This unit comprised, amongst others, an infantry company and eleven remaining light tanks.[35]

The vanguard left by truck, but most of the men had to move on foot, due to a shortage of trucks. The companies left at considerable intervals. Following the movement of the infantry, Major Teerink's battle staff relocated in their vehicles, leapfrogging to the village Tjileuleuj initially.[36] The retreat was covered by 10-4 R.I., the 'Ambonese' company, with a screen of posts in the terrain, and a machine gun section of 4-Inf. V (two machine guns), reinforced with two "tankbuksen" (2-cm calibre anti-armour rifles), and one anti-armour gun, next to the road.

At about 09:00 hrs 10-4 R.I. withdrew and also began to march towards Tjileuleuj. Around noon the machine gun section, commanded by SM J.B. Heffelaar, brought up the rear. He had a truck to move the anti-armour gun and several packhorses for the machine guns. Somewhere between 14:00 hrs and 15:00 hrs, the rearguard reached Tjileuleuj a few kilometres down the road. From here the troops were transported by truck to the Tambakan tea enterprise a few kilometres north of the three-forked crossroads at Djalantjagak, where 10-4 R.I. had taken over the covering role by now. A few Japanese Ki-48 bombers had bombed the tea enterprise and damaged or destroyed a considerable number of Teerink Group's vehicles dispersed there.[37]

Securing the tea enterprise did not quite go according to the book. By 14:30 hrs panic broke out among part of the Ambonese Company. What happened was that in response to an air raid on Andir the heavy anti-aircraft artillery had begun to fire to the north of the airbase. A number of the exceedingly nervous men took the explosion clouds for paratroopers and began to flee.[38] Men from the Mobile Unit at Djalantjagak, managed to check the panic and send the soldiers back.[39] In the afternoon the bulk of 10-4 R.I. left Tambakan early for the three-forked crossroads in trucks, only to be sent back just north of it by Captain J.H.J. Brendgen, the commander of the infantry company of the Mobile Unit. When SM Heffelaar arrived at Tambakan, the men of the rearguard of 10-4 R.I. were getting ready to withdraw, leaving behind as much as possible of their equipment. In order to prevent this, SM Heffelaar's section blocked the road.[40]

The companies 2-Inf. II and 1-Inf. V (reinforced with machine gun and mortar sections from 4-Inf. II and 4-Inf. V, respectively) had already assembled at around 13:00 hrs at Tambakan. After a short rest 2-Inf. II left first, and after the arrival of 10-4 R.I., 1-Inf. V followed. These units had been attacked several times on their way to Tambakan by pairs of Ki-51 fighter aircraft that had machine-gunned them. The men had got used to it by now, and there were no casualties.[41] The 1st Battery of A. II Bg. (1-A. II Bg.) at Tambakan, under operational command of Teerink, was withdrawn during the morning behind the Tjiater fortification.

There were no suitable positions for the battery in the terrain north of Djalantjagak, and south of Djalantjagak and Segalaherang the terrain was relatively open with tea shrubs. If the battery took up position there, the Japanese air force would have a field day, according to Teerink, who did not need any artillery support anymore.[42]

The battery received the order to fall back on Lembang, just before the 3rd Hiko Dan carried out a raid on the two three-forked crossroads near Djalantjagak that it would have to pass (see below). By the time the battery had loaded up, the raid was over. In view of possible attacks from the air, the vehicles drove at great intervals and not in a column, but they were not attacked. The battery arrived in the early afternoon in the vicinity of Lembang, where it came once more under command of Captain P.E. Hendriksz, the CO of A. II Bg.[43]

Japanese air attacks on the Mobile Unit and 2-A. II Bg.

From about 07:45 hrs onwards the 3rd Hiko Dan had been attempting to neutralise the apparently regrouping enemy motorised unit (Teerink Group and Mobile Unit) and to prevent a renewed attack on Soebang. A pair of Ki-48s first bombed the dispersed vehicles of Teerink Group near the Tambakan tea enterprise. Several vehicles went up in flames after direct hits and many were damaged and could not be used anymore. Early in the morning Ki-51s had carried out reconnaissance sorties of the road from Lembang, via the Tjiater fortification to Soebang, targeting traffic on the road several times. One of their targets had been the bus with medical personnel of A. II Bg., which had been machine-gunned just south of the western crossroads near Djalantjagak, but those on board had been able to get off in time. However, the Ki-51s had also detected the position of the Mobile Unit.[44]

The infantry of the Mobile Unit covered the two tactically impor-tant crossroads near Djalantjagak and had established positions nearby and positioned anti-armour guns. The command post of Captain G.J.

Wulfhorst (the commander of the Mobile Unit) was located a kilometre south of the western crossroads in a tea shed. Dispersed along the roads near Djalantjagak and to the south of this village were the vehicles, camouflaged as well as possible, of the combat train and the light tanks, armoured vehicles and other rolling stock of the Mobile Unit.[45]

Two pairs of Ki-48 light bombers raided the positions near the two crossroads at about 08:00 hrs. There, next to the road, the Mobile Unit had positioned five 'fighting vehicles' with manned machineguns, damaged in the fight on 2 March and towed from Soebang, as a makeshift casemate. Two of these light tanks were riddled with bullets. Of the operational tanks, however, three were lost, along with a few trucks. There were no casualties.[46]

One to two kilometres to the south of the Mobile Unit positions the 2nd Battery of A. II Bg., a mountain battery that had been put under operational command of the Commander of the Mobile Unit, had been located north of the village of Tjiater since the morning of 4 March. It had been accommodated in a house and some sheds of the Tjiater tea enterprise, with four guns in a well-concealed position in the terrain. In spite of this good camouflage, the battery was discovered by a pair of Ki-51s and subsequently machine-gunned in the tea fields. The men of the battery had seen how the Mobile Unit had been bombed earlier in the morning, but at around 09:00 hrs it was their turn. Twice a pair of Ki-48s light bombers attacked them, while Ki-51 fighter aircraft machine-gunned them in the intervals and afterwards. The material damage was light, though, and there were no casualties. Apparently the camouflage was of some use, for the two Ki-48s only scored near misses.[47]

In the early afternoon command of 2nd Battery was again transferred to the commander of A. II Bg. The commander of the Mobile Unit did not have any use for artillery, either, and, after consulting with the artillery commander of Bandoeng Group, Captain Hendriksz ordered a move in the direction of Lembang. This message, however, did not reach the battery commander, Captain F.W.H. Twiss, until after 14:00 hrs. In the course of the late afternoon the battery moved to a wood opposite the Tankoeban Prahoe hotel, where the last vehicles arrived at about 18:00 hrs. Twiss thought movement by daylight somewhat risky, as the road to the Tjiater fortification was by now replete with vehicles, with Japanese reconnaissance planes flying past regularly. The vehicles, which had left at one-minute intervals, were not attacked, however, and they all arrived safely.[48]

The 3rd Hiko Dan had its hands full by now with the execution of other assignments. It had to support Egashira Group, with reconnaissance flights and, if necessary, bombing raids, in its continued advance from Tjikampek, which had been taken around noon, to Krawang. Besides, Major-General Endo, the commander of the 3rd Hiko Dan, wanted a new bombing raid on Andir as soon as possible to neutralise the remaining allied air forces there. When Egashira did not meet with any resistance worth mentioning and the weather over the Bandoeng plateau had cleared up somewhat, Ki-48s and Ki-43 fighters carried out attacks on Andir airbase between 14:30 hrs and 15:30 hrs (see below). Only when the aircraft had returned to Kalidjati was there capacity available again for new attacks on the enemy motorised unit south of Soebang. Major Egashira could still fend for himself.

The KNIL retreat in the afternoon and evening of 4 March

Major-General Pesman initially considered the Mobile Unit and Teerink Group positions a forward defence line of the Tjiater fortification, from where a new attack on Soebang could be launched in due course. In a meeting at General Headquarters, however, Pesman was ordered to concentrate on the defence of the Bandoeng plateau during the retreat of the West Group. In time, it would be assessed whether a breakout from the Tjisomang fortification by the reinforced Inf. IX was a possibility.

Subsequently, in the course of the afternoon Pesman took the decision to pull back the Mobile Unit and Teerink Group behind the Tjiater position, in order to let his reserves recuperate somewhat there. Teerink Group was ordered to make quarters at Lembang; the Mobile Unit was directed to Tjikidang. By that time the remaining eight light tanks had already been sent to the Military Motor Service at Bandoeng for urgent maintenance. As Bandoeng Group had no flatbeds to transport the 'fighting vehicles' to the front, the light tanks with their tracks had made so much mileage that they were no longer serviceable.[49] At about 16:00 hrs Captain Wulfhorst and Major Teerink received their orders for the retreat. At that time Teerink Group was still in the middle of a phased movement to Segalaherang and Djalantjagak. Late in the afternoon 2-Inf. II was the first to arrive there.[50]

In the second half of the afternoon the 3rd Hiro Dan carried out renewed attacks on the infantry columns. At about 17:00 hrs two Ki-48s attacked the vehicles of 1-Inf. V, which had been dispersed along the road near Djalantjagak, destroying a number of trucks. There was one fatal casualty among the infantry in the tea shrubs near the eastern crossroads.[51]

Shortly after that, two Ki-48s attacked the column of 2-Inf. II, which had been the first to be ordered to pull back from its positions near Segalaherang to Lembang. There were several casualties and a number of vehicles were lost.[52]

Major Teerink arrived at Djalantjagak between 18:00 hrs and 19:00 hrs and he also issued the orders to retreat to 10-4 R.I., 1-Inf. V and the reinforced section of Heffelaar's. At Djalantjagak Captain G.G. Kerkkamp rejoined his company (10-4 R.I.), after having retreated in the evening of 3 March after the first attack on Soebang with part of his command group together with a section (a group of about 15 men) of Inf. V. This group, however, had become disoriented in the dark and the rain and had wandered far off the road. With considerable difficulty the group of about 20 stragglers managed to find its way back to the main road on 4 March, where it encountered several men with the anti-armour gun of the rearguard. The group went through the terrain towards the western three-forked crossroads near Djalantjagak, where it waited for the companies that would be coming in their direction from Tambakan. Somewhat prior to this, Captain W.M. Wensel, the commander of 2-Inf. II, had shown up again, after having gone missing the entire night. Shortly after 19:00 hrs the above-mentioned companies began their withdrawal, passing the burnt-out vehicles of 2-Inf. II along the road.[53]

In the course of the evening the companies passed the Tjiater fortification, the last rearguards of Teerink Group and the Mobile Unit following shortly after midnight. In the mean time, engineers had blown up a bridge near Segalaherang by order of Bandoeng Group, which prevented the Japanese from making use of the direct route via an enterprise road from Kalidjati to Segalaherang.[54] Teerink Group had been withdrawn successfully and without any losses worth-mentioning. The retreat had been conducted professionally. Only 10-4 R.I. was in bad shape due to its completely collapsed morale. This company had already been out of control in the night of 3 on 4 March, and, as described above, during the following afternoon panic had struck again.

Support missions of the 3rd Hiko Dan (4 March)

From sunrise onwards Ki-51 assault aircraft of the 27th Sentai carried out a number of reconnaissance missions towards Poerwakarta in support of Wakamatsu Group. At around 07:45 hrs a pair of Ki-48 light bombers raided the first line of the Tjisomang fortification. The advance of Wakamatsu and the occupation of Poerwakarta were unopposed. In fact the Japanese troops were pursuing 2-R.I., which had been routed the previous day from Kalidjati with the help of extensive air raids. Wakamatsu Group (coming from Kalidjati), however, was too late to be able to definitively take out Colonel C.G. Toorop's troops. The last KNIL troops had already withdrawn behind the Tjisomang fortification when the first Japanese soldiers entered Poerwakarta at 04:00 hrs.[55]

In the early morning the 27th Sentai commenced flying missions in order to find back the enemy motorised unit south of Soebang. Although it had been attacked successfully the previous day, it had not been definitively taken out, and Colonel Shoji considered it to be a major threat for his positions at Kalidjati and Soebang. There was only one pair of Ki-51s up at any given time, but the flights were constantly being relieved over the battle ground. Any targets that were spotted were also machine-gunned. In the morning the attacks concentrated on the infantry on foot or in vehicles near Tjileuleuj and Tambakan and on the Mobile Unit and the 2nd Battery of A. II Bg. near Djalantjagak and Tjiater. In the afternoon the 27th Sentai carried out reconnaissance missions for Egashira Group, during which the pilots also kept an eye on any possible enemy activity from the Tjisomang fortification, which lay in Egashira's back.[56]

As said above, securing Poerwakarta was intended to allow Egashira battle group to advance safely (from Pamanoekan) via Soebang and Sadang to Tjikampek. After taking the deserted Tjikampek (around noon) this battle group was to occupy Krawang and to secure the bridge across the Tjitaroem River near Gedoenggedeh. This bridge was reached by the vanguard at around 18:00 hrs, but when the men approached it, it was blown up. The advance of the battle group had been virtually unopposed. Only at Krawang at around 16:00 hrs they assaulted an enemy infantry company, the (unmotorised) 1st Company of Inf. X, commanded by Captain H.C.J.G. Schmidt, which was taking a rest on their way to Gedoenggedeh. Apart from a few men the company was lost.[57]

The absence of any opposition during Egashira's advance gave the commander of the 3rd Hiko Dan the opportunity to carry out a renewed attack on Andir airfield (see below). The remaining allied combat aircraft still formed a major threat for his aircraft at Kalidjati and as such for the continued support of Colonel Shoji's troops.

The large traffic bridge across the Tjitaroem River near Krawang, which was blown up by KNIL troops in the face of a Japanese vanguard on 4 March 1942. (Private collection, P.C. Boer)

The Ki-51s carried out a large number of successful reconnaissance sorties, but were less fortunate when carrying out attacks. Several vehicles of the KNIL had been taken out by means of strafing on the roads between Lembang and Tambakan, but the retreat of Teerink Group was conducted with minimal losses. By now, the men had got used to Japanese single-engine planes and knew that they were only in danger when the aircraft went into a dive and when the unit was in the line of their dive. Only in 10-4 R.I. the chaos kept increasing, but this was only very indirectly related to the actions of the 3rd Hiko Dan.

The Ki-48 light bombers of the 75th Sentai caused more damage when they carried out six missions in a total of 12 sorties against vehicles near the Tambakan tea plantation, the Mobile Unit, 2-A. II Bg. and (in the late afternoon) the companies 2-Inf. II and 1-Inf. V. The first mission took off at around 07:30, which was late due to an air raid on Kalidjati by three Hurricanes (already described). The 75th Sentai had only few operationally serviceable aircraft left and probably flew the missions with only six Ki-48s.[58] It is not known whether also Ki-43 fighter aircraft were deployed for the protection of the bombers. It is likely, however, that the Japanese fighters were pro-tecting Kalidjati air base during the attacks of the 75th Sentai by flying combat air patrols.[59]

The success of the bombing raids was also limited, however. Teerink Group lost several tens of trucks and other vehicles, especially in the vicinity of Tambakan. There were only few fatalities and a small number of wounded, besides. There were no casualties among the Mobile Unit, but here, too, the material damage done was relatively great. Apart from 2 light tanks, used as a casemate, which had already been damaged once before on 2 March, 3 of the 11 still operational fighting vehicles were lost. On top of that a few trucks were destroyed.

A new Japanese air raid on Andir (4 March)

At first the weather in the afternoon was bad over Andir and a large part of the Bandoeng plateau, with clouds and rain showers. As soon as it began to improve somewhat, 14 Ki-48 light bombers of the 75th and 90th Sentais, escorted by 6 Ki-43 fighter aircraft attacked Andir completely unexpectedly. The 14 bombers probably were all the Ki-48s that were still operationally serviceable after the strafings of 242 Squadron.[60]

In the morning the 3rd Hiko Dan, after an earlier raid by three Hurricanes, had again been taken by surprise by a fighter sweep of 242 Squadron at around 09:00 hrs, carried out this time, as described above, by seven Hurricanes. The remaining allied air capacity needed to be taken out as soon as possible if the 3rd Hiko Dan was to con-tinue operating from Kalidjati. With the still available fighter aircraft it was impossible to defend the base. The Shoji detachment was still extremely vulnerable and heavily dependent on the support from the air of the 3rd Hiko Dan. In fact, the support to Shoji was to be stepped up as of 4 March and Major-General Endo was no doubt severely concerned by the situation.[61]

After a first strafing run by some of the Ki-43s, the bombers carried out three runs, bombing the southern as well as the northern part of Andir with light fragmentation bombs and fire bombs. In between and at the end of the bombing runs the fighters carried out strafings, targeting, amongst others, the anti-aircraft positions around the air base and again the aircraft parked near the Noordhangaar.[62]

The air raid was reasonably successful, the Japanese pilots reporting that five enemy aircraft had gone up in flames. Of the fighter aircraft parked near the Noordhangaar all of the four (not used) Brewster-Buffalo fighters and the one surviving Curtiss H-75A Hawk of 1-Vl.G.V (not used, either) had to be written off. In the vicinity of the Noordhangaar a further Hurricane of the ML was hit, the only fighter of this type the ML had left. The aircraft, coming from 2-Vl.G.IV, whose wobbling propeller had been repaired in the night of 2 on 3 March, had been damaged on 3 March in the Japanese air raids and in the night of 3 on 4 March and the morning after had been repaired again. It was now finally standing ready to be committed, but instead it went completely up in flames. In the southern end of Andir near the Technical Service several Glenn Martins and Hudsons received bullet and fragmentation damage. A Fokker transport plane, which had been parked near the complex of the Koninklijke Nederlands-Indische Luchtvaartmaatschappij–Royal Netherlands Indies Airline (KNILM) in the south-east of the base went up in flames. The Brewsters of 1-Vl.G.V and the Hurricanes of 242 Squadron in the northern and southern part of Andir, respectively, incurred no or only light damage, although one Hurricane of 242 Squadron was eventually lost due to damage which had escaped notice (see below).[63]

In the evening the Technical Service picked up the damaged fighter aircraft near the Noordhangaar. The Hawk, the Hurricane of the ML and all of the Buffaloes were to be cannibalised, but two other RAF Buffaloes were partially disassembled and subsequently modified as much as possible to the standard of the ML Brewsters. The work, however, would not be completed before the capitulation.[64]

The afternoon and night missions of the ML and the RAF (4 March)

When the Japanese attacked Andir, two Hurricanes were just about ready to take off on an armed reconnaissance mission for Bandoeng Group. The pilots headed for a trench and could do little else than wait the air raid out. When the all-clear had been given, Flt Lt B.J. Parker and Plt Off Fitzherbert took off at around 15:45 hrs. The latter noticed the cooling fluid come flowing out of the engine of the Hurricane which was climbing out in front of him and gestured to Parker that he had to return. His cockpit almost immediately filled itself with smoke, but Parker still managed to make a belly landing at Andir, his Hurricane missing by a hair's breadth a Glenn Martin of 2-Vl.G.III, which having just come of repairs, was being loaded with bombs. The fighter aircraft was a write off, the entire belly of the plane being destroyed. A small fragment had damaged the cooling fluid pipe of the engine of the Hurricane. No further attempt at flying another reconnaissance mission was made.[65]

In the late afternoon a CW-22 reconnaissance plane of Vk.A.1, crewed by Sergeant-Major R.E. Nobbe and observer Elt H.P.C. Kiliaan, was to carry out a reconnaissance mission and was on the point of taking off. In the vicinity of Poerwakarta and Sadang no enemy activity whatsoever was noticeable. On the road leading from the north (the direction of Soebang) to the Tjiater fortification they saw the KNIL troops of Teerink Group. There was no Japanese advance in the direction of Tjiater as yet.[66]

In the late afternoon there was one operationally serviceable bomber at Andir, a Glenn Martin of 2-Vl.G.III. The two other aircraft of this afdeling had received damage during the latest Japanese attack and were to be repaired that evening.[67] There were three operationally serviceable Glenn Martins of 1-Vl.G.II and two Vildebeestes of 36 Squadron RAF at Tasikmalaja. JAC had all available bombers reassigned for missions to Kalidjati. However, due to heavy rain showers and poor visibility, it was decided to cancel the raids of the Glenn Martins, which were planned to take place around sunset.[68]

The aircraft of 36 Squadron RAF took off after 22:00 hrs with ten minute's intervals. Visibility over Kalidjati, however, was still very bad and the crews did not manage to score any results. In the early morning of 5 March a second mission was to be flown, to be followed at sunrise on 5 March by a mission of the Glenn Martins.[69]

Results for both belligerents and the situation in the evening of 4 March

4 March 1942 was a sort of transition day, on which both General Headquarters and Colonel Shoji changed their strategy. Shoji had to give up his primary assignment, the severing of the connection between Batavia and Bandoeng, due to a timely demolition of a bridge near Gedoenggedeh. Just like the 3rd Hiko Dan, he found himself in a tricky situation with his regimental battle group and decided to commence his attack on Bandoeng. As a result of the failure of the recapture of Kalidjati by the reinforced 2-R.I., Bandoeng Group of the KNIL had too few troops to make a successful stand on the Bandoeng plateau. For this reason the army commander took the decision to withdraw West Group in its entirety and all at once on to the plateau. This was a complex logistical operation, which would take several days

to complete. The retreat began in the afternoon of 4 March and the first units of West Group were expected to be combat ready again on 10 March. Bandoeng Group refrained from carrying out a(n) (second) attack on Soebang and withdrew its mobile reserves, the Mobile Unit and Teerink Group south of Soebang, on the plateau.

Giving up the western part of western Java brought along the execution of elaborate demolitions. Thus, the harbour complex of Tandjoeng Priok, Batavia's harbour, had to be destroyed, along with the airfields near Batavia (Tjililitan and Kemajoran) and Buitenzorg (Semplak). The demolition of the military airfields of Tjililitan and Semplak was completed in the afternoon of 4 March. Several damaged or incomplete aircraft that could not be made airworthy in time, were also destroyed.[70]

The remaining allied combat aircraft were concentrated at Andir on 4 March (all fighter aircraft and part of the bombers) and at Tasikmalaja (most of the bombers), the new airfield which was still partially under construction. In its air raids on Andir the 3rd Hiko Dan temporarily put five bombers out of action, while one Hurricane of the ML and several fighter aircraft that were not in actual use were destroyed. Due to damage which had been missed, one Hurricane of the RAF was lost. Before this, 242 Squadron RAF had carried out an armed reconnaissance mission and a subsequent fighter sweep against Kalidjati, which proved to be extremely successful. Seven fighter aircraft, bombers and reconnaissance planes of the 3rd Hiko Dan were lost or were severely or considerably damaged. Furthermore, probably one Ki-43 was lost in an aerial combat, for the loss of two allied Hurricanes.

The attrition had decreased the capacity for providing air support for the allied air forces as well as the 3rd Hiko Dan. At Java Air Command the number of operationally serviceable fighters and bombers had decreased to 15 in the morning of 5 March. The first reinforcements, 27 P-40 fighter aircraft of which 24 were being assembled, however, were expected to become gradually operational no sooner than around 10 March. The 3rd Hiko Dan had already sustained substantial losses at Kalidjati on 2 and 3 March and for this reason the 64th and 90th Sentais had been transferred from Palembang to Kalidjati, after all. In spite of the losses of 4 March the air brigade still had 26 operationally serviceable fighter aircraft and bombers available in the morning of 5 March.

* * *

CHAPTER 4.3
The Battle on 5 March 1942

Introduction

On 4 March 1942 Major-General Pesman, the commander of Bandoeng Group, was told by the army commander that West Group was to be transferred to his area of command in its entirety and within several days. After a consolidation and reorganisation there would be one force, able to defend the Bandoeng plateau and strong enough to carry out offensive sallies against the Japanese. The latter actions were to be directed first and foremost against the enemy who had landed at Eretan Wetan. In the early hours of 5 March it was decided that Major-General W. Schilling of West Group would be given command of the force, upon which Pesman tendered his resignation. He remained in function for the time being.

As Schilling's main force would not be arriving until 6 and 7 March and could not be deployed for the first four days after that, it fell to Bandoeng Group to "fill the gaps" for a number of days. The Tjisomang and Tjiater fortifications needed to be reinforced to such an extent that a Japanese break-through to the Bandoeng plateau could be prevented for the short term. That a Japanese attack would be coming via one of the passes, was a firm conviction held at General Headquarters (AHK) as well as the staff of Bandoeng Group.[1]

After fending off the allied attack on Kalidjati (on 3 March, see the previous part: The Battle of Kalidjati) Colonel Shoji had focussed on severing the connection between Batavia and Bandoeng, but had been forced to give up that effort on 4 March. Egashira battle group got stranded at the destroyed bridge across the Tjitaroem and had to be withdrawn by Shoji. He deemed it very likely that the allies would regroup their forces on the Bandoeng plateau under cover of a front they had established north of Bandoeng. Indeed, this was exactly what General Headquarters was busy doing. Shoji intended to disrupt this concentration, which would be so dangerous for his detachment, by attacking Bandoeng via the Tjiater pass as soon as possible with the help of the 3rd Hiko Dan.[2]

Shoji was in a hurry, for his detachment still found itself in a tricky situation. The allied ground forces that had attacked on 3 March had only partially been taken out. The allied air forces had succeeded in putting part of the combat aircraft of the 3rd Hiko Dan at Kalidjati out of action. A few more successful fighter sweeps and bombing raids and the air support for Shoji would not come down to much anymore. Colonel Shoji deemed that his best defence was to go on the attack.

The radio communication between Colonel Shoji and the staff of the Japanese 16th Army at Serang in western Java finally became operational in the morning of 5 March, and only then did it become clear that Shoji had decided to launch his attack. In the west enemy troop movements in the direction of Bandoeng had been observed in the evening of 4 March. The staff of the Japanese 16th Army assumed that the KNIL troops defending Bandoeng were being reinforced and it feared that the enemy would be able to stop Shoji's advance in the Tjiater pass, and subsequently carry out a counter-offensive. Nevertheless, Shoji's decision to attack was approved.[3]

The troops at the Tjisomang fortification had already been reinforced by Pesman on 4 March (see the previous chapter) and the required reinforcements for the Tjiater fortification arrived in the vicinity of Bandoeng on 4 March. It was the infantry battalion Inf. L.H. XXI, transferred by General Headquarters from central Java. On 4 March Pesman withdrew the battalion Inf. IV (minus), which he had committed against Eretan Wetan, from Tomo to Soemedang, so that it was somewhat nearer to hand and the fortification near Tjiadas Pangeran, which dominated the eastern access to the plateau, could be reinforced.[4]

Pesman would need all the help he could get, but after the transfer of Inf. L.H. XXI there was not much General Headquarters could do for him. However, from the morning of 5 March all remaining air forces were "fully at the disposal" of Bandoeng Group during daylight hours. The Java Air Command (JAC) interpreted this order of General Headquarters to refer to all fighter aircraft, for the time being. The bombers did not stand any chance of survival in operations around Bandoeng during the largely cloudless mornings and early afternoons. They operated in conformity with earlier standing orders from JAC, which allowed them to fly only in the evenings and nights, towards sunrise and in the late afternoons (if there was enough cover of clouds), unless they could be given an escort of fighter aircraft.[5]

Until sunrise and after sunset the bombing raids on Kalidjati were to continue as usual, but the intervention of General Headquarters meant that during the day any further fighter sweeps against Kalidjati would be out of the question. This was reason enough for Major-General L.H. van Oyen, the commander of JAC, to protest strenuously, but in vain. In JAC's view it was precisely the execution of fighter sweeps against Kalidjati that was the most sensible thing that could be done for the troops. Besides, there would be no more fighter aircraft available for air defence. In itself this was not a disaster, as timely warning had become impossible by now, due to the absence of most air warning posts and the dismantlement of the British radar stations near Batavia. A timely warning of the fighter aircraft of approaching enemy air forces had become impossible.[6]

JAC did not have many combat aircraft left, but in consultation with Bandoeng Group it planned several missions, whose times and place of execution were to be determined later by the Operations section of the staff of the Group. In order make all this go smoothly, the liaison officer Elt H.F. Zeylemaker was going to be assisted by an RAF fighter pilot, Flt Lt V.B. de la Perelle of BRITAIR, who had flown Hurricanes in 258 Squadron. The two officers were to phone in the information needed for the execution of the missions to the ML Command and BRITAIR, respectively.[7]

The situation for the allied air forces was grim, indeed. Thus, by now there was a great shortage of spare parts for the Brewster fighter aircraft and for these aircraft there were no replacement engines any-more. For the Hurricanes spare propellors were completely lacking. There was no oxygen available in the whole of Java for the use in fighter and bomber aircraft. The Vildebeestes light bombers were 'just service-able', and the number of available combat aircraft of all types had decreased drastically over the past few days. On 5 March, at the begin-ning of the day, JAC had the following numbers of aircraft available:[8]

Table 25

Unit	Assigned	Operationally Serviceable	Remarks
242 Squadron	7	4	
1-Vl.G.V	6	3	Two for major repairs at TD One in rep. at Pameungpeuk
1-Vl.G.I	1	0	

Table 25 continued

Unit	Assigned	Operationally Serviceable	Remarks
1-Vl.G.II	3	3	At Tasikmalaja
2-Vl.G.III	3	2	
3-Vl.G.III	3	0	All planes at the TD
36 Squadron	4	3	At Tasikmalaja
Total	27	15	

Allied early morning bombing missions

In the extremely early hours, between 03:00 hrs and 05:00 hrs, the three operationally serviceable Vildebeestes of 36 Squadron at Tasik-malaja carried out (for the second time that night) individual attacks with 50-kilogramme fragmentation bombs on Kalidjati airfield. The mission was led by Flt Lt R.J. Allanson (other pilots unknown). On their return the pilots reported to have caused several fires.[9] According to a Japanese source, one staff reconnaissance plane (Ki-15 or Ki-46) of the 50th Chutai received damage.[10]

By sunrise 1-Vl.G.II at Tasikmalaja was to take over from 36 Squadron, raid Kalidjati airfield with two aircraft, and with the one remaining aircraft attack any targets that might present themselves on the road from Soebang towards the Tjiater position. The latter mission had been planned by JAC in the late evening of 4 March, in conformity with a request for air support from Bandoeng Group. The staff of the Group had requested an armed reconnaissance of the road in connection with a possible Japanese advance. One Glenn Martin, however, had sunk deep into the mud in its pen and there was no tractor available to pull the aircraft out. Upon this, Tlt P.E. Straatman and Tlt C.J.H. Samsom decided to attack Kalidjati with the remaining two Glenn Martins, because this was obviously the more important objective. During the taxiing to the beginning of the runway the air-craft of Sgt W.J. Hofmyster's crew got stuck into the mud. In the end, Tlt Straatman took off alone.[11]

In first light his aircraft approached Kalidjati, where, in spite of the early hour, the bomber was intercepted by patrolling Ki-43 fighter aircraft and after a short chase, set on fire. Straatman and his bombar-dier Sgt H. Feisma were killed, the wireless operator and the seriously burned air gunner landed by parachute, but only the latter, Private R. Gefas, in territory which was still in KNIL hands. Corporal J.P.E. Knops was caught by the Japanese and later killed or executed.[12]

Allied morning reconnaissance missions (5 March)

Apart from the Glenn Martin of the Straatman crew, a CW-22 reconnaissance plane of Vk.A.1 was up. The (unknown) crew of the aircraft, which was flying via Poerwakarta and Sadang in the direction of Kalidjati, aborted their mission when in the first light they spotted Japanese fighter aircraft (possibly Ki-51 assault aircraft, however). Up to now the Japanese air forces had never operated this early in the day and it was clear that something was afoot.[13]

In part on the basis of the reconnaissance report of Vk.A.1 and a report on the lost Glenn Martin of the Straatman crew, Major-General Pesman directed his only immediately available infantry reserve, Inf. L.H. XXI, from Bandoeng to the Tankoeban Prahoe hotel at around 07:00 hrs. This hotel was located at about 5 kilometres from the Tjiater fortification, which was only sparsely manned with a reinforced infantry company, the 2nd Company of the Ist Infantry Battalion (2-Inf. I), commanded by Captain M. Kooistra. Apart from that, some several kilometres behind the position a mountain artillery battery was positioned. Pesman wanted his infantry reinforcements to be close at hand.[14]

The first day operation by JAC from Andir was a reconnaissance mission by order of General Headquarters, flown by two Glenn Martins of 2-Vl.G.III escorted by two Hurricanes of 242 Squadron. General Headquarters was worried about new landings on the north coast as a reinforcement for the Japanese troops that had landed at Eretan Wetan. Shortly before 05:00 hrs the two fighter aircraft (pilots unknown) took off from Andir. The Glenn Martins of 2-Vl.G.III (with crews led by Elt L. Gosma and Sgt J. Bos), however, were having technical problems and finally took off by 05:30 hrs, when it was becoming light. In the mean time, the two Hurricanes could not be called back as radio communication was impossible. The result was that the Glenn Martin patrol had to carry out part of their planned reconnaissance mission of a coastal area of some 50 kilometres on both sides of Cape Pamanoekan (some 40 kilometres west of Eretan Wetan) and a coastal road running parallel to it without an escort. At around 06:15 hrs the British pilots had to return because they were running out of fuel. In the mean time, Andir was being raided (see below).

The reconnaissance mission went well and the Glenn Martins landed safely at Andir at around 08:00 hrs. They had not discovered any Japanese activity. On its way back the patrol was supposed to have raided Kalidjati with nine 50-kilogramme fragmentation bombs per aircraft. This, however, proved to be impossible as Kalidjati was completely hidden from view by a thick layer of clouds. It would be the last operation carried out by ML bombers.[15]

As the requested "aerial reconnaissance" (by a Glenn Martin from Tasikmalaja) could not take place, a patrol from the Tjiater position left for a reconnaissance along the road in the direction of Soebang at around 05:00 hrs. It consisted of a group of approximately 15 men on a truck, escorted by an armoured vehicle of the Mobile Unit for fire support. Several dispatch riders came along to report back the results of the reconnaissance. The entire group was commanded by Ensign H. de Vries. The possible Japanese advance was there, but the patrol did not get a chance to report it.

By 08:00 hrs the truck got stuck in a ditch near the tea enterprise of Tambakan north of Segalaherang as a result of a quick strafing by three Ki-43 fighter aircraft. The dismounted group were making a reconnaissance in the direction of the enterprise, while the truck was being made ready to roll. The armoured vehicle had gone into cover nearby, its machine gun pointing at the road. Subsequently, the patrol was attacked by two Ki-51s, which appeared to be flying ahead of the Japanese vanguard. The group made contact with the enemy at some eight kilometres south of Soebang. The armoured vehicle was fired at by a Japanese tank and put out of action, but its crew managed to escape into the terrain. De Vries and several of his subordinates died in the clash. Only a few men made it to the rear area of the Tjiater fortification in the evening, having made a long detour along the first line of the position which, by that time, was in Japanese hands.[16]

The preparations on both sides (5 March)

Around sunrise the Japanese Army air force began its operation in support of the attack on the Tjiater fortification. It was to be carried out from Soebang by Wakamatsu battle group, reinforced with a mountain artillery battery (four 7.5-cm guns).[17] The 27th Sentai made several reconnaissance flights. Ki-43 fighter aircraft were protecting

Kalidjati airfield and Wakamatsu's assembly area near Soebang, and, in doing so, shot down the Glenn Martin of the Straatman crew. Several Ki-48s were on stand-by to be able to quickly deal with any possible KNIL counter-actions. There was, however, no allied activity at all on the ground, upon which an air raid was carried out with six aircraft in total on Andir airfield.[18]

Between approximately 06:00 hrs and 06:30 hrs Japanese fighter aircraft raided Andir, followed by bombers. The first to attack were four Ki-43 fighter aircraft of the 59th Sentai, which machine gunned parked aircraft and anti-aircraft artillery positions. Then came two Ki-48 bombers of the 75th Sentai. The damage to the aircraft of the RAF and ML was not so bad this time, the bombers of 1-Vl.G.I and 2-Vl.G.III receiving some fragmentation damage, and only one aircraft, of 2-Vl.G.III, being lost after having been set ablaze.[19]

The men of the RAF, the ML and the anti-aircraft artillery of the KNIL and the British Army did not get any warning time at all. The air warning circles had disintegrated and the Air Defence Command Bandoeng had only a few warning posts left. By the time an air raid report came in, the enemy planes could usually already be seen at Andir. This time, too, the Japanese were totally unexpected. The anti-aircraft artillery managed to bring out some fire at them, and reported hits on all six Japanese aircraft, but none of them were shot down. The allied fighter aircraft did not take off when the all-clear was given, as they had been taken off air defence by now.[20] There was only one Hurricane that took off after the first attack of the Ki-48s.

Two fighter aircraft of 242 Squadron were on readiness for carrying out any possible assignments when the Japanese attack began. After the first bomb run of the Ki-48s, Sgt I.D. Newlands took off in one of these aircraft. He was back on the ground within five minutes, due to glycol vapours (of cooling fluid) in the cockpit. Afterwards it appeared that the filler cap of the reservoir had not been screwed on properly. Newlands managed to dive into a trench just in time when the Ki-48s were again dropping bombs from a low altitude in their second attack. This time they were successful. Most bombs fell on or around the complex of buildings and hangars in the south-western part of Andir where the Glenn Martin afdelingen 1-Vl.G.I and 2-Vl.G.III and Vk.A.1 were accommodated. The Glenn Martin of 2-Vl.G.III, mentioned above, went up in flames, the heat of the fire causing the machine gun in the nose of the aircraft to begin to fire spontaneously, exactly over the trench in which Newlands was hiding. Afterwards,

Flt Lt I. Julian was not amused; if Newlands had managed to get up into the air, he would almost certainly have been shot down.[21]

At around 07:00 hrs Colonel Shoji reported to Major-General Endo of the 3rd Hiko Dan that he was on the point of beginning his advance, upon which two Ki-51 assault aircraft made a reconnaissance of the route of advance, the road leading from Soebang to the village of Tjiater. During their reconnaissance mission the crews discovered and fired at the vehicles and men of the patrol which had been sent out from the Tjiater position. The advance guard of the battle group left Soebang at around 08:00 hrs; an hour later came the first air raid on the Tjiater position in preparation of the Japanese ground attack.[22]

Shortly after 09:00 hrs Captain Kooistra telephoned the staff of Bandoeng Group and reported that no news had come back from the reconnaissance patrol he had sent out earlier that morning, and that an air raid was being carried out on his position. Major-General Pesman and his staff concluded from this that the Japanese ground attack on the Tjiater position was about to begin. The air forces, however, were only ordered to carry out a reconnaissance for Bandoeng Group.[23]

In the mean time, the three available Brewsters and four more operationally serviceable Hurricanes were kept ready for take off. There came, however, no requests for (direct) support of the ground forces. When this was beginning to raise a few eyebrows in the course of the morning, Captain J.H. van Helsdingen, the commander of 1-Vl.G.V, called ML Command to see whether there were really no requests. It appeared to be so, upon which Van Helsdingen proposed at 09:00 hrs to carry out at least a strafing on Kalidjati at dusk, as he felt it would be irresponsible towards everyone involved to keep the still available fighter aircraft on the ground. Even Colonel E.T. Kengen the commander of ML Command could not give him any combat assignments, however.

Only when it became clear, after 09:00 hrs, that a Japanese attack on the Tjiater fortification was imminent, did the request for the already mentioned reconnaissance come in. By 10:00 hrs 242 Squadron RAF received orders for an armed reconnaissance of the road leading from Soebang to Tjiater, upon which at around 10:00 hrs two Hurricanes, flown by Flt Lt B.J. Parker and Plt Off W.M. Lockwood, took to the air. The remaining fighter aircraft stayed on the ground, which the fighter pilots at Andir found rather strange.[24]

The road reconnaissance had priority, but the pilots had permission to attack "particularly favourable targets presented by the Japanese army".[25] Although the peaks of the mountains surrounding the Preanger plateau were hidden by clouds, visibility was excellent at lower altitude. The two RAF pilots carefully flew just below the clouds in the direction of Kalidjati and then began flying down the road towards the south. Parker did the actual reconnaissance at low altitude and Lockwood flew behind him at higher altitude and considerable distance for cover. There was no enemy traffic on the road. In view of the danger of attacks from the air the Japanese used the roads as much as possible at night and the troops advacing the Tjiater fortification probably had already got as far as the foothills leading up to the plateau. On approaching the hills, Parker spotted two aircraft circling some 100 metres above the ground. They appeared to be twin-engine bombers, whose crews were unaware of the presence of the British aircraft.

Parker had little trouble shooting down a Ki-48, but the second one escaped into the direction of Kalidjati, upon which Parker and Lockwood returned to Andir. Suddenly, however, four Ki-43 fighter aircraft came diving down from high altitude at Parker. Lockwood, who was flying somewhat behind and higher escaped, but Parker was chased by one of the Ki-43s right across Andir airfield. In the mean time, the other Ki-43s began firing at the anti-aircraft positions along the flight terrain. By now it was around 10:30 hrs. Parker made a very tight turn around the complex of buildings and hangars in the south-western part of Andir and subsequently headed back to Andir via the centre of the Bandoeng. At a low altitude he again flew from east to west across the airfield at top speed, hoping that this time the anti-aircraft artillery would open up fire at his pursuer. The anti-aircraft guns did indeed fire, but also at Parker's Hurricane. He was fired at by the 2-cm and 12.7-mm anti-aircraft sections which took his aircraft for a Navy O, but fortunately they missed. Then, these KNIL sections as well as 4-cm Bofors guns of 48 LAA, fired at the Ki-43, which quickly disappeared from the scene without pursuing his chase of Parker, probably unharmed. Somewhat later both Hurricane pilots landed safely at Andir which had been bombed in the mean time.[26]

The Ki-48 that had been shot down by Parker crashed burning right in front of the Tjiater fortification, an enormous morale boost for the men manning the position, who had already shot down one Ki-48 earlier themselves (see below).[27] The four Ki-43s had been en route to Andir when they spotted Parker. The Japanese fighter pilots formed the escort of 12 Ki-48s and had flown ahead for a strafing run of the base. The Ki-43 pilot had to abandon his pursuit of Parker as the Ki-48s were closing in for their bombing raid of Andir.[28]

In the night of 4 on 5 March the last of the withdrawing KNIL troops passed the Tjiater fortification, after which there were no more troops between the position and Soebang. In principle, therefore, the allied fighter aircraft would have been able to bomb and shoot all the Japanese targets off the road, without any coordination problems and with some of their own aircraft for top cover. Such a mission had been planned by JAC, involving the Brewsters armed with 50-kilogramme fragmentation bombs. After a preliminary armed road reconnaissance to be carried out by 242 Squadron, the Brewsters and Hurricanes would have been in the position to conduct an attack of the road leading from Soebang to the fortification. Major-General Pesman, however, followed his own fashion of force protection, to be able to commit the scarce remaining fighter aircraft for direct ground support if the troops in the fortification requested it. At first, the Operations section of his staff did not take any initiative with regard to the deployment of the air forces, but left it to the position commander. A missed opportunity.[29]

A final bombing raid on Andir

At around 11:00 hrs the Japanese Army air force carried out a last attack from Kalidjati on Andir air base. This time 12 Ki-48 bombers bombed the airfield in two runs from a high altitude (approximately 5,000 metres), outside the reach of most of the anti-aircraft artillery. In between the raids and afterwards, the four Ki-43s which had attacked Parker and Lockwood carried out strafings, making especially the buildings in the southern part and the anti-aircraft artillery positions and the groups of pens for aircraft along the edges of the terrain their targets. The air raid lasted for about 30 minutes, during which the heavy anti-aircraft artillery (8-cm of the KNIL and 9-cm of the British Army) did not score any hits.

Most of the bombs fell in the south-western part of the airfield, but also the complex of the Koninklijke Nederlands-Indische Luchtvaartmaatschappij–Royal Netherlands Indies Airline (KNILM) in the south-east received several hits. The Japanese used light frag-mentation bombs that smashed straight through the roofs of the hangars, sometimes causing great damage to the aircraft parked in there. At the KNILM a Douglas DC-5 which was in repairs, having been damaged on 3 March, was hit, sustaining serious damage from bomb fragments and splinters from the roof of the hangar it was in.[30]

The two remaining bombers of 2-Vl.G.III (the M-520 and the M-521) received medium to heavy damage. The heavily damaged air-craft would be stripped for spare parts and a wing in the evening, in order for the Technical Service to be able to repair the less damaged one. Two CW-22s of Vk.A.1 were total losses, and the remaining two aircraft of this afdeling received light damage. In the south-eastern part of Andir, furthermore, a Grumman G-21 amphibious aircraft of the KNILM, also in repairs, incurred considerable damage. This plane had been intended for an evasion attempt to Ceylon. Like the two CW-22s of Vk.A.1, this aircraft would still be repaired, but under Japanese supervision. The fighter aircraft of 1-Vl.G.V and 242 Squadron escaped unharmed. The allied fighters, incidentally, were not sent out any more in response to Parker's report that there were no targets on the road from Soebang to the Tjiater fortification.[31]

The Tjiater fortification

The Tjiater fortification, on the mountain slopes of the northern end of the pass across the Goenoeng Tankoebang Prahoe (volcano) at an altitude of more than 1,000 metres above sea level, had been designed for an infantry regiment (three battalions), and consisted of some outposts, a few positions for infantry weapons connected by a trench and a casemate with a 5-cm gun, and more to the rear (higher up the mountain) a first and second line of casemates, accommodations and infantry battle positions, all connected by trenches. The first line had a front width of about two kilometres, with a barbed wire obstacle along its full length. In front of the first line was a ravine with the Tji Pangasahan rivulet running at the bottom. Right across and in front of the position ran the road from Lembang to Soebang, winding and twisting along the mountain down in northerly direction (see the sketch on p. 406).

As was said above, the position was only manned by a reinforced company, which made infiltration into the position relatively easy, especially in the dark. Although the position had a considerably front width it did not link up with any natural obstacles. That made it possible to by-pass the whole complex, even though that would not be simple due to the rugged terrain.[32]

The position itself and the area behind it were manned by the 'European' company of the Ist Infantry Battalion (2-Inf. I, commanded

by Captain M. Kooistra, who was also the position commander), reinforced with a section (platoon) of Landstorm (older enlisted men) with
two 6.5-mm machine guns, a platoon (four 6.5-mm machine guns) and
a mortar section (two 8-cm mortars) of the machine gun company of
Inf. I (4-Inf. I), three to five anti-armour guns (some of which were
new portable American equipment), a number of dispatch riders, a
section of search lights, engineers (for laying and disposing of mines
and obstacles and, if need be, carrying out demolitions) and a signals
unit with telephone operators and wireless operators for the long-range
radio (LARA) for communication with the staff of Bandoeng Group
and short-range radio (KARA) for the communication between Captain
Kooistra's command post and the first line.

Moreover, in the night of 4 and 5 March two so-called South-
African armoured vehicles, belonging to the rear guard of the Mobile
Unit had been left behind in the fortification for any reconnaissance
tasks that might be required on 5 March. They were four-wheel Marmon
Herrington armoured vehicles, assembled in South Africa, with a
turret which was open at the top, armed with one 6.5-mm machine
gun and a crew of two men.

In front of the fortification proper the above-mentioned 5-cm
gun was positioned in a pillbox, manned by personnel of the mountain
artillery who had been seconded to 2-Inf. I. This gun was able to fire
on part of the lower road, across which an obstacle consisting of two
rows of train rail sections could be set up.[33]

At the southern end of the Tjiater pass a new fortification was
under construction, the so-called Wates fortification, whose second
line was to lie at the entrance to the pass, where there was a three-
forked crossroads, the starting point of the road through the pass in
the direction of Soebang, as well as a tourist toll road leading towards
the crater of the Tankoebang Prahoe. At the beginning of the toll road
there was a tollbooth with a gate across the road, which lent its name
to the three forked crossroads: 'Tolhek' (Toll Gate) crossroads. Along
the toll road and somewhat to the west of the Tolhek crossroads the 3rd
Battery of A. II Bg. (commanded by Captain E.G.K.L. Vos de Wael)
was positioned. One of the artillery observers of the battery, Lieutenant
A.F.X.E.J. Vos de Wael, LL.M., was in the first line of the fortification
in the morning of 5 March with the second-in-command of 2-Inf. I,
Lieutenant P.J.J. Quanjer. With them in the position was also a liaison
officer of A. II Bg. (Lieutenant J. de Jonge, Esq.). Together with a few
men of the command group of 2-Inf. I and some signal personnel

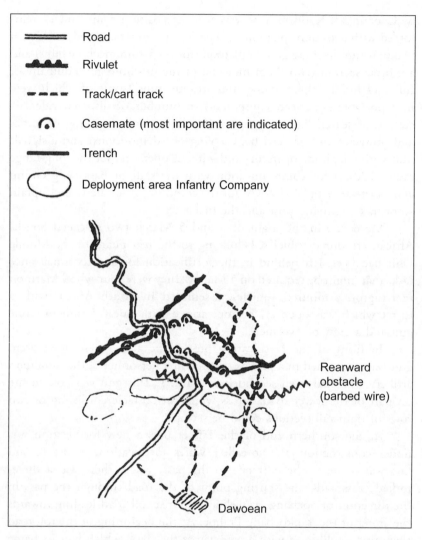

═════ Road

▄▄▄▄▄ Rivulet

▄ ▄ ▄ ▄ Track/cart track

⌒ Casemate (most important are indicated)

━━━━━ Trench

⬭ Deployment area Infantry Company

Rearward
obstacle
(barbed wire)

Dawoean

Sketch (not to scale) of the Tjiater fortification and the rear area, by P. van Meel, based on contributions of several veterans of A. II Bg. and 2-Inf. I.

Quanjer was manning a forward command post. Lieutenant Vos de Wael had his own telephone line to his battery.[34]

The first line of the Tjiater fortification was not fully manned. This was impossible with only one reinforced company and, on top of that, making the neglected position operational again had only been undertaken from 27 February with the arrival of 2-Inf. I (belonging to

4-R.I., and coming from central Java). The intention had been to re-place the position by the above-mentioned newly-to-be-constructed Wates fortification, whose first line was planned some two to three kilometres south of the Tjiater fortification somewhat higher up in the southern end of the mountain pass across the Tankoebang Prahoe and about 500 metres north of the Tolhek three-forked crossroads. There had hardly been any progress yet in the construction work on that position at the time of the Japanese landings, however, as priority had been given to the construction and improvement of a variety of coastal fortifications. In the mean time, the Tjiater fortification was not maintained anymore, and in spite of all the efforts of the 2-Inf. I personnel, only part of the position was operational to some extent on 5 March. One reason for this was that after the Japanese landings the hired Indonesian workmen failed to turn up any longer.[35]

Of the part of the first line that could be used again only a sort of kernel position in the centre of the old Tjiater fortification could be occupied, with a front of several hundred metres wide to the left and right of the road from Lembang to Soebang, which ran right through the position. The unoccupied flanks of the position were secured with minefields. The second line was almost finished, but was not occupied, not even in case of an alert, due to a lack of troops.[36]

The two batteries of A. Bg. II, which had been detached earlier to the Mobile Unit and Teerink Group (see the previous chapter), were situated in the vicinity of the Tankoeban Prahoe hotel, and somewhat south of Lembang, respectively. The staff of the mountain artillery battalion was also located near the hotel. In the morning of 5 March all three batteries were organised back into their old battalion structure. The 1st and 2nd Batteries came under the command again of battalion commander Captain P.E. Hendriksz, who ordered the commander of the 2nd Battery to prepare for taking up positions in the vicinity of the 3rd Battery. For the time being, the 1st Battery would remain where it was and in reserve, somewhat to the south of Lembang near the so-called Ursone farm.[37]

The Battle of the Tjiater Pass, Day 1 (5 March 1942)

Japanese air actions during the morning hours

Since around 06:30 hrs the 27th Sentai of the 3rd Hiko Dan had been continually engaged in carrying out reconnaissance missions of the fortification itself and the area to the south as far as Lembang. Everything the Ki-51 crews could find in the line of military activities, field fortifications, vehicles, etc., was meticulously mapped, while several targets in the vicinity of Lembang (among which there were various improvised positions near the encampment area of Teerink Group) were machine gunned by Ki-51s and bombed by Ki-48s. Besides, a number of Ki-51s machine gunned the KNIL barracks at Tjimahi, a large complex encompassing, among others, the Depot Mobiele Artillerie–Mobile Artillery Depot and a military hospital and in which also the regimental staff of 48 LAA of the British Army had been accommodated. There were also attacks on a section of 239 Battery (77 HAA, two 9-cm anti-aircraft guns) in the direct vicinity of the barracks and a section of this battery (also two 9-cm guns) at Lembang.[38] As was said above, at around 09:00 hrs the first air raid on the Tjiater fortification began with an initial machine gun attack on the trenches from an extremely low altitude by Ki-43 fighter aircraft, followed by several bombing raids carried out by Ki-48s of the 75th and 90th Sentais.

The first mission of the Japanese air brigade was flown by seven Ki-48s (two pairs and one threesome), escorted by seven Ki-43 fighter aircraft. A second morning mission consisted of six Ki-48s and seven Ki-43s. Apart from that, there was a constant presence of a flight of two Ki-51s in the target area. After having carried out their initial reconnaissance tasks, these aircraft took care of the target tracking and dropped several light bombs. As there was no opposition from the air, the Ki-43 fighter aircraft also carried out several strafings. Up to 12:00 hrs the occupants of the Tjiater fortification were under constant bombing and machine gun attacks. With the exception of two aircraft, the Ki-48s, however, were withdrawn in the course of the morning and subsequently committed in the bombing raid on Andir by 12 aircraft of this type around 11:00 hrs, already described above.[39]

At around 12:00 hrs the aircraft of the 3rd Hiko Dan were withdrawn north of Tjiater and shortly after that Japanese motorised infantry, supported by a number of light tanks, opened the attack. Although the Japanese pilots began operating at an increasingly lower altitude in the course of the morning, due to an almost total absence of anti-aircraft fire, the 3rd Hiko Dan managed to inflict only little damage in the fortification. The concrete casemates proved to be of excellent quality and the two-metre deep trenches and underground shelters offered sufficient protection during the machine gun attacks by the Ki-43s and Ki-51s. There were only a few casualties as a result of bomb fragments.

The machine gunners of 4-Inf. I and the Landstorm, on the other hand, managed to shoot down one of the low-flying Ki-48s in the morning. Under loud cheers of the men in the fortification the bomber crashed into the ravine in front of their position and blew up. A second aircraft was hit some time later by the machine gunner of the remaining armoured vehicle, which was operating from the road running right through the fortifiaction in the direction of Soebang. This was an enormous boost for morale, especially because the men had been able to see how the two aircraft had been hit. As already described above, at around 10:15 hrs a Hurricane shot a second Ki-48 down.[40] Incidentally, the Japanese air actions were resumed after around 13:00 hrs, but this time they were directed against targets in the entire rear area of the fortification, the Wates fortification still under construction, the environment of the three-forked Tolhek cross-roads and the surroundings of Lembang (see below).

The Land Battle Begins

At around 12:00 hrs the land battle for the Tjiater fortification began. At that moment the first enemy vehicles were spotted at some 800 metres' distance from the first line of the position. At first, the battle developed well for the KNIL. The 5-cm gun firing from the casemate in front of the actual fortification set fire to a number of light tanks and vehicles of the Japanese vanguard, which had been held up by the tank obstacle of train rail sections across the road. Subsequently, the fire was redirected against the enemy infantry, which by this time had put a number of machine guns into position in the side terrain. The brigade (group of about 15 men) positioned near the tank obstacle had just managed to put the first row of train rail sections up when they had to make a run for it, taking cover for the Japanese mortar and machine gun fire. Normally, that job did not take much time, but they were hindered by the tenacious attacks of one Ki-51, whose crew also dropped a light bomb. A machine gun of 4-Inf. I in the line of outposts covered their retreat.

At around 13:00 hrs also 3rd Battery of A. II Bg. opened fire on the Japanese vehicle column and after that on the Japanese infantry alongside the road. Only one battery (four guns) was available at that moment, which made the artillery fire not very effective, in spite of the high firing rate achieved by the gun crews. In the mean time, the Japanese infantry had begun to climb the hill leading up to the casemate which held the gun and the infantry positions and trench adjacent to it.[41]

At 15:00 hrs after a few hours of battle, the approximately 50 men in these forward posts were withdrawn, the 5-cm gun was destroyed and the bridge in the road in front of the fortification was blown up. This bridge spanned the ravine right in front of the fortification, through which ran the Tji Pangasahan rivulet. Its demolition blocked a Japanese motorised advance, for the time being. Also several other crossings over the rivulet (pedestrian crossings for the employees of the tea factory of the plantation in which the position was situated) were destroyed. One of the two anti-armour guns that were positioned on the stretch of road behind the bridge and in front of the first line was lost in an attack from a Ki-51. The machine gun team commanded by SM J.C. Hanssens had been covering the retreat from the forward posts, but ran into trouble on their return. Near the bridge a nervous Landstorm soldier fired at the sergeant-major, who died of his wounds the next day. The incident made a deep impression on the (mostly young) conscripts and regular soldiers in the first-line positions.

The retreat came just in time, for at around 15:15 hrs the enemy reached the forward posts, upon which the Japanese infantry began to make a crossing of the Tji Pangasahan on both sides of the demolished bridge. When the enemy had come within range, fire from the first line of the fortification was opened by the two mortars. The fields of fire of the six own machine guns were partially limited, as two of them had been positioned in casemates. The mortar fire was well aimed. The screams of the Japanese wounded could be heard in the higher positions of the first line.[42] Initially, the reinforced 2-Inf. I did not get into trouble and the men were generally well protected against enemy rifle fire and machine gun fire in the casemates, the open 'schutters kuilen'–rifle men battle positions (larger dug-outs for a group of rifle gunners) and the emplacements of the machine guns and mortars. At around 15:00 hrs, however, a Japanese mortar shell hit a casemate that held a machine gun. The shell struck near the embrasure, destroying the machine gun and killing the machine gun team of four manning it. Under cover of its own mortar fire the Japanese infantry was approaching, climbing the slope on which the first line of the fortification was situated. At around 15:30 hrs Kooistra's first line in the centre of the fortification had to be given up, the Japanese having forced their way into the unmanned part of the first line to the left and right of the company. From there Japanese patrols attempted to get behind the sections of 2-Inf. I and the positions of the machine gun company. There was heavy exchange of fire.[43]

The men fell back on the central part of the second line of case-mates, battle positions, shelters and trenches, some 400 to 500 metres further to the back (but hardly higher) to the left and right of the road. Some personnel no longer needed and several casualties were withdrawn from the fortification. There were some groups of soldiers who got isolated and at least ten men were unable to get out of the first line in time and were forced to spend the night there. The positions in the second line were much less advantageous, as they gave a poor view on the first line, abandoned by now, and no view on the terrain in front of it, due to the dense foliage between the first and second lines. Because of this, the artillery observers were faced with an impossible situation and on top of that the telephone lines to the three-forked Tolhek crossroads (the southern end of the Tjiater pass) and Lembang had gone dead. The overground lines mostly ran along the roads and were vulnerable to enemy mortar fire and bombard-ments. The search lights and the short-distance radio could not be evacuated from the first line and had to be destroyed. Moreover, one anti-armour gun was lost in the retreat. Kooistra still had a radio vehicle equipped with a LARA in his rear area, but that afternoon no radio traffic with Bandoeng was possible due to atmospheric interference. He had become dependent on dispatch riders for his communication.[44]

Shortly after the withdrawal, six so-called South-African armoured vehicles arrived at the position. The two platoons of Marmon Herring-ton armoured vehicles of the same type as the two vehicles of the Mobile Unit that had been attached earlier to the position were the first reinforcements to arrive. Their commanding officer was Captain E. van Dongen.[45]

Captain Kooistra gave him an update of the situation, upon which Van Dongen advanced over the road (the only way to operate due to the heavy terrain) towards the abandoned centre of the first line of the fortification, which appeared to have been occupied by the enemy in the mean time. Almost immediately the armoured vehicles came under enemy machine gun fire. The crews tried to locate the Japanese firing positions, but during the fight the Japanese infantry advanced under cover of the dense foliage on the armoured vehicles and tried to throw hand grenades into the turrets which were open at the top. There was hardly any room for manoeuvre for the unwieldy armoured vehicles with their turning circles of as much as 14 metres. Van Dongen, who had been standing upright in his turret, was killed by a hand grenade in the first few minutes of the fight. In the end two armoured vehicles were lost, while the others retreated. They were first stationed in the vicinity of the village Dawoean and eventually sent back to Lembang, but they were later used to carry out several reconnaissance missions.[46]

Captain Kooistra fell back with his command group from the second line to a location behind the fortification, near a three-forked crossroads, where a small road leading to Dawoean joined the main road (see the situation sketch of the Tjiater fortification). In the mean time, at around 15:00 hrs he reported by phone to the staff of Bandoeng Group that his first line had been encircled and he had asked once again for infantry reinforcements. He was told that they were on their way and that he had to hold out and receive the new troops. The first reinforcements to arrive after the armoured vehicles of Van Dongen, however, were artillery.[47]

Shortly after 15:00 hrs Captain F.W.H. Twiss, the commanding officer of 2-A. II Bg., was ordered to take up positions with his battery, which was at that moment situated near the Tankoeban Prahoe hotel, adjacent to (east of) the 3rd Battery. The 2nd Battery moved in between two air raids and arrived at the three-forked Tolhek crossroads, some two kilometres away, between around 15:00 hrs and 16:00 hrs. Traffic had congested at the three-forked crossroads and the battery had to find itself a way by all sorts of vehicles of infantry units. Subsequently, Twiss went forward himself and met up with his colleague Vos de Wael, commanding officer of the 3rd Battery, who was on his way back from a meeting with Captain Kooistra. The latter had no immediate need for any artillery fire as he did not have any specific target to fire on. Besides, it was impossible to establish observer positions anyway, due to a lack of usable telephone connections.[48]

After consultation with Captain Hendriksz (the commanding officer of A. II Bg.), Twiss and Hendriksz went over to Kooistra's command post. The latter repeated what he had said to Vos de Wael. He was in bad need of infantry, not artillery. After some persuasion and by referring to the instructions from the artillery commander of Bandoeng Group, they managed to get Kooistra to agree on "map firing" on the road in front of his fortification, in particular with a view to boosting the morale of his own troops. The two officers did

Part of a 7.5-cm gun of the mountain artillery during a pre-war exercise. The small-calibre, but accurate, guns had a high rate of fire and could be disassembled completely for transport on horseback (eight loads). During the war the mountain guns were mostly transported on trucks. (Private collection, P.C. Boer)

not return to the three-forked Tolhek crossroads until 17:00 hrs. Both batteries then began to deliver harassing fire periodically on the road and the side terrain in front of the fortification. Of necessity this was map firing, for, as was said above, the communication lines with the observers of 3-A. II. Bg. (who were still in the second line) had been severed. They had to wait for their return to get new ideas for the establishment of observer positions outside the Tjiater fortification itself and possibilities for artillery support.[49]

At around 15:30 hrs the Japanese aircraft disappeared. Rain began to fall and apparently the aircraft were called back. By 16:00 hrs the rain came pouring down and the rapidly increasing humidity shrouded the Tjiater position in fog. When the rain subsided and the fog was thinning about half an hour later, the Japanese had firmly established itself in the first line of the fortification. Japanese mortars (grenade launchers) were firing at the second line, while the Japanese infantry occasionally directed rifle fire and some machine gun fire on the positions of 2-Inf. I. Only the mortar fire was really harassing and caused several casualties. The Kooistra company, however, was well protected in the second line and the Japanese infantry was unable to get them out of there.[50]

The exchange of fire continued until sunset, with the two batteries of A. II Bg. firing occasionally until well into the evening and night. This was harassing the Japanese to a considerable extent. Rain began to fall again at around 17:30 hrs, and by the time darkness fell it had become a downright down pour in the Tjiater fortification.[51]

The Japanese air operations in the afternoon of 5 March

As was mentioned above, at around 13:00 hrs the Japanese air raids were resumed, but further to the south this time. The 3rd Hiko Dan continued flying its sorties in support of the advancing troops and carried out scores of sorties which would nowadays be called battle field air interdiction. Targets in the vicinity of the three-forked Tolhek crossroads were repeatedly bombed. Ki-48s were committed first against the artillery, which had been positioned to the west of the three-forked crossroads. The Japanese knew that somewhere in the rear area of the fortification artillery must be located, but the guns were perfectly camouflaged among the young kina trees and were not detected. This was partly due to the tactics employed by the mountain artillery. Whenever Japanese aircraft were approaching, firing was stopped and everyone went into cover. This made it impossible to spot any muzzle fire coming from the guns. As soon as the aircraft had left, firing was immediately resumed. As a result the Ki-48s kept on bombing the wrong locations.[52]

In the afternoon the 3rd Hiko Dan carried out two missions, with six Ki-48s and seven Ki-43 fighter aircraft each time, and simultaneously maintained a constant presence of two Ki-51s from patrols relieving each other. It was not until around 15:00 hrs that the first allied aircraft would appear again over the Tjiater position, a CW-22 reconnaissance plane of Vk.A.1.[53]

On 5 March the 3rd Hiko Dan flew a total of 48 air support sorties with Ki-51s and Ki-48s, plus another 28 fighter sorties. The 27th Sentai carried out 11 missions in all, flying a total of 23 sorties with Ki-51 assault aircraft. The 75th and 90th Sentais carried out four missions, in total 25 sorties with Ki-48 light bombers, and the 59th and 64th Sentais also flew four missions with a total of 28 sorties of Ki-43 fighter aircraft. The fighters flew combat air patrols over the area of operations and from time to time carried out low-level attacks on targets on the ground. The Japanese were not hindered by any opposition from the air in the afternoon. To the relief of the commander of the 3rd Hiko Dan there were no air raids on Kalidjati airfield during the entire day. The enemy air forces on Andir, however, had not been completely taken out yet.[54]

Infantry reinforcements for the Tjiater pass

In part on the basis of the reconnaissance report of the crew of Vk.A.1, which had flown a reconnaissance mission for his staff in the early hours of 5 March, Major-General Pesman at around 07:00 hrs ordered the commanding officer of Inf. L.H. XXI, Lieutenant-Colonel B.C.D. Drejer to move to the Tangkoeban Prahoe hotel as soon as possible. Drejer was to keep his battalion ready there to reinforce the manning of the fortification. At this time, Bandoeng Group still reckoned with the possibility of the Japanese main attack coming from the direction of Poerwakarta via the Tjisomang fortification after all. The battalion, which had only arrived at Bandoeng from central Java on 3 and (mostly) on 4 March, subsequently moved in some 60 vehicles from Bandoeng in the direction of the Tangkoeban Prahoe hotel, at a distance of some five kilometres from the fortification. Drejer then drove over to the Tjiater fortification with several men of his battalion staff in order to consult with Captain Kooistra and to reconnoitre the situation.[55]

The vehicles were positioned alongside the road in chessboard manner, allowing other traffic to pass. The men of L.H. XXI went into cover in the terrain next to the road when some Japanese aircraft passed at high altitude, but soon relaxed when no air raids followed and the military traffic on the road kept going on. The unit had no battle experience. Inf. L.H. XXI was a battalion including a company of short-term volunteers of the Mankoe Negoro auxiliary corps and a machine gun company (minus), which only encompassed two machine gun platoons (eight machine guns in total) and an incomplete mortar platoon (three or four mortars).

The unit had only been brought up to strength after the mobilisation in central Java (late December 1941) and had subsequently begun

to train as an operational battalion. By the end of February 1942, however, their training programme had been all but completed. There had
also been several exercises together with artillery and reconnaissance
planes of the ML. Morale was excellent and there was also a strong
cohesion, but the battalion had had to stomach a number of very
exhausting moves in central Java and from there to Bandoeng.[56]

Very nervous by now, Lieutenant-Colonel Drejer did not return
to his battalion until well into the afternoon. He had been in the thick
of several Japanese air raids and a subsequent attack on the first line of
the fortification. Japanese fire had prevented him from returning to his
unit at first.[57]

Subsequently, at around 13:30 hrs, shortly after Kooistra's report
that the Japanese attack had begun, Pesman gave the order to direct
virtually all infantry and artillery he had at his disposal at Lembang and
surroundings to the Tjiater fortification or the vicinity of the three-forked
Tolhek crossroads. Among them were Teerink Group (whose 10-4 R.I.
company, however, was tasked with guard duties at Lembang), the
above-mentioned two platoons of 'South-African' armoured vehicles,
commanded by Captain E. van Dongen, and a detachment commanded by Lieutenant-Colonel H. van Altena, consisting of cadets of
the Koninklijke Militaire Academie–Royal Netherlands Military Academy (KMA) at Bandoeng, reserve officer candidates of the so-called
CORO (Corps Opleiding Reserve Officieren–Reserve Officers Training
Corps) and Ambonese recruits from the 3rd Infantry Depot at Lembang
(ex Gombong), originally intended as anti-para troops.

Three sections of cadets and CORO students formed up an
improvised company, under command of Captain J.L. Paardekoper,
and three sections of Ambonese recruits constituted an improvised
company, commanded by Sub-Lieutenant L.Z. Siahaya. Furthermore,
Van Altena had a machine gun platoon consisting of cadets.[58] The
armoured vehicle platoons were the first to arrive in the position and
conducted the fight, described above, during which Van Dongen died
and two vehicles were lost. An order for an armed (air) reconnaissance
of the road from Soebang to Tjiater (issued at around 13:30 hrs) could
not be carried out (see below).

The Van Altena detachment was the first to move and was located
as direct reserve some three kilometres behind the Tjiater fortification
around and to the north of the three-forked Tolhek crossroads. About
500 metres to the north of the crossroads lay the first line of the Wates
fortification (under construction), which, though not fully finished,

was now occupied and arranged as a fortified position as well as possible. Near the three-forked crossroads, where the second line of the Wates fortification had been planned, Colonel W.J. de Veer, the commanding officer of the 4th Infantry Regiment (4-R.I.), to whom Major-General Pesman had given command of this mixed bag of units in and near the two fortifications and the rear area, established his command post. The units of Teerink Group and 2-Inf. I originally came from his regiment.

The command post of Teerink Group had been established in the Villa Zonneweelde hotel at Lembang. It was not completely abandoned but, by order of Bandoeng Group, manned as a reserve command post. The 1st Battery of A. II Bg. (commanded by Lieutenant F.L. Kroesen) remained stationed as reserve near the Ursone farm, somewhat to the south of Lembang. In case of a Japanese break-through this battery was to close off the access roads around Lembang in an anti-armour role, and one section (two guns) already got into position east of Lembang along the road to Tjikidang in the afternoon.[59]

The first movements of Teerink Group into the direction of the fortification were spotted by Japanese aircraft crews. Up to four times pairs of Ki-51s attacked the vehicles in the vanguard of Teerink Group, though with little success. In his account, written after the war, Sergeant-Major J.B. Heffelaar (4-Inf. V) stated, "The bombs were thrown extremely inaccurately." The other movements were not hindered by air raids.[60]

Pesman sent Captain J.R. Kraan of his staff to the Tjiater fortification by blitzbuggy (jeep), in order to consult with Kooistra about the coordination of the deployment of the reinforcements. The captain of the General Staff arrived at the fortification in the course of the afternoon. Kooistra, however, was not in his command post. He kept shuttling to and fro between his command post and the front line, where he was right then. The somewhat older Kooistra showed great empathy with his men and the fact that he was with them regularly had a positive effect on morale, which was still good. Due to Japanese fire, Kraan could not enter the position and drove back over the road to the Tangkoeban Prahoe hotel, where he hoped to meet with Colonel De Veer.[61]

At around 15:00 hrs he arrived at the three-forked Tolhek crossroads, where he met with Sergeant-Major Heffelaar, who had taken up positions to the left and right of the road with his two machine guns, and whose truck had got stuck with its front wheels in a ditch alongside the road in an air raid. Even Captain Van Dongen, who just happened to be passing, could not dislodge the truck with one of his armoured vehicles. Incidentally, Heffelaar lent his armourer to Van Dongen, as one of the armoured vehicle crews lacked a machine gunner. Together with part of the command group of 4-Inf. V, the sergeant-major with his section formed the point of the vanguard of Teerink Group.[62]

The arrival of the infantry reinforcements at the Tjiater fortification

The infantry reinforcements which had been promised to Kooistra did arrive, but they were late. Certainly from 15:00 hrs onwards the road from Lembang to the Tjiater fortification was blocked by an enormous traffic jam, the last vehicles of which were standing already in front of the Tangkoeban Prahoe hotel and which stretched as far as several hundred metres beyond the three-forked Tolhek crossroads, near the hairpin bend in the road which led through the first line of the Wates fortification. All the traffic in the direction of the Tjiater fortification had to make use of one narrow road, which had absolutely insufficient capacity for the purpose. Before the above-mentioned hour columns had been forced to a halt because of abandoned vehicles having been left standing on the road during air raids. Nevertheless, the traffic in the direction of the Tjiater fortification kept moving, albeit slowly. Around 15:30 hrs the 2nd Battery of A. II Bg. found itself a way towards its new position near the three-forked crossroads. At the same time along the Tolweg towards the crater of the Tankoebang Prahoe (volcano) to the west of the three-forked crossroads the vehicles of the ammunition train and the signals section of A. II Bg. had to be positioned. Trucks of infantry units and vehicles of the mountain artillery soon formed an inextricable jumble. By that time, however, the first infantry companies had already passed the three-forked crossroads.[63]

A location to the left and right of the main road, near the village Dawoean, had by now been designated as reception area for the units of Teerink Group and Inf. L.H. XXI. Sergeant-Major Heffelaar and some volunteers of his machine gun section (with one machine gun) and some men from the command group of 4-Inf. V, led by Lieutenant G.J. Assink, arrived as vanguard, one shortly after the other, from around 16:15 hrs. For the time being, Heffelaar took up position just behind the rear (barbed wire) obstacle of the Tjiater fortification, to the left (west) of the road. Neither he nor Lieutenant Assink had received any instructions from Major Teerink. They did not know that by now a reception area had been designated for the reinforcements. From the Tjiater fortification the sound of rifle fire could be heard. Their first real confrontation with the battle came in the form of several wounded Landstorm troopers with rifle wounds who came walking down the road leading from the fortification.[64]

Somewhat later Captain Kooistra came walking down the road with his command group in order to establish a new command post and to coordinate the first reception of the reinforcements. Shortly after that the mortar platoon of Inf. L.H. XXI arrived by bus. Some 13 men joined Heffelaar, after a fruitless search for suitable positions for their mortars in the terrain. The other half of Heffelaar's machine gun section had remained behind in an (unfinished) casemate near the three-forked Tolhek crossroads. As was described above, their truck had ended up in a ditch and only Heffelaar had been able to go ahead in a commandeered private car of the staff of A. II Bg., together with some volunteers and the one machine gun. The luxury car was used to transport the wounded Landstorm troopers to the rear for further medical treatment.[65]

Reinforced with two machine guns, Lieutenant M.P.A. den Ouden arrived with a section consisting of CORO students at around 17:00 hrs and he was directed by Kooistra to the south-eastern part of his second line. This reinforced section had been charged with guard duties at the three-forked Tolhek crossroads and, after having been relieved, had been ordered to go to the fortification. Around 17:00 hrs 1-Inf. V (Europeans) of Teerink Group arrived in the assembly area, commanded by Lieutenant J.C.A. Faber, who had received instructions from Major Teerink on his way there. For the time being, his company took up positions alongside the road. The rear (barbed wire) blockade of the Tjiater fortification was situated at half an hour's walk down the road and in the distance the men could hear rifle fire.[66]

Faber went to see Kooistra in his command post and was asked by the latter shortly after 18:00 hrs to inspect the terrain to the west of the second line of the fortification with his company and to make a sweep in northerly direction, which was to bring him near the west flank of the first line that had been taken by the Japanese. With darkness falling, Faber did not think this was a good idea and decided to stick to Major Teerink's orders as closely as possible, which came down to waiting for the arrival of three other companies in the assembly area and then take up agreed positions west (left) of 2-Inf. I.[67] Soon two other companies began arriving by truck and bus, first 2-Inf. L.H. XXI (Soedanese) and then 1-Inf. L.H. XXI (Europeans). Kooistra also consulted with the commanders of these units, asking them after the instructions they had received. 1- and 2-Inf. L.H. XXI were to take up positions east (right) of 2-Inf. I. Kooistra explained the situation in the fortification and asked the three company commanders to take up positions as quickly as possible left and right of the road, behind the rear blockade of the Tjiater fortification. The Japanese were behind the first line and had by now infiltrated the unoccupied sections of the second line, preventing the reinforcements from entering the fortification. Attempting to do this anyhow, with darkness setting in, was deemed to be an unacceptable risk by Kooistra.[68]

In response to Kooistra's cry for help, the three companies, led by Faber's, moved up the road at short intervals towards their designated locations. To the west of the road, 1-Inf. V subsequently went to take up positions beyond the barbed wire obstacles in the pouring rain and deepening dusk.[69] The taking up of positions by the companies of Inf. L.H. XXI was less successful. Their unfamiliarity with the terrain, the lack of maps and the, by now, total darkness and pouring rain made that everything that could go wrong in the taking up of positions did go wrong.

The main force of 2-Inf. L.H. XXI (two infantry sections, reinforced with machine guns), the second to arrive at around 18:15 hrs, commanded by Captain J.B. Doedens, took a wrong turning on their way to their position to the east of the road. When they suddenly began to receive Japanese fire, some men in the company started to make a run for it. At around 19:00 hrs Captain A.C.J. de Thouars, the commanding officer of 4-Inf. V (machine guns and mortars), met Captain Doedens who was busily engaged in trying to reassemble his company again. It was not until sunrise that the company could finally take up positions. De Thouars had been on his way to the fortification as one of his machine gun platoons (four 6.5-mm machine guns) had been assigned as reinforcement to 1-Inf. V. He also went to see Heffelaar and told him that (with his one 6.5-mm machine gun) he had been put under command of Faber too.[70]

The third company to arrive, 1-Inf. L.H. XXI (reinforced with machine guns), commanded by Captain A.F. Avink, in the mean time, took up positions next to 1-Inf. V, to the east of the road. But his went wrong, too. The company went a bit too far north, passed the position of 1-Inf. V., and took a path taking them in a north-easterly direction. The men of 1-Inf. V heard rifle fire and a quarter of an hour later the company came back over the road, having suffered a few casulties due to Japanese fire. After a short rest, Avink withdrew to the assembly area and only took up the agreed position with his company next to 1-Inf. V to the east of the road by sunrise.[71]

At around 20:00 hrs the main force of 2-Inf. II (Javanese) of Teerink Group and the command group of this company, among whom was the company commander, Captain W.M. Wensel, arrived by truck. A machine gun platoon (= two sections with two machine guns each) of the machine gun company 4-Inf. II of Teerink Group had been assigned to them as reinforcement. The two infantry sections, led by Lieutenant H.W. van Pelt and Ensign Th. Meyer, took up positions left of 1-Inf. V with their front facing in north-westerly direction. For the time being, Captain W.M. Wensel remained in the assembly area with his command group and received the third infantry section there, commanded by Warrant Officer H.A. Nuse, which had been sent to the position after all. Nuse took up provisional positions west of the road and behind 1-Inf. V. Only in the early hours of 6 March were Wensel's command group and Nuse's section led to their intended positions by guides of 1-Inf. V.[72]

Most infantry sections of 1-Inf. V, 2-Inf. II and 1- and 2 Inf. L.H. XXI had been reinforced with a section of two 6.5-mm or 7.7-mm machine guns of their respective machine gun companies. The mortar sections of these companies, however, were kept in the vicinity of the Tolhek by order of Colonel De Veer or withdrawn to Tolhek, respectively.[73]

In the mean time, a part of the reinforced 2-Inf. I had been withdrawn from the fortification in conformity with orders from Captain Kooistra, who assumed that the Japanese would not undertake an assault during the night in unfamiliar terrain, and that therefore he could send as many of his men as possible for a badly needed rest period to Dawoean. This small village had been evacuated earlier to accommodate the encampment of some of the men manning the fortification and to store supplies. A nearby complex of drying sheds of the Tjiater tea company had also been taken in use. It was impossible to spend the night in the fortification (which lay at an altitude of more than 1,000 metres) due to the cold and humidity (there was regular rain and fog). The personnel of 2-Inf. I had had hardly any rest since 1 March and, due to an order to move, which was then rescinded, and the retreat of Teerink Group, they had had very little sleep. If they had not been tasked to man guard posts, they had been employed working on the fortification itself, which had to be made suitable to accommodate a regiment and up to and including 4 March the men had been occupied maintaining the trenches, clearing fields of fire and expanding obstacles.[74]

Lieutenant Quanjer was the first to withdraw from the second line with his section at around 18:00 hrs. Near the rear blockade they ran into Faber's company. It must have been a strange meeting, Quanjer marching along the road, while Faber was moving tactically. Quanjer's leaving the fortification puzzled Faber. In total some 100 men left for Dawoean, including the personnel of the machine gun platoon and the mortar section of 4-Inf. I, who began arriving in the village from around 19:30 hrs. Including Lieutenant Den Ouden's section, which had been located on the south-eastern flank, some 130 men (three sections) remained behind in the centre of the second line. They had at least four machine guns, operated by CORO students and Landstorm troopers, and on top of that there was at least one anti-armour gun in position. On arrival at Dawoean, Quanjer arranged the accommodation for the drivers and the other train personnel of Teerink Group and Inf. L.H. XXI and accommodated personnel and vehicles in the village and in the complex of sheds of the tea enterprise nearby, where also a part of 2-Inf. I had been accommodated.[75]

In the mean time, Lieutenant D. ter Brugge of Staff Inf. V had established Major Teerink's command post some 150 metres north of the three-forked Tolhek crossroads. Signals personnel of Bandoeng Group laid a telephone line to this command post in the afternoon of 5 March, which became operational at around 18:00 hrs.[76] Accompanied by several members of his staff, Teerink soon went to the Tjiater fortification and he arrived in the assembly area approximately between 20:30 hrs and 21:00 hrs. He then went to meet with Captain Kooistra, who appeared to have gone to Dawoean to see Quanjer. Major Teerink talked to him there, upon which he immediately left with Kooistra to have an urgent consultation with Colonel De Veer (see below).[77]

At around 19:00 hrs the commander of A. II Bg. was ordered by Colonel De Veer to make available as many officers as possible to disentangle the traffic chaos at Tolhek, which took the assigned teams of A. II Bg. many hours, but at around 04:00 hrs in the morning of 6 March the road was completely empty again. The last to have been sent on were the trucks of the combat trains (with ammunition) and then the trucks of the baggage trains (with food) for the infantry in and near the Tjiater fortification. In the mean time, the batteries of A. II Bg. had collected ammunition with their own trucks, which the personnel of the ammunition train of A. II Bg., unable to get through the traffic jam in the dark and the pouring rain, had been forced to unload in the yard of a house at Lembang.[78]

For the time being, communication was maintained by dispatch riders who kept going to and fro on motor bikes and in jeeps and commandeered private cars between the various command posts and the Tjiater fortification. It was vital that new telephone line be laid as quickly as possible in the morning of 6 March. The anti-armour defence also still needed seeing to, while Colonel De Veer had asked the artillery commander of Bandoeng Group for permission to reposition the 1st Battery of A. II Bg. to the new first line. Thus, if the situation required, part of them could also be committed in an anti-armour role. That permission did not come until the morning of 6 March, when the road leading towards the position could not be used anymore. Furthermore, on the request of Bandoeng Group Java Air Command had reassigned a section of 12.7-mm and a section of 2-cm anti-aircraft guns, both coming from the abandoned Maospati (Madioen) airfield in central Java, as a reinforcement of the Tjiater fortification. Incidentally, at Lembang already a section of 239 Battery (77 HAA) with two 9-cm guns had been stationed.[79]

Most of the infantry men behind the Tjiater fortification spent the night in plant holes (cylindrical fertiliser holes one metre in depth) for kina tree saplings, ideal foxholes, though cold and humid. Every man had his own foxhole, with enough room in it for a second, if need be. However, they got no sleep at all, what with own and enemy activities. All through the night there was constant toing and froing on the road of units arriving, while the Japanese occasionally blew up mines in the forward terrain, and, judging by the loud hammering they were busy repairing the bridge across the ravine that ran right in front of the Tjiater fortification. On top of that the KNIL's own artillery fired at locations in front of the fortification at regular intervals.[80]

On the arrival of extra reinforcements (see below), the sections of 2-Inf. I and the CORO section of Lieutenant Den Ouden, were evacuated from the fortification in the early morning of 6 March at around 04:00 hrs. However, this was only partially possible, as a small number of men had been surrounded by Japanese infantry and could not be reached anymore. Subsequently, most of the men in the second line left for Tolhek.[81] A group of about four men, armed with an anti-tank weapon, carried out a patrol around the former first line of the fortification.[82]

Colonel De Veer's plan

Colonel De Veer arrived in the vicinity of the three-forked Tolhek crossroads in the afternoon and established himself in a makeshift command post, for the time being without any telephone connection with the staff of Bandoeng Group. Only in the morning of 6 March was this connection established (via the PTT telephone exchange at Lembang). Taking up the command post, incidentally, was not so simple because, as was mentioned above, an enormous traffic jam of all sorts of vehicles near Tolhek had developed, so, accompanied with his adjutant, De Veer had to walk there from the Tankoeban Prahoe hotel. Together with Major Teerink and Lieutenant-Colonel Van Altena, Colonel De Veer had devised a plan during a consultation in the hotel for the positioning of the infantry reinforcements and their deployment for the next morning. Captain J. R. Kraan of the staff of Bandoeng Group was also present.[83]

The companies 1-Inf. V and 2-Inf. II (minus) of Teerink Group and 1-Inf. L.H. XXI and 2-Inf. L.H. XXI (minus), all reinforced with machine guns, were to take up positions to the west (left) and to the east (right) of Kooistra's company, respectively. These units were to advance at daybreak (6 March) up to about a kilometre north of the Tjiater fortification, in order to relieve some of the pressure on the Kooistra company. The Paardekoper 'company' and 3-Inf. L.H. XXI (reinforced with machine guns) were to take up positions approximately 500 metres north of Tolhek, left and right of the road (in the Wates fortification under construction) and the 'company' of Ambonese recruits was to form the reserve near the three-forked Tolhek crossroads itself. The third sections of 2-Inf. II and 2-Inf. L.H. XXI were to remain deployed to the west of the three-forked crossroads to secure the artillery. Lieutenant-Colonel Drejer of Inf. L.H. XXI, on his way back to his unit, passed the hotel towards the end of the consultation on this plan and in this way could be informed in time of its contents. Only Kooistra was not present as he could not be contacted in the Tjiater fortification.[84]

At around 19:30 hrs Major-General Pesman arrived, upon which a new meeting was convened with the subordinate commanders, in the course of which De Veer's plan was somewhat adjusted. Intelligence from Bandoeng Group showed that in front of the unoccupied flanks of the first line of the Tjiater fortification minefields had been laid. Besides, the general had abandoned all offensive plans, and therefore the companies were not to advance beyond the line in which 2-Inf. I had taken up positions. Furthermore, the general promised a 'fresh' battalion, as reinforcement and partial relief for the troops, and he asked De Veer to hold the southern access to the Tjiater pass at any cost.[85]

Pesman had just returned from a conference at General Headquarters (AHK), chaired by Lieutenant-General H. ter Poorten, the KNIL army commander, also Commander-in-Chief ABDA Area. The navy and air force commanders had also been present, as had been the most senior Dutch and British subordinate commanders and several staff officers of, amongst others, AHK. During this meeting, which had begun at 18:00 hrs the following was agreed on in general terms.

- The situation is very precarious, the Tjiater fortification has been all but breached, the morale of many KNIL units is low and Bandoeng may fall before long.
- The troops from Batavia and Buitenzorg cannot be used for a counter-offensive in the coming four days.
- An attempt will be made to still deal a blow to the enemy at Lembang.
- There will be no fighting in Bandoeng in view of the large numbers of refugees in the city.

The participants of the meeting also discussed the possibilities for continuing the battle by means of a guerrilla, in case Bandoeng fell.[86]

As was mentioned above, at around 21:00 hrs Major Teerink and Captain Kooistra met in the encampment of 2-Inf. I in Dawoean, after which they both went to see Colonel De Veer, as the adjusted plan for the reinforcement of the fortification could not be executed, either. The Japanese had advanced so far that it had become impossible to enter the fortification area and occupy in the dark the second line parts not occupied by Kooistra's company. For that reason, Kooistra had ordered the companies of Teerink Group and Inf. L.H. XXI to take up positions behind the barbed wire fence that formed the rear cover of the Tjiater position.[87]

In consultation with Teerink and Kooistra De Veer adjusted his plan to the circumstances. The infantry reserves of Teerink Group and

Inf. L.H. XXI, were moved forward and arrived at the Tjiater fortification in the middle of the night as yet. The units involved were the third section of 2-Inf. II, the third section of 2-Inf. L.H. XXI and 3-Inf. L. H. XXI. The latter unit was filled almost completely with short-term volunteers of the Mangkoe Negoro reserve corps. It acted as the reserve behind 1- and 2- Inf. L.H. XXI and was also tasked with the security of Lieutenant-Colonel Drejer's command post. As was said above, Kooistra's company was subsequently evacuated from the second line of the fortification in the morning of 6 March at around 04:00 hrs. De Veer had Kooistra brief him elaborately on the battle that had been going on and the local circumstances and was quite frankly astonished that 2-Inf. I was still in the position. He complimented Koositra on his brave tenacity.[88]

The men of Teerink Group and Inf. L.H. XXI were now to take over the defence from positions directly behind the Tjiater fortification (a line behind the former position of Kooistra's company). It was assumed that the Japanese would try to go round the second line of the fortification, rather than through it. To this end, sappers of the engineer detachment of 2-Inf. I were to lay mines and block the road.[89] In the Wates fortification (under construction) and the vicinity of the three-forked Tolhek crossroads of Teerink Group a machine gun platoon of 2-Inf. II stayed behind, together with a mortar platoon (minus) of 2-Inf. II, a section of anti-armour guns (two guns), a machine gun platoon of 4-Inf. V, half a section of machine guns of 4-Inf. V (one machine gun of the Heffelaar section) and a mortar platoon (minus) of 4-Inf. V. Of Inf. L.H. XXI only the mortar platoon (minus) stayed behind there.[90]

De Veer also informed Major-General Pesman, who at the conference mentioned above had maintained that the defence of the northern access to the Tjiater pass was to be considered almost completely breached. During the conference the participants had also discussed the low morale of many KNIL units. Pesman was pleasantly surprised with the actions of 2-Inf. I and asked De Veer to express to Kooistra his pleasure with the company ("not running away, but bravely holding out").[91]

Allied air support during the daylight hours (5 March)

There were targets in abundance in the morning of 5 March for the allied fighter aircraft; in a manner of speaking, the road from Soebang to the Tjiater position was full with them. The staff of Major-General Pesman at Bandoeng, however, was not informed about this, but, in principle, this was not necessary, anyway. There was only one avenue of approach for Major Wakamatsu, and how vulnerable motorised units on that road were had become painfully clear for Teerink Group only hours before (see the previous chapter). Attached to the staff of Major-General Pesman as liaison officers were Lieutenant H.F. Zeylemaker of the ML and Flight Lieutenant V.B. de la Perelle of the RAF, especially for the processing of the requests for air support and the giving of advice with regard to honouring the requests. 2-Inf. I, however, did not request any support from the air and the advice from the two liaison officers to take the initiative to deploy the fighter aircraft at readiness at Andir airfield fell on deaf ears with the head of Operations of the staff. As was described above, only by 10:00 hrs did he order a new reconnaissance mission. A planned attack by 242 Squadron and 1-Vl.G.V was cancelled, as by this time there were no more targets on the road from Soebang to Tjiater.[92]

That the fortification commander, Captain Kooistra, had felt no need for air support during the morning was understandable to some extent, in view of the reported course of the battle; after all, his reconnaissance patrol might still be on the way back and risked being attacked by own aircraft. Colonel De Veer, however, who had been given command over all the troops in the two fortifications and their rear area, did not request it either. Initially, it was thought at Bandoeng that this was caused by communication problems, as the radio connections were extremely poor due to the atmospheric and geographic conditions. Besides, the telephone lines between the three-forked Tolhek crossroads and the Tjiater fortification broke down shortly after 15:00 hrs (probably due to a Japanese bombardment). In the evening of 5 March, during Pesman's visit, it appeared that in De Veer's opinion a request for air support had been unnecessary. He probably simply lacked information on the conditions in the first line.[93]

The runway at Andir could still be used after the above-mentioned Japanese air raid, carried out between around 11:00 hrs and 11:30 hrs, and no allied fighter aircraft had been taken out of action in it. Finally, in the early afternoon, around 13:30 hrs, the Operations section of the staff of Bandoeng Group gave an order for air support, but due to air alerts and a lack of cloud cover, the allied fighter aircraft could not take to the air. Ki-43 fighters and also Ki-51 assault aircraft had been flying regularly over the hills north of Andir and occasionally into the direction of the air base itself, triggering off repeated air alerts. There were, however, no attacks. Given the (incorrectly) assumed great Japanese air superiority (all Ki-43s and Ki-51s were taken for Navy Os) and the small number of own fighter aircraft, it was thought at BRITAIR that the only course of action was to wait for cover of cloud before 242 Squadron and 1-Vl.G.V could carry out the requested reconnaissance and attack.

The assignment that was to be carried out by 242 Squadron was postponed. 1-Vl.G.V, at readiness with its three Brewsters loaded up with 50-kilogramme bombs, ready to attack targets discovered by the British, remained at readiness. Zeylemaker was a bit upset by this. Lieutenant-Colonel H.A. Reemer, head of Operations and Chief of Staff, thought the RAF and ML were suffering from unfounded fear of the Japanese, but he did not want to hear that he himself had made no attempt whatsoever in the morning to commit JAC aircraft in an offensive role.[94]

At around 14:45 hrs there was sufficient cover of cloud and Tlt W. Jessurun of Vk.A.1 took off from Andir in his CW-22 for a reconnaissance mission on behalf of Bandoeng Group. The order for this reconnaissance mission had already been issued at around 13:00 hrs, after a telephone conversation between Major-General Pesman and Captain Kooistra, who had reported the start of the Japanese ground attack. No Japanese activity was visible from the air in the environment of Poerwakarta and Sadang. This was different near the Tjiater fortification at around 15:00 hrs, although the fight seemed to have come to an end. In any case, there were no more Japanese aircraft up in the air near the position.[95]

Second Lieutenant Jessurun and mechanic Sergeant C.J. Alard, who had been assigned as air gunner, saw a column of KNIL soldiers march away south from the first line, and a kilometre further up the road a column of Japanese soldiers going north, almost as if there had been a signal "end of battle". It was a peculiar sight. The road north of Tjiater was deserted. When Jessurun reported the results of his reconnaissance by telephone after landing, his report was received with scepticism. They had better have another good look the next morning. The fighter aircraft of 242 Squadron and 1-Vl.G.V were not sent out as the road was empty and the position of own troops could not be verified.[96]

A Japanese air raid on Tasikmalaja (5 March)

At around 16:00 hrs Major-General Endo, the commanding officer of the 3rd Hiko Dan, decided to carry out a mopping up operation to take out the remaining allied air forces as soon as the weather improved. Upon this, 12 Ki-48 bombers and 4 Ki-43 fighter aircraft attacked Tasikmalaja between around 16:30 hrs and 17:00 hrs. The air raid, however, failed, probably because the weather was still very bad at Tasikmalaja with heavy clouds. Apparently, the runway was the target of the Ki-48s, but all the bombs missed it (by far) and no damage was done. In the mean time, the remaining Ki-43 fighter aircraft of the 59th and 64th Sentais provided a cover for Kalidjati airfield, but an attack on the latter air base did not come.[97]

A blunder by General Headquarters (AHK)

In hindsight, making available all the remaining allied air forces to the commander of Bandoeng Group must be considered a blunder. Although this was only partially realised at the JAC, the ML Command and BRITAIR, the air forces were quite successful in suppressing the Japanese operations from Kalidjati. JAC's strategy, which consisted of evening and night bombing missions and periodic fighter sweeps by daylight, had resulted in the 3rd Hiko Dan having only 10 to 11 operationally serviceable fighter aircraft (of the 19 that had been flown over to Kalidjati) left on 5 March. In other words, there was no great Japanese air superiority whatsoever, at least not in terms of fighter aircraft.

At Palembang there were still a number of Ki-43s of the 59th and 64th Sentais, but they could not be committed at the time of the battle. The airfield near Palembang was of vital importance for the Japanese supplies, but it had already shown itself to be vulnerable to enemy air attacks in February 1942. Apart from the local air defence at Palembang, the part of the 3rd Hiko Shudan remaining at Palembang (among which a detachment of light bombers of the 75th and 90th Sentais of the 3rd Hiko Dan) was responsible for the support of the Japanese main force which had landed in the far west of Java. For this reason the fighter aircraft of the 1st and 11th Sentais of the 12th Hiko Dan were kept at Palembang and Tanjoengkarang and could not be spared for the reinforcement of Kalidjati.[98]

The aircraft groups of the 3rd Hiko Dan could dispose of the following total of operationally serviceable aircraft (with in parentheses the original number of aircraft flown over to Kalidjati): 10 to 11 Ki-43 fighter aircraft (19), approximately 15 Ki-48 light bombers (30) and approximately 14 Ki-51 assault aircraft (16). There was one more operationally serviceable Ki-15 or Ki-46 reconnaissance aircraft (4) left. Only the Ki-51 assault aircraft had all survived the allied air raids, although several aircraft had been damaged in allied air raids and by anti-aircraft fire on 2 and 3 March.[99]

The 3rd Hiko Dan did not have any warning systems, such as radar and listening posts at Kalidjati and could only protect Kalidjati air base against enemy air raids, in daylight only, by carrying out new bombing raids and strafings of Andir (and later Tasikmalaja) and flying combat air patrols. The Japanese, however, also needed their Ki-43 fighter aircraft for the protection of the somewhat vulnerable Ki-48 light bombers, and, in brief, had a serious shortage of fighter aircraft.

JAC could not exploit this situation because of the interference of General Headquarters, against the advice of Major-General Van Oyen, the JAC commander. Van Oyen was of the opinion that the remaining air forces would be committed most efficiently in the continuance of the actions against Kalidjati and he would have wanted to keep this indirect air support up for as long as possible. The number of fighter aircraft that was still left would be too small to attack Kalidjati on a regular basis and to provide simultaneous support to the KNIL troops. Real direct support of the ground troops, close air support, in which support would be provided right in front of the forward line of own troops, incidentally, was, generally speaking, impossible, unless there was a forward line of own troops whose location was precisely known. On 5 March 1942 this was the case near the Tjiater fortification until around 15:00 hrs.

Close air support had never been practised by the ML before the war, procedures were lacking and the necessary means of communication were not available anymore. The few radio vehicles of the ML with equipment suitable for telephony had all been lost. Besides, there were no crystals for the radios in the RAF fighters to have them work at the frequencies of the KNIL. The ground forces had no experience in requesting air support for more direct support and, consequently, did not request such support via the staff of Bandoeng Group.[100]

As was mentioned above, General Headquarters did agree with the continuance of the evening and night air raids on Kalidjati. In the late evening of 5 March JAC was ordered to carry out a bombing mission against Japanese targets on the road from Soebang to the Tjiater pass. This was probably the outcome of Major-General Pesman's visit to Colonel De Veer. The Glenn Martins of the ML were the only suitable aircraft for this mission, which was to be carried out the next morning by sunrise.[101]

Continuing the night bombardments on Kalidjati (5 March)

In the evening of 5 March three Vildebeest light bombers took off from Tasikmalaja at around 22:00 hrs to carry out bombing raids on Kalidjati (individually). The pilots were Flg Off R.R. Lamb, Flg Off B.A. Gotto and Sgt B. Appleby. A fourth plane had to stay behind, as one Glenn Martin of 1-Vl.G.II had got stuck in the mud, right in front of the Vildebeest's pen. In the attack Appleby's plane was hit by anti-aircraft fire and he did not manage to reach Tasikmalaja to make an emergency landing, upon which the two crew members successfully used their parachutes. They returned to their squadron the next day. The pilot was killed. Visibility was bad and the bombs were dropped over the dispersal areas of Kalidjati. The crew members claimed to have hit a building and probably four aircraft. These may, however, have been allied aircraft that had been left behind. In fact, some damage had indeed been inflicted, but the Japanese had also lost ten men.[102]

After the Japanese bombing raids not a single Glenn Martin was operationally serviceable at Andir. Three aircraft of 3-Vl.G.III were still in repairs at the Technical Service at Andir and were not ready until the evening and night of 6 March. The other two Glenn Martin afdelingen at Andir, 1-Vl.G.I and 2-Vl.G.III, had only one aircraft left each, which were both in repairs and would remain so for the coming two days. The two aircraft of 1-Vl.G.II at Tasikmalaja were still stuck in the mud in the evening of 5 March.[103] Due to the rapid advance of the Japanese main force from the west and the retreat of West Group to the Bandoeng plateau, Tjikembar airfield was evacuated on 5 March. Vk.A.1 (the two patrols under operational command of West Group) was transferred to Tasikmalaja. The afdeling did not fly any missions from there anymore, however. The convoy with the majority of the ground personnel did not arrive at its destination until 7 March.[104]

Allied results and the situation at the end of the day (5 March)

The men of the reinforced company 2-Inf. I of the KNIL held out from the afternoon of 5 March 1942 in the Tjiater fortification and blocked the advance of the Japanese battle group of Major Wakamatsu until their withdrawal in the early hours of 6 March. Thanks to their tenacity, the companies 1-Inf. V and 2-Inf. II could take up positions in time to the left behind 2-Inf. I. Only 1- and 2-Inf. L.H. XXI had not been able anymore to take up their positions to the right behind 2-Inf. I due to darkness and rainfall, and would only do so in the early morning of 6 March. During the course of the morning also some anti-armour of Teerink Group, 1st Battery of A. II Bg. and two sections of anti-aircraft artillery would be moved to the new first line. These delays caused a dangerous gap in the defence.

The allied air forces of JAC had not been able to contribute much to the defence of the Tjiater fortification. This was, however, in part due to the fact that during daylight the remaining aircraft were fully made available to Bandoeng Group, whose staff subsequently refrained from committing the combat aircraft against the Japanese advance in the morning of 5 March. Only 242 Squadron had flown a reconnaissance mission with two Hurricanes of the road from Soebang to the fortification. The mission cost the 3rd Hiko Dan one Ki-48. In the mean time, there were no Japanese targets on the road anymore.

The Japanese air forces at Kalidjati in fact did not contribute much to the advance of Major Wakamatsu's battle group, either, in spite of a great number of sorties. The air raids on the fortification in the morning of 5 March only caused a few casualties there and hardly did any damage. The lucky downing of a Ki-48 bomber and the hitting of a second by machine gunners in the fortification, on the contrary, boosted morale among the defenders of the KNIL. Although Waka-matsu held the first line of the fortification and parts of the second in the evening of 5 March, he could not dislodge the defenders in the centre of the second line.

The Japanese as well as the allied air forces suffered losses on this day. A reconnaissance plane of the 50th Chutai had been damaged during a night bombing raid on Kalidjati and one Ki-48 bomber had been shot down by a Hurricane. As was said above, machine gunners in the Tjiater position had shot down a second Ki-48, while a third one had been damaged. One Glenn Martin and a Vildebeest were shot down near Kalidjati by Ki-43s and anti-aircraft artillery, respectively. Two Japanese air raids on Andir airbase cost the allies a Glenn Martin bomber and two CW-22 reconnaissance aircraft. The capability of JAC to give support to its own troops during the coming days had become even slighter due to these losses.

Everything would depend on the way things developed the following day. A great shortage of troops within Bandoeng Group, causing an insufficient defence of the southern access to the Tjiater pass, amongst others, and the almost total absence of own air support, however, forced the conclusion on the defenders that the chances of being able to hold on to the Tjiater pass, even the southern access to the pass, were slim.

***

CHAPTER 4.4

The Battle on 6 March 1942

Introduction

The inhabitants of Bandoeng and the thousands of refugees in the town having come from Singapore, Malaya and the different parts of the Indonesian archipelago could hear the guns of the two batteries of the mountain artillery fire periodically all through the night. The battle came, for many once again, dangerously close. The servicemen, too, who were reporting for duty at Andir airfield at 05:00 hrs, were doing so precisely at the moment that the thunder of the guns in the hills in the north was plainly audible. The final battle had begun and it was taking place in the Tjiater pass. From sunrise they could see Japanese assault aircraft and bombers fly over the vicinity of Lembang. When the Ki-48s came close enough the anti-aircraft artillery would open fire. The enemy aircraft, however, always turned away in time and no attack on Andir followed. In the afternoon, incidentally, the anti-aircraft artillery at Andir was still reinforced somewhat by the coming into position of a section of three 12.7-mm machine guns and a section of two 2-cm guns arriving from Madioen in central Java. The two sections had originally been intended for the Tjiater fortification, but could not be moved safely anymore in the morning. Also the anti-aircraft guns and machine guns (with the exception of the 8-cm guns) from the KNIL at Tandjong Priok and Batavia were on their way to Bandoeng by train. They would arrive too late for redeployment, however.[1]

For the troops at the Tjiater fortification the battle began shortly after sunrise. As described in the previous chapter, a new first line had been formed behind the evacuated Tjiater fortification. At the other end of the Tjiater pass, some three kilometres to the south, the Wates position (under construction) had been established as best as the circumstances allowed and manned with infantry sections consisting of reserve officer candidates, Royal Netherlands Military Academy (KMA) cadets and Ambonese recruits, reinforced with several machine guns and the occasional anti-armour gun. The second line of this fortification under construction was located at the so-called three-forked Tolhek crossroads. Apart from an infantry covering force (reinforced with machine guns and mortars), this was also the location of the command posts of Colonel W.J. de Veer (commander of the two fortifications and the rear area) and Major C.G.J. Teerink (commander of Teerink Group, the reserve of Bandoeng Group), and to the west of the three-forked crossroads, along the Tolweg to the crater of the Goenoeng Tankoebang Prahoe (volcano), the two above-mentioned batteries of the IInd Battalion Mountain Artillery (A. II Bg.). At 06:00 hrs the first Japanese attack on the troops behind the Tjiater fortification began.

The balance of strength

On the Dutch side in the new first line in the northern end of the Tjiater pass there were four regular infantry companies reinforced with machine gun platoons and one company of short-term volunteers of the auxiliary Mankoe Negoro Corps. Including the train personnel of these companies in the rear area, this amounted to a force of some 950 men. Up against them was a Japanese infantry battalion (minus), Wakamatsu battle group, which consisted of approximately 1,000 men, including train personnel, but without the added artillery battery and several detachments which had been left behind (amongst others, the occupation of Kalidjati). Differences in manpower, however, were not what mattered most. It was the difference in armament and, in particular, air support which played a deciding role in the outcome of the battle. In contrast to the KNIL units the Japanese units had mortars (grenade launchers) and were in positions from where these could effectively be deployed and also had a small number of light tanks at their disposal. On top of that, Wakamatsu could bank on the maximum support of the combat aircraft of the 3rd Hiko Dan. The Japanese artillery battalion would play no role whatsoever in the battle.[2]

Although the KNIL used the term new 'first' line, there was no line behind that. If the Japanese broke through the defence of the northern end of the pass, the road to Bandoeng was virtually open to them. The troops in and near the southern end of the pass, some 400 men, only formed a relatively small reserve. On top of that, the bulk of them were not experienced infantrymen, but cadets and reserve officer candidates originally coming from various arms and services and recruits, organised in improvised sections. The staff of Bandoeng Group had done what little it could do for Colonel De Veer and had scraped all (mobile) infantry together it could find and had sent it to his area of command.

In the morning of 6 March the following orders were issued: battalion Inf. IV (minus one infantry company and part of the machine gun company) were to relocate from Soemedang to a location in the vicinity of Lembang, two infantry companies coming from the west coast of Sumatra (arrived at Bandoeng on 5 March) were also to relocate to a location near Lembang, 'battalion De Vries' (an incomplete battalion commanded by Major B.P. de Vries, consisting of three incomplete infantry companies and an incomplete machine gun company, composed of remaining elements of Inf. X, Inf. XIV and Inf. V, see the previous part: The Battle of Kalidjati) at Tjimahi, was to relocate to Lembang and battalion Inf. IX (Tjisomang position) was to be kept ready to move to Tjisaroea after sunset. These units were to form an improvised defence line near Lembang.[3]

The order to the 'battalion De Vries' was first rescinded after a plea by its commander with the staff of Bandoeng Group and then at around 18:00 hrs changed into a relocation after sunset with two companies to Tjikidang. The third company plus the machine gun company, a section of engineers from 2nd Infantry Regiment (2-R.I.) and a makeshift infantry company, patched together at the last possible moment, came under the command of Major K. Anten (commander of Inf. XV). The reorganised Inf. XV received orders around 18:00 hrs to move to a location near Lembang.[4]

The number of air operations that could be carried out on this day from Andir and Tasikmalaja in support of the troops in the Tjiater pass was limited. All combat aircraft of Java Air Command were still fully at the disposal of Bandoeng Group during the hours of daylight, but the number of operationally serviceable aircraft had dwindled considerably from March 4 onwards. The number of operationally serviceable fighter aircraft, 11 to 12 in the morning of 4 March, seven

The Tankoebang Prahoe volcano (in top centre), photographed from the direction of Lembang. The picture clearly shows how the Bandoeng plateau was surrounded by mountains. (Private collection, P.C. Boer)

in the morning of 5 March, was eight at 05:00 hrs in the morning of 6 March. The liaison officers of the ML and RAF at the staff of Bandoeng Group, however, were ready to phone through the take off times of the missions which had been planned by JAC on behalf of Bandoeng Group in the evening of 5 March.[5]

Failed bomber missions

Due to sheer bad luck not a single bomber mission could be carried out in the early morning of 6 March (until sunrise). The planned missions with Vildebeest and Glenn Martin bombers were all cancelled. One mission to Kalidjati of 36 Squadron RAF did not go through because both fuel pumps of the unit failed to work and fuelling up the Vildebeestes by hand took too much time.[6]

The action of 1-Vl.G.II at Tasikmalaja with two aircraft by sunrise against targets on the road from Soebang to the Tjiater position was also cancelled as both planes were stuck in the mud, one of which on a taxi route, right in front of a Vildebeest pen. For the same reason the latter plane had not been able to join in the night raid on 5 March on Kalidjati (see the previous chapter).

By now the RAF had towed away the Glenn Martin of the crew of Sgt W.J. Hofmyster and a heavy tractor of the RAF was standing ready in the early morning near the pen with the stuck aircraft of the crew of Tlt C.J.H. Samson. It was the 'lead' plane, equipped with the bomb sight. The operator of the tractor, however, was nowhere to be found and SM H.F. de Koning, who had to prepare this plane and was to come along as air gunner, could not get the machine with which he was unfamiliar to work. Not even by giving full throttle on both aircraft engines did he manage to make the stuck Glenn Martin move. Disappointed the crew went back to their accommodation.[7]

By sunrise the 3rd Hiko Dan attacked Tasikmalaja with five Ki-48s of the 90th Sentai, escorted by four Ki-43 fighters of the 64th Sentai. The bombers attacked the runway from a relatively low altitude, but hit the road running along the airfield. The fighters fired at the flight terrain and put the local labourers who were working for the Engineers doing the ground work for an extension of the runway to flight. There was no damage to the airfield or aircraft.[8]

Allied morning fighter reconnaissance missions

At daybreak on 6 March JAC had two, later three (operationally serviceable) Brewsters and six Hurricanes at its disposal at Andir. The Brewster B-395 'E', which had stranded at Pameungpeuk on 4 March with engine trouble, had been repaired by now and was added to the operational strength of 1-Vl.G.V this morning. At 242 Squadron several Hurricanes had come out of repairs in the previous evening and at 05:00 hrs the squadron had six operationally serviceable aircraft available.[9]

By 05:00 hrs a Falcon of Vk.A.1 was to have taken off for a reconnaissance mission in the direction of Tjiater, but this assignment could not go through. The two remaining CW-22s of Vk.A.1 (see the previous chapter) after the latest bombing raid on Andir could not leave their pens because craters had not been filled up and wreckage had not been cleared away yet. Incidentally, on the advice of ML Command the Falcon reconnaissance aircraft were not deployed anymore after the cancellation of the morning reconnaissance mission, in view of the Japanese air superiority and the vulnerability of these slow planes.[10]

Subsequently, the staff of Bandoeng Group combined the reconnaissance with a mission that was to be carried out by 242 Squadron.
In the early morning the squadron was ordered to fly a mission with
all available aircraft to the Lembang-Tjiater area. The idea was to bind
the Japanese air forces, thus giving the troops in the Tjiater position
who had been under continuous attacks from the air the previous day,
some respite. 1-Vl.G.V (initially only with two aircraft) was kept at
readiness to bomb and machine gun any possible targets on the road
from Soebang to the Tjiater position. At around 08:00 hrs, when after
several rain showers some considerable cloud had formed over the
plateau, the Hurricanes took to the air.[11] A protest against the nature of
the mission from the commanding officer of 242 Squadron at BRITAIR
had been to no avail. BRITAIR, just like the ML Command, had
hardly any say with regard to the operational control of the units.[12]

The mission of 242 Squadron was led by Sqn Ldr I. Julian.
Recently promoted, Julian assumed command of the squadron on
this day. Sqn Ldr R.E.P. Brooker was to be evacuated to Australia
by Lodestar transport plane of the ML. The other pilots were: Flt Lt
B.J. Parker, Plt Off W.M. Lockwood, Plt Off E.C. Gartrell, Plt Off
R.T. Bainbridge and Sgt G.J. King. The latter, who had started as the
penultimate plane, got in trouble right after take off due to engine
failure. He made an emergency landing during which his Hurricane
was lost, but he survived the crash without as much as a scratch. His
pair lead Bainbridge returned to Andir after having made certain that
King had survived the crash.

Making use as much as possible of the clouds, Julian and Gartrell
flew towards Lembang, whereas Parker and Lockwood went into the
direction of Tjiater first. Both pairs encountered a patrol of three
Ki-48 bombers. Julian and Gartrell were convinced they had shot down
one Ki-48 and a probable second, respectively. Gartrell's Hurricane,
however, was hit by fire from one of the bombers, upon which the
pilot made a precautionary landing at Tasikmalaja. Lockwood and
Parker claimed one Ki-48 each, with Parker confirming that the plane
hit by his colleague had crashed burning into the jungle. In actual fact,
two Ki-48s in total had been shot down and one at least had been
damaged. Japanese fighter aircraft were nowhere to be seen.[13]

One of the British fighter pilots, probably Julian himself, made
a fly-by of the Tjiater fortification. On his return Julian reported by
phone that the KNIL troops were engaged in battle and that (probably
Japanese) troops were outflanking the fortification in the west. There

was no activity or fighting in the eastern section of the first line, nor was there any enemy traffic on the road from Soebang to Tjiater, leaving no targets for the Brewsters, as a consequence. Back at Andir, the Hurricanes were kept on readiness, but the squadron did not receive a new combat order until the afternoon.[14]

The Brewsters had already been bombed up with two 50-kilogramme fragmentation bombs per aircraft well before sunrise. The pilots, led by Elt P.A.C. Benjamins, were still waiting for their battle orders in the Noordhangaar when the Hurricanes were taking off. Every 30 minutes the mechanics of 1-Vl.G.V fired up the engines of the fighter aircraft, but the battle orders did not come. Across the field, at 242 Squadron, the fact the Brewsters were not committed even gave rise to the rumour that the ML fighter aircraft were being fitted out with extra fuel tanks in order to evacuate to Australia. The rumour was quickly dispelled, but 1-Vl.G.V was not to get any battle orders whatsoever on 6 March.[15]

Continued Japanese air actions (6 March)

At around 05:30 hrs the Japanese resumed their attack on the Tjiater fortification, being supported from the start by the Ki-51 assault aircraft, the Ki-48 light bombers and the Ki-43 fighter aircraft of the 3rd Hiko Dan at Kalidjati. These air forces were committed in a fashion which today still looks rather modern. In the target area there was a continuous presence of two to four Ki-51s, relieving each other. Apart from that, the 75th and 90th Sentais, escorted by fighter aircraft from the 59th and 64th Sentais, flew five missions on this day, each lasting some two and a half hours, covering the entire period of daylight hours. The first mission of the 75th and 90th Sentais consisted of 13 Ki-48 light bombers (five sections of two or three aircraft), escorted by seven Ki-43 fighter aircraft, which were flying combat air patrols over the area of operations to intercept any possible enemy fighters and occasionally machine gunning targets on the ground. That they would not always be able to intercept enemy fighter aircraft could not be avoided, as the area of operations was too big and the number of their own fighters too small.

The crews of the Ki-51s tried to spot pockets of resistance and artillery, passing on the coordinates of these targets to their own troops or Ki-48s. In the rear area of the positions in the Tjiater pass they reconnoitred the enemy reserves, logistic units, command posts, etc., and directed Ki-48s towards them, too. One or two patrols of Ki-48s would carry out attacks, while the others would fly holding patterns north of the Tjiater fortification between Tjiater and Soebang. The Ki-51s also dropped some light bombs themselves (the assault aircraft could hold a bomb load of 200 kilogrammes) and machine gunned troops on the ground, sometimes to fix enemy units until the Ki-48s could take them out. Also, the civilian infra-structure in the area, such as the sheds of the enterprises, a small village evacuated by the KNIL and several hotels were bombed.[16]

The Japanese infantry in the first line could not communicate directly with the aircraft, other than by signal cloth. It was possible to transmit radio messages via a small forward command post of the 3rd Hiko Dan, a liaison officer of one of the air groups with a few signals personnel and a radio, which went along with Major Wakamatsu's battalion command post. But the Japanese, too, had trouble with their radio communication. The Ki-51 passed on urgent messages via message cylinders they dropped from their planes. In fact, they were facing similar communication problems to those of the KNIL troops. The Japanese system for 'ground-air' cooperation worked reasonably well, albeit that on this day, too, the Japanese did not manage to take out the guns of the mountain artillery.

The Japanese Sentais dropped hundreds of bombs on 6 March, as a result of which not only many vehicles and other materiel were lost, but also the morale of the defenders was eroded and there were many casualties. Gradually, everything was breaking down. Movements had become extremely dangerous and food could not be brought up any more. Telephone lines had been bombed to shreds and dispatch riders with their motor bikes or jeeps were machine gunned off the roads by the Japanese Ki-51s.[17]

The ground battle at the Tjiater position on day 2 (6 March)

The companies of Teerink Group and Inf. L.H. XXI that had arrived in the evening of 5 March were defending the Tjiater pass from positions behind the second line of the Tjiater fortification. The occupied part of the second line was evacuated by 2-Inf. I at around 04:00 hrs after the arrival of extra reinforcements. To the west of the road (in plant holes and ditches) 2-Inf. II and 1-Inf. V of Teerink Group had taken up positions; to the east of the road the three companies of the Inf. L.H. XXI battalion. As described in the previous chapter, during the night

Colonel De Veer had adjusted his plan for the defence in consultation with Major C.G.J. Teerink and Captain M. Kooistra (the commanding officer of 2-Inf. I).[18]

The Japanese ground attack concentrated on the units to the west of the road. Inf. L.H. XXI was tackled from the air, which allowed the Japanese to attack the troops to the west of the road with superior numbers. As described in the previous chapter, the men of Inf. L.H. XXI had gone forward as late as the early hours of the morning and had arrived at their deployment areas by first light. At around 05:00 hrs some Japanese patrols fired at the 1st Company of Captain K.F. Avink and possibly also the 2nd Company, commanded by Captain J.B. Doedens. By that time, 1-Inf. L.H. XXI, to the east of the road and on the left flank of the battalion, had only just begun to organise and take up battle positions. At the same time they could hear heavy rifle and machine gun fire to the west of the road.

Lieutenant-Colonel B.C.D. Drejer, the commanding officer of Inf. L.H. XXI, concluded that Japanese had broken through the position to his west and that his battalion was being outflanked, upon which he tried to withdraw his troops in an orderly fashion. It was his intention to take up new positions more to the south. However, in reality there was no Japanese attack going on, just yet. It was just men of 2-Inf. II and 1-Inf. V firing intensely at several Japanese patrols, it taking a while for fire discipline to be re-established in these units (see below). This had completely misled Drejer, who neglected to check on the situation to the west of the road.[19]

Some elements of the companies of Inf. L.H. XXI were probably south of, or passed during their movement, the imaginary line in the terrain south of which the 3rd Hiko Dan could attack at will. Men to the west of the road observed a single-engine plane (Ki-51) fly over the sector of Inf. L.H. XXI, upon which they saw three or four aircraft of the same type carry out diving attacks. Somewhat later several Ki-48 bombers attacked Dawoean and surroundings, dead south of Inf. L.H. XXI, the location of, amongst others, the forward elements of the battle train with a substantial number of trucks loaded with ammunition. The morale of the men, eroded as it had been by exhausting movements and a sleepless night in the cold of the high Tjiater pass, broke during the air raids.

The withdrawal of Inf. L.H. XXI disintegrated in chaotic flight through the terrain towards the Tankoeban Prahoe hotel, and from there along the road to Lembang, although an occasional brigade (group of

about 15 men) of 1-Inf. L.H. XXI held its position in the terrain to
the east of the road, south of the original positions this company had
taken up. There were also several losses in the companies as a result
of the Japanese air attacks. In late March 1942 teams of POWs of
the KNIL buried many dozens of mortal remains near the Tjiater
fortification, a small number of which to the east of the road and at
Dawoean and surroundings. At around 14:00 hrs an (unknown) officer
of the battalion reported to Colonel De Veer and stated that Inf. L.H.
XXI had "flowed back".[20]

In the early morning also the men of 2-Inf. I who had remained
in Dawoean marched up towards the Tjiater fortification, led by
Lieutenant P.J.J. Quanjer, in order to (partially) relieve the troops in
the second line. These troops, however, appeared to have been withdrawn in the mean time. Near the second line of the fortification
Quanjer encountered Captain Kooistra, who had come to pick up
the rest of his company and who had received new instructions from
Colonel De Veer. In the mean time, the personnel that had been
evacuated from the second line had been deployed as reserve near
the Wates position (the section of reserve officer candidates led by
Lieutenant M.P.A. de Ouden), and near the Tankoeban Prahoe hotel
(the sections of 2-Inf. I), respectively. Also, the rest of the men of
2-Inf. I were to move to the latter location and to take up positions
south of the hotel.[21]

When Quanjer and Kooistra were discussing the situation, the
sections suddenly found themselves under fire. It was decided to withdraw the men groupwise in the first instance to an assembly area near
the three-forked Tolhek crossroads. The sections of the machine gun
company took along two mortars and several machine guns, complete
with ammunition. These men were the last to leave as their carrier horses
still needed to be loaded up. One of the horses was killed. Because of
enemy air activity the groups retreated in part through the terrain.[22]
The road from the Tjiater fortification to the Wates fortification was
largely a 'hollow road', with trees on both sides, making any traffic on
the road hard to discern form the air. The stretch of the road that ran
just south of the Tjiater fortification, however, ran through more open
terrain and was covered by Japanese fire.[23]

The journey meant many hours of walking and as the men came
closer to the Wates fortification, the danger from the air increased.
Japanese aircraft flying over forced them to go into cover from time
to time. One flight of Ki-48 bombers subsequently bombed targets

near the Tolhek crossroads and caused even more delay. At around 14:00 hrs only 16 men so far (among whom Quanjer) had made it to the assembly location, and most men of the machine gun and mortar sections followed only hours later. At least one mortar and one machine gun came into position near the three-forked crossroads once more in the course of the afternoon.[24]

The attack on the two companies west of the road (6 March)

Thanks to the effort of the 3rd Hiko Dan to the east of the road, Major Wakamatsu could concentrate his troops against the enemy to the west of the road. There the attack came at the very moment that bread, which had been brought up in the extremely early hours of the morning by personnel of the baggage trains, was being distributed. They had also brought coffee and tea. When the men of 2-Inf. II and 1-Inf. V came out of their covers at around 05:30 hrs, 'cold, stiff, tired and miserable', to collect their breakfast, a Japanese patrol and a brigade on the left flank of 1-Inf. V opened fire almost simultaneously. Everyone jumped back into their plant holes and ditches quick as lightning, but the first men had already fallen. Section commander Ensign Th. Meijer of 2-Inf. II wrote in his post-war account, "… everybody began to fire like madmen". It took a while before fire discipline had been re-established and the friendly fire cost a few dead and wounded; nor did the fire of the Japanese infantry (probably several reconnaissance patrols) miss its effect. At 1-Inf. V one of the men who were just collecting their bread dropped mortally wounded into the bread basket, and in the first fire contact at least six men in total were killed. At around 06:00 hrs the Japanese infantry launched its attack.[25]

The men of 2-Inf. II and 1-Inf. V were somewhat at a disadvantage because in front of their own positions, which lay in kina garden, there were tea shrubs with an occasional tree among them. This provided good cover for the Japanese infantry. From this cover the Japanese were able to throw hand grenades and to position a few light machine guns under cover. The defenders, however, managed to push the Japanese infantry back by delivering discriminate fire into the tea shrubs and crowns of the trees. The barbed wire fence behind the Tjiater fortification had not stopped the Japanese for long, as in several places there were still small bridges across the barbed wire for the tea pickers, which the KNIL personnel had not been able to remove.[26]

A Madsen light machine gun ("karabijn mitrailleur") of the Infantry during
KNIL demonstrations at Andir on 30 April 1940. (Private collection, P.C.
Boer)

The section of 2-Inf. II which had been positioned on the right
flank got into trouble during the first Japanese attack. The Japanese
infantry tried to drive a wedge between the positions of 2-Inf. II and
1-Inf. V and pushed a part of the section of Lieutenant H.W. van
Pelt from its position. Van Pelt immediately reacted and "borrowed"
a machine gun from the section of Sergeant-Major J.B. Heffelaar
on the left flank of 1-Inf. V. With the help of Heffelaar order was
restored and the gap in the defence closed. Only, when it was over
the command group of company commander Captain W.M. Wensel
had disappeared. They appeared to have retreated for the enemy fire.[27]
The first attack was repelled, as was the heavier second one at around
08:30 hrs. It took a while before it came, but the reason for this
delay soon emerged. The Japanese had called in aircraft. From around
08:00 hrs (probably four) Ki-51s of the 3rd Hiko Dan carried out
machine gun attacks on the positions of both companies. The coordination was flawless, but not really difficult as the forward line of own
troops was clearly visible in the terrain from the air. Like the ground
attacks, the strafings caused a number of dead and wounded. The
attacks of the Japanese infantry came mainly from the north-west in

an attempt to envelop 2-Inf. II and 1-Inf. V, which failed. When their second attack also bogged down, however, the Japanese committed three light tanks and a new attack followed at around 09:15 hrs, supported by tank and mortar fire.[28]

From the road (a position near the barbed wire fence behind the Tjiater fortification) the tanks fired at the positions of both companies, while at the same time the mortars began to fire. It rained shrapnel and clods of earth onto the men in the plant holes and other cover. The number of killed and heavily wounded began to rise rapidly. The enemy infantry subsequently tried to envelop 2-Inf. II from the left, while attacking both companies frontally. This attack, too, could still be repelled, but it was all the companies could take. The enemy tank and mortar fire had caused many casualties and the remaining infantry men of 2-Inf. II and 1-Inf. V did not have much ammunition left anymore. Wounded who had been sent back to the road in order to be evacuated to the rear, came under enemy fire there and had a hard time getting themselves into safety. An armoured vehicle of Van Dongen's squadron, sent out by Colonel De Veer to restore contact with the first line and to reconnoitre the situation there was riddled with bullets, the two-man crew being killed.[29]

The sections of 2-Inf. II, which had been thinned out as a result of losses and the dispatching of the wounded, were the first to retreat behind 1-Inf. V back to the road, leaving much of their equipment behind. The retreat was orderly; the machine guns of the machine gun sections were destroyed before leaving. The road was under machine gun fire, but had to be crossed in order to be able to retreat via the terrain to the east of the road, which was not lying under fire. Lieutenant Van Pelt, who had taken over command after the disappearance of Captain Wensel, had sent word to his colleague Lieutenant J.C.A. Faber of 1-Inf. V, who remained in position with his sections for a while to cover 2-Inf. II's retreat.[30]

The retreat of 1-Inf. V itself was less successful. Faber had already drawn the conclusion that a new attack would certainly be successful and for that reason gave the order to withdraw at around 10:00 hrs. After all, he had not heard from either of the two dispatch riders, whom he had sent with requests for reinforcements and orders for the combat train to resupply him with ammunition. Afterwards both men appeared to have been killed. One by one, his sections began crossing the road in groups into the safer terrain to the east of the road, where the Japanese infantry was not active yet. The machine gun sections fired as much of their remaining ammunition as they could, and then, before they left, destroyed their machine guns.[31]

A number of men of the section of Sub-Lieutenant Schouten on the left flank and of the section of Sergeant-Major J.G. Meeuwissen that had been positioned in the right front, 20 to 25 men in total, and the section of Lieutenant W. Postema, which had been positioned in the right rear in its entirety (some 39 men), found they were surrounded and got involved in man-to-man fights. It was around 11:00 hrs that the last men surrendered. During the crossing of the roads by the groups which had managed to get away, there were several wounded.[32]

The retreat of the escaped brigades, machine gun sections and command groups through the terrain to the east of the road was difficult (the terrain being hilly and partially heavily forested), but without contact with the enemy. They did encounter a few brigades (groups of about 15 men) of 1-Inf. L.H. XXI, though, which were still faithfully holding their positions. At around 14:00 hrs the first small groups of men arrived at the Tankoeban Prahoe hotel, among them Sub-Lieutenant Schouten and Sergeant-Major Heffelaar. Most groups, however, went around the three-forked Tolhek crossroads and Lembang because of the Japanese air raids and a later Japanese ground attack, and went on through the terrain towards Bandoeng. After a two-day's walk Lieutenant Faber, with approximately 25 men arrived there. He had some 50 exhausted men left of his company. After the war Faber was awarded the Militaire Willems-Orde (Knight of the Military Willems Order) for his excellent leadership during the battle.[33]

The Japanese infantry collected the POWs. Together with the men of 2-Inf. I and the Landstorm section assigned to them, who had been surrounded in the second line of the fortification, the total came up to 75 men. A few men managed to hide from the Japanese and escape later. At the last moment two men of A. II Bg. were added to the group of POWs. They were tied together with their own puttees (leg bandages) and taken away by the Japanese infantry. Some 500 metres to the west of the road and 150 metres south of the Tji Panghasahan rivulet they were machine gunned. Only four men survived this war crime, the Japanese taking them for dead. Two men, who had been taken from the group shortly before to act as guides, managed to escape (see below).[34]

An isolated small group of six men of 2-Inf. I which had been left behind in a dug-out in the evacuated first line of the Tjiater fortification, passed the hill with the victims in the early evening after a wearisome detour around the fortification. They could not do much for the wounded and after bandaging some of them and leaving behind some first-aid dressings, they went on their way.[35]

The reconnaissance patrol of 2-Inf. I (see the previous chapter) had not been successful. By sunrise the men lay hidden among the tea shrubs in position with their anti-tank gun, at a distance of some 70 to 100 metres from the bridge in front of the Tjiater fortification which had been repaired by the Japanese. When the first Japanese tank appeared, the gun blocked. While a new shell was inserted, the tank raced across the bridge, followed by dozens of Japanese infantrymen. The group kept hidden under the tea shrubs and managed to escape when darkness set in.[36]

The losses in 2-Inf. II and 1-Inf. V were heavy. According to the initial estimate of the company commanders, some 30 to 50 men, respectively (not including the above-mentioned POWs) had fallen on the battlefield. A small number of missing showed up again later. There were at least 20 wounded lying in various hospitals on 8 March. After the capitulation they were joined by several more, who had been collected by KNIL personnel under surveillance of the Japanese. The groups of volunteers who were burying their fallen comrades there at the end of March, also found a seriously wounded survivor who could be taken to hospital in time. When in 1948 the last killed-in-action were reburied the KNIL Gravendienst–War Graves Service calculated a total of around 120 killed in 1-Inf. V and 2-Inf. II (including the murdered POWs of 1-Inf. V).[37]

The situation at the Wates fortification and the three-forked Tolhek crossroads in the morning and early afternoon of 6 March

In the morning Colonel De Veer had had two armoured vehicles of Van Dongen's squadron relocated from Lembang to the three-forked crossroads; a dangerous undertaking. In spite of several attacks from the air by Ki-51s, both vehicles reached their destination safely, upon which both vehicle commanders, an ensign and a sergeant, were briefed at De Veer's command post. At around 09:00 hrs one of the vehicles left for the first line for a reconnaissance of the situation behind the Tjiater fortification. The crew never returned.[38]

At around 09:30 hrs De Veer received a message from the staff of Bandoeng Group to the effect that allied aircraft had spotted a Japanese advance to the west of the road, through the terrain, in order to outflank the new forward line of own troops (2-Inf. II, 1-Inf. V and Inf. L.H. XXI). The report came from Squadron Leader I. Julian, who (as was described above) had been carrying out a reconnaissance flight in a Hurricane. Communications with the troops in the first line had not been re-established as yet, and De Veer did not have a clue about the course of the battle. That it was still in full swing was clearly audible in the southern end of the pass. De Veer seriously reckoned with the possibility that, after their advance through the terrain to the west of the road, the enemy troops would also attempt to outflank the Wates fortification and launch an attack on the three-forked Tolhek cross-roads from the west. As he did not know how far the forward enemy units had already progressed, he ordered a reconnaissance of the terrain to the west of the three-forked crossroads at around 10:00 hrs in order to prevent any possible infiltrations of Japanese groups (see below).

A short while later, between 10:00 hrs and 10:30 hrs, De Veer's telephone connection between his command post and the staff of Bandoeng Group, which ran through the PTT exchange at Lembang, was broken. The Lembang exchange and a crucial part of the line net-work were lost in a Japanese bombardment, and the damage could not be repaired anymore. The telephone lines with Teerink's command post, some 150 metres north of the three-forked Tolhek crossroads, and the back-up command post in the Zonneweelde hotel had also been severed. There was still the radio vehicle with the long-distance radio (LARA), but radio traffic was impossible because of atmospheric interference. The result was that the regimental commander had be-come entirely dependent on dispatch riders for his communication.[39]

The Wates fortification (under construction) some 500 metres north of the three-forked Tolhek crossroads and the crossroads itself with De Veer's command post there, were defended by men of Captain Paardekoper's and of Sub-Lieutenant L.Z. Siahaya's improvised companies (see the previous chapter). The location of the Wates forti-fication on a mountain ridge was extremely strategic and during the battle it consisted of some 12 casemates roughly in an ellipse shape, most of which, however, had not been completely finished yet. All other projected casemates so far only existed on paper. The road winded through the position in a large loop. The ground work prior to the construction of communication trenches and emplacements for infantry weapons had been started but hardly any progress had been made. The complex was surrounded by a barbed wire fence, though. Some infantry positions, among which that of the section of cadets of Lieutenant A. Luteijn (approximately 50 men) in a tea garden to the west of the road, lay in front of the outer casemates.[40]

In the centre of the Wates fortification, to the left and right of the road, there was a section of reserve officer candidates of the Corps Opleiding Reserve Officieren–The Reserve Officers Training Corps (CORO), commanded by Lieutenant C. Veenendaal (approximately 50 men) and in the terrain to the east of this section there was a reinforced section (about 60 men) of Ambonese recruits. The fire support consisted of not more than a few machine guns and some anti-armour defence, probably one anti-armour gun and a few tank rifles (2-cm calibre anti-tank rifles). As reserve, some 200 metres north of the three-forked crossroads, there was the CORO section of Lieutenant M.P.A. den Ouden, which had been withdrawn from the Tjiater fortification.[41]

At around 10:00 hrs Luteijn's section of cadets was ordered to pull back some 100 metres and to make a front facing to the west (in connection with a possible attack). This order did not come through correctly and Luteijn ended up taking up positions to the south-west at some distance from the three-forked crossroads, not seeing an enemy the entire day, upon which he made a phased withdrawal on Lembang. Between 12:00 hrs and 12:30 hrs, however, the first Japanese patrols appeared near the Wates fortification and the CORO section received some, not very intensive, machine gun fire. In the afternoon own mortars fired from positions near the three-forked crossroads at the Japanese who had advanced up to the positions which Luteijn had vacated.

Some men of the CORO section had just left, and by order of Captain Paardekoper, who had been assigned as the commanding officer of both 'student' companies, were carrying out a reconnaissance to the east of the road, in north-easterly direction. It took them two hours on the outward and two hours on the homeward stretch through the heavy terrain, but they did not encounter any enemy or friendly troops. At around 16:00 hrs the entire section was deployed again in the Wates fortification, which, after Luteijn's departure, had been manned by the CORO section and the reinforced Ambonese recruits section, with the above-mentioned (probably two) machine guns and some anti-armour defences. The total number of men, including the section of Den Ouden, which had been positioned as reserve along the

stretch of road between the Wates fortification and the three-forked
Tolhek crossroads, amounted to approximately 180.[42]

At around 13:00 hrs Colonel De Veer sent a report on the course
of the battle to the staff of Bandoeng Group by dispatch rider. The
situation was extremely uncertain, but there was every likelihood that
the new first line behind the Tjiater fortification had been breached
and the enemy had advanced as far as the Wates fortification through
the terrain to the west of the road. Based on De Veer's report, Major-
General Pesman reported to General Headquarters at around 14:00 hrs
that the men in the southern end of the pass would be able to hold
out a further 24 hours at best. The number of troops still available in
Bandoeng Group was too small to repel an enemy attack. The first large
unit of West Group, Blackforce, was still fully occupied in moving to
Oedjoengbroeng and would not be able in time to come to assistance
as mobile reserve.[43]

Near the three-forked Tolhek crossroads the second line of the
Wates fortification had been projected, but at the time of the Japanese
landings in Java it consisted of little more than a few (unfinished)
casemates and a tank trap in the road. In the mean time, it had been
extended with a number trenches and barbed wire obstacles. Near the
three-forked crossroads and its direct vicinity two sections (some 80
men in total) of Ambonese recruits had been deployed for the defence
of the southern end of the pass and the safeguarding of the command
posts. Their commanders were Sub-Lieutenant L.Z. Siahaya and
Lieutenant A Karreman (the latter coming from the CORO), respectively. The IInd Battalion Mountain Artillery had some organic security
personnel and saw to its own security.

The fire support consisted of a mortar platoon (minus) of 4-Inf. V
(four mortars), commanded by Sergeant-Major W. Koster, a machine
gun platoon of 4-Inf. V (two sections with four machine guns in
total), half a machine gun section of 4-Inf. V (one machine gun of the
Heffelaar section in a casemate at the three-forked road itself) and a
machine gun platoon of 4-Inf. II (four machine guns). Some distance
to the south of the three-forked crossraods there was probably the
mortar platoon (minus) of 4-Inf. L.H. XXI (three or four mortars). The
number of men at and near the three-forked cross-roads amounted to
a total of approximately 150.[44]

Around the Tankoeban Prahoe hotel, along the road from the
three-forked crossroads to Lembang, the troops that acted as the
reserve and security for the forward elements of the combat trains with

ammunition, the dressing station located in the hotel and the forward stocks of fuel, mines, etc., were located. They consisted of two sections of 2-Inf. I (withdrawn from the Tjiater fortification and short of men due to losses), one infantry section, consisting of recruits and led by CORO students, which had had too little training as yet to do other than security tasks, a machine gun platoon (KMA-cadets, commanded by Lieutenant H.J. Lublink Weddink, probably minus one section) of the Paardekoper company and a mortar platoon (minus) probably of 4-Inf. II. The rear area proper was in and around Lembang, where there were some garrison facilities.[45]

The deployment of A. II Bg. near the three-forked Tolhek crossroads

In the morning the 3rd Hiko Dan carried out several bombardments on or near the three-forked Tolhek crossroads. They were in part aimed at the positions of A. II Bg. None of the bombs, however, hit their targets. Lieutenant A.F.X.E.J. Vos de Wael LLM, observer of the 3rd Battery, had been the first to go forward in the early morning and reported back that he had found an observer post and needed a telephone line. It took a while before permission was given to go up to the first line because of the confusing situation and the fact that they had to wait for the arrival of the armoured vehicles from Lembang. At around 09:00 hrs Lieutenant A.V. Vosveld of the signals unit of A. II Bg. gave the necessary instructions to Corporal J.C. Hoogstraten. The infantry had established a new first line behind the Tjiater fortification and a telephone team had to lay a telephone line as soon as possible to the observer post established by now. An armoured vehicle drove in front to reconnoitre.[46]

Somewhat later in the morning Lieutenant J. de Jonge Esq. and gunner J. de Vries drove up to the first line to establish a second observer post. In the mean time, the telephone personnel of A. II Bg. were laying out a telephone line along the road (with the help of a purpose-made sidecar motorcycle). Having arrived at some 500 metres behind the Tjiater fortification, De Jonge and De Vries stopped their jeep behind a barbed wire fence that had been erected there by own troops during the night. Suddenly, the bullets were flying from everywhere. It was impossible to go ahead and when the shooting subsided somewhat they headed back full speed. By this time it was around 10:00 hrs.[47]

A battery of the Mountain Artillery during a pre-war exercise on the Bandoeng plateau. (Private collection, P.C. Boer)

A few hundreds metres further south while driving up they had encountered two telephone technicians who were working on the telephone line. The two were nowhere to be seen anymore, probably because they had gone into cover in a ditch along the road. Both found themselves among Japanese infantry and together with Corporal Hoogstraten they fell into Japanese hands. The latter had gone to pick them up with a motor cycle after an emergency call they had sent by phone. Just when he was on the point of picking them up, Japanese infantry fired at the small group. Telephone technician W. Koster was killed and the motor cycle broke down. Hoogstraten and telephone technician W.G. Heyman fired back until their ammunition ran out and then they took cover in the ditch, where they were discovered around 13:00 hrs. They were added to the group of approximately 75 infantry POWs mentioned above that was led down the road by several Japanese. Hoogstraten and one of the infantrymen were taken from the group to serve as guides for the Japanese. Both managed to escaped in the evening.[48]

In the night of 5 on 6 March and in the morning of 6 March both batteries of A. II Bg. gave periodic harassing fire on known co-ordinates in the terrain and on the road in front of the Tjiater position. Somewhat later in the morning the 2nd Battery (Captain F.W.H. Twiss) gave discriminate fire at the road and the side terrain, after they had managed to get an observer with a radio up a slope of a mountain to the east of the three-forked crossroads. Around 09:45 hrs, however, the radio communication between the guns and the observer suddenly went dead. The radio communication went through the radio vehicle of the signals unit of A. II Bg., which had been dispersed together with other vehicles (among which there were ammunition tenders) in a camouflaged location along the Tolweg to the west of the positions of the batteries. When Twiss went to see what had happened at the Tolweg, he saw the enormous havoc and found that all the personnel had gone.[49]

Afterwards, it appeared that Lieutenant Vosveld had ordered to set fire to all the vehicles and had withdrawn all his personnel in small groups through the difficult and confusing terrain in the direction of Lembang. Like the battery commanders, Vosveld had got a message to the effect that the Japanese were probably outflanking the position and would attack the three-forked Tolhek crossroads from the West.[50]

In the early morning the first bombs fell very close to the location of the signals unit and in the direct vicinity of the three-forked crossroads there were still several fires burning. Among them was a fire in a complex of sheds under construction along the Tolweg. At around 09:45 hrs Hoogstraten reported that the two telephone technicians who were busy laying new telephone lines to the first line had got themselves positioned among the Japanese as far as some 700–800 metres south of the Tjiater fortification. Shortly after this a friendly machine gun near the three-forked crossroads opened fire briefly.

In the stress and chaos of the moment Vosveld drew the (mistaken) conclusion that he had to move fast in order to bring his men into safety. He fell into Japanese hands later in the day while roaming around in the terrain with two telephone technicians. After having been taken along for a considerable period of time the two telephone technicians were killed with bayonets and Vosveld was left behind for dead. He was found on 8 March and survived.[51]

By order of Colonel De Veer the gunners of both the batteries of A. II Bg. were deployed shortly after 10:00 hrs as infantry. They carried out a reconnaissance in the thick growth of the slopes of the

Tankoebang Prahoe in westerly direction (to the north and south of the Tolweg up to two to three kilometres away from their position) and did not even see a single Japanese. One of the guns with a complete gun team had been positioned near the three-forked crossroads as anti-armour defence next to the road. Every battery left a small group of men behind for security, with one gunner with a demolition charge for every gun.

The situation near the first line was extremely unclear. Taking into account Hoogstraten's report, the Japanese infantry had already passed the first line, but whether their own infantry was still there was unknown. According to De Veer, continued shelling of parts of the terrain and the road in front of the Tjiater fortification by mountain artillery had little point any more, especially as their own air reconnaissance had reported an empty road. At 17:00 hrs the first guns were manned again.

The situation at the Wates fortification and the three-forked crossroads in the afternoon of 6 March

In the early afternoon there was still complete uncertainty at De Veer's command post about what had gone on near the Tjiater fortification. All communication had been severed and Japanese bombers were carrying out continuous air raids on targets in the area of the three-forked crossroads and also to the south of it. Sometimes these raids were carried out by groups of two or three aircraft, sometimes a single bomber dropped its load on a specific target. Thus, in the beginning of the afternoon the casemate which contained the machine gun of the section of 4-Inf. V near the three-forked crossroads was attacked by one Ki-48. The fortification received a direct hit, damaging the gun and causing two wounded.[52] A number of other Ki-48s attacked Major Teerink's command post and destroyed it, killing or seriously wounding several men. Major Teerink himself, having just returned from a visit to the Wates fortification with Captain Paardekoper, was killed in the air raid, too.[53]

The remainders of 2-Inf. II and 1-Inf. V withdrew through the heavy terrain, their route taking them across the mountain slopes east of the three-forked crossroads to the vicinity of the Tankoeban Prahoe hotel. As they were retreating there was initially no news from these units.[54]

The remaining armoured vehicle, commanded by Sgt L.W. Sibbald (Van Dongen Squadron), carried out a reconnaissance in the direction of the first line, but did not return. Afterwards it appeared that on its way back the vehicle had been attacked by a Japanese Ki-43 or Ki-51 and broken down. The crew survived the attack, but had to go back to the three-forked Tolhek crossroads on foot.[55]

The first information on the battle of 2-Inf. II and 1-Inf. V came at around 15:00 hrs, when Sub-Lieutenant Schouten of 1-Inf. V reported back to De Veer. In the morning Schouten had told Sergeant-Major Heffelaar that the situation was critical and that he was allowed to withdraw, but the advancing Japanese and the heavy firing had prevented him from reaching his own section. He had been forced to withdraw along with Heffelaar and a few men of his own section. Schouten did not know whether any troops had stayed behind in the first line, and if so, how many. He had passed an occasional brigade of 1-Inf. L.H. XXI to the east of the road during his retreat, but apart from them there were no further friendly troops there. Probably the Japanese were on their way, however, and most likely they would come in tanks along the road.[56]

De Veer briefly conferred with his staff and sub-commanders to see how the three-forked crossroads and the Wates fortification could be reinforced. Subsequently, at around 16:00 hrs, Captain Paardekoper received the order to organise the defence around the three-forked crossroads. The sections in the Wates fortification and the Den Ouden section were ordered to move to the three-forked crossroads. The only infantry reserve that could still be brought up was 10-4 R.I. (Teerink Group) at Lembang. This company, which had lost the confidence of almost everybody (see Chapter 4.2), was bombed by a few Ki-48s during its move up, upon which it withdrew on its own initiative. The sections responsible for the security of the Tankoeban Prahoe hotel and the many vehicles and supplies in the area had already been bombed at around 15:30 hrs, during which four men had been killed and several wounded. De Veer dispatched Lieutenant-Colonel H. van Altena to the staff of Bandoeng Group to explain the situation there and to press for a speedy arrival of the promised infantry battalion (see the previous chapter).[57]

Van Altena left at around 16:30 hrs. On his way over he passed the machine gun platoon of the Paardekoper company, one section of which was blocking the road near the hotel. He sent these men to the three-forked crossroads, too. All along the road, from the hotel to the south, even beyond Lembang, he saw soldiers on retreat. These were mostly small groups of men of Inf. L.H. XXI, who seemed to be on their way to Bandoeng, in chaos and not heeding anyone's orders. Groups of 2-Inf. I personnel were on their way to a collection point south of the hotel where Captain Kooistra had established a temporary command post.[58]

At 17:00 hrs while Paardekoper was still engaged in organising the defence, moving the Den Ouden section, the Japanese began their expected attack from the west on the three-forked crossroads. By this time, it had been thoroughly prepared by means of bombardments and strafings. Also, the 3rd Hiko Dan carried out bombardments in the environment of Lembang and the town itself, one of the targets there being the garrison kitchens, from where the food to the front troops was supplied. The kitchens were completely destroyed, forcing the men to resort to combat rations from the supplies in the battalion combat trains. The Japanese air activities, however, made it virtually impossible to bring them up.

There was also an attack on the position of 1-A. II Bg., near the Ursone farm south of Lembang. This attack was carried out by a number of Ki-48s and took place at around 15:00 hrs. One man was killed and a vehicle and some of the ammunition which was stacked next to the road were lost by direct hits. The section of 1-A. II Bg. which had been deployed as anti-armour defence east of Lembang did not suffer any losses in the attack. One of the two guns, however, was damaged and could not be used anymore. In the evening the section was pulled back to Ursone.[59] The battalion Inf. IV was attacked by 17:00 hrs at several kilometres from Lembang.

This battalion (minus) had been ordered in the morning by the staff of Bandoeng Group to move via Bandoeng to positions to the north of Lembang, but needed to be re-assembled first. Inf. IV was deployed near the Soemedang position and belonged to the force that was guarding the easterly access to the plateau. The men could find cover in the terrain just in time, and except for a few wounded, there were no casualties during the bombardment. A few of the parked trucks dispersed along the road, however, were lost and the road itself was also damaged in several places.[60]

Air support for the KNIL on day 2 (6 March)

After the morning mission flown by 242 Squadron the three operationally serviceable Hurricanes and all available Brewsters had been on readiness at Andir, idly. The number of operationally serviceable Brewsters increased to five in the course of the day. No combat orders were received by the units and only after the war would it become clear what had happened. Communications with the troops of Colonel De Veer had been severed at a crucial moment. Many, but not all, radio vehicles had been lost in the Japanese air raids, while the atmospheric conditions continued to be very poor. For that reason, in the morning of 6 March, a telephone line was laid between the PTT telephone exchange at Lembang and Colonel De Veer's command post near the three-forked Tolhek crossroads for the communication with Bandoeng Group. At around 10:00 hrs De Veer requested air support via this line from the staff of Bandoeng Group.[61]

Upon this Elt H.F. Zeylemaker, the ML liaison officer in the staff asked for precise target information and the position of own troops. This information was to follow as soon as possible. In the mean time, Zeylemaker and his RAF colleague Flight Lieutenant De la Perelle issued the necessary warning orders, on behalf of Pesman, to ML Command and BRITAIR. The idea was to first have the fighter aircraft carry out a support mission and at a later moment, when there was enough cover of cloud, have the two (at that moment) operationally serviceable Glenn Martins at Tasikmalaja carry out (if needed with an escort of fighters) an attack on the road from Soebang to the Tjiater position. Although during the earlier mission flown by 242 Squadron no targets had been observed on the road, the bombers could still render the road unsuitable as a supply route. The specific information from De Veer did not come. At around 10:30 hrs the telephone line with his command post broke down; the result of a Japanese air raid, it appeared later. It proved to be impossible to repair the line, and it was decided not to issue 1-Vl.G.V and 242 Squadron with any combat orders.[62]

A second attempt

In the afternoon a second attempt was made. The three Hurricanes took off at around 16:30 hrs for a patrol north of Bandoeng. Their assignment was to search the sector between Bandoeng and Tjiater for Japanese air activity and to attack any possible enemy aircraft that might find themselves in this area. In the mean time, the Brewsters were ready for take off for an attack on ground targets.

At around 15:30 hrs Colonel De Veer sent a dispatch rider with the available information on the course of the battle to Bandoeng

Group and requested air support. After having received this information, Zeylemaker conferred with Captain J.D. de Riemer of the ML Command, upon which it was again decided not give 1-Vl.G.V (and also 1-Vl.G.II at Tasikmalaja) any combat orders. It was absolutely unclear where and against what the ML pilots were to direct their attacks. It was even unknown whether there were any own troops near the Tjiater fortification. Only on the morning of 7 March did the confirmation come that the Japanese had driven the KNIL troops out of the Tjiater pass.[63]

While the mechanics of 1-Vl.G.V kept on firing up the engines of the Brewsters every half hour, 242 Squadron were flying their patrol north of Bandoeng. Julian, Parker and Lockwood immediately encountered Japanese aircraft. Lockwood was in the trailing plane and suddenly he spotted two aircraft. His warning over the radio was not heard and he turned away on his own for an identification. They appeared to be single-engine two-seater dive bombers (Ki-51s). He had to break off his attack on one of the two planes when the rear gunner managed to hit the radiator of his Hurricane. Lockwood landed safely at Andir.

Julian and Parker, in the mean time, had pursued their patrol, but after about half an hour in flight they suddenly found two Japanese fighter aircraft on their tails. Julian escaped and made it safely to Andir, but Parker's fighter received hits in the tail section, in a wing tank and in the plate of armour behind the pilots' seat. Parker made an emergency landing at Pameungpeuk. He had been lucky. There was a hole in the plate of armour, but the thick canvas harnass of his parachute (supplied by the ML) had stopped most of the fragments. The flight surgeon of the ML looked after the pilot and mechanics of the ML at the base made makeshift repairs to the Hurricane the following day, so that it could be flown over to Andir.[64]

In the mean time, Java Air Command had decided to relocate 242 Squadron to Tasikmalaja and to re-equip it with 12 Curtiss P-40E fighter aircraft, which were being assembled in the auxiliary workshop of the Technical Service of the ML there. The relocation of the remaining (three at the time) still operationally serviceable Hurricanes was to take place the following morning. There was already a damaged fighter at Tasikmalaja and also the Hurricane at Pameungpeuk was to be flown from there to this airfield. However, this aircraft had an accident while taking off in the morning of 7 March and was a total loss. The first P-40s would be ready in a couple of days. Tasikmalaja was also reinforced with anti-aircraft artillery and British ground defence personnel. In the afternoon of 5 March 1942 already two Troops of 21 LAA (eight 4-cm guns in total) had been sent from Andir to Tasikmalaja and in the afternoon of 6 March the complete 48 LAA, 239 Battery of 77 HAA, plus two 'infantry companies' (12 and 15 Battery) of 6 HAA left Bandoeng and Tjimahi. Also 49 Battery of 48 LAA (ex Kalidjati) which had been converted into infantry after the evacuation of Tjikembar and for this reason had already come under the command of the commanding officer of 6 HAA on 5 March, came along.[65]

The ground battle in the late afternoon and evening of 6 March

As was said above, the Japanese launched an attack at the three-forked Tolhek crossroads at 17:00 hrs. The infantry was approaching the three-forked crossroads through the terrain along the Tolweg, so it had to get past the positions of A. II Bg. After its reconnaissance towards the west the 2nd Battery had just manned the guns once more when the first mortar shell landed, upon which the guns were loaded with anti-personnel and soft targets shells. After the first volley, rapid fire was used on the gently sloping hill covered in kina saplings, down which the Japanese were advancing. The gun positions, however, began to receive heavy mortar and machine gun fire, and one gun after the other was taken out. There were several wounded and at least six men were killed. Within half an hour the first Japanese had infiltrated the positions and the guns had to be destroyed with a demolition charge, where this was still possible.[66]

The personnel of the 3rd Battery could not reach their position anymore. Captain Vos de Wael had got as far as 200 to 300 metres away from it when he encountered some of the men he had left behind, who told him that the battery had just been taken by the enemy. During this conversation the men were fired at by machine guns. Vos de Wael went in south-easterly direction, behind the artillery positions and found the rest of the men he had left behind and the men of the 2nd Battery who had managed to pull back along the road. In the mean time, Colonel De Veer and Major Teerink had died in battle along with many others.[67]

In the attack on the three-forked crossroads itself, the section of Ambonese recruits of Lieutenant Karreman was the first to engage in battle. Karreman was killed almost immediately and a part of his section was taken out. De Veer personally organised a counter-attack and to that end assembled several dozens of men around him. In the counter-attack not only he and his adjutant Captain F.H.F. Taatgen were killed, but also several tens of soldiers, mostly Ambonese recruits, were killed or wounded. They had counter-attacked with great fervour. Among the dead were also a number of infantrymen who had returned from the Tjiater fortification. The counter-attack had been successful and the three-forked crossroads and its direct environment remained in their own hands. Paardekoper took over command.[68]

At around 17:30 hrs the re-assembled personnel of both batteries of A. II Bg., commanded by Vos de Wael, as the battalion commander had been wounded, made an attempt to drive the Japanese from their own positions, during which action again a few gunners were killed. The opposition was so strong that they did not succeed in reaching the positions. When darkness fell, they pulled back under fire to the three-forked crossroads, where Captain Paardekoper had taken up positions with the remaining infantrymen.

Around 18:00 hrs the all-round defence of the three-forked cross-roads had been completed and 'Wates' had been evacuated success-fully. In the mean time, mortar fire had kept the Japanese at bay. At around 19:30 hrs Captain Vos de Wael and ten other volunteers from A. II Bg. joined the defenders. The other gunners went back to Lembang and from there to Bandoeng about half an hour later. The Japanese units did not make a second attempt to take the three-forked crossroads, probably because of the darkness. A reconnaissance along the Tolweg later in the evening showed that the Japanese troops even had retreated some distance, which allowed the KNIL troops to bring many wounded and dead within their position.[69]

Shortly before the Japanese attack on the three-forked crossroads Colonel De Veer had dispatched Lieutenant J.C. Stravers with Sergeant A.C. Worst of his command staff to Bandoeng Group, in order to request for medical aid for the defenders of the Wates fortification and the three-forked crossroads. Paardekoper did not have any medical orderlies, there were no emergency bandage packages, and doctors and medical personnel of the field dressing station in the Tankoeban Prahoe hotel were not allowed to go up to the first line. Around 21:30 hrs Paardekoper received a handwritten order, actually intended for Colonel De Veer, to hold out to the last man. The message also stated that in the course of the evening two companies coming from the west coast of Sumatra were expected, followed by three quarters of a not specified company. The latter unit probably was the infantry company of the Mobile Unit. These reinforcements never arrived.[70]

In the evening of 6 March by order of Major-General Pesman a defence line, under command of Lieutenant-Colonel H. van Altena, was improvised near Lembang. North-east of Lembang Inf. IV (minus) took up positions (behind a bridge in the road leading to Tolhek) and in a line south-west, south and south-east of Lembang a mixed bag of units, among which were Inf. IX and the two above-mentioned companies coming from Padang (west coast of Sumatra). For the rest there were only remnants of units that had only little combat strength left: the infantry companies formed of men of Inf. X, Inf. XIV and Inf. XV, that by now had been reorganised in the newly-formed battalions (minus) Inf. X and Inf. XV. Furthermore, there was the infantry company of the Mobile Unit, the remnants of the improvised companies that had been fighting the Japanese near the three-forked Tolhek crossroads and the section of cadets of Lieutenant Luteijn. At around 05:00 hrs on 7 March all units had taken up their positions, with the exception of Inf. XV. Shortly after midnight Paardekoper received orders to pull back to the Ursone farm, to the south of Lembang. The phased withdrawal, by truck with taking along all the wounded, began at around 02:00 hrs and went without any problems. The improvised position around the three-forked crossroads could be outflanked and isolated, and for this reason it was pointless to try and keep troops there. It was also possible to withdraw many of the supplies stored near the Tankoeban Prahoe hotel. The strong rear guard near the three-forked Tolhek crossroads did not have any contact with the Japanese either during its phased withdrawal via the hotel to Lembang.[71]

In the evening Major Wakamatsu held the environment of the Wates fortification and had taken the artillery positions along the Tolweg. However, he had to report to Colonel Shoji (who by now was in Djalantjagak) that by nightfall the enemy had "not entirely been taken out". Only during the night did his troops secure the pass. In the early morning the positions near the three-forked crossroads were found abandoned.[72]

In the evening of 6 March Colonel Shoji decided to launch his attack on Bandoeng in the early hours of the next morning, before the enemy could regroup. He moved up Egashira battle group from Soebang, which was to commence the attack via the road along the Tankoeban Prahoe hotel to Lembang. Wakamatsu battle group was to mop up the enemy to the west of the road and advance through the terrain in the direction of Lembang from positions just south of the three-forked Tolhek crossroads.[73]

The battle of the Tjiater pass on 5 and 6 March had cost some 300 dead, missing and wounded on the Dutch side. In 1948, after having recovered and reburied the mortal remains, the War Graves Service of the KNIL counted around 180 dead, including those who had succumbed of wounds later and a number of unknown Indonesian soldiers. Of this total, around 50 men had died at or near the three-forked crossroads and its vicinity. The Japanese losses amounted to about 200 dead and wounded. The battle had been fierce, and especially the men of 2-Inf. I, 2-Inf. II, 1-Inf. V, 4-Inf. II, 4-Inf. V, A. II Bg. and the reserve officer candidates and Ambonese recruits had put up an excellent fight. It had been in vain, though.[74]

Bandoeng Group of the KNIL, as well as Java Air Command, had come to the end of their tether. Although the units of West Group were pouring onto the plateau by now, they could not be deployed the first few days to come. The new P-40 fighter aircraft of JAC at Bandoeng and Tasikmalaja were still being assembled. In the second half of the afternoon of 6 March 1942 General Headquarters was definitively forced to conclude that the race against time had been lost. They had needed just a few days more. The last preparations were made for the departure by transport aircraft to Australia of a group of government representatives and senior civil servants in the night of 6 on 7 March. Several staff officers of General Headquarters were given permission to join the party. At around 02:15 hrs Major-General Van Oyen and his adjutant Lieutenant H. Creutzberg LL.M were among the passengers of the penultimate Lockheed Lodestar to take off from the concealed Boeabatoeweg landing strip in south Bandoeng.[75]

The use of Air power on day 2 (6 March)

In particular it was the almost total lack of air support on the allied side and the abundant own air support that enabled the Japanese taking of the Tjiater pass. By making a creative use of Air power the troops of Major Wakamatsu, managed to breach the first line in the northern end of the Tjiater pass, albeit with heavy losses. The 3rd Hiko Dan put the KNIL battalion on the east flank to flight, virtually without the help of own infantry. This took about five sorties of Ki-51 assault aircraft.

There were a further circa four Ki-51 sorties against the enemy troops on the west flank.

On 6 March the 3rd Hiko Dan sent out a total of 70 sorties in support of Colonel Shoji: 21 Ki-51 sorties (ten missions), 28 Ki-48 sorties of the 75th Sentai and 21 Ki-48 sorties of the 90th Sentai. These 49 bomber sorties were flown in five missions. Most of the sorties were interdiction missions, directed against enemy troops with which there was no direct contact in combat. As cover for the Ki-48s some 30 fighter sorties were flown over the area of operations. To a modest extent the Ki-43 pilots also carried out strafings of soldiers and vehicles on the roads. The final two missions of the 75th and 90th Sentais, flown on the afternoon of 6 March, each only counted seven Ki-48s, with six Ki-43 fighters flying combat air patrols during both missions.

However, the losses were relatively heavy with two Ki-48s downed (plus several damaged aircraft). The operations of 242 Squadron with regard to the suppression of Japanese air activity had been reasonably effective, but this had little impact on the outcome of the battle because of the relatively large numbers of available Ki-48s (about 18) and Ki-51s (about 14). Because the allied air forces had stopped their bombing raids and, most importantly, fighter sweeps against Kalidjati, the operational strength of the 3rd Hiko Dan had not been eroded any further and the air brigade had instead been able to repair a number of damaged Ki-48s and to add to its strength. There only remained a shortage of fighter aircraft.[76]

The KNIL had had to go virtually without air support on 6 March. Through sheer bad luck and failing communications the allied air forces had not been able to fly any bomber sorties whatsoever, and a mere seven fighter sorties, which were combat air patrols combined with reconnaissance. They had, however, not suffered any losses, with the exception of an accident with one Hurricane. In the evening and night of 6 March the ML and RAF did not fly any more missions.

In the late afternoon of 6 March JAC was disbanded and its tasks were handed over to the Operations section of General Headquarters, the personnel being transferred to various other staffs and units. There was no further need for an operational coordination with regard to the deployment of ML and RAF units, given the small number of remaining units and aircraft. BRITAIR and COIC also closed their doors. The personnel of BRITAIR and the RAF/RAAF personnel of COIC left for Tasikmalaja, including Flight Lieutenant V.B. de la

Perelle of BRITAIR, who had been detached with the Operations section of Bandoeng Group. The Operations Staff of JAC, so busily engaged in mission planning in late February and early March, had hardly anything left to do. Besides, all the air forces that were still left remained at the disposal of Bandoeng Group during daylight hours and were also controlled by the staff of that Group.[77]

In relation with this matter Major-General Van Oyen, the commander of JAC, fell out with Major-General Pesman, the commander of Bandoeng Group. Van Oyen had already objected on 5 March and reiterated his protest more forcefully in the morning of 6 March against what he considered the injudicious deployment of the combat aircraft during daylight hours. In the morning of 5 March the combat aircraft had not been committed against the Japanese advance towards the Tjiater position, while the enemy troops could only make use of one narrow road and, had they been attacked, would have suffered considerable losses. The allied fighters had also been barred from flying fighter sweeps against Kalidjati.

Apart from necessary reconnaissance missions, Major-General Pesman had wanted to use the allied fighter aircraft to bind the Japanese aircraft over the battlefield and thus boost the morale of his troops, which were exposed to continuous attacks from the air. Van Oyen, who, in this respect, had the full support of Air Vice-Marshal Maltby (commander of BRITAIR) considered this to be inefficient and a waste of aircraft and crews. By means of fighter sweeps the few allied fighters could, albeit indirectly, be of much more assistance to the troops and the chances of own losses would be considerably smaller. The army commander, however, supported Pesman. By way of compromise, JAC was given permission to carry out a fighter attack on Kalidjati in the early evening.[78]

As was mentioned above, Major-General Van Oyen was assigned on 6 March to evacuate by transport aircraft to Australia along with a group of government representatives and senior civil servants. He had been approached about this before, but he only wanted to leave with the very last plane. It was to be the penultimate aircraft. General Headquarters had prepared a partial capitulation and was going to send a negotiator to the Japanese lines as soon as Lembang was in danger of falling. The reason for this was that by order of the Governor-General of the Netherlands East-Indies it was forbidden to fight in and around Bandoeng (a city which was full of refugees). Van Oyen was ordered by the army commander to take up command of all the KNIL units and men present in Australia. These were mainly ML units, which had to be organised in such a way as to enable a continuation of the struggle from Australia with the allied forces.[79]

At Tasikmalaja the crews of 36 Squadron and 1-Vl.G.II were on stand-by to carry out bombing assignments. After the closing down of JAC, General Headquarters, however, gave no orders to the air forces. At Andir 1-Vl.G.V was standing ready with the five operationally serviceable Brewsters available at that moment to carry out a low level attack in the evening twilight on Kalidjati. The attack was cancelled. The evening and night bombardments on Kalidjati in conformity with the JAC strategy were also discontinued.[80] At the end of the day on 6 March the various afdelingen and squadrons had the following numbers of assigned and operationally serviceable aircraft at their disposal:[81]

Table 26

Unit	Assigned	Operationally Serviceable	Remarks
242 Squadron	5	3	
1-Vl.G.V	5	5	
2-Vl.G.IV	0	0	Awaiting re-equipment
36 Squadron	3	2	
1-Vl.G.II	2	2	
3-Vl.G.III	3	0	
1-Vl.G.I	1	0	Awaiting re-equipment
2-Vl.G.III	1	0	Ibid.
Total	20	12	

Logistic problems at the ML and RAF

Whereas on the Japanese side the number of operationally serviceable aircraft could be kept up, in spite of losses, it was rapidly decreasing on the allied side. Not only had the number of operationally serviceable aircraft on the allied side become very small, the possibilities for giving air support were decreasing fast for logistical reasons. Thus, ML Command insisted on not committing 1-Vl.G.V unnecessarily, as there were no more spare engines for the Brewsters and hardly any specific spare parts left. The situation was so serious that on 4 March a small team of mechanics, led by fighter pilot Ensign F. Pelder, had been sent by car to the deserted (and already destroyed on their arrival) Semplak near Buitenzorg. They were to collect as many spare parts left behind and still usable as could be found on this former home base of Vl.G.V. The next day Pelder returned to Andir with a truck load full of spare parts, but 1-Vl.G.V would nevertheless only be able to carry out operations for a few days more. There was enough ammunition and fuel for the Brewsters.[82]

The situation was slightly better at 242 Squadron, as most of the Hurricanes had come into use as late as February 1942, which made them six months younger than the average Brewster of the ML. The spare part situation was reasonable, although some spare parts were very scarce indeed, and there were no more spare propellers. The squadron had been able to evacuate much materiel from Tjililitan to Andir and also 81 Repair and Salvage Unit of the RAF had been evacuated in time from Tjililitan. The ML was still capable of providing the squadron with 100 octane fuel (the Brewsters used 91 octane fuel), but was unable to supply oxygen for use by the pilots at high altitude. The only oxygen factory in Java had been destroyed shortly after the Japanese landings and already as early as 5 March the ML had exhausted its store.[83]

The situation was equally serious with regard to the bombers. 36 Squadron already used the qualification 'just serviceable' to describe the situation of the ready aircraft. There were hardly any spare parts left for the Vildebeestes and all remaining aircraft were already up for major maintenance on 6 March. However, no more facilities existed in Java to do it, making it practically impossible to operate with the Vildebeestes any longer.[84]

Even for the Glenn Martins certain spare parts had become scarce. When the war broke out the ML had relatively large stores of specific aircraft and engine spare parts for all types of Glenn Martins (WH-1, -2, -3 and -3A), but the intensive use had caused them to dwindle rapidly. Thus, there were only a few spare engines for the WH-3 and -3A types left. The one remaining Glenn Martin of 1-Vl.G.I, the WH-3 M-542, had been repaired with partially hand-made spare parts. Likewise, at 2-Vl.G.III, the broken aileron of the WH-2 (either the M-520 or the M-521) that had been damaged on 5 March had to be replaced by a hand-made wooden one.[85]

In spite of all this, the ML would nevertheless carry out a mission with the remaining Brewster fighter aircraft to support the troops at Lembang the next day. Subsequently, in the morning of 8 March 1942 two Hurricanes carried out another road reconnaissance in support of the concentration of the allied troops at Garoet.

Summary of the events of 6 March 1942

The course of the land battle went unfavourably for the KNIL, but not dramatically so. In the evening of 6 March, however, there were insufficient troops left for a successful defence of the southern end of the Tjiater pass (Wates fortification and the three-forked Tolhek cross-roads). The new first line, which had been established during the night of 5 and 6 March, directly behind the Tjiater fortification in the northern end of the pass, was breached by the Japanese in the morning of 6 March after heavy fighting. Early in the morning the combat aircraft of the 3rd Hiko Dan had for the most part driven the troops of Inf. L.H. XXI from the area to the east of the road to Lembang and at around 10:00 hrs the companies of Teerink Group to the west of the road had to withdraw because of heavy losses and the fact that the ammunition for the infantry could not be suppleted anymore. Victory had not come easily for the troops of Major Wakamatsu.

The Japanese had learned from their earlier failed attempts (on 5 March) to breach the first and second lines of the KNIL in the Tjiater fortification and wanted to avoid bogging down in the pass. Wakamatsu's troops, therefore, went through the difficult terrain on the slopes of the Goenoeng Tankoebang Prahoe (volcano) to the southern end of the pass. Although Japanese patrols had been keeping the men in the Wates fortification (under construction) occupied since 12:30 hrs, this position, too, was outflanked and a direct attack from the west on the three-forked Tolhek crossroads was launched.

The attack was carefully prepared by means of bombardments and strafings, mainly carried out by the Ki-48 bombers and the Ki-51 assault aircraft of the 3rd Hiko Dan. Systematic attacks on anything that looked like reserves, artillery, supply units and command posts and direct attacks on the defenders in the positions in the southern end of the pass caused a large number of dead and wounded and pre-vented the scarce reserves the KNIL had from being moved close to the three-forked crossroads.

Not until 17:00 hrs did the Japanese attack on the three-forked crossroads come, the batteries of the mountain artillery somewhat to the west of the three-forked crossroads being the first to come under fire. The attack failed, in part because of a counter-attack carried out under personal command of Colonel De Veer. Together with several other men De Veer was killed and many others were wounded. The Wates fortification and its second line near the three-forked crossroads stayed in Dutch hands. The Japanese made no further attempts to attack during the night. The last defenders in 'Wates' withdrew around 18:00 hrs to the three-forked crossroads. Shortly after midnight Captain Paardekoper, who had taken over command of the defenders after the death of Colonel De Veer, was ordered to pull back on Lembang, where in the mean time a new defence line was being improvised. The positions around the three-forked crossroads could be outflanked and had to be given up. By sunrise on 7 March the Japanese infantry found the positions had been abandoned.

The remaining combat aircraft of JAC, in particular the fighter aircraft, had hardly been committed during the daylight hours of 6 March and if they had seen any action, it had mostly been in an inefficient manner. Although the fighter aircraft of the RAF shot down a few Ki-48 bombers over the battle field, JAC could have done much more for the troops by flying fighter sweeps against Kalidjati. In the period from 2 March up to and including 4 March the 3rd Hiko Dan saw its numbers of operationally serviceable aircraft decrease by the day. When, after 4 March the fighter sweeps against Kalidjati stopped, the KNIL troops were faced with an increase in the number of sorties that the 3rd Hiko Dan could fly in support of Colonel Shoji's troops. The fall-out about the deployment of the allied fighter aircraft between Major-Generals Van Oyen and Pesman, however, had been decided to the advantage of the latter by the army commander. In the late afternoon of 6 March 1942 JAC and also BRITAIR closed their doors. For all practical purposes, the battle for the Bandoeng plateau was over.

* * *

CHAPTER 4.5
The Battle on 7 March 1942

Introduction

In the morning of 7 March 1942 at around 09:30 hrs a meeting was convened at the Algemeen Hoofdkwartier–General Headquarters (AHK) on the strategy to be pursued. Apart from the army commander,

Lieutenant-General H. ter Poorten, the meeting was attended by Major-Generals R. Bakkers (Chief of Staff), W. Schilling and J.J. Pesman, Colonel E.T. Koppen, the artillery commander of West Group, and Lieutenant-Colonel W.P. van Veen, the Deputy Chief of the General Staff. How could the enemy at Lembang still be dealt a blow? A problem was the explicit wish of the Governor-General that there would be no fighting in Bandoeng and its direct surroundings. The positions at Lembang were already so close to Bandoeng that the artillery could not be used anymore without the battlefield becoming extended towards the edge of the town.

Schilling's troops were still not ready to be deployed and Pesman's only 'fresh' troops at Lembang were the reinforced Inf. IX battalion and two companies coming from Sumatra. The other units at Lembang had not much combat strength left in them due to the earlier fighting. There were hardly any allied aircraft left to give support and there was a massive enemy air superiority. The new P-40 fighter aircraft of Java Air Command were not ready yet. In short, it was impossible that the position at Lembang would hold for a long time, but that was not the intention, anyway.

Already in the afternoon of 6 March General Headquarters had concluded, on the basis of a report on the course of the battle from Major-General Pesman, that the battle against time had been lost. The southern end of the pass could not be held with such small numbers of troops, and as Pesman had predicted, the positions there had to be given up in the very early hours of the morning on 7 March.

The retreat of West Group

In the evening of 4 March the retreat of West Group was already in full swing. At around 18:30 hrs that night Blackforce broke off the fight near Leuwiliang, where up to that moment the Japanese had been successfully repelled, the enemy troops having suffered considerable losses. Under cover of rain fall the allied brigade fell back on Soekaboemi, where the main force arrived in the early hours of 5 March.

Apart from some small skirmishes, the KNIL units defending the line Batavia-Buitenzorg to the north of the brigade, had not seen any combat yet, and because of the retreat to the Bandoeng plateau they would not see any in the future. A unit that did engage with the enemy was a rearguard of Inf. XI, in positions near a river crossing at Tjibadak, along the route to Soekaboemi, when they made contact

Map of the Lembang defence line and the Japanese advance

with the Japanese Sato battle group in the night of 6 on 7 March. The
Japanese reported losses.[1]

The retreat of West Group went via Buitenzorg and was at
first conducted in a reasonably orderly fashion. This changed when
the columns began to move from Buitenzorg to Bandoeng and its
surroundings. It grew into chaos that did not end in disaster only
because of the heavily clouded weather and almost total absence of
Japanese air activity. Schilling's division staff first moved to Buitenzorg
on 5 March and from there to Patjet. Major-General Schilling arrived
at Bandoeng on 6 March at around 11:30 hrs. By order of General
Headquarters the main force of the Blackforce was concentrated that
day at Oedjoengbroeng, to the east of Bandoeng. On 7 March also
some of the KNIL units of West Group arrived on the plateau, among
which was the main force of Inf. XI.[2]

After having been informed by the staff of Bandoeng Group about the course of the battle on the plateau, Schilling was invited the next morning to attend the meeting at General Headquarters, in order to give his view on the continuation of the battle. Schilling advocated a continuation of the battle at Lembang, but his ideas were not shared by most of the other attendants of the meeting. In particular Major-General Bakkers and Major-General Pesman saw nothing in his plans, mostly because of the explicit wish of the Governor-General which prevented the defenders from committing their artillery and an almost total absence of own air support.

On the basis of a draft capitulation order already written on 6 March it was decided to offer a partial capitulation of the troops on the plateau only, as soon as Lembang was in danger of falling. In connection with this it was also decided to withdraw all usable troops which had not been engaged in the fight as yet from the plateau within 24 hours.[3]

The defence of the Lembang position still only served a very limited objective, which was creating enough time for a timely reorganisation of all unengaged troops into guerrilla combat groups to the south of the plateau. As early as 3 March the Governor-General had received instructions from the Dutch Government in London with regard the continuance of the struggle. One of the instructions referred to the prohibition of a total surrender. The fighting was to continue to the utmost and at an appropriate moment to change over into guerrilla warfare. Already in the afternoon of 6 March Schilling had begun to make preparations for a possible guerrilla to the south of Soekaboemi. After the conference on 7 March he had all movements in easterly direction stopped and began to concentrate the main force of the KNIL element of West Group in the environment of Tjiandoer as a preparation of the guerrilla war. At 19:00 hrs Schilling left Bandoeng with his staff. Blackforce left in the night of 7 on 8 March for the area near Garoet in order to continue the battle to the south-east of Bandoeng.[4]

The position at Lembang

In the evening of 6 March Major-General Pesman gave Lieutenant-Colonel H. van Altena the command of a new position to be established by him at Lembang. Under his command came Inf. XV (minus), two companies coming from Sumatra, as well as the troops that were to be withdrawn from the three-forked Tolhek crossroads (see the previous chapter). In front of Van Altena's troops and on his flanks (not under his command) came Inf. IV (minus), the reinforced Inf. IX and Inf. X (minus). Inf. IV (minus) was the first to take up positions to the north-east of Tjiboerial in the late afternoon and early evening of 6 March.[5]

The remnants of the improvised companies at the three-forked Tolhek crossroads, under command of Captain J.L. Paardekoper, retreated without any problems in the direction of Lembang in the very early hours of 7 March. At around 05:00 hrs the sections of reserve officer candidates, KMA cadets and Ambonese recruits had taken up positions again near and east of the Ursone farm, somewhat south of Lembang. The KMA cadets section, commanded by Lieutenant A. Luteijn, which had already arrived at Lembang on 6 March, took up positions in the northern edge of the small town.[6]

At around 02:00 hrs Inf. XV (minus), under command of Major K. Anten, arrived at Lembang. This unit consisted of remnants of 2-R.I., which had been defeated on 3 March in the attack on Kalidjati (see the previous part: The Battle of Kalidjati). The battalion (minus) was given a sector south-west of Lembang, north of the village Batoereok, but would never take up this position. Near Batoereok there were already two companies coming fom Padang (west coast of Sumatra), commanded by Captain H.M.C.H. Bremmer and Captain T.A. Willemse, who were now, however, going to defend a sector west of Batoereok which partially ran along the road from this village to the village Tjitespong.[7]

Inf. X (minus), commanded by Major B.P. de Vries, also composed of remnants of 2-R.I., arrived at Tjikidang, east of Lembang, at around 05:00 hrs, where already the infantry company of the Mobile Unit (ME) was positioned, under command of Captain J.H.J. Brendgen. The reinforced Inf. IX, commanded by Major J.W.G.A. Hoedt, had been withdrawn from the Tjisomang fortification and had arrived at Tjisaroea in the night of 6 on 7 March. The reinforcements assigned to this battalion consisted of one battery of A. I. Bg., an extra infantry section, several machine gun and mortar sections and an anti-armour section. At the staff of Bandoeng Group this was called Hoedt Group. This unit subsequently moved somewhat in easterly direction towards the village Tjitespong, some two kilometres as the crow flies west of Lembang. At the time of the Japanese attack on Palembang and Banka this unit was located in Banka and Billiton. It had not been committed then, but had suffered losses during the retreat to Java from Japanese air raids on the evacuation ships. After this, it had been taken in reserve.

Hoedt Group was to carry out a counter-attack against the Japanese flank, but a proposal to commence the attack immediately after the movement was rejected by the staff of Bandoeng Group. Instead, the Hoedt Group as well as Inf. X were given the order to reconnoitre the start position for a counter-attack on the west and east flank of the expected enemy assault force, respectively, which was to begin as soon as the Japanese attack on Lembang had started. In the mean time, the two battalions were to patrol intensively in the forward terrain.[8]

The available allied air support

The air support during daylight hours that could still be provided to the KNIL troops was extremely limited. At Andir there were five Brewsters of 1-Vl.G.V operational and at Tasikmalaja there were two Glenn Martin bombers of 1-Vl.G.II and two Vildebeestes of 36 Squadron RAF. In the early morning a further three Glenn Martins of 3-Vl.G.III and the three operationally serviceable Hurricanes of 242 Squadron were sent to the latter base.[9]

At around 05:00 hrs the patrol of 3-Vl.G.III landed at Tasikmalaja with the Tlt P.J.P. van Erkel, Tlt J. Coblijn and Vdg M.P. Bosman crews. Their orders were to be on stand-by for a bombing assignment. The Technical Service at Andir had delivered the three aircraft in the course of the night after repairs of the bomb damage incurred on 3 March. In the dark one of the Glenn Martins got off the runway due to a brake that blocked, rammed a barbed wire obstacle and incurred damage to the right wing. A second got a bamboo mat, used to strengthen the muddy taxiway but which had got loose, in one of its propellers during taxiing. The plane was not damaged but it took a while to remove the bits and pieces of the mat, which had wound itself around the propeller hub. Then it appeared the Glenn Martin had sunk in the mud and needed to be pulled out again.[10]

242 Squadron took off from Andir shortly after 3-Vl.G.III. Five of the pilots of this unit had by now evacuated to Australia with the very last Lodestar at around 03:00 hrs. They were Sqn Ldr R.E.P. Brooker, Sgt G.J. King and three wounded or sick pilots: Plt Off T.W. Watson, Sgt J.A. Sandeman Allen and Sgt G. Hardie. On board of the transport plane were also Elt H.H.J. Simons of 1-Vl.G.V and Elt K. Akkerman an observer of 1-Vl.G.I, plus seven civil servants. The three Hurricanes left Andir at around 05:00 hrs, led by Sqn Ldr I. Julian. His trailing pilots were Plt Off W.M. Lockwood and Sgt I.D. Newlands.

The rear-party of the ground crew left for Tasikmalaja somewhat later in the morning. The aircraft had just been dispersed and covered with branches at their new base when the Japanse Army air force bombed Tasikmalaja for the last time at 05:30 hrs.[11]

Japanese air action on day 3 (7 March)

Ten Ki-48s of the 75th Sentai, escorted by six Ki-43 fighter aircraft of the 59th Sentai carried out the attack. This time the results were better (see the description of the attack carried out on 6 March described in the previous chapter). The Japanese concentrated on the pens holding aircraft. Two of the recently arrived Glenn Martins of 3-Vl.G.III went up in flames, and on top of that a Vildebeest of 36 Squadron RAF, a Lockheed L212 trainer of the Vlieg- en Waarnemersschool–Flying and Observer School (VWS) of the ML and one of the four Hurricanes at the airfield were total losses.[12]

In the morning of 7 March Colonel Shoji consolidated his positions and the preparations for the advance on Lembang were started. Reconnaissance flights of the 27th Sentai showed that the KNIL had established new defence lines there. Apart from Wakamatsu Group, Shoji now also committed Egashira Group, which had just been taken back from Gedonggede to Soebang. This had taken a considerable period of time, as not only the distance was relatively large, but also because the movement of the units of the battle group had to take place as much as possible after sunset, in view of the still present danger of allied air attacks.

The concentration at Soebang was only completed in the night of 6 on 7 March. For this reason, the attack on Lembang could not begin before the afternoon of 7 March. Egashira marched up along the road of the Tjiater pass in the direction of Bandoeng, whereas Wakamatsu went through the terrain to the west of this road. Wakamatsu's advance was through difficult terrain and for that reason went slowly. At around 15:30 hrs the Japanese troops launched their attack on Inf. IV near Tjiboerial to the north-east of Lembang.[13]

In the morning (from around 06:00 hrs onwards) the air support of the 3rd Hiko Dan had initially consisted only of reconnaissance and attack missions on the KNIL troops near Lembang by Ki-51 assault aircraft, of which at any time there were only two to four airborne. This could, therefore, hardly be termed intensive air raids on troops. It had changed between 10:00 hrs and 11:00 hrs when the support by the 75th and 90th Sentais with Ki-48 light bombers began. In the late morning and in the afternoon the two sentais flew three missions with 15 aircraft each time. The 59th and 64th Sentais carried out combat air patrols over the area of operations, the first two missions with nine Ki-43s and the last mission with seven fighters. Two fighter aircraft were lost shortly after 15:00 hrs in aerial combat (see below). All in all, the 3rd Hiko Dan put in a maximum effort.[14]

Flights of Ki-48s also supported Colonel Shoji's troops indirectly by bombing several positions of the KNIL in the south-east and south-west of the plateau and several road and railway junctions. Thus, in the afternoon a number of Ki-48s bombed Padalarang railway yard. By these actions the transport of supplies and movement of reinforcements was effectively restrained, as was the shipment of supplies in westerly direction to Tjiandoer on behalf of the guerrilla force that Schilling was forming.[15]

On this day Japanese combat aircraft made a few flights over the direct vicinity of Andir. In the early morning the first of these planes appeared, but no attack followed. The anti-aircraft artillery could only fire a couple of rounds before they disappeared again. In the afternoon Japanese Ki-48s approached from the direction of Lembang. This time

Kawasaki Ki-48 bombers of the type operated by the 75th and 90th Sentais. (Private collection, William H. Bartsch)

the 8-cm Bofors guns of the Andir North position as well as those of Andir South fired at the bombers, which quickly turned away and the anti-aircraft artillery did not score any hits. Andir was not attacked, but in all probability this had not been the intention in the first place.

Late in the afternoon a new formation of Ki-48s approached the base from the direction of Lembang and this time Andir was successful. One Ki-48 was lost from fire from the 8-cm section of the Andir North position. The men of Andir North saw bits and pieces coming off the plane and later ML personnel found wreckage of the exploded plane to the north of the base. Shortly after this, the anti-aircraft gunners saw how a formation of Ki-48s was bombing a target in Bandoeng. At around 17:00 hrs four bombers of the 75th Sentai bombed the southern part of the centre of the town, the so-called Aloon-aloon (a square with a large stretch of grass). A mosque and a public shelter received direct hits. The staff of Bandoeng Group and General Headquarters interpreted the attack as a demonstrative warning.[16]

The land battle in the afternoon of 7 March

In the afternoon the 3rd Hiko Dan kept up its thorough preparations of the coming advance of Colonel Shoji's troops on Lembang. The intensity of air attacks was staged up, and apart from an occasional group of Ki-48s, Ki-51s carried out many dive attacks with light bombs and machine guns. In support of these attacks Ki-43s now began to carry out low-level attacks on ground targets. The Ki-51s and Ki-43s mainly concentrated their attacks on dug-in enemy infantry. The air raids on the exhausted troops were very effective. In spite of the fact that there were only few casualties, morale suffered terribly form the continuous attacks from the air. When it began to rain at around 16:00 hrs and the aircraft had to be taken back, Shoji's troops launched their attack. Within a few hours the resistance melted away almost completely.

Battalion Inf. IV (minus one company and a machine gun platoon, which were at Bandoeng, and half of the mortar platoon, which was left at Soemedang, but strengthened with a section of three anti-tank guns) defended a position behind a small river spanned by a demolished bridge in the road from Tjiboerial in the direction of the Tankoeban Prahoe hotel and Tolhek. Behind the bridge in the terrain left and right of the road was the 1st Company, Menadonese and Ambonese soldiers, commanded by Captain Mulder, minus a section, but strengthened by a machine gun platoon and a machine gun section (six 6.5-mm machine guns in total) and an anti-tank group of one anti-tank gun positioned on the road and a few tank rifles (2-cm anti-tank rifles) next to the road. The road from Tjiboerial to this position had a mountain ridge on the west side and a bamboo wood on the other side. In this wood the 3rd Company (minus a section), Timorese soldiers, commanded by Elt Kingma, was positioned, supported by two machine guns and (positioned near Tjiboerial) a mortar group with three mortars. From the edge of the wood there was a good view over the empty fields between the wood and the small river the Japanese were expected to cross. Close to Tjiboerial, in a bend in the road, two more anti-tank guns were positioned. The command group of Inf. IV was near a crossroads on the edge of Tjiboerial, where also an infantry section was positioned as a reserve. Another infantry section guarded the road from Tjiboerial to Boeabathoe. From around 07:00 hrs the troops were attacked several times by dive bombing and strafing Ki-51s. Also Ki-48 bombers carried out at least one attack. Between 15:00 hrs and 15:30 hrs the first Japanese patrols appeared, upon which the defenders opened up fire immediately. At the same time two Brewsters of the ML carried out an attack on the Japanese troops which were approaching the bridge along the road from the direction of the Tankoeban Prahoe hotel. The fighter aircraft were, however, driven away by enemy fighters (see below). Then, the Japanese infantry attack began. It was repelled by intense firing.

By 16:00 hrs, in light rain, the Japanese attacked again in force and this time the infantry was preceded by three light tanks, which shot up the positions. Also mortars (grenade launchers) were brought up. The Japanese used the same tactics as during the breach of the line occupied by Teerink Group behind the Tjiater fortification. The intensive Japanese tank and mortar fire seemed especially targeted at the fire support of the 1st Company, as it destroyed all the anti-tank weapons and destroyed or rendered unserviceable most of the machine guns. There were several dead and wounded. The Japanese infantry was prevented from crossing the small river, but at approximately 16:30 hrs the fight was almost over. A couple of Ki-51s started dive bombing and shooting up the positions again. Captain Mulder was personally operating the last serviceable machine gun. He directed a dispatch rider to the command post at Tjiboerial with the message that he would have to withdraw at short notice because the Japanese were repairing the bridge and would cross with tanks. The battalion commander immediately gave his companies the order to withdraw. When the attacks stopped, Mulder's troops retreated along the road.[17]

The battalion had been at it continually since 1 March, and, after having carried out two attacks on the Japanese landing area at Eretan Wetan (see the previous part: The Battle of Kalidjati), had been moved to and fro. Due to a movement first to Tomo (4 March), then to Soemedang (5 March) and finally Lembang (6 March), many of the men in the unit had hardly slept for three consecutive nights. The battalion commander, Lieutenant-Colonel L. Vriesman, had warned Major-General Pesman in a telephone conversation in the morning of 7 March that his battalion would probably not be able to resist long in case of a Japanese attack and ought to be relieved in the afternoon. Vriesman was ordered to hold out as long as possible, as there were no troops to relieve him. Vriesman used the initial success to pull his companies back, an operation that went by the book, orderly and with taking along equipment and ammunition. Group by group the infantrymen pulled back on the assembly area with the vehicles. Afterwards it was realised that the mortar group was missing, but the group (mistakenly not warned) made good its escape by truck and on foot.[18]

At around 17:00 hrs the first column of Inf. IV vehicles (of the trains at Lembang) left for Bandoeng. Vriesman stopped at Lieutenant-Colonel Van Altena's command post at the Ursone farmhouse to report the withdrawal of his battalion to Pesman. The telephone line had been down for some time now, and radio communication had been impossible for an hour now (probably due to atmospheric circumstances). Vriesman, exhausted as he was, had a serious quarrel with his colleague Van Altena, who reproved him for having retreated without good reason. At about 17:30 hrs Major-General Pesman, who had moved to a command post in the Isola hotel near Lembang, reported to General Headquarters that the Lembang line had been breached.[19]

In the course of the afternoon the battalions Inf. X (minus) and Inf. XV (minus), composed of the remnants of 2-R.I., largely fell back on Bandoeng on their own initiative. Inf. XV disintegrated almost completely under the impact of the enemy air attacks. Major Anten failed to get his companies take up the assigned positions in the tea and kina gardens north of the village Batoereok. His vanguard had already been put to flight in the morning after an attack by Ki-51 assault aircraft, leaving behind several loaded and fully operational machine guns, and from 10:00 hrs onwards his companies on their way to their positions were bombed by Ki-48s.[20]

The two companies which had been reinforced with machine gun sections were assembled by Anten around noon in the village Tjihideung at some one and a half kilometre west of the asphalt road to Lembang. Even this failed to some extent. Some of the men at Tjihideung refused to stay there when Japanese planes were spotted once more and left for Bandoeng. These were mainly men of the original Inf. XIV, which, after the failed attack on Kalidjati (see the previous part: The Battle of Kalidjati) and a march through the terrain which had lasted several days, could only be reassigned again on 6 March.[21]

Inf. X (minus) made contact with the Japanese in the afternoon, when at around 16:00 hrs they received fire coming from a northerly direction, probably from several Japanese patrols. Major De Vries ordered to take up the starting position for a counter-attack on the Japanese flank which had been reconnoitred earlier. However, when groups of men coming from the Tjiater fortification came passing through their positions, complete sections of Inf. X joined them spontaneously in their retreat. Only the section of Menadonese soldiers, coming from the original Inf. X (Captain Ohl's 2nd Company) remained in their positions. Like the other battalion commanders, De Vries was ordered at around 18:00 hrs to break off the battle, and with the remaining Menadonese men he marched back to Bandoeng after darkness had set in.[22]

Hoedt Group (the reinforced Inf. IX battalion) to the west of Lembang was ready to launch a counter-attack on the enemy's west flank. There was intensive patrolling by a number of detachments in the forward terrain in order to intercept any Japanese infiltrating patrols. But there were none whatsoever. The terrain to the north-east of the starting position of the battalion was difficult and the advance of Wakamatsu Group lagged behind that of Egashira Group. Only from 17:00 hrs was there fire contact with Japanese patrols. When darkness set in, in the pouring rain, several sections tried to take out Japanese patrols, but they were unsuccessful. Hoedt was ordered to cease firing at 18:00 hrs. Under cover of darkness Major Hoedt withdrew via Lembang. The own troops at Lembang appeared to have already fallen back (see below), upon which Inf. IX moved to Tjimahi.[23]

The air support for the KNIL on day 3 (7 March)

In the morning of 7 March the team of fighter pilots of 1-VI.G.V, commanded by Elt P.A.C. Benjamins, at Andir was relieved by Capt.

J.P. van Helsdingen, with a team of eight pilots mostly coming from the former 2-Vl.G.V. At around 05:00 hrs the 'fresh' pilots reported in the Noordhangaar, upon which Van Helsdingen asked for volunteers for the four Brewsters that were still available. The fifth assigned fighter aircraft had caught fire during the warming-up of the engine and could not be used for the time being. All pilots volunteered and the afdeling commander appointed: Elt A.G. Deibel, Vdg J.F. Scheffer, Vdg P.R. Jolly and Sgt G.M. Bruggink. The other pilots were sent to their quarters, for the time being. Tlt P.A. Hoyer stayed in case the fifth Brewster would come available in the course of the day. This proved to be out of the question, however. Van Helsdingen left for the ML Command by car to see what assignments could be expected of them.[24]

At around 09:30 hrs in the morning of 7 March an assignment for air support from Major-General Pesman came in at the ML Command and BRITAIR. Japanese aircraft were attacking the defence line of the KNIL near Lembang. Colonel E.T. Kengen (commander of ML Command and acting commander ML, and promoted in the beginning of March to nominal Major-General, without being aware of this) advised against the execution of the action. It was already broad daylight and the skies were full of Japanese aircraft. Kengen was convinced that the few remaining fighters were very unlikely to be able to effectuate any relief for the ground forces and that such an attack would probably cost the lives of most of the pilots that were assigned to it. Pesman, however, had a message sent to the effect that it was his most express wish that the order be executed. When Van Helsdingen heard this at the ML Command he shouted, "The assignment will be carried out, but it is suicide." After some discussion, the afdeling commander drove back to Andir.[25]

The attack was to take place around noon. In the course of the morning Elt H.F. Zeylemaker phoned Captain P. Valk, the station commander at Tasikmalaja, on behalf of Pesman, and ordered him to have the still available Hurricanes of 242 Squadron rendezvous with the Brewsters of 1-Vl.G.V near the target area at 12:00 hrs, an order which he rescinded again shortly before the take-off time. In the mean time, Van Helsdingen had agreed with Pesman to fly the mission at a later time, as he wanted to wait for more suitable weather conditions (clouds) to give a chance of survival to the pilots of his patrol. In a telephone conversation the general personally gave Van Helsdingen permission to do this, as, on second thoughts, the commander of

Bandoeng Group realised that there was not the slightest chance of success and he showed an understanding of the great risk the fighter pilots would be facing. He asked Van Helsdingen to try and see if he could fly the mission in such a way as to boost the morale of the own troops a little, which (according to a message of Van Altena) had rock-bottomed by now.[26]

Sqn Ldr Julian at Tasikmalaja saw nothing in the mission and, when given the choice by Zeylemaker, chose not to take part. The British pilots were extremely tired, there were only a few Hurricanes and pilots available anymore, and the ground personnel had not yet arrived.[27]

The knights' flight

Although Van Helsdingen had been barred since 2 March by the ML Command from flying along operationally as a result of a lack of experienced afdeling commanders, he assigned himself as patrol commander and took over Vdg Jolly's aircraft. The latter was already sitting in his cockpit and had to get out again. At 15:00 hrs the four Brewsters took off for a strafing of the Japanese troops to the north-east of Lembang. By now there was heavy cloud over Bandoeng. The take-off did not go smoothly. For unknown reasons Van Helsdingen broke off his take-off from the short north-south runway and susbsequently taxied along with the other aircraft to the main runway. After this, the take-off of the patrol went without problems, Deibel (in the B-3110, Van Helsdingen's usual plane) and Scheffer (in the B-395 E) trailing and at an altitude some 200 metres higher than Van Helsdingen and Bruggink (in the B-3101 and B-3120, respectively).[28]

Shortly after take-off Deibel and Scheffer encountered a Ki-48 bomber. Deibel fired at the plane until it was visibly hit and disappeared out of sight in a steep dive. Almost immediately after this nine Ki-43s appeared, a patrol of three coming from the direction of the Tangkoebang Prahoe volcano, another three-plane patrol from the direction of Boerangrang mountain and a third patrol from a position west of Boerangrang mountain.[29]

Three of the Japanese fighters went after Van Helsdingen and Bruggink, who had just reached the road north of Tjiboerial leading to the Tankoeban Prahoe hotel and had begun to machine gun the Japanese infantry there. They could not make a second strafing run. Bruggink accelerated and warned Van Helsdingen with hand gestures

Sketch of an 8-cm anti-aircraft gun of "Andir Noord" by O.A.O. Kreefft with the four Brewsters in the air leaving for the final mission of 1-Vl.G.V. (Private collection, P.C. Boer)

that they were having fighter aircraft on their tails. He broke away to the right and then escaped in a ravine to the east of the road. Bruggink returned safely and with an undamaged plane via the plateau to the east of Bandoeng to Andir, where he was the last to land.[30]

Two of the three Ki-43s had dived down for an attack on the two Brewsters. Just like Bruggink Van Helsdingen had gone down to tree top level, a dangerous manoeuvre in the rough climbing terrain and with the clouds hanging very low against the mountain. Apparently, he did not follow Bruggink into the ravine and went missing. His plane has never been found.[31]

Deibel and his wing man Scheffer were attacked by three or four Ki-43s after they had been able to surprise the third Japanese patrol. Deibel first attacked the middle of these three Ki-43s, which was hit and when down sidewise. Subsequently, he attacked the leading fighter plane, whose pilot had just begun a sharp turn. Before the Ki-43 was in an attacking position, however, Deibel had got the plane in his sights. Constantly firing he raced headlong towards it, pulled up just in time and shot over the cockpit of his opponent at a distance of some two metres. The visibly hit Ki-43 went down and Deibel pulled up and went for cover in a thin cloud. When the ML pilot came out of the cloud and wanted to recharge the blocking nose machine guns of his Brewster, he suddenly saw another Ki-43s arc of fire. His plane was hit in the oil tank and oil came streaming over his canopy and also into the cockpit. His opponent had gone, and Deibel saw no Ki-43s or Brewsters anymore.[32]

Deibel dived into a ravine and managed to put his damaged plane on the ground at Andir. During the landing a damaged wheel flew off the B-3110, which got off the runway in a ground loop and was damaged on the wing. Scheffer landed about a minute after him, not having scored any hits in the aerial battle with the six Japanese fighter aircraft. After a short fight he had dived into a cloud in order to escape from the superiority in numbers. His Brewster remained undamaged. Scheffer confirmed that one of the Ki-43s had indeed been shot down by Deibel. He also reported that Deibel had shot down the Ki-48 but observers at Andir who had followed the fight did not see a crash.[33]

The aerial battle cost the 3rd Hiko Dan two Ki-43s and two pilots, for whom after the capitulation of the KNIL a small monument was erected. Pilot Sgt Yasuhiko Sakakibara of the 59th Sentai was one of the casualties, whose plane, the 3rd Hiko Dan thought at the time, had been downed by anti-aircraft fire. An unknown pilot of the 64th Sentai was also killed. It is possible that one of these pilots flew into the terrain in the chase of Captain Van Helsdingen. The plane chasing Van Helsdingen was fired at (but without visible result) by several machine gunners of Inf. IV.[34] The circumstances for aerial combat close to the ground were extremely unfavourable. Bruggink had had all the luck in the world when, having dived into the ravine, he was confronted with a wall of low clouds hanging against the mountain at the end of it. He narrowly missed the mountain face when he climbed out through the clouds at full throttle.[35]

The first thing the ML fighter pilots got to hear when they returned at Andir was, "You have been up for nothing, we are going to capitulate." By now the news had reached Andir that a staff officer had been sent to the Japanese troops at Lembang with a white flag to negotiate. The personnel of the ML afdelingen largely withdrew to their commandeered quarters in Bandoeng, waiting for the cessation of hostilities, which was probably going to take place the following day.[36]

The last flight of 1-Vl.G.V was going to go into history as the knights' flight. By Koninklijk Besluit–Royal Decree (K.B.) of 14 July 1948 Nr 5 Lieutenant Deibel, Ensign Sheffer (posthumously) and Sergeant Bruggink were entered into the registers of the Militaire Willems-Orde–Military Willems-Order (MWO) as Knights 4th class for valour, skill, and loyalty shown on 7 March 1942. By the same Royal Decree Captain Van Helsdingen, who had earlier been appointed to Knight 4th class, was promoted posthumously to Knight of the Military Willems-Order 3rd class. The above for "... once more distighuishing himself in battle by exceptional acts of valour, skill and loyalty....".[37]

The end of the ground war

The troops of Lieutenant-Colonel Van Altena, south of Lembang, did not come into action anymore. After the report of the retreats the interpreter Captain J. Gerharz, present at Pesman's command post in the Isola hotel, on behalf of Major-General Pesman gave the order to Van Altena to cease fire at 18:00 hrs and to pull back on Bandoeng. Around 18:30 hrs the Japanese units occupied the northern edge of Lembang. An hour later Gerharz arrived with a white flag at a Japanese commandpost in the first line.[38]

In the evening of 7 March the troops near Lembang withdrew to Bandoeng and subsequently moved partially to Tjimahi. The remaining battery of A. II Bg. (1-A. II Bg. with three operational guns left) had already been pulled back on 6 March towards the southern edge of Bandoeng, and accommodated near the Tegallega race course. On 7 March Lieutenant-Colonel G.J. Reerink, the artillery commander in the staff of Bandoeng Group, announced that A. II Bg. would not be deployed anymore for the time being.[39] Japanese troops of Egashira Group occupied Lembang in the course of the evening and Wakamatsu Group subsequently advanced to the high terrain south of this town, from which they could look down on Bandoeng.[40] The capitulation was only a matter of time and it would be impossible to limit it exclusively to the troops on the Bandoeng plateau.

The main force of the West Group (minus Blackforce), insofar it had already arrived on the plateau, had been sent away from there to the vicinity of Tjiandjoer. The troop movements went on throughout the evening and night. Major-General Schilling himself left Bandoeng

The house near Kalidjati airfield where the capitulation talks took place. (Private collection, P.C. Boer)

with his staff at 19:00 hrs. The conditions for a guerrilla war, however, were not favourable and the combative Schilling already had to give up his attempts to continue the battle from an area south of Soekaboemi on 8 March. Blackforce and the RAF and British Army personnel who had come along with the brigade capitulated together with the KNIL. In the morning of 9 March 1942 the allied unit commanders received the conditions of capitulation, effective as of that day. In order to prevent any misunderstandings the allied troops formally surrendered on 12 March 1942.[41]

The end of the air war

On this day the 3rd Hiko Dan supported the troops with a total of 90 sorties. The 27th Sentai flew 20 sorties (ten missions), the 75th and 90th Sentais 45 sorties (three missions) together and the 59th and 64th Sentais flew 25 fighter sorties as cover for the bombers. Furthermore, as desribed above, the 75th Sentai bombed a target in Bandoeng with four Ki-48s.[42]

The allied air forces had come to the end of their tether on 7 March 1942. In the late afternoon the situation with regard to the assigned and serviceable aircraft was as follows:[43]

Table 27

Unit	Assigned	Operationally Serviceable	Remarks
Bombers			
1-Vl.G.I	1	0	
1-Vl.G.II	2	2	
2-Vl.G.III	1	0	
3-Vl.G.III	1	0	
36 Squadron	2	2	
Fighter aircraft			
1-Vl.G.V	2	2	
2-Vl.G.IV	3	0	2 P40s airworthy, but not operationally serviceable
242 Squadron	4	2	
Total	16	8	

There were two further Glenn Martins (the M-523 of 2-Vl.G.III and the M-585 of 1-Vl.G.II) at the Technical Service which were almost ready after major repairs, but still needed to made operationally serviceable at the afdelingen.

Detachments of Vl.G.I and Vl.G.III were at Bangalore in British India and at Archerfield in Australia, respectively, to take over new North American B-25 Mitchell bombers. Only a few aircraft had been handed over, however, and the crews had not yet started transition training. An estimate of the ML was that by the end of March 1942 the first B-25s would be operational from NEI airfields. On 7 March the first three P-40s for 2-Vl.G.IV were flown in at Andir, one of which went back to the Technical Service with engine trouble. On this day one of the assembly teams shipped two of the new planes over to Andir from a location on the edge of Bandoeng to assemble the wings at the Technical Service. The ML Command assumed that the fighter pilots of the ML, used to flying American materiel, would need only a few days of training on this type.[44]

It was too late. In the afternoon of 7 March, shortly after 16:00 hrs Colonel Kengen began a round of telephone calls with the various commanders at Andir ordering them that, without any message to the contrary, at 18:00 hrs a start should be made with rendering unserviceable the remaining aircraft there. Via the commander of Tasikmalaja he ordered 1-Vl.G.II to evacuate the one Glenn Martin for which a bomb bay tank was available there to Australia. That same afternoon 36 Squadron RAF was given permission by Air Commodore W.E. Staton of BRITAIR (now at Tasikmalaja) to try and evacuate the two remaining Vildebeestes to Birma.[45]

At 1-Vl.G.I the one remaining Glenn Martin, the M-542, was almost ready after extensive repairs. A bomb bay tank was waiting to be built in, so that an attempt could be made to evacuate the aircraft to Australia. The order for this came from Kengen, who wanted to evacuate as many ML personnel as possible to Australia with it, in order to reinforce the Vliegschool–Flying School and the Vl.G.III detachment at Archerfield, which had moved there earlier. With bleeding hearts the mechanics set about destroying all the fabric rudder panels and slashed the tyres. Personnel of the RAF still built in the tank the next day and started repairing the destroyed fabric of the ailerons, elevator and rudder. The Station Commander of the RAF at Andir, however, forbade the evacuation attempt for fear of reprisals of the Japanese against those who would stay behind.[46]

One Glenn Martin of 1-Vl.G.II, with a crew of 3-Vl.G.III and several passengers on board, was the only one to evacuate in the night of 7 March. This aircraft, the M-585, had just been fitted out with new engines at the Technical Service, but still required some minor repairs. In the afternoon of 7 March Elt A.B. Wolff, the commander of 3-Vl.G.III, asked Colonel Kengen for permission to fly the plane to Australia. He got it, but at around 16:30 hrs Kengen ordered him to take off as soon as possible, but in any case before 18:00 hrs, and if necessary to go to Tasikmalaja first to finish the repairs. This, however, was impossible in view of the nature of the repairs and the building in the bomb bay tank. Kengen did not rescind this order, but gave his unofficial blessing. The M-585 took off at 23:45 hrs, with Tlt Van Erkel and Elt Wolff as first and second pilot, respectively, and seven crew members and passengers. The plane reached Broome in northern Australia safely. Among the passengers was the future army commander KNIL Captain S.H. Spoor.[47]

On 8 March at 01:45 hrs the two Vildebeestes took off from Tasikmalaja. The Glenn Martin of the Hofmeyster crew, the bomb bay tank built-in but not yet connected, remained on the ground. In the end, neither the pilots of 1-Vl.G.II, nor those of Vk.A.1, dared to make an evacuation attempt to Australia. They had no maps, or any intelligence on the wind and their fuel would just be sufficient at best. RAF personnel, however, were interested in giving it a shot.[48]

In the morning of 8 March 1942 the base commander Captain P. Valk received the order to render unserviceable the remaining aircraft. In many cases this was done extremely thoroughly. Also the 12 P-40s that were being assembled were destroyed. The Glenn Martin of the Samson crew of 1-Vl.G.II was first battered with an axe, a hammer and other tools and later fired at with one of aircraft's taken-out 7.7-mm machine guns. RAF personnel kept on making an attempt to finish the work on the aircraft of the Hofmeyster crew until after the capitulation. This effort had to be abandoned as several senior RAF officers feared reprisals against the personnel that would be left behind after an evacuation attempt.[49]

In the early morning of 8 March 1942 242 Squadron still flew an armed reconnaissance with the only two remaining operationally serviceable Hurricanes on behalf of the British and Australian units that were concentrated in the environment of Garoet. After their return these aircraft were also destroyed.[50]

$$* * *$$

CHAPTER 4.6
Analysis and Conclusions

Endo's and Shoji's gamble

The location of the Japanese Shoji regimental battle group, behind the allied lines near Batavia and Buitenzorg and in a position that made it impossible for the Japanese main force, which had landed much farther to the west to lend any support, was vulnerable. If something went wrong, Shoji could be defeated, his superiors feared. The plan to capture Kalidjati airfield (without own air support) on the first day of the landings, however, worked out well and in the late afternoon of 2 March 1942 the 3rd Hiko Dan of the Japanese Army air force stationed the first fighter and assault aircraft at the base. Colonel Shoji frankly admitted that the survival of his troops largely depended on the air support of the 3rd Hiko Dan. That air brigade, commanded by Major-General Endo, however, had been manoeuvred in an extremely vulnerable position at Kalidjati.

In contrast to what Japanese believed initially, the allied air forces had not been defeated at all. For this reason, the Japanese Army air force, in cooperation with the Navy air force, organised a large-scale air raid against Andir airfield. It took a considerable period of time to arrange the planning for this attack, but at the end of the morning of 3 March over 50 bombers escorted by fighter aircraft from Palembang in southern Sumatra, Celebes and Bali, attacked Andir. The base was severely damaged and several aircraft were lost. Nevertheless, the Japanese soon found that the results were insufficient.

The attack on Andir did result in the closure of the base for the rest of the day (3 March), though, which prevented the ML, the RAF and RAAF from lending air support to KNIL troops that were carrying out a major attack directed at recapturing Kalidjati air base. This attack was repelled by the 3rd Hiko Dan without committing Japanese ground forces. The KNIL troops that had been involved in the attack, however, had not been taken out sufficiently and especially the enemy motorised unit (the Mobiele Eenheid–Mobile Unit and Teerink Group of the KNIL) south of Soebang formed a source of concern for Shoji.

Subsequently, on 4 March, Colonel Shoji committed Egashira Group to carry out his primary mission, the severing of the line Batavia-Bandoeng. After occupying Tjikampek, this reinforced battalion (minus) was to advance on Krawang and the large road bridge near Gedoenggede. The action failed when the KNIL blew up the bridge in front of the Japanese vanguard's eyes. Wakamatsu Group, deployed to secure Egashira's advance on Tjikampek, was largely withdrawn to Kalidjati and Soebang as soon as possible on the same day, in view of the danger of a renewed allied attack on Soebang.

Already on 4 March it was obvious that there were still considerable allied air forces left, and the vulnerability of the 3rd Hiko Dan at Kalidjati became apparent when Hurricanes of the RAF shot down a Ki-43 fighter aircraft and destroyed or damaged a number of Ki-48 bombers and other aircraft on the ground there. Because of this the 3rd Hiko Dan carried out renewed air raids against Andir on 4 and 5 March and against Tasikmalaja airfield on 6 and 7 March.

For Colonel Shoji's troops as well as the aircraft groups of Major-General Endo the danger of new attacks remained present. Their positions were and remained vulnerable. If the enemy got the opportunity to consolidate his troops, Shoji feared envelopment and saw only one way out: an attack on Bandoeng as soon as possible, a move comparable to Field Marshal Rommel's desert war approach in northern Africa. In spite of the obvious risks attached to this manoeuvre, he got permission from his superiors, albeit in retrospect. On 5 March Shoji attacked the Tjiater pass from the direction of Soebang with all the air support he could get from Endo.

The relative strength in the air

The 3rd Hiko Dan did not have any warning systems, there were no radar or listening posts and it could only try to prevent attacks on Kalidjati by carrying out bombing raids on enemy air bases and flying combat air patrols, and that only during the day. The Japanese air brigade, however, was faced with a serious shortage of fighter aircraft as a result of the allied air raids on 2, 3 and 4 March. This shortage became acute when on 5 March the missions in support of the ground troops in their advance on Bandoeng began, when the protection of Kalidjati air base as well as the vulnerable Ki-48 bombers was to be carried out by as few as 10 or 11 Ki-43s.

At that moment the ML and the RAF had available seven and a day later even nine operationally serviceable Brewsters and Hurricanes. So, with regard to the fighter aircraft, there was no (great) Japanese air superiority. However, the Java Air Command did not realise this, especially because the Japanese Ki-51 assault aircraft, single-engine Army Co-operation aircraft which were relatively slow but very manoeuvrable, were often taken for fighter aircraft.

On the allied side, on the contrary, there was a great shortage of operationally serviceable bombers to carry out air raids on Kalidjati in the evening and nightly hours and around sunrise and sunset. In the morning of 4 March JAC had 13, but one day later only eight operationally serviceable bombers at its disposal. After the arrival of the 90th Sentai at Kalidjati, the 3rd Hiko Dan had approximately 14 to 15 operationally serviceable Ki-48 light bombers on 4 and 5 March. The normal payload of the Ki-48 was 300 kilogrammes, that of the Glenn Martins of the ML and Vildebeestes of the RAF 450 kilogrammes, when armed with 50-kilogramme fragmentation bombs. This resulted in a Japanese air superiority as of 5 March already measured in terms of numbers and dropping capacity.

Kalidjati was a very large base, with plenty of possibilities for spreading out aircraft in several dispersal areas. Taking the 3rd Hiko Dan out of action by means of bombing raids, therefore, implied a large number of sorties. Given the small quantities of allied bombers, generating such numbers at short notice was impossible. With daylight fighter sweeps, however, the number of sorties against Kalidjati was increased considerably, which constituted at least a partial compensation for the effects of the Japanese air superiority.

The strategy of General Headquarters and the relative strength on the ground

The almost complete loss of the reinforced 2-R.I. (about 3,500 men) during the failed recapturing of Kalidjati, caused a serious shortage of troops on the side of the allied land forces in western Java. General Headquarters (AHK) opted for a withdrawal of West Group (amongst others consisting of 1-R.I. and the allied Blackforce brigade) from the western part of western Java (the Buitenzorg-Batavia line), in order to commit it on the Bandoeng plateau as a reinforcement of Bandoeng Group. This was an extremely complex movement over large distances through mountainous terrain which began on 4 March. The first units were concentrated on the plateau on 6 March, but could not be deployed for the first four days. It fell to Bandoeng Group, therefore, to stop the gaps for the time being, that is, denying the Japanese access to the plateau by defending the passes. West Group and Bandoeng Group were to be combined into one battle group, which would not only be able to defend the plateau, but which would also be capable of carrying out sallies to neutralise the Japanese units. First on the list was the regimental battle group of Colonel Shoji, which had landed at Eretan Wetan.

In the battle for the access to the plateau the KNIL had superiority in numbers of ground troops. The regimental battle group of Shoji only amounted to some 3,000 men, including the combat train. At the time of the Japanese landings in Java Bandoeng Group of the KNIL had approximately 5,900 battle-ready troops, a number which increased further in the days following to about 9,000 men, although the remnants of the reinforced 2-R.I. and one of the three infantry companies of Teerink Group (the reserve of Bandoeng Group) included in these numbers had little combat value left after the failed attack on Kalidjati on 3 March.

In contrast to Colonel Shoji's troops, however, the KNIL troops could not be concentrated and had to defend multiple passes. In principle the Japanese attack could take place along three different routes, of which the one via Poerwakarta and the Tjisomang fortification, as well as that from Soebang via the Tjiater fortification were the most probable. The KNIL defended the passes from well prepared positions and in order to approach them the Japanese could only make use of narrow roads, often without much side terrain, with (wet) rice paddies on one or both sides. The route to Bandoeng the least hazardous for the Japanese was that through Soebang via the Tjiater pass and Lembang. Shoji's attack remained a very risky affair. The Japanese Army air force, however, proved that air power could amply outweigh the above-mentioned disadvantages when the ground forces are focused on and trained on cooperation with the air arm. This was hardly the case in the KNIL, although the Air support coordination on staff level was up to the mark.

The strategy of Java Air Command

The greatest threat for Shoji consisted of the vulnerable position of the 3rd Hiko Dan at Kalidjati, and, by extension, the still remaining allied air forces. Java Air Command was fully aware of this. On 2 March 1942 ML Command had drafted a report on the strength of the enemy who had landed at Eretan Wetan, which concluded that it came down to only 5,000 maximum, or rather 4,000 men, and that, given this relative weakness, it would make the Japanese heavily dependent on support from their air forces. In the morning of 5 March General Headquarters had sent out air reconnaissance missions to establish that the enemy force had not been reinforced in the mean time. Already from 2 March onwards JAC had pursued the strategy of carrying out maximum bombing missions in the evenings and nights and around sunrise and sunset and flying periodic fighter sweeps against Kalidjati during the hours of daylight. On top of that the ML and RAF were flying support missions for the KNIL during the day, mostly armed reconnaissance sorties. The strategy proved to be effective and the 3rd Hiko Dan at Kalidjati saw its numbers of operationally serviceable aircraft decrease as a result of enemy air attacks. Of the enemy aircraft transferred to Kalidjati in the period of 2 March up to and including 4 March 1942, 69 in total, only about 41 were operationally serviceable at the beginning of the day on 5 March. Apart from that the Japanese Army air force lost a number of transport planes. The commander of the 3rd Hiko Dan was very anxious with regard to any renewed fighter sweeps. They did not come, however.

On 4 March the remaining allied air forces were so small in numbers that the JAC commander wanted to commit them in a concentrated fashion only. For his primary objective he chose the Japanese combat aircraft stationed at Kalidjati. By putting out of action as many Japanese aircraft as possible the KNIL could be supported in an efficient manner, albeit indirectly. As soon as the Japanese troops began their advance on Bandoeng or were concentrated prior to an attack, the air forces would shift their focus of attention towards the Japanese ground forces. The KNIL and the ML and the RAF in western Java were not trained in requesting and delivering close air support, respectively, while no radio contact was possible from the ML and RAF fighters with the troops on the ground. Consequently, giving more direct support to the ground forces was impossible unless the exact location of the forward line of own troops was unambiguously clear.

Initially, General Headquarters welcomed Major-General Van Oyen's proposal, but the commander of Bandoeng Group, Major-General Pesman, objected with the army commander. The consequence of this 'quarrel of the generals' was that as of 5 March the remaining combat aircraft were made fully available to Bandoeng Group during daylight hours. To an extent JAC had been out-manoeuvred.

The battle of the Tjiater pass

The battle of the Tjiater pass lasted two days and began on 5 March 1942 at around 09:00 hrs with the first Japanese air raid on the Tjiater fortification in the northern end of the pass. The battle for possession of the pass ended in the early hours of 7 March with the Japanese troops entering the (by now deserted) KNIL positions in the southern end of the pass. Japanese troops of the battle group commanded by Major Wakamatsu fought themselves a way through the Tjiater fortification on 5 and 6 March, and subsequently launched an attack on the positions of the KNIL in the southern entrance to the Tjiater pass near the so-called three-forked Tolhek crossroads.

In the afternoon of 5 March Wakamatsu Group (approximately 1,000 men, including the support units) attacked the reinforced

2-Inf. I (about 250–300 men) of the KNIL. They put up an excellent defence and managed to hold out in the second line of the Tjiater fortification. In the night of 5 and 6 March the company had the section of the second line they occupied still firmly in their hands.

In the late afternoon and evening of 5 March a new defence line was established directly behind the second line of the fortification. Some of the reinforcements that had been moved up, however, were able to take up their positions only by daybreak of 6 March. Besides, in the morning of 6 March the anti-armour and anti-aircraft defences and signals with the first line still needed to be established. This was not to be, however. Soon after sunrise on 6 March the Japanese infantry again attacked.

To the west of the road running through the Tjiater fortification Teerink Group (two companies) had taken up positions and to the east of the same road was Inf. L.H. XXI (two companies and a company minus), around 950 men in total, including the support units. At the southern end of the Tjiater pass another position was improvised, with a first line in the Wates fortification, which was still under construction, and a second line near the three-forked Tolhek crossroads, where the second line of the Wates fortification had been planned. Due to a lack of troops in Bandoeng Group 'Wates' and 'Tolhek' were manned by a mere 400 troops (apart from the two mountain artillery batteries positioned near the three-forked crossroads), mostly KMA cadets, reserve officer candidates and Ambonese recruits of an Infantry Depot.

On 5 March the 2-Inf. I was not bothered too much by air attacks from the 3rd Hiko Dan and even managed to shoot down a Ki-48 bomber and to hit another. Besides, the troops witnessed a Ki-48 being shot down in front of their position by a British Hurricane. The impact on the battle from the 3rd Hiko Dan, however, changed radically the following day. Wakamatsu was confronted by a strongly defended prepared position and with the help of a forward command post of the 3rd Hiko Dan, which moved along with his own battalion staff, in the morning of 6 March committed Ki-51 assault aircraft and Ki-48 bombers against the enemy troops to the east of the road. This allowed him to concentrate his troops against Teerink Group to the west of the road, which at that moment lacked both anti-aircraft and anti-armour defences.

The opposition of the two companies, which had been reinforced with machine gun sections, however, was tenacious. It took an air raid by Ki-51s and an action of several tanks to break the resistance. At around 10:00 hrs, having suffered severe losses and it being impossible to be resupplied with ammunition, Teerink Group had to disengage from the fight. To the east of the road Inf. L.H. XXI had already been chased out of their positions by air raids. The extremely exhausted men, coming from central Java, who had been on the move since 1 March and had scarcely enjoyed any rest and had had to spend the night out in the cold of the elevated Bandoeng plateau, had already been receiving the first Japanese fire while they were still taking up their positions in the early morning. When shortly after this the 3rd Hiko Dan attacked, their morale broke and the majority of the men took flight.

The main force of Wakamatsu Group advanced through the difficult, very hilly terrain to the west of the road in southerly direction and around the Wates fortification. The Japanese avoided using the road through the Tjiater fortification in order to prevent the advance from bogging down inside the pass. In the mean time, the 3rd Hiko Dan made an effort to take out the defence of the southern end of the pass and as many of the enemy artillery, reserves, logistic units, command posts and the like in the rear area as possible. In view of the time Wakamatsu needed to accomplish his advance through the heavy terrain, the air brigade could take ample time for this. The Ki-51s and especially the Ki-48s wreaked havoc, causing dozens of casualties and susbstantially eroding the morale of the defenders. At around 17:00 hrs came the expected attack on the three-forked Tolhek crossroads, which was defended mainly by reserve officer candidates and Ambonese recruits. The Japanese attack failed. In a successful counter-attack, however, Colonel W.J. de Veer, the commander of the troops in the fortifications and the rear area, was among those who lost their lives.

Shortly after midnight on 7 March the remaining defenders fell back on Lembang, where a new defence line was improvised. In fact this was only intended to gain some more time before the enemy would be offered a partial capitulation of the troops on the plateau. Tolhek was too easy to envelop and isolate and was abandoned without a further fight. Both the KNIL troops and Colonel Shoji's troops suffered considerable losses in the battle of the Tjiater pass. Given their means and the enemy air superiority, the KNIL troops, with the exception of Inf. L.H. XXI, had performed well. The defenders had hardly seen any of their own air forces on 6 March, which had quite devastated morale.

Cooperation between ground and air forces

Up to 5 March the ML afdelingen and the RAF squadrons supported the KNIL mainly indirectly by means of attacks against Kalidjati airfield, which had been taken in use by the 3rd Hiko Dan. The intention was to lower as much as possible the number of operationally serviceable Japanese combat aircraft, a strategy which was successful. General Headquarters did communicate on the activities and results of the air forces with Bandoeng Group, but the latter did not pass this on to the commanders of the sub-ordinate KNIL units. Had this been done in any more or less elaborate way, the disadvantage of JAC's strategy with regard to the morale of the KNIL troops might well have been partially compensated for. The troops in the Tjiater position were aware that allied aircraft attacked Kalidjati regularly as they looked down on the base from their posts high up on the edge of the plateau. In the southern end of the Tjiater pass and farther south, nobody saw anything of the efforts of the crews of the allied air forces.

The course of the land battle on 5 and 6 March was closely related to the deployment of Air power by both the belligerents. As was mentioned above, this deployment on the allied side, at least during daylight, was the responsibility of the KNIL, more particularly the staff of Bandoeng Group. The commander of the troops in the Tjiater fortification and subsequently the commander of the troops in the area of operations (the fortifications in the Tjiater pass and the rear area) could request air support through this staff. The head of Operations of the staff of Bandoeng Group also gave direct orders to the ML and RAF. Inside the staff there were liaison officers of the ML and RAF to coordinate and advise on the deployment of the air forces. In particular the deployment of fighter aircraft by the KNIL, however, can be characterised as too little and inefficient, whereas the deployment of the combat aircraft for air support with the Japanese opponent can only be called abundant and efficient.

In view of the number of still available aircraft (on 6 March, for example, there were still eight fighter aircraft available at 05:00 hrs), the ML and RAF actually flew only few assignments in support of the troops. The execution of several assignments could not go through because of bad weather, a Japanese air raid, not being able to identify any targets in a preparatory reconnaissance, or lack of information on the position of own troops. As the survey below will indicate, however, most fighter aircraft were on stand-by for most of the daylight periods. The numbers of bomber sorties also stated in it exclusively refers to attacks on Kalidjati carried out in the evenings and nights or early mornings until sunrise. Several sorties with Glenn Martins of the ML against targets on the road from Soebang to the Tjiater fortification were cancelled because the bombers were stuck in the mud at Tasikmalaja (one sortie by sunrise on 5 March and two by sunrise on 6 March).

Table 28 Numbers of sorties of allied fighter aircraft and bombers

	Fighters		Bombers		Total	Remarks
	ML	RAF	ML	RAF		
5 March	0	4	3	6	13	
6 March	0	9	0	0	9	Two sorties aborted
7 March	4	0	0	0	4	
8 March	0	2	0	0	2	

During the fighting for the Tjiater pass and Lembang the allied air forces carried out the following support missions for the KNIL (Bandoeng Group).

Realised support missions (aircraft actually taking off):

5 March: two sorties by 242 Squadron (armed road reconnaissance Lembang-Tjiater).

6 March (morning): six sorties by 242 Squadron (binding of enemy aircraft and reconnaissance; one crashed during take off and one returned).

6 March (afternoon): three sorties by 242 Squadron (binding of enemy air forces and reconnaissance).

7 March: four sorties by 1-Vl.G.V (strafing of enemy troops north-east of Tjiboerial).

The situation at the 3rd Hiko Dan on 5 and 6 March was a completely different one. The operationally serviceable aircraft flew large numbers of sorties. Besides, the Japanese aircraft were committed more efficiently, according to a tested doctrine for air-ground cooperation. The 3rd Hiko Dan carried out the following number of sorties in support of the advance on Bandoeng:

Table 29   Numbers of sorties of Japanese combat aircraft at Kalidjati

	Ki-51	Ki-48	Ki-43	Total	Remarks
5 March	23	25	28	76	
6 March	21	49	ca 30	ca 100	
7 March	20	45	25	90	
8 March	–	–	–	–	Only 'demonstration flights'

The allied fighter aircraft were occasionally deployed for carrying out armed road reconnaissance missions and on 6 March for binding enemy aircraft over the battlefield. They were NOT deployed by Bandoeng Group to carry out attacks against the Japanese troops that were approaching the Tjiater fortification from Soebang in the morning of 5 March, nor were they assigned to fly fighter sweeps against Kalidjati. In particular the latter type of attack had proved to be very effective on 3 and 4 March in putting Japanese aircraft out of action. The commander of Bandoeng Group, however, was against such a deployment and wanted to keep the fighters in reserve for support missions to his troops. Because the air attacks against Kalidjati stopped the 3rd Hiko Dan was able to keep the number of operationally serviceable aircraft up to standard, in spite of the losses it had suffered, as the survey below indicates:

Table 30   Estimated numbers of operationally serviceable fighters and bombers 3rd Hiko Dan at Kalidjati (KD)

	Fighters	Bombers	Remarks
4 March	10	14	After fighter sweep by 242 Sq
5 March	11	15	
6 March	11	18	
7 March	11	18	
8 March	11	18	

Numbers of transferred and lost fighter aircraft and bombers

To KD	19	30	In period 2–4 March 1942 (incl.)
Total loss	7	7	In period 2–7 March 1942 (incl.)

Conclusions

With their attack on Bandoeng via the Tjiater pass Colonel Shoji and Major-General Endo took a considerable risk. However, in all probability, not launching an attack was deemed a greater risk by both commanders. Kalidjati might have to be evacuated by the 3rd Hiko Dan, with all the consequences of such a move for Shoji's troops. Success or failure of the advance through the Tjiater pass heavily depended on air support, while the 3rd Hiko Dan found itself in an extremely vulnerable position at Kalidjati of all places, the allied fighter sweeps, in particular, wreaking havoc. These, however, stopped on 4 March, which allowed the 3rd Hiko Dan to fly a large number of sorties in support of Colonel Shoji's troops as of 5 March. Because of this, his advance was so successful, even though the Japanese troops faced some tenacious resistance in several places.

The inefficient use of the few remaining allied fighter aircraft, as he saw it, caused Major-General Van Oyen (the JAC commander) to fall out with Major-General Pesman, the commander of Bandoeng Group. The latter found support from the army commander and as of 5 March the combat aircraft (in actual fact, only the fighters) came exclusively at the disposal of Bandoeng Group during daylight hours. In hindsight it can be concluded that Van Oyen was right in his choice for a more concentrated deployment of the few remaining combat aircraft. A controversy such as the one between Van Oyen and Pesman, incidentally, was by no means unique during World War II. In the period between 1939 and 1942, for instance, there was a constant struggle going on between the German *Wehrmacht* and *Luftwaffe* on the organisation of the 'ground-air' coordination, which was only decided in favour of the *Luftwaffe* in 1942.[1]

The efficiency of the deployment of the remaining allied fighter aircraft dissipated as of 5 March. If the strategy advocated by JAC had been adopted, this would have led to air raids on the Japanese troops advancing on the Tjiater fortification in the morning of 5 March and to more fighter sweeps against Kalidjati. This might have given the KNIL troops in the Tjiater pass the opportunity to hold out a few days longer, as it would have given them more time to reinforce and organise the new first line behind the Tjiater fortification. It would have taken three or four more days on 6 March for the most important units of

West Group (the Blackforce brigade the first among them) to become operational again and to get the new P-40 fighter aircraft being assembled at Andir and Tasikmalaja operational.

Making the air forces exclusively available to Bandoeng Group during daylight must, in hindsight, be qualified as a blunder of General Headquarters. The outcome of the final battle for western Java would, with the allied navy gone, the allied air forces almost gone (the evacuated Americans not having heard of again until 6 March) and no help from the allies to be expected, have been the same had General Headquarters decided otherwise and Bandoeng Group operated differently. It is, however, very likely that Colonel Shoji's troops would have bogged down if the allied air forces had been deployed more efficiently. In that case the difficult retreat of West Group to the Bandoeng Plateau would not have been in vain.

PART 5

⋙⋘

Conclusions

※※※

Conclusions

Introduction

The final battle for Java in the period of 18 February up to and including 7 March 1942 mainly took place over southern Sumatra and Banka, in the eastern part of the Java Sea and over and in western Java and is marked by four major clashes with the Japanese opponent. First of all, there was the battle for air superiority over western Java in the period between 18 February up to and including 27 February 1942, which was followed by the Battle of the Java Sea on 27 February 1942. Both major allied operations, intended to prevent a Japanese invasion of Java, failed. After this it fell to the allied land forces, mainly consisting of KNIL troops, supported by the remaining air forces, to try and make the Japanese invasion fail. In the night of 28 February on 1 March 1942 Japanese troops made simultaneous landings on various locations in western Java and eastern Java. The battle of Java that subsequently developed took place mainly in western Java, where the bulk of the KNIL and the allied land forces had been concentrated.

The Japanese, too, laid the emphasis of the battle in the west, in the realisation that at Bandoeng and its surroundings the largest concentration of allied headquarters and military installations was situated. The battle for Bandoeng would be decisive. Following the landings two battles were fought in western Java for possession of Kalidjati air base (28 February up to and including 3 March 1942) and the Tjiater pass (5 March up to and including 7 March 1942), respectively. The outcomes of these battles, subsequently, made a capitulation unavoidable.

The battle for air superiority

The Counter air operation (as it would nowadays be called) conducted by the allied air forces and anti-aircraft artillery from 18 February up to and including 27 February 1942, was directed at a postponement

503

of the Japanese invasion by extending the period the Japanese would need to gain air superiority over western Java. In modern terms the operation involved an attrition strategy, a type of approach that is known nowadays for the time it takes before the first results become visible and the abundant reserves of aircraft needed. This was also realised at ABDAIR, and later JAC, but there was no alternative. The whole thing depended on the edge resulting from the fact that the Japanese could only spread out the targets for the allied bombers to a very limited extent and from the reinforcement of Java's air defences with British radar stations and installations for radio direction finding. With the help of the allied intelligence services two main targets were defined. It was believed that a concentrated deployment of own means could hit the enemy the hardest. These two centres of gravity (in the modern lingo) were the aircraft fuel stores at Palembang and the Japanese combat aircraft stationed there. The latter were engaged by allied bombers as well as allied fighters and anti-aircraft artillery over western Java.

In hindsight, this selection of targets appears to have been spot on and the set-up of the Counter air operation in itself is exemplary for what can still be achieved with a limited quantity of own means. The results mainly involved the destruction of the bulk of the aircraft fuel stored at Palembang which had fallen into Japanese hands and the destruction or extended putting out of action of around 20 bombers and 25 fighter aircraft of the Japanese Army air force by the allied anti-aircraft artillery, in aerial combat and by means of bombing raids of Palembang airfield, known as Palembang I. On a total of approximately 140 enemy fighter aircraft and bombers stationed at Palembang I (on 23 February 1942) this not a bad result by any standard. This is especially so, when it is realised that the British radar in western Java did not become operational before 26 February 1942, which means that until that moment the allied fighter aircraft could not be concentrated to intercept the Japanese air raids. However, more time was needed to bring the loss percentage of the Japanese up to a critical level. Time which was not given to the allies.

The simultaneous Japanese air offensive to acquire air superiority over western Java from Palembang was an official success, but in practice it did not lead to the expected measure of (almost total) air superiority. Especially in the Japanese Navy, which only wanted to commit its ships in a situation of own air superiority, this led to some raised eyebrows. Time and again in their attacks against Java the Army air force combat aircraft encountered enemy fighter aircraft and enemy bombers kept flying bombing missions, alone or in small formations, against Palembang I. The Japanese, however, were under pressure of time, and, in view of the logistical situation the Japanese army, could not afford to postpone the planned invasion of Java for too long. On 23 February 1942 the Army had agreed to delaying the invasion by two days on request of the Navy, on condition, however, that this postponement would be the last. Although the allied air forces had not been fully neutralised by the end of February, this limited air superiority would have to do. The same logistical reasons made relatively high losses of the Army air force acceptable. Further delay would allow the allies to reinforce Java even more and would rapidly lower the chances of a successful invasion. Java, however, was the final objective of the Japanese operations in the Pacific.

In view of the problems the Japanese were facing, it can be concluded (in hindsight) that the quantity of the resources available to the allies in their air offensive was too small. In particular the British in the ABDAIR days had been convinced of this from the start, but Major-General Van Oyen, commander of JAC as of 22 February 1942, believed that by committing all available resources it might just be possible to push the invasion back a little. This postponement could give the allies the time they needed to reinforce Java with the available American fighter aircraft standing ready in Australia. Van Oyen and his staff were convinced that the Japanese Army and Army air force must be facing logistical problems, and therefore the target selection of the Counter air operation was partially based on this assumption. They had misjudged somewhat, however, that the time pressure for the Japanese was so great, and, as a result of that, their readiness to take risks and accept losses.

As early as 25 February 1942 the first Japanese invasion fleet had been spotted by an allied flying boat and Van Oyen knew that he had been mistaken. The discovery of this invasion fleet in the Macassar Straits directly led to the second major clash, the battle of the Java Sea. Flying boats of JAC continually monitored Japanese ship movement as far north as possible. As soon as an invasion fleet was spotted, the overall allied defence plan dictated, the naval squadron would leave port to engage it.

The battle of the Java Sea

The allied navy was defeated in the battle of the Java Sea after a protracted battle which can be divided into the so-called day and night fights. The battle was not lost as a result of a lack of direct air support from allied fighter aircraft. During the day fight Rear-Admiral Doorman was the only party with air support. A total of 15 allied fighter aircraft (which in part had recently been transferred from western to eastern Java) ensured an allied local air superiority for most of the day fight, preventing the enemy from using his float planes for artillery observation. Also during the night fight the Japanese had no advantage in the air. The only Japanese float plane that was up during the most crucial stage of the night fight did not have a functioning radio connection. Doorman, however, was facing an enemy superiority of heavy cruisers and destroyers and eventually perished in the night fight.

That he engaged this superior force, rather than the Japanese transport fleet, is also related to Air power, in particular the allied reconnaissance capability generated by flying boats and bombers of Java Air Command. This capability was small due to earlier combat and a shortage of reserve crews for the flying boats, while also bad weather hindered the reconnaissance sorties. Moreover, there were also the capacity constraints in the Signals service of the Royal Netherlands Navy, which caused delays in the transmission of reconnaissance reports to Doorman. Thus, in the evening of 27 February 1942 communication broke down at a crucial moment and Doorman did not receive the position of the enemy transport fleet in time. The Combined Striking Force perished with great loss of lives and the role of the allied navy in the defence of Java was played out, the remaining units evacuating to Ceylon or Australia.

In the evening of 28 February 1942 the bombers of JAC began intensive air raids against the Japanese invasion fleets. In the mean time, a second invasion fleet had been discovered in the west. As of the morning of 1 March 1942 JAC also committed its fighter aircraft against the Japanese landing operations.

The battle of Kalidjati

In the west the emphasis lay on attacking the Japanese landing operation near Eretan Wetan, as it formed a great threat for the large air base Kalidjati, which lay close to the coast. In the first instance the landing operation was only attacked by air forces. The keeping, and subsequent recapturing by the KNIL, of Kalidjati lay at the core of the deployment of the air forces up to and including 3 March 1942.

Although JAC determined its strategy within the general instructions of the KNIL army commander, who also was the allied

Commander-in-Chief ABDA Area, it was narrowly directed at the support of the actions of the land forces as of 1 March 1942. Besides, the results of reconnaissance missions carried out by the allied air forces filled the wide gaps in the combat intelligence of the land forces. Needless to say, this had a great impact on the deployment of the land forces. The so-called Air support coordination was conducted according to a system developed by the British, first introduced in northern Africa in the second half of 1941, and was very modern for that time. This system of requesting and granting air support had already been used successfully for the support of allied naval forces.

Japanese commanders at various levels deliberately took several considerable risks in the final battle for western Java. The invasion took place at a moment when the Japanese Army air force had only established a limited air superiority over western Java. In order to help force a quick decision the Japanese Army subsequently landed a detachment (regimental battle group) commanded by Colonel Shoji at Eretan Wetan in western Java. This location was not very suitable for a landing, as it was behind the main allied lines and far from the Japanese main force, which had landed much farther to the west near Merak and in the Bay of Bantam. The landing operation could only succeed if the nearby large allied airfield of Kalidjati could be captured immediately and quickly put to use by the Japanese Army air force for air support purposes. It worked out well for the Japanese, but allied actions to recapture Kalidjati stood a good chance of success. A first attempt by the Mobile Unit of the KNIL on 2 March 1942 came to within an inch of success. On 3 March the main attack was launched, supported with several secondary operations. The Japanese Army, however, was extremely lucky that an earlier planned very heavy bombing raid on Andir air base, from which all the support missions were to be flown for the allied troops, who (four to five hours behind schedule) were advancing on Kalidjati, came just at the right time. The allied local air superiority, which had existed up to that moment, evaporated all at once.

In order to survive with his relatively small detachment, Shoji depended heavily on Air power, in this case the 3rd Hiko Dan of the Japanese Army air force. Equally dependent on Air power (the fighters, bombers and reconnaissance planes of the ML, RAF and RAAF) were the KNIL troops of the allied land forces, who, unlike Shoji's battalions (with earlier campaigns in southern China and the capture of Hong Kong under their belts) for the most part had only little combat experience and who had to defend a large area with relatively small numbers. Most of the KNIL troops that carried out the attack on Kalidjati on 3 March, virtually all the reserves the allied land forces had available, were defeated and put to flight by the continuous Japanese air attacks carried out from Kalidjati. In particular the psychological effects of the air raids that kept on going for hours at a time played a large role in this. Andir was in ruins and was closed for the rest of the day, making it impossible for the allied air forces to give any support whatsoever.

There were no further troops for a renewed recapturing attempt, unless they were taken away from western Java and the cities of Batavia and Buitenzorg were given up. This is precisely what the General Headquarters of the KNIL army commander decided. West Group was relocated in a phased movement to the Bandoeng plateau to be combined with Bandoeng Group. The still remaining air forces in the west, too, along with as much of the anti-aircraft artillery as could be managed, were mostly relocated to Andir. This withdrawal onto the Bandoeng plateau was in accordance with the overall strategy for the defence of Java agreed on in February 1942.

The battle of the Tjiater pass

In the mean time, the Japanese Shoji detachment still found itself in a predicament. The captured Kalidjati proved to be very dangerous as all allied air forces had not been taken out of action by far. A part of Shoji's air support had been put out of action due to allied air raids on Kalidjati on 2, 3 and 4 March 1942. Furthermore, an allied motorised unit to the south of Soebang was still intact. Colonel Shoji chose to attack in order to prevent envelopment from regrouping allied troops. He launched his attack on Bandoeng on 5 March 1942 via the Tjiater pass. The risk of his troops bogging down in the pass and then being defeated, however, was quite real, which made Shoji once more heavily dependent on air support. He got it on a generous scale, but only after heavy fighting against a tenaciously defending KNIL did he manage to force access to the Bandoeng plateau.

By now there were hardly any allied air forces available due to repeated Japanese air raids on Andir and later also Tasikmalaja. Moreover, from 5 March 1942 onwards the remaining allied air forces were exclusively at the disposal of Bandoeng Group of the KNIL for support in the defence of the Bandoeng plateau. This deployment was less successful and in fact the conclusion is justified that committing the remaining fighter aircraft by Bandoeng Group was injudicious. Keeping up the indirect air support to the KNIL by means of bombing raids on Kalidjati during the nightly hours and fighter sweeps against this base during the day, in combination with attacks of fighter aircraft on Japanese targets on the road from Soebang to Tjiater might indeed have led to a bogging down of Shoji's troops.

On 7 March the fight was over. Bandoeng Group had insufficient troops to stop the Japanese for long and units of West Group, the first elements of which had arrived on the plateau on 6 March, would not be able to deploy operationally for the first few days to come. Once more, a calculated Japanese risk had caused time pressure on the allies. With the capture of the pass the road to Bandoeng lay open to the Japanese troops. Not only were all important allied military and civilian headquarters located in the city, there were also thousands of refugees. The Governor-General of the Netherlands East Indies therefore had stated his express wish that there would be no fighting in and around Bandoeng. Thus, losing the pass meant losing Java.

In conclusion

Holding out on the Bandoeng plateau and conducting sallies from there, as was laid down in the defence plans for western Java, never materialised. The fight for Java ended with the capitulation of the KNIL and allied units, effective as of 9 March 1942, followed three days later (to prevent any misunderstandings) by a complete surrender of the allied armed forces. The edge of the Japanese forces had been slim, however. Only a limited form of air superiority was attained at the time of the Japanese landings and although after the battle of the Java Sea the Japanese naval forces had realized supremacy at sea, there was no strategic reserve force that could quickly be transported to West Java in case anything did go wrong during the ground war. Japanese commanders at different levels took some deliberate risks that turned out well for them and which each time brought great time pressure to the allies. Besides an element of luck, the Japanese successes had much to do with the efforts of the Army and Navy air force. The availability of air support on both sides had played a crucial role in the outcome of the land battle. When the entire final battle in the period between 18 February 1942 and 7 March 1942 is considered, the crucial role of Air power emerges and when all is taken into account there is only one final conclusion. The loss of Java was to a high extent a matter of Air power.

Notes

Introduction

1. Boer, *Borneo*, 117–8; De Jong, 11a, I, 2e helft, 761–76.
2. Wavell, *Despatch*; De Jong, 11a, I, 2e helft, 866, 778–9.
3. Wavell, *Despatch*; De Jong, 11a, I, 2e helft, 851, 865–6.
4. Wavell, *Despatch*; for the air battle over eastern Java, see: Boer, *Indië*, chapter 7.
5. De Jong, 11a, I, 2e helft, 865–6, 870, 873.
6. De Jong, 11a, I, 2e helft, 872; interviews with H. Creutzberg and W. Mulder.
7. Boer, *Indië*, 123–4; Bosscher, 2, 272.
8. Boer, *Indië*, 123–4; Maltby, *Report*, 1394; interviews with H. Creuzberg and W. Mulder; correspondence of S.H.A. Begemann (via W. Mulder).
9. Ibid.; for a description of these procedures, see the H.F. Zeylemaker's notes 'Beschrijving oorlogsoperaties' (March 1942, via A. van Aarem and J. Mossou).
10. See, for instance, Maltby, *Report*, 1396, section 523 for a concise summary.
11. Interviews with H. Creutzberg, F.R. Lettinga and A.B. Wolff; correspondence of S.H.A. Begemann (via W. Bosman).
12. Wavell, *Despatch*; interview with H. Creutzberg; correspondence of S.H.A. Begemann (via W. Bosman).
13. Interviews with H. Creutzberg, F.R. Lettinga, P.A. Hoyer and A.B. Wolff; NEI Order of battle information (available aircraft/crews) (AIR 23/4716, PRO, via Mark Haselden); ABDACOM Situation Reports and Dutch Operations Reports (summaries) (Veuger/De Smalen collection, SLH).
14. Nortier, *et al.*, *Java*, 57–8; Rear Admiral F.W. Coster, Verslag betreffende de krijgsverrichtingen te land in Nederlands-Indië, 20 May 1942, E, 1 (Marinestaf, Historische Sectie Bc–8/1, IMH).
15. Ibid.
16. Ibid.; for the composition of West Group, see Nortier, *et al.*, *Java*, 308–9, attachment 4.
17. Ibid.; 'Beschrijving oorlogsoperaties' H.F. Zeijlemaker (March 1942, via A. van Aarem and J. Mossou) with regard to the date of Pesman taking command. For the composition of Bandoeng Group, see Nortier *et al.*, *Java*, 308–9, attachment 5.

18. See Part 1; for the discovery of the convoy, see, for instance, Maltby, *Report*, 1396.
19. See Part 1.
20. Ibid.; see Part 2 for the operations of the fighter aircraft in eastern Java and of the bombers in the west in (helping in) the search for the 'western' invasion fleet.
21. See Part 2.
22. See Part 3.
23. See Part 4.

Chapter 1A.1

1. Maltby, *Report*, 1393 and 1414; De Jong, 11a, I, 2e helft, 867, 888; Shores, 2, 385; correspondence author with J.G. Bücker; Rapport Kengen, 41 (Ward collection, SLH); interview with H. Creutzberg; correspondence of S.H.A. Begemann (via W. Bosman). See Part 2 for the P-40s of the USAAF.
2. Maltby, *Report*, 1393; ABDACOM Situation Reports and Dutch Operations Reports (summaries) (Veuger/De Smalen collection, SLH; henceforth ABDACOM/Dutch reports); NEI Order of battle information (available aircraft/crews) (AIR 23/4716, PRO, via Mark Haselden; henceforth, NEI ORBAT); interview with P.A. Hoyer; correspondence of S.H.A. Begemann (via W. Bosman).
3. Maltby, *Report*, 1393; NEI ORBAT; ABDACOM/Dutch reports; interviews with P.G. Tideman, W. Boxman and J.B.H. Bruinier.
4. Rapport Kengen, 41 (Ward collection, SLH); correspondence author with J.G. Bücker; interview with F.R. Lettinga.
5. Schotborg (editor), *Nederlands Indië contra Japan*, IV, 109; Maltby, *Report*, 1414.
6. Interviews with P.A. Hoyer and H. Creutzberg; correspondence of S.H.A. Begemann (via W. Bosman); Maltby, *Report*, 1414, the short-range (25-nM) GL-sets were of little value for early warning purposes and were becoming operational from 27 February, only to be destroyed the next day; see also Shores, 2, 191.
7. See Part 2.
8. Maltby, *Report*, 1393; interview with W. Boxman; correspondence of S.H.A. Begemann (via W. Bosman).
9. Boer, *Indië*, 261–6; interview with H. Creutzberg. The RAF expected no reinforcements whatsoever of the bomber fleet, the ML was to equip the first afdeling with North American B-25 Mitchell medium bombers in March 1942 and the USAAF was to station a first medium-bomber squadron fitted out with Martin B-26 Marauders in Java during that same month.
10. Correspondence author with P.D. Gifford and T. Kelly; Shores, 2, 191–2; Maltby, *Report*, 1392–3; Boer, *Indië*, 50, 136. In Java 39 Hurricanes arrived

with a British convoy which was originally destined for Singapore and a further four arrived in the freighter *Phrontis*, which had transported the aircraft to Singapore, coming back from there during the evacuation of the town with the aircraft and most of the other stores still on board. Of these 43, the RAF flew 14 aircraft to Palembang I, in the first instance, followed by another nine Hurricanes just prior to the fall of southern Sumatra. Subsequently, 12 aircraft were transferred to the ML.

11. History of 226 Group (via AHB); Kelly, *Hurricane over the jungle*, 166.

12. Correspondence author with P.D. Gifford (data from his logbook); Shores, 2, 191.

13. Correspondence author with P.D. Gifford (data from his logbook); NEI ORBAT; ABDACOM/Dutch reports; A.A.M. van Rest's notes (his pocket book).

14. Maltby, *Report*, 1393 (Maltby consistently calls 242 Squadron, 232 Squadron, this mistake has been copied in Boer, *Indië*; in fact the squadron was designated as 232 Squadron only the first few days after its formation and from 22 February 1942 onwards it was designated 242 Squadron); Beauchamp, *Escape from Singapore*, 85–6; Bezemer, *Nederlandse Koopvaardij*, 721.

15. Lieutenant-Colonel J.V.O. Macartney-Filgate M.C., 'The 48th Light Anti-Aircraft Regiment Royal Artillery in the Dutch East Indies, February–March 1942' (via J. Mulders, henceforth Report 48 LAA); W. Schilling verslag (dossier NIcJ 12/1, IMG); Nortier *et al.*, *Java*, 306–7, attachment 4.

16. NEI ORBAT; the strength mentioned in a report of the 1st Division to General Headquarters, see also Hoogenband, van den and Schotborgh (editors), *Nederlands-Indië contra Japan*, VII, 22 (though not dated there), probably concerns the number of serviceable Hurricanes of 232 Squadron on 20 February 1942 only; interviews with C.W.A. Oyens and J.C. Benschop.

17. Maltby, *Report*, 1393 (erroneously dates the coming into operation of 605 Squadron on 23 February 1942, however); NEI ORBAT; correspondence with P.D. Gifford and T. Kelly; Kelly, *Hurricane over the jungle*, 181; Fabricius, *Brandende aarde*, 124.

18. NEI ORBAT (states eight available aircraft for 232 Squadron, this, however, is only the number available for air defence); A.A.M. van Rest's notes (his pocket book, he wrote, "T[jililitan]21/18", I have assumed that these are the numbers of assigned and serviceable Hurricanes); see also, Maltby, *Report*, 1393.

19. Maltby, *Report*, 1393; interviews with P.A. Hoyer, J.B.H. Bruinier and B. Wink.

20. Description of command structure by P.A. Hoyer; W. Schilling report (dossier NIcJ 12/1, IMG); report T.C.N. Canter-Visscher (dossier Canter-Visscher, Ward collection, SLH); Maltby, *Report*, 1393, section 498; Report 48 LAA; diary entries of and e-mails with explanations from O.A.O. Kreefft.

21. NEI ORBAT; ABDACOM/Dutch reports; Boer, *Indië*, 137–8 (is partially incorrect); further information provided by J.B.H. Bruinier and W. Boxman.

22. NEI ORBAT; ABDACOM/Dutch reports; further information provided by W. Boxman and J. van Os. In late February 1942 the Interceptor unit was considered by the ML Inspection an independent afdeling, temporarily reduced in strength, operating separately from 2-Vl.G.IV at Kalidjati and Ngoro. This had probably to do with the plan to absorb the patrol in the newly to be formed (with P-40s) 1-Vl.G.IV. All the personnel, however, belonged to 2-Vl.G.IV administratively and also Elt Boxman was assigned administratively (as of 20 February) to 2-Vl.G.IV. This remained so until the end of the battle.

23. NEI ORBAT; ABDACOM/Dutch reports; A.A.M. van Rest's notes (his pocket book); interviews with P.G. Tideman, B. Wink and W. Boxman.

24. Ibid.; interviews with R.M.H. Hermans, P.A. Hoyer,T. van der Muur, A.E. Stoove, P.R. Jolly and F. Pelder. An eleventh Brewster destined for 2-Vl.G.V (ex-3-Vl.G.IV) was at the Technical Service depot at Andir for major repairs (damage from a belly landing near Palembang in January 1942). A 12th aircraft (ex-3-Vl.G.IV) was at the Technical Service depot for modifications of the wing tanks, which, however, necessitated a complete wing change. The repair section of 2-Vl.G.V was at Semplak (Buitenzorg).

25. Military History Office, Senshi Sosho (Series of Military History of World War II), 34 (after this, Senshi Sosho, 34), 503–4.

26. Senshi Sosho, 34, 542, 546; Military History Office, Senshi Sosho (Series of Military History of World War II), 26 (henceforth, Senshi Sosho, 26), 649, 652, 468, 564.

27. Senshi Sosho, 34, 504; Senshi Sosho, 26, 652, 468, 564.

28. Senshi Sosho, 34, 542, 551.

29. Senshi Sosho, 26, 468, 564.

30. Senshi Sosho, 34, 546.

31. Senshi Sosho, 26, 628, 646–9.

32. See Part 3 for a more detailed description of the anti-aircraft units at Bandoeng and Andir.

Chapter 1A.2

1. Boer, *Indië*, 155; interviews with J.B.H. Bruinier and P.G. Tideman; correspondence author with G.M. Bruggink.

2. Ibid. See also Shores, 2, 215 (the event described by Shores is dated by Tideman and Bruinier on the day before the first air raid on Andir).

3. ABDACOM Situation Reports and Dutch Operations reports (summaries) (Veuger/De Smalen Collection, SLH; henceforth, ABDACOM/Dutch reports); NEI Order of battle information (available aircraft/crews) (AIR

23/4716, PRO, via Mark Haselden; henceforth, NEI ORBAT); A.A.M. van Rest's notes (his pocket book). The Hawks are never included on the surveys of strengths, but were constantly operationally serviceable, according to P.G. Tideman. The aircraft were hardly used, however, due to operational limitations. The type was not to be used for air defence tasks anymore and the two aircraft could in fact only be used to carry out armed reconnaissance missions. The term available signified availability for normal operations. So, there were often more aircraft serviceable than available. Thus, serviceable aircraft could be assigned for training purposes or convoy protection. The number of serviceable aircraft of 242 Squadron on 19 February, for instance, was 12, while only 8 were available.

4. Boer, *Indië*, 157; Shores, 2, 204; correspondence author with P.D. Gifford (former fighter pilot 488 Squadron).

5. Military History Office, Senshi Sosho (Series of Military History of World War II), 34, 548 (henceforth, Senshi Sosho, 34); Boer, *Indië*, 156.

6. Boer, *Indië*, 156; further information provided by G.M. Bruggink, P.C. 't Hart and P.A. Hoyer. In A.G. Deibel's report from 1946 (dossier Deibel, Ward collection, SLH), mistakenly eight fighter aircraft are mentioned. This incorrect number has since been copied in various publications (including the Military Willems-order recommendation of Deibel himself).

7. Ibid.

8. Interview with R.A. Sleeuw; report by P.A. Hoyer regarding the recovery of Kuijper and Groot's mortal remains.

9. Boer, *Indië*, 157; interview with F. Pelder.

10. Dutch Operations Reports, provisional reports (AIR 23/4725, PRO, via Mark Haselden); Boer, *Indië*, 156.

11. Correspondence author with P.C. 't Hart.

12. Boer, *Indië*, 156.

13. Dutch Operations Reports, provisional reports (AIR 23/4725, PRO, via Mark Haselden); Rear Admiral F.W. Coster, Verslag betreffende de krijgsverrichtingen te land in Nederlands-Indië, 20 May 1942, F, 13 (Marinestaf, Historische sectie, Bc-8/1, IMH; henceforth, Verslag Coster, with regard to the claims mentions only the two 'Navy Os' of Deibel, as in the operations report, as 't Hart and Scheffer could not be debriefed yet at the time of the writing of the original provisional report); further information provided by P.C. 't Hart, R.A. Sleeuw and P.A. Hoyer.

14. Interview with R.A. Sleeuw (was in contact at the time with KNIL officers of 1st Division about the discovered wreckage) and P.A. Hoyer (attached shortly after the air battle to the local Air Officer Commanding Captain C. Terluin, who collected all reports of army, police and navy on discovered wreckage).

15. War diary 64th Sentai (via Military History Department, National Institute for Defense Studies, Tokyo) and Senshi Sosho, 34, 548.

16. Interviews with P.A. Hoyer, P.R. Jolly, F. Pelder, H. Huijs and T. van der Muur; correspondence author with G.M. Bruggink; see also Boer, *Indië*, 156–7.

17. Report A.G. Deibel, 1946 and military register A.G. Deibel (dossier Deibel, Ward collection, SLH).

18. Dutch Operations Report, provisional report (AIR 23/4725, PRO, via Mark Haselden); interview with T. van der Muur; Verslag Coster, F, 13 (erroneously only mentions the three Hudsons and the two Sikorskys, as in the original provisional report); see also Shores, 2, 203–4.

19. Hagens, *De KNILM vloog door*, 97; Shores, 2, 203–4.

20. Boer, *Indië*, 156; further interview with T. van der Muur; see also Shores, 2, 203–4.

21. Boer, *Indië*, 157 and further information given by R.A. Sleeuw and P.A. Hoyer; Hoogenband, van den and Schotborgh (editors), *Nederlands-Indië contra Japan*, VII, 14.

22. Interviews with P.G. Tideman, P.A. Hoyer and R.A. Sleeuw; Shores, 2, 204; G.J. de Haas in his report from 1946 (dossier De Haas, Ward collection, SLH) states that the Hurricanes intercepted the Japanese aircraft over the coast, but according to P.D. Gifford (former fighter pilot 488 Squadron) the attempt failed. Also in other reports no mention is made of an interception.

23. Military History Office, Senshi Sosho (Series of Military History of World War II), 26, 621 (henceforth, Senshi Sosho, 26).

24. Report P.G. Tideman, 1946 (dossier Tideman, Ward collection, SLH) and further information provided by P.G. Tideman.

25. Interview and correspondence with P.G. Tideman, H.H.J. Simons and A.E. van Kempen.

26. Description based on information provided by H.H.J. Simons, P.A.C. Benjamins and A.E. van Kempen.

27. Boer, *Indië*, 157 (gives a partially incorrect and incomplete rendering); further information provided by P.A.C. Benjamins, A. Bergamin, A.E. van Kempen, J.P. Adam and W. Boxman; H.H.J. Simons, 'Java-Drama' in *Remous*, May 1943 (Ward collection, SLH).

28. Ibid.

29. A.A.M. van Rest's notes (his pocket book); description by P.A.C. Benjamins, A.E. van Kempen, W. Boxman and H.M. Haye; see also Boer, *Indië*, 157–8.

30. Boer, *Indië*, 158.

31. Interviews and correspondence with P.G. Tideman and H.H.J. Simons; see also H.H.J. Simons, 'Java-Drama' in *Remous*, May 1943 (Ward collection, SLH).

32. Correspondence author with J.P. Adam.

33. Ikuhiko Hata *et al.*, 292; Dutch Operations Reports (AIR 23/4725, PRO, via Mark Haselden); Boer, *Indië*, 158 and further information provided

by A.E. van Kempen, J.P. Adam, H.H.J. Simons and P.A.C. Benjamins; correspondence author with P.G. Tideman.

34. Description by W. Boxman; interview with H.M. Haye.

35. Dutch Operations Reports (AIR 23/4725, PRO, via Mark Haselden); A.A.M. van Rest's notes (his pocket book).

36. Ibid.; Verslag Coster, F, 13; and Boer, *Indië*, 158 do not give a complete rendering.

37. Description by H.M. Haye; the date of the event appears from NEI ORBAT for 19 and 20 February 1942 (difference of one aircraft).

38. Interviews with R.A. Sleeuw and P.A. Hoyer, see also notes 14 and 33; information received from CWGC; with regard to the Hudson, see also Shores, 2, 214.

39. Senshi Sosho, 34, 548.

40. Interviews with P.A. Hoyer and R.A. Sleeuw; correspondence of author with P.C. 't Hart; data 64th Sentai Association (via Military History Department, National Institute for Defense Studies, Tokyo); Senshi Sosho, 34, 548.

41. War diary 64th Sentai (via Military History Department, National Institute for Defense Studies, Tokyo).

42. Ibid.; AAFHS 29A; see also Shores, 2, 208.

43. Senshi Sosho, 34, 548.

44. Correspondence author with P.G. Tideman.

45. Interviews with H.H.J. Simons, A.E. van Kempen, A. Bergamin, B. Wink and P.A.C. Benjamins. The fighter aircraft of 1-Vl.G.V were equipped with a modern American N2A reflector-sight in the first half of February 1942.

Chapter 1A.3

1. ABDACOM Situation Reports and Dutch Operations Reports (summaries) (Veuger/De Smalen collection, SLH; henceforth ABDACOM/Dutch reports); NEI Order of battle information (Available aircraft/crews) (AIR 23/4716, PRO, via Mark Haselden; henceforth NEI ORBAT), states serviceable strengths of the ML afdelingen; A.A.M. van Rest's notes (his pocket book); Van Rest did not only note the strengths of the ML afdelingen at Andir and Kalidjati, but also 'T [jililitan]14', I have assumed this to be the number of serviceable Hurricanes.

2. Shores, 2, 211; interviews with F. Pelder and P.R. Jolly.

3. Interviews with R.A. Sleeuw and P.A. Hoyer (both confirm that of the three claimed fighter aircraft the wreckage of one single-engine plane was found); see also report of W. Boxman, 1946 (via W. Bosman), refers to three crashed planes "in the Bantam area", claimed by the RAF pilots. Observers on the ground quickly confirmed via the 1st Division that these were probably two downed Japanese single-engine reconnaissance planes, after which the

RAF changed the claims to two. Only one wreckage was found afterwards, however.

4. NEI ORBAT; interview with W. Boxman; correspondence with P.G. Tideman.

5. Interviews with F. Pelder and P.R. Jolly; Military History Office, Senshi Sosho (Series of Military History of World War II), 26 (henceforth Senshi Sosho, 26), 621.

6. Senshi Sosho, 26, 646.

7. Interviews with F. Pelder and P.R. Jolly; Shores, 2, 211.

8. Interview with P.A. Hoyer and R.A. Sleeuw.

9. Military register E.H.C. Cleuver (Ward collection, SLH); see also Kelly, *Hurricane over the jungle*, 207, letter by Vincent.

10. Interviews with F. Pelder and P.R. Jolly; Boer, *Indië*, 159 (erroneously states that the aircraft of 2-Vl.G.V operated from Tjisaoek).

11. Military History Office, Senshi Sosho (Series of Military History of World War II), 34, 548; Boer, *Indië*, 116 (erroneously mentions two heavily damaged Glenn Martins and erroneously fails to mention the destroyed Lockheed L212), 159 (mentions an incorrect number of fighter aircraft of 1-Vl.G.V); correspondence author with P.G. Tideman regarding his report from 1946 (dossier Tideman, Ward collection, SLH).

12. See Part 1B.

13. Interviews with C.A.M. Koopmans and J.B.H. Bruinier; Boer, *Indië*, 137 (erroneously mentions the wrong name for the commander of RAF detachment 2-Vl.G.IV). David was a former engineering officer of 243 Squadron RAF.

14. Interviews with J.B.H. Bruinier, R.A.D. Anemaet and H. Creutzberg.

Chapter 1A.4

1. ABDACOM Situation Reports and Dutch Operations Reports (summaries) (Veuger/De Smalen collection, SLH; henceforth ABDACOM/Dutch reports); NEI Order of battle information (available aircraft/crews) (AIR 23/4716, PRO, via Mark Haselden; henceforth NEI ORBAT); A.A.M. van Rest's notes (his pocket book with regard to numbers of serviceable fighter aircraft 1-Vl.G.V).

2. Boer, *Indië*, 159; further data provided by P.A.C. Benjamins, A.E. van Kempen, H.H.J. Simons, A. Bergamin, W. Boxman and H.M. Haye.

3. Ibid.; interview with J. van Os.

4. Ibid. The death of Tlt Dekker is sometimes dated on 24 February 1942. This, however, is in contradiction to the data of the Gravendienst KNIL-War graves service KNIL (currently with OGS), while the loss of two ML fighter aircraft instead of one is confirmed by the AHQFE operations summary (AIR 24/504, PRO, via Mark Haselden). The original Dutch

operations report, quoted by Rear Admiral F.W. Coster, Verslag betreffende de krijgsverrichtingen te land in Nederlands-Indië, 20 May 1942 (Marinestaf, Historische sectie, Bc-8/1, IMH; henceforth verslag Coster), F, 13, mentions the loss of one (own) fighter, but the reports used were the provisional summaries and these did not mention any missing aircraft.

5. Military History Office, Senshi Sosho (Series of Military History of World War II), 34, 549 (henceforth Senshi Sosho, 34).

6. Ibid.; report Tideman, 1946 (dossier Tideman, Ward collection, SLH); further interview with P.G. Tideman (dated for me again the events mentioned in his report and gave further details); correspondence and interview with J.P. Adam.

7. Correspondence and interview with J.P. Adam; interview with A.E. van Kempen.

8. Concise report of Capt. Van Rest, Fort Leavenworth, May 1942, IX–X (dossier van Rest, Ward collection, SLH); Van Rest's notes (his pocket book); correspondence and interviews with P.G. Tideman and A.E. van Kempen; interviews with H.H.J. Simons, A. Bergamin, W. Boxman and H.M. Haye.

9. Van Kempen, *Mijn Verhaal*, 55–6.

10. Boer, *Indië*, 159–60 (does not give an entirely correct description); further data provided by H.H.J. Simons and P.A.C. Benjamins; correspondence of P.G. Tideman (with thanks to Chr. Shores), see also Shores, 2, 215.

11. Senshi Sosho, 34, 549; correspondence author with P.G. Tideman, with regard to his report from 1946 (dossier Tideman, Ward collection, SLH); see also Shores, 2, 215.

12. Correspondence author with P.A.C. Benjamins.

13. Ibid.

14. Ibid.

15. Data provided by the Military History Department of the National Institute for Defense Studies (Tokyo); Van Rest's notes (his pocket book, only mentions Tideman's plane as confirmed claim); interviews with P.G. Tideman and P.A.C. Benjamins; Verslag Coster, F, 13, mentions a total claim of five for the fighter aircraft, this, however, is probably the claim of the anti-aircraft artillery at Kalidjati, viz. four bombers hit and one probable, see Part 1B.

16. Senshi Sosho, 34, 549; War diary 64th Sentai (via Military History Department, National Institute for Defense Studies, Tokyo).

17. Ibid.; correspondence author with P.A.C. Benjamins.

18. Van Rest's notes (his pocket book); Concise report of Capt. Van Rest, Fort Leavenworth, May 1942, IX–X (dossier van Rest, Ward collection, SLH); correspondence author with P.A.C. Benjamins.

19. Data 64th Sentai Association (via Military History Department, National Institute for Defense Studies, Tokyo).

20. Van Rest's notes (his pocket book); correspondence and interview with B. Wink.

21. NEI ORBAT; interview with P.A. Hoyer; see also Shores, 2, 215.

Chapter 1A.5

1. See for instance De Jong, 11a, I, 2e helft, 879 and Bezemer, *Nederlandse Koopvaardij*, 705–6; see also Maltby, *Report*, 1392.

2. Bosscher, 2, 272.

3. NEI Order of battle information (available aircraft/crews) (AIR 23/4716, PRO, via Mark Haselden; henceforth NEI ORBAT) states the available aircraft/crews of the RAF Squadrons; Van Rest's notes (his pocket book) states the strengths of the afdelingen at Andir/Kalidjati.

4. See for instance Maltby, *Report*, 1392.

5. De Jong, 11a, I, 2e helft, 879; Bezemer, *Nederlandse Koopvaardij*, 705–6.

6. Ibid.

7. Maltby, *Report*, 1399 (erroneously mentions 1 March 1942 as date of transfer); see also Shores, 2, 216.

8. Bezemer, *Nederlandse Koopvaardij*, 705–6; Cull *et al.*, 200–1; correspondence author with P.D. Gifford; Fabricius, *Brandende aarde*, 124.

9. Interviews with P.A. Hoyer and R.A. Sleeuw.

10. Ibid.; correspondence author with T. Kelly; see also Shores, 2, 217.

11. Interviews with P.A. Hoyer and R.A. Sleeuw; correspondence author with T. Kelly.

12. Ibid.; Shores, 2, 217.

13. NEI ORBAT; correspondence author with T. Kelly; Shores, 2, 192, 219.

14. Japanese monograph 69; Lieutenant-Colonel J.V.O. Macartney-Filgate M.C., 'The 48th Light Anti-Aircraft Regiment Royal Artillery in the Dutch East Indies, February–March 1942' (via J. Mulders); Schotborgh (ed.), *Nederlands-Indië contra Japan*, IV, 139.

15. See Part 1B.

16. Shores, 2, 219; correspondence author with T. Kelly; interview with P.A. Hoyer.

17. Interview with P.A. Hoyer; correspondence author with T. Kelly.

18. Ibid.; Shores, 2, 219.

19. Fabricius, *Brandende aarde*, 118–9; Kelly, *Battle for Palembang*, 150–2.

20. Correspondence author with B. Wink.

21. Interview with H. Creutzberg (then lieutenant-adjutant of Van Oyen).

22. Ibid.; Boer, *Indië*, 123–4.

23. Ibid.; in Shores, 2, 227–8, the impression is given that BRITAIR took over the ABDAIR building on 24 February 1942; this is incorrect and wrongly dated. Also Maltby, *Report*, 1394 does not describe this altogether correctly, the "last minute additions" of RAF personnel that Maltby mentions are in fact an addition of the strongly reduced staff of the COIC.

24. Interviews and correspondence with H. Creutzberg, W. Mulder, A.A.M. van Rest, P.A.C. Benjamins, A.B. Wolff and F.R. Lettinga; see for COIC also Bosscher, 2, 205.

25. Interviews with H. Creutzberg, F.R. Lettinga, A.B. Wolff and P.A. Hoyer; Boer, *Indië*, 172.

26. Japanese Monograph 69; A.A.M. van Rest's notes (his pocket book).

27. Military History Office, Senshi Sosho (Series of Military History of World War II), 26, 645.

28. A.A.M. van Rest's notes (his pocket book), only mentions a claim for a reconnaissance float plane on 23 February; further data provided by T. Kelly (dates the mission on 22 February); Shores, 2, 211–2, dates the mission on 20 February 1942. In view of the above and bearing in mind the date on which the Japanese reconnaissance float planes arrived at Banka, I have concluded that 23 February is the right date for the events described by Shores.

29. The 1st Division of the KNIL at Batavia reported no wreckage on the land and that the KM had reported that a patrol boat had not been able to find any wreckage of downed enemy aircraft (P.A. Hoyer, at the time attached to the local Air Officer Commanding for the fighter aircraft at Batavia, Capt. C. Terluin).

30. Correspondence author with C. Busser; interview with A. Bergamin.

31. See Part 1B.

32. Boer, *Indië*, 161; further data provided by W. Boxman and B. Wink.

33. Boer, *Indië*, 161; correspondence author with B. Wink.

34. Boer, *Indië*, 161; Rapport Kengen, 53 (Ward collection, SLH); interview with J.A.J. Oonincx.

35. Preserved part of Operations Report JAC (via A.B. Wolff); interviews with P.R. Jolly and P.A. Hoyer.

36. See Part 1B.

Chapter 1A.6

1. Preserved part of Operations Report JAC, with anonymous notes on numbers of assigned aircraft (via A.B. Wolff); A.A.M. van Rest's notes (his pocket book). The Hawks are not mentioned separately; according to P.G. Tideman, the two aircraft were constantly combat ready, but they were never committed because of the restrictions imposed to the operational use (not to be used for air defence).

2. Kelly, *Hurricane over the jungle*, 205, 207, letter by Vincent; G.M. Bruggink's notes (his pocket book); interviews and correspondence with P.R. Jolly, P.G. Tideman and F.R. Lettinga (at the time commander of Tjisaoek); Boer, *Indië*, 16.

3. Cull *et al.*, 204.

4. A.A.M. van Rest's notes (his pocket book), see also Concise report of Capt. Van Rest, Fort Leavenworth, May 1942 (Ward collection, SLH); correspondence author and further interview with B. Wink; interview with G.J. de

Haas. According to W. Boxman he did not fly along during this aerial combat (the first after the death of Tlt D. Dekker).

5. G.M. Bruggink's notes (his pocket book); correspondence author with G.M. Bruggink; interview with P.R. Jolly.

6. Operations Report, see note 1; A.A.M. van Rest's notes (his pocket book); Boer, *Indië*, 161–2 (gives a wrong number of Brewsters taking off and an incorrect mentioning of the pilots of 1-Vl.G.V involved); further data provided by G.J. de Haas, P.A.C. Benjamins and B. Wink.

7. Interviews and correspondence with P.A.C. Benjamins, H.H.J. Simons and A.E. van Kempen.

8. Correspondence and further interviews with P.G. Tideman and B. Wink (his aircraft was used for firing tests at Samarinda II).

9. Operations Report, see note 1; A.A.M. van Rest's notes (his pocket book); see also Concise report of Capt. Van Rest, Fort Leavenworth, May 1942 (Ward collection, SLH); Rear Admiral F.W. Coster, Verslag betreffende de krijgsverrichtingen te land in Nederlands-Indië, 20 May 1942 (Marinestaf, Historische sectie, Bc–8/1, IMH; henceforth Verslag Coster), F, 14; interview with B. Wink.

10. Boer, *Indië*, 192; further data provided by G.M. Bruggink.

11. Military History Office, Senshi Sosho (Series of Military History of World War II), 34 (henceforth Senshi Sosho, 34), 552; Japanese monograph 69; Lieutenant-Colonel J.V.O. Macartney-Filgate M.C., 'The 48th Light Anti-Aircraft Regiment Royal Artillery in the Dutch East Indies, February–March 1942' (via J. Mulders, henceforth Report 48 LAA).

12. P.C. Boer, 'Het vliegtuigmaterieel en de materieelverliezen van de ML/KNIL in de periode mei 1940–mei 1942' (unpublished manuscript); Verslag Coster, F, 14; erroneously mentions only three B-17s and one fighter aircraft damaged.

13. Diary O.A.O. Kreefft and e-mail correspondence author with O.A.O. Kreefft.

14. Operations Report, see note 1; Verslag Coster, F, 14; Report 48 LAA.

15. Japanese Monograph 69; Senshi Sosho, 34, 552; Operations Report, see note 1; Maltby, *Report*, 1394, section 506; Verslag Coster, F, 14; Shores, 2, 222–3, gives incorrect information with regard to the losses of the RAF and RAAF.

16. Senshi Sosho, 34, 552; the Japanese claim in all likelihood includes probables; Report 48 LAA.

17. Interview with J.B.H. Bruinier and A. Kok.

18. Operations Report, see note 1; Coster, F, 14; Shores, 2, 224–5; interview with P.A. Hoyer (at the time attached to the local Air Officer Commanding of the fighter aircraft at Batvavia, Captain C. Terluin); correspondence with T. Kelly.

19. Operations Report, see note 1; Report 48 LAA (confirms the statement in various interviews that the formation approaching Kalidjati consisted of 20

Ki-48s); Verslag Coster, F, 14; Shores, 2, 224–5; Senshi Sosho, 34, 552; Japanese Monograph 69; data received from the Military History Department, National Institute for Defense Studies, Tokyo. The Japanese publications are not quite complete and clear with regard to the raids carried out on 24 February 1942. It is clear from Japanese documents that 21 Ki-48s in total took off from Palembang, 16 of which were to attack Kalidjati and 5 Tandjong Priok (see also Senshi Sosho, 34). The attack on Tandjong Priok, according to all Dutch sources and the Report of 48 LAA, was only carried out with four Ki-48s, however. This leads me to conclude that the Hutton section probably shot one of them down.

20. Shores, 2, 248 (dated incorrectly, however, on 28 February 1942, according to Dutch as well as Japanese data, Tjililitan was submitted to one bombing raid and that was on 24 February 1942).

21. Operations Report, see note 1; Verslag, Coster, F, 14; Shores, 2, 224–5, 247–8 (dated incorrectly, however, on 28 February 1942, see remark in note 20; Senshi Sosho, 34, 552; Japanese Monograph 69.

22. Report 48 LAA; Operations Report, see note 1; Verslag Coster, F, 14; Senshi Sosho, 34, 552. The Japanese bomber crews claimed to have set fire to a larger plane and two smaller ones. No Hurricanes were lost in the bombing raid, but possibly one or two militarised light planes of the MVAF were.

23. Operations Report, see note 1; Verslag Coster, F, 14; Report 48 LAA; Senshi Sosho, 34, 552.

24. Japanese Monograph 69; this mission is not mentioned in Senshi Sosho, 34, 552; Report 48 LAA.

25. Shores, 2, 236 (dated incorrectly on 27 February 1942, Vincent's visit took place on the same day as his visit to Tjisaoek, which was on 24 February 1942); Operations Report, see note 1; correspondence author with T. Kelly.

26. Shores, 2, 236 (dated incorrectly, see remark in note 25).

27. Operations Report, see note 1; Verslag Coster, F, 14; Report 48 LAA.

28. Diary entry O.A.O. Kreefft and e-mail with explanation from O.A.O. Kreefft.

29. Shores, 2, 236 (dated incorrectly, see remark in note 25); interview with H. Creutzberg (Vincent called BRITAIR about the departure of 2-Vl.G.V, and created quite a stir; afterwards it appeared that BRITAIR did know about the departure).

30. Senshi Sosho, 34, 552; Military History Office, Senshi Sosho (Series Military History of World War II), 26, 646.

31. Report 48 LAA; interview with P.A. Hoyer; Senshi Sosho, 34, 552; Japanese Monograph 69; data received from the Military History Department, National Institute for Defense Studies, Tokyo. Preserved documents of the Army air force do not mention all losses incurred; Dutch and British sources, however, show that there were indeed such losses. Salvaged parts of crashed Ki-48 bombers were collected at Andir and at Tjililitan, at Kalidjati the Battery of 48 LAA put a piece of a shot down Ki-48 on display.

Chapter 1A.7

1. Boer, *Indië*, 165, 175–6; interview with H. Creutzberg.
2. Ibid.
3. The allied bomber deployment is described in Part 1B.
4. Boer, *Indië*, 163; Military History Office, Senshi Sosho (Series of Military History of World War II), 26 (henceforth Senshi Sosho, 26), 646.
5. Correspondence author with T. Kelly; Shores, 2, 228: Boer, *Indië*, 158, 163.
6. Ibid.
7. Shores, 2, 228.
8. Lieutenant-Colonel J.V.O. Macartney-Filgate M.C., 'The 48th Light Anti-Aircraft Regiment Royal Artillery in the Dutch East Indies, February–March 1942' (henceforth Report 48 LAA, via J. Mulders); Boer, *Indië*, 158; correspondence author with T. Kelly; interview with P.A. Hoyer. The 1st Division of the KNIL later confirmed that one Japanese 'fighter' had crashed.
9. Senshi Sosho, 26, 628, 649; Report 48 LAA.
10. Boer, *Indië*, 158, 163; Shores, 2, 228.
11. Rear Admiral F.W. Coster, Verslag betreffende de krijgsverrichtingen te land in Nederlands-Indië, 20 May 1942, F, 14 (Marinestaf, Historische sectie, Bc–8/1, IMH; henceforth Verslag Coster).
12. Bosscher, 2, 272.
13. Bosscher, 2, 272, 299.
14. Military History Office, Senshi Sosho (Series of Military History of World War II), 34 (henceforth Senshi Sosho, 34), 552.
15. Boer, *Indië*, 125, 162–3; interview with H. Creutzberg.
16. Boer, *Indië*, 125, 162–3; further information provided by A. Kok, H.J. Mulder and J.C. Jacobs.
17. Ibid.
18. Ibid.
19. Senshi Sosho, 34, 552.
20. Report 48 LAA; interview with J. Hendriks; see also Boer, *Indië*, 125, 163.
21. Senshi Sosho, 34, 552; Senshi Sosho, 26, 646; Report 48 LAA; interview with J. Hendriks.
22. Following a discussion with R.A.D. Anemaet.
23. Bosscher, 2, 273; Unclassified report of 17th Pursuit Squadron (P) activity in Java 14 January–February 1942 (AFHRA, Maxwell AFB, via G.J. Casius); interviews and correspondence with H.H.J. Simons and B. Wink; see also the report of H.H.J. Simons, 1946 (dossier Simons, Ward collection, SLH).
24. Ibid.
25. A.A.M. van Rest's notes (his pocket book); correspondence and interviews with P.G. Tidmeman, P.A.C. Benjamins, A. Bergamin; A.E. van Kempen, G.J. de Haas, J.P. Adam and J.C. Benschop.

26. Ibid.
27. Senshi Sosho, 26, 618; Senshi Sosho, 34, 551.
28. Senshi Sosho, 34, 553.
29. P.C. Boer, 'Het vliegtuigmaterieel en de materieelverliezen van de ML/KNIL in de periode mei 1940–mei 1942' (unpublished manuscript).
30. Senshi Sosho, 26, 631.
31. Senshi Sosho, 34, 551.

Chapter 1A.8

1. See Part 2.
2. Ibid.
3. A.A.M. van Rest's notes (his pocket book); interviews with R.A.D. Anemaet.
4. Boer, *Indië*, 164 (gives partially incomplete and incorrect information on the number of aircraft); A.A.M. van Rest's notes (his pocket book); interviews with W. Boxman, H.M. Haye and G.J. de Haas.
5. P.C. Boer, 'Het vliegtuigmaterieel en de materieelverliezen van de ML/KNIL in de periode mei 1940–mei 1942' (unpublished manuscript).
6. Cull *et al.*, 208; interview with P.R. Jolly.
7. See Part 2.
8. A.A.M. van Rest's notes (his pocket book); Kelly, *Hurricane over the jungle*, 204, Vincent's letter.
9. Military History Office, Senshi Sosho (Series of Military History of World War II), 34 (henceforth Senshi Sosho, 34), 553; Japanese Monograph 69.
10. Lieutenant-Colonel J.V.O. Macartney-Filgate M.C., 'The 48th Light Anti-Aircraft Regiment Royal Artillery in the Dutch East Indies, February–March 1942' (henceforth Report 48 LAA, via J. Mulders); A.A.M. van Rest's notes (his pocket book); correspondence author with T. Kelly; interview with H. Creutzberg; see also Shores, 2, 235.
11. Shores, 2, 235; interviews with H. Creutzberg and P.A. Hoyer.
12. Maltby, *Report*, 1398, section 547; Report 48 LAA; correspondence author with T. Kelly; see also Kelly, *Hurricane over the jungle*, 198; Shores, 2, 246 (dated incorrectly after 226 Group History); 226 Group History (AHB, dates Vincent's visit incorrectly on 28 February 1942).
13. Report 48 LAA; Kelly, *Hurricane over the jungle*, 198; Shores, 2, 246 (however, dated incorrectly on 28 February 1942).
14. Rear Admiral F.W. Coster, Verslag betreffende de krijgsverrichtingen te land in Nederlands-Indië, 20 May 1942 (Marinestaf, Historische sectie, Bc-8/1, IMH; henceforth Verslag Coster), F, 15 (confirms that in total "probably" five Japanese aircraft … [were] … shot down); interview with P.A. Hoyer.
15. Hagens, 131; Report 48 LAA (dated incorrectly on 28 February 1942, probably in conformity with a JAC Operations Report on 27 February that appeared the next day, see note 21); interview with J. Coblijn.

16. Fabricius, 118–9; Maltby, *Report*, 1398, section 547.

17. Military History Office, Senshi Sosho (Series of Military History of World War II), 26 (henceforth Senshi Sosho, 26), 645, 649; Senshi Sosho, 34, 553.

18. Senshi Sosho, 26, 619; Bosscher, 2, 229.

19. Boer, *Indië*, 165; Bosscher, 2, 300.

20. Bosscher, 2, 262–3; Boer, *Indië*, 165 incorrectly states that Tandjong Priok was attacked.

21. JAC Operations Report (AIR 23/12344, PRO, via Mark Haselden) dated 28 February 1942, but, taking into account the Dutch Weermacht communiqué (collection Veuger/De Smalen, SLH) and Coster, see below, describes the events at Semplak of 27 February 1942; Verslag Coster, F, 15; Schotborgh (ed.), *Nederlands-Indië contra Japan*, IV, 141; see also Shores, 2, 235 (incorrectly mentions three Dutch planes that were lost); interview with P.A. Hoyer.

22. See Part 2.

23. See Part 1B.

Chapter 1A.9

1. Military History Office, Senshi Sosho (Series of Military History of World War II), 34 (henceforth Senshi Sosho, 34), 624–8, tables 29 up to and including 31 (losses and additions fighter aircraft per month).

2. Ibid. In Senshi Sosho, 34 there are many references to the logistic situation. The Japanese army called the fuel supply "critical" and did its utmost to capture Palembang with its large stores of aircraft fuel intact, see for instance Senshi Sosho, 34, 498–503, 550. As for the stores and usage of the Army air force, see Senshi Sosho, 34, 643–6.

3. Vliegveldgids Nederlands-Indië–Airfield guide Netherlands-Indies (Ward collection, SLH); interviews with A.B. Wolff, P.A. Hoyer, P.A.C. Benjamins and H. Creutzberg.

4. Discussion on this subject with former ML fighter pilots P.A. Hoyer and A.E. Stoove; correspondence with P.G. Tideman.

5. The Ki-43 appeared to have a light construction, without armour for the pilot and without self-sealing fuel tanks.

6. Interview with L.A.R. Adam, the repairs on the American Douglas A-24 dive bombers were given priority.

7. See for instance Kelly, *Hurricane over the jungle*, 186. The Navy O could operate over 8,000 metres, but only with oxygen for the pilot. The Yamamada fighter group did not have this.

8. Interviews and correspondence with P.A.C. Benjamins, A.E. van Kempen and W. Boxman.

9. Ibid.; see also Rapport Kengen, 42 (Ward collection, SLH) and Spick, *Allied Fighter Aces, The Air Combat Techniques of World War II.*

10. See for instance the biographies in Ikuhiko Hata *et al.*, *Japanese Army Air Force fighter units and their aces, 1931–1945*, 188ff.

11. As for the results of the allied bombers see Part 1B.

12. See for instance Military History Office, Senshi Sosho (Series Military History of World War II), 26, 649 for the supply problems at Palembang II.

13. In conformity with note 11.

Chapter 1B.1

1. J.J. Nortier, 'De gevechten bij Palembang in februari 1942', *Militaire Spectator* 154 (1985): 7, 8, 312–25 and 355–68.

2. Ibid.

3. Ibid.

4. Ibid.

5. Boer, *Indië*, 95–6.

6. Ibid., 99–100.

7. Ibid., 97, 104–110; interview with A.B. Wolff (pointed out to me that the mission led by him on 17 February was targeted at Japanese ships in the Moesi delta and not the BPM refinery or its tank park).

8. In conformity with note 1.

9. Rear Admiral F.W. Coster, Verslag betreffende de krijgsverrichtingen te land in Nederlands-Indië, 20 May 1942 (Marinestaf, Historische sectie, Bc–8/1, IMH; henceforth Verslag Coster), D, 5.

10. Ibid.; Hoogenband, van den and Schotborgh (ed.), *Nederlands-Indië contra Japan* (henceforth NIcJ), VII, 19–20; Boer, *Indië*, 102.

11. Hoogenband, van den (ed.), NIcJ, III, 124–6, 168; De Jong, 11a, I, 2e helft, 860–3; Helfrich, I, 351.

12. Hoogenband, van den (ed.), NIcJ, III, 128–9; Verslag Coster, D, 5–6; interview with W. Mulder.

13. For a brief survey see for instance Bezemer, 273–84.

14. For a brief survey of the missions to Bali see Boer, *Indië*, 166–8.

15. Wavell, *Despatch*, section 28 (confirms the force planning with regard to the RAF/RAAF); correspondence of S.H.A. Begemann (via W. Bosman); interviews with H. Creutzberg, A.B. Wolff and F.R. Lettinga.

16. ABDACOM Situation reports and Dutch Operations Reports (summaries) (Veuger/De Smalen collection, SLH; henceforth ABDACOM/Dutch reports); NEI Order of battle information (available aircraft/crews) (AIR 23/4716, PRO, via Mark Haselden; henceforth NEI ORBAT); correspondence with A.D.M. Moorrees; information from J. Holmes (via A.D.M. Moorrees) with regard to movements of 36 and 100 Squadron.

17. Maltby, *Report*, 1393, section 496–7.

18. Maltby, *Report*, 1393, section 497 (mentions a number of 26 Blenheims and an incorrect, too high, number of operationally serviceable Hudsons); Shores, 2, 193 (mentions a number of 29 Blenheims, this number is confirmed by several RAF veterans of the squadrons at Kalidjati and has been copied by me as correct).

19. NEI ORBAT; Maltby, *Report*, 1393, section 498. The number of operationally serviceable aircraft was sometimes higher, as aircraft that had been assigned for training or special operations, such as convoy protection, were not counted as available.

20. Boer, *Indië*, 81 (erroneously mentions 13 February 1942 as the date of transfer for 2-Vl.G.I, this must be 12 February 1942); furthermore, it is not mentioned that along with the 1-Vl.G.I patrol also two Glenn Martins of 2-Vl.G. I were temporarily stationed at Malang.

21. Boer, *Indië*, 82–3.

22. Ibid., 83–5.

23. Ibid., 85; NEI ORBAT. Interviews show that with regard to the ML the number of operationally serviceable aircraft was equal to the number of available aircraft.

24. Boer, *Indië*, 261–3; interviews with H. Creutzberg and W. Mulder.

Chapter 1B.2

1. ABDACOM Situation Reports and Dutch Operations Reports (summaries) (Veuger/De Smalen collection, SLH); NEI Order of battle information (available aircraft/crews) (AIR 23/4716, PRO, via Mark Haselden; henceforth NEI ORBAT); Shores, 2, 193–4; Maltby, *Report*, 1393, section 497; interviews with A.D.M. Moorrees, T. van der Muur and P.A. Hoyer.

2. NEI ORBAT; A.B. Wolff's notes (his pocket book) and H.J. Weijschede notes (his pocket book); Maltby, *Report*, 1394, section 504 (mentions the mission, but dates it incorrectly on 19 February 1942); interviews with A.D.M. Moorrees, C.J.H. Samson and G. Cooke; correspondence author and further interview with F.R. Lettinga.

3. Shores, 2, 199; interview with T. van der Muur.

4. Shores, 2, 199–200.

5. Ibid. (Shores erroneously mentions Sidell, whose reconnaissance mission did not take place until 19 February, see also Shores, 2, 203); Maltby, *Report*, 1393, section 503; interview with T. van der Muur.

6. Interviews with J.C. Benschop and T. van der Muur.

7. AAFHS 29 A; Edmonds, 342.

8. Ibid.

9. Maltby, *Report*, 1393, section 501; interview with J.V.C. Wyllie.

10. Interviews with C.W.A. Oyens and J.C. Benschop.

11. NEI ORBAT; interviews with G. Cooke, K.B.A. Karssen, B. Erkelens, T. van den Dolder, M. Jassies, R.A. Maassen, and H.E. van Wijk.

12. Questionnaire R. de Senerpont Domis (Ward collection, SLH); interview with G. Cooke.

13. Rapport Kengen, 49 (Ward collection, SLH; states incorrectly that the overall command passed on to the RAF); further interviews with F. Stapel and F. J.W. den Ouden; correspondence author with A.D.M. Moorrees.

14. Ibid.

15. NEI ORBBAT; A.B. Wolff's notes (his pocket book); correspondence author with F.R. Lettinga and J.G. Bücker.

16. Boer, *Indië*, 113; further interview with A.B. Wolff and J. Coblijn.

17. Boer, *Indië*, 113 (after Senshi Sosho, 34, see below, mentions erroneously 4,800 litres); Military History Office, Senshi Sosho (Series Military History of World War II), 34 (henceforth Senshi Sosho, 34), 550, mentions erroneously 4,800 litres; data received from the public information office of Shell with regard to the contents of the storage tanks.

18. Boer, *Indië*, 113; further interview with J.H. Wetzels and R. Timmermans.

19. Shores, 2, 199 (event dated incorrectly, see 203), 203; interview with T. van der Muur.

20. Shores, 2, 203; Rear Admiral F.W. Coster, Verslag betreffende de krijgsver-richtingen te land in Nederlands-Indië, 20 May 1942, F, 13 (Marinestaf, Historische sectie, Bc-8/1, IMH).

21. AAFHS 29A (states the good weather as the reason for aborting the mission); account of the mission by F.R. Lettinga (correspondence author with F.R. Lettinga); interviews with W. de Vrij (at the time mechanic-air gunner assigned to the Lettinga crew) and M.F. Noorman van der Dussen.

22. Ibid.

23. Correspondence author with A.D.M. Moorrees; Shores, 2, 204 and further information provided by Chr. Shores (Shores erroneously mentions M.K. Holland as the pilot of one of the Blenheims); interview with J.V.C. Wyllie (confirms that he and not M.K. Holland flew the lead plane of 84 Squadron and with Bennett as air gunner); Maltby, *Report*, 1394 and Boer, *Indië*, 114 give incorrect information.

24. Shores, 2, 204–7; interview with J.V.C. Wyllie.

25. Ibid.; Senshi Sosho, 34, 550.

26. Shores, 2, 206.

27. AAFHS 29A, confirms as the total claim of the P I raid, two enemy fighters downed; Shores, 2, 207; Senshi Sosho, 34, 550.

28. Boer, *Indië*, 114

29. Ibid.

30. Ibid.

31. Ibid.

32. Boer, *Indië*, 114–5; further interviews with H.J. Burgers and D. Brouwer.

33. Verslag B.P. de Vries (Dossier NIcJ 5/74, IMG).

34. Ibid.; Bosscher, 2, 251.

Chapter 1B.3

1. ABDACOM Situation Reports and Dutch Operations Reports (summaries) (Veuger/De Smalen collection, SLH; henceforth ABDACOM/Dutch reports); NEI Order of battle information (available aircraft/crews) (AIR 23/4716, PRO, via Mark Haselden; henceforth NEI ORBAT); information with regard to 27 and 34 Squadrons received from Chr. Shores; see also Shores, 2, 212 (according to ABDAIR Reports the reorganisation of the Hudsons squadrons, contrary to what Shores states, took place on 21 February 1942, however, with transfer of aircraft next day).

2. NEI ORBAT; A.B. Wolff's notes (his pocket book); correspondence author with F.R. Lettinga and J.G. Bücker.

3. Diary entries F.H. van Onselen (his pocket book); correspondence author with R.C. Schäftlein; interviews with A.B. Wolff and K. van Gessel. At the time it was concluded that one of the four tanks had been hit by the Van Erkel crew (on 19 February) and the other three by the Schäftlein patrol.

4. Interviews with J. Coblijn and M.P. Bosman; correspondence author with M.P. Bosman; Military History Office, Senshi Sosho (Series Military History of World War II), 34 (henceforth Senshi Sosho, 34), 550, states: "the fire in the fuel tank [farm] was stirred up once more".

5. Original operations summary 2-Vl.G.III missions; Rear Admiral F.W. Coster, Verslag betreffende de krijgsverrichtingen te land in Nederlands-Indië, 20 May 1942 (Marinestaf, Historische sectie, Bc-8/1, IMH; henceforth Verslag Coster) F, 14 (states the result of 2-Vl.G.III in conformity with the operations summary); Senshi Sosho, 34, 546 (discovery Tandjoengkarang airfield).

6. Bosscher, 2, 252; Maltby, *Report*, 1391, sections 478 and 479 (in all probability refers to the sorties of 2-Vl.G.III and earlier reconnaissance flights by Hudsons).

7. Maltby, *Report*, 1394, section 505; Shores, 2, 212, mentions four direct hits on ships (this is not confirmed by any document, however).

8. Shores, 2, 205–6, however, dated incorrectly on 19 February 1942; Maltby, *Report*, 1394, section 505, mentions "severe fighter opposition" of fighters having taken off from PI.

9. Original combat report of the mission (with thanks to G.J. Casius).

10. Ibid.

11. Logbook J. van Kruiselbergen; interviews with F.J.W. de Ouden, J. van Kruiselbergen, D.T. de Bont, F. van de Broek and W. Bohre.

12. Senshi Sosho, 34, 548; Japanese Monograph 69; Verslag Coster, F, 14; interviews with A.D.M. Moorrees, J. van Kruiselbergen, C.J.H. Samson, F.J.W. den Ouden, K.B.A. Karssen, F. van den Broek and D.T. de Bont.

13. Lieutenant-Colonel J.V.O. Macartney-Filgate M.C., 'The 48th Light Anti-Aircraft Regiment Royal Artillery in the Dutch East Indies, February–March 1942' (henceforth Report 48 LAA, via J. Mulders); interviews with J. Tap and J. Hendriks; correspondence with A.D.M. Moorrees.

Chapter 1B.4

1. Helfrich, I, 373; Rear Admiral F.W. Coster, Verslag betreffende de krijgsverrichtingen te land in Nederlands-Indië, 20 May 1942 (Marinestaf, Historische sectie, Bc-8/1, IMH; henceforth Verslag Coster) D, 5–6; interviews with W. Mulder and A.B. Wolff.

2. Bosscher, 2, 304 (states that the missions were carried out in the nights of 23 to 24 and 24 to 25 February); G.F. Rijnders (his logbook, flew along 22 February in the Y-69 of Groep Vliegtuigen 17 of the MLD); Helfrich, I, 375. According to Helfrich the MLD was given orders to lay magnetic mines in the evening of 20 February and the missions were carried out on 22 and 23 February 1942. This is in conformity with G.F. Rijnders. One of the committed aircraft was lost in the early morning of 23 February 1942 on landing at Tandjong Priok, with five crew members perishing. This was the Y-47 of GVT 18 (information via N. Geldhof, IMH).

3. Lieutenant-Colonel J.V.O. Macartney-Filgate M.C., 'The 48th Light Anti-Aircraft Regiment Royal Artillery in the Dutch East Indies, February–March 1942' (henceforth Report 48 LAA, via J. Mulders); interviews with J. Tap and J. Hendriks; correspondence author with A.D.M. Moorrees.

4. Description of Semplak by T. van der Muur; interviews with T. van der Muur and C.W.A. Oyens.

5. ABDACOM Situation reports and Dutch Operations Reports (summaries) (Veuger/De Smalen collection, SLH); NEI Order of battle information (available aircraft/crews) (AIR 23/4716, PRO, via Mark Haselden); ABDAIR message with regard to units to be evacuated (Veuger/De Smalen collection, SLH); A.B. Wolff's notes (his pocket book).

6. Questionnaire H.E. van Thiel (Ward collection, SLH); Verslag Coster, F, 14; interview with H.E. van Thiel.

7. Interview with K. van Gessel; diary entries F.H. van Onselen (his pocket book).

8. Shores, 2, 214; information received from the Commonwealth War Graves Commission (for dates of death of those involved see <www.cwgc.org>); personnel of Vl.G.V which helped load the bombs confirm that in the first instance two Hudsons took off, I have, however, been unable to find any further particulars or results of these reconnaissance flights.

9. Shores, 2, 214.

10. Military History Office, Senshi Sosho (Series Military History of World War II), 34 (henceforth Senshi Sosho, 34), 550; correspondence author and further interview with F.R. Lettinga.

11. Boer, *Indië*, 117.
12. Ibid.; further interviews with F.J.W. den Ouden and W. Bohre.
13. Maltby, *Report*, 1394, section 505; Shores, 2, 214, however, mentions an incorrect take off time; interviews with F.J.W. den Ouden, C.J.H. Samson and K.B.A. Karssen.
14. Shores, 2, 214.
15. Boer, *Indië*, 118; Senshi Sosho, 34, 549; Japanese Monograph, 69.
16. Boer, *Indië*, 118 (gives incorrect information on the Japanese losses); further interviews with G.A. van Cattenburch and K.B.A. Karssen; correspondence author with A.D.M. Moorrees.
17. Boer, *Indië*, 118; AHQFE Reports (AIR 24/504, PRO, via Mark Haselden); Report 48 LAA.

Chapter 1B.5

1. ABDACOM Situation Reports and Dutch Operations Reports (summaries) (Veuger/De Smalen collection, SLH); NEI Order of battle information (available aircraft/crews) (AIR 23/4716, PRO, via Mark Haselden; henceforth NEI ORBAT); A.B. Wolff's notes (his pocket book); interviews with A.B. Wolff and F.R. Lettinga.
2. See for instance De Jong, 11a, I, 2e helft, 879; see also Maltby, *Report*, 1392.
3. Bosscher, 2, 272.
4. See for instance Maltby, *Report*, 1392.
5. Bezemer, *Nederlandse Koopvaardij*, 705–6; Maltby, *Report*, 1399 (mentions erroneously 1 March 1942 as the date of transfer of 205 Squadron); see also Shores, 2, 216.
6. Bezemer, *Nederlandse Koopvaardij*, 705–6; De Jong, 11a, I, 2e helft, 879.
7. Interviews with A.B. Wolff, P.A. Hoyer and R.A. Sleeuw.
8. See for instance Gillison, 437–8; Shores, 2, 212 and Cull *et al.*, 199–201.
9. A.B. Wolff's notes (his pocket book); interviews with A.B. Wolff and J. Coblijn; the information on the deployment of 3–Vl.G.III on 22 February 1942 in Boer, *Indië*, 119 is incorrect (date of the mission concerned is incorrect).
10. Account of the reconnaissance flight by H.M. Franken and further interview with H.M. Franken; interviews with F.R. Lettinga, W. de Vrij and M.F. Noorman van der Dussen. Boer, *Indië*, 118–9, gives incorrect information on the deployment of 2-Vl.G.III. Franken's mission was dated incorrectly on 21 February 1942.
11. Military History Office, Senshi Sosho (Series Military History of World War II), 26, 646.
12. Shores, 2, 217.
13. Boer, *Indië*, 119.

14. This mission has incorrectly been left out in Boer, *Indië*, 119; further interviews with F.J.W. den Ouden and W. Bohre (at the time air gunner in the lead plane).

15. Shores, 2, 217; Maltby, *Report*, 1394, section 505, dates incorrectly, however, on 21 February 1942.

16. Gillison, 438; Shores, 2, 217; Boer, *Indië*, 118, after Maltby, *Report*, 1394, section 505, incorrectly dates the mission on 21 February 1942.

17. Rear Admiral F.W. Coster, Verslag betreffende de krijgsverrichtingen te land in Nederlands-Indië, 20 May 1942 (Marinestaf, Historische sectie, Bc-8/1, IMH; henceforth Verslag Coster), F, 13; Japanese Monograph 69; Shores, 2, 217–8. It must be remarked that the Japanese attack is mentioned in Japanese Monograph 69, but not in Military History Office, Senshi Sosho (Series Military History of World War II), 34. The aircraft lost at Semplak are specified with serial numbers in an ABDAIR message (via G.J. Casius, copied in, amongst others, Shores, 2, 217).

18. Verslag Coster, F, 13; Schotborgh (ed.), *Nederlands-Indië contra Japan*, IV, 139; Japanese Monograph 69; interview with J. van Breemen (at the time KNILM).

19. Interview with H. Creutzberg (at the time Lieutenant-Adjutant to Van Oyen).

20. Correspondence author with B. Wink; interview with C.W.A. Oyens.

Chapter 1B.6

1. Preserved part of a JAC Operations Report, with anonymous notes on the number of assigned aircraft (via A.B. Wolff); A.B. Wolff's notes (his pocket book).

2. Military History Office, Senshi Sosho (Series Military History of World War II), 34 (henceforth Senshi Sosho, 34), 550.

3. Operations Report, see note 1; A.B. Wolff's notes (his pocket book, confirms the hit); correspondence author with M.P. Bosman.

4. Operations Report, see note 1; L.H. van Onselen's notes (his pocket book); interview with K. van Gessel.

5. Operations Report, see note 1; Boer, *Indië*, 120, gives incorrect information; interview with M.F. Noorman van der Dussen; see also questionnaire J. Bos (Ward collection, SLH).

6. Operations Report, see note 1; Boer, *Indië*, 119–20.

7. Boer, *Indië*, 119–20.

8. Operations Report, see note 1; Rear Admiral F.W. Coster, Verslag betreffende de krijgsverrichtingen te land in Nederlands-Indië, 20 May 1942 (Marinestaf, Historische sectie, Bc-8/1, IMH), F, 14; according to F. Stapel (staff of Kalidjati air station) there was great enthusiasm at the time about the results and several congratulations of higher commanders were received. Preserved

Japanese documents state only the losses incurred on the ground of the 12th Hiko Dan at P I and not those of the 3rd Hiko Dan. Because of this no losses are reported in Senshi Sosho, 34 for 23 February 1942 (Military History Department, National Institute for Defense Studies, Tokyo).

9. Operations report, see note 1; Maltby, *Report*, 1394, section 507; Shores, 2, 220; interviews with H. Creutzberg and W. Mulder. See the remarks in [8].
10. Operations report, see note 1; Shores, 2, 220.

Chapter 1B.7

1. Preserved part of a JAC Operations Report, with anonymous notes on the number of assigned aircraft (via A.B. Wolff).
2. Rear Admiral F.W. Coster, Verslag betreffende de krijgsverrichtingen te land in Nederlands–Indië, 20 May 1942 (Marinestaf, Historische sectie, Bc–8/1, IMH; henceforth Verslag Coster), F, 14; Military History Office, Senshi Sosho (Series Military History of World War II), 34 (henceforth Senshi Sosho, 34), 552; Japanese Monograph 69; interview with M.F. Noorman van der Dussen.
3. Operations Report, see note 1; Verslag Coster, F, 14; correspondence author with M.P. Bosman.
4. Military History Office, Senshi Sosho (Series Military History of World War II), 26 (henceforth Senshoi Sosho, 26), 646; Senshi Sosho, 34, 551.
5. Operations report, see note 1; L.H. van Onselen's notes (his pocket book); see also questionnaire L.H. van Onselen (Ward collection, SLH); Verslag Coster, F, 14; interview with J. Coblijn.
6. Ibid.; data received from the Dutch War Graves Foundation (OGS); interviews with former class mates of the Mechanics School of P. van der Zee and with A.B. Wolff (his CO).
7. Senshi Sosho, 34, 552; Japanese Monograph 69.
8. Japanese Monograph 69 (the mentionings in Senshi Sosho, 34 are not complete).
9. Verslag Coster, F, 14; Lieutenant-Colonel J.V.O. Macartney-Filgate M.C., 'The 48th Light Anti-Aircraft Regiment Royal Artillery in the Dutch East Indies, February–March 1942' (henceforth Report 48 LAA, via J. Mulders); interviews with K. Akkerman, K.B.A. Karssen and C.J.H. Samson.
10. Interview with J.V.C. Wyllie.
11. Bosscher, 2, 304; Honselaar, 196; Senshi Sosho, 34, 551 (the Ki-43 pilots claimed to have downed two four-engine flying boats near Noordwachter); Senshi Sosho, 26, 646 (the Japanese Navy pilots claimed to have downed one of the two Dorniers). In view of the rather large number of Ki-43 pilots involved, an over-claim is not unlikely, in contrast to the claim of the Japanese Navy O pilots. Therefore, I have concluded that it is most likely that one Dornier was shot down by Ki-43 pilots and one by Navy O pilots.

Chapter 1B.8

1. Preserved part of a JAC Operations Report, with anonymous notes on the number of assigned aircraft (via A.B. Wolff); as for the RAF/RAAF strength see the comparable state in Maltby, *Report*, 1394, section 509.

2. Operations Report, see note 1; see also Rear Admiral F.W. Coster, Verslag betreffende de krijgsverrichtingen te land in Nederlands-Indië, 20 May 1942 (Marinestaf, Historische sectie, Bc–8/1, IMH; henceforth Verslag Coster), F, 14, last paragraph (date in margin absent), gives a somewhat abbreviated version of the mission account from the operations report; account of the mission by H.M. Franken; Boer, *Indië*, 121, erroneously dates this mission on 24 February and states assigned crews incorrectly; Boer, *Indië*, 124 (incorrectly mentions that a Blenheim was intercepted).

3. Account of the mission by H.M. Franken; interview with F.R. Lettinga.

4. Ibid.; Military History Office, Senshi Sosho (Series Military History of World War II), 34 (henceforth Senshi Sosho, 34), 552 (the downed aircraft was mistakenly identified as a Hudson at the time); Verslag Coster, F, 14.

5. Operations Report, see note 1; see also Verslag Coster, F, 14; Senshi Sosho, 34, 552; letter of Th. Magnee to a relative in Batavia (written at Kaleander around 27 February 1942 and received late March 1942 (Ward collection, SLH).

6. Interviews with F.R. Lettinga and J.G. Bücker.

7. Interviews with A.B. Wolff, G. Cooke, C.J.H. Samson and K. Akkermans; Boer, *Indië*, 125, incorrectly states that 3-Vl.G.III did not have any operationally serviceable aircraft.

8. Shores, 2, 222; Boer, *Indië*, 124.

9. Senshi Sosho, 34, 552; Military History Office, Senshi Sosho (Series Military History of World War II), 26 (henceforth Senshi Sosho, 26), 646, confirms the emergency landing at sea of the Ki-43; Lieutenant-Colonel J.V.O. Macartney-Filgate M.C., 'The 48th Light Anti-Aircraft Regiment Royal Artillery in the Dutch East Indies, February–March 1942' (henceforth Report 48 LAA, via J. Mulders); interviews with J. Hendriks, C.J.H. Samson, K. Akkermans and G. Cooke; Shores, 2, 222.

10. Operations Report, see note 1; Maltby, *Report*, 1394, section 509; Shores, 2, 222–3, dated incorrectly, however, on 24 February 1942 (the account of the Japanese raid in two waves, one of which on low altitude, points at 25 February 1942).

11. Shores, 2, 222–4; Senshi Sosho, 34, 552, does not mention the fight (no account has been preserved, Military History Department, National Institute for Defense Studies, Tokyo).

12. Operations report, see note 1.

13. Ibid.

Chapter 1B.9

1. For a concise summary see for instance Maltby, *Report*, 1394, section 523.
2. Boer, *Indië*, 165, 176; interviews with H. Creutzberg and W. Mulder.
3. Ibid.
4. The allied fighter deployment is described in Part 1A.
5. Military History Office, Senshi Sosho (Series Military History of World War II), 26 (henceforth Senshi Sosho, 26), 618 and Military History Office, Senshi Sosho, 34 (henceforth Senshi Sosho, 34), 551.
6. Senshi Sosho, 34, 553.
7. P.C. Boer, "Het vliegtuigmaterieel en de materielverliezen van de ML/KNIL in de periode mei 1940–mei 1942" (unpublished manuscript).
8. Senshi Sosho, 26, 631.
9. Senshi Sosho, 34, 551.

Chapter 1B.10

1. Interviews with A.B. Wolff, H. Creutzberg and W. Mulder; see also Helfrich, I, 351.
2. Preserved part of a JAC Operations Report, with anonymous notes on the number of assigned aircraft (via A.B. Wolff).
3. Operations Report, see note 2; interviews with C.J.H. Samson and W. Mulder.
4. Boscher, 2, 277–8, 299; Morrison, 338; Shores, 2, 233; Helfrich, I, 395–6; data with regard to the deployment of MLD flying boats received from N. Geldhof, IMH; interviews with H. Creutzberg and W. Mulder.
5. Ibid.
6. Operations Report, see note 2; account of the mission by M.F. Noorman van der Dussen.
7. Helfrich, I, 351; interviews with A.B. Wolff, C.J.H. Samson and F. Stapel. Several of the photographs (not preserved) were put up at Lieutenant-Colonel Zomer's command post at Kalidjati. The estimate of the percentage of destroyed storage capacity was made known at the time by the ML Command (correspondence of S.H.A. Begemann, via W. Bosman; interview with F. Stapel).
8. Helfrich, I, 395–6; Shores, 2, 233; interviews with H. Creutzberg, W. Mulder and F. Stapel.
9. Ibid.
10. Operations Report, see note 2; correspondence author with R.C. Schäftlein (11-02-1988) and M.P. Bosman (4-10-1987); interview with K. van Gessel.
11. Correspondence author with R.C. Schäftlein (11-02-1988) and M.P. Bosman (4-10-1987); interview with R. Haasjes.

12. Correspondence author with M.P. Bosman (4-10-1987); interview with R. Haasjes.
13. Correspondence author with M.P. Bosman (3-4-1988).
14. In conformity with note 4.
15. Honselaar, *Vleugels van de vloot*, 196–200.
16. Military History Office, Senshi Sosho (Series Military History of World War II), 34, 553.
17. In conformity with note 15.
18. Interviews with H. Creutzberg and W. Mulder.
19. Boer, *Indië*, 176; Bosscher, 2, 274.
20. Boer, *Indië*, 177; Bosscher, 2, 277–8.
21. Boer, *Indië*, 260; Shores, 2, 234; Edmonds, 408, 412 (erroneously dates departure of Kota Gede on 28 February 1942); Bezemer, *Nederlandse Koopvaardij*, 721.
22. Boer, *Indië*, 264–5.
23. Correspondence with Chr. Shores; interviews with G. Cooke, K. Akkerman, C.J. Gilin, F.J. W. den Ouden, D.T. de Bont and J. van Kruiselbergen.

Chapter 1B.11

1. Bosscher, 2, 277–8; Morison, 338; Shores, 2, 233; Helfrich, I, 395–6; data with regard to the deployment of MLD flying boats received from N. Geldhof, IMH; interviews with H. Creutzberg and W. Mulder.
2. Honselaar, 196–7; interviews with H. Creutzberg and W. Mulder; Bosscher, 2, 299; Helfrich, I, 395–6. See also Bosscher, 2, 593, note 163, the text of the two telegrams does not relate to the western, but the eastern invasion fleet.
3. Interviews with H. Creutzberg and A.B. Wolff.
4. Interviews with H. Creutzberg and W. Mulder; Helfrich, I, 394; Bosscher, 2, 275.
5. Preserved part of a JAC Operations Report, with anonymous notes on the number of assigned aircraft (via A.B. Wolff).
6. Operations Report, see note 5 and Maltby, *Report*, 1396, section 530; Shores, 2, 237; interviews with W. Mulder and C.J.H. Samson.
7. Boer, *Indië*, 128–9; further interviews with A.H. Erdkamp and A.B. Wolff; interview with P.G. Tideman.
8. Boer, *Indië*, 128–9.
9. Ibid.
10. Ibid.; interviews with P.G. Tideman and A.B. Wolff.
11. Correspondence author and interview with F.R. Lettinga; interview with W. de Vrij.
12. Ibid.
13. Ibid.; Operations report, see note 5.
14. Operations Report, see note 5; Shores, 2, 237.

15. Rear Admiral F.W. Coster, *Verslag betreffende de krijgsverrichtingen te land in Nederlands-Indië*, 20 May 1942 (Marinestaf, Historische sectie, Bc-8/1, IMH) F, 15; interview with J.V.C. Wyllie and his account of the mission; interviews with H. Creutzberg and W. Mulder.
16. Boer, *Indië*, 127; interview with J. Stemerdink.
17. Military History Office, Senshi Sosho (Series Military History of World War II), 26, 628; interviews with H. Creutzberg, W. Mulder and A.B. Wolff.
18. Boer, *Indië*, 194; Maltby, *Report*, 1396–97; interviews with A.B. Wolff and H. Creutzberg.
19. Interviews with H. Creutzberg, C.J.H. Samson, A.B. Wolff, F.J.W. den Ouden and J. Coblijn.
20. Boer, *Indië*, 129 and further interviews with J.C.H. Samson and J. van Loggem.

Chapter 1B.12

1. The Blenheim Mark Is were (with Vildebeestes and Albacores of 36 Squadron) mainly deployed for reconnaissance of the north coast of western Java, but possibly also one or two times for carrying out reconnaissance flights of the roads from Oosthaven to Palembang in southern Sumatra. It is estimated that the Mark Is in the period described did not fly more than ten operational sorties and for the rest they were used only for transport and training flights. The south coast of western Java was regularly reconnoitered by the ML with Lockheed L212-trainers of the 4th Reconnaissance afdeling at Pameungpeuk.
2. Various surveys of strengths show that the 59th and 64th Sentais did not receive any replacement aircraft in the event of losses (Military History Department, National Institute for Defense Studies, Tokyo). In the Senshi Sosho volumes 34 and 26 published by the Military History Office there are several references with regard to the logistic situation. The Japanese army called the supply of fuels "critical" and did its utmost to capture the large aircraft fuel stores at Palembang intact. See for instance Senshi Sosho, 34, 498–503 and 550, and 643–6 for the stores and usage of the Army air force; see Senshi Sosho, 34, 624–8; tables 29 up to and including 31 for the losses and replacements of aircraft.
3. See for instance Senshi Sosho, 26, 649, with regard to the supply problems at Palembang.

Chapter 2.1

1. For the discovery of the convoy see for instance Maltby, *Report*, 1396.
2. AAFHS 29A; Unclassified report of 17th Pursuit Squadron (P) activity in Java 14 January–February 1942 (AFHRA, Maxwell AFB, via G.J. Casius;

henceforth Report 17 PS); correspondence and further interview with H.H.J. Simons, interviews with H. Creutzberg, B. Wink and J.B.H. Bruinier. There was no 303-inch ammunition, hydraulic oil and oxygen for the Hurricanes at Ngoro. There were also no crystals for the board radios. Boer, *Indië*, 174, erroneously states that the Simons patrol was transferred on 24 February.

3. Bosscher, 2, 273; Report 17 PS; correspondence and further interview with H.H.J. Simons; interview with B. Wink. Boer, *Indië*, 175, erroneously states that 12 P-40s took off.

4. Report 17 PS; Rear-Admiral F.W. Coster, Verslag betreffende de krijgsverrichtingen te land in Nederlands-Indië, 20 May 1942 (Marinestaf, Historische sectie, Bc-8/1, IMH), F, 15; Winslow, 116; Schotborgh (ed.), *Nederlands-Indië contra Japan* (henceforth NIcJ), IV, 141 (erroneously suggests that the fighters were involved in the failure of the bombing raid); correspondence and further interview with H.H.J. Simons; see also Shores, 2, 234.

5. Military History Office, Senshi Sosho (Series Military History of World War II), 26 (henceforth Senshi Sosho, 26), 630; due to the absence of a Japanese combat report the American claim cannot be verified.

6. Interviews with G.J. de Haas and H. Huys; see also G.M. Bruggink's report (1946, Ward collection, SLH). A seventh Brewster returned with trouble to Andir and did not arrive until 28 February 1942 (pilot H. Huys).

7. Bosscher, 2, 277–8, 299; Morison, 338; Shores, 2, 233; Helfrich, I, 395–6; data with regard to the deployment of MLD flying boats received from N. Geldhof, IMH; interviews with H. Creutzberg and W. Mulder.

8. Ibid.

9. Interviews with H. Creutzberg and W. Mulder; Elt H.F. Zeylemaker (at the time Staff Bandoeng Group KNIL) describes the procedures in his notes "Beschrijving oorlogsoperaties H.F. Zeylemaker" from March 1942 (via A. van Aarem and J. Mossou).

10. Honselaar, 196–7; interviews with H. Creutzberg and W. Mulder; Bosscher, 2, 299; Helfrich, I, 395–6. See also Bosscher, 2, 593 note 163, the text of the two telegrams does not relate to the western, but the eastern invasion fleet.

11. Operations Journal 19th Bomb. Group, 8 Dec. 1941–19 March 1942 (AFHRA, Maxwell AFB, via G.J. Casius), 60; interviews with H. Creutzberg and A.B. Wolff; Bosscher, 2, 274 (probably the committed heavy bomber is meant here; Bosscher, however, erroneously states that no aircraft could be made available). See also AAFHS 29A for the mission of the LB-30, take off time was 00:35 hrs, landing 06:25 hrs.

12. Interviews with H. Creutzberg and W. Mulder; Helfrich, I, 394; Bosscher, 2, 275.

13. Interviews with H. Creutzberg and W. Mulder, G.J. de Haas, and P.G. Tideman; Bosscher, 2, 600, note 251; A.A.M. van Rest's diary entry (his

pocket book), Van Rest noted, "All Brewsters made available for permanent protection of fleet."

14. See Part 1A.
15. Interviews with H. Creutzberg and W. Mulder, J. Geverdinck and J.C. Benschop.
16. AAFHS 29A; Preserved part of a JAC Operations Report, with anonymous notes on the number of assigned aircraft (via A.B. Wolff); data logbook W.P. van der Baars (at the time GVT 7) and letters of KLTZ W. P. Petschi dated 7 January 1955 and OVL 1 B. Sjerp dated 1 October 1947 with regard to GVT 7 (via N. Geldhof, IMH).
17. Honselaar, 196–201. After the war it became clear that the flying boat had been shot down by Japanese fighter aircraft.
18. Operations Report, see note 16 and Maltby, *Report*, 1396, section 530; Shores, 2, 237; interviews with W. Mulder and C.J.H. Samson.
19. See Part 1B.
20. Ibid.
21. Senshi Sosho, 26, 628; interviews with H. Creutzberg, W. Mulder and A.B. Wolff.
22. Gillison, 434, 436; NIcJ, IV, 113; Bosscher, 298–9; data with regard to convoy MS 5 received from G. Busby (e-mail correspondence August–September 2004 with a survey of data from American and Australian primary sources); e-mail correspondence with W.H. Bartsch (July 2009).
23. De Jong, 11a, I, 2e helft, 887–8.
24. Bosscher, 2, 298–9; Bezemer, 327; data with regard to GVT 5 received from N. Geldhof, IMH; see also Shores, 2, 240. Morison, 360–1, gives an incorrect account, which has been copied entirely or partially in a number of later publications (see for instance Edmonds, 417–8).
25. Bosscher, 2, 298–9; Messimer, 265; Shores, 2, 240–1.
26. Interviews with H. Creutzberg and P.G. Tideman.
27. Interviews with J.C. Benschop (at the time Technical Service at Andir and responsible for the TD personnel at Tjilatjap, J.G. Bücker (at the time 2-Vl.G.III and responsible for the expansion of Tjisaoek for the American squadrons) and J. Geverdinck (at the time CO of the infantry section that had to help with offloading). The Chief of Staff of South Group KNIL was to be present to welcome the Americans of the Langley.
28. In conformity with note 25; Senshi Sosho, 26, 662; data with regard to GVT 5 received from N. Geldhof, IMH.
29. In conformity with note 25.
30. Bosscher, 2, 277–8.
31. AAFHS 29A; Operations Journal 19th Bomb. Group, 8 Dec. 1941–19 March 1942 (AFHRA, Maxwell AFB, via G.J. Casius); Edmonds, 422; interview with W. Mulder; Bosscher, 2, 274 (erroneously states that no American bomber could be made available) and 278.

32. Correpondence and further interview with H.H.J. Simons, interviews with B. Wink and G.J. de Haas; see also the reports of H.H.J. Simons and G.J. de Haas (1946, Ward collection, SLH). Boer, *Indië*, 175–6, does not mention this correctly and dates erroneously. The reader is advised that the reports of Simons and De Haas contain errors, and I received corrections from both.

33. Ibid.; Bosscher, 2, 279 (Bosscher erroneously assumes that the aircraft flying over the war ships were Japanese); account of the course of the flight, the discovery of the Japanese 'reconnaissance plane' and the return flight to Ngoro by B. Wink (1984).

34. Bosscher, 2, 279 and 599, note 233; correspondence and further interviews with H.H.J. Simons, interview with B. Wink.

35. Bosscher, 2, 279; AAFHS 29A; Operations Journal 19th Bomb. Group, 8 Dec. 1941–19 March 1942 (AFHRA, Maxwell AFB, via G.J. Casius); see also Shores, 2, 238 and Helfrich, I, 400 (wrongly notes that it was not confirmed that the attacking planes were American; HQ V Bomber Command at Djocjakarta sent an apology to Doorman through JAC and ABDA-FLOAT).

36. Bosscher, 2, 599, note 233 (as explained in the text, this note relates to two different things).

37. Senshi Sosho, 26, 662; AAFHS 29A; Operations Journal 19th Bomb. Group, 8 Dec. 1941–19 March 1942 (AFHRA, Maxwell AFB, via G.J. Casius); war diary Tainan Kokutai (via Military History Department, National Institute for Defense Studies, Tokyo), the Japanese pilot who tried to intercept reported a "flying boat"; Bosscher, 2, 279; see also Shores, 2, 238 (only Japanese "sea time" not translated to Mid Java Time).

38. Bosscher, 2, 279; Operations Journal 19th Bomb. Group, 8 Dec. 1941–19 March 1942 (AFHRA, Maxwell AFB, via G.J. Casius).

39. Bosscher, 2, 280; information on flying boat operations on 26–27 February 1942 received from N. Geldhof, IMH (February 1985).

40. Senshi Sosho, 26, 622; war diary Tainan Kokutai (via Military History Department, National Institute for Defense Studies, Tokyo); information on flying boat operations on 26–27 February 1942 received from N. Geldhof, IMH (February 1985).

41. Bosscher, 2, 281, 601 note 256 (H. Dorré makes it look in his post-war account as if his flying boat was attacked by fighter aircraft); Honselaar, 203–4 (quoting from the report of the sergeant observer of the Y-45; this shows that this aircraft was not attacked by fighter aircraft, but by a catapult plane launched from a cruiser).

42. Interviews with H. Creutzberg and W. Mulder; Bosscher, 2, 208 and 541, note 129; KTZ ret. G.G. Bozuwa, 'De Reconnaissance Group (ABDA Air) van het Supreme Command (te Bandoeng) van 10 januari tot 1 maart 1942' (undated report, probably from 1946, via N. Geldhof, IMH).

Chapter 2.2

1. Bosscher, 2, 281; information on the deployment of the Japanese cruiser reconnaissance planes received from the Military History Department, National Institute for Defense Studies (Tokyo).

2. Bosscher, 2, 280–1 and 601, note 255; Winslow, 116 and 137, the remaining cruiser reconnaissance plane of *Houston* was flown to Tandjong Priok on 28 February 1942 to be taken on board again there, see also Shores, 2, 249. The Walrus plane of *Exeter* appeared to be still on board when the ship arrived around midnight of 27 on 28 February at Soerabaja (though damaged from gun blast), see for instance Morison, 343. The Walrus of *Perth* was also still on board when the ship arrived at Tandjong Priok, see for instance Air Britain Aeromilitaria, Spring 2005.

3. In conformity with note 1.

4. Military History Office, Senshi Sosho (Series Military History of World War II), 26 (henceforth Senshi Sosho, 26), 662.

5. Bosscher, 2, 282; information on the deployment of the Japanese cruiser reconnaissance planes received from the Military History Department, National Institute for Defense Studies (Tokyo).

6. See Part 1B.

7. Interviews with H. Creutzberg and W. Mulder.

8. Interviews with H. Creutzberg, G.J. de Haas and A.J.A. Geurtz (at the time ML liaison officer with 17 PS).

9. Interview with G.J. de Haas; Unclassified report of 17th Pursuit Squadron (P) activity in Java 14 January–February 1942 (AFHRA, Maxwell AFB, via G.J. Casius); see also Shores, 2, 239.

10. Bosscher, 2, 282 and 602, note 273 (what is stated here is incorrect, only the Hurricanes were limited operationally serviceable due to the lack of crystals for their radios); interview with A.J.A. Geurtz (got questions at the time from Ente van Gils).

11. Bosscher, 2, 282 and 602, note 267.

12. Ibid., 282.

13. AAFHS 29A; Bosscher, 2, 602, note 273 (states the take off times as they were passed on at the time to the Naval Commander Soerabaja); Edmonds, 422, (erroneously mentions 4:15 p.m. as the take off time for the A-24s, according to several of the interviews with P-40 pilots from 1945 and later, however, this was the time over target); interview with G.J. de Haas (stated that Kiser was informed by telephone that the A-24s had taken off on the agreed time); see also Shores, 239.

14. Operations Journal 19th Bomb. Group, 8 Dec. 1941–19 March 1942 (AFHRA, Maxwell AFB, via G.J. Casius) erroneously states that eleven P-40s were committed as escorts); AAFHS 29A (this mission survey often only mentions the American missions, as in this case); Unclassified Report

of the 17th Pursuit Squadron (P) activity in Java 14 January–February 1942 (AFHRA, Maxwell AFB, via G.J. Casius), 11 (the text was drafted later after the arrival of the squadron in Australia, no combat report of the mission on 27 February 1942 has been preserved); interviews with G.J. de Haas, H.H.J. Simons, B. Wink and L.J. Johnsen; correspondence with G.M. Bruggink and H.H.J. Simons; interview with C.A. Vonk (1946, via W. Bosman). The reader is advised that the reports of G.J. de Haas and H.H.J. Simons drafted in 1946 (Ward collection, SLH) contain errors and were drafted in mutual consultation on 15 April 1946 (I received corrections from both).

15. After (very similar) accounts of H.H.J. Simons, B. Wink, C.A. Vonck and L.J. Johnsen. The Operations Journal 19th Bomb. Group, 8 Dec. 1941–19 March 1942 (AFHRA, Maxwell AFB, via G.J. Casius), 60, text derived from the original combat reports mentions an attack time of 16:47 hrs. According to the interviewed fighter pilots it was a flight of several minutes from the location of the sea battle to the location of the Japanese transport fleet. At 16:38 hrs (he wrote the time down) L.J. Johnsen (17 PS) passed over both naval squadrons at an altitude of 7,500 metres, taking several pictures with his private camera. B. Wink, too, states approximately 16:30 hrs as the time at which he arrived over the two fighting war fleets.

16. Ibid.; Kiser's radio messages also reached the KM and apparently also ABDA-FLOAT, see Helfrich, I, 415, first paragraph. This text cannot be but derived from Kiser's radio messages, even if his American English seems to have been translated rather clumsily and Helfrich added the names of Japanese ships. In doing so, Helfrich did not realise that the fighter pilots thought that *Haguro* and *Nachi* were battle ships. Where Helfrich mentions an enemy cruiser burning it was in all probability in actual fact a light cruiser or destroyer.

17. Information on the deployment of the Japanese cruiser reconnaissance planes received from the Military History Department, National Institute for Defense Studies (Tokyo, via P.G. Tideman), confirms that during the day battle no Japanese cruiser floatplanes were near the area of the sea battle.

18. Rear-Admiral F.W. Coster, Verslag betreffende de krijgsverrichtingen te land in Nederlands-Indië, 20 May 1942 (Marinestaf, Historische sectie, Bc-8/1, IMH), F, 15 (erroneously mentions British dive bombers); Bosscher, 2, 610, note 356; interviews with G.J. de Haas, H.H.J. Simons and B. Wink; correspondence author with H.H.J. Simons and G.M.Bruggink.

19. In conformity with note 17; see also Bosscher, 2, 610, note 358. Taking a reconnaissance float plane on board again was a time-consuming process. It was preceded by a reconnaissance flight by the plane of the surrounding area and ended with the cruiser coming to a (near) complete stop to be able to lift the float plane out of the water by a crane and place it back on a catapult.

20. Bosscher, 2, 281–8.

21. Boscher, 2, 288 and 610, note 349, 609–10, note 346.

22. Bosscher, 2, 288–9; interview with W. Mulder (confirms that this was checked also in Bandoeng).
23. Messimer, 268–9; information on flying boat operations on 26–27 February 1942 received from N. Geldhof, IMH (February 1985); Bosscher, 2, 289–90; letter of G.F. Rijnders dated 25 March 1986 (via N. Geldhof, IMH).
24. Ibid.
25. Bosscher, 2, 288–92; data received from the Dutch Oorlogsgraven Stichting–War Graves Foundation (OGS).
26. Messimer, 269; letter of G.F. Rijnders dated 25 March 1986 (via N. Geldhof, IMH); see also Bosscher, 2, 292. According to H. Creutzberg JAC received the news of the defeat of the naval squadron between 04:00 hrs and 05:00 hrs.

Chapter 2.3

1. Interviews with H. Creutzberg and W. Mulder.
2. Boer, *Indië*, 190–2. The CL (local AOC), Major C.J.J.M. Waltmann, was the operational commander of both 2-Vl.G.III and 3-Vl.G.III.
3. In conformity with note 1; Maltby, *Report*, 1397; preserved part of a JAC Operations Report, with anonymous notes on the number of assigned aircraft (via A.B. Wolff).
4. Interviews with H. Creutzberg and W. Mulder; Maltby, *Report*, 1396, section 533; letter dated 25 March 1986 and logbook entries of G.F. Rijnders (via N. Geldhof, IMH).
5. AAFHS 29A; Operations Journal 19th Bomb. Group, 8 Dec. 1941–19 March 1942 (AFHRA, Maxwell AFB, via G.J. Casius). The LB-30s were vulnerable in fighter attacks as they lacked self-sealing fuel tanks and were relatively lightly armed.
6. Interviews with H. Creutzberg, A.B. Wolff, F.J.W. den Ouden and J. Coblijn.
7. In confomity with note 1, A.A.M. van Rest's notes (his pocket book).
8. See for instance Helfrich, I, 433–4; interviews with G.J. de Haas, B. Wink and H.H.J. Simons.
9. Operations Report, see note 3; A.A.M. van Rest's notes (his pocket book, confirms strength of 1-Vl.G.V); Edmonds, 427 (confirms strength of 17 PS). The two Curtiss H-75 Hawks of 1-Vl.G.V were operationally serviceable only to a very limited extent (for instance not for air defence) and were not considered operational (interview with P.G. Tideman).
10. A.A.M. van Rest's notes (his pocket book); interviews with P.G. Tideman and P.R. Jolly.
11. In conformity with note 10; Shores, 2, 247.
12. Bezemer, *Zeven Zeeën*, 363; Winslow, 136.
13. Interviews with P.G. Tideman and P.R. Jolly.
14. Interviews with P.R. Jolly and W. Boxman.

15. Operations Report, see note 3; Shores, 2, 247.
16. Bosscher, 2, 300; Roskill, II, 16; see also Helfrich, I, 422.
17. Operations Report, see note 3; Shores, 2, 249.
18. Winslow, 136.
19. Winslow, 137; Shores, 2, 249.
20. AAFHS 29A; Edmonds, 427; correspondence and further interview with H.H.J. Simons; interviews with B. Wink, G.J. de Haas and C.A. Vonck (1946 via W. Bosman).
21. Ibid.
22. Ibid.; Saikada, 85; war diary Tainan Kokutai (via Military History Department, National Institute for Defense Studies, Tokyo).
23. Interviews with H.H.J. Simons and H. Huys.
24. See for instance Helfrich, I, 434.
25. Winslow, 138; Maltby, *Report*, 1396; Hoogenband, van den and Schotborgh (ed.), *Nederlands-Indië contra Japan*, VII, 29; Helfrich, I, 439; Shores, 2, 247.
26. Operations Report, see note 3; Shores, 2, 247.
27. Boer, *Indië*, 192.
28. Ibid., 194.
29. Ibid., 194, 196; further interviews with J. Coblijn and F.J.W. den Ouden.

Chapter 2.4

1. Information on flying boat operations on 26–27 February 1942 received from N. Geldhof, IMH.
2. Helfrich, I, 384–5, 400, 403–4. Helfrich's remarks and conclusions on the air support (see also 409–10) in actual fact are far from correct and, reading his memoirs, it feels as if Helfrich worked in complete isolation from his staff at the time. It seems impossible to me, however, that he did not know about the agreements that were made between staff officers of ABDA-FLOAT and JAC on the air support. The number of eight (Dutch) fighter aircraft that Helfrich mentions (I, 403) very probably refers to the seven not fully operationally serviceable Hurricanes and the one Brewster fighter left behind at Ngoro. The American bomber he mentions (I, 409) is the lead A-24 dive bomber.
3. Bosscher, 2, 610, note 358, 289–90; for data on numbers and types of aircraft of the committed Japanese cruiser aircraft, see for instance Okumiya and Horikoshi, *Zero, the story of the Japanese Navy Air Force, 1937–1945*.
4. Bosscher, 2, 613, note 385.

Chapter 3.1

1. See for instance Nortier *et al.*, *Java*, 293, attachment 1.
2. See Part 1A.

3. The indication minus is used when an organic element of a certain unit, such as a complete company of a battalion or a Troop of an anti-aircraft Battery, was not assigned. In contrast, when elements from other units had been attached to that particular unit, the term reinforced unit (minus) is used.

Chapter 3.2

1. See Part 1.
2. Ibid. See also Chapter 3.6, note 42, for a concise description of the system of Air Support coordination.
3. Nortier *et al.*, *Java*, 57–8; Rear-Admiral F.W. Coster, Verslag betreffende de krijgsverrichtingen te land in Nederlands-Indië, 20 May 1942 (Marinestaf, Historische sectie, Bc-8/1, IMH; henceforth Verslag Coster), E, 1. The reader is advised that the Technical Service of the ML also had two smaller workshops (technical depots) at Madioen and Djocjakarta and two so-called auxiliary workshops (sub depots) at Kalidjati and Malang. In February 1942 another auxiliary workshop was established at the new airfield at Tasikmalaja.
4. Ibid.
5. Ibid.; for the composition of West Group see Nortier *et al.*, *Java*, 306–7, attachment 4; Lieutenant-Colonel J.V.O. Macartney-Filgate M.C., 'The 48th Light Anti-Aircraft Regiment Royal Artillery in the Dutch East Indies, February–March 1942' (via J. Mulders, henceforth Report 48 LAA). The indication minus is used when an organic element of a certain unit, such as a complete company of a battalion or a Troop of an anti-aircraft Battery, was not assigned. In contrast, when elements from other units had been attached to that particular unit, the term reinforced unit (minus) is used.
6. Report 48 LAA; Maltby, *Report*, 1395.
7. Maltby, *Report*, 1395; interviews with F.R. Lettinga and P.A. Hoyer.
8. In conformity with note 5.
9. For the composition of Bandoeng Group see Nortier *et al.*, *Java*, 308–9, attachment 5. Originally also an East Group was to be formed. Until the end of the battle, however, Bandoeng Group's area of operations also included the area assigned to East Group. According to H.F. Zeylemaker, 'Beschrijving oorlogsoperaties H.J. Zeylemaker' (March 1942, via A. van Aarem and J. Mossou), Pesman assumed command on 26 February 1942. The KNIL battalions were numbered consecutively. 1st Infantry Battalion (Inf. I), 2nd Infantry Battalion (Inf. II), etc. The designations had no relation with the regiment a particular battalion had been assigned to. The regiments, too, were numbered consecutively, 1st Infantry Regiment (1-R.I.), 2nd Infantry Regiment (2-R.I.), etc.
10. Verslag Coster, E. 2; Report 48 LAA.

11. After descriptions of A. van Aarem and J. Mossou; description of the training for tactical and artillery observer by A. van Aarem; A.J. van der Heijden's logbook notes; correspondence author with J. Staal.

12. Boer, *Borneo*, 46; further information provided by B. Wink (at the time one of the forward air controllers avant la letter at Vl.G.V). Maintaining radio communications with the ML bombers was possible at the battalion level, but this was not practised during the war and there were no procedures for it.

13. See for instance Nortier *et al.*, *Java*, 50, 503; description by F.L. Kroesen; interview with A.H. Holslag. In *Java*, Nortier gives a somewhat outdated picture and in fact sketches the period of before the middle of 1940. Later, and especially in 1941, a great many radio operators were trained at the Engineers at Tjimahi, among them classes especially dedicated to the ML. Also, in the course of 1941 much signals equipment came in, among which there were dozens of short-wave radios and many tactical radios to be used by the infantry battalions, among others. The radios were in part built at the Engineers with the help of imported parts.

14. Boer, *Borneo*, 46.

15. 'Beschrijving oorlogsoperaties H.F. Zeylemaker' (March 1942, via A. van Aarem and J. Mossou); interview with H. Creutzberg.

16. Interviews with P.A.C. Benjamins, P.A. Hoijer, J.B.H. Bruinier and B. Wink.

17. Interview with H. Creutzberg.

18. Military History Office, Senshi Sosho (Series of Military History of World War II), 34 (henceforth Senshi Sosho, 34), various mention; information on the deployment of Ki-51s received from the Military History Department, National Institute for Defense Studies, Tokyo.

19. Ibid.

20. See Part 1.

21. Reconstruction on the basis of a preserved part of a JAC Operations Report, with anonymous notes on the number of assigned aircraft (via A.B. Wolff) and A.A.M. van Rest's notes (his pocket book). The ML afdelingen belonged administratively to a Vliegtuiggroep–Aircraft Group, an administrative corps stationed at a particular air base. Ist Vliegtuiggroep, Vl.G.I, was originally stationed at Andir, the IInd, Vl.G.II, at Malang, the IIIrd Vliegtuiggroep, Vl.G.III, at Tjililitan, etc. Each Vliegtuiggroep had two or three (Vliegtuig)afdelingen. Vl.G.III, for instance, originally consisted of three afdelingen, 1-Vl.G.III (the 1st Vliegtuigafdeling of IIIrd Vliegtuiggroep), 2-Vl.G.III and 3-Vl.G.III. Only the reconnaissance afdelingen were numbered consecutively.

22. P.C. Boer, 'Het vliegtuigmaterieel en de materieelverliezen van de ML/KNIL in de periode mei 1940–mei 1942' (unpublished manuscript).

23. In conformity with note 21; Maltby, *Report*, 1398; see also Part 1A.

24. Maltby, *Report*, 1398 (Maltby erroneously states that both squadrons were amalgamated on 28 February, see, however, for instance Kelly, *Hurricane*

over the jungle, 204, 208); preserved parts of JAC documents show that the combined squadron was designated as 242 Squadron and not as 232 Squadron as Maltby states in his *Report*. This error was copied in various later publications, including Boer, *Indië*.

25. Various military registers of service personnel 2-Vl.G.V and military register A.A.M. van Rest (SLH).

26. Not counted are the numbers of Glenn Martins WH-1, which were not deemed to be combat worthy.

27. See for instance Shores, 2, 45, with regard to the original strength of the RAF Blenheim squadrons which arrived in Sumatra in February 1942 and Gillison, 152, with regard to the RAF and RAAF squadrons at Singapore.

28. See Part 1B.

29. See Chapter 3.4.

30. Data provided by Air Marshal ret. (Indonesian Air Force) Raden S. Suryadarma; 'Beschrijving oorlogsoperaties H.F. Zeylemaker' (March 1942, via A. van Aarem and J. Mossou); Boer, *Indië*, 205; P.C. Boer, 'Het vliegtuigmaterieel en de materieelverliezen van de ML/KNIL in de periode mei 1940–mei 1942' (unpublished manuscript, the replacement CW-22s were assigned to the Vliegschool–Flight School at Kalidjati); Boer, *Indië*, 205 (states erroneously that Vk.A.2 flew the remaining CW-22s over on 2 March and incorrectly mentions J. Mossou as one of the pilots); further interview with J. Mossou (left from Djocjakarta to Andir by road) and A. van Aarem.

31. Ibid.

32. See Part 4; Boer, *Indië*, 223–5.

33. Boer, *Indië*, 261–3, 264–6.

34. Report 48 LAA; data from O.A.O. Kreefft's diary (at the time A. III Ld. at Andir); interviews with J. Tap and J. Hendriks (at the time A. III Ld. at Kalidjati); Nortier *et al.*, *Java*, 308–9, attachment 5; see also Klinkert *et al.*, 236–7; data with regard to the organisation of the British anti-aircraft units in Java received via the RAF Air Historical Branch; N.E.I. Existing A.A. Defenses, doc. WO 193/933, 37 (PRO, concerns January 1942). See also Maltby, *Report*, 1394, section 506 and 1395, section 520.

35. Report 48 LAA; verslag W. Schilling (dossier NIcJ 12/1, IMG); see also Nortier *et al.*, *Java*, 306–7, attachment 4.

36. Report 48 LAA.

Chapter 3.3

1. Military History Office, Senshi Sosho (Series of Military History of World War II), 26 (henceforth Senshi Sosho, 26), 643–4; Military History Office, Senshi Sosho (Series of Military History of World War II), 34 (henceforth Senshi Sosho, 34), 553–4; Japanese Monograph 66.

2. Ibid.

3. Japanese Monograph 66 and further information received from Military History Department, National Institute for Defense Studies (Tokyo); see also Nortier *et al.*, *Java*, 102–3, attachment 2.
4. Ibid.
5. Ibid.
6. Data on the Ki-51 and Army Co-operation received from the Military History Department, National Institute for Defense Studies (Tokyo), 1985.
7. Ibid.
8. After a description of the training of the artillery observers by A. van Aarem. For the description of the U-lap system (also in use after the war) see G.J. Burgers, *6 AVRA Squadron*, 221–2.
9. Senshi Sosho, 34, 624–6, tables 29 and 30. Remark: the 1st and 11th Sentais had in total 54 Ki-27s, the 27th Sentai had 27 Ki-51s in total. The number of combat ready aircraft is an estimate. The percentages non-combat ready aircraft normally lay between 30 and 40 per cent for the fighter aircraft and bombers. Here and there non-combat ready aircraft had been left behind on airfields in Malacca that still needed to be turned in for major repairs. Also due to a lack of spare parts these percentages were relatively high. The combat readiness in the units at Palembang was relatively good, due to the transfer of only combat ready aircraft and the arrival of a number of replacement aircraft around the date of the transfer to Palembang. It even improved somewhat before the transfer to Kalidjati began.
10. Senshi Sosho, 26, 712–3.
11. Senshi Sosho, 34, 555; Japanese Monograph 69.
12. Maltby, *Report*, 1396–97; interviews with A.B. Wolff and H. Creutzberg; correspondence author with F.R. Lettinga.
13. Hoogenband, van den and Schotborgh (ed.), *Nederlands-Indië contra Japan* (henceforth NIcJ), VII, 54–5.
14. Preserved part of Operations Report JAC, with on it anonymous notes on numbers of assigned aircraft (via A.B. Wolff); Rear-Admiral F.W. Coster, Verslag betreffende de krijgsverrichtingen te land in Nederlands-Indië, 20 May 1942 (Marinestaf, Historische sectie, Bc–8/1, IMH), E, 3 (henceforth Verslag Coster), erroneously mentions the deployment of all still available air forces against the Japanese fleet at Indramajoe.
15. Maltby, *Report*, 1396.
16. Operations Report, see note 14; interviews with H. Creutzberg, F.J.W. den Ouden and J. van Loggem; correspondence author with F.R. Lettinga; Shores, 2, 251–2.
17. Senshi Sosho, 26, 644; Shores, 2, 251–2 (however, mentions an incorrect take off time; darkness fell in Java at around 18:30 hrs).
18. Operations Report, see note 14; Shores, 2, 250; AAFHS 29A (confirms numbers of Blenheims).

19. Operations Report, see note 14; Shores, 2, 250; description of weather conditions by J. van Kruiselbergen, M.F. Noorman van der Dussen and H.M. Franken.

20. Ibid.; Shores, 2, 252; Gillison, 441.

21. Operations Report, see note 14; Shores, 2, 250.

22. Operations Report, see note 14; Shores, 2, 250–2 (however, mentions wrong take off times on p. 252).

23. Ibid.; interview with C.J.H. Samson (who, immediately after the departure of the British bombers, flew a Glenn Martin to Andir).

24. AAFHS 29A; Shores, 2, 250–2 (erroneously mentions Rankasbitung as location of Sayer's emergency landing); interviews with F. Stapel, J. van Kruiselbergen and M.F. Noorman van der Dussen; correspondence author with B. Wink.

25. Boer, *Indië*, 195–6. The given times have been derived from J. van Kruiselbergen's logbook and further interviews with J. van Kruiselbergen and M.F. Noorman van der Dussen.

26. Ibid.

27. In conformity with note 25; Operations Report, see note 14.

28. Boer, *Indië*, 192–3.

29. Boer, *Indië*, 193.

30. Ibid.; Operations Report, see note 14.

31. In conformity with note 30.

32. In conformity with note 29.

33. Boer, *Indië*, 193–4.

34. Ibid.

35. Helfrich, *Memoires*, I, 439; Japanese Monograph 66, as well as Senshi Sosho, 34, 544, erroneously mention attacks by six enemy bombers at 23:00 hrs (Mid Java Time); Operations Report, see note 14. The four Bleinheims probably already arrived at Andir in the course of the morning of 28 February (interview O.A.O. Kreefft).

36. Senshi Sosho, 34, 554; Senshi Sosho, 26, 663–4, 672–5.

37. Operations Report, see note 14; interviews with J. van Kruiselbergen and M.F. Noorman van der Dussen. The Blenheim at Andir went to Pameungkeuk to "shelter" there on 1 March 1942 and remained there until it was destroyed in an air raid on 3 March 1942.

38. Operations Report, see note 14; AAFHS 29A; Gillison, 441; Maltby, *Report*, 1397; Verslag Coster, F, 15.

39. Senshi Sosho, 26, 729.

40. Senshi Sosho, 26, 644.

Chapter 3.4

1. Rear-Admiral F.W. Coster, Verslag betreffende de krijgsverrichtingen te land in Nederlands-Indië, 20 May 1942 (Marinestaf, Historische sectie, Bc-8/1, IMH; henceforth Verslag Coster) E, 2–3.

2. This is not mentioned in Verslag Coster, but appears from the information that the staff of the CL (local AOC) at Kalidjati received and is confirmed in Maltby, *Report*, 1397, section 537.
3. Interview with H. Creutzberg.
4. Ibid.; 'Beschrijving oorlogsoperaties H.F. Zeylemaker' (March 1942, via A. van Aarem and J. Mossou).
5. Interview with H. Creutzberg and correspondence of S.H.A. Begemann (via W. Bosman).
6. Interview with H. Creutzberg; see also De Jong, 11a, I, 2e helft, 977.
7. Interview with H. Creutzberg; data provided by Air Marshal ret. (Indonesian Air Force) Raden S. Suryadarma.
8. Interview with H. Creutzberg; Maltby, *Report*, 1397, section 537.
9. 'Beschrijving oorlogsoperaties H.F. Zeylemaker' (March 1942, via A. van Aarem and J. Mossou); interviews with H. Creutzberg, and F. Stapel; correspondence with J.H. van Balen. With the help of radio vehicles the radio network was expanded if need be. Thus, then Warrant Officer J.H. van Balen was sent with a radio vehicle from Tjililitan to Tjisaoek in February 1942.
10. 'Beschrijving oorlogsoperaties H.F. Zeylemaker' (March 1942, via A. van Aarem and J. Mossou); interviews with H. Creutzberg and F. Stapel; Maltby, *Report*, 1397; see also Shores, 2, 468–9, Appendix III, this is the literal text of the investigative report of Air Vice-Marshal Maltby on the fall of Kalidjati from March 1942.
11. These units are not reported in Nortier *et al.*, *Java*, 308–9, attachment 5, probably because they were only partially motorised and therefore were not designated as mobile troops. Data on the composition and strength derived from A.B. Wolff (who knew several men in the battalions), F. Stapel and Maltby, *Report*, 1395, section 520.
12. Boer, *Indië*, 201–2 (does not give an entirely correct account of the first mission and mentions several incorrect names of the pilots involved); Van Kempen, *Mijn verhaal*, 59–60 (erroneously dates on 28 February); A.A.M. van Rest's notes (his pocket book).
13. Van Kempen, *Mijn verhaal*, 59; interviews with A.E. van Kempen, A.E. Stoové, J.P. Adam and correspondence and interview with P.A.C. Benjamins.
14. Van Kempen, *Mijn verhaal*, 60; interviews with A.E. van Kempen, A.E. Stoové, P.R. Jolly, J.P. Adam; A.A.M. van Rest's notes (his pocket book); report P.G. Tideman, 1946 (dossier Tideman, Ward collection, SLH); correspondence and interview with P.A.C. Benjamins.
15. Ibid.
16. Ibid.
17. Ibid.; A.A.M. van Rest's notes (his pocket book, gives concise results and specificies committed fighter aircraft); see also Verslag Coster, F, 16.
18. In conformity with note 14.

19. Ibid.

20. Ibid.

21. After an account of the events by H.M. Franken and F.F. de Haan, at the time pilot and mechanic, respectively, of the M-523; F.V. Rühl's diary entries (via G.J. Hagens).

22. A.A.M. van Rest's notes (his pocket book).

23. Shores, 2, 297–8; Maltby, *Report*, 1397; Gillison, 441–2.

24. Preserved part of Operations Report JAC, with on it anonymous notes on numbers of assigned aircraft (via A.B. Wolff); Shores, 2, 292–3.

25. Ibid.

26. Kelly, *Hurricane over the jungle*, 200–2; correspondence author with T. Kelly.

27. Operations Report, see note 24.

28. In conformity with note 26.

29. War diary 1st Air Group (via Military History Department, National Institute for Defense Studies, Tokyo); see also Shores, 2, 294.

30. Shores, 2, 294; Kelly, *Hurricane over the jungle*, 202.

31. Military History Office, Senshi Sosho (Series of Military History of World War II), 26, 713; Kelly, *Hurricane over the jungle*, 202.

32. Operations Report, see note 24; Maltby, *Report*, 1398, section 550 (incorrectly mentions three destroyed F1Ms in total, very probably on the basis of claims by Kelly and Fitzherbert, see also note 85).

33. Boer, *Indië*, 201. Another aircraft of the afdeling had been standing heavily damaged at Tjileungsir since 27 February 1942 and was transferred to the Technical Service, which wrote if off a few days later.

34. Operations Report, see note 24 and an account by L. Kroes.

35. Ibid.; Boer, *Indië*, 201.

36. 'Beschrijving oorlogsoperaties H.F. Zeylemaker' (March 1942, via A. van Aarem and J. Mossou); Boer, *Indië*, 205.

37. Boer, *Indië*, 197–8; further interview with F. Stapel (at the time duty NCO in the CL command post).

38. Interview with C.J.H. Samson.

39. In conformity with note 37.

40. Boer, *Indië*, 198.

41. Ibid.; J. van Kruiselbergen's logbook; further interviews with J. van Kruiselbergen and F.J.W. den Ouden. The time of landing of the Glenn Martins given in *Indië*, 198 is incorrect.

42. In conformity with note 40.

43. Ibid. and further interview with F. Stapel; Maltby, *Report*, 1397, section 537.

44. Nortier *et al.*, *Java*, 105. Not mentioned, erroneously, is that Inf. IV. got the order to attack Eretan Wetan instead of occupying the Tomo position, see notes 93 up to and including 95. The whole story is described incorrectly

in Verslag Coster, E. 3, and in the post-war account of Major-General R. Bakkers (dossier NIcJ 17/6, IMG).

45. Boer, *Indië*, 198–9 and further interview with F. Stapel.

46. Ibid.

47. Ibid.; Shores, 2, 296–7 and 468–9, appendix III (literal text of the investigative report of Air Vice-Marshal Maltby on the fall of Kalidjati, March 1942).

48. Report L.J. Prummel (dossier NIcJ 13/6, IMG). Interviews with former members of 84 Squadron (via Chr. Shores) and 1-Vl.G.II (H.J. Hofmyster) show that the Van den Berkhof section had withdrawn (probably after the blocking of the road to Pasir Boengoer) and had taken up new positions along the road to Poerwakarta at some 10 kilometres west of Kalidjati. See also Shores, 2, 301 and report of J.R.J. Rugebregt (dossier NIcJ 13/64, IMG also states that Van den Berkhof blocked the road to Poerwakarta).

49. Lieutenant-Colonel J.V.O. Macartney-Filgate M.C., 'The 48th Light Anti-Aircraft Regiment Royal Artillery in the Dutch East Indies, February–March 1942' (henceforth Report 48 LAA, via J. Mulders). For the ground defence training of the heavy anti-aircraft artillery units of the British Army see for instance the report of the commander 6 Heavy Anti-Aircraft Regiment (dossier NIcJ 5/55, IMG), who fought with his unit at Palembang in February 1942.

50. Report L.J. Prummel (dossier NIcJ 13/62, IMG); interviews with F. Stapel and A. Servaas. In his post-war account Prummel erroneously states that many of the gunners arrived without any weapons. He probably confuses this with the often unarmed British refugees who were later received to the south of the base.

51. In conformity with the debriefing of the country guards in the command post of the CL Kalidjati (A. Servaas and F. Stapel, at the time present as picket officer and duty NCO, respectively). In his post-war report (NIcJ 17/6, IMG) Major-General R. Bakkers wrote that the country guards who had been positioned between Eretan Wetan and Soebang hurriedly ran away on the approach of the enemy and even neglected to warn Kalidjati. This is incorrect. Several 'warning detachments' were taken out without having had the opportunity to warn (one country guard of these detachment later arrived at Kalidjati, after all) and the two country guards of the post that was nearest to Soebang did warn, as is described in the text.

52. Shores, 2, 296 (confirms that the RAF and RAAF personnel at Soebang were warned, but mentions an incorrect time); Gillison, 442; Schotborgh (ed.), *Nederlands-Indië contra Japan*, IV, 147; interview with F. Stapel.

53. Japanese Monograph 66; see also Nortier *et al.*, *Java*, 103 and De Jong, 11a, I, 2e helft, 972–3, as well as L.J. Prummel's reports (dossier NIcJ 13/62, IMG) and J.R.J. Rugebregt (13/64, IMG).

54. In conformity with the debriefing of the country guards in the command post of the CL Kalidjati, see note 51. Captain Prummel was also present at this debriefing and did not believe the country guards when they said that the Landstorm company (in his eye incapable of doing so) had engaged the Japanese, see also his post-war account (dossier NIcJ 13/62, IMG). RAF personnel saw the Landstorm company pass the gates of Kalidjati during their withdrawal in the direction of Poerwakarta, see Shores, 2, 297; several dossiers war crimes investigation Australian National Archives, statements 1946 (via J. Mulders).

55. Report H.J. Heijligers (dossier NIcJ 13/63, IMG). The time of the battle with elements of the Japanese vanguard, given in this post-war account, does not match the times from other sources and with the moment of return of the fighters that flew by. Although the country guards who drove to Kalidjati (see note 51) reported having passed the position of Heijligers, the latter does not mention this.

56. Dossiers war crimes investigation (see note 54), statement Major-General Shoji, 1947; Japanese Monograph 66; see also Nortier *et al.*, *Java*, 103 and De Jong, 11a, I, 2e helft, 973.

57. Boer, *Indië*, 199.

58. Dossiers war crimes investigation (see note 54), statement H.G. Christian, 1946; Boer, *Indië*, 199 and further interview with F. Stapel. *Indië*, 199 gives an incorrect time of arrival of the country guards at the command post of the CL. See also L.J. Prummel's report (dossier NIcJ 13/62, IMG), confirms the telephoned message to the CL that Kalidjati did not run any immediate danger.

59. Versalg L.J. Prummel (dossier NIcJ 13/62, IMG) and verslag J.R.J. Rugebregt (dossier NIcJ 13/64, IMG); interview with F. Stapel. Rugebregt's report gives incorrect times, which are not in accordance with those mentioned in interviews with former ML and RAF personnel. The time given of the attack on Kalidjati in the text is also confirmed in Japanese sources.

60. Boer, *Indië*, 199.

61. Shores, 2, 296–7; further data received from Chr. Shores from his correspondence with former RAF and RAAF servicemen involved; further interview with F. Stapel.

62. Shores, 2, 296–7. See also the investigative report of Air Vice-Marshal P.C. Maltby on the fall of Kalidjati, drafted in March 1942, included in its entirety in Shores, 2, 468–9, appendix III.

63. Boer, *Indië*, 199–200. Personnel of 1-Vl.G.II were later questioned by a KNIL officer on the withdrawal of the Van den Berkhof section, which appeared to go against the orders of the company commander.

64. Gillison, 442; Shores, 2, 297–8.

65. Shores, 2, 298–301.

66. In conformity with note 64.
67. In conformity with note 65.
68. Boer, *Indië*, 200.
69. Ibid.
70. Ibid.; Verslag L.J. Prummel (dossier NIcJ 13/62, IMG); interviews with J.A. Woutersz and H. E. van Wijk; dossiers war crimes investigation, see note 54, statement J.C. Oostveen, 1946. RAF Prisoners of War later cleared the bodies of the KNIL infantrymen around Kalidjati village (data received from Chr. Shores from his correspondence with former RAF and RAAF servicemen involved).
71. Boer, *Indië*, 200.
72. Ibid. and further interviews with J.A. Woutersz and H.E. van Wijk.
73. Dossiers war crimes investigation, see note 54; Shores, 2, 301.
74. Interview with J. Tap; see also *Stabelan*, 4de jaargang, 4, 15 April 1978, 44–7.
75. Verslag L.J. Prummel (dossier NIcJ 13/62, IMG) and verslag J.R.J. Rugebregt (NIcJ 13/64, IMG).
76. Shores, 2, 468–9, appendix III (investigative report Maltby); interview with F. Stapel.
77. Ibid.; the incorrect impression stems from Maltby, *Report*, 1397, which has been copied in, amongst others, Gillison, 442; dossiers war crimes investigation, see note 54.
78. Shores, 2, 468–9, appendix III (investigative report Maltby); dossiers war crimes investigation, see note 54; Report 48 LAA; M. Godfrey, 'The years that the locusts have eaten, War diary and sermons of Rupert Godfrey 1941–1945' (via J. Mulders); see also Maltby, *Report*, 1397, section 541.
79. P.C. Boer, 'Het vliegtuigmaterieel en de materieelverliezen van de ML/KNIL in de periode mei 1940–mei 1942' (unpublished manuscript); Boer, *Indië*, 201 (does not give complete information). Twenty Ryan STM-2 trainers were already crated and fell into Japanese hands on a railway siding near Bandoeng after the capitulation.
80. Boer, *Indië*, 201; Honours list Royal Netherlands Air Force. Of the militarised civilian personnel of the Technical Service and the mechanics of aircraft afdelingen and the Flight School working in the auxiliary workshop of the Technical Service the following were killed: reserve second lieutenant H.J. van Pesch (TD), Sgt mechanic J. Kläring, Sgt mechanic W.F.H. Crasbeek, aircraft specialist B.A. van der Engh (militarised TD), aircraft specialist K.A. Talens (militarised TD) and about five Indonesian personnel of the TD whose names are not known. At Kalidjati around 2 March 1942 the Japanese executed Sergeant-Major mechanic M.H. Smeets, under whose command the Glenn Martin of 1-Vl.G.I was repaired (the Honours list incorrectly gives 5 March as the date).
81. Boer, *Indië*, 201.

82. Operations Report, see note 24; Boer, *Indië*, 203 (mentions an incorrect number of aircraft); Verslag Coster, E, 3; Maltby, *Report*, 1398, section 552.

83. Japanese Monograph 66.

84. Operations Report, see note 24; Shores, 2, 293.

85. Operations Report, see note 24; Shores, 2, 294–5, 302. The war diary of the 1st Air Group (Military History Department, National Institute for Defense Studies, Tokyo) shows that two of the four F1Ms remained in the end.

86. Operations Report, see note 24; Shores, 2, 294–5.

87. War diary of the 1st Air Group (Military History Department, National Institute for Defense Studies, Tokyo); see also Shores, 2, 295.

88. Japanese Monograph 66.

89. Maltby, *Report*, 1398, section 548, erroneously states that the amalgamation of the squadrons took place on 28 February 1942. See for instance Kelly, *Hurricane over the jungle*, 203, 208 for the correct course of events.

90. Operations Report, see note 24; A.A.M. van Rest's notes (his pocket book); Boer, *Indië*, 203–4 (does not give a completely correct description); Van Kempen, *Mijn verhaal*, 61; correspondence and interviews with P.G. Tideman, P.A.C. Benjamins and A.E. van Kempen.

91. 'Beschrijving oorlogsoperaties H.F. Zeylemaker' (March 1942, via A. van Aarem and J. Mossou); brief account by W.A.N. Eduard, 1946 (via W. Bosman); correspondence and interviews with P.G. Tideman, P.A.C. Benjamins and A.E. van Kempen.

92. 'Beschrijving oorlogsoperaties H.F. Zeylemaker' (March 1942, via A. van Aarem and J. Mossou); correspondence and interviews with P.G. Tideman, P.A.C. Benjamins (confirm that the raid was intended as a support of an attack by the KNIL).

93. Nortier, *et al.*, *Java*, 104–5; statement L. Vriesman and reports of P.F. Post and B.E. Rijborz (dossier NIcJ 14/9, IMG); interviews with H.L. Schroeders and J.J. Cnoops (via P. van Meel). The reader is advised that *Java*, 105 does not present a correct picture of the deployment of Inf. IV.

94. Ibid.

95. Ibid.

96. Boer, *Indië*, 207; J. van Kruiselbergen's logbook; further interview with J. van Kruiselbergen.

97. Boer, *Indië*, 207; further interviews with J. van Kruiselbergen and M.F. Noorman van der Dussen.

98. Hagens, *De KNILM vloog door*, 139; Maltby, *Report*, 1396, 1398.

99. Shores, 2, 246.

100. Hagens, *De KNILM vloog door*, 139.

101. Boer, *Indië*, 207.

102. Verslag Coster, E, 3; Shores, 2, 298, 300.

103. Interview with H. Creutzberg.

104. Operations Report, see note 24; Boer, *Indië*, 204.

105. Ibid. and further interview with C.J.H. Samson (confirmed the composition of the patrol of 1-Vl.G.II).
106. In conformity with note 105 and further interview with J. van Loggem.
107. A.A.M. van Rest's notes (his pocket book); Van Kempen, *Mijn verhaal,* 62–3.
108. Interview with H. Creutzberg; 'Beschrijving oorlogsoperaties H.F. Zeylemaker' (March 1942, via A. van Aarem and J. Mossou).
109. Ibid.; Nortier, *et al., Java,* 114–5.
110. Nortier, *et al., Java,* 115.
111. Ibid.
112. Interviews with H. Creutzberg and A.H. Holslag; Nortier, *et al., Java,* 115; Verslag G.J. Wulfhorst, 1946 (dossier NIcJ 13/28, IMG) and G.H.O. de Wit, 'De mobiele eenheid van het Javaleger (dec. '41–mrt. '42)' deel 1 en 2, *Stabelan,* 6e jaargang, 4, 14 februari 1980 resp. 5, 15 April 1980.
113. Van Kempen, *Mijn verhaal,* 62–3.
114. Ibid.

Chapter 3.5

1. Nortier, *et al., Java,* 109; Rear-Admiral F.W. Coster, Verslag betreffende de krijgsverrichtingen te land in Nederlands-Indië, 20 May 1942 (Marinestaf, Historische sectie, Bc–8/1, IMH; henceforth Verslag Coster) E, 4–5.
2. Nortier, *et al., Java,* 109–10; interview with H. Creutzberg; data about the strength of Teerink Group in conformity with information received from J.J. Nortier.
3. Boer, *Indië,* 205 (however, gives an incomplete survey of the Vk.A.1 sorties flown from Tjikembar); interview with H. Creutzberg; data provided by Air Marshal ret. (Indonesian Air Force) Raden S. Suryadarma (sortie survey Vk.A.1 Tjikembar).
4. Interview with H. Creutzberg; 'Beschrijving oorlogsoperaties H.F. Zeylemaker' (March 1942, via A. van Aarem and J. Mossou).
5. Interview with H. Creutzberg; Maltby, *Report,* 1397 (confirms that a KNIL battalion had already been ordered to carry out a counter-attack on Eretan Wetan on 1 March); interview with F. Stapel (also confirms that on 1 March at around 07:00 hrs the CL at Kalidjati heard from the ML Command that the battalion at Cheribon had been ordered to launch a counter-attack on Eretan Wetan).
6. Interview with H. Creutzberg; 'Beschrijving oorlogsoperaties H.F. Zeylemaker' (March 1942, via A. van Aarem and J. Mossou), confirms that initially it was thought at the staff of Bandoeng Group that only a Japanese vanguard had arrived at Kalidjati, which the ME could easily deal with.
7. In conformity with note 4; Nortier, *et al., Java,* 109; Verslag Coster, E, 4.

8. Interview with H. Creutzberg; C.J.M. Kretschmer de Wilde's notes (written during his time as a POW, via W. Bosman); correspondence of S.H.A. Begemann (via W. Bosman).

9. Ibid.

10. Nortier, *et al.*, *Java*, 102–3; Japanese Monograph 66; further data received from the Military History Department, National Institute for Defense Studies (Tokyo).

11. Interview with H. Creutzberg (confirms that the Vildebeest torpedo bombers were re-assigned as night bombers); Boer, *Indië*, 209; Verslag Coster, F, 16; Military History Office, Senshi Sosho (Series of Military History of World War II), 26 (henceforth Senshi Sosho, 26), 730 (erroneously mentions air raids by 12 aircraft in total); preserved part of JAC Operations Report with anonymous notes on numbers of assigned aircraft (via A.B. Wolff).

12. Boer, *Indië*, 209; further information provided by F.J.W. den Ouden, D.T. de Bont, L. Gosma, K. van Gessel and J.H. Wetzels; Operations Report, see note 11, specifies the results in conformity with Coster, see note 11, albeit that Coster speaks of direct hits on three other ships, which were in fact near misses.

13. A.A.M. van Rest's notes (his pocket book); Boer, *Indië*, 210 (does not give a completely correct survey of the missions flown by 242 Squadron, after Maltby, *Report*, incorrectly designated as 232 Squadron); interview with H. Creutzberg; Verslag Coster, F, 16 (Coster erroneously uses the term "bombed and machine gunned", the Hurricanes did not carry any bombs in the East Indies). 2-Vl.G.IV personnel later talked to several RAF pilots, who told them about their successful morning mission.

14. Boer, *Indië*, 210 (does not give an entirely correct account of the mission); further information provided by A.E. van Kempen, P.A.C. Benjamins, A. Bergamin and A.E. Stoové (who confirmed that he did not fly along); A.A.M. van Rest's notes (his pocket book, confirms that the mission served as "infantry support").

15. Interviews with A.E. van Kempen, P.A.C. Benjamins, A. Bergamin, G.J. de Haas and P.R. Jolly.

16. Interviews with W. Boxman and H.M. Haye; A.A.M. van Rest's notes (his pocket book); 'Beschrijving oorlogsoperaties H.F. Zeylemaker' (March 1942, via A. van Aarem and J. Mossou).

17. Data provided by Air Marshal ret. (Indonesian Air Force) Raden S. Suryadarma; Shores, 2, 319, erroneously dates this mission on 4 March 1942; Maltby, *Report*, 1398, section 551 (the text, however, stands between two sections that refer to events on 1 March); Boer, *Indië*, 210 (gives an incorrect account of the mission).

18. Shores, 2, 308; data provided by Air Marshal ret. (Indonesian Air Force) Raden S. Suryadarma (confirms the missing of one of the British pilots and

the number of sorties flown by 242 Squadron); Maltby, *Report*, 1398, section 551.

19. Boer, *Indië*, 215 (does not give an entirely complete survey of the activities of Vk.A.1); data provided by Air Marshal ret. (Indonesian Air Force) Raden S. Suryadarma (sortie survey Vk.A.1 Tjikembar); further interview with C.W. Bilderbeek; verslag A. van Hessen (dossier Van Hessen, Ward collection, SLH).

20. Boer, *Indië*, 215.

21. Ibid., 215, 232.

22. Nortier, *et al.*, *Java*, 65–8.

23. 'Beschrijving oorlogsoperaties H.F. Zeylemaker' (March 1942, via A. van Aarem and J. Mossou); Verslag Coster, F, 16.

24. Ibid., Shores, 2, 308, erroneously mentions a "dawn take off"; Maltby, *Report*, 1398, section 554.

25. 'Beschrijving oorlogsoperaties H.F. Zeylemaker' (March 1942, via A. van Aarem and J. Mossou); Verslag Coster, F, 16; Boer, *Indië*, 210 (does not give an entirely correct picture of the mission).

26. 'Beschrijving oorlogsoperaties H.F. Zeylemaker' (March 1942, via A. van Aarem and J. Mossou).

27. Ibid.; Verslag Coster, F, 16; Japanese Monograph 66; Nortier, *et al.*, *Java*, 116, erroneously states that this air support was not planned. According to Zeylemaker, the staff of Bandoeng Group had requested the road reconnaissance missions earlier. In order carry these out on the basis of the reconnaissance results of Vk.A.1, the reports of the Falcon crews were not only passed on to the staff of Bandoeng Group, but simultaneously to the ML Command, the General Headquarters, JAC and also RecGroup and the COIC.

28. Shores, 2, 308; see also Maltby, *Report*, 1398, section 554. No crashed Japanese fighter aircraft was reported or found, there was only a report of a downed (Ki-48) bomber (Air Marshal ret. Raden S. Suryadarma).

29. Interviews with H. Creutzberg and J.B.H. Bruinier; 'Beschrijving oorlogsoperaties H.F. Zeylemaker' (March 1942, via A. van Aarem and J. Mossou).

30. Nortier, *et al.*, *Java*, 116; interviews with then aviation radio operator students from the ML training at Andir, who had been made available to the KNIL to man the mobile radio stations; A.H. Holslag, R.L. van Motman, C. Holtrop and M.J.M. Verkaar.

31. Military History Office, Senshi Sosho (Series of Military History of World War II), 34 (henceforth Senshi Sosho, 34), 554–5; Japanese Monographs 66 and 69; Senshi Sosho, 26, 698–9.

32. Senshi Sosho, 34, 554–5.

33. Senshi Sosho, 34, 554; see also Senshi Sosho, 34, 537, table 24.

34. Boer, *Indië*, 211; futher interviews with P.A.C. Benjamins.

35. A.A.M. van Rest's notes (his pocket book); Boer, *Indië*, 209–10, does not give an entirely correct account of the mission; further interviews with A. Bergamin, W. Boxman and P.A.C. Benjamins; 'Beschrijving oorlogsoperaties H.F. Zeylemaker' (March 1942, via A. van Aarem and J. Mossou, confirms that Zeylemaker gave the take off order by telephone when Inf. IV had reported they were about to open the attack).

36. After accounts of the mission by P.G. Tideman, A. Bergamin and W. Boxman; P.A.C. Benjamins confirmed that during the briefing they had been told to avoid Soebang and Kalidjati.

37. Shores, 2, 309; data provided by Air Marshal ret. (Indonesian Air Force) Raden S. Suryadarma.

38. After an account of the mission by P.A.C. Benjamins.

39. Ibid.

40. Ibid.

41. Ibid.; interview with P.R. Jolly; A.A.M. van Rest's notes (his pocket book).

42. Operations Report, see note 11; Boer, *Indië*, 212 (gives an incorrect time of the raid); further interview with C.J.H. Samson; Senshi Sosho, 34, 555.

43. Ibid.; questionnaire L.N. Bieger (dossier Bieger, Ward collection, SLH, Bieger erroneously dates his mission on 1 March 1942); Verslag Coster, F, 16; 'Beschrijving oorlogsoperaties H.F. Zeylemaker' (March 1942, via A. van Aarem and J. Mossou).

44. Maltby, *Report*, 1398; Shores, 2, 309; A.A.M. van Rest's notes (his pocket book). Interviews with the ML pilots involved in the alert take off show that 242 Squadron had landed about a quarter of an hour earlier.

45. Ibid.; data provided by Air Marshal ret. (Indonesian Air Force) Raden S. Suryadarma (confirms that Tjililitan was eventually evacuated in the morning of 4 March).

46. Interview with H. Creutzberg; 'Beschrijving oorlogsoperaties H.F. Zeylemaker' (March 1942, via A. van Aarem and J. Mossou).

47. Nortier, *et al.*, *Java*, 116–9; Hoogenband, van den and Schotborgh (ed.), *Nederlands-Indië contra Japan* (henceforth NIcJ), VII, 62–4; Japanese Monograph 66; Senshi Sosho, 34, 556; Senshi Sosho, 26, 699.

48. Nortier, *et al.*, *Java*, 119; NIcJ, VII, 63; Japanese Monograph 66; report of interview with J.L.W. Rhaesa (collectie Veuger/De Smalen, SLH).

49. Japanese Monograph 66; Senshi Sosho, 26, 699.

50. Nortier, *et al.*, *Java*, 119; verslag F.W.H. Twiss (dossier NIcJ 13/30, IMG); report of interview with J.L.W. Rhaesa (at the time commander of one of the infantry sections, collectie Veuger/De Smalen, SLH); F.L. Kroesen, 'De oorlogsgeschiedenis van A. II Bg. (dec. '41-mrt. '42)', *Stabelan*, 4e jaargang, 1, 31 augustus 1977.

51. Interview with A.H. Holslag; 'Beschrijving oorlogsoperaties H.F. Zeylemaker' (March 1942, via A. van Aarem and J. Mossou); G.H.O. de Wit, 'De mobiele eenheid van het Javaleger', *Stabelan*, 6e jaargang, 5, 15 april 1980.

52. Nortier, *et al.*, *Java*, 120; NIcJ, VII, 60–2; Verslag Coster, E, 4; strength in conformity with data provided by Col. (ret.) J.J. Nortier.

53. Nortier, *et al.*, *Java*, 120; NIcJ, VII, 62; interview with J.B. Heffelaar (via P. van Meel).

54. De Jong, 11a, I, 2e helft, 989; NIcJ, VII, 64; verslag J. B. Heffelaar, *Stabelan*, 15e jaargang, 3, 1 maart 1989; verslag D.H. Stephan (dossier NIcJ 13/73, IMG).

55. NIcJ, VII, 59; Nortier, *et al.*, *Java*, 120. Afterwards H.F. Zeylemaker attributed it all to exhaustion among the staff officers. The staff of Bandoeng Group was too small to work in shifts and regular breaks were not observed. Zeylemaker himself was not involved in the planning of the land operations.

56. Verslag J.B. Heffelaar, *Stabelan*, 15e jaargang, 3, 1 maart 1989; further interview with J.B. Heffelaar (via P. van Meel); interviews with H.M. Haye and W. Boxman, confirmed that the air cover consisted of only two fighter aircraft, what is stated in *Java*, p. 120 (probably derived from the verslag Stephan, see note 54), is therefore incorrect. According to F.L. Kroesen, the commander of A. II Bg. reported to the staff of Bandoeng Group on the departure of Inf. V that this battalion, contrary to what had been announced at the issuing of the deployment orders for the 1st and 2nd Battteries, had not left immediately after the departure of the Mobile Unit. See 'De oorlogsgeschiedenis van A. II Bg.', *Stabelan*, 3e jaargang, 5, 8 juni 1977. At the staff, this report "did not make a big impression" (which makes sense as the staff had only issued orders to Teerink Group around 23:00 hrs) and the officers present only spoke some soothing words. "They will make contact with Captain Wulfhorst soon enough", Lieutenant T.H. Bakker of the staff said, according to F.L. Kroesen.

57. Interview with W. Boxman; Nortier, *et al.*, *Java*, 120; verslag D.H. Stephan (dossier NIcJ 13/73, IMG).

58. Nortier, *et al.*, *Java*, 120–1; verslag J.B. Heffelaar, *Stabelan*, 15e jaargang, 3, 1 maart 1989; verslag J.C.A. Faber (dossier NIcJ 13/80, IMG); P.J.J. Jonker, 'Ooggetuigeverslag massa-fusilering Tjiater', *Stabelan*, 23e jaargang, 3, 3 maart 1997.

59. Ibid.

60. Interview with then aviation radio operator students from the ML training at Andir, who had been made available to the KNIL to man the mobile radio stations: A.H. Holslag, R.L. van Motman, C. Holtrop and M.J.M. Verkaar; Verslag Coster, E, 5 (erroneously states that Teerink "rushed to help", Teerink, however, reported by radio that he was going to do that).

61. F.L. Kroesen, 'De oorlogsgeschiedenis van A.II Bg.', *Stabelan*, 3e jaargang, 5, 8 juni 1977.

62. Ibid.; data collected by F.L. Kroesen about the war operations of A. II Bg. (via P. van Meel).

63. Ibid.
64. Ibid.; interview with J.B. Heffelaar (via P. van Meel).
65. In conformity with note 61; Nortier, *et al.*, *Java*, 121–2; Verslag Coster, E, 5.
66. Verslag Coster, E, 4–5; Japanese Monongraph 66; Nortier, *et al.*, *Java*, 111–2.
67. Nortier, *et al.*, *Java*, 110; strength of Vriesman's unit derived from data provided by J.J. Nortier.
68. Verslag P.F. Post (dossier NIcJ 14/9, IMG); verslag B.E. Rijborz (dossier NIcJ 14/9, IMG); verslag F.B.R. Soentken (dossier NIcJ 13/9, IMG); interviews with H.L. Schroeders and J.J. Cnoops (via P. van Meel). The interviews show that Inf. IV already arrived at Kadanghaoer in the afternoon of 1 March 1942, somewhere between 15:00 hrs and 16:00 hrs, what is stated in *Java*, 110 is therefore incorrect, see also note 69.
69. Ibid.; H.L. Schroeders, *Stabelan*, 11e jaargang, 4, 15 februari 1985; J.J. Cnoops, *Stabelan*, 8e jaargang, 2, 22 oktober 1981; interviews with ML pilots involved, see note 35; the reports of the KNIL personnel (NIcJ 13/9 and 14/9, IMG) are somewhat confusing. When asked, both H.L. Schroeders and J.J. Cnoops confirmed, however, that Inf. IV launched an attack on the Japanese bridgehead on two consecutive days, in the morning and afternoon, respectively. The attack of the battalion on Eretan Wetan in the morning of 2 March is also mentioned in the 'Beschrijving oorlogsoperaties H.F. Zeylemaker' (March 1942, via A. van Aarem and J. Mossou). The description in *Java*, 110 is therefore incorrect.
70. Verslag F.B.R. Soentken (dossier NIcJ 13/9, IMG); interviews with H.L. Schroeders and J.J. Cnoops (via P. van Meel).
71. A.A.M. van Rest's notes (his pocket book); Boer, *Indië*, 212 (gives an incorrect account and partially incorrect names of the pilots involved); interviews with A.E. van Kempen, W. Boxman and H.M. Haye.
72. Ibid.
73. After descriptions by P.G. Tideman and A.E. van Kempen.
74. Interviews with P.R. Jolly, W. Boxman and H.M. Haye. Due to the low number of remaining fighter aircraft, an earlier standing order to avoid enemy superior numbers had recently been reaffirmed by the commander JAC. ML Command and BRITAIR had subsequently also emphasised that the fighter pilots must not take any risks (interview with H. Creutzberg).
75. Correspondence and interview with P.G. Tideman and A.E. van Kempen.
76. Senshi Sosho, 34, 555.
77. In conformity with note 75.
78. Senshi Sosho, 34, 555; 'Beschrijving oorlogsoperaties H.F. Zeylemaker' (March 1942, via A. van Aarem and J. Mossou); P.C. Boer, 'Het vliegtuigmaterieel en de materieelverliezen van de ML/KNIL in de periode mei 1940–mei 1942' (unpublished manuscript).
79. Senshi Sosho, 34, 555; Japanese Monograph 69.

80. P.C. Boer, 'Het vliegtuigmaterieel en de materieelverliezen van de ML/KNIL in de periode mei 1940–mei 1942' (unpublished manuscript).

81. Boer, *Indië*, 214–5 (does not give an entirely correct description); A.A.M. van Rest's notes (his pocket book); Shores, 2, 310 (erroneously states that Brooker was to lead this mission). Senshi Sosho, 34, 555, states that six Hurricanes carried out the attack at 17:30 hrs, without mentioning the ML fighter aircraft.

82. Ibid.

83. Verslag G.J. de Haas, 1946 (dossier De Haas, Ward collection, SLH); interview with W. Boxman.

84. Shores, 2, 310; Senshi Sosho, 34, 555.

85. Senshi Sosho, 34, 555; A.A.M. van Rest's notes (his pocket book); interview with W. Boxman.

86. Various military registers former personnel of 2-Vl.G.V, military register A.A.M. van Rest (SLH).

87. Anonymous notes on preserved part of Operations Report, see note 11.

88. Interviews with H. Creutzberg, A.B. Wolff and M.P. Bosman.

89. After a description by M.P. Bosman.

90. Senshi Sosho, 26, 712–3; information concerning the 1st Air Group received from the Military History Department, National Institute for Defense Studies (Tokyo); see also Shores, 2, 309.

91. Questionnaire Bieger (dossier Bieger, Ward collection, SLH); interview with C.J.H. Samson; Boer, *Indië*, 213, incorrectly states that also Bieger's aircraft was intercepted.

92. Interview with C.J.H. Samson; verslag J.F. Samola, 1946 (dossier Samola, Ward collection, SLH); preserved part of Operations Report JAC, with on it anonymous notes on numbers of assigned aircraft, see note 11.

93. Boer, *Indië*, 213–4 (erroneously states that three Glenn Martins attacked instead of two); Operations Report, see note 11.

94. Operations Report, see note 11; Verslag Coster, F, 16; interview with A.B. Wolff; Senshi Sosho, 34, 555, only mentions the loss of a transport plane. According to the Military History Department, National Institute for Defense Studies (Tokyo) no documents have survived with data on the losses of the 59th Sentai and the deployment of this unit from Kalidjati, with the exception of the very concise summary for the late afternoon of 2 March copied in Senshi Sosho, 34, 555. See also Chapter 3.6 notes 79 and 80.

95. Boer, *Indië*, 213–4 (gives an incorrect time for the return at Andir); Operations Report, see note 11; Senshi Sosho, 34, 555; further interview with F. van den Broek.

96. Ibid.; G.J. Hagens, *De KNILM vloog door*, 161 (in view of the time, the DC 3 must have been the aircraft of the Hulsebos crew and not that of the Smirnoff crew as is stated in *Indië*, 214).

97. Boer, *Indië*, 214, gives incorrect information with regard to the deployment of 36 Squadron; data received from J.W. Holmes (via A.D.M. Moorrees); see also Harry Woodman, '*The Weybridge beast*' (confirms that 36 Squadron only attacked for the first time in the night of 3 March). The weather conditions are confirmed by former ground personnel of 1-Vl.G.I, see also G.J. Hagens, *De KNILM vloog door*, 161.

Chapter 3.6

1. Preserved part of Operations Report JAC, with on it anonymous notes on numbers of assigned aircraft (via A.B. Wolff); A.A.M. van Rest's notes (his pocket book). The remarks in the survey in the text concern the number of assigned aircraft.
2. Personnel of 3-Vl.G.III saw the CW-22 take off, it has, however, not been possible to determine the crew; 'Beschrijving oorlogsoperaties H.F. Zeylemaker' (March 1942, via A. van Aarem and J. Mossou); data provided by Air Marshal ret. (Indonesian Air Force) Raden S. Suryadarma.
3. Operations Report, see note 1; account of the mission by M.P. Bosman; interview with R. Haasjes; H.F. Zeylemaker's notes, see note 2, these show that the first sortie was flown by order of the General Headquarters.
4. Ibid.
5. Interviews with H.M. Haye and G.R. Schilling (at the time a mechanic in 2-Vl.G.IV); verslag W. Boxman, 1946 (via W. Bosman); interview with H. Creutzberg (confirms objective of mission).
6. P.C. Boer, 'Het vliegtuigmaterieel en de materieelverliezen van de ML/KNIL in de periode mei 1940–mei 1942' (unpublished manuscript).
7. Operations Report, see note 1; interviews with A.G.J. de Jong and L. Gosma; correspondence author with F.R. Lettinga (at the time commander 2-Vl.G.III); Rear-Admiral F.W. Coster, Verslag betreffende de krijgsverrichtingen te land in Nederlands-Indië, 20 May 1942 (Marinestaf, Historische sectie, Bc–8/1, IMH), F, 16.
8. Correspondence and interviews with P.G. Tideman, P.A.C. Benjamins, J.P. Adam and G.J. de Haas; verslag G.J. de Haas, 1946 (dossier De Haas, Ward collection, SLH); verslag P.G. Tideman, 1946 (dossier Tideman, Ward collection, SLH); A.A.M. van Rest's notes (his pocket book, confirms the number of ML fighter aircraft and the deployment of six Hurricanes); interview with H. Creutzberg (confirms objective of mission). The reader is advised that Shores, 2, 315, erroneously does not mention this mission and does not make a distinction between the first and second 242 Squadron mission to Kalidjati on 3 March 1942.
9. Correspondence and interviews with P.G. Tideman and J.P. Adam.
10. Correspondence and interviews with P.A.C. Benjamins and G.J. de Haas; verslag G.J. de Haas, 1946 (dossier De Haas, Ward collection, SLH).

11. After an account by P.A.C. Benjamins; Military History Office, Senshi Sosho (Series of Military History of World War II), 34 (henceforth Senshi Sosho, 34), 556, erroneously mentions attacks by four Hurricanes and one Buffalo, followed by a B-17 bomber raid (aircraft recognition was not the strongest point of the Japanese ground personnel); Senshi Sosho, 34, 626, table 30 aircraft losses March 1942 (according to this table no Ki-21 bombers were lost, only transport versions of this bomber).

12. Operations Report, see note 1; interviews with J. Coblijn, J.H. Wetzels and J. van Loggem; Verslag Coster, F. 16; see also the questionnaire SLH in dossier Wetzels (Ward collection, SLH).

13. Operations Report, see note 1; interviews with C.J.H. Samson and J. van Loggem; verslag J.F. Samola (1946) and verslag H.J. Otten (1946) (Ward collection, SLH, Veuger/De Smalen collection, SLH, respectively). The Japanese airfield personnel erroneously reported an attack by a Hurricane prior to the attack by the two Glenn Martins, see Senshi Sosho, 34, 556.

14. Ibid.; Honours list Royal Netherlands Air Force.

15. Operations Report, see note 1; interviews with D.T. de Bont and T.C.L. Croes; combat report mission M-542 (March 1942; copy present in dossier De Bont, Ward collection, SLH). This aerial combat is not reported in Senshi Sosho, 34, as the data on the deployment of the 59th Sentai on 3 March have not been preserved (Military History Department, National Institute for Defense Studies, Tokyo).

16. Ibid.; P.C. Boer, 'Het vliegtuigmaterieel en de materieelverliezen van de ML/KNIL in de periode mei 1940–mei 1942' (unpublished manuscript).

17. Interview with H. Creutzberg; 'Beschrijving oorlogsoperaties H.F. Zeylemaker' (March 1942, via A. van Aarem and J. Mossou).

18. Correspondence and interviews with P.G. Tideman and J.P. Adam; data provided by Air Marshal ret. (Indonesian Air Force) Raden S. Suryadarma; Maltby, *Report*, 1398, section 555 does not completely correctly state that 242 Squadron "... was airborne throughout the morning, repelling Japanese air attacks". In the text following events of 3 and 4 March are mixed up.

19. Interview with H. Creutzberg (confirms deployment of the entire squadron); A.A.M. van Rest's notes (his pocket book, mentions the landing of nine Hurricanes); 'Beschrijving oorlogsoperaties H.F. Zeylemaker' (March 1942, via A. van Aarem and J. Mossou); Shores, 2, 309 (however, incorrectly dated, the shooting down of W. Boxman took place on 3 March), 315–6 (Shores erroneoulsy does not mention this mission and does not make a distinction between the first and second 242 Squadron mission to Kalidjati on 3 March 1942 and mentions an incorrect number of fighter aircraft).

20. Senshi Sosho, 34, 555–6; Shores, 2, 315–6 (mentions an incorrect number of fighter aircraft); verslag O.H. Wöhe, 1946 (at the time A. II Bg., servicemen in the Tjiater position saw the aerial combat and counted 14 or 15 fighter aircraft in total, one of which crashed on the spot).

21. Shores, 2, 315–6 and data received from Chr. Shores from his correspondence with former pilots involved; A.A.M. van Rest's notes (his pocket book, noted the landing of nine Hurricanes). Maltby, *Report*, 1398, section 555 2nd part is incorrectly dated and in fact concerns 4 March 1942. The aerial combat is not mentioned in Senshi Sosho, 34, as the data on the deployment of the 59th Sentai on 3 March have not been preserved. There are no data preserved on losses on the ground either (Military History Department, National Institute for Defense Studies, Tokyo).

22. Verslag O.H. Wöhe, see note 20, states that the KNIL troops in the Tjiater position saw four or five aircraft go ablaze on the flight terrrain. This count was made by an artillery officer-observer with his azimuth instrument by means of the rising smoke colums. Shores, 2, 315, mentions a twin-engine plane and a bowser set on fire by Flt Lt Parker. Sqn Ldr Brooker at the time reported that his fighter pilots had managed to take out at least 12 enemy bombers and a few transport planes (interview with H. Creutzberg). Some of the twin-engine planes on fire were probably transport aircraft. According to Creutzberg and in view of the great importance attached to the correctness of the data pilots were subsequently carefully debriefed and Brooker's original claim had been downscaled somewhat.

23. Diary entries of and interview with J.C. Taffijn, as well as diary entries of and e-mail correspondence with O.A.O. Kreefft (at the time A. III Ld. 'Andir Noord'); Lieutenant-Colonel J.V.O. Macartney-Filgate M.C., 'The 48th Light Anti-Aircraft Regiment Royal Artillery in the Dutch East Indies, February–March 1942' (via J. Mulders, after this Report 48 LAA); Verslag Coster, F, 16; Senshi Sosho, 34, 555–6. Further interviews with witnesses on the ground shows that 17, 7, 19, and 9 bombers attacked Andir consecutively. The bombing raid on Tjimahi is confirmed, amongst others, in Coster, F, 16 and verslag W. Boxman, 1946 (via W. Bosman). The war diaries of the units of the Japanese Navy air force further show that the Kanoya Kokutai committed 25 G4Ms in total and the Takao Kokutai 24 G4Ms (Military History Department, National Institute for Defense Studies, Tokyo), see also Military History Office, Senshi Sosho (Series of Military History of WW II), 26 (henceforth Senshi Sosho, 26), 711. It is therefore concluded that six G4Ms attacked Tjimahi. Boer, *Indië*, 231, gives a partially incorrect description of the bombing raid on Andir and erroneously states that 242 Squadron evacuated to Pameungpeuk.

24. Senshi Sosho, 26, 711; Report 48 LAA; description of the bombing raid by O.A.O. Kreefft and J.C. Taffijn.

25. Shores, 2, 309; correspondence with P.G. Tideman and P.A.C. Benjamins.

26. A.A.M. van Rest's notes (his pocket book); verslag W. Boxman, 1946 (via W. Bosman) and interview with W. Boxman; verslag H.H.J. Simons, 1946 (dossier Simons, Ward collection, SLH); correspondence and interviews with P.G. Tideman and P.R. Jolly.

27. Ibid.
28. Correspondence and interviews with P.A.C. Benjamins; description by W. Boxman, see also dossier Boxman (Ward collection, SLH); letter Air Marshal ret. (Indonesian Air Force) Raden S. Suryadarma to SLH dated 28 February 1974; interviews with P.R. Jolly, F.J. de Wilde and P.G. Tideman.
29. War diary Tainan Kokutai (via Military History Department, National Institute for Defense Studies, Tokyo); see also Shores, 2, 316.
30. Verslag H.H.J. Simons, 1946 (dossier Simons, Ward collection, SLH); Senshi Sosho, 34, 556; Verslag Coster, F, 16; interview with P.R. Jolly; questionnaire A. Rozema (dossier Rozema, Ward collection, SLH).
31. Senshi Sosho, 34, 556.
32. Report 48 LAA; diary entries and further interview with O.A.O. Kreefft; Honours list Royal Netherlands Air Force.
33. Shores, 2, 317–8; Boer, *Indië*, 234–5 (in view of the reactions received is not entirely correct); interview with J.C. Taffijn. Gillison, 442, incorrectly dates the big bombing raid on Andir on 2 March 1942.
34. Boer, *Indië*, 235 (in view of the reactions received is not entirely correct); P.C. Boer, 'Het vliegtuigmaterieel en de materieelverliezen van de ML/ KNIL in de periode mei 1940–mei 1942' (unpublished manuscript); e-mail correspondence with O.A.O. Kreefft; Senshi Sosho, 34, 556, states that the 90th Sentai "penetrated Bandoeng airfield", it is concluded that this unit only operated with nine Ki-48s and that it was the Kanoya Kokutai that also attacked Tjimahi, see note 23.
35. Boer, *Indië*, 234–5 (in view of the reactions received is not entirely correct); P.C. Boer, 'Het vliegtuigmaterieel en de materieelverliezen van de ML/KNIL in de periode mei 1940–mei 1942' (unpublished manuscript); further interviews with A.B. Wolff and M.P. Bosman.
36. Ibid.; Shores, 2, 239 (probably after Gillison, see note 33, incorrectly dated on 2 March); data received from G.J. Hagens.
37. Boer, *Indië*, 234–5. Tasikmalaja was a large airfield with many possibilities for dispersal of aircraft. However, it was still under construction and the stocking up of bombs, fuel, etc. was still going on. The airfield was not threatened by the Japanese advance over land. There were no other airfields available to transfer the planes coming from Andir to, as the bases that were still in use were too small, too wet, or could offer too few possibilities for dispersal of parked aircraft. Tjililitan was deemed too vulnerable for stationing bombers there and was gradually evacuated from 2 March 1942 onwards.
38. Maltby, *Report*, 1598–9 (sections 555–6, incorrectly dated on 3 March, for dating of the announcement in which Batavia was declared an "open city" see for instance De Jong, 11a, I, 2e helft, 999); report 48 LAA; verslag A. van Hessen (dossier Van Hessen, Ward collection, SLH); data provided by Air Marshal ret. (Indonesian Air Force) Raden S. Suryadarma.

39. Correspondence with B. Wink.
40. Nortier, *et al.*, *Java*, 124–5; verslag C.G. Toorop (dossier NIcJ 13/27, IMG); J.J. Nortier, 'De gevechten bij Palembang in februari 1942', *Militaire Spectator*, 154 (1985) 7, 312 ff and 154 (1985) 8, 355 ff; data provided by Air Marshal ret. (Indonesian Air Force) Raden S. Suryadarma (1975), with regard to Javanese soldiers serving in Inf. X and Inf. XV (confirmed that relatively many Indonesian servicemen had already served for a longer period of time); personnel strength of the reinforced 2–R.I. in conformity with data received from J.J. Nortier.
41. Verslag C.G. Toorop (dossier NIcJ 13/27, IMG); see also Hoogenband, van den and Schotborgh (ed.) *Nederlands-Indië contra Japan* (henceforth NIcJ), VII, 65–7 and Verslag Coster, E, 4.
42. Nortier, *et al.*, *Java*, 125–6; 'Beschrijving oorlogsoperaties H.F. Zeylemaker' (March 1942, via A. van Aarem and J. Mossou). Requests for air support were normally sent around 22:00 hrs from the Group staff to General Headquarters (AHK), where after approval of the operational plans (for the deployment of the ground forces) for the coming day, the priorities were determined and the requests were fully or partially approved by the liaison officer of the ML and JAC, Lieutenant-Colonel W.J. van Gulik. The latter had by that time received a survey of the expected availability of air forces for the next day. Between 23:00 hrs and 24:00 hrs the ML liaison officer at the Group staff would get a message back on whether the air support would actually be given. JAC assigned resources to approved requests and made a general mission planning. BRITAIR and the ML Command translated this planning into operational orders for the units. This is how it also went on this occasion, on the understanding that in consultation between General Headquarters and JAC the combat aircraft for the support of 2-R.I. would be on readiness as of 08:00 hrs and would take off "on call".
43. Nortier, *et al.*, *Java*, 126–8; NIcJ, VII, 68–9.
44. 'Beschrijving oorlogsoperaties H.F. Zeylemaker' (March 1942, via A. van Aarem and J. Mossou), confirms that the reconnaissance messages were transmitted by radio to Toorop.
45. Nortier, *et al.*, *Java*, 128–9; NIcJ, VII, 69–70.
46. In conformity with note 44; interview with H. Creutzberg (confirmed that 242 Squadron was deployed in its entirety for support of 2-R.I.).
47. In conformity with note 44; see also Verslag Coster, E, 5. Zeylemaker confirms that this message was transmitted by radio to Toorop.
48. Nortier, *et al.*, *Java*, 129–30; NIcJ, VII, 70–1; Verslag Coster, E, 5; Senshi Sosho, 34, 556; Japanese Monographs 66 and 69; further information from the Military History Department, National Institute for Defense Studies (Tokyo).
49. Senshi Sosho, 34, 556.

50. Ibid.; interview with H. Creutzberg. The arrival of the Japanese aircraft and the attack by the Hurricanes was observed from the Tjiater position (verslag O.H. Wöhle, see note 20) and was also reported to staff Bandoeng Group, see 'Beschrijving oorlogsoperaties H.F. Zeylemaker' (March 1942, via A. van Aarem and J. Mossou).

51. Senshi Sosho, 34, 556; Nortier, *et al.*, *Java*, 130; NIcJ, VII, 70–1; Verslag Coster, E, 5.

52. Nortier, *et al.*, *Java*, 130; NIcJ, VII, 70–1; verslag B.P. de Vries (dossier NIcJ 12/43, IMG); data provided by Air Marshal ret. (Indonesian Air Force) Raden S. Suryadarma, see note 40. Contrary to what was suggested in, amongst others, the post-war account of battalion commander De Vries, the number of wounded in Inf. X was fairly high because bombs fell unexpectedly amongst the vehicles and the servicemen who were unloading them. In such circumstances one does not wait for orders, but one flees into the side terrain for safety.

53. Senshi Sosho, 34, 556; Nortier, *et al.*, *Java*, 128–30.

54. Senshi Sosho, 34, 556.

55. 'Beschrijving oorlogsoperaties H.F. Zeylemaker' (March 1942, via A. van Aarem and J. Mossou).

56. Senshi Sosho, 34, 556; Nortier, *et al.*, *Java*, 130; NIcJ, VII, 71.

57. Ibid.

58. Nortier, *et al.*, *Java*, 130; verslag C.G. Toorop (dossier NIcJ 13/27, IMG); verslag J.H. Wessel (dossier NIcJ 13/39, IMG).

59. Ibid.; NIcJ, VII, 71; Verslag Coster, E,5; 'Beschrijving oorlogsoperaties H.F. Zeylemaker' (March 1942, via A. van Aarem and J. Mossou); data with regard to the death of Captain J.H. Scheffer received from J.J. Nortier; data provided by Air Marshal ret. (Indonesian Air Force) Raden S. Suryadarma, see note 40.

60. Data Prof. dr. N. Beets (at the time reserve medical officer at Sadang, via Indonesian Department NIOD); see also De Jong, 11a, I, 2e helft, 993–4; Nortier, *et al.*, *Java*, 130; NIcJ, VII, 71.

61. P.C. Boer, 'Psychologische effecten van het luchtwapen', *Carré*, 20 (1997) 10, 10 ff; see also Verslag Coster, E, 5 (concludes that the morale of the troops broke down completely due to a lack of sleep, exhaustion, bad nourishment and the fact that it was their first combat experience); verslag Baar van Slangenburgh (dossier NIcJ 13/44, IMG).

62. Nortier, *et al.*, *Java*, 130; NIcJ, VII, 71; verslag J.H. Wessel (dossier NIcJ 13/39, IMG). Amongst others, then Major-General R. Bakkers (dossier NIcJ 17/6, IMG) wrote after the war that it was in particular the Indonesian servicemen whose morale dropped and that there were many desertions among the Indonesian soldiers. This, however, must be considered a rationalisation after the fact. Indonesian as well as European troops fled on 3 March and the story that European soldiers followed the Indonesian

servicemen after some time is a fable. What is true, though, is that many Indonesian troops showed up only after some time, as initially they dared not leave their cover and thus missed the retreat.

63. Ibid.; Verslag Coster, E, 5; 'Beschrijving oorlogsoperaties H.F. Zeylemaker' (March 1942, via A. van Aarem and J. Mossou).

64. In conformity with note 60; verslag J.H. Wessel (dossier NIcJ 13/39, IMG); Verslag Coster, E, 5.

65. Verslag D.H. Stephan (dossier NIcJ 13/73, IMG); verslag J.B. Heffelaar in *Stabelan*, 15e jaargang, 3, 1 maart 1989 and further interview with J.B. Heffelaar (via P. van Meel).

66. Nortier, *et al.*, *Java*, 122.

67. Ibid., 122–3; verslag J.B. Heffelaar, *Stabelan*, 15e jaargang, 3, 1 maart 1989; Senshi Sosho, 34, 556.

68. Verslag D.H. Stephan (dossier NIcJ 13/73, IMG); interviews with then aviation radio operator students from the ML training at Andir, who had been made available to the KNIL to man the mobile radio stations: A.H. Holslag, R.L. van Motman, C. Holtrop and M.J.M. Verkaar.

69. Nortier, *et al.*, *Java*, 123–4; F.L. Kroesen, 'De oorlogsgeschiedenis van A. II Bg.', *Stabelan*, 4e jaargang, 1, 31 augustus 1977; P.J.J. Jonker, 'Ooggetuigenverslag massa-fusilering Tjiater', *Stabelan*, 23e jaargang, 3, maart 1997; interview with J.B. Heffelaar (via P. van Meel); Verslag Coster, E, 5; Senshi Sosho, 34, 556; Japanese Monograph 66.

70. Nortier, *et al.*, *Java*, 123; verslag J.B. Heffelaar in *Stabelan*, 15e jaargang, 3, 1 maart 1989 and interview with J.B. Heffelaar (via P. van Meel).

71. Nortier, *et al.*, *Java*, 123–4; P.C. Boer, 'Psychologische effecten van het luchtwapen', *Carré*, 20 (1997)10, 10 ff.

72. Nortier, *et al.*, *Java*, 123–4; verslag D.H. Stephan (dossier NIcJ 13/73, IMG); interview with J.B. Heffelaar (via P. van Meel).

73. Nortier, *et al.*, *Java*, 124; verslag D.H. Stephan (dossier NIcJ 13/73, IMG); verslag F.H. Wolthuis, 1946 (dossier NIcJ 14/7, IMG); Verslag Coster, E, 5.

74. NIcJ, VII, 68; statement L. Vriesman, 1947 (dossier NIcJ 14/9, IMG); Verslag Coster, E, 4; interview with J.J. Cnoops (via P. van Meel).

75. Statement L. Vriesman, 1947 (dossier NIcJ 14/9, IMG); verslag J.J. Cnoops, *Stabelan*, 8e jaargang, 2, 22 oktober 1981 and further interview with J.J. Cnoops (via P. van Meel).

76. Ibid.

77. Ibid.; 'Beschrijving oorlogsoperaties H.F. Zeylemaker' (March 1942, via A. van Aarem and J. Mossou).

78. Japanese Monograph 66; Verslag Coster, E, 5; Nortier, *et al.*, *Java*, 111 (Nortier *et al.*, 110, incorrectly suppose that Inf. IV only carried out an attack on 3 March 1942, see, however, Chapter 3.5 and relevant notes).

79. Senshi Sosho, 34, 555–7; Japanese Monographs 66 and 69; statements Kiyoshi Kanzaki and Hyoichi Sadaka, 1947 (war crimes investigation files,

Australian National Archives); further information from the Military History Department, National Institute for Defense Studies (Tokyo). Senshi Sosho, 34 states that on 3 and 4 March 1942 16 fighter aircraft, 30 light bombers, 16 assault aircraft and four reconnaissance planes were "in operation from Kalidjati". These totals do not include the fighter aircraft of the Navy air force. Very likely they are the aircraft flown over to Kalidjati on 2, 3, and 4 March, minus the Ki-43s of the 59th Sentai that had been lost in the allied air raids on 2 and 3 March. As for the Navy fighters, see Senshi Sosho, 26, 711 (on take off from Palembang II at around 07:45 hrs MJT one of the four aircraft was damaged). On the deployment of the fighter aircraft of the 59th and 64th Sentais at Kalidjati (3–4 March 1942) no data have survived (Military History Department, National Institute for Defense Studies, Tokyo). The data on the arrival of the aircraft of the 3rd Hiko Dan on 3 and 4 March are derived from a statement drafted by Hyiochi Sadaka (war crimes investigation files, Australian National Archives), in 1942 the personal pilot of Major-General Endo, and data received from the Military History Department, National Institute for Defense Studies (Tokyo) from several documents used in the composition of Senshi Sosho, 34 (Senshi Sosho, 34, 555–7).

80. Senshi Sosho, 34, 556; Japanese Monographs 66 and 69. In the early morning of 4 March 1942 six Ki-43s of the 59th Sentai carried out an attack on Andir, see Part 4, it is likely that for this attack all available operationally serviceable fighter aircraft were committed.

81. Ibid.

82. P.C. Boer, 'Psychologische effecten van het luchtwapen', *Carré*, 20 (1997) 10, 10 ff.

83. S.T. Hosner, Rand 1996, Study prepared for the United States Air Force, Project Air Force MR-576-AF, 101–7.

84. Sir Basil Liddell Hart and Barrie Pitt (ed.), *Standaard Geschiedenis van de Tweede Wereldoorlog*, Antwerpen-Utrecht, 1968, 1, 222.

85. In conformity with note 83.

86. Ibid., 152 ff.

87. In conformity with note 82.

Chapter 4.1

1. See Part 3.
2. See Chapter 4.2
3. Nortier, *et al.*, *Java*, 100–2, 133 and 308–9, attachment 5.
4. Ibid., 298–9.
5. In conformity with note 2; see Part 3 for the losses inflicted on the 3rd Hiko Dan on 2 and 3 March 1942. The numbers of operationally serviceable Japanese aircraft at Kalidjati have been estimated by me on the basis of the descriptions in the various chapters of losses inflicted by the allies.

Chapter 4.2

1. Nortier, *et al.*, *Java*, 88–9; verslag W. Schilling (dossier NIcJ 12/1, IMG); Rear-Admiral F.W. Coster, Verslag betreffende de krijgsverrichtingen te land in Nederlands-Indië, 20 May 1942 (Marinestaf, Historische sectie, Bc-8/1, IMH; henceforth Verslag Coster), E, 6; verslag R. Bakkers (NIcJ 17/6, IMG).

2. Ibid.

3. See for instance Nortier, *et al.*, *Java*, 88–92.

4. Ibid., 132; interview with C.A. Heshusius.

5. Hoogenband, van den and Schotborgh (ed.), *Nederlands-Indië contra Japan* (henceforth NIcJ), VII, 73; 'Beschrijving oorlogsoperaties H.F. Zeylemaker' (March 1942, via A. van Aarem and J. Mossou).

6. Nortier, *et al.*, *Java*, 131–2; 'Beschrijving oorlogsoperaties H.F. Zeylemaker' (March 1942, via A. van Aarem and J. Mossou).

7. NIcJ, VII, 42; Japanese Monograph 66; Military History Office, Senshi Sosho (Series of Military History of World War II), 34 (henceforth Senshi Sosho, 34), 557.

8. Nortier, *et al.*, *Java*, 172; interview with C.A. Heshusius; Verslag Coster, E, 6.

9. Preserved part of Operations Report JAC, with anonymous notes on numbers of assigned aircraft (via A.B. Wolff). The strength concerned the situation of 05:00 hrs. At around 06:00 hrs the strength had risen somewhat (numbers in parentheses). The remarks relate to the numbers in the Assigned column. For the strengths of RAF and RAAF, see the identical statement in Maltby, *Report*, 1399.

10. Shores, 2, 325 (incorrectly dates mission in the night of 4 on 5 March); Operations Report, see note 9; data from report I.W. Hutcheson (via Chr. Shores).

11. Operations Report, see note 9; Maltby, *Report*, 1399; Shores, 2, 325; interview with H. Creutzberg; correspondence author with H.F. de Koning (witnessed the arrival of the Vildebeestes at Tasikmalaja); Boer, *Indië*, 239, erroneously mentions that the reconnaissance mission was flown from Tasikmalaja and that a Vildebeest was destroyed on leaving Tjikembar. This happened earlier on leaving Tjikampek on 1 March.

12. Operations Report, see note 9; Boer, *Indië*, 235, 238; further information received from C.J.H. Samson, M.E. Wernicke and H.F. de Koning.

13. Boer, *Indië*, 238, 246; De Jong, part 11a, I, 2e helft, 978; Rapport Kengen, 36 (Ward collection, SLH); Lieutenant-Colonel J.V.O. Macartney-Filgate M.C., 'The 48th Light Anti-Aircraft Regiment Royal Artillery in the Dutch East Indies, February–March 1942' (henceforth Report 48 LAA, via J. Mulders).

14. Boer, *Indië*, 238.

15. In conformity with note 9; interview with H. Creutzberg. Boer, *Indië*, 238 erroneously states that the Hudsons could not be committed as there were

no British bombs at Andir. Besides, an incorrect number of assigned aircraft is stated. The Hudsons used bombs from the ML stocks (assembled in the NEI but with imported American cases).

16. Maltby, *Report*, 1399; Shores, 2, 310.
17. 'Beschrijving oorlogsoperaties H.F. Zeylemaker' (March 1942, via A. van Aarem and J. Mossou); interview with H.H.J. Simons, see also his report from 1946 (dossier Simons, Ward collection, SLH). Personnel of 2-Vl.G.III saw the CW-22s take off, I have, however, not been able to identify the crews.
18. Diary entries J.C. Taffijn (at the time 1-Vl.G.V) and interview with J.C. Taffijn; diary entries O.A.O. Kreefft (at the time A. III Ld. Andir North) and e-mail from O.A.O. Kreefft with explanations; correspondence author with F.R. Lettinga (at the time commander of 1-Vl.G.III).
19. Interviews with P.A.C. Benjamins, R.A. Sleeuw, T. van der Muur and D.T. de Bont; correspondence author with F.R. Lettinga; diary entries O.A.O. Kreefft and his e-mail with explanations. See for instance Boer, *Indië*, 241–2, for the escape of the B-17 to Australia. Boer, *Indië*, 239, gives partially incorrect information on the fighter aircraft parked near the Noordhangaar.
20. See Part 3.
21. Verslag H.H.J. Simons, 1946 (dossier Simons, Ward collection, SLH); further information provided by H.H.J. Simons; 'Beschrijving oorlogsoperaties H.F. Zeylemaker' (March 1942, via A. van Aarem and J. Mossou).
22. 'Beschrijving oorlogsoperaties H.F. Zeylemaker' (March 1942, via A. van Aarem and J. Mossou); verslag G.J. de Haas, 1946 (dossier De Haas, Ward collection, SLH); further information provided by H.H.J. Simons; interview with H. Huys.
23. 'Beschrijving oorlogsoperaties H.F. Zeylemaker' (March 1942, via A. van Aarem and J. Mossou); Operations Report, see note 9; Boer, *Indië*, 239; Shores, 2, 308 (mission incorrectly dated on 2 March).
24. Operations Report, see note 9; Shores, 2, 319–20 (however, states a wrong number of Hurricanes); Boer, *Indië*, 239; Senshi Sosho, 34, 557. The allied fighter pilots consistently mistook the Ki-43s for A6M Navy O fighters.
25. Military History Office, Senshi Sosho (Series of Military History of World War II), 26 (henceforth Senshi Sosho, 26), 711; Senshi Sosho, 34, 557; see Part 3, Chapter 3.6, note 79. The data stated in Shores, 2, 310, 318 are partially incorrect.
26. Shores, 2, 320.
27. Verslag O.H. Wöhle, 1946 (at the time A. II Bg.); Operations Report, see note 9; Shores, 2, 320–1.
28. Ibid. A report of the 59th and 64th Sentais for this day has not been preserved (Military History Department, National Institute for Defense Studies, Tokyo) and Senshi Sosho, 34 of the Japanese staff work series does not mention this aerial combat for this reason. The losses incurred on the ground,

as well as the claims of the Japanese fighter pilots, are stated in a document from the Japanese groundstaff at Kalidjati and are reported in Senshi Sosho, 34 (p. 557).

29. Operations Report, see note 9; Senshi Sosho, 34, 557; verslag O.H. Wöhe, states that KNIL personnel in the position did not see any fighter aircraft crash and quotes an anonymous officer-observer of the mountain artillery who witnessed the aerial combat and followed it through his azimuth instrument. This witness reported that one of the Japanese fighter aircraft landed at Andir rather soon again, possibly with combat damage. A (probably hit) Hurricane came gliding by. A comparison of known dated losses and the total losses of Ki-43s in the period between 1 and 10 March shows that in the night of 2 on 3 March, on 3 March and on 4 March four Ki-43s were lost in total (Senshi Sosho, 34, 626, table 30 and 628, table 31; data provided by the Military History Department, National Institute for Defense Studies, Tokyo). On the basis of data from Dutch sources I have concluded that of the four Ki-43s only one was lost on 4 March 1942.

30. 'Beschrijving oorlogsoperaties H.F. Zeylemaker' (March 1942, via A. van Aarem and J. Mossou).

31. Interview with H. Creutzberg.

32. In conformity with note 30.

33. Ibid.; interview with P.A.C. Benjamins; e-mail received from O.A.O. Kreefft with regard to weather conditions on 4 March, amongst others; interview with C.A. Heshusius.

34. In conformity with notes 30 and 31.

35. 'Beschrijving oorlogsoperaties H.F. Zeylemaker' (March 1942, via A. van Aarem and J. Mossou); verslag D. H. Stephan (NIcJ 13/73, IMG); verslag F.H. Wolthuis (NIcJ 14/7, IMG).

36. Verslag D.H. Stephan (NIcJ 13/73, IMG); interview with J.B. Heffelaar (via P. van Meel).

37. J.B. Heffelaar, 'De strijd te Soebang en Tjiater v/m 1 maart 1942 t/m 7 maart 1942', *Stabelan*, 15e jaargang nr. 3, 1 maart 1989 and interview with J.B. Heffelaar (via P. van Meel). According to Heffelaar the time of arrival at Tjileuleuj is incorrectly stated in his report from 1946, which formed the basis for the above-mentioned article.

38. Bijkerk, 154; interview with J.B. Heffelaar (via P. van Meel).

39. Interview with G.H.O. de Wit, see also his article 'De Mobiele Eenheid van het Javaleger (dec. '41–mrt '42), deel 1', *Stabelan*, 6e jaargang nr. 4, 14 februari 1980, 9.

40. In conformity with note 37. J. H.J. Brendgen, *Belevenissen van een KNIL-officier*, 18, however, dates the events incorrectly.

41. 'Beschrijving oorlogsoperaties H.F. Zeylemaker' (March 1942, via A. van Aarem and J. Mossou); verslag D.H. Stephan (NIcJ 13/73, IMG).

42. F.L. Kroesen, 'De oorlogsgeschiedenis van AIIBg', *Stabelan*, 4e jaargang nr. 2, 15 november 1977, 6–7; data collected by F.L. Kroesen with regard to the war history of A. II Bg. (via P. van Meel).

43. F.L. Kroesen, 'De oorlogsgeschiedenis van AIIBg', *Stabelan*, 4e jaargang nr. 2, 15 november 1977, 8.

44. Senshi Sosho, 34, 557; F.L. Kroesen, 'De oorlogsgeschiedenis van AIIBg', *Stabelan*, 4e jaargang nr. 2, 15 november 1977, 7–8.

45. Interview with G.H.O. de Wit; F.L. Kroesen, 'De oorlogsgeschiedenis van AIIBg', *Stabelan*, 4e jaargang nr. 2, 15 november 1977, 7.

46. In conformity with note 39, see also F.L. Kroesen, 'De oorlogsgeschiedenis van AIIBg', *Stabelan*, 4e jaargang nr. 2, 15 november 1977, 7.

47. Verslag F.W.H. Twiss (NIcJ 13/70, IMG); data collected by F.L. Kroesen with regard to the war history of A. II Bg. (via P. van Meel).

48. Ibid.

49. In conformity with note 39.

50. Interview with G.H.O. de Wit; verslag D.H. Stephan (NIcJ 13/73, IMG).

51. In conformity with note 37.

52. Ibid.

53. Ibid.; P.J.J. Jonker, 'Ooggetuigeverslag Massa-fusilering Tjiater', *Stabelan*, 23e jaargang nr. 3, maart 1997.

54. F.L. Kroesen, 'De oorlogsgeschiedenis van AIIBg', *Stabelan*, 4e jaargang nr. 2, 15 november 1977 and 4e jaargang nr. 3, 25 januari 1978; data collected by F.L. Kroesen with regard to the war history of A. II Bg. (via P. van Meel); verslag H.J. Heijligers (NIcJ 13/63, IMG).

55. 'Beschrijving oorlogsoperaties H.F. Zeylemaker' (March 1942, via A. van Aarem and J. Mossou); Senshi Sosho, 34, 557; Japanese Monograph 69; data with regard to the deployment of the 3rd Hiko Dan received from the Military History Department, National Institute for Defense Studies, Tokyo.

56. Verslag D.H. Stephan (NIcJ 13/73, IMG); P.J.J. Jonker, 'Ooggetuigeverslag Massa-fusilering Tjiater', *Stabelan*, 23e jaargang nr. 3, maart 1997; interview with J.B. Heffelaar (via P. van Meel); F.L. Kroesen, 'De oorlogsgeschiedenis van AIIBg', *Stabelan*, 4e jaargang nr. 2, 15 november 1977; verslag F.W.H. Twiss (NIcJ 13/70, IMG).

57. For an account of the events see Nortier *et al.*, *Java*, 88–9.

58. In conformity with note 55.

59. The description of the aircraft that carried out the machine gun attacks shows they had a fixed landing gear; therefore, they were not Ki-43s but Ki-51 assault aircraft.

60. Senshi Sosho, 34, 557; diary entries O.A.O. Kreefft with explanations by O.A.O. Kreefft.

61. Senshi Sosho, 34, 557.

62. Diary entries O.A.O. Kreefft and an e-mail with explanations from O.A.O. Kreefft; report 48 LAA; interviews with P.A.C. Benjamins and T. van der Muur.

63. Senshi Sosho, 34, 557; interviews with P.A.C. Benjamins and T. van der Muur (confirms that in the morning of 4 March all four Buffaloes and the H-75A were still parked near the Noordhangaar); correspondence author with F.R. Lettinga; data from correspondence with RAF veterans received from Chr. Shores; e-mail from J. Hagens, 4 April 2004.

64. P.C. Boer, 'Het vliegtuigmaterieel en de materieelverliezen van de ML/KNIL in de periode mei 1940–mei 1942' (unpublished manuscript).

65. Shores, 2, 321; interviews with F.R. Lettinga and J.W. Giezen.

66. 'Beschrijving oorlogsoperaties H.F. Zeylemaker' (March 1942, via A. van Aarem and J. Mossou); data from correspondence of S.H.A. Begemann (via W. Bosman); recommendation Oorlogsherinneringskruis–War Memory Cross (OHK) R. E. Nobbe (dossier Nobbe, Ward collection, SLH).

67. Correspondence author with F.R. Lettinga; interview with A.B. Wolff (confirmed that the three aircraft of his afdeling were still at the Technical Service).

68. Correspondence author with H.F. de Koning; interviews with C.J.H. Samson, M.E. Wernicke and W.J. Hofmyster; Operations Report, see note 9.

69. Operations Report, see note 9; Maltby, *Report*, 1399; interviews with C.J.H. Samson, M.E. Wernicke and W.J. Hofmyster.

70. Data provided by Air Marshal ret. (Indonesian Air Force) Raden S. Suryadarma; interview with B. Wink.

Chapter 4.3

1. Nortier, *et al.*, *Java*, 88–90; Rear-Admiral F.W. Coster, Verslag betreffende de krijgsverrichtingen te land in Nederlands-Indië, 20 May 1942 (Marinestaf, Historische sectie, Bc-8/1, IMH; henceforth Verslag Coster), E, 6; 'Beschrijving oorlogsoperaties H.F. Zeylemaker' (March 1942, via A. van Aarem and J. Mossou).

2. Japanese Monograph 66; Nortier, *et al.*, *Java*, 88–9, 131–2.

3. Nortier, *et al.*, *Java*, 82; Japanese Monograph 66.

4. Verslag Coster, E, 6; interviews with H.L. Schroeders and J.J. Cnoops (via P. van Meel). The designation L.H., left half, in Inf. L.H. XXI is an historical one and refers to the original 'half battalion' that formed the core of the unit.

5. Nortier, *et al.*, *Java*, 138; 'Beschrijving oorlogsoperaties H.F. Zeylemaker' (March 1942, via A. van Aarem and J. Mossou); interview with H. Creutzberg.

6. Interview with H. Creutzberg; letter Th. C.N. Canter Visscher dated 2 October 1946 (Ward collection, SLH).

7. In conformity with note 5; Maltby, *Report*, 1399.

8. Preserved part of Operations Report JAC, with on it anonymous notes on numbers of assigned aircraft (via A.B. Wolff). The strength concerned the situation of 05:00 hrs (the so-called start of day strength).

9. Operations Report, see note 8; Maltby, *Report*, 1399; Military History Office, Senshi Sosho (Series of Military History of World War II), 34 (henceforth Senshi Sosho, 34), 557. Senshi Sosho, 34 states that at 03:30 hrs and at 04:15 hrs, respectively, one aircraft carried out the attack, the Japanese data, however, were not conspicuous for their completeness. As a rule per aircraft the bombs were thrown in more than one run, so that the number of attacking planes was difficult to determine during the night.

10. Senshi Sosho, 34, 557. From Japanese statements on aircraft captured after the capitulation in Java it can be concluded that a number of the aircraft left behind by RAF/RAAF and the ML had gone lost or were damaged.

11. Boer, *Indië*, 242; further information provided by C.J.H. Samson and H.F. de Koning.

12. Ibid.; Honours list Royal Netherlands Air Force.

13. 'Beschrijving oorlogsoperaties H.F. Zeylemaker' (March 1942, via A. van Aarem and J. Mossou).

14. Ibid.; Nortier, *et al.*, *Java*, 140.

15. Boer, *Indië*, 242–3; battle report of the mission (dossier Gosma, Ward collection, SLH, verbatim copy of the original carbon copy).

16. Nortier, *et al.*, *Java*, 138; Stichting Stabelan, *Tanda Mata KNIL*, 133.

17. Nortier, *et al.*, *Java*, 134; Japanese Monograph 66.

18. Senshi Sosho, 34, 557.

19. Interview and correspondence with F.R. Lettinga; interview with A.B. Wolff; interview with J.W. Giezen (at the time a mechanic of the aircraft of 2-Vl.G.III that went up in flames); interview with J.G. Bücker. The M-542 of 1-Vl.G.I, damaged in an air raid on 4 March, again sustained some damage.

20. In conformity with note 6.

21. Shores, 2, 237; interview with J.W. Giezen.

22. Senshi Sosho, 34, 557; verslag M. Kooistra (NIcJ 13/78, IMG).

23. Verslag M. Kooistra (NIcJ 13/78, IMG); 'Beschrijving oorlogsoperaties H.F. Zeylemaker' (March 1942, via A. van Aarem and J. Mossou).

24. Boer, *Indië*, 243.

25. Shores, 2, 325–7; Maltby, *Report*, 1399.

26. Lieutenant-Colonel J.V.O. Macartney-Filgate M.C., 'The 48th Light Anti-Aircraft Regiment Royal Artillery in the Dutch East Indies, February–March 1942' (henceforth Report 48 LAA, via J. Mulders); Shores, 2, 325–7; diary O.A.O. Kreefft and e-mail from O.A.O. Kreefft (personnel of Andir North saw the pursuit of the Hurricane).

27. Verslag Coster, E, 7.

28. Senshi Sosho, 34, 557; diary O.A.O. Kreefft and e-mail from O.A.O. Kreefft; data with regard to the deployment of the 3rd Hiko Dan in March 1942 received from the Military History Department, National Institute for Defense Studies, Tokyo.

29. 'Beschrijving oorlogsoperaties H.F. Zeylemaker' (March 1942, via A. van Aarem and J. Mossou).

30. Senshi Sosho, 34, 557; Report 48 LAA; e-mails O.A.O. Kreefft to author; diary entries of J.C. Taffijn and further interview with J.C. Taffijn.

31. Boer, *Indië*, 243 (incorrectly dates the bombarment on 4 March); correspondence with F.R. Lettinga; interviews with C.J. Alard, J.G. Bücker and A.G.J. de Jong; diary F.V. Rühl (via G.J. Hagens); Shores, 2, 327.

32. After descriptions by F.L. Kroesen and E. Vermeesch (via P. van Meel).

33. F.L. Kroesen, 'De oorlogsgeschiedenis van AIIBg', *Stabelan*, 4e jaargang nr. 3, 25 januari 1978, 3.

34. Ibid., 4e jaargang nr. 2, 15 november 1977, 8.

35. In conformity with notes 32 and 33.

36. Ibid.

37. F.L. Kroesen, 'De oorlogsgeschiedenis van AIIBg', *Stabelan*, 4e jaargang nr. 2, 15 november 1977, 6–10.

38. Senshi Sosho, 34, 557; Japanese Monograph 69; data with regard to the deployment of the 27th Sentai received from the Military History Department, National Institute for Defense Studies, Tokyo; Nortier, *et al.*, *Java*, 138; Hoogenband van den and Schotborgh (ed.), *Nederlands-Indië contra Japan*, (henceforth NIcJ), VII, 74; interviews with J.B. Heffelaar (via P. van Meel).

39. Verslag M. Kooistra (NIcJ 13/78, IMG) and verslag P.J.J. Quanjer (NIcJ 13/79, IMG); Senshi Sosho, 34, 557; Japanese Monograph 69; data with regard to the deployment of the 3rd Hiko Dan in March 1942 received from the Military History Department, National Institute for Defense Studies, Tokyo.

40. Verslag P.J.J. Quanjer (NIcJ 13/79, IMG).

41. F.L. Kroesen, 'De oorlogsgeschiedenis van AIIBg', *Stabelan*, 4e jaargang nr. 3, 25 januari 1978, 6; Stichting Stabelan, *Tanda Mata KNIL*, 124.

42. Verslag P.J.J. Quanjer (NIcJ 13/79, IMG); Stichting Stabelan, *Tanda Mata KNIL*, 124; further interview with E. Vermeesch (via P. van Meel). In the book mentioned Vermeesch writes that the anti-armour gun had been abandoned by the men. According to reactions received, the team of the anti-armour gun, however, retreated after an attack by a Ki-51, during which the gun was damaged and became unserviceable.

43. Verslag P.J.J. Quanjer (NIcJ 13/79, IMG); interview with E. Vermeesch (via P. van Meel).

44. Ibid.; F.L. Kroesen, 'De oorlogsgeschiedenis van AIIBg', *Stabelan*, 4e jaargang nr. 3, 25 januari 1978, 7.

45. Nortier, *et al.*, *Java*, 140 (erroneously mentions seven armoured vehicles, see note 46); J.B. Heffelaar, 'De strijd te Soebang en Tjiater', *Stabelan*, 15e jaargang nr. 3, 1 maart 1989, 4 and further interview with J.B. Heffelaar (via P. van Meel); interview with C.A. Heshusius. The remaining ME armoured vehicle went back to the ME in the course of the morning.

46. Verslag P.J.J. Quanjer (NIcJ 13/79, IMG) and verslag M. Kooistra (NIcJ 13/78, IMG); C.A. Heshusius, *KNIL Cavalerie, 1814–1950*, 74–5, erroneously mentions seven armoured vehicles. This error originates from a mistake in the Bronzen Kruis–Bronze Cross recommendation of L.W. Sibbald, orginally armourer in the machine gun section of Sergeant-Major J.B. Heffelaar; further interview with C.A. Heshusius. The Van Dongen reconnaissance squadron originally had ten armoured vehicles, three of which, under command of Heshusius, were directed to the Tjisomang position and one of which was given an unknown destination.

47. 'Beschrijving oorlogsoperaties H.F. Zeylemaker' (March 1942, via A. van Aarem and J. Mossou) states that Kooistra made contact around 15:00 hrs with the head of Operations of the staff. J.B. Heffelaar 'De strijd te Soebang en Tjiater', *Stabelan*, 15e jaargang nr. 3, 1 maart 1989, 4 and further interview with J.B. Heffelaar (via P. van Meel).

48. Data with regard to the war history of A. II Bg. collected by F.L. Kroesen (via P. van Meel); see also F.L. Kroesen, 'De oorlogsgeschiedenis van AIIBg', *Stabelan*, 4e jaargang nr. 3, 25 januari 1978, 6–7.

49. Ibid.

50. Verslag P.J.J. Quanjer (NIcJ 13/79, IMG) and an account of the battle and the circumstances on 5 March by E. Vermeesch (via P. van Meel).

51. Ibid.; verslag F.W.H. Twiss (NIcJ 13/70, IMG); P.J.J. Jonker, 'Ooggetuigeverslag Massa-fusilering Tjiater', *Stabelan*, 23e jaargang nr. 3, maart 1997, 24 (it is pointed out that Jonker consistently predates all events by one day).

52. Verslag F.W.H. Twiss (NIcJ 13/70, IMG); F.L. Kroesen, 'De oorlogsgeschiedenis van AIIBg', *Stabelan*, 4e jaargang nr. 3, 25 januari 1978, 7; data with regard to the war history of A. II Bg. collected by F.L. Kroesen (via P. van Meel).

53. Senshi Sosho, 34, 557; Japanese Monograph 69; data with regard to the deployment of the 3rd Hiko Dan received from the Military History Department, National Institute for Defense Studies, Tokyo.

54. Ibid.

55. Nortier, *et al.*, *Java*, 133, 140 (the text relating to Inf. L.H. XXI on the latter page is mainly derived from H. van Altena's account, which contains quite a few errors; thus, it is not correct that the vehicles of the battalion blocked the road); statement B.C.D. Drejer (NIcJ 13/48, IMG); 'Beschrijving oorlogsoperaties H.F. Zeylemaker' (March 1942, via A. van Aarem and J. Mossou); interview with J.B. Heffelaar (via P. van Meel), confirms that the troops of Inf. L. H. XXI were later transported by truck and bus to the Tjiater position.

56. Interview with J.B. Heffelaar (via P. van Meel), see also his 'De strijd te Soebang en Tjiater 1942', *Stabelan*, 15e jaargang nr. 3, 1 maart 1989, 3; F.L. Kroesen, 'De oorlogsgeschiedenis van AIIBg', *Stabelan*, 4e jaargang nr. 3, 25 januari 1978, 5; Nortier, *et al.*, *Java*, 155, 181; NIcJ, VII, 102, 114–5; interview with J. Staal with regard to the contribution of Vk.A.3 of the ML to the training of the companies of Inf. XXI. The 'European' company 1-L.H. XXI partially consisted of conscripts, partially of European regular soldiers.

57. Verslag H. van Altena (NIcJ 13/26, IMG).

58. Nortier, *et al.*, *Java*, 140–1; 'Beschrijving oorlogsoperaties H.F. Zeylemaker' (March 1942, via A. van Aarem and J. Mossou).

59. Nortier, *et al.*, *Java*, 141.

60. Interview with J.B. Heffelaar (via P. van Meel), see also his article (see note 56); Verslag H. van Altena (NIcJ 13/26, IMG).

61. Ibid.; Nortier, *et al.*, *Java*, 142.

62. Interview with J.B. Heffelaar (via P. van Meel), see also his article (see note 56).

63. Nortier, *et al.*, *Java*, 143.

64. J.B. Heffelaar, 'De strijd te Soebang en Tjiater 1942', *Stabelan*, 15e jaargang nr. 3, 1 maart 1989, 4; further interview with J.B. Heffelaar (via P. van Meel).

65. Ibid.

66. Ibid.; Nortier, *et al.*, *Java*, 143; verslag J.C.A. Faber (NIcJ 13/80, IMG); P.J.J. Jonker, 'Ooggetuigeverslag Massa-fusilering Tjiater', *Stabelan*, 23e jaargang nr. 3, maart 1997, 24.

67. Verslag J.C.A. Faber (NIcJ 13/80, IMG); interview with J.B. Heffelaar (via P. van Meel), see also his article mentioned in note 56.

68. Verslag J.C.A. Faber (NIcJ 13/80, IMG); verslag M. Kooistra (NIcJ 13/78, IMG); P.J.J. Jonker, 'Ooggetuigeverslag Massa-fusilering Tjiater', *Stabelan*, 23e jaargang nr. 3, maart 1997, 24.

69. Verslag J.C.A. Faber (NIcJ 13/80, IMG); P.J.J. Jonker, see note 68; *De Opmaat* 6, 2 (2000): 31.

70. Nortier, *et al.*, *Java*, 144; interview with J.B. Heffelaar (via P. van Meel); see also NIcJ, VII, 77; according to former servicemen of A. II Bg., a section of Soedanese soldiers had been assigned for security tasks, but it was sent to the Tjiater position together with a section of 2-Inf. II in the very early hours of 6 March (data with regard to the war history of A. II Bg. collected by F.L. Kroesen (via P. van Meel).

71. Interview with J.B. Heffelaar (via P. van Meel), see also his article mentioned in note 56, 4. According to Heffelaar the times mentioned by him should be one hour earlier. The company that Heffelaar saw come by consisted of European soldiers and therefore was 1-Inf. L.H. XXI and not 2-Inf. L.H. XXI, as Nortier *et al.*, *Java*, suggests.

72. Nortier, *et al.*, *Java*, 144; verslag H. W. Van Pelt (NIcJ 14/4, IMG) and statement Th. Meyer (NIcJ 13/52, IMG); interview with J.B. Heffelaar (via P. van Meel), confirms that the Nuse section did not come into position until the early morning of 6 March.
73. Interview with J.B. Heffelaar (via P. van Meel). Heffelaar ran into servicemen from various mortar sections in the vicinity of the Tolhek three-forked crossroads. The machine gun section of Inf. L.H. XXI had 7.7-mm, instead of the normal 6.5-mm machine guns.
74. Nortier, *et al.*, *Java*, 147 (withdrawal of CORO section of Elt M.P.A. de Ouden); verslag M. Kooistra (NIcJ 13/78, IMG) and verslag P.J.J. Quanjer (NIcJ 13/79, IMG); description by E. Vermeesch (via P. van Meel).
75. Verslag M. Kooistra (NIcJ 13/78, IMG) and verslag P.J.J. Quanjer (NIcJ 13/79, IMG); verslag A. de Bruin (at the time Landstorm corporal, via A.B. Wolff), confirms that three sections reinforced with machine guns remained behind. When he wanted to (partially) relieve these sections the following morning, Quanjer found that they were no longer in the 2nd line. J.C.A. Faber, commander 1-Inf. V, was not aware of the fact that the 2nd line had remained occupied and levelled heavy, but unjustified, criticism at M. Kooistra after the war, as he thought that the 2nd line was abandoned on his arrival. The Commissie Gedragingen–Behaviour Commission of the KNIL army commander, however, ascertained that Kooistra's company had been evacuated as it had been relieved by newly arriving companies (see dossier NIcJ 13/76, IMG). Nortier, *et al.*, *Java*, 144, too, voices Faber's erroneous view.
76. Verslag D.H. Stephan (NIcJ 13/73, IMG).
77. Verslag M. Kooistra (NIcJ 13/78, IMG) and verslag P.J.J. Quanjer (NIcJ 13/79, IMG).
78. F.L. Kroesen, 'De oorlogsgeschiedenis van AIIBg', *Stabelan*, 4e jaargang nr. 3, 25 januari 1978, 9; data with regard to the war history of A. II Bg. collected by F.L. Kroesen (via P. van Meel).
79. Diary Artilleriecommando Groep Pesman (dossier NIcJ 14/18, IMG); data with regard to the war history of A. II Bg. collected by F.L. Kroesen (via P. van Meel); 'Beschrijving oorlogsoperaties H.F. Zeylemaker' (March 1942, via A. van Aarem and J. Mossou) confirms that anti-aircraft sections returning from Madioen were destined in the first instance to reinforce the Tjiater position; diary O.A.O. Kreefft, confirms that the anti-aircraft artillery eventually took up positions at Andir.
80. Nortier, *et al.*, *Java*, 145; interview with J.B. Heffelaar (via P. van Meel); P.J.J. Jonker, 'Ooggetuigeverslag Massa-fusilering Tjiater', *Stabelan*, 23e jaargang nr. 3, maart 1997, 24; 'Voor vorstin and vaderland', *De Opmaat* 6, 2 (2000): 31. According to Heffelaar no one at the time realised that the Japanese were blowing up their own (KNIL) mines, as no one was familiar with the sound of such a mine explosion.

81. Nortier, *et al.*, *Java*, 147; verslag A. de Bruin (via A.B. Wolff); print out of list of Tjiater KIAs, obtained from J.J.Teeuwisse, Oorlogsgravenstichting–War Graves Foundation (OGS).

82. *De Opmaat* 6, 5 (2000): 37 (letter J. Nieuwenhof).

83. Nortier, *et al.*, *Java*, 142–3; verslag R. Froijen (NIcJ 13/43, IMG).

84. Nortier, *et al.*, *Java*, 142; Verslag Coster, E, 6–7; see note 70 with regard to the staying behind of two infantry sections. H. van Altena (NIcJ 13/26, IMG) in his account mentions the remnants of the Teerink Group. Apart from a few machine gun sections and mortars there were no remnants of infantry of Teerink Group at the three-forked crossroads or its vicinity. I therefore have concluded that it must have been 3-Inf. L.H. XXI.

85. Nortier, *et al.*, *Java*, 143; verslag H. Van Altena (NIcJ 13/26, IMG); Van Altena mentions a time of 19:00 hrs, soldiers who guarded the three-forked crossroads, however, give a time of around 20:00 hrs for Pesman's arrival.

86. Verslag Coster, E, 7; Maltby, *Report* 1400.

87. Verslag M. Kooistra (dossier NIcJ 13/78, IMG).

88. Nortier, *et al.*, *Java*, 144; data with regard to the war history of A. II Bg. collected by F.L. Kroesen (via P. van Meel). The bringing up of the reserves of the three-forked crossroads and vicinity to the Tjiater position was witnessed by various men of A. II Bg., see note 70. 'Beschrijving oorlogsoperaties H.F. Zeylemaker' (March 1942, via A. van Aarem and J. Mossou) and Verslag Coster, E, 7. Major J.M.R. Sandberg, Esq of the General Headquarters, evacuated to Australia in the night of 6 on 7 March 1942, wrote chapter 7 for this report in April or May 1942, and stated, "… the Kooistra company, which had fought extremely well…."According to Zeylemaker there was even mention at the staff of a very lofty decoration for Kooistra. Sadly enough, after the war, due to F.C.A. Faber (who had seen the withdrawal of the Quanjer section from the 2nd line) and H. van Altena (whose information was only second-hand) the absolutely unjustified idea took hold that Kooistra had left the Tjiater position against the orders. See note 75.

89. It could not be ascertained whether actually any mines were laid, although personnel of A. II Bg. stumbled upon own barbed wire obstacles put across the road in the night of 6 March, see the following chapter. See also the reports of M. Kooistra (NIcJ 13/78, IMG) and P. J.J.Quanjer (NIcJ 13/79, IMG).

90. Interview with J.B. Heffelaar (via P. van Meel).

91. 'Beschrijving oorlogsoperaties H.F. Zeylemaker' (March 1942, via A. van Aarem and J. Mossou), see also the remark in note 88; see also Verslag Coster, E, 7.

92. 'Beschrijving oorlogsoperaties H.F. Zeylemaker' (March 1942, via A. van Aarem and J. Mossou).

93. Nortier, *et al.*, *Java*, 143; 'Beschrijving oorlogsoperaties H.F. Zeylemaker' (March 1942, via A. van Aarem and J. Mossou), confirms that De Veer had informed Pesman that he had no need for air support.

94. In conformity with note 92.
95. Ibid.; interview with C.J. Alard.
96. Boer, *Indië*, 243; further information provided by C.J. Alard.
97. Senshi Sosho, 34, 557; interviews with W.J. Hofmyster and M.E. Wernicke.
98. Data with regard to the deployment of the 3rd Hiko Dan received from the Military History Department, National Institute for Defense Studies, Tokyo.
99. Ibid. The estimates have been made on the basis of Dutch and Japanese data of known lost aircraft of the 3rd Hiko Dan (mentioned in the text of the chapters), with the supposition that in the attack on Andir all remaining operationally serviceable Ki-48s were committed.
100. Correspondence of S.H.A. Begemann (via W. Bosman); 'Beschrijving oorlogsoperaties H.F. Zeylemaker' (March 1942, via A. van Aarem and J. Mossou); interview with H. Creutzberg.
101. Ibid.
102. Report I.W. Hutcheson (via Chr. Shores); statement Chiko Yoshitake, 1946 (war crimes investigation files, Australian National Archives); Shores, 2, 328; Maltby, *Report*, 1399, section 563; data with regard to the deployment of the 3rd Hiko Dan received from the Military History Department, National Institute for Defense Studies, Tokyo. The Japanese data preserved are incomplete and it is not clear whether Japanese aircraft were damaged or lost. On the basis of Japanese statements of captured aircraft it is certain, however, that several aircraft left behind by the RAF/RAAF and ML at Kalidjati were lost or damaged.
103. Interview with A.B. Wolff; correspondence and interview with F.R. Lettinga; interviews with C.J.H. Samson and M.E. Wernicke; correspondence with H.F. de Koning.
104. Boer, *Indië*, 243–4.

Chapter 4.4

1. Diary entries O.A.O. Kreefft and further e-mail correspondence with O.A.O. Kreefft; interview with P.A.C. Benjamins. The anti-aircraft artillery coming from Madioen was initially to be deployed near the Tjiater position, but could not be moved safely anymore.
2. Data on KNIL strength derived from J.J. Nortier; data with regard to the composition of the force landed at Eretan Wetan received from the Military History Department, National Institute for Defense Studies, Tokyo and data received from L.F. de Groot with regard to the strength of the Shoji regimental battle group, as provided after the war by Major-General Shoji (statement Shoji, war crimes investigation files, Batavia special court).
3. Rear-Admiral F.W. Coster, Verslag betreffende de krijgsverrichtingen te land in Nederlands-Indië, 20 May 1942 (Marinestaf, Historische sectie,

Bc-8/1, IMH; henceforth Verslag Coster), E, 7; verslag B.J. de Vries (dossier NIcJ 12/43, IMG) and verslag H. van Altena (NIcJ 13/26, IMG); see also Hoogenband, van den and Schotborgh (ed.), *Nederlands-Indië contra Japan* (henceforth NIcJ), VII, 79.

4. Verslag B.J. de Vries (NIcJ 12/43, IMG) and verslag H. van Altena (NIcJ 13/26, IMG).

5. 'Beschrijving oorlogsoperaties H.F. Zeylemaker' (March 1942, via A. van Aarem and J. Mossou).

6. Shores, 2, 328.

7. Boer, *Indië*, 248–9; further information provided by H.F. de Koning and C.J.H. Samson, the event described in Boer, 242 (middle) is incorrectly dated.

8. Military History Office, Senshi Sosho (Series of Military History of World War II), 34 (henceforth Senshi Sosho, 34), 559; data with regard to the deployment of the 3rd Hiko Dan in March 1942 received from the Military History Department, National Institute for Defense Studies, Tokyo; Boer, *Indië*, 249.

9. Preserved part of Operations Report JAC, with on it anonymous notes on numbers of assigned aircraft (via A.B. Wolff); P.C. Boer, 'Het vliegtuigmaterieel en de materieelverliezen van de ML/KNIL in de periode mei 1940–mei 1942' (unpublished manuscript).

10. Boer, *Indië*, 243; further information provided by C.J. Alard.

11. Operations Report, see note 9; 'Beschrijving oorlogsoperaties H.F. Zeylemaker' (March 1942, via A. van Aarem and J. Mossou).

12. Shores, 2, 330.

13. 'Beschrijving oorlogsoperaties H.F. Zeylemaker' (March 1942, via A. van Aarem and J. Mossou); Shores, 2, 330–1; Senshi Sosho, 34, 626, table 30, losses March 1942 (in fact period 1–10 March), after deduction of known losses on other dates, two Ki-48s remain.

14. 'Beschrijving oorlogsoperaties H.F. Zeylemaker' (March 1942, via A. van Aarem and J. Mossou).

15. Shores, 2, 330; interview with P.A.C. Benjamins.

16. Senshi Sosho, 34, 559; Japanese Monograph 69; data with regard to the deployment of the 3rd Hiko Dan in March 1942 received from the Military History Department, National Institute for Defense Studies, Tokyo; data from various reports of KNIL service personnel (dossiers NIcJ, IMG); data with regard to the war history of A. II Bg. collected by F.L. Kroesen (via P. van Meel).

17. Nortier *et al.*, *Java*, 148; data with regard to the deployment of the Ki-51s received from the Military History Department, National Institute for Defense Studies, Tokyo; data with regard to the war history of A. II Bg. collected by F.L. Kroesen (via P. van Meel).

18. Nortier *et al.*, *Java*, 142–4.

19. Statements B.C.D. Drejer and H. van Altena (NIcJ 13/48, IMG); NIcJ, VII, 77, erroneously assumes that only 1-Inf. L.H. XXI was present (see previous chapter).

20. Data with regard to the deployment of the 3rd Hiko Dan in March 1942 received from the Military History Department, National Institute for Defense Studies, Tokyo, the 27th Sentai claimed to have cleared the eastern side of the Tjiater front of enemies; interviews with J.B. Heffelaar and P.J.J. Jonker (via P. van Meel), according to Heffelaar, the unknown officer he met after his interview with De Veer, was either a lieutenant of a captain, and definitely not a lieutenant-colonel; verslag H. van Altena (NIcJ 13/26, IMG), confirms that until around 14:00 hrs there was not a single message from the eastern side of the first line; Verslag Coster, E, 7, erroneously states that "later that morning" a message came about the withdrawal of Inf. L.H. XXI. See also Nortier *et al., Java*, 145.

21. Verslag P.J.J. Quanjer (NIcJ 13/79, IMG) and verslag M. Kooistra (NIcJ 13/78, IMG); see also Nortier *et al., Java*, 145.

22. Ibid. Personnel of A. II Bg. saw a number of men from 4-Inf. I arrive at the three-forked crossroads (F.L. Kroesen, via P. van Meel). See also A.C. Worst's report (NIcJ 14/20, IMG).

23. After descriptions by F.L. Kroesen and O.H. Wöhe.

24. Verslag P.J.J. Quanjer (NIcJ 13/79, IMG) and verslag A.C. Worst (NIcJ 14/20, IMG).

25. Nortier *et al., Java*, 145–6; verslag Th. Meyer (NIcJ 13/35, IMG); *De Opmaat* 6, 2 (2000): 31–2; P. J.J. Jonker, 'Ooggetuigeverslag massa-fusilering Tjiater', *Stabelan*, 23e jaargang nr. 3, maart 1997, 24.

26. Ibid.; interview with J.B. Heffelaar (via P. van Meel).

27. J.B. Heffelaar, 'De strijd te Soebang en Tjiater v/m 1 maart 1942 t/m 7 maart 1942', *Stabelan*, 15e jaargang nr. 3, 1 maart 1989, 4; further interview with J.B. Heffelaar (via P. van Meel). In his article Heffelaar mistakely wrote that he had been ordered to move by a lieutenant of Inf. L.H. XXI, but this should be a lieutenant of 2-Inf. II.

28. Verslag of F.C.A. Faber (NIcJ 13/80, IMG); P.J.J. Jonker, 'Ooggetuigeverslag massa-fusilering Tjiater', *Stabelan*, 23e jaargang nr. 3, maart 1997, 24; interview with J.B. Heffelaar (via P. van Meel); see also *De Opmaat* 6, 2 (2000): 32 (experiences of P.B. de Lizer of 1-Inf. V).

29. Ibid.; see also Nortier *et al., Java*, 146–7; it was probably this armoured vehicle that was found back by the team of volunteers burying the dead there after the battle, as described in 'De ziekenverpleger alias the bobberlap', *Stabelan*, 16e jaargang nr. 1, 31 augustus 1999, 29.

30. Nortier *et al., Java*, 147; interview with J.B. Heffelaar (via P. van Meel).

31. In conformity with note 28.

32. Ibid.; print out of Tjiater KIAs, obtained from J.J. Teeuwisse, Oorlogsgravenstichting–War Graves Foundation (OGS), december 2003; see also verslag J.G. Meeuwissen (NIcJ 13/67, IMG).

33. Nortier *et al.*, *Java*, 147; verslag F.C.A. Faber (NIcJ 13/80, IMG), verslag H.W. van Pelt (NIcJ 14/4, IMG) and verslag J.P. Buys (NIcJ 14/14, IMG); interview with J.B. Heffelaar (via P. van Meel) and his article, see note 27.

34. *De Opmaat* 6, 2 (2000): 31–4; P.J.J. Jonker, 'Ooggetuigeverslag massafusilering Tjiater', *Stabelan*, 23e jaargang nr. 3, maart 1997, 24–5; *Stabelan*, 4e jaargang nr. 2, 15 november 1977, 'Gesprek met Hoogstraten over 6 maart Tjiater', 49–53. Apart from J.C. Hoogstraten (A. II Bg.) the following persons (of 1-Inf. V) survived the mass execution: P. Vroomen (escaped after having been appointed as guide with Hoogstraten), P.J.J. Jonker, Moes (initials unknown), D. van Swieten and P.B. de Lizer. A few men managed to hide during the surrender, amongst whom were Van Leeuwen, the bugler of the command group of 1-Inf. V, mentioned by Jonker. The location is in conformity with the notes on the archive cards of the Gravendienst KNIL–War graves service KNIL, copies of which are to be found at the Oorlogsgravenstichting–War Graves Foundation (OGS).

35. Stichting Stabelan, *Tanda Mata KNIL*, 125–6.

36. *De Opmaat* 6, 5 (2000): 37, letter to the editor from J. Nieuwenhof.

37. Data received from Prof. dr. N. Beets (at the time medical officer). The number of approximately 50 for 1-Inf. V is confirmed in the report of J.C.A. Faber (NIcJ 13/80, IMG); 'De ziekenverpleger alias de bobberlap', *Stabelan*, 16e jaargang nr. 1, 31 augustus 1999, 29.

38. Data collected by F.L. Kroesen with regard to the war history of A. II Bg. (via P. van Meel), probably derived from an interview with P.E. Hendriksz. The killed armoured vehicle crew was probably the crew that was found back by one of the recovery teams, see *Stabelan*, 16e jaargang nr. 1, 31 augustus 1999, 29.

39. Nortier *et al.*, *Java*, 148 (the anonymous source mentioned there was in fact Squadron Leader Julian, as described in the text); F.L. Kroesen, 'De oorlogsgeschiedenis van AIIBg', *Stabelan*, 4e jaargang nr. 4, 15 april 1978, 12; 'Beschrijving oorlogsoperaties H.F. Zeylemaker' (March 1942, via A. van Aarem and J. Mossou); interviews with then aviation radio operator students from the ML training at Andir, who had been made available to the KNIL to man the mobile radio stations: R.L. van Motman, A.H. Holslag, C. Holtrop and M.J.M. Verkaar; verslag R. Froijen (NIcJ 13/43, IMG).

40. After descriptions by F.L. Kroesen and O.H. Wöhe; Nortier *et al.*, *Java*, 148.

41. Nortier *et al.*, *Java*, 147–9.

42. Ibid.; data collected by F.L. Kroesen with regard to the war history of A. II Bg. (via P. van Meel).

43. Verslag Coster, E, 7–8; 'Beschrijving oorlogsopraties H.F. Zeylemaker' (March 1942, via A. van Aarem and J. Mossou).

44. Nortier *et al.*, *Java*, 147–9; interviews with J.B. Heffelaar (via P. van Meel) and O.H. Wöhe; data collected by F.L. Kroesen with regard to the war history of A. II Bg. (via P. van Meel).

45. Interview with J.B. Heffelaar (via P. van Meel); data collected by F.L. Kroesen with regard to the war history of A. II Bg. (via P. van Meel); verslag H. van Altena (NIcJ 13/26, IMG) and verslag M. Kooistrax (NIcJ 13/78, IMG).

46. F.L. Kroesen, 'De oorlogsgeschiedenis van AIIBg', *Stabelan*, 4e jaargang nr. 2, 15 november 1977, 47–54 and nr. 4, 15 april 1978, 11–2; data collected by F.L. Kroesen with regard to the war history of A. II Bg. (via P. van Meel).

47. Ibid.

48. F.L. Kroesen, 'De oorlogsgeschiedenis van AIIBg', *Stabelan*, 4e jaargang nr. 2, 15 november 1977, 52.

49. Verslag F.W. Twiss (NIcJ 13/70, IMG); F.L. Kroesen, 'De oorlogsgeschiedenis van AIIBg', *Stabelan*, 4e jaargang nr. 4, 15 april 1978, 11.

50. F.L. Kroesen, 'De oorlogsgeschiedenis van AIIBg', *Stabelan*, 4e jaargang nr. 4, 15 april 1978, 11–2.

51. Ibid.; data collected by F.L. Kroesen with regard to the war history of A. II Bg. (via P. van Meel).

52. J.B. Heffelaar, 'De strijd te Soebang en Tjiater v/m 1 maart 1942 t/m 7 maart 1942', *Stabelan*, 15e jaargang nr. 3, 1 maart 1989, 4 and further interview with J.B. Heffelaar (via P. van Meel).

53. Verslag A.C. Worst (NIcJ 14/20, IMG), J.C. Stravers and A.C. Worst had already been sent to the staff of Bandoeng Group prior to the Japanese attack on the three-forked crossroads and reported Major Teerink's death there (mentioned in 'Beschrijving oorlogsoperaties H.F. Zeylemaker', March 1942, via A. van Aarem and J. Mossou). Therefore Teerink cannot have died in the counter-attack led by De Veer, as reported in, amongst others, Nortier *et al.*, *Java*, 150.

54. Interview with J.B. Heffelaar (via P. van Meel).

55. Ibid.; C.A. Heshusius, *KNIL-Cavalerie*, 75. It must be remarked that the text of the recommendation for the Bronzen Kruis–Bronze Cross of L.W. Sibbald contains several errors.

56. Interview with J.B. Heffelaar (via P. van Meel); see also NIcJ, VII, 78.

57. Ibid.; verslag H. van Altena (NIcJ 13/26, IMG) and verslag J.L. Paardekoper (NIcJ 13/31, IMG).

58. Verslag H. van Altena (NIcJ 13/26, IMG). J.B. Heffelaar encountered several men of 2-Inf. I near the hotel (interview with J.B. Heffelaar); see also verslag M. Kooistra (NIcJ 13/78, IMG).

59. F.L. Kroesen, 'De oorlogsgeschiedenis van AIIBg', *Stabelan*, 4e jaargang nr. 4, 15 april 1978, 14–5.

60. In conformity with note 51.

61. 'Beschrijving oorlogsoperaties H.F. Zeylemaker' (March 1942, via A. van Aarem and J. Mossou); Nortier *et al.*, *Java*, 147; verslag R. Froijen (NIcJ 13/43, IMG).

62. 'Beschrijving oorlogsoperaties H.F. Zeylemaker' (March 1942, via A. van Aarem and J. Mossou); interview with P.A.C. Benjamins.

63. Shores, 2, 331; 'Beschrijving oorlogsoperaties H.F. Zeylemaker' (March 1942, via A. van Aarem and J. Mossou).

64. Shores, 2, 331.

65. Ibid.; Boer, *Indië*, 252; ML personnel that witnessed the arrival of the Hurricanes at Tasikmalaja, confirm that there were three aircraft. Also P. Valk, at the time base commander, confirms the number in his post-war report (Ward collection, SLH); Maltby, *Report*, 1399, section 568, states the strength of the squadron on 7 March to be five aircraft. I have concluded that this must have been the total strength, including a damaged aircraft that had arrived earlier on 6 March and the damaged plane at Pameungpeuk (Flt Lt B.J. Parker survived the crash in the early morning of 7 March 1942 and left for Tasikmalaja via Andir by car); Lieutenant-Colonel J.V.O. Macartney-Filgate M.C., 'The 48th Light Anti-Aircraft Regiment Royal Artillery in the Dutch East Indies, February–March 1942' (via J. Mulders).

66. F.L. Kroesen, 'De oorlogsgeschiedenis van AIIBg', *Stabelan*, 4e jaargang nr. 4, 15 april 1978, 12–3.

67. Ibid.

68. Verslag J.L. Paardekoper (NIcJ 13/31, IMG).

69. In conformity with note 65; verslag J.L. Paardekoper (NIcJ 13/31, IMG); data collected by F.L. Kroesen with regard to the war history of A. II Bg. (via P. van Meel).

70. Nortier *et al.*, *Java*, 150.

71. Verslag H. van Altena (NIcJ 13/26, IMG) and verslag J.L. Paardekoper (NIcJ 13/31, IMG); data collected by F.L. Kroesen with regard to the war history of A. II Bg. (via P. van Meel); in his post-war report Paardekoper mentions evacuating the dead. This is incorrect. Men killed within the position were buried in a temporary grave there.

72. Japanese Monograph 66.

73. Ibid.

74. Data provided by Prof. dr. N. Beets (at the time medical officer); data provided by J.J. Teeuwisse, Oorlogsgravenstichting–War Graves Foundation (OGS), December 2003 and a print out of the Tjiater KIAs, OGS, December 2003; statement Major-General Shoji made for his post-war (war crimes) trial (via L.F. de Groot).

75. Boer, *Indië*, 247–8; Verslag Coster, E, 8.

76. Senshi Sosho, 34, 558; Japanese Monograph 69; data with regard to the deployment of the 3rd Hiko Dan in March 1942 received from the Military History Department, National Institute for Defense Studies, Tokyo.

77. Correspondence of S.H.A. Begemann (via W. Bosman); military register L.H. van Oyen (Ministry of Internal Affairs, The Hague, with thanks to the afdeling Beleidsontwikkeling DGP, Ministry of Defence, The Hague); Maltby, *Report*, 1401.

78. Interviews with H. Creutzberg and P.A.C. Benjamins; 'Beschrijving oorlogsoperaties H.F. Zeylemaker' (March 1942, via A. van Aarem and J. Mossou); correspondence author with H.H.J. Simons.

79. Boer, *Indië*, 247.

80. Report I.W. Hutcheson (at the time commanding officer of 36 Squadron, via Chr. Shores); interviews with C.J.H. Samson, M.E. Wernicke, J. Coblijn, W. Bosman, A.H. Erdkamp and R. Haasjes; correspondence author with H.H.J. Simons.

81. P.C. Boer, 'Het vliegtuigmaterieel en de materieelverliezen van de ML/KNIL in de periode mei 1940–mei 1942' (unpublished manuscript); report I.W. Hutcheson (via Chr. Shores); Maltby, *Report*, 1399, section 564 (the strength of 36 Squadron mentioned here is probably that of operationally serviceable aircraft on 6 March end of day, that is, 19:00 hrs), 1399, section 568.

82. Boer, *Indië*, 244; interviews with P.A.C. Benjamins, P.A. Hoyer, F. Pelder and T. van der Muur.

83. Shores, 2, 325.

84. Maltby, *Report*, 1399, section 560.

85. Boer, *Indië*, 253, 281.

Chapter 4.5

1. Nortier *et al.*, *Java*, 88–92, 97; Japanese Monograph 66, mentions the fight with KNIL troops near Tjibadak. According to Air Marshal (Indonesian Air Force) ret. Raden S. Suryadarma (at the time ML and JAC liaison officer in Schilling's staff) it was a fight with the rear guard of Inf. XI.

2. Nortier *et al.*, *Java*, 88; Rear-Admiral F.W. Coster, Verslag betreffende de krijgsverrichtingen te land in Nederlands-Indië, 20 May 1942 (Marinestaf, Historische sectie, Bc-8/1, IMH; henceforth Verslag Coster), E, 6, 8.

3. Nortier *et al.*, *Java*, 92–5.

4. Ibid.

5. Nortier *et al.*, *Java*, 151–2.

6. Ibid.

7. Ibid.

8. Ibid.; Verslag Coster, E, 8–9; see also verslag R. Bakkers (NIcJ 17/6, IMG), Bakkers incorrectly assumed that Inf. IX had been ambushed.

9. Interviews with P.A.C. Benjamins, P.A. Hoyer, P.R. Jolly, C.J.H. Samson, M.E. Wernicke and W.J. Hofmyster; correspondence with H.F. de Koning; Maltby, *Report*, 1399; verslag P. Valk (dossier Valk, Ward collection, SLH).

10. A.B. Wolff, 'verslag betreffende de vlucht van de M–585 van Andir naar Melbourne op 8 maart 1942 en de daaraan voorafgaande voorbereidingen', 30 June 1945 (report of the flight of the M-585 from Andir to Melbourne on 8 March 1942 and the preparations leading up to it, 30 June 1945, Ward collection, SLH); interviews with A.B. Wolff, J. Coblijn, M.P. Bosman,

R. Timmermans and A.H. Erdkamp; Boer, *Indië*, 248–9, incorrectly dates the arrival of the Glenn Martins on 6 March.

11. Correspondence author with H.H.J. Simons; interview with K. Akkerman; Shores, 2, 336 (mentions wrong numbers of aircraft); verslag P. Valk (dossier Valk, Ward collection, SLH). Both Valk and the personnel of 1-Vl.G.II and 3-Vl.G.III who witnessed the arrival of the fighter aircraft mention the arrival of three Hurricanes.

12. Military History Office, Senshi Sosho (Series of Military History of World War II), 34 (henceforth Senshi Soho, 34), 559; Japanese Monograph 69; verslag A.B. Wolff dated 30 June 1945, see note 10; Boer, *Indië*, 251–2, erroneously states that the Glenn Martin that was damaged on landing received renewed damage during the bombing raid. According to A.H. Erdkamp (the mechanic of the plane) the aircraft left behind by 3-Vl.G. III incurred heavy damage on the right wing on landing, which required the coming over of a Technical Service team from Andir. In the text of *Indië*, 251, the other aircraft that were lost during the air raid have not been mentioned by mistake.

13. Hoogenband, van den and Schotborgh (ed.), *Nederlands-Indië contra Japan* (henceforth NIcJ), VII, 81; Nortier *et al.*, *Java*, 152; data with regard to the deployment of the 3rd Hiko Dan in March 1942 received from the Military History Department, National Institute for Defense Studies, Tokyo.

14. Senshi Sosho, 34, 559; Japanese Monograph 69; data with regard to the deployment of the 3rd Hiko Dan in March 1942 received from the Military History Department, National Institute for Defense Studies, Tokyo.

15. Nortier *et al.*, *Java*, 96.

16. Senshi Sosho, 34, 559; Diary O.A.O. Kreefft and e-mail received from O.A.O. Kreefft; 'Beschrijving oorlogsoperaties H.F. Zeylemaker' (March 1942, via A. van Aarem and J. Mossou); interviews with P.A. Hoyer and P.R. Jolly; F.L. Kroesen, 'De oorlogsgeschiedenis van AIIBg', *Stabelan*, 4e jaargang nr. 5, 30 juni 1978, 6, however, erroneously mentions 18 bombers (this number probably refers to an intimidation flight flown by the 3rd Hiko Dan on 8 March).

17. Interview with J.C. Hoogstraten (via P. van Meel), see also F.L. Kroesen, 'De oorlogsgeschiedenis van AIIBg', *Stabelan*, 4e jaargang nr. 2, 15 november 1977, 53–4; interviews with H.L. Schroeders and R.G. Kloër (via P. van Meel); verslag R.G. Kloër published in J.M. van Wijk et al, *Dwangarbeid in 't midden der gevaren*, 1999.

18. Nortier *et al.*, *Java*, 153 (gives an incorrect account); interviews with H.L. Schroeders and R.G. Kloër (via P. van Meel); verslag R.G. Kloër published in J.M. van Wijk *et al.*, *Dwangarbeid in 't midden der gevaren*, 1999; 'Beschrijving oorlogsoperaties H.F. Zeylemaker' (March 1942, via A. van Aarem and J. Mossou).

19. Nortier *et al.*, *Java*, 153; verslag H. van Altena (NIcJ 13/26, IMG); Verslag Coster, E, 8–9.
20. Nortier *et al.*, *Java*, 152–3; verslag H. van Altena (NIcJ 13/26, IMG).
21. Ibid.
22. Nortier *et al.*, *Java*, 152.
23. Nortier *et al.*, *Java*, 153.
24. Boer, *Indië*, 249–50.
25. Ibid., 250; 'Beschrijving oorlogsoperaties H.F. Zeylemaker' (March 1942, via A. van Aarem and J. Mossou).
26. Ibid.
27. Ibid.
28. Boer, *Indië*, 250–1; correspondence author with G.M. Bruggink and e-mail received from G.M. Bruggink.
29. Ibid.; interviews with P.A. Hoyer and P.R. Jolly (followed the fight from Andir).
30. Boer, *Indië*, 251; correspondence author with G.M. Bruggink and e-mail received for G.M. Bruggink.
31. Correspondence author with G.M. Bruggink and e-mail received for G.M. Bruggink. According to former servicemen of Inf. IV two Japanese fighter aircraft followed the Brewsters down. How the fight close to the ground ended, they could not see.
32. Verslag A.G. Deibel, 1946 (dossier Deibel, Ward collection, SLH).
33. Ibid.; interviews with P.A. Hoyer, P.R. Jolly, F. Pelder and A.E. van Kempen.
34. Data received from the Military History Department, National Institute for Defense Studies, Tokyo. The small monument is mentioned in various reports of ML pilots, see for instance the verslag W. Boxman, 1946 (via W. Bosman), which confirms that, "At the time of the capitulation ceremony on the Tjiater two Japanese pilots [were] buried...." After the capitulation an officer of the 64th Sentai inquired with, amongst others, Tideman after the fate of a pilot of the 64th Sentai who had gone missing on 7 March.
35. Correspondence author with G.M. Bruggink.
36. Boer, *Indië*, 251.
37. Register Militaire Willems-Orde-register of the knights of the Military Willems-Order (copies at SLH, Ward collection).
38. Nortier *et al.*, *Java*, 154; NIcJ, VII, 81, 91; Senshi Sosho, 34, 559, with regard to the time of arrival of Gerharz at the Japanese lines.
39. F.L. Kroesen, 'De oorlogsgeschiedenis van AIIBg', *Stabelan*, 4e jaargang nr. 5, 30 juni 1978, 7.
40. Japanese Monograph 66; Senshi Sosho, 34, 559.
41. Nortier *et al.*, *Java*, 97–9; see also NIcJ, VII, 81–4.
42. Senshi Sosho, 34, 559.
43. P.C. Boer, 'Het vliegtuigmaterieel en de materieelverliezen van de ML/KNIL in de periode mei 1940–mei 1942' (unpublished manuscript); Maltby,

Report, 1399, section 568 (Referring to 242 Squadron that, "by the evening only two aircraft remained". This probably concerns the number of combat ready aircraft).

44. P.C. Boer, 'Het vliegtuigmaterieel en de materieelverliezen van de ML/KNIL in de periode mei 1940–mei 1942' (unpublished manuscript).

45. Boer, *Indië*, 249, 252 (incorrectly dates this); Shores, 2, 338–9, gives a description of the evasive effort. Eventually, it ended in emergency landings along the west coast of southern Sumatra.

46. Boer, *Indië*, 251, Shores, 2, 438–9.

47. Boer, *Indië*, 251, 267–8; verslag A.B. Wolff dated 30 June 1945, see note 10.

48. Boer, *Indië*, 252; Shores, 2, 439.

49. Boer, *Indië*, 255; Shores, 2, 439 (Shores erroneously concludes here that the aircraft was "possibly the DB–7"); P. Valk also began to fear reprisals and had the remaining personnel of 1-Vl.G.II later park the two Glenn Martins of 1-Vl.G.II in a hangar. The damaged aircraft of 3-Vl.G.III that had been left behind at Tasikmalaja was set ablaze by retreating RAF personnel on 8 March 1942.

50. Maltby, *Report*, 1399; Shores, 2, 339.

Chapter 4.6

1. W. Murray, 'The Luftwaffe Experience, 1939–1941', in *Case studies in the development of Close Air Support*.

❦

ATTACHMENT 1

Abbreviations

A	Afdeling–Battalion [Artillery or Anti-aircraft artillery]
AAFHS	Army Air Force Historical Studies
AFHSO	Air Force Historical Studies Office
ABDA	American-British-Dutch-Australian [HQ]
ABDA-AIR	Headquarters allied air forces
ABDAIR	as above
ABDACOM	Headquarters allied supreme commander
ABDA-FLOAT	Headquarters allied naval forces
AHK	Algemeen Hoofdkwartier–General Headquarters
AHQFE	Air Headquarters Far East
Bg	Bergartillerie–Mountain Artillery
Capt	Captain
Cav	Cavalerie–Cavalry
CL	Commandant Luchtstrijdkrachten–local Air Officer Commanding
COIC	Combined Operations and Intelligence Centre
CWGC	Commonwealth War Graves Commission
Elt	Eerste luitenant–Lieutenant
Flg Off	Flying Officer [=Elt]
Flt Lt	Flight Lieutenant [=Kap]
GHQ	General Headquarters
GVT	Groep Vliegtuigen–Aircraft Group [of MLD]
HAA	Heavy Anti-Aircraft Regiment
Hw	Houwitser(s)
HQ	Headquarters
IMG	Instituut Militaire Geschiedenis–Military History Institute Royal Netherlands Army, presently part of the NIMH

IMH	Instituut Maritieme Historie–Maritime History Institute Royal Netherlands Navy, presently part of the NIMH
Inf	Infanterie–Infantry [Battalion]
JAC	Java Air Command
Kap	Kapitein–Captain
KARA	Korte afstand radio [Short range radio]
KB	Koninklijk Besluit–Royal Decree
KMA	Koninklijke Militaire Academie–Royal Netherlands Military Academy
KNIL	Koninklijk Nederlands-Indisch Leger–Royal Netherlands Indies Army
KNILM	Koninklijke Nederlands–Indische Luchtvaartmaatschappij–Royal Netherlands Indies Airline
KLu	Koninklijke Luchtmacht–Royal Netherlands Air Force
KM	Koninklijke Marine–Royal Netherlands Navy
Kol	Kolonel–Colonel
Kpl	Korporaal–Corporal
KTZ	Kapitein-ter-zee–Captain [Navy=Colonel]
LAA	Light Anti-Aircraft Regiment
LARA	Lange afstand Radio–Long range radio
LAS	Landmachtstaf–Staff Royal Netherlands Army
Lbs	Pound [British]
Ld	Luchtdoelartillerie–Anti–aircraft artillery
ME	Mobiele Eenheid–Mobile Unit
MJT	Midden Java Tijd–Central Java Time zone (GMT + 7.5 hrs)
ML	Militaire Luchtvaart–Army Aviation Corps [of the KNIL]
MLD	Marineluchtvaartdienst–Naval Air Service [of the KM]
MVAF	Malayan Volunteer Air Force
NEI	Netherlands East Indies
N.I.	Nederlands-Indië–Netherlands Indies
NIMH	Netherlands Institute for Military History of the Netherlands Defence Academy
NIOD	Nederlands Instituut voor Oorlogsdocumentatie– Netherlands Institute for War Documentation
NIcJ	Nederlands-Indië contra Japan–Netherlands Indies contra Japan

OGS	Oorlogsgraven Stichting–War Graves Foundation
ORBAT	Order of battle
OVL	Officier-vlieger–Pilot Officer [MLD]
PatWing	Patrol Wing
Pla	Afdeling Pantser-en luchtafweergeschut–Anti-armour and anti-aircraft Battalion
Plt Off	Pilot Officer [=Tlt]
Plv	Plaatsvervangend–Deputy
PRO	Public Records Office
PS	Pursuit Squadron
PTT	Post, telefoon en telegraaf (postal, telephone and telegraph)
RAAF	Royal Australian Air Force
RAF	Royal Air Force
RecGroup	Reconnaissance Group
Ret	Retired
R.I.	Regiment Infanterie–Infantry Regiment
RMWO	Ridder Militaire Wilems-Orde–Knight in the Military Willems Order
RNLMA	Royal Netherlands Military Academy
Sgt	Sergeant
Sld	Soldaat–Private
SLH	Sectie Luchtmachthistorie–Air Force History Unit of the Staff of the Commander-in-Chief Royal Netherlands Air Force, presently part of NIMH
SM	Sergeant-majoor
Sq	Squadron
Sqn Ldr	Squadron Leader [=Major]
TD	Technische Dienst [of the ML]
Tlt	Tweede luitenant–2nd Lieutenant
U/S	Unserviceable
USAAF	United States Army Air Force
Vd	Veldartillerie–Field Artillery
Vdg	Vaandrig–Ensign [ML and KNIL]
Vk.A.	Verkenningsafdeling–Reconnaissance squadron
Vl.A.	Vliegtuigafdeling–Squadron [of ML]
Vl.G.	Vliegtuiggroep–Aircraft Group [Wing of ML]
VPA	Verbandplaatsafdeling–Field Dressing Station
Wnd	Waarnemend–Acting
2 Lt	Second Lieutenant [=Tlt]

※※

ATTACHMENT 2

Data on the Most Important Aircraft Used

Legend:
 [a] number of engines * thrust [hp]
 [b] max. speed [kilometres/hour]
 [c] cruising speed
 [d] climbing speed
 [e] maximum range
 [f] armament
 [g] bomb load
 (a–e in conformity with factory data)

Brewster B339D
 Single seat fighter; low decker with retractable landing gear.
 [a] 1 * 1.200 hp / take off
 [b] 545 km/hr at 5.000 m
 [c] 450 km/hr at 5.000 m
 [d] 6.000 m / 7 min, 0 sec
 [e] 1.700 km
 [f] 2 * 7.7 mm / 2 * 12.7 mm machineguns
 [g] 100 kg

Hawker Hurricane IIB
Single seat fighter; low decker with retractable landing gear.
 [a] 1 * 1.280 hp / take off
 [b] 550 km/hr at 6.400 m
 [c] 475 km/hr at 6.400 m
 [d] 6.080 m / 7 min, 30 sec
 [e] 1.127 km

[f] 8 * 7.7 mm machineguns [as employed on Java]

[g] none [as employed on Java]

Nakajima Ki-43-Ia Army 1

Single seat fighter; low decker with retractable landing gear.

[a] 1 * 970 hp / 3.400 m

[b] 495 km/hr at 4.000 m

[c] 320 km/hr at 2.500 m

[d] 5.000 m / 5 min, 30 sec

[e] 1.200 km

[f] 1 * 7.7 mm and 1 * 12.7 mm [firing brisant granades] machine guns

[g] none [as deployed above Java]

Glenn Martin Model 139 / WH-2

Four to five crew medium-bomber; mid decker with retractable landing gear.

[a] 2 * 840 hp / 2.650 m

[b] 359 km/hr op 3.000 m

[c] 270 km/hr op 3.000 m

[d] 3.000 m / 8 min, 15 sec

[e] 2.247 km

[f] 3 * 7.7 mm machine guns

[g] 1.000 kg

Glenn Martin Model 166 / WH-3A

Four to five crew medium-bomber; mid decker with retractable landing gear.

[a] 2 * 900 hp / 2.000 m

[b] 388 km/hr at 3.000 m

[c] 300 km/hr at 3.000 m

[d] 3.000 m / 4 min, 54 sec

[e] 2.565 km

[f] 3 * 7.7 mm machineguns

[g] 1.000 kg internal [plus 1.000 kg external for short distances]

Kawasaki Ki-48-I Army 99

Four crew light bomber; mid decker with retractable landing gear.

[a] 2 * 980 hp / 3.000 m

[b] 480 km/hr at 3.500 m

[c]   350 km/hr at 3.500 m
[d]   5.000 m / 9 min, 0 sec
[e]   2.400 km
[f]   3 * 7.7 mm machineguns
[g]   300 kg [max. 400 kg over short distances]

Mitsubishi Ki-51 Army 99
Two seat attack and army co-operation aircraft; low decker with fixed undercarriage.
[a]   1 * 950 hp / 2.300 m
[b]   424 km/hr at 3.000 m
[c]   unknown
[d]   5.000 m / 9 min, 55 sec
[e]   1.060 km
[f]   3 * 7.7 mm machineguns
[g]   200 kg

Curtiss-Wright CW-22 Falcon
Two seat tactical reconnaissance aircraft; low decker with retractable landing gear.
[a]   1 * 420 hp / 430 m
[b]   346 km/hr at 760 m
[c]   314 km/hr at 760 m
[d]   570 m / 1 min, 0 sec
[e]   833 km
[f]   2 * 7.7 mm machineguns
[g]   100 kg [with reduced fuel load]

ﷻ

ATTACHMENT 3

Data on the Composition of the Most Important Type of KNIL Units

Infantry

A KNIL Infantry battalion consisted of staff elements, trains, three Infantry companies and a Machinegun company. During the war period it had a statutory strength of 850 men. The Infantry companies each had a statutory strength of 188 men and consisted of a staff element, trains and three Infantry sections of 47 men each. Each section, apart from the CO and deputy CO consisted of three brigades of 15 men each. The Machinegun company consisted of three platoons of machineguns each consisting of two sections with two 6.5 mm machineguns each (so the company had 12 machineguns in total) and a mortar platoon with six 8 cm mortars (three sections with two mortars each). Usually also a so called Tankbuksgroep with two to three 2 cm anti-tank rifles was attached.

Cavalry

A KNIL motorised Cavalry eskadron (=squadron) had a statutory strength of 123 men (without trains) and consisted of staff elements (including one White scout car equipped as a command vehicle with radio and some jeeps armed with Madsen light machine guns), trains, two jeep platoons, a platoon equipped with armoured cars (one White scout car and three Alvis Strausslers) and a motorised platoon of heavy machine guns (four 12.7 mm machine guns). A jeep platoon was equipped with 11 jeeps of which eight were armed (two 6.5 mm machine guns and six Madsen light machine guns).

Artillery

A KNIL motorised Artillery afdeling (=battalion) had a statutory strength of 419 men and consisted of staff elements, trains and three batteries. Each battery had a statutory strength of 84 men and consisted of staff elements, trains and four artillery pieces. The battery was composed of two sections with two artillery pieces each.

Bibliography

Books and printed reports

Beauchamp, G. *Escape from Singapore*, Ontario, 1985.

Bezemer, K.W.F. *Geschiedenis van de Nederlandse Koopvaardij in de Tweede Wereldoorlog*, Amsterdam/Brussel, 1986.

—————. *Zij vochten op de zeven zeeën, verrichtingen en avonturen van de Koninklijke Marine in de tweede wereldoorlog*, Zeist, 1964.

Bijkerk, J.C. *Vaarwel tot betere tijden, documentaire over de ondergang van Nederlands-Indië*, Franeker, 1974.

Boer, P.C. *De Luchtstrijd rond Borneo*, Houten, 1987.

—————. *De luchtstrijd om Indië*, Houten, 1990.

Bosscher, Ph.M. *De Koninklijke Marine in de tweede wereldoorlog, 2*, Franeker, 1986.

Brendgen, J.H.J. *Belevenissen van een K.N.I.L-officier in de periode 1942–1950*, s.p., s.a.

Burgers, G.J. *Het 6 ARVA Squadron in Nederlands-Indië: 1946–1950; Brochures Sectie Luchtmacht Historie nr. 14*, 's-Gravenhage, 2002.

Cull, Brian *et al. Buffalo's over Singapore*, London, 2003.

Edmonds, W.D. *They fought with what they had*, Boston, 1951.

Gillison, D. *Royal Australian Air Force 1939–1942, Australia in the war of 1939–1945, 3, Air, Volume 1*, Canberra, 1962.

Hagens, G.J. *De KNILM vloog door…; Java's evacuatie, 1942*, Haarlem, 1972.

Helfrich, C.E.L. *Memoires van C.E.L. Helfrich, Luitenant-Admiraal b.d., Eerste deel, De Maleise Barriere*, Amsterdam-Brussel, 1950.

Heshusius, C.A. *KNIL-Cavalerie, 1814–1950. Geschiedenis van de Cavalerie en de pantsertroepen van het Koninklijk Nederlands-Indische Leger*, Sectie Krijgsgeschiedenis KL, Den Haag, s.a.

Hoogenband, C. van den and Schotborgh, L. (eds.). *Nederlands-Indië contra Japan, Deel VII: De strijd op Java*, Den Haag, 1961.

Honselaar, L. (bewerker) *Vleugels van de vloot. De geschiedenis van de Marine-luchtvaartdienst*, Rotterdam, 1950.

Jong, L. de *Nederlands-Indië, I, eerste en tweede helft. Het Koninkrijk der Nederlanden in de Tweede Wereldoorlog, 11a*, Leiden, 1984.

Kelly, T. *Hurricane over the jungle*, London, 1977.

Kempen, A.E. van *Mijn verhaal. Een verhaal uit vele rond de tweede wereldoorlog*, s.p., 1989.

Klinkert, W., Otten, R.U.M.M. and Plasmans, J.F. *75 jaar Luchtdoelartillerie, 1917–1992*, Den Haag, 1992.

Maltby, Sir Paul. *Report of the air operations during the campaign in Malaya and the Netherlands East Indies 8 December 1941 to 12 March 1942*, London, 1948.

Meel, P. van (ed.). *Tanda Mata KNIL*, Stichting Stabelan, Dordrecht, 1984.

Messimer, D.R. *In the hands of fate: The story of Patrol Wing Ten 8 December 1941– 11 May 1942*, Annapolis, 1985.

Military History Office of the Defence Agency's Defence College. *Senshi Sosho, 34* [*Army AirDrive to the Southern Pacific Area*], Tokyo, 1970.

_____. *Senshi Sosho, 26* [*Naval Drive to Dutch East Indies and Bay of Bengal*], Tokyo, 1969.

Morison, S.E. *The Rising Sun in the Pacific: History of United States Naval Operations in World War II, Volume III*, Boston, 1951.

Murray, W. *Case Studies in the development of Close Air Support*, s.p., 1990.

Nortier, J.J., Kuijt, P. and Groen, P.M.H. *De Japanse aanval op Java*, Amsterdam, 1994.

Okumiya, M. and Horikoshi, J. *Zero, the story of the Japanese Navy Air Force, 1937–1945*, London, 1957.

Roskill, S.W. *The War at Sea 1939–1945, Volume II, The period of balance*, London, 1956.

Schotborgh, L. (ed.). *Nederlands-Indië contra Japan, Deel IV: De verrichtingen van de Militaire luchtvaart bij de strijd tegen de Japanners in en om de archipel, in samenwerking met bondgenootschappelijke luchtstrijdkrachten*, 's-Gravenhage, 1956.

Shores, Christopher and Cull, Brian. *Bloody Shambles, Volume Two, The Defence of Sumatra to the Fall of Burma*, London, 1993.

Spick, M. *Allied Fighter Aces: The Air Combat Techniques of World War II*, London: Mechanicsburg, 1997.

Wavell, Sir Archibald. *Despatch by the Supreme Commander of the ABDA Area to the Combined Chiefs of Staff on Operations in the South-West Pacific 15 January 1942 to 25 February1942*, London, 1948.

Weal, E.C., Weal, J.A. and Barker, R.F. *Combat aircraft of World War II*, London, 1977.

Wijk, J.M. van *et al. Dwangarbeid. In 't midden der gevaren*, Barneveld, 1999.

Willmott, H.P. *Empires in the Balance. Japanese and Allied Pacific Strategies to April 1942*, London, 1982.

Winslow, W.G. *The Ghost of the Java Coast* (*Saga of the U.S.S. Houston*), Sattelite Beach, Florida, 1974.

Reports

Army Air Force Historical Studies 29A: Summary of Air Actions in the Philippines and the Netherlands East Indies, 7 December 1941–26 March 1942. Assistant-Chief of Air Staff, Intelligence-Historical Division, Washington, D.C., 1945 [can be obtained via AFHSO, Bolling AFB, DC, USA].

Coster, F.W., Schout-bij-nacht, Commandant der Marine in Australië. Verslag betreffende de krijgsverrichtingen in Nederlands-Indië te land, attachment to nota No S.65, 20 May 1942 to ZE de Minister van Marine [can be obtained via NIMH, The Hague, The Netherlands].

Japanese Monograph nr. 66: Invasion of the Netherlands East Indies Washington D.C., 1948 [can be obtained via Library of U.S. Congress, DC, USA].

Japanese Monograph nr. 69: Air Operations in the Invasion of the Netherlands East Indies Washington D.C., 1948 [can be obtained via Library of U.S. Congress, DC, USA].

Articles

Boer, P.C., "Psychologische effecten van het luchtwapen", in *Carré*, 20 (1997) 10.

Nortier, J.J., "De Afdeling Operaties van het Algemeen Hoofdkwartier KNIL in 1941/42", in *Militaire Spectator*, 156 (1987) 9.

_____., "De gevechten bij Palembang in februari 1942", in *Militaire Spectator*, 154 (1985) 7 and 8.

Simons, H.H.J. "Java-Drama", in *Remous*, Jackson, May 1943.

Warden III, John, A., "The Enemy as a System", in *Air Power Journal*, 9 (Spring 1995) 2.

Different authors, articles and published reports from the period 1946–47, in *Stabelan, Periodiek van de Stichting Vriendenkring oud KNIL Militairen*, volumes 1974 up to and including 1999, different numbers.

Archives

Instituut Militaire Geschiedenis van de Koninklijke Landmacht [Military History Institute of the Royal Netherlands Army, presently part of the Netherlands Institute for Military History, The Hague, The Netherlands]. Dossiers [files] from the collection Nederlands-Indië contra Japan [Netherlands East Indies contra Japan].

Sectie Luchtmachthistorie van de Staf Bevelhebber der Luchtstrijdkrachten [Air Force History Unit of the Staff of the Commander-in-Chief of the Royal Netherlands Air Force, presently part of the Netherlands Institute for Military History, The Hague, The Netherlands]. Dossiers [files] from the collections Ward and Veuger/De Smalen.

Documents obtained from private persons

Aarem, A. van en Mossou, J. 'Beschrijving oorlogsoperaties H.F. Zeylemaker', notities van Elt vl wnr Zeijlemaker [description of war operations, diary notes of Lieutenant H.F. Zeijlemaker], March 1942.

Bont, D.T. Original combat report mission with M-542 on 3 March 1942.

Kreefft, O.A.O. Diary notes and drawings in his military pocket book, period December 1941–March 1942.

Kruiselbergen, J. van. Pilots logbook period December 1941–March 1942.

Rest, A.A.M. van. Notes on the actions and availability of fighters kept in his military pocket book up to and including 3 March 1942.

Taffijn, J.C. Diary notes in his military pocketbook, December 1941–March 1942.

Wolff, A.B. Parts from JAC Operations Reports, period 23 February 1942–6 March 1942.

Index